■ THE RESOURCE FOR THE INDEPENDENT TRAVELER

"The guides are aimed not only at young budget travelers but at the indepedent traveler; a sort of streetwise cookbook for traveling alone."

—The New York Times

"Unbeatable; good sight-seeing advice; up-to-date info on restaurants, hotels, and inns; a commitment to money-saving travel; and a wry style that brightens nearly every page."

—The Washington Post

"Lighthearted and sophisticated, informative and fun to read. [Let's Go] helps the novice traveler navigate like a knowledgeable old hand."

—Atlanta Journal-Constitution

"A world-wise traveling companion—always ready with friendly advice and helpful hints, all sprinkled with a bit of wit."

—The Philadelphia Inquirer

■ THE BEST TRAVEL BARGAINS IN YOUR PRICE RANGE

"All the dirt, dirt cheap."

—People

"Anything you need to know about budget traveling is detailed in this book."

—The Chicago Sun-Times

"Let's Go follows the creed that you don't have to toss your life's savings to the wind to travel—unless you want to."

—The Salt Lake Tribune

■ REAL ADVICE FOR REAL EXPERIENCES

"The writers seem to have experienced every rooster-packed bus and lunar-surfaced mattress about which they write."

—The New York Times

"Value-packed, unbeatable, accurate, and comprehensive."

—The Los Angeles Times

"[Let's Go's] devoted updaters really walk the walk (and thumb the ride, and trek the trail). Learn how to fish, haggle, find work—anywhere."

—Food & Wine

LET'S GO PUBLICATIONS

TRAVEL GUIDES

Australia 8th Edition
Austria & Switzerland 12th edition
Brazil 1st edition
Britain & Ireland 2005
California 10th edition
Central America 9th edition
Chile 2nd edition
China 5th edition
Costa Rica 2nd edition
Eastern Europe 2005
Ecuador 1st edition **NEW TITLE**
Egypt 2nd edition
Europe 2005
France 2005
Germany 12th Edition
Greece 2005
Hawaii 3rd edition
India & Nepal 8th edition
Ireland 2005
Israel 4th edition
Italy 2005
Japan 1st edition
Mexico 20th edition
Middle East 4th edition
Peru 1st edition **NEW TITLE**
Puerto Rico 1st edition
South Africa 5th edition
Southeast Asia 9th edition
Spain & Portugal 2005
Thailand 2nd edition
Turkey 5th edition
USA 2005
Vietnam 1st edition **NEW TITLE**
Western Europe 2005

ROADTRIP GUIDE

Roadtripping USA **NEW TITLE**

ADVENTURE GUIDES

Alaska 1st edition
New Zealand **NEW TITLE**
Pacific Northwest **NEW TITLE**
Southwest USA 3rd edition

CITY GUIDES

Amsterdam 3rd edition
Barcelona 3rd edition
Boston 4th edition
London 2005
New York City 15th Edition
Paris 13th Edition
Rome 12th edition
San Francisco 4th edition
Washington, D.C. 13th edition

POCKET CITY GUIDES

Amsterdam
Berlin
Boston
Chicago
London
New York City
Paris
San Francisco
Venice
Washington, D.C.

LET'S GO

ECUADOR
INCLUDING THE GALÁPAGOS ISLANDS

August Dietrich Editor
Lindsay E. Crouse Associate Editor

Researcher-Writers
Megha Doshi
Abe Kinkopf
Ben Robbins
Anna Walters

Nick Kephart Map Editor
Emma Nothmann Managing Editor

ST. MARTIN'S PRESS ✿ NEW YORK

Maps by David Lindroth copyright © 2005 by St. Martin's Press.

Let's Go: Ecuador Copyright © 2005 by Let's Go, Inc. All rights reserved. Printed in the United States of America. No part of this book may be used or reproduced in any manner whatsoever without written permission except in the case of brief quotations embodied in critical articles or reviews. Let's Go is available for purchase in bulk by institutions and authorized resellers. For information, address St. Martin's Press, 175 Fifth Avenue, New York, NY 10010, USA. www.stmartins.com.

Distributed outside the USA and Canada by Macmillan, an imprint of Pan Macmillan Ltd. 20 New Wharf Road, London N1 9RR
Basingstoke and Oxford
Associated companies throughout the world
www.panmacmillan.com

ISBN: 0-312-33562-8
EAN: 978-0312-33562-8
First edition
10 9 8 7 6 5 4 3

Let's Go: Ecuador is written by Let's Go Publications, 67 Mount Auburn Street, Cambridge, MA 02138, USA.

Let's Go® and the LG logo are trademarks of Let's Go, Inc.
Printed in the USA.

CONTENTS

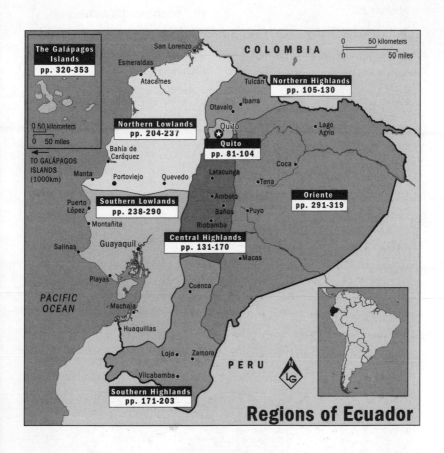

The Galápagos
Islands
pp. 320-353

0 50 kilometers
0 50 miles

TO GALÁPAGOS
ISLANDS
(1000km)

PACIFIC
OCEAN

San Lorenzo

Esmeraldas

Atacames

Bahía de
Caráquez

Manta

Puerto
López

Montañita

Salinas

Guayaquil

Playas

Machala

Huaquillas

Portoviejo

Quevedo

Otavalo

Quito

Latacunga

Ambato

Baños

Riobamba

Loja

Vilcabamba

COLOMBIA

0 50 kilometers
0 50 miles

Tulcán

Ibarra

Northern Highlands
pp. 105-130

Northern Lowlands
pp. 204-237

Quito
pp. 81-104

Lago
Agrio

Coca

Tena

Oriente
pp. 291-319

Southern Lowlands
pp. 238-290

Puyo

Central Highlands
pp. 131-170

Macas

Cuenca

Zamora

PERU

Southern Highlands
pp. 171-203

Regions of Ecuador

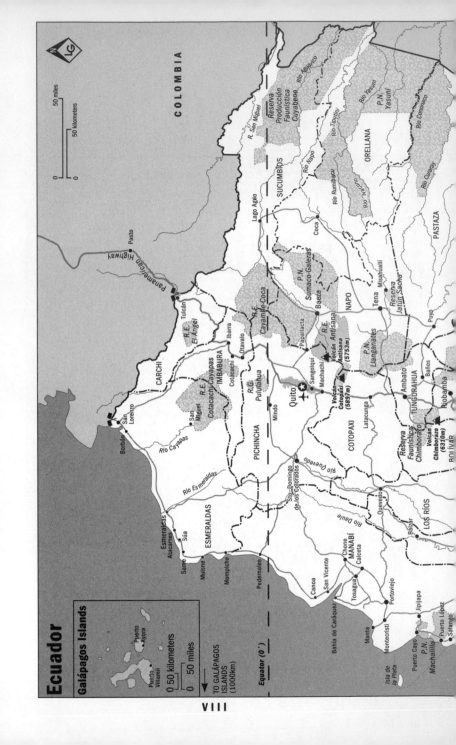

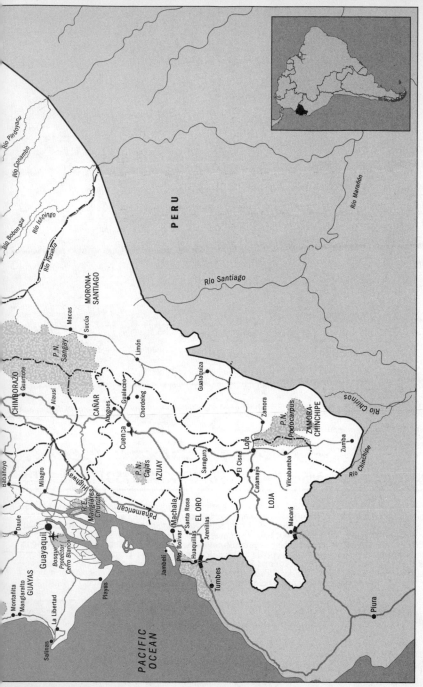

HOW TO USE THIS BOOK

COVERAGE LAYOUT. Jungle, mountain, and beach: *Let's Go: Ecuador, 1st edition* has covered all the bases. This book has broken Ecuador into eight regions, each based on geography and culture. It begins with Quito and then travels north to south through the Highlands and then the Lowlands. Next it traverses west to the Oriente, reviewing it, again, north to south. It ends in the Pacific Ocean with the Galápagos. Along the way, major cities serve as hubs from which to branch out to surrounding towns and parks. Black tabs at the side of each page and an extensive index in the back further organize the book.

TRANSPORTATION INFO. Sections on international, intercity, and local transportation will help you get around. Wherever possible, we list destinations, durations, departure times, and fares, in that order, for airplanes, trains, buses, boats, and taxis. A typical listing: Buses depart to: **Quito** (2½hr., M-Sa 1pm, US$4).

COVERING THE BASICS. Use our Essentials chapter to learn the facts about traveling to and around Ecuador. It'll also give the basics on how to stay safe, how to store money and valuables, and what to pack. Check out Discover for suggested itineraries, the Life and Times section for a crash-course on history and culture, the Alternatives to Tourism chapter for information on less conventional ways to travel, such as studying or volunteering, and the Appendix for some helpful Spanish phrases.

SCHOLARLY ARTICLES. Let's Go solicits articles from experts on interesting subjects. In this edition, articles discuss Ecuador's dollarization process (see p. 59) and the challenges of protecting the Galápagos's delicate ecosystem (see p. 341). A third article relates some lessons learned on an archaeological dig (see p. 79).

PRICE DIVERSITY. To help you pick establishments that best fit your budget, we have compiled a price diversity chart that ranks establishments ❶ to ❻. We assigns one of these numbers to each food or accommodations establishment reviewed. Pricier establishments receive higher numbers. Check out the table on p. xii for specifics. In addition, note that the order of each town's or city's establishments denotes its quality. To our absolute favorites, we give the Let's Go thumbs-up (🖐).

FEATURES. *Let's Go: Ecuador, 1st edition* also offers short slices of information on a wide array of interesting topics. Look to the margins for brief articles on culinary delights—from bananas (see p. 219) to ants (see p. 305)—the inside scoop on cheap buys (see p. 93), and important community projects and other recent news.

A NOTE TO OUR READERS. The information for this book was gathered by *Let's Go* researchers from May through August of 2004. Each listing is based on one researcher's opinion, formed during his or her visit at a particular time. Those traveling at other times may have different experiences since prices, dates, hours, and conditions are always subject to change. You are urged to check the facts presented in this book beforehand to avoid inconvenience and surprises.

PRICE RANGES>>ECUADOR

Our researchers list establishments in order of value from best to worst; our favorites are denoted by the Let's Go thumbs-up (📖). Since the best value is not always the cheapest price, however, we have also incorporated a system of price ranges, based on a rough expectation of what you'll spend. For **accommodations,** we base our range on the cheapest price for which a single traveler can stay for one night. For **restaurants** and other dining establishments, we estimate the average amount a traveler will spend. The table tells you what you'll *typically* find in Ecuador at the corresponding price range; keep in mind that no system can allow for every individual establishment's quirks, and you'll typically get more for your money in smaller towns. In other words: expect anything.

ACCOMMODATIONS	RANGE	WHAT YOU'RE *LIKELY* TO FIND
❶	under US$4	A basic budget hotel, featuring running water, a bed, shared bath, and probably some insect friends. The lucky few may be blessed with hot water, TV, private bath, or a fan.
❷	US$4-8	Cleaner, likely to have hot water, may have private bath. Fan likely. TV for the fortunate. Perhaps an insect—it just wants to be your friend. May offer tourist services.
❸	US$8-14	Similar to 2, with more amenities and usually in a quieter part of town. A/C more likely, TV, private bath, fridge, more attractive, and cleaner. Some offer tourist services, Internet, and breakfast.
❹	US$14-25	Near resort- or business hotel-style accommodation. Usually excellent service, all the amenities, and prime location. The staff may well provide tourist services.
❺	over US$25	Can we say really nice business hotel or resort? If it's a 5 and doesn't have what you want, you paid too much.

FOOD	RANGE	WHAT YOU'RE *LIKELY* TO FIND
❶	under US$3	In small towns, the restaurants are homey and generally serve a daily *menú* with large portions. Portions get smaller in larger cities.
❷	US$3-5	Local joints, sometimes hole-in-the-wall establishments, but will have seating. *Menús*, again, are the norm.
❸	US$5-6	All the expected dishes in a slightly more pleasant setting. No lack of new and exciting gastronomic options.
❹	US$6-8	Often catered to tourists. More exotic or western dishes available. May be better prepared, or at least appear to be.
❺	over US$8	The freshest meat and fish cooked to perfection. Excellent service should be a part of the experience. It better be worth writing home about.

ABOUT LET'S GO

GUIDES FOR THE INDEPENDENT TRAVELER

At Let's Go, we see every trip as the chance of a lifetime. If your dream is to grab a machete and forge through the jungles of Brazil, we can take you there. If you'd rather bask in the Riviera sun at a beachside cafe, we'll set you a table. We write for readers who know that there's more to travel than sharing double deckers with tourists and who believe that travel can change both themselves and the world—whether they plan to spend six days in London or six months in Latin America. We'll show you just how far your money can go, and prove that the greatest limitation on your adventures is not your wallet, but your imagination. After all, traveling close to the ground lets you interact more directly with the places and people you've gone to see, making for the most authentic experience.

BEYOND THE TOURIST EXPERIENCE

To help you gain a deeper connection with the places you travel, our researchers give you the heads-up on both world-renowned and off-the-beaten-track attractions, sights, and destinations. They engage with the local culture, writing features on regional cuisine, local festivals, and hot political issues. We've also opened our pages to respected writers and scholars to hear their takes on the countries and regions we cover, and asked travelers who have worked, studied, or volunteered abroad to contribute first-person accounts of their experiences. We've also increased our coverage of responsible travel and expanded each guide's Alternatives to Tourism chapter to share more ideas about how to give back to local communities and learn about the places you travel.

FORTY-FIVE YEARS OF WISDOM

Let's Go got its start in 1960, when a group of creative and well-traveled students compiled their experience and advice into a 20-page mimeographed pamphlet, which they gave to travelers on charter flights to Europe. Four and a half decades later, we've expanded to cover six continents and all kinds of travel—while retaining our founders' adventurous attitude toward the world. Our guides are still researched and written entirely by students on shoestring budgets, experienced travelers who know that train strikes, stolen luggage, food poisoning, and marriage proposals are all part of a day's work. This year, we're expanding our coverage of South America and Southeast Asia, with brand-new *Let's Go: Ecuador*, *Let's Go: Peru*, and *Let's Go: Vietnam*. Our adventure guide series is growing, too, with the addition of *Let's Go: Pacific Northwest Adventure* and *Let's Go: New Zealand Adventure*. And we're immensely excited about our new *Let's Go: Roadtripping USA*—two years, eight routes, and sixteen researchers and editors have put together a travel guide like none other.

THE LET'S GO COMMUNITY

More than just a travel guide company, Let's Go is a community. Our small staff comes together because of our shared passion for travel and our desire to help other travelers see the world. We love it when our readers become part of the Let's Go community as well—when you travel, drop us a postcard (67 Mt. Auburn St., Cambridge, MA 02138, USA) or send us an e-mail (feedback@letsgo.com) to tell us about your adventures and discoveries.

For more information, visit us online: www.letsgo.com.

RESEARCHER-WRITERS

Megha Doshi
Southern Lowlands, Galápagos

A *Let's Go: Southeast Asia* and *Costa Rica* veteran, she made Ecuador the last notch in a well worn belt. Before island-hopping about the Galápagos, she surfed her way down the southern half of the Pacific coast. But Megha's not all fun-in-the-sun; at every stop along the way, she wrote reams of splendid new coverage—all while making time for a daily run. She's one hardcore RW—boxing in her spare time—and passionate about saving the environment.

Abe Kinkopf
Quito, Central Highlands, Southern Highlands

Having already written a book *and* a play, Abe filled a notebook per week out of habit. He has an instinct for discovering cozy hotels, delicious food, and gorgeous cathedrals—as well as adding witty commentary at every chance he got: his book was on jokes, and his play was a comedy. And, though it might have even seemed to him that all he did was write, he did a lot of talking, too. In the end, he probably learned about as many inside scoops as the locals knew. Oh, and he raps. Keep an ear out for Father Abraham.

Ben Robbins
Oriente, Southern Highlands, Southern Lowlands

Rafting through the dense Ecuadorian jungle was a new experience for this physics student from New York. So was being delayed for hours when his bus driver decided it was time for lunch—or to heave a hut-sized boulder from the middle of the road. Luckily, penning hilarious and thorough prose was old news—a task he managed to accomplish in the shadow of several active volcanos. He also partied till dawn, explored Quichua villages, and even discovered his favorite drug, Cipro.

Anna Walters
Northern Highlands, Northern Lowlands

This relentless researcher found hidden nook after forgotten cranny all over the northern half of Ecuador. It couldn't have hurt that she made numerous friends at every stop along the way; most of the time locals just treated her as family. Her beautiful Spanish even talked upstart tour guides into leading her around multiple Northern Lowlands towns free of charge. And then she stumbled upon Mompiche—an as-of-yet undiscovered surfer town; or, as locals call it, the next Montañita.

ACKNOWLEDGMENTS

LET'S GO

TEAM ECUADOR THANKS: Emma, who made it all possible, showing us the way and standing ready to help all along it; Nick for making maps that even the IGM of Ecuador doesn't have; Jeremy for writing hilarious emails; and Teresa for late-night company.

AUGUST THANKS: Emma—she's incredible; Lindsay, a paper-editing machine and a stalwart with a smile; Ashley, who gave the pod a dose of Andean tranquility; Dan for keeping it real; Luke for keeping it lively; Joel for advice; Jeremy for sloshball; Shelley for pulling the night shift with me; Chris for making the barbecues possible; Riley, Todd, and Craig; Mom and Dad for making sure I didn't go hungry, and Andrew and Cynth to share my stories with; Montreal for the greatest weekend ever; and my RWs for working themselves to the bone till the end.

LINDSAY THANKS: August Reich Dietrich—an amazing boss with an amazing name; you made this job fun! Emma for having all the answers; Ashley for making our pod a llama amusement park for a day; Teresa for keeping calm in the face of "excitement;" Luke for Top Gun; Dan for Pau-Latina; the family back in RI, for encouragement; Danila for the check-ins that kind of happened; Mike for Roadtrips and making gnocchi and helping me out; and the RWs, whose amazing adventures and relentless dedication left us all inspired.

NICK THANKS: August and Lindsay for the words beside the maps; Abe for an outstanding job in Quito; Anna for cartographic wonders; Ben for finding the mysterious boundaries of all of the national parks; and Megha for amazing maps of Guayaquil.

Editor
August Dietrich
Associate Editor
Lindsay E. Crouse
Managing Editor
Emma Nothmann
Map Editor
Nick Kephart
Typesetter
Amelia Aos Showalter

Publishing Director
Emma Nothmann
Editor-in-Chief
Teresa Elsey
Production Manager
Adam R. Perlman
Cartography Manager
Elizabeth Halbert Peterson
Design Manager
Amelia Aos Showalter
Editorial Managers
Briana Cummings, Charlotte Douglas, Ella M. Steim, Joel August Steinhaus, Lauren Truesdell, Christina Zaroulis
Financial Manager
R. Kirkie Maswoswe
Marketing and Publicity Managers
Stef Levner, Leigh Pascavage
Personnel Manager
Jeremy Todd
Low-Season Manager
Clay H. Kaminsky
Production Associate
Victoria Esquivel-Korsiak
IT Director
Matthew DePetro
Web Manager
Rob Dubbin
Associate Web Manager
Patrick Swieskowski
Web Content Manager
Tor Krever
Research and Development Consultant
Jennifer O'Brien
Office Coordinators
Stephanie Brown, Elizabeth Peterson

Director of Advertising Sales
Elizabeth S. Sabin
Senior Advertising Associates
Jesse R. Loffler, Francisco A. Robles, Zoe M. Savitsky
Advertising Graphic Designer
Christa Lee-Chuvala

President
Ryan M. Geraghty
General Manager
Robert B. Rombauer
Assistant General Manager
Anne E. Chisholm

Study Spanish at Academia Kolumbus

Individual and Minigroup Classes

Experienced Teachers

Internships, Volunteering

Salsa Classes, Excursions

Academia Kolumbus
Guanguiltagua N34-596
Quito - Ecuador
Phone: +593/2/2445684
info@academia-kolumbus.com
www.academia-kolumbus.com

DISCOVER ECUADOR

From trail-weary trekkers to lifelong Quiteños, everyone agrees that this corner of South America is a land of extremes. Ecuador is rich with culture, whirls under head-spinning political fluctuations, and dazzles the imagination with some of the world's most astounding geographical diversity. To the east, chilly Andean slopes plummet into the humid Amazon Basin, while in the west, snow-crowned peaks fall to some of the most pristine beach on earth. Indeed, this is a region brimming with superlatives: modern-day Quito was once the northern capital of one of the wealthiest empires in history; the Galápagos are home to the world's largest tortoise population; Volcán Cayambe is the closest point on earth to the stars—yes, even closer than Everest. Offering myriad opportunities for the adventurous of heart and the inquisitive of mind—from beach-bumming to jungle-tripping, museum-hopping to llama-spotting—Ecuador has many secrets to share.

Of course, a look at the foreign media paints Ecuador as even more extreme than it is. If CNN told the story of Ecuador, almost every day in recent years would appear a nausea-inducing roller coaster, with drug wars spilling over the Colombian border, oil-companies destroying acres of land once teaming with life, and indigenous communities striking out against their poor standards of living. In reality, beyond major city centers, life progresses as usual: calmly, coolly, slowly. Ecuador is a place where everything gets done in its own time; if not today, then *mañana, sin falta*.

DIGITS...

NUMBER OF MIDDLES OF THE WORLD: 2, Mitad del Mundo and the town of Cayambe

NUMBER OF SPECIES OF GALÁPAGOS GIANT TORTOISES: 11

NUMBER OF VOLCANOES: 280

NUMBER OF ACTIVE VOLCANOES: 18

PERCENTAGE OF TOTAL LAND AREA THAT IS PROTECTED: 39.2

WHEN TO GO

Though its name may imply hot and humid, Ecuador spans three disparate climates (coast, Sierra, and jungle) that keep things interesting. Nonetheless, two main seasons divide the Ecuadorian year: the **dry winter** from June to September and the **wet summer** from December to April. Along Ecuador's Pacific **coast,** the sweltering heat reflects tropical norms, but bring a sweater—or twelve—for trips

...AND DATA

FAVORITE RODENT CONSUMED IN ECUADOR: Guinea pig *(cuy)*
CLOSEST POINT TO HEAVEN ON EARTH: Volcán Chimborazo (6310m)
LONGEST MOUNTAIN RANGE IN THE WORLD: The Andes
SIXTH COUNTRY IN THE WORLD TO ABOLISH CAPITAL PUNISHMENT: Ecuador (1897)
10TH HIGHEST CITY IN THE WORLD: Quito

into the **Sierra.** The best time to visit the Highlands is during the winter, when clear skies make for drier and happier hiking. The **jungle** (called the "Oriente"), on the other hand, is always wet and warm, never below 77% humidity. The jungle can become utterly impenetrable during the rainy months (Dec.-Apr.).

In the **Galápagos Islands,** hot, rainy weather prevails from January through April, while the rest of the year is dry and cool with the water a chilly 20°C (68°F) or lower. As expected, the temperature gets warmer farther north toward the **equator.** Ecuadorian coasts tend to be warm year-round. Here, the ideal visiting months are between seasons—March through May, when rainfall lightens, and November through December, when the temperature warms. Be aware that during the busy months of July, August, and December, prices for accommodations and transportation rise significantly. All things considered, the **best month** to visit is May: tourist traffic is light, the climate is moderate, and the seas are calm. For wave-lovers, the Galápagos **surfing** season is December through February. If you're there for the animals, research nesting patterns to avoid disappointment. For more specifics, see the climate chart (see p. 16).

Local **festivals and holidays** are another seasonal variation to keep in mind when planning your trip. Go for some crazy fun, but be prepared for crowded accommodations and lots of people. The most important nation-wide holidays are Christmas, Semana Santa (Easter week), Inti Raymi (June 24), and Independence Day (May 24). See the appendix for other festivals and holidays (see p. 354).

WHAT TO DO

Ecuador offers something for everyone. The sections below highlight some of the reasons to visit this country; for more specific regional attractions, see the **Highlights** section at the beginning of each chapter.

JUNGLE JOURNEYS

The Oriente offers the outdoorsy traveler—the contemplative Henry Thoreau-type or the extreme X-Games-type—everything that he desires. Want to go kayaking? Head to Tena (see p. 295) for world-class class IV+ rapids (and anything below) where internationally renowned kayakers have been heading for only the past few years. How about some volcano-scaling or jungle-trekking? Make the jaunts up to the **Antisana Ecological Reserve** (see p. 294) or down to **Parque Nacional Sangay** (see p. 157). Most traditional indigenous culture resides within the Oriente, as well. Head to Quichua, Shuar, Siecoya, Huaorani, and many other communities spread throughout the Oriente. Many communities have ecotourist lodges set up to handle large business retreats and others offer rooming and activities for solo travelers. Most of these communities are only a few kilometers from major Oriente cities, such as Tena, Puyo, and Macas. Others are much deeper into the forest, such as the Achuar of **Yasuní Nacional Park** (see p. 306). Watch shaman demonstrations; go on jungle treks to find medicinal herbs; swing like Tarzan from long, green vines; or howl like a monkey from the top of the rainforest canopy. The best incentive yet—your having fun and learning about the jungle can translate to a sustainable life for indigenous communities of the Oriente. Be an ecotourist and enable the continuation of a slowly vanishing but ancient culture.

MOTHER NATURE'S HOT TUB

So, you've been hiking for days, up to 5000m plus and down again multiple times. You've been city hopping all the way down central Ecuador from **Quito** (see p. 81) to **Guayaquil** (see p. 263). You thought, hey, why can't I, why can't I, and hopped on a giant, older-than-your-great-grandfather tortoise for a ride (please, please, do not do this). And, now you're tired. Well, Ecuador and Mother Nature teamed up a few million years ago to make the world's first—and still the best— hot tubs. At **Baños** (see p. 150), **Papallacta** (see p. 293), and a handful of other places, you can ease those tired bones in pools of steaming, lava-heated water. Many believe the pools have therapeutic value, even healing power. One thing's certain: you won't be complaining when your body goes limp after about 5min. of hot springs-lounging.

WALKING ON CLOUDS

Yes, it is possible at one of Ecuador's many cloud forests. For the size of country it is, Ecuador has a lot of protected forest (see **Digits...**, p. 1), some of which is actually in the clouds. Four major reserves are within 2hr. of Quito: **Reserva Geobotánica Pululahua** (see p. 114), the **Bellavista Cloud Forest Reserve** (see p. 115), **Reserva Maquipucuna** (see p. 116), and **Reserva Los Cedros** (see p. 118). All of these reserves have—you guessed it—cloud forests. These only exist above 1500m, territory usually reserved for hardier plants and animals due to the harsher, drier environment. Around the equator, however, the climate is so wet that a much lusher evergreen environment thrives. Definitely spend a day—or a month—wandering through the

TOP TEN WATERFALLS

10. Alto Macuma: Crystal clear water flows from these cascades outside of Ma█████p. 310. They come wit█████ly formed water slides, as well.

9. Cugusha Falls: In Parque Nacional Sangay (see p. 157). Take a guide, set up camp, and swim in the river.

8. Cascada Ponderosa: In Parque Nacional Podocarpus (p. 186. An easy path leads to this waterfall.

7. Hola Vida: At Hola Vida (see p. 309). Take a walk behind the falls and contemplate nature's beauty.

6. Cascadas San Miguel: The first of 20 falls in Río Verde (see p. 156) that gush over sleek, black volcanic rock.

5. Cavernas de Logroño: The trip to this 30m subter█████an waterfalls is exciting but also dangerous; rains from the hills flood the cave (see p. 315) quickly.

4. Cascada Escondida: A hike in Hola Vida (See p. 309) through chest-deep water leads to it.

3. Pailón del Diablo (Devil's Cauldron): Terrifyingly tall, this waterfall in Río Verde crashes into Río Pastaza far below.

2. Cascadas Gran Edén (Cascadas de Latas): Slide into the pristine pool at the base of these "Tin Falls" on one of the naturally formed slides near Tena (see p. 295).

1. San Rafael Falls: north of Baeza (see p. 292). The most voluminous falls in Ecuador crash down 130m.

forests. You may just fall in love with them and decide to stay for a year, volunteering (see **Alternatives to Tourism: Environmental Conservation,** p. 74) to preserve these havens of biodiversity.

LIVING THE (WILD)LIFE

Fed up with laws that claim Creationism is just as valid an explanation for life on earth as the theory of evolution? Don't want to rely on Charles Darwin for all your facts? Then, head on down to Ecuador to make your own decisions about who came from what. Enormous tortoises, probably older than you'll ever be, slowly plod their ways around the Galápagos. Iguanas, blue-footed boobies, and finches galore (along with a whole lot of other animals found only in the **Galápagos**) make up the rest of the islands' population. That is, except for humans, most of whom reside there making a living off of tourism, and some of whom live there as fishermen (see **Poaching in the Galápagos,** p. 341).

But this fun does come with a high price tag. Government regulation and the little space available for permanent residence or simply vacationing on the Galápagos has made the islands less of a budget traveler's destination. Fear not; a few animals (iguanas and blue-footed boobies, to name a couple) still roam the mainland and coastal islands. **Isla de la Plata** (see p. 246) got the nickname "poor man's Galápagos" for its veritable menagerie of tropical, Galápagos-variety animals in a less pricey locale. Animals this uniquely exotic aren't found anywhere else in the world.

SAVING MOTHER NATURE

Ecuador's been doing a good job with this. Yes, there is logging. Yes, there is oil drilling. Nonetheless, Ecuador has established more than 10 major national parks and many smaller ones—in a country about the size of the US state of Nevada. Its largest, **Yasuní Nacional Park** (see p. 306), shares the same border that the northern Oriente shares with Colombia and Peru. Most who visit this park are scientists conducting research of some sort. But the Oriente contains other national parks, such as **Antisana Ecological Reserve** (see p. 294), **Parque Nacional Llanganates** (see p. 160), **Jatun Sacha Ecological Reserve** (see p. 304), **Parque Nacional Sangay** (see p. 157), and more. Parks deeper into the jungle offer more nature-watching and jungle-trekking activities than those farther west that offer more mountain climbing and lake hiking. Ecuador has also protected territory in the south. **Parque Nacional Podocarpus** (see p. 186), down near **Loja, Zamora,** and **Vilcabamba,** offers hikes along streams and up mountains. Slightly west of Podocarpus is the **Puyango Petrified Forest** (see p. 283) that gives a glimpse of what Ecuador must have looked like a few million years ago. Here nature-lovers will find scenes of flora and fauna, frozen since time immemorial. A little ways north, just outside of Cuenca, is **Parque Nacional Cajas** (see p. 182). Working up the coast by **Guayaquil** (see p. 263), trekkers and animal-lovers will find **Reserva Ecológica Manglares Churute** (see p. 281), **Bosque Protector Cerro Blanco** (see p. 279), **Pueblo Ecológico Alandaluz** (see p. 249), and **Parque Nacional Machalilla** (see p. 243), all great places to wander through. Up north, parks higher in altitude but lower in latitude offer gorgeous hikes through lush and verdant forest through drier and rockier terrain, all the way up to snow-capped peaks and lava-spewing craters. For these experiences, head to **Reserva Cotacachi-Cayapas** (see p. 209), **Reserva Maquipucuna** (see p. 116), **Reserva Los Cedros** (see p. 118), **Reserva Geobotánico Pululahua** (see p. 114), and the **Bella Vista Cloud Forest Reserve** (see p. 115).

BEACH BUMMIN'

No, not all of Ecuador is rapid-riding, peak-bagging, monkey-spotting, or *artesanía*-buying. Ecuador has beaches, too—with quite the hoppin' party scene. From **Jambelí** (see p. 290) down south to **Atacames** (see p. 212) way up north, Ecuador has some of the best beaches in the world. And, it has enough for everyone. Don't like beaches crowded with other tourists and bothersome hagglers? Don't worry. *Let's Go* has found some amazingly pristine and quiet sand. Indeed, our coverage has added **Mompiche,** a beach town only sprung up within the last two years (see p. 220). For partiers, the beaches at **Montañita** (see p. 249) and **Atacames** are the best. Be forewarned that those beaches are less than tranquil, but, thankfully, that means they offer a lot of wild times. For those with a little more cash to burn, set up camp at the eco-friendly lodge at **Hostería Ecológica Alandaluz** (see p. 249) and hang out at its nearly virgin beaches or daytrip to Montañita. But fear not, budget travelers! In and around Montañita inexpensive hotels and hostels abound. True fiesta-fiends should make sure Atacames is at the top of their lists. This town is known throughout Ecuador for throwing the **best parties.**

On the other hand, for some peace and quiet, **Playa Escondida** (see p. 218), not too far from Atacames, really is a "hidden beach." The few who know about it respect it for its tranquility. Get away from it all to rejuvenate here. Or, for a slightly more up-beat time at a place that offers more than just beach, travel to **Bahía de Caráquez** (see p. 225). At Ecuador's coastal mid-point, this city on the shore is a great place to set up a base. Stay for a few days and explore daytrips to beach towns up and down the coast.

▧ LET'S GO PICKS: THE BEST OF ECUADOR

BEST HIGHS: Chimborazo (see p. 162), closest earthly point to heaven; **Cotopaxi** (see p. 136), the world's highest active volcano.

BEST MISNOMERS: Panama hats (see p. 234), headgear actually from Ecuador.

BEST WALK ON THE PREHISTORIC WILD SIDE: Puyango Petrified Forest (see p. 283), where you can wander around 120 million-year-old fossilized Arcadia trees and examine other Triassic Period sea creatures.

BEST RELIGIOUS INTERPRETATION: According to paintings in Quito, Christ ate *cuy* (guinea pig) for his Last Supper.

BEST NEW BEACH: Mompiche (see p. 220), where waves are plentiful and people are sparse.

BEST HAVEN FOR SURF: Montañita (see p. 249), where the parties rock, and the waves roll—all day, everyday.

BEST VIRTUAL GALÁPAGOS: Isla de la Plata (see p. 246), the "poor man's Galápagos."

BEST ARCHITECTURE: La Basílica (see p. 95), where there's a jaw-dropping view of La Virgen from either of the 78m-tall towers.

BEST SPOT TO HOP BETWEEN HEMISPHERES: Mitad del Mundo (see p. 102), at latitude 0°0'0", where an army of hemisphere straddlers dances on the equator, and mothers tell their children to "get back in this hemisphere, right now!"

BEST COUNTRYSIDE ESCAPE: Latacunga Loop (see p. 142), where tranquil life can slow the gait of any big city denizen.

BEST PAMPERING: Baños (see p. 150), where the hot water never runs out. **Papallacta** (see p. 293), where the baths are even better than in Baños.

BEST WHITEWATER: Tena (see p. 295), at a confluence of rivers with world-class rapids.

BEST JUNGLE JUICE: Chicha, a potent concoction of yucca plant fermented by wads of spittle—the Amazonian drink of choice. Cheers!

DISCOVER

SUGGESTED ITINERARIES

CLIMB EVERY MOUNTAIN

PACIFIC OCEAN
COLOMBIA
Cotacachi
Otavalo
Ibarra
Quito
Machachi
Latacunga
Ambato
ECUADOR
Baños
Riobamba
Ingapirca
Cuenca
Cajas
Loja
Vilcabamba
PERU

CLIMB EVERY MOUNTAIN (FOR ABOUT 2 MONTHS)

There's no better way to start a trip in Ecuador than with a week-long stay in **Quito** (see p. 81, 7 days). All its modern amenities make for an easy way to ease into Ecuadorian life. Don't worry about the toothpaste left at home or the lack of hot water commonplace in many other regions of Ecuador—Quito has all that. But it also has some of the most beautiful churches and historic colonial architecture in all of South America. You'll need at least a full week to see the magnificent **La Basílica** (see p. 95), daytrip to **Mitad del Mundo** (see p. 102), wander through **Old Quito,** and visit innumerable other sights. Plus a slow-paced week at 2800m will help acclimate lungs to the mountain air. Travel next to **Otavalo** (see p. 106, 2 days) where *everything's* sold at the Saturday Market. From here take a jaunt up to **Ibarra** (see p. 126, 6 days) for its peaceful parks. Use it as a base from which to visit **San Antonio** (see p. 129) and pick up exquisitely carved, wooden chests and statues. Spend another of the six days visiting **Valle del Choza,** the next at **La Esperanza** (see p. 126), a third conquering **Volcán Imbabura** (see p. 126), and a final day in **Ilumán** (see p. 122) to rest up from the hike. Then travel south, making a few stops along the way back to Quito. First travel a bit to the west to **Cotacachi** (see p. 124, 1 day). If you're up for it, do a little hiking on nearby **Volcán Cotacachi** (see p. 125). Next travel to the town of **Cayambe** (see p. 122, 2 days) where you'll actually be on the equator—in a less hokey environment than Mitad del Mundo—and in close proximity to **Volcán Cayambe** (see p. 122). Then travel straight down to **Machachi and Aloasí** (see p. 131, 4 days) for a first taste of Andes *tranquilo* and a good base to hike **Volcanoes Rumiñahui** (see p. 134) and **Cotopaxi** (see p. 136). (Between hikes, you could even head back to Quito.) Now take a short drive down the Panamerican Hwy. to **Latacunga** (see p. 138, 2 days). From here, set up a base from which to daytrip, or begin to town-hop around the **Latacunga Loop** (see p. 142). Spending time in the north is best. First, hop on over to **Chugchilán** (see p. 144, 3 days) where mountain serenity overtakes villagers and visitors alike. From **Isinlivi** (see p. 145, 2 days), the next town over, set out to peak one or both of the **Ilinizas** (see p. 137), then head on over to **Saquisilí** (see p. 145, 2 days) for a market that means business. From here, jump on a bus to **Ambato** (see p. 146, 1 day) to see an homage to Juan Montalvo, a Literary hero of Ecuador, or, if you come in February, stay for the largest carnival thrown in the whole country. Spend a day enjoying the *artesanía* at **Salasaca** (see p. 149) and then **Pelileo** (see p. 150) before moving on to **Baños** (see p. 150, 7 days), the city for outdoor activity and indoor pampering. Hike, bike, and bathe around town, but beware the temperamental **Volcán Tungurahua;** it's likely to erupt at any moment. Then spend a day mesmerized by the waterfalls at **Río Verde** (see p. 156), a city in limbo—not quite moutains, not quite jungle. Next stop: **Riobamba** (see p. 163, 2 days). Spend a day to check out the city, and another to peak **Volcán Chimborazo** (see p. 162), before heading into **Parque Nacional Sangay** (see p. 157, 3 days) for mountain-climbing, swamp-trekking, and thermal bath-seeking. Keep your eyes peeled for the Andean Tapir, an elusive animal found only here. Next on the list is without a doubt **Cuenca** (see p. 171, 4 days) for the last big city of the Ecuadorian Andes. From here daytrip to the ruins of **Ingapirca** (see p. 179) up north and then to nearby **Baños** (see p. 181, 1 day), not to be confused with the larger Baños to the north. Find good fishing and hiking at **Parque Nacional Cajas** (see p. 182, 2 days) just slightly to the west. Then save time for the towns of **Gualaceo** (see p. 180, 1 day), **Chordeleg** (see p. 180, 1 day), and **San Juan** (see p. 181, 1 day) before journeying farther south to **Saraguro** (see p. 199, 1 day). Next visit **Loja** (see p. 190, 3 days), the largest of the southern cities, to set up base for some daytripping. Your first stop needs to be **Vilcabamba** (see p. 194, 3 days), a town with beautiful character that is also a great place from which to visit **Parque Nacional Podocarpus** (see p. 186), the southern Highlands' gorgeous protected forest. Pause in **Catamayo** (see p. 201, 1 day) before getting even better rest in **Catacocha** (see p. 202, 2 days). Now, go catch a home-bound plane in Guayaquil.

LET'S GO TO THE BEACH

Tonchigüe Atacames
Muisne
Pedernales
Canoa
Manta   Bahía de
         Caráquez
Puerto   Puerto Cayo
López   Salango   ECUADOR
         Montañita
         Salinas

COLOMBIA

Quito

PACIFIC
OCEAN

PERU

LET'S GO TO THE BEACH! (FOR TWO AND A HALF MONTHS!)

Fly into **Quito** (see p. 81), but then head straight to **Atacames** (see p. 212, 7 days) for the absolute best party spot in Ecuador. Hit the beach not for the sand or the water (though both are spectacular) but for the dusk-till-dawn and all-day-long craziness. But, good beaches in Ecuador don't necessarily have to come with the same booze-fest hysteria found in Atacames. Four other spots just to the south—the northernmost one within walking distance—offer escapes (almost) as tranquil as Highlands towns. **Súa** (see p. 216, 2 days) offers a nice beach, better budget accommodations, and short hikes to coves with good views of Atacames. **Same** (see p. 217, 2 days) is the next beach down, and more upscale. It's well-groomed beaches, however, more than compensate. A short drive south will encounter **Playa Escondida** (see p. 218, 2 days), a beautiful spot to swim in the ocean or take long walks on the beach. In fact, a nice hike from Playa Escondida leads all the way to **Tonchigüe** (see p. 218, 2 days), the last of Atacames's neighboring beaches. Save laying out on the sand for later in the trip—fishing-town Tonchigüe's perk is very cheap, but very fresh, seafood. A little farther down, ferry over to the car-free island of **Muisne** (see p. 219, 4 days), where dreams are realized with horse rides at dusk, along virgin beach. But then again, the true virgin beach is back on the mainland, about an hour south at **Mompiche** (see p. 220, 3 days). Black sand, big waves, a few surfers, and inexpensive lodging call this place "home"—and "the next Montañita." Though the last epithet remains to be seen, nothing stands to stop it. Once satisfied, continue on down the coast to **Pedernales** (see p. 221, 1 day). Sort of like Tonchigüe, this town has little to offer in the way of beaches, but it does host the largest market on the west coast. Pick up some goods on the way to **Canoa** (see p. 222, 5 days), one of the most relaxing getaways Ecuador has to offer. Sip daiquiris; lay back in a hammock; then roll on down to **Bahía de Caráquez** (see p. 225, 7 days). This upscale town still offers a lot for the budget traveler. Don't lounge away each day here; the town's got a lot to see—the last remaining dry tropical forest in Ecuador, for example. South from here, go hang-gliding and paragliding at **Crucita** (see p. 229, 3 days). For good beaches and better nightlife, progress to **Manta** (see p. 230, 4 days) where sailors compliment the normal mix of locals and tourists. Take a breather a little ways inland at **Montecristi** (see p. 234, 1 day) and don a locally woven Panama hat before leaving for **Puerto Cayo** (see p. 248, 2 days) to spend a couple of days more on a small-town beach. Then scoot on down to **Puerto López** (see p. 243, 4 days) for some salsa-filled nights (mainly during high-season) and sun-soaked days. Use it as a base to venture into **Parque Nacional Machalilla** (see p. 243, 3 days) for tropical dry forest excursions, boating trips to Isla de la Plata, and pristine beach. The next link in the chain of beaches is **Salango** (see p. 248, 3 days), a great place for snorkeling and scuba diving, as well as learning about the many ancient cultures that used to inhabit its shores. Next head to the not-so-budget but certainly eco-friendly beachfront resort of **Hostería and Pueblo Ecológico Alandaluz** (see p. 249, 4 days). Make sure to go on its interesting ecotours. For a time almost as crazy as the one at Atacames but with better beach, keep moving on to **Montañita** (see p. 249, 7 days). Lounge, surf, wall-climb, paraglide: this town's got it all. Then, after a week of utter debauchery, head to the quiet beach at **Valdivia** (see p. 253, 1 day), before heading to **Ayangue** (see p. 253, 1 day) for a second day of tourist-free tranquility. Pace a little too slow? It's time to get a place at **Salinas** (see p. 254, 4 days), one of the nicest—and most expensive—beaches in Ecuador. Now that you've blown your budget, it's time to head home.

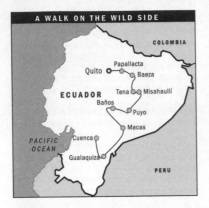

A WALK ON THE WILD SIDE (FOR ABOUT A MONTH AND A HALF) First fly into **Quito** (see p. 81) and hop on a bus bound for **Papallacta** (see p. 293, 4 days) in the Oriente. This town has a knack for easing foreigners into Ecuadorian life. Just kick back and relax at its hot spring baths after a day or two of hiking through verdant forest. Drive on down the road a little ways to **Baeza** (see p. 292, 4 days) for a good base from which to explore the **San Rafael Falls** (see p. 295), **Volcán Reventador** (see p. 294), and the rest of the **Antisana Ecological Reserve** (see p. 294). Spend some time in **Tena** (see p. 295, 10 days) in the only big city (very large town) of the Oriente. At a confluence of rivers that offer some of the best rafting in the world, Tena has plenty of outdoor activities to offer. Use it as an entry point to visit indigenous communities and the deeper regions of the jungle. Not too far north from Tena is **Archidona** (see p. 301), a good place to pick up supplies before spending time (5 days) camping out, staying in local cabañas, or searching for **Petroglyphs** (see p. 301). For a thorough

cross-section of what the Oriente has to offer, move on to **Selva Viva** (see p. 302, 3 days) where an incredible variety of rehabilitating animals live. Be sure to visit the local indigenous community of Runa Huasi. Then drive on over to **Misahuallí** (see p. 303, 1 day) for a taste of the jungle within the borders of a town before heading into the rainforest for a daytrip or longer. **Jatun Sacha** (see p. 304, 2 days) is a jungle that offers contemplative hikes. Find **Puyo** (see p. 306, 3 days) a bit south. Spend time in its outskirts at **Hola Vida** and **Dique de Mera** before heading out to **Baños** (see p. 150, 5 days) for nightly dips in hot springs baths after daily adventures of hiking, biking, riding, and rafting. Then get back on the bus and speed on over to **Macas** (see p. 310, 6 days) for small town atmosphere with all the amenities of a larger city. Use it as a starting point for longer jungle treks, visits to local Shuar communities, or hikes through **Parque Nacional Sangay** (see p. 313). Go on excursions to **Cuevas de Los Tayos** (see p. 314), **Guapu Archaeological Complex** (see p. 314), **Sevilla Don Bosco** (see p. 314), **Tsurakú Community Biological Station and Reserve** (see p. 314), and the **Alto Macuma** (see p. 315) waterfalls. Finish up the Oriente by town-hopping through **Sucúa** (see p. 315, 1 day), **Méndez** (see p. 317), and **Gualaquiza** (see p. 317, 1 day), and then head on over for some big city living in **Cuenca** (see p. 171, 3 days) before heading home.

ULTIMATE ECUADOR! (FOR ABOUT THREE MONTHS) Fly into **Quito** (see p. 81, 7 days) and ease into life in Ecuador. Visit **Mitad del Mundo** (see p. 102) one day and hike **Volcán Pichincha** (see p. 101) another. Take a bus just north to **Mindo** (see p. 111, 7 days) where ecotourism and outdoor adventures abound. Visit the surrounding protected forests: first head to **Reserva Geobotánica Pululahua** (see p. 114), the next day wander over to the **Bellavista Cloud Forest Reserve** (see p. 115), the following day visit **Reserva Maquipucuna** (see p. 116), and the day after that go over to **Reserva Los Cedros** (see p. 118). Spend a day or more at any one. Make sure to save at least one day to explore the **Cochasquí Archaeological Park** (see p. 119), including its 15 truncated pyramids. Then relocate to **Otavalo** (see p. 106, 3 days), a town with great markets that is also a good base for exploring the surrounding

ULTIMATE ECUADOR!

area. One day, visit **Lagunas de Mojandas and Fuya Fuya** (see p. 119). Another, explore **Las Cascadas de Peguche** (see p. 121). Then head to **Cotacachi** (see p. 124, 4 days), the leatherwork capital of Ecuador, that will also serve as a good base from which to hike **Volcán Cotacachi** (see p. 124). Next head to the **Intag Cloud Forest** (see p. 125) and walk on clouds. Next on the list must be **Ibarra** (see p. 126, 3 days), which may be used as a base from which to hike **Volcán Imbabura** (see p. 126), to take many other daytrips, or for a pleasant visit before heading southward again. Before stressing the body too much more, soak in the hot spring baths in **Papallacta** (see p. 293, 2 days). Then move on to **Baeza** (see p. 292) leave your luggage and daytrip to the **San Rafael Falls** (see p. 295). Return to the Andes to **Machachi and Aloasí** (see p. 131, 4 days)— either town is a good base to hike **Volcán Rumiñahui** (see p. 134) and to visit **Parque Nacional Cotopaxi** (see p. 134), where serious hikers will find **Volcán Cotopaxi** (see p. 136) pleasantly challenging. Then, why not bag **The Ilinizas** (see p. 137)? Spend less than a week traveling around the northern half of the **Latacunga Loop** (see p. 142, 5 days), beginning at **Chugchilán** (see p. 144, 2 days); then hike over to **Isinliví** (see p. 145, 1 day), ending at **Saquisilí** (see p. 145, 1 days), for its Saturday market. **Ambato** (see p. 146, 2 days) is the best next stop before going wild in **Baños** (see p. 150, 7 days), where every night hot spring baths will rejuvenate weary bodies. Just a daytrip away is **Río Verde** (see p. 156, 1 day), a town with over 20 waterfalls. Travel over to **Riobamba** (see p. 163, 4 days), a good starting point for

climbing at least part of **Volcán Chimborazo** (see p. 162). Continue on to **Cuenca** (see p. 171, 4 days), and then to **Loja** (see p. 190, 2 days), on the way to **Vilcabamba** (see p. 194, 2 days), where locals believe they drink from a fountain of youth. Drive northward to **Guayaquil** (see p. 263, 4 days), the largest city in Ecuador. Then fly to the **Galápagos** (see p. 320, 7 days) for a cruise around the archipelago. Fly back and go straight to **Montañita** (see p. 249, 5 days), surfers' heaven. Travel up the coast a little ways to **Hostería and Pueblo Ecológico Alandaluz** (see p. 249, 4 days). From here, beach hop up the coast to **Bahía de Caráquez** (see p. 225, 3 days), **Canoa** (see p. 222, 2 days), and **Mompiche** (see p. 220, 2 days), ending at **Atacames** (see p. 212, 3 days) for some hardy partying before heading home.

ECUADOR IN 2 WEEKS

QUICK TRIP: THE ESSENTIALS OF ECUADOR IN 2 WEEKS

Fly into **Quito** (see p. 81, 2 days), and then move on quickly to **Chugchilán** (see p. 144, 1 day), a peaceful mountain escape. Next head on down to **Baños** (see p. 150, 2 days) for a couple of days of relaxation in hot springs. **Cuenca** (see p. 171, 2 days) is a bit of a bus ride south. Try to make time to see the ruins at **Ingapirca** (see p. 179). From there head to **Guayaquil** (see p. 263, 1 day) before going to the beach at **Montañita** (see p. 249, 2 days). Head up the coast to **Mompiche** (see p. 220, 2 days), *Let's Go*'s new find this year, with black sand and killer waves. Go all out during the last couple of vacation days at **Atacames** (see p. 212, 2 days), before hopping on a plane back home.

ESSENTIALS

PLANNING YOUR TRIP

ENTRANCE REQUIREMENTS
Passport (p. 11). Required for all visitors.
Visa (p. 12). Not required for visitors of any English-speaking nations.
Inoculations (p. 20). Travelers arriving from areas currently at risk for yellow fever may be required to show documentation of a yellow fever vaccination. No other inoculations are required, but several are recommended for those traveling to more rural and humid parts of the region.
Work Permit (p. 12). Required for all foreigners planning to work in Ecuador.
Driving Permit (p. 30). Required for all foreigners planning to drive in Ecuador.

EMBASSIES AND CONSULATES

ECUADORIAN CONSULAR SERVICES ABROAD

Australia: Embassy of Ecuador, 11 London Cct., 1st fl., Law Society Building, Canberra ACT 2601, Australia (☎2 6262 5282; fax 6262 5285).

Canada: Embassy of Ecuador, 50 O'Connor St. #316, Ottawa, ON K1P 6L2, Canada (☎613-563-8206; mecuacan@rogers.com).

New Zealand: Consulate of Ecuador, Ferry Building 2nd fl., Quay St., Auckland, New Zealand (☎09 309 0229; fax 303 2931).

United Kingdom and Northern Ireland: Embassy of Ecuador, Flat 3B, 3 Hans Crescent, Knightsbridge, London SW1X OLS, UK (☎020 7584 1367; fax 020 7823 9701).

US: Embassy of Ecuador, 2535 15th St. NW, Washington, D.C. 20009, US (☎202-234-7200; www.ecuador.org).

CONSULAR SERVICES IN ECUADOR

IN QUITO
Bolivia, Eloy Alfaro 2432 (☎2244 830; fax 2244 833), at Fernando Ayarza. Open M-F 8:30am-1pm.

Canada, 6 de Diciembre 2816, 4th fl. (☎2232 040; quito@dfait.maeci.gc.ca), at Paul Rivet. Open M-Th 9am-4pm, F 9am-1pm.

Ireland, Antonio de Ulloa 2651 (☎2451 577; fax 2269 862), at Rumipamba. Open M-F 9am-1pm.

Peru, El Salvador 495 (☎2252 582), at Irlanda. Open M-F 9am-1pm and 3-5pm.

UK (☎2970 800 or 2970 801; fax 2970 807), at Naciones Unidas and República de El Salvador, 14th fl. Open M-Th 8am-noon and 2-3pm, F 8-11:30am.

US (☎2562 890; fax 2502 052), at 12 de Octubre and Patria. Open M-F 8am-12:30pm and 1:30-5pm.

IN GUAYAQUIL

Canada, Córdova 812 (☎2563 580; fax 2314 562), off Manuel Rendón, 21st fl., Of. 4. Open M-F 9am-noon.

Germany (☎2206 867), at Las Monjas and Carlos J. Arosemena.

Sweden (☎2254 111; fax 2254 159), at Via Daule Km6½.

UK, Córdova 623 (☎2560 400 or 2563 850; weekend emergency cell 09 9429 107; fax 2562 641), in the Edificio de Agripac at Padre Solano. Open M-F 8am-6pm.

US (☎2323 570; 24hr. emergency cell 02 9321 152; www.usembassy.org.ec), at 9 de Octubre and García Moreno. Open M-F 7:30am-4:30pm.

TOURIST OFFICES

IN QUITO

■**The South American Explorers (SAE),** Jorge Washington 311 (☎/fax 2225 228; www.saexplorers.org), at Leonidas Plaza, New Town. Canny, English-speaking staff offers honest info. Event listings, lending library, storage, and **maps** galore. First-time visitors should peruse the recommendation sheets (US$1-1.50) of SAE's preferred hostels and restaurants, some great alternatives to tourism (see p. 70), and first-hand reports of crime against tourists. Always looking for **volunteers.** Membership US$50, couples US$80. Open M-W and F 9:30am-5pm, Th 9:30am-8pm, Sa 9am-noon.

Corporation Metropolitana de Turismo (CMT; ☎2551 566), at Reina Victoria and Cordero, New Town, in the park, at the glass kiosk with blue and white trim. Open M-F 9am-5pm. **Branches** at the airport (☎3300 163; open daily 8am-12:30am, depending on flight schedules); in Old Town (García Moreno N12-01 and Mejía; ☎2572 566 or 2283 480; open M-Sa 9am-6pm, Su 9am-4pm); at Museo Nacional del Banco Central (open Tu-Su 9am-5pm). CMT offers **maps** and info on hotels, transport, events, and tours.

Oficina Información Turística (☎2586 591), on Plaza Grande, Old Town. Talk to professional navy-blue-clad officers, either at the office on Pasaje Arzobispal, at the kiosk in the plaza, or on the street. English- and Spanish-speakers provide city info and run 4 tours daily (US$12, children US$4). 2 nocturnal tours provide an alternative to exploring Old Town alone. Price includes admission to churches. Open daily 8:30am-5pm.

Ministerio de Turismo, Eloy Alfaro N32-300, 3rd fl. (☎2507 555; www.vivecuador.com), across from Parque la Carolina, New Town, in a state office. Provides **maps** and info on tours and lodging. Open daily 8:30am-12:30pm and 1:30-5pm.

IN GUAYAQUIL

Ministry of Tourism (☎2568 764; fax 2562 544), at Pichincha and Icaza, 6th fl., across from Banco del Pacífico in the large tan building adorned with paintings. Excellent maps of Guayaquil Centro, the northern suburbs, and Ecuador. Open M-F 9am-5pm.

Dirección Municipalidad de Turismo (☎2524 100, ext. 3477; www.guayaquil.gov.ec), at Malecón and 9 de Octubre in the Municipal building, has information about sights, festivals, cultural events, and museums. Some English spoken. Open M-F 9am-5pm.

DOCUMENTS AND FORMALITIES

PASSPORTS

REQUIREMENTS

Citizens of Australia, Canada, Ireland, New Zealand, the UK, and the US need valid passports to enter Ecuador and to re-enter their home countries. In general, Ecuador does not allow entrance if the holder's passport expires in under six months; returning home with an expired passport is illegal and may result in a fine.

ESSENTIALS

NEW PASSPORTS

Citizens of Australia, Canada, Ireland, New Zealand, the UK, and the US can apply for a passport at any passport office and many post offices and courts of law. Any new passport or renewal application must be filed well in advance of the departure date, though most passport offices offer rush services (about two weeks) for a very steep fee. Citizens living abroad who need a passport or renewal should contact the nearest passport office of their home country.

PASSPORT MAINTENANCE

Photocopy the page of your passport with your photo, as well as your visas, traveler's check serial numbers, and any other important documents. Carry one set of copies in a safe place, apart from the originals, and leave another set at home. If you lose your passport, immediately notify the local police and the nearest embassy or consulate of your home government. To expedite its replacement, you will need to know all information previously recorded and show ID and proof of citizenship. In some cases, a replacement may take weeks to process, and it may be valid only for a limited time. In an emergency, ask for immediate temporary traveling papers that will permit you to re-enter your home country.

VISAS AND WORK PERMITS

VISAS

As of August 2004, for stays shorter than 90 days, citizens of Australia, Canada, Ireland, New Zealand, the UK, the US only need a valid passport to enter Ecuador. Visas are required for longer stays. Double-check entrance requirements at the nearest embassy or consulate of Ecuador (see p. 10) before departure. US citizens can also consult http://travel.state.gov/foreignentryreqs.html.

IDENTIFICATION

When you travel, always carry at least two forms of identification on your person, including a photo ID; a passport and a driver's license or birth certificate is usually adequate. Never carry all of your IDs together; split them up in case of theft or loss, and keep photocopies of all of them in your luggage and at home.

STUDENT, TEACHER, AND YOUTH IDENTIFICATION

The **International Student Identity Card (ISIC)**, the most widely accepted form of student ID, provides discounts on some sights, accommodations, food, and transport; access to a 24hr. emergency helpline; and insurance benefits for US cardholders. To find ISIC discounts on accommodations, restaurants and more, head to the "Discounts" section of www.isic.org. Applicants must be full-time secondary or post-secondary school students at least 12 years of age. Because of the proliferation of fake ISICs, some services (particularly airlines) require additional proof of student identity. The **International Teacher Identity Card (ITIC)** offers teachers the same insurance coverage as the ISIC and similar but limited discounts. For travelers who are 25 years old or under but are not students, the **International Youth Travel Card (IYTC)** also offers many of the same benefits as the ISIC.

Each of these cards costs US$22 or equivalent. ISIC and ITIC cards are valid through the academic year in which they are issued; IYTC cards are valid for one year from the date of issue. Many student travel agencies (see p. 26) issue the cards; for a list of issuing agencies or more information, see the **International Student Travel Confederation (ISTC)** website (www.istc.org).

CUSTOMS

Upon entering Ecuador, you must declare certain items from abroad and pay a duty on the value of those articles if they exceed the allowance established by Ecuador's customs service. Upon departure, you might have to pay a value-added tax of 12% on each purchase made during your visit. In addition, a 10% tax for restaurant and accommodation services rendered may be imposed. Note that goods and gifts purchased at **duty-free** shops abroad are not exempt from duty or sales tax; "duty-free" merely means that you need not pay a tax in the country of purchase. Upon returning home, you must likewise declare all articles acquired abroad and pay a duty on the value of articles in excess of your home country's allowance. In order to expedite your return, make a list of any valuables brought from home and register them with customs before traveling abroad, and be sure to keep receipts for all goods acquired abroad. Note that coca leaves, legal throughout the Andes, are not generally appreciated by customs officials in countries of lower altitudes; **coca leaves are illegal in the US and Australia.**

MONEY

CURRENCY AND EXCHANGE

Take note that Ecuador has adopted the US dollar as its national currency. The currency chart below is based on August 2004 exchange rates between U.S. dollars and Australian dollars (AUS$), Canadian dollars (CDN$), European Union euros (EUR€), New Zealand dollars (NZ$), British pounds (UK£). Check a currency converter (www.xe.com or www.bloomberg.com) or a large newspaper for the latest exchange rates.

Store your money in a variety of forms; ideally, at any given time you will be carrying some cash, some traveler's checks, and an ATM and/or credit card.

US DOLLARS	
AUS$ = US$0.71	US$ = AUS$1.42
CDN$ = US$0.74	US$ = CDN$1.34
EUR€ = US$1.23	US$ = EUR€0.81
NZ$ = US$0.63	US$ = NZ$1.58
UK£ = US$1.84	US$ = UK£0.54

TRAVELER'S CHECKS

Traveler's checks are one of the safest and least troublesome means of carrying funds. American Express and Visa are the most recognized brands. Many banks and agencies sell them for a small commission. Check issuers provide refunds if the checks are lost or stolen, and many provide additional services, such as toll-free refund hotlines abroad, emergency message services, or stolen credit card assistance. Though accepted in Quito, Guayaquil, and Cuenca, all currencies other than the dollar are hassles. After dollarization, few currency exchange places stuck around. In smaller cities, if traveler's checks are accepted, the commission on cashing them is even higher. American Express traveler's cheques are most readily accepted. Ask about toll-free refund hotlines and the location of refund centers when purchasing checks, and always carry emergency cash.

American Express: Checks available with commission at select banks, at all AmEx offices, and online (www.americanexpress.com; US residents only). AmEx cardholders can also purchase checks by phone (☎ 888-269-6669). Checks available in Australian, Canadian, Euro, Japanese, UK, and US currencies. For purchase locations or more information, contact AmEx's service centers: in Australia ☎800 68 80 22; in New Zealand 0508 555 358; in the UK 0800 587 6023; in the US and Canada 800-721-9768; in Ecuador first dial 1 800 999 119, and then 888 937 2639; elsewhere call the US collect at +1 801-964-6665.

Visa: Checks available (generally with commission) at banks worldwide. AAA offers commission-free checks to its members. For the location of the nearest office, call Visa's service centers: in the UK ☎0 800 89 50 78; in the US 800-227-6811; elsewhere, call the UK collect at +44 173 331 8949. Checks available in Canadian, Japanese, Euro, UK, and US currencies.

Travelex/Thomas Cook: Issues V traveler's checks. Members of AAA and affiliated automobile associations receive a 25% commission discount on check purchases. In the US and Canada call ☎800-287-7362; in the UK call 0800 62 21 01; elsewhere call the UK collect at +44 1733 31 89 50.

CREDIT, DEBIT, AND ATM CARDS

Where accepted, **credit cards** often offer superior exchange rates—up to 5% better than the retail rate used by banks and other currency exchange establishments. Credit cards may also offer services such as insurance or emergency help and are sometimes required to reserve hotel rooms or rental cars. **Mastercard, Visa,** and **Diners Club** are the most welcomed; **American Express** cards work at some ATMs. Credit cards are accepted readily throughout most of mainland Ecuador (except for the smallest of towns) but not in the Galápagos.

ATMs are prevalent in larger cities of Ecuador, such as Quito, Guayaquil, and Cuenca. Smaller towns and rural communities have fewer ATMs, but all but the tiniest towns have ATMs, with at least one open 24hr. The Galápagos have few ATMs. Depending on your home bank's system, you can most likely access your personal bank account from abroad. ATMs get the same wholesale exchange rate as credit cards, but there is often a limit on the amount of money you can withdraw per day (usually around US$500). There is typically also a surcharge of US$1-5 per withdrawal, and most banks charge a foreign transaction fee of US$1-5. Be sure to check with your bank about additional fees prior to your departure. Take note that in Ecuador PINs longer than four digits may not work. Before you go, ask your bank if the first four digits of your PIN will be sufficient to use your ATM card, or request a new four-digit PIN to use while in Ecuador.

Debit cards are as convenient as credit cards but have an immediate impact on your funds. They can be used wherever its associated credit card company is accepted, yet the money is withdrawn directly from the holder's checking account. Debit cards often also function as ATM cards and can be used to withdraw cash from associated banks and ATMs throughout Ecuador. The two major international money networks are **Cirrus** (US ☎800-424-7787 or www.mastercard.com) and **Visa/PLUS** (US ☎800-843-7587 or www.visa.com). Banco de Guayaquil owns both Cirrus and Visa/PLUS ATMs throughout Ecuador. More banks own Cirrus ATMs and, overall, there are more Cirrus ATMs in Ecuador.

GETTING MONEY FROM HOME

If you run out of money while traveling, the easiest and cheapest solution is to have someone back home make a deposit to the bank account linked to your credit card or ATM card. Failing that, consider one of the following options. The online **International Money Transfer Consumer Guide** (http://international-money-transfer-consumer-guide.info) may also be of help.

WIRING MONEY

It is possible to ask a bank back home to wire money to a bank in Ecuador by **bank money transfer.** This is the cheapest and slowest way to transfer cash—usually taking several days or more. Larger banks and those accustomed to wiring charge smaller fees. Note that some banks may only release your funds in local currency, potentially sticking you with a poor exchange rate; inquire about this in advance. Money transfer services like **Western Union** are faster and more convenient than bank transfers—but also much pricier. Western Union has many locations world-wide. To find one, visit www.westernunion.com, or call: in Australia ☎800 501 500, in Canada 800-235-0000, in the UK 0800 83 38 33, in the US 800-325-6000, or in Ecuador 800 989 898. Western Union offices are common throughout Ecuador. Money transfer services are also available at **American Express, Thomas Cook,** and **Viamericas** (www.viamericas.com) offices.

US STATE DEPARTMENT (US CITIZENS ONLY)

In serious emergencies only, the US State Department will forward money within hours to the nearest consular office, which will then disburse it according to instructions for a US$30 fee. If you wish to use this service, you must contact the Overseas Citizens Service division of the US State Department (☎317-472-2328; nights, Sundays, and holidays 202-647-4000).

COSTS

The cost of your trip will vary considerably depending on where you go, how you travel, and where you stay. The most significant expense will probably be your round-trip **airfare** to Ecuador (see p. 26) and a **railpass** or **bus pass.** Before you go, spend some time calculating a reasonable daily **budget.**

STAYING ON A BUDGET

To give you a general idea, a bare-bones day in Ecuador (camping or sleeping in hos-tels/guesthouses, buying food at supermarkets) would cost about US$15; a slightly more comfortable day (sleeping in hostels/guesthouses and the occasional budget hotel, eating one meal per day at a restaurant, going out at night) would cost US$20; and for a luxurious day, the sky's the limit. Don't forget to factor in emergency reserve funds (at least US$200) when planning how much money you'll need. Keep in mind that cost of living is slightly higher in big cities, and lower in small towns and rural areas; the Highlands and Galápagos are the most expensive (no less than US$20 per day), the Oriente the least (tight budget US$7-8 per day).

TIPS FOR SAVING MONEY

Some simpler ways include searching out opportunities for free entertainment, splitting accommodation and food costs with trustworthy fellow travelers, and buying food in supermarkets rather than eating out. Bring a sleepsack (see p. 16), and do your laundry in the sink (unless you're explicitly prohibited from doing so). That said, don't go overboard. Though staying within your budget is important, don't do so at the expense of your health or a great travel experience.

TIPPING AND BARGAINING

Generally, **tipping** is not common and not expected, although some fancier restau-rants include a small (5-10%) tip on the bill. It is also rare to tip for services, but on occasion it is appropriate to tip for maid service or for a guide or porter; in many cases, these people count on a small bonus. Tips are expected on some tours.

In some places it's okay to **bargain,** and a little practice can make it worth the effort. Bargaining for rooms works best in the low season and it's not hard to get prices lowered at markets or from street vendors. It is also acceptable to bargain with taxi drivers, though an excessively low first bid may send the *tax-ista* on his way without you. While bargaining is the norm, travelers need not bargain down to a price that is clearly unreasonable. In countries such as

Ecuador where the cost of living is already dirt cheap, the discount of pennies or a dollar received by a foreigner might mean a lot more in the pocket of a local vendor. A good rule of thumb is to ask a local what the price should be, and then bargain from special *gringo* prices. Advertised prices in restaurants and shops are generally non-negotiable.

TAXES

Ecuadorian businesses charge a **sales tax (IVA)** of 12%, which you should expect to appear on the bill. The real whammy, though, hits the traveler on the way out with airport/departure taxes (in Guayaquil, US$10; in Quito, US$25).

Temp. (°C/°F) Precipitation (mm)	January			April			July			October		
	°C	°F	mm	°C	°F	mm	°C	°F	mm	°C	°F	mm
Guayaquil	26.2	97.2	224	26.7	80.1	180	24.0	75.2	1.9	24.4	75.9	2.8
Loja	15.9	60.6	84	16.3	61.3	89	14.8	58.6	52	16.2	61.2	61
Quito	13.6	56.5	90	13.5	56.3	165	13.6	56.5	29	13.2	55.8	94
San Cristóbal	25.0	77.0	60	25.9	78.6	75	22.4	72.3	7.4	22.0	71.6	6.2

PACKING

Pack lightly: Lay out only what you absolutely need, then take half the clothes and twice the money. Remember that weather in Ecuador is extremely variable and elevation dependent. Be prepared for frigid nights in the Highlands and extreme humidity in the jungle. The Travelite FAQ (www.travelite.org) is a good resource for tips on traveling light. The online **Universal Packing List** (http://upl.codeq.info) will generate a customized list of suggested items based on your trip length, the expected climate, your planned activities, and other factors. If you plan to do a lot of hiking, also consult **Camping and the Outdoors,** p. 37.

Luggage: If you plan to cover most of your itinerary by foot, a sturdy **frame backpack** is unbeatable. For the basics on buying a pack, see p. 40. Toting a **suitcase** or **trunk** is fine if you plan to live in 1 or 2 cities and explore from there but not a great idea if you plan to move around frequently. In addition to your main piece of luggage, a **daypack** is useful.

Clothing: No matter when you're traveling, it's a good idea to bring a warm jacket or wool sweater, a rain jacket (Gore-Tex® is both waterproof and breathable), sturdy shoes or hiking boots, and thick socks. Flip-flops or waterproof sandals are must-haves for grubby hostel showers. You may also want 1 outfit for going out, and maybe a nicer pair of shoes. If you plan to visit religious or cultural sites, remember that you will need modest and respectful dress. Veer away from tank tops and shorts. Clothing should keep you cool by day and warm at night. Buy rubber boots for wet weather in the Oriente.

Sleepsack: Some hostels require that you either provide your own linen or rent sheets from them. Save cash by making your own sleepsack: fold a full-size sheet in half the long way, then sew it closed along the long side and one of the short sides.

Converters and Adapters: In Ecuador, electricity is 120-127 volts AC. All of North America operates at 120 volts. Americans and Canadians need only buy an adapter (which changes the shape of the plug; US$5). The extra 7 volts should not require them to buy converters (which change the voltage; US$20-$30). Citizens of Australia, New Zealand, the UK, and any other nation with electricity different from 120 volts do need to buy converters. Don't make the mistake of using only an adapter (unless appliance instructions explicitly state otherwise). For more on all things adaptable, check out http://kropla.com/electric.htm.

Toiletries: Toothbrushes, towels, cold-water soap, talcum powder (to keep feet dry), deodorant, razors, tampons, and condoms are often available but may be difficult to find; bring extras. Contact lenses are likely to be expensive and difficult to find, so bring enough extra pairs and solution for your entire trip. Also bring your glasses and a copy of your prescription in case you need emergency replacements. If you use heat-disinfection, either switch temporarily to a chemical disinfection system (check first to make sure it's safe with your brand of lenses), or buy a converter to 220/240V. It's also a good idea to carry a small roll of toilet paper with you; many places don't provide it.

First-Aid Kit: For a basic first-aid kit, pack bandages, a pain reliever, antibiotic cream, a thermometer, a Swiss Army knife, tweezers, moleskin, decongestant, motion-sickness remedy, diarrhea or upset-stomach medication (Pepto Bismol or Imodium), an antihistamine, sunscreen, insect repellent, burn ointment, and a syringe for emergencies (get an explanatory letter from your doctor). Always remember to pack sharp items in checked luggage rather than in your carry-on to avoid delaying bag searches.

Film: Film and developing are of poor quality in Ecuador. Consider bringing enough film for your entire trip and developing it at home. Despite disclaimers, airport security X-rays can fog film, so buy a lead-lined pouch at a camera store or ask security to hand-inspect it. Always pack film in your carry-on luggage, since higher-intensity X-rays are used on checked luggage. If you plan on taking a lot of pictures, airmail your film home, labelling it "Exposed Film. Do not X-ray."

Other Useful Items: For safety purposes, you should bring a **money belt** and small **padlock.** A plastic water bottle, compass, waterproof matches, pocketknife, sunglasses, sunscreen, and hat may also prove useful. Quick repairs of torn garments can be done on the road with a needle and thread; also consider bringing electrical tape for patching tears. If you want to do laundry by hand, bring detergent, a small rubber ball to stop up the sink, and string for a makeshift clothes line. Other things you might forget are sealable **plastic bags** (for food, damp clothes, soap, shampoo, and other spillables); an **alarm clock;** safety pins; rubber bands; a flashlight; earplugs; garbage bags; and a small **calculator.** A cell phone can be a lifesaver (literally) on the road (see p. 36).

Important Documents: Don't forget your passport, traveler's checks, ATM and/or credit cards, adequate ID, and photocopies of all of the aforementioned in case these documents are lost or stolen (see p. 12). Also check that you have any of the following that might apply to you: a hosteling membership card (see p. 37); driver's license (see p. 12); travel insurance forms; ISIC card (p. 12).

SAFETY AND HEALTH

GENERAL ADVICE

In any type of crisis situation, the most important thing to do is **stay calm.** Your country's embassy abroad (see p. 10) is usually your best resource when things go wrong; registering with that embassy upon arrival in the country is often a good idea. The government offices listed in the **Travel Advisories** box below can provide information on the services they offer their citizens in case of emergencies abroad.

DRUGS AND ALCOHOL

A meek "I didn't know it was illegal" will not suffice. While in Ecuador, you are subject to Ecuador's laws, and it is your responsibility to familiarize yourself with these before leaving. The US and Ecuador have teamed up in the War on Drugs; those caught in possession of drugs can expect extended pre-trial detention in poor prison conditions and a lengthy prison sentence if convicted. If you carry pre-

ESSENTIALS

scription drugs while you travel, it is vital to have the prescriptions themselves and a note from a doctor, both readily accessible at borders. Also be aware that some prescription drugs and traditional herbal remedies readily available in Ecuador may be illegal in your home country. Coca-leaf tea, for example, though easy to acquire in Ecuador, is illegal in many nations, including the US.

Drinking in Latin America is not for amateurs; non-tourist bars are often strongholds of machismo. When someone calls you "amigo" and orders you a beer, bow out quickly unless you want to match him glass for glass in a challenge. Female travelers should also be wary of people who offer to buy them drinks. Avoid public drunkenness; it can jeopardize your safety and earn the disdain of locals.

SPECIFIC CONCERNS

NATURAL DISASTERS

Be ready for the worst. Ecuador's climate can be very unpredictable. Read daily updates on the status of active volcanoes. In the Oriente, heavy rain and mudslides fell trees and roll boulders that can block roads for days or longer.

VOLCANO ERUPTIONS. Ecuador has many volcanos, though few are active. **Guagua Pichincha** erupted in 1998, but has since been fairly inactive. **Reventador** (see p. 294) exploded in 2002, and, though still active, is not a serious threat. Watch out for **Tungurahua** (see p. 146), which has a history of extreme volatility. Ecuador has set its alert status to orange: it is dangerous and needs to be monitored, but it does not present an immediate threat.

HEAVY RAINS. Ecuador is wettest from December through May. Heavy rains that cause flooding and landslides fall sporadically during this period. In more remote areas, roads may disappear for months. Check with locals and your local consular services about road conditions in jungle and rural areas before heading to them.

DEMONSTRATIONS AND POLITICAL GATHERINGS

Since dollarization, many complain about the lack of money and jobs. The indigenous population historically has been short-ended, and the government has a pension for corruption. Angry groups often voice their complaints in the form of political gatherings and public demonstrations, though these events tend not to be violent. Insurgents will often block thoroughfares, such as the Panamerican Hwy. around Quito, to make their voices heard.

TERRORISM

The box on travel advisories lists offices to contact and webpages to visit to get the most updated list of your home country's government's advisories about travel. Most international terrorism in Ecuador comes from Colombia. Civil workers from many different nations have been kidnapped and even murdered near Ecuador's border with Colombia. National terrorism is of the social unrest variety. Any tourist in Ecuador should always be aware of local uprisings.

PERSONAL SAFETY

EXPLORING AND TRAVELING

To avoid unwanted attention, try to blend in as much as possible. Respecting local customs (in many cases, dressing more conservatively than you would at home) may placate would-be hecklers. Familiarize yourself with your surroundings before setting out, and carry yourself with confidence. Check maps

ESSENTIALS

in shops and restaurants rather than on the street. If you are traveling alone, be sure someone at home knows your itinerary, and never admit that you're by yourself. When walking at night, stick to busy, well-lighted streets, and avoid dark alleyways. If you ever feel uncomfortable, leave the area as quickly and directly as you can.

There is no sure-fire way to avoid every threatening situation you might encounter while traveling, but a good **self-defense course** will give you concrete ways to react to unwanted advances. **Impact, Prepare, and Model Mugging** can refer you to local self-defense courses in the US (☎800-345-5425; www.impactsafety.org). Workshops (1½-3hr.) start at US$75; full courses (20-25hr.) run US$350-400.

If you are using a **car,** learn local driving signals and wear a seatbelt. Children under 18kg should ride only in specially designed carseats, available for a small fee from most car rental agencies. Study route maps before you hit the road, and if you plan on spending a lot of time driving, consider bringing spare parts. If your car breaks down, wait for the police to assist you. For long drives in desolate areas, invest in a cellular phone and a roadside assistance program (see p. 36). Park your vehicle in a garage or well traveled area, and use a steering wheel locking device in larger cities. Sleeping in your car is one of the most dangerous (and often illegal) ways to get your rest. For info on the perils of hitchhiking, see p. 32.

POSSESSIONS AND VALUABLES

Never leave your belongings unattended. Bring your own **padlock** for hostel lockers, and don't ever store valuables in any locker. Be particularly careful on buses and trains; horror stories abound about determined thieves who wait for travelers to fall asleep. Carry your backpack in front of you where you can see it. When alone, use good judgment in selecting a train compartment: never stay in an empty one, and use a lock to secure your pack to the luggage rack. Try to sleep on top bunks with your luggage stored above you (if not in bed with you), and keep important documents and other valuables on your person.

There are a few steps you can take to minimize the financial risk associated with traveling. First, bring as little with you as possible. Second, buy a few combination padlocks to secure your belongings either in your pack or in a hostel or train station locker. Third, carry as little cash as possible. Keep your traveler's checks and ATM/credit cards in a money belt—not a "fanny pack"—along with your passport and ID cards. Fourth, keep a small cash reserve separate from your primary stash. This should be about US$50 sewn into or stored in the depths of your pack, along with your traveler's check numbers and important photocopies.

In large cities **con artists** often work in groups and may involve children. Beware of certain classics: sob stories that require money, rolls of bills "found" on the street, mustard spilled (or saliva spit) onto your shoulder to distract you while they snatch your bag. Some furtively slice packs with razors and wait for valuables to fall out. **Never let your passport and your bags out of your sight.** Beware of **pickpockets** in city crowds, especially on public transportation. Also, be alert in public telephone booths: If you must say your calling card number, do so very quietly; if you punch it in, make sure no one can look over your shoulder.

If you will be traveling with electronic devices such as a laptop computer or a PDA, check whether your homeowner's insurance covers loss, theft, or damage when you travel. If not, you might consider purchasing a low-cost, separate insurance policy. **Safeware** (☎ US 800-800-1492; www.safeware.com) specializes in covering computers and charges US$90 for 90-day comprehensive international travel coverage up to US$4000. Do keep in mind that there are few places to use laptops outside of the larger cities of Ecuador. If you plan to do most of your traveling in small towns and other remote areas, consider leaving laptops and other electronic devices at home. Unusable gadgets become extra, uncomfortable weight quickly.

PRE-DEPARTURE HEALTH

In your **passport,** write the names of any people you wish to be contacted in case of a medical emergency, and list any allergies or medical conditions. Matching a prescription to a foreign equivalent is not always easy, safe, or possible, so if you take prescription drugs, consider carrying up-to-date, legible prescriptions or a statement from your doctor stating the medication's trade name, manufacturer, chemical name, and dosage. While traveling, be sure to keep all medication with you in your carry-on luggage. For tips on packing a basic **first-aid kit** and other health essentials, see p. 40.

IMMUNIZATIONS AND PRECAUTIONS

Travelers should make sure that the following vaccines are up to date: MMR (for measles, mumps, and rubella); DTaP or Td (for diphtheria, tetanus, and pertussis); IPV (for polio); Hib (for *haemophilus* influenza B); and HepB (for Hepatitis B). Adults traveling to the developing world on trips longer than four weeks should consider the following additional immunizations: Hepatitis A vaccine and/or immune globulin (IG), an additional dose of Polio vaccine, typhoid and cholera vaccines, particularly if traveling off the beaten path, as well as a meningitis vaccine, Japanese encephalitis vaccine, rabies vaccine, and yearly influenza vaccines. While yellow fever is only endemic to parts of South America, Ecuador may deny entrance to travelers arriving from these zones without a certificate of vaccination (see p. 10). For recommendations on immunizations and prophylaxis, consult the CDC (see below) in the US or the equivalent in your home country, and check with a doctor for guidance.

INSURANCE

Travel insurance covers four areas: medical/health problems, property loss, trip cancellation/interruption, and emergency evacuation. Though regular insurance policies may extend to travel-related accidents, you may consider purchasing separate insurance if the cost of potential trip cancellation, interruption, or emergency medical evacuation is greater than you can absorb. Prices for travel insurance purchased separately generally run about US$50 per week for full coverage, while trip cancellation/interruption may be purchased separately at a rate of US$3-5 per day depending on length of stay. **Medical insurance** (especially uni-

PRE-DEPARTURE HEALTH ■ 21

INOCULATION REQUIREMENTS AND RECOMMENDATIONS
Centers for Disease Control (CDC) maintains a very comprehensive and detailed database of information for people traveling abroad. As of June 2004 they recommend protection against the following diseases:

Hepatitis A: ask your doctor about Harvix or an injection of **immune globulin.**

Hepatitis B: if you might be exposed to blood, have sexual contact on the road, stay more than 6 months in the region, or be exposed through medical treatment. Infants and 11- to 12-year-olds who have not gone through the series of HepB vaccinations should.

Malaria: travelers to the coast, jungle, or rural areas may want to take weekly prescription anti-malarial drugs.

Rabies: if you might be exposed to animals through your work or recreation.

Typhoid: particularly if you are visiting rural areas in Ecuador.

Yellow fever vaccination: if you will be traveling outside urban areas

Tetanus-diptheria and measles: booster doses as needed.

versity policies) often covers costs incurred abroad. **US Medicare** does not cover foreign travel. **Canadian** provincial health insurance plans increasingly do not cover foreign travel; check with the provincial Ministry of Health or Health Plan Headquarters for details. **Homeowners' Insurance** often covers theft during travel and loss of travel documents (passport, plane ticket, railpass, etc.) up to US$500.

ISIC and **ITIC** (see p. 12) provide basic insurance benefits to US cardholders, including US$100 per day of in-hospital sickness for up to 60 days and US$5000 of accident-related medical reimbursement (see www.isicus.com). Cardholders have access to a toll-free 24hr. helpline for medical, legal, and financial emergencies overseas. **American Express** (US ☎ 800-528-4800) grants most cardholders automatic collision and theft car rental insurance and ground travel accident coverage of US$100,000 on flight purchases made with the card.

INSURANCE PROVIDERS
STA (see p. 26) offers a range of plans that can supplement your basic coverage. Other private insurance providers in the US and Canada include: **Access America** (☎ 800-284-8300; www.accessamerica.com); **Berkely Group** (☎ 800-797-4514; www.berkely.com); **Globalcare Travel Insurance** (☎ 800-821-2488; www.globalcare-cocco.com); **Travel Assistance International** (☎ 800-821-2828; www.europ-assistance.com); and **Travel Guard** (☎ 800-826-4919; www.travelguard.com). **Columbus Direct** (☎ 020 7375 0011; www.columbusdirect.co.uk) operates in the UK and **AFTA** (☎ 02 9264 3299; www.afta.com.au) in Australia.

USEFUL ORGANIZATIONS AND PUBLICATIONS
The US **Centers for Disease Control and Prevention** (**CDC;** ☎ 877-FYI-TRIP; fax 888-232-3299; www.cdc.gov/travel) maintains an international travelers' hotline and an informative website. The CDC's comprehensive booklet *Health Information for International Travel* (The Yellow Book), an annual rundown of disease, immunization, and general health advice, is free online or US$29-40 via the Public Health Foundation (☎ 877-252-1200; http://bookstore.phf.org). Consult the appropriate government agency of your home country for consular information sheets on health, entry requirements, and other issues for various countries (see p. 19). For quick information on health and other travel warnings, call the **Overseas Citizens Services** (☎ 888-407-4747 M-F 8am-8pm; after-hours 202-647-4000; 317-472-2328 from overseas), or contact a passport agency, embassy, or consulate abroad. For information on medical evacuation services and travel insurance firms, see the US

government's website at http://travel.state.gov/medical.html or the **British Foreign and Commonwealth Office** (www.fco.gov.uk). For general health info, contact the **American Red Cross** (☎ 800-564-1234; www.redcross.org).

STAYING HEALTHY

Common sense is the simplest prescription for good health while you travel. Drink lots of fluids to prevent dehydration and constipation. Though locals may drink tap water, use caution if you choose to do so. It may contain bacteria or other chemicals a traveler's stomach cannot handle. To be safe, drink bottled water or purify your own. Steer clear of street vendor food; it may set even the hardiest of stomachs on fire. In the same vein, eat meat only if it is thoroughly cooked.

Always be sure to wear sturdy, broken-in shoes and clean socks. Especially if you're camping, check socks and shoes for bugs before putting them on. Keeping socks packed away and tapping out shoes should keep your feet bug bite free.

ONCE IN ECUADOR

ENVIRONMENTAL HAZARDS

Heat exhaustion and dehydration: Heat exhaustion leads to nausea, excessive thirst, headaches, and dizziness. Avoid it by drinking plenty of fluids, eating salty foods (e.g. crackers), abstaining from dehydrating beverages (e.g. alcohol and caffeinated beverages), and always wearing sunscreen. Continuous heat stress can eventually lead to heatstroke, characterized by a rising temperature, severe headache, delirium and cessation of sweating. Victims should be cooled off with wet towels and taken to a doctor.

Sunburn: Always wear sunscreen (SPF 30 is good) when spending excessive amounts of time outdoors. If you are planning on spending time near water, in the desert, or in the snow, you are at a higher risk of getting burned—even through clouds. If you get sunburned, drink more fluids than usual and apply an aloe-based lotion. Severe sunburns can lead to sun poisoning, a condition that affects the entire body, causing fever, chills, nausea, and vomiting. Sun poisoning should always be treated by a doctor.

Hypothermia and frostbite: A rapid drop in body temperature is the clearest sign of overexposure to cold. Victims may also shiver, feel exhausted, have poor coordination or slurred speech, hallucinate, or suffer amnesia. *Do not let hypothermia victims fall asleep.* To avoid hypothermia, keep dry, wear layers, and stay out of the wind. When the temperature is below freezing, watch out for frostbite. If skin turns white or blue, waxy, and cold, do not rub the area. Drink warm beverages, stay dry, and slowly warm the area with dry fabric or steady body contact until a doctor can be found. Especially when in the Andes, be aware of getting too cold.

High altitude: Allow your body a couple of days to adjust to less oxygen before exerting yourself. Note that alcohol is more potent and UV rays are stronger at high elevations.

INSECT-BORNE DISEASES

Many diseases are transmitted by insects—mainly mosquitoes, fleas, ticks, and lice. Be aware of insects in wet or forested areas, especially while hiking and camping; wear long pants and long sleeves, tuck your pants into your socks, and use a mosquito net. Use insect repellents such as DEET and soak or spray your gear with permethrin (licensed in the US only for use on clothing). **Mosquitoes**—responsible for malaria, dengue fever, yellow fever, and Japanese encephalitis, among others—can be particularly dangerous in wet, swampy, or wooded areas. **Ticks**—responsible for Lyme and other diseases—are more of a nuisance of the outdoors than a threat to life in Ecuador. In Ecuador, mosquitoes and ticks are most prevalent in rural and jungle areas. Far fewer of these bugs make it to cities and towns, especially those of the Highlands.

Malaria: Transmitted by *Anopheles* mosquitoes that bite at night. The incubation period varies 10 days-4 weeks. Early symptoms include fever, chills, aches, and fatigue, followed by high fever and sweating, sometimes with vomiting and diarrhea. See a doctor for any flu-like sickness that occurs after travel in a risk area. To reduce the risk, use mosquito repellent, particularly in the evenings and when visiting forested areas. See a doctor at least 4-6 weeks before a trip to a high-risk area to get up-to-date malaria prescriptions and recommendations. A doctor may prescribe oral prophylactics, like **mefloquine** or **doxycycline.** Be aware that mefloquine can have very serious side effects, including paranoia, psychotic behavior, and nightmares.

Dengue fever: An "urban viral infection" transmitted by *Aedes* mosquitoes, which bite during the day rather than at night. The incubation period is 3-14 days, usually 4-7 days. Early symptoms include a high fever, severe headaches, swollen lymph nodes, and muscle aches. Many patients also suffer from nausea, vomiting, and a pink rash. If you experience these symptoms, see a doctor immediately, drink plenty of liquids, and take fever-reducing medication such as acetaminophen (Tylenol). *Never take aspirin to treat dengue fever.* There is no vaccine available for dengue fever.

Venezuelan equine encephalitis: Another mosquito-borne disease, most prevalent during the rainy season in rural, agricultural areas near rice fields and livestock pens. Most cases have mild flu-like symptoms of fever, chills, headaches, abdominal pains. If the disease progresses to the central nervous system, symptoms include delirium, fear of light, and disorientation. If the disease does progress to the CNS, coma and death follow within a week. Though rarely fatal, go to a hospital as soon as any symptoms appear. There is a vaccine for VEE, but the best way not to be infected is by taking the proper precautions. Use mosquito repellents containing DEET, and sleep under mosquito nets.

Yellow fever: A viral disease transmitted by mosquitoes; derives its name from one of its most common symptoms, the jaundice caused by liver damage. While most cases are mild, the severe ones begin with fever, headache, muscle pain, nausea, and abdominal pain before progressing to jaundice, vomiting of blood, and bloody stools. While there is no specific treatment, there is an effective vaccine that offers 10 years of protection. International regulations require proof of vaccination for travel to Ecuador from nations with yellow fever outbreaks.

Other insect-borne diseases: Lymphatic filariasis is a roundworm infestation transmitted by mosquitoes. Infection causes enlargement of extremities and has no vaccine. **Leishmaniasis** is a parasite transmitted by sand flies. Common symptoms are fever, weakness, and swelling of the spleen, as well as skin sores weeks to months after the bite. There is a treatment, but no vaccine. **CHAGAS disease (American trypanomiasis)** is another relatively common parasite transmitted by the cone nose and kissing bug, which infest mud, adobe, and thatch. Its symptoms are fever, heart disease, and later, an enlarged intestine. There is no vaccine and limited treatment.

FOOD- AND WATER-BORNE DISEASES

Be sure that your food is properly cooked and the water you drink is clean. Peel fruits and vegetables and avoid tap water (including ice cubes and anything washed in tap water, like salad). Watch out for food from markets or street vendors that may have been cooked in unhygienic conditions. Other culprits are raw shellfish, unpasteurized milk, and sauces containing raw eggs. Buy bottled water, or purify your own water by bringing it to a rolling boil or treating it with **iodine tablets;** note, however, that some parasites such as *giardia* have exteriors that resist iodine treatment, so boiling is more reliable. Always wash your hands before eating or bring a quick-drying purifying liquid hand cleaner. Rural areas of Ecuador are at the greatest risk of having unclean water supplies.

Traveler's diarrhea: Results from drinking contaminated water or eating uncooked and contaminated foods. Symptoms include nausea, bloating, and urgency. Try quick-energy, non-sugary foods with protein and carbohydrates to keep your strength up. Over-the-counter anti-diarrheals (e.g. Imodium) may counteract the problems. The most dangerous side effect is dehydration; drink 8 oz. of water with ½ tsp. of sugar or honey and a pinch of salt, try uncaffeinated soft drinks, or eat salted crackers. If you develop a fever or your symptoms don't go away after 4-5 days, consult a doctor. Consult a doctor immediately for treatment of diarrhea in children.

Dysentery: Results from a serious intestinal infection caused by certain bacteria in contaminated food or water. The most common type is bacillary dysentery. Symptoms include bloody diarrhea (sometimes mixed with mucus), fever, and abdominal pain and tenderness. Bacillary dysentery generally only lasts a week, but it is highly contagious. Amoebic dysentery, which develops more slowly, is a more serious disease and may cause long-term damage if left untreated. A stool test can determine which kind you have; seek medical help immediately. Dysentery can be treated with the drugs norfloxacin or ciprofloxacin (commonly known as Cipro). If you are traveling in high-risk (especially rural) regions, consider obtaining a prescription before you leave home. Dehydration can be a problem; be sure to drink plenty of water or eat salted crackers.

Cholera: An intestinal disease caused by bacteria in contaminated food. Severe diarrhea, dehydration, vomiting, and muscle cramps are symptoms. If left untreated, it may be deadly—even within a few hours. Antibiotics are available, but the most important treatment is rehydration. There is no vaccine available in the US.

Hepatitis A: A viral infection of the liver acquired primarily through contaminated water, including through shellfish from contaminated water. Symptoms include fatigue, fever, loss of appetite, nausea, dark urine, jaundice, vomiting, aches and pains, and light stools. The risk is highest in rural areas and the countryside, but it is also present in urban areas. Ask your doctor about the Hepatitis A vaccine (Havrix or Vaqta) or an injection of immune globulin (IG; formerly called gamma globulin).

Giardiasis: Transmitted through parasites (microbes, tapeworms, etc. in contaminated water and food) and acquired by drinking untreated water from streams or lakes. Symptoms include diarrhea, abdominal cramps, bloating, fatigue, weight loss, and nausea. If untreated it can lead to severe dehydration.

Schistosomiasis: A parasitic disease caused when the larvae of certain freshwater snail species penetrate unbroken skin. Symptoms include an itchy localized rash, followed in 4-6 weeks by fever, fatigue, headaches, muscle and joint aches, painful urination, diarrhea, nausea, loss of appetite, and night sweats. To avoid it, don't swim in fresh water in areas with poor sanitation; if exposed to untreated water, rub the area vigorously with a towel and apply rubbing alcohol.

Typhoid fever: Caused by the salmonella bacteria; **common in villages and rural areas in South America.** While mostly transmitted through contaminated food and water, it may also be acquired by direct contact with another person. Early symptoms include a persistent, high fever, headaches, fatigue, loss of appetite, constipation, and sometimes a rash on the abdomen or chest. Antibiotics can treat typhoid, but a vaccination (70-90% effective) is recommended.

OTHER INFECTIOUS DISEASES

Rabies: Transmitted through the saliva of infected animals; fatal if untreated. By the time symptoms (thirst and muscle spasms) appear, the disease is in its terminal stage. If you are bitten, wash the wound thoroughly, seek immediate medical care, and try to have the animal located. A rabies vaccine, which consists of 3 shots given over a 21-day period, is available and recommended for developing world travel but is only semi-effective. Rabies is often transmitted through dogs.

Hepatitis B: A viral infection of the liver transmitted via blood or other bodily fluids. Symptoms, which may not surface until years after infection, include jaundice, loss of appetite, fever, and joint pain. It is transmitted through activities like unprotected sex, injections of illegal drugs, and unprotected health work. A 3-shot vaccination sequence is recommended for health-care workers, sexually-active travelers, and anyone planning to seek medical treatment abroad; it must begin 6 months before traveling.

AIDS and HIV: For detailed information on Acquired Immune Deficiency Syndrome (AIDS) in Ecuador, call the US Centers for Disease Control's 24hr. hotline at ☎800-342-2437, or contact the Joint United Nations Programme on HIV/AIDS (UNAIDS), 20, ave. Appia, CH-1211 Geneva 27, Switzerland (☎+41 22 791 3666; fax 22 791 4187). Note that Ecuador denies visas for work or study to those who test positive for HIV or AIDS. Contact the consulate of Ecuador for information.

Sexually transmitted diseases (STDs): Gonorrhea, chlamydia, genital warts, syphilis, herpes, and other STDs are more common than HIV and can cause serious complications. **Hepatitis** B and C can also be transmitted sexually. Though condoms may protect you from some STDs, oral or even tactile contact can lead to transmission. If you think you may have contracted an STD, see a doctor immediately.

OTHER HEALTH CONCERNS

MEDICAL CARE ON THE ROAD

Travelers in rural areas will find understaffed hospitals that lack the capacity to treat serious sickness or injury. Some small town hospitals offer helicopter service to the nearest big city, but do not count on it. If you are concerned about obtaining medical assistance while traveling, you may wish to employ special support services. The *MedPass* from **GlobalCare, Inc.,** 6875 Shiloh Rd. East, Alpharetta, GA 30005, USA (☎800-860-1111; www.globalcare.net), provides 24hr. international medical assistance, support, and medical evacuation resources. The **International Association for Medical Assistance to Travelers (IAMAT;** US ☎716-754-4883, Canada ☎519-836-0102; www.cybermall.co.nz/NZ/IAMAT) has free membership, lists English-speaking doctors worldwide, and offers detailed info on immunization requirements and sanitation. If your regular **insurance** policy does not cover your trip, consider purchasing additional coverage (see p. 20).

Those with medical conditions (such as diabetes, allergies to antibiotics, epilepsy, heart conditions) may want to obtain a **Medic Alert** membership (first year US$35, annually thereafter US$20), which includes a stainless steel ID tag, among other benefits, like a 24hr. collect-call number. Contact the Medic Alert Foundation, 2323 Colorado Ave, Turlock, CA 95382, USA (☎888-633-4298; outside US 209-668-3333; www.medicalert.org).

WOMEN'S HEALTH

Women traveling in unsanitary conditions are vulnerable to **urinary tract (including bladder and kidney) infections.** Over-the-counter medicines can sometimes alleviate symptoms, but if they persist, see a doctor. **Vaginal yeast infections** may flare up in hot and humid climates. Wearing loosely fitting trousers or a skirt and cotton underwear will help, as will over-the-counter remedies like Monostat or Gynelotrimin. Bring supplies from home if you are prone to infection, as they may be difficult to find on the road. And, since **tampons, pads,** and reliable **contraceptive devices** are sometimes hard to find when traveling, bring supplies with you. **Abortion** is legal in Ecuador under certain conditions; contact Family Care International for more information on women's health in Ecuador (Manuel Larrea 115 and Santa Prisca, CONEISA bldg., 8th fl., Of. 846; ☎/fax 2283 978; marthajl@uio.satnet.net).

GETTING TO ECUADOR

BY PLANE

When it comes to airfare, a little effort can save you a bundle. If your plans are flexible enough to deal with the restrictions, courier fares are the cheapest. Tickets bought from consolidators and standby seating are also good deals, but last-minute specials, airfare wars, and charter flights often beat these fares. The key is to hunt around, be flexible, and ask persistently about discounts. Students, seniors, and those under 26 should never pay full price for a ticket.

AIRFARES

Airfares to Ecuador peak between mid-June and mid-September; holidays are also expensive. The cheapest times to travel are during the North American winter months. Midweek (M-Th morning) round-trip flights run US$40-50 cheaper than weekend flights, but they are generally more crowded and less likely to permit upgrades. Not fixing a return date ("open return") or arriving in and departing from different cities ("open-jaw") can be pricier than round-trip flights. Patching one-way flights together is the most expensive way to travel. Flights to Ecuador's major cities, Quito and Guayaquil, will tend to be cheaper.

Fares for round-trip flights to Quito from the US or Canadian east coast cost US$720, US$630 in the low season (Oct. and Jan.-May); from the US or Canadian west coast US$850/$690; from the UK UK£760/£570; from Australia AUS$4020/$3460.

If Ecuador is only one stop on a more extensive globe-hop, consider a round-the-world (RTW) ticket. Tickets usually include at least five stops and are valid for about a year; prices range US$3400-5000. Try **Northwest Airlines/KLM** (US ☎800-447-4747; www.nwa.com) or **Star Alliance,** a consortium of 22 airlines including United Airlines (US ☎800-241-6522; www.staralliance.com).

BUDGET AND STUDENT TRAVEL AGENCIES

While agents specializing in flights to Ecuador can make your life easy, they may not spend the time to find you the lowest possible fare—they get paid on commission. Travelers holding **ISIC** and **IYTC cards** (see p. 12) qualify for discounts from student travel agencies. Most flights from budget agencies are on major airlines, but in peak season some may sell seats on less reliable chartered aircraft.

STA Travel, 5900 Wilshire Blvd., Ste. 900, Los Angeles, CA 90036, USA (24hr. reservations and info ☎800-781-4040; www.sta-travel.com). A student and youth travel organization with over 150 offices worldwide including US offices (☎800-781-4040) in big cities. Ticket booking, travel insurance, railpasses, and more. Walk-in offices are located throughout Australia (☎03 9349 4344), New Zealand (☎09 309 9723), and the UK (☎0870 1 600 599).

Travel CUTS (Canadian Universities Travel Services Limited), 187 College St., Toronto, ON M5T 1P7, Canada (☎416-979-2406; www.travelcuts.com). Offices across Canada and the US including Los Angeles, New York, Seattle, and San Francisco.

USIT, 19-21 Aston Quay, Dublin 2, Ireland (☎01 602 1777; www.usitworld.com), Ireland's leading student/budget travel agency, has 22 offices throughout Northern Ireland and the Republic of Ireland.

COMMERCIAL AIRLINES

Commercial airlines' lowest regular offer is the **APEX** (Advance Purchase Excursion) fare, which provides confirmed reservations and allows "open-jaw" tickets. Generally, reservations must be made seven to 21 days ahead of departure, with seven- to 14-day minimum stay and 90-day maximum-stay restrictions. These fares carry hefty cancellation and change penalties (fees rise in summer). Book peak-season APEX fares early. Use **Microsoft Expedia** (msn.expedia.com) or **Travelocity** (www.travelocity.com) to get an idea of the lowest published fares, then use the resources outlined here to try and beat those fares. Low-season fares should be appreciably cheaper than the **high-season** (mid-June to mid-Sept.) ones listed here.

TICKET CONSOLIDATORS

Ticket consolidators, or **"bucket shops,"** buy unsold tickets in bulk from commercial airlines and sell them at discounted rates. The best place to look is in the Sunday travel section of any major newspaper (such as the *New York Times*), where many bucket shops place tiny ads. Call quickly, as availability is typically extremely limited. Not all bucket shops are reliable, so insist on a receipt that gives full details of restrictions, refunds, and tickets, and pay by credit card (in spite of the 2-5% fee) so you can stop payment if you never receive your tickets. For more info, see www.travel-library.com/air-travel/consolidators.html.

Travel Avenue (☎800-333-3335; www.travelavenue.com) searches for best available published fares and then uses several consolidators to attempt to beat that fare. **NOW Voyager,** 315 W. 49th St. Plaza Arcade, New York, NY 10019, USA (☎212-459-1616; www.nowvoyagertravel.com), arranges discounted flights, mostly from New York, to Barcelona, London, Madrid, Milan, Paris, and Rome. Find more tickets online at **Cheap Tickets** (☎800-652-4327; www.cheaptickets.com), **Flights.com** (www.flights.com), and **TravelHUB** (www.travelhub.com). Keep in mind that these are just suggestions to get you started in your research; Let's Go does not endorse any of these agencies. As always, be cautious, and research companies before you hand over your credit card number.

CHARTER FLIGHTS

Charters are flights a tour operator contracts with an airline to fly extra loads of passengers during peak season. Charter flights fly less frequently than major airlines, make refunds particularly difficult, and are almost always fully booked. Schedules and itineraries may also change or be cancelled at the last moment (as late as 48hr. before the trip, and without a full refund), and check-in, boarding, and baggage claim are often much slower. However, they can also be cheaper.

Discount clubs and fare brokers offer members savings on last-minute charter and tour deals. Study contracts closely; you don't want to end up with an unwanted overnight layover.

BY BUS

Flying to Ecuador is most common, but overland routes from North and Central America are possible. They are also very inconvenient. From North and Central America, buses go as far south as Panama. In South America, they stop in Colombia. Between Panama and Colombia is a region of jungle impenetrable to roads. Unless you are ready to trek over 200km through this dense jungle (known as the Darien Gap), stick to flying.

BORDER CROSSINGS

TO COLOMBIA

Relatively straightforward and heavily policed border crossing to Colombia occurs at **Tulcán.** Nevertheless, Let's Go does not recommend travel near Ecuador's border with Colombia due to recent kidnappings and murders in this area.

TO PERU

The border-crossing at **Macará** (see p. 202), Ecuador to Piura, Peru is more pleasant than the crossing from **Huaquillas** (see p. 284), Ecuador to Tumbes, Peru.

GETTING AROUND ECUADOR

BY PLANE

Ecuador's major airline is **TAME** (toll free ☎1 800 555 999, in Quito ☎2509 375), which runs international and domestic flights. Flights on the mainland are usually cheap (US$40-100), though they can cost more between the larger cities. Expect flights to the Galápagos to be very expensive (US$300-450). As a general guideline, purchase tickets a few days before departure—at least a week in advance for flights between large destinations—and call to confirm 72hr. before the flight. **Arrive at least 2hr. early for both domestic and international flights.** Often, flights are overbooked and, despite holding a *billete* (ticket), a passenger may be bumped off the flight for not having *cupo*, roughly translated as "a reservation." Ask the ticketing agent if you have both. If you don't have *cupo*, it is still possible to fly standby if you arrive 3hr. early. Flights tend to leave early in the morning, so arrive a few hours earlier to guarantee a seat. Airlines often offer lower "promotional fares" from November to March. For specific flight, airline, and airport information, see the **Practical Information** section in individual cities with access to an airport.

 AIRCRAFT SAFETY. The airlines of developing world nations do not always meet safety standards. The *Official Airline Guide* (www.oag.com) and many travel agencies can tell you the type and age of aircraft on a particular route. The **International Airline Passengers Association** (US ☎800-821-4272, UK ☎020 8681 6555) provides region-specific safety information. The **Federal Aviation Administration** (www.faa.gov) reviews the airline authorities for countries whose airlines enter the US. **US State Department** travel advisories (☎202-647-5225; http://travel.state.gov/travel_warnings.html) sometimes involve foreign carriers, especially when terrorist bombings or hijackings may be a threat.

TO THE GALÁPAGOS ISLANDS. During the high season (June 15-Aug. 31 and Dec. 1-Jan. 5), round-trip tickets cost US$393 from Quito and US$347 from Guayaquil; low-season fairs dip to about US$336 from Quito and US$302 from Guayaquil. Getting last-minute flights to and from Puerto Ayora can be hard during the high season and just before and after these dates. Buying a ticket does not assure flying on a specific day; flights tend to be overbooked.

BY BUS

While bus travel is the cheapest and most reliable way to get around Ecuador, it can still be daunting. Buses along the well-paved Panamerican Hwy. promise a reasonably tame journey; elsewhere, prepare for anything. Coaches crammed with people and luggage whip around hairpin turns through thick clouds on the edges of cliffs. And, as soon as you muster the courage to open your eyes again, a bus coming from the opposite direction swerves past on a one-lane dirt highway overlooking oblivion. Inland, there are virtually no paved highways and the quality of dirt roads varies from smooth to non-stop bumps.

Night buses are common in Ecuador, but think twice before hopping on. Most bus accidents occur at night, either because of adverse conditions or because bus drivers fall asleep. Whenever possible, opt for the daytime trip. It may be the most important decision you'll ever make.

Buses normally leave town from the **terminal terrestre** (bus station), and run between most destinations frequently enough that it is practical just to show up at the terminal and board the next bus headed your way. On popular routes, it is wise to buy a ticket at least one day in advance. In more rural places it may be necessary to flag down a passing bus—this is the only time when bargaining is necessary, as unpublished prices are up to the discretion of the person taking the money. The vehicles themselves vary quality, from open-air trucks to sparkling new Mercedes-Benz mega-buses. A general guideline: the longer the route, the nicer the bus will be. Some bus companies offer different classes of travel, ranging from the most basic; to middle-of-the-line with videos, bathrooms, and air conditioning; to the most luxurious with reclining seats and meals (sometimes referred to as imperial service or royal service). One peculiar aspect of bus travel is that the buses rarely get "full." Drivers are often happy to pack as many passengers/ chicken crates as they can into the aisles or even hanging out the doors and windows. If the buses get really full in Ecuador, drivers will occasionally let passengers ride on the roof, an especially amazing (and certainly dangerous) experience in the mountains. It is a good idea to keep your bags and belongings with you if at all possible, although luggage is usually stored on the roof or below the bus. If you store luggage, make sure to get a baggage claim ticket.

BY TRAIN

Railroad travel is not the most convenient, cheapest, or quickest way to get around, but it can be a comfortable alternative to buses. While the tracks run the length of Ecuador, much of this distance is in disrepair due to mudslides, El Niño, and other natural damage. Nevertheless, there are several stretches that have been repaired and maintained. The most traveled stretch lies between Guayaquil and Alausí (see p. 170). The most enticing—and perhaps dangerous—aspect of trains in Ecuador is roof-riding. Let's Go does not recommend roof-riding. For info on prices and travel times, check the **Practical Information** sections of each town.

BY TAXI AND CAR

Taxis are convenient, especially when you are in a hurry or traveling to places where buses don't venture. They are commonly used for travel between towns or to outlying destinations. It is usually cheaper to arrange for a taxi to drop you off and pick you up at an out-of-the-way spot than it is to rent a car. When taking a taxi, always agree on the price beforehand—few taxis have meters and drivers often charge more for unsuspecting tourists. Beware of advice given by taxi drivers—their recommendations are often biased; in particular, they may be lying if they tell you your chosen lodging is full. In the jungle the regular taxi is replaced by the mototaxi—a motorcycle with a two- or three-person open-air cart attached to the back. These are cheaper and in smaller cities they are the only option.

You can also travel by **colectivo,** often a VW van that travels regular routes and picks up numerous passengers, falling in between taxis and buses in price, speed, and size. The destination is usually indicated on the bus or car itself and advertised by a man yelling the town's name over and over again. There are no scheduled stops on colectivos; when you want to get off, shout *"bajo aquí"* repeatedly.

ESSENTIALS

ESSENTIALS

TRICKY TRANSPORT TERMINOLOGY
auto: a car.
coche: also a car.
carro: a loosely used term, generally applied to buses, never to cars.
colectivo: leaves when full or when someone pays for the empty seats.
camioneta: a pickup truck that can act as a colectivo, depending on location and number of passengers.
taxi: these tend not to have meters; fix a price before you step in.
mototaxi: a Frankensteinian motorcycle/tricycle/taxi hybrid; best for short distances; known to haul goats.
micro: a small bus.
autobús: a bus for inter-city/transcontinental trips.
económico: a standard, cheap, no-nonsense bus.
bus cama: the opposite of *económico;* a luxury bus that features reclining seats, a bathroom, and a movie; runs direct.
especial: halfway between *económico* and *bus cama.*

RENTING

Driving a car in Ecuador can be a Herculean feat. Road conditions are poor in the cities and terrifying in the outskirts; roadside assistance is poor at best. Furthermore, there is almost no need to rent a car, as public transportation goes nearly everywhere. If you do find the need to rent, a motorbike may be a better option. **Car rental** will cost between US$30-80 per day (try Budget for good deals), the roads and drivers can be very scary, and a car is one more thing to worry about getting stolen. If you plan to drive, you should have an **International Driving Permit (IDP).** It will be indispensable if you're in a situation (e.g. an accident or being stranded in a smaller town) where the police do not speak English, as information on the IDP is printed in Spanish. Your IDP, valid for one year, must be issued in your own country before you depart. An application for an IDP usually must include one or two photos, a current local license, an additional form of identification, and a fee.

DRIVING PRECAUTIONS. When traveling in the summer or in the desert, bring substantial amounts of water (a suggested 5L of **water** per person per day) for drinking and for the radiator. For long drives to unpopulated areas, register with police before beginning the trek, and again upon arrival at the destination. Check with the local automobile club for details. When traveling for long distances, make sure tires are in good repair and have enough air, and get good maps. A **compass** and a **car manual** can also be very useful. You should always carry a **spare tire** and **jack, jumper cables, extra oil, flares, a flashlight (torch),** and **heavy blankets** (in case your car breaks down at night or in the winter). If you don't know how to **change a tire,** learn before heading out—especially if you are planning on traveling in deserted areas. Blowouts on dirt roads are exceedingly common. If you do have a breakdown, **stay with your car;** if you wander off, there's less likelihood trackers will find you.

If you rent, lease, or borrow a car, you will need a **green card,** or **International Insurance Certificate,** to certify that you have liability insurance and that it applies abroad. Green cards can be obtained at car rental agencies, car dealers (for those leasing cars), some travel agents, and some border crossings. Rental agencies may require you to purchase theft insurance in countries that they consider to have a high risk of auto theft.

Cheaper cars tend to be less reliable and harder to handle on difficult terrain. Less expensive 4WD vehicles in particular tend to be more top heavy, and are more dangerous when navigating particularly bumpy roads.

RENTAL AGENCIES

You can generally make reservations before you leave by calling major international offices in your home country. However, there are occasionally discrepancies between the information provided by different offices. Try checking with both numbers to make sure you get the best price and accurate information. Local desk numbers are included in town listings; for home-country numbers, call your toll-free directory. To rent a car from most establishments in Ecuador, you must be at least 25 years old. Some agencies permit those aged 21-24 to rent. In such cases, agencies tend to charge an additional insurance fee. Policies and prices vary from agency to agency. Small local operations occasionally rent to people under 21, but be sure to ask about the insurance coverage and deductible, and always check the fine print. Rental agencies in Ecuador include:

Avis, in Quito, at the airport (☎2255 890; open daily 6:30am-11:30pm). In Guayaquil, at the airport (☎2287 906; open daily 7am-10pm); downtown at Av. de las Americas (☎2285 498; open M-F 9am-6pm).

Budget, in Quito, at the airport (☎2467 756; open M-Sa 7am-10pm, Su 8am-10pm); at Av. Amazonas 1409 at Colón (☎2237 026; open M-F 8am-8pm, Sa 8am-2pm, Su 10am-4pm). In Guayaquil, at the airport (☎2288 510; open M-F 7am-10pm, Sa-Su 8am-7pm); at Av. de las Americas #900 at C. N (☎2284 559; open M-F 8:30am-7:30pm, Sa 8:30am-12:30pm); at García Moreno at Hurtado, in front of the Oro Verde Hotel (☎2328 571; open M-F 9am-5pm).

Hertz, in Quito, at the airport (☎2254 257; open M-F 7am-8pm, Sa-Su 8am-5pm); at C. Cordero 433 at Av. 12 de Octubre (☎2569 130; open M-F 8am-8pm, Sa 8am-1pm). In Guayaquil, at the airport (☎2293 011; open daily 7am-10:30pm); at 9 de Octubre and Garcia Moreno in Oro Rent a Car (☎2327 895; open M-F 8am-8pm, Sa 8am-1pm).

COSTS AND INSURANCE

Rental car prices start at around US$40 per day from international companies. Expect to pay more for larger cars and for 4WD. Cars with **automatic transmission** can cost twice as much a day as standard manuals (stick shift), and in some places, automatic transmission is hard to find in the first place. It is virtually impossible, no matter where you are, to find an automatic 4WD.

Many rental packages offer unlimited kilometers, while others offer 200km per day with a surcharge of approximately US$0.35 per km after that. Return the car with a full tank of petrol to avoid high fuel charges at the end. Be sure to ask whether the price includes theft and collision **insurance.** Remember that if you are driving a conventional vehicle on an **unpaved road** in a rental car, you are almost never covered by insurance; ask about this before leaving the rental agency. Beware that cars rented on an **American Express** or **Visa/MasterCard Gold or Platinum** credit cards in Ecuador might not carry the automatic insurance that they would in some other countries; check with your credit card company. Insurance plans almost always come with an **excess** (or deductible) of around US$2000 for conventional vehicles. This means you pay for all damages up to that sum, unless they are the fault of another vehicle. The excess you will be quoted applies to collisions with other vehicles; collisions with non-vehicles, such as trees ("single-vehicle collisions"), will cost you even more.

Large international chains often allow **one-way rentals,** picking up in one city and dropping off in another. There is usually a minimum hire period and sometimes an extra drop-off charge of several hundred dollars.

BY BOAT

Large **cargo ships** travel the rivers that connect many towns in the jungle. These usually have two decks: a lower one for cargo and an upper one for passengers. The latter features a few toilets and showers, several cramped and windowless cabins (bedding is not provided), and often a canteen selling biscuits, soda, toilet paper, and other "necessities." The **kitchen** can be found below, where the cook often scoops water straight from the river to prepare the rice, fish, or soup—many passengers become ill from the food, so it may be wise to bring your own. Either way, you'll need your own bowl and utensils as well as enough water to last you more days than the captain projects. Every passenger also makes use of his or her own **hammock** and hanging rope, which are best installed as far from the bathrooms, the engine, and the lights, as possible. Hammocks are available in markets all over the jungle, in both string and cloth varieties. The cloth sort—though somewhat more expensive—provides far greater protection against intrusive elbows or feet. Other useful items include toilet paper, a chain with which to attach your bag to a pole while you sleep, a clothesline on which to hang wet towels, and a sleeping bag or blanket—constant wind makes sleeping on deck quite chilly at night.

Boats accepting passengers hang **chalkboards** from their bows, announcing their intended destination and departure times. However, while most reach their destination, few depart on time. They often hang around the port for weeks, stuffing themselves with cargo; the boat that looks most ready to sink under the weight of its load will probably be the next to leave. There's no need to arrange a "ticket" ahead of time, as these boats don't take reservations; but it may be a good idea to establish a price with the captain. Someone will collect the passage fee (depends on length of journey and usually includes 3 meals per day) once the boat has embarked. The fee may be reduced if you wish to bring your own food. However, a tiny private cabin will raise the price—again, arrangements should be made with the captain before departure. It's also worth going down to the port beforehand to search for a boat without your backpack; travelers who arrive at the ports with their luggage often find themselves being pulled in every direction by touts. And should your chosen vessel not depart the day you board? Sling your hammock anyway and spend the night in port. The first people on board may have to wait the longest, but they also receive first choice in hammock location.

Although cargo boats may be a more romantic mode of travel, speedboats connect some destinations in a much more practical time frame (and a much higher price). Speedboats often serve meals.

BY THUMB

 Let's Go never recommends hitchhiking as a safe means of transportation, and none of the information presented here is intended to do so.

Let's Go strongly urges travelers to consider the risks before they choose to hitchhike. In Ecuador, there is little need to hitchhike; buses go almost everywhere. Nonetheless, trucks often pick up passengers to make a little extra money. Usually truckers charge the same rate as taxis; sometimes they charge more. Be sure to settle on a price before getting in. If hitchhiking, use common sense and go with your gut; if something does not feel right or safe, you're better off waiting.

KEEPING IN TOUCH

BY MAIL

SENDING MAIL HOME FROM ECUADOR

Airmail is the best way to send mail home from Ecuador. **Aerogrammes,** printed sheets that fold into envelopes and travel via airmail, are available at post offices. Write *"por avión"* on the front. Most post offices will charge exorbitant fees or simply refuse to send aerogrammes with enclosures. **Surface mail** is by far the cheapest and slowest way to send mail. It takes one to two months to cross the Atlantic and one to three to cross the Pacific—good for heavy items you won't need for a while. In general, to reach the US, *certificada* (certified) takes 15 days, *ordinaria* (ordinary) takes eight days, and *correo expreso* (express mail) takes less than 8 days. Mail usually takes three additional days to reach Europe or Australia. **DHL** is expensive but only takes three days.

SENDING MAIL TO ECUADOR

To ensure timely delivery, mark envelopes "airmail," "par avion," or "por avión." In addition to the standard postage system, **Federal Express** (www.fedex.com; Australia ☎ 13 26 10; Canada and US 800-463-3339; Ireland 1800 535 800; New Zealand 0800 733 339; UK 0800 123 800) handles express mail services from most countries to Ecuador; for example, they can get a letter from New York to Ecuador in two days for US$50, and from London to Ecuador in two days for UK£37.60.

Australia: Allow 6-7 days for regular airmail to Ecuador. Postcards and letters up to 20g cost AUS$1; packages up to 0.5kg AUS$12, up to 2kg AUS$45. EMS can deliver mail in 3-5 days AUS$49. http://www1.auspost.com.au.

Canada: Allow 6-10 days for regular airmail to Ecuador. Postcards and letters up to 20g cost CDN$0.95; packages up to 0.5kg CDN$8.50, up to 2kg CDN$29. Purolator International can get a letter to Ecuador in 2-4 days for CDN$40. www.canadapost.ca/personal/rates/default-e.asp.

Ireland: Allow 5-7 days for regular airmail to Ecuador. Postcards and letters up to 20g cost €0.32; packages up to 0.5kg €8.50, up to 2kg €28.30. Swiftpost International can get a letter to Ecuador in 4-6 days for €34. www.letterpost.ie.

New Zealand: Allow 5-10 days for regular airmail to Ecuador. Postcards and letters up to 20g cost NZ$1-9; packages up to 0.5kg NZ$19, up to 2kg NZ$59. International Express can get a letter to Ecuador in 2-5 days for NZ$41. www.nzpost.co.nz/nzpost/inrates.

UK: Allow 3-5 days for regular airmail to Ecuador. Letters up to 20g cost UK£0.70; packages up to 0.5kg UK£5, up to 2kg UK£18.50. UK Airsure delivers letters a day faster for UK£4 more. www.royalmail.co.uk/calculator.

US: Allow 4-7 days for regular airmail to Ecuador. Letters up to 1 oz. cost US$0.80; packages up to 1 lb. US$9.25, up to 5 lb. US$28. US Express Mail takes 3-5 days and costs US$22. http://ircalc.usps.gov.

RECEIVING MAIL IN ECUADOR

There are several ways to arrange pick-up of letters sent to you by friends and relatives while you are abroad. Mail can be sent via **Poste Restante** (General Delivery; *Lista de Correos* in Spanish) to almost any city or town in Ecuador with a post office, and is fairly reliable. Address *Poste Restante* letters like so:

Napoleon BONAPARTE
Lista de Correos
City, Ecuador

The mail will go to a special desk in the central post office—unless you specify a post office by street address or postal code. It's best to use the largest post office, since mail may be sent there regardless. Bring your passport (or other photo ID) for pick-up; there may be a small fee, though if there is, it should not exceed the cost of domestic postage. If the clerks insist that there is nothing for you, have them check under your first name as well. Let's Go lists post offices in the **Practical Information** section for each city and most towns. If you know a specific address, make sure that you include the phone number of the destination: name, intersection of streets, telephone number, city, Ecuador.

BY TELEPHONE

CALLING HOME FROM ECUADOR

A **calling card** is probably your cheapest bet. Calls are billed collect or to your account. You can frequently call collect without even having a company's calling card just by calling their access number and following the instructions. **To call home with a calling card,** contact the operator for your service provider in Ecuador by dialing the toll-free access number (listed below in the second column).

COMPANY	TO OBTAIN A CARD, DIAL:	(ANDINATEL) TO CALL ABROAD, DIAL:	(PACIFICTEL) TO CALL ABROAD, DIAL:
AT&T (US)	800-364-9292	999 119	800 225 528
Canada Direct	800-561-8868	999 175	999 175
MCI (US)	800-777-5000	999 170	800 999 170

Making direct international calls from pay phones is difficult. Few pay phones in Ecuador allow calling card calls. Without a calling card, you'll find yourself dropping coins as quickly as your words. Prepaid cards and sometimes major credit cards can be used for direct international calls, but they are generally less cost-efficient. Placing a collect call through an international operator is even more expensive. You can place collect calls through the service providers listed above even if you don't have one of their phone cards. Before settling on a calling card plan, be sure to research your options in order to pick the one that best fits both your needs and your destination.

CALLING WITHIN ECUADOR

Prepaid phone cards (available at street vendors, supermarkets, and pharmacies), which carry a certain amount of phone time depending on the card's denomination, save time and money. The computerized phone will tell you how much time, in units, you have left on your card. Another kind of prepaid telephone card comes with a Personal Identification Number (PIN) and a toll-free access number. Call the access number and follow the directions on the card. These cards can be used to

ESSENTIALS

> **PLACING INTERNATIONAL CALLS.** To call Ecuador from home or to call home from Ecuador, dial:
>
> 1. The **international dialing prefix.** To call from **Australia,** dial 0011; **Canada** or the **US,** 011; **Ireland, New Zealand,** or the **UK,** 00; **Ecuador,** 00.
> 2. The **country code** of the country you want to call. To call **Australia,** dial 61; **Canada** or the **US,** 1; **Ireland,** 353; **New Zealand,** 64; the **UK,** 44; **Ecuador,** 593.
> 3. The **city/area code.** Let's Go lists the city/area codes for cities and towns in Ecuador opposite the city or town name, next to a ☎. If the first digit is a zero (e.g., 020 for London), omit the zero when calling from abroad (e.g., dial 20 from Canada to reach London).
> 4. The **local number.**

make international as well as domestic calls. MCI calling cards rarely work in Ecuador except at select Andinatel phone booths. Purchase calling cards in Ecuador to be sure they work. If they exist, coin operated phones are extremely rare.

CELLULAR PHONES

Ecuador has two different cellular networks: BellSouth and Porta Cellular. **Bell-South** operates on the AMPS system and **Porta Cellular,** the TDMA system. Each operates in the 800Mhz range. Most phones outside of the Americas operate on the GSM standard, also at 800Mhz. Thus, it is unlikely that phones from countries outside of North or South America will function in Ecuador. Additionally, few US cell phones still use the TDMA system, having transferred to CDMA (Sprint and Verizon) or GSM (Cingular, T-Mobile, and soon AT&T). In addition, many US phones operate at the higher 1900Mhz frequency.

But don't be disheartened. Cell phone usage is extremely common in Ecuador, with coverage in more densely populated areas (much of the Highlands and Southern Lowlands get coverage). It is relatively inexpensive to acquire a cell phone in Ecuador—you can pay for service by the minute or month.

TIME DIFFERENCES

Ecuador is 5hr. behind Greenwich Mean Time (GMT); 1hr. behind New York; 2hr. ahead of Vancouver and San Francisco; 15hr. behind Sydney; 17hr. behind Auckland (NZ). Ecuador ignores **daylight saving time.** A good source for this info is www.worldtimeserver.com.

BY EMAIL AND INTERNET

Though in some places it's possible to forge a remote link with your home server, in most cases this is a much slower (and thus more expensive) option than taking advantage of free **web-based email accounts** (e.g., www.hotmail.com, google.gmail.com, www.yahoo.com—or in Ecuador, www.latinmail.com). **Internet cafes** are listed in the **Practical Information** sections of most cities. For lists of additional cybercafes in Ecuador, check out www.cybercafes.com, www.goecuador.com, or http://cybercafe.katchup.co.nz. Increasingly, travelers find that taking their **laptop computers** on the road with them can be a convenient option for staying connected. Laptop users can call an Internet service provider via a modem using long-distance phone cards specifically intended for such calls. They may also find Internet cafes that allow them to connect their laptops to the Internet. For information on insuring your laptop while traveling, see p. 19.

ACCOMMODATIONS

HOSTELS AND OTHER LODGING

Hostel rooms are small and simple. Bathrooms may be private or communal. Most places include a lounge area or courtyard. They sometimes have kitchens and utensils for your use, bike or moped rentals, storage areas, transportation to airports, breakfast and other meals, laundry facilities, and Internet access. There can be drawbacks: some hostels have a curfew, don't accept reservations, impose a maximum stay, or, less frequently, require that you do chores. Reservations are generally only necessary for big festivals and in cities with a large number of tourists. Hotels are the most expensive (and most luxurious) option, followed by *hostales*, *residenciales*, and *alojamientos*. In Ecuador, a dorm bed in a hostel will average US$3-8. Hostel and hotel owners frequently require guests to present a passport number upon checking in. There is occasionally a lockout time before which you must return to the hotel or hostel. If you get locked out, you can try to wake the owner or receptionist, but don't expect a cheerful greeting.

Many accommodations offer **matrimonials**—rooms for two people with a double or queen-sized bed rather than the two twin beds—that often cost less than a traditional double. Hostels with dorm-style accommodations are rarely found outside of capital cities. Budget accommodations generally include sheets, blankets, and that's about it—bring your own towels.

Both hotels and hostels may offer laundry service for a fee, they may have a place where guests can do their own laundry (sometimes a washtub and a clothes line), or there may be no laundry facilities at all. It is expected everywhere that after you've finished your business, you **throw your toilet paper into the waste basket**—*not* the toilet. **Hot water** can be something of a luxury. **Electric showers** usually provide a short (about 1min.) burst of hot water (and occasionally minor shocks), available 24hr. **Thermal showers** have a separate hot-water knob and a set time (usually early morning) when you can take a shower.

BOOKING HOSTELS ONLINE. One of the easiest ways to ensure you've got a bed for the night is by reserving online. Click to the **Hostelworld** booking engine through **www.letsgo.com,** and you'll have access to bargain accommodations from Argentina to Zimbabwe with no added commission.

Besides camping, Ecuador offers bed and breakfasts as well as resorts. **Bed and breakfasts** operate much the same way as hostels. Boarders may rent singles, doubles, or even triples; prices may be by the bed or by the room. Most **resorts** offer higher-end living. Budget travelers may choose to look elsewhere. However, some indigenous communities of the Oriente have set up affordable ecotourist compounds, some of which are set up as resorts. The overall price may be a lot higher than a night at a hostel, but the complete package comes with so much more: food, lodging, outdoor activities, even shaman demonstrations.

CAMPING AND THE OUTDOORS

Camping is possible in Ecuador, but it is most frequently an option for hikers along trails or in national parks rather than in established campsites in towns. Some parks and reserves have designated camping areas and some more fre-

quently climbed mountains have *refugios* (rustic shelters) at various elevation levels. Closer to town, tourist recreation centers sometimes have space for camping next to pools, restaurants, and discos. Let's Go will always mention if camping is an option. The **Great Outdoor Recreation Pages** (www.gorp.com) provides excellent information for travelers planning on camping or spending time in the outdoors.

LEAVE NO TRACE. Let's Go encourages travelers to embrace the "Leave No Trace" ethic, minimizing their impact on natural environments and protecting them for future generations. Trekkers and wilderness enthusiasts should set up camp on durable surfaces, use cookstoves instead of campfires, bury human waste away from water supplies, bag trash and carry it out with them, and respect wildlife and natural objects. For more detailed information, contact the **Leave No Trace Center for Outdoor Ethics,** PO Box 997, Boulder, CO 80306, USA (☎800-332-4100 or 303-442-8222; www.lnt.org).

The non-profit **South American Explorers (SAE)** is widely recognized as the ultimate source of travel information on Ecuador. This well-respected outfit (with clubhouses in Lima and Cusco, Peru; Quito, Ecuador; and Ithaca, New York) provides information about outdoor experiences, discount airfares, trip planning, and travel conditions. Contact SAE at 126 Indian Creek Rd., Ithaca, NY 14850, USA (☎607-277-0488; www.samexplo.org).

USEFUL PUBLICATIONS AND RESOURCES

A variety of publishing companies offer hiking guidebooks to meet the educational needs of novice or expert. For information about camping, hiking, and biking, write or call the publishers listed below to receive a free catalog.

Sierra Club Books, 85 Second St., 2nd fl., San Francisco, CA 94105, USA (☎415-977-5500; www.sierraclub.org), publishes general resource books on hiking and camping.

The Mountaineers Books, 1001 SW Klickitat Way, Ste. 201, Seattle, WA 98134, USA (☎206-223-6303; www.mountaineersbooks.org), boasts over 600 titles on hiking, biking, mountaineering, natural history, and conservation.

South American Explorers, Jorge Washington 311 at Leonidas Plaza, Apt. 17-21-431, Eloy Alfaro, Quito, Ecuador (☎2225 228; www.samexplo.org). To non-members, it sells general information packets on Ecuador and the Galápagos. Members who visit the clubhouse in Quito have access to helpful information on the outdoors of Ecuador.

NATIONAL PARKS

Thirty-nine percent of Ecuador's total land area consists of protected national forest. Towns serve as access points to the majority of national parks in the Highlands and westward. Many, but far from all, have ranger stations. And those that have them often lack rangers to man them. In the end, rangers play a secondary role to guides. In many parks, guides are required, and in nearly all parks, they are highly recommended. Most often, Let's Go lists pertinent guides in reviews of the nearest towns. Respectable guides know the land well and will make sure that wilderness treks remain less than dangerous. Few trails—only those in the most highly touristed parks—are well maintained. Quito offers myriad tour companies that will lead treks into nearly any national park in Ecuador. When choosing a guide, be sure to shop around. Especially in smaller towns, costs of wilderness expeditions are not set. In addition, make sure to check what the total price includes: food, necessary gear, park entrance fee, etc.

WILDERNESS SAFETY

THE GREAT OUTDOORS

Staying warm, dry, and well-hydrated is key to a happy and safe wilderness experience. For any hike, prepare yourself for an emergency by packing a first-aid kit, a reflector, a whistle, high energy food, extra water, raingear, a hat, and mittens. For warmth, wear wool or insulating synthetic materials designed for the outdoors. Cotton is a bad choice since it dries painfully slowly.

Check **weather forecasts** often and pay attention when hiking, as weather patterns can change suddenly. Always let someone—either a friend, your hostel, a park ranger, or a local hiking organization—know when and where you are hiking. Know your physical limits and do not attempt a hike beyond your ability. See p. 40 for information on outdoor ailments and medical concerns.

CAMPING AND HIKING EQUIPMENT

WHAT TO BUY

Good camping equipment is both sturdy and light. North American suppliers tend to offer the most competitive prices.

Sleeping Bags: Most sleeping bags are rated by season; "summer" means 30-40°F (around 0°C) at night; "four-season" or "winter" often means below 0°F (-17°C). Bags are made of **down** (warm and light, but expensive, and miserable when wet) or of **synthetic** material (heavy, durable, and warm when wet). Prices range US$50-250 for a summer synthetic to US$200-300 for a good down winter bag. **Sleeping bag pads** include foam pads (US$10-30), air mattresses (US$15-50), and self-inflating mats (US$30-120). Bring a **stuff sack** to store your bag and keep it dry.

Tents: The best tents are free-standing (with their own frames and suspension systems), set up quickly, and only require staking in high winds. Low-profile dome tents are the best all-around. Worthy 2-person tents start at US$100, 4-person at US$160. Make sure your tent has a rain fly and seal its seams with waterproofer. Other useful accessories include a **battery-operated lantern**, a plastic **groundcloth**, and a nylon **tarp.**

Backpacks: Internal-frame packs mold well to your back, keep a lower center of gravity, and flex adequately to allow you to hike difficult trails, while **external-frame packs** are more comfortable for long hikes over even terrain, as they carry weight higher and distribute it more evenly. Make sure your pack has a strong, padded hip-belt to transfer weight to your legs. There are models designed specifically for women. Any serious backpacking requires a pack of at least 4000 in³ (16,000cc), plus 500 in³ for sleeping bags in internal-frame packs. Sturdy backpacks cost US$125-420—your pack is an area where it doesn't pay to economize. On your hunt for the perfect pack, fill up prospective models with something heavy, strap it on correctly, and walk around the store to get a sense of how the model distributes weight. Either buy a **rain cover** (US$10-20) or store all of your belongings in plastic bags inside your pack.

Boots: Be sure to wear hiking boots with good **ankle support.** They should fit snugly and comfortably over 1-2 pairs of **wool socks** and a pair of thin **liner socks.** Break in boots over several weeks before you go to spare yourself blisters.

Other Necessities: Synthetic layers, like those made of polypropylene or polyester, and a pile jacket will keep you warm even when wet. A **space blanket** (US$5-15) will help you to retain body heat and doubles as a groundcloth. Plastic **water bottles** are vital; look for shatter- and leak-resistant models. Carry **water-purification tablets** for when you can't boil water. Although most campgrounds provide campfire sites, you may want to bring a small **metal grate** or **grill.** For those places that forbid fires or the gathering of firewood, you'll need a **camp stove** (the classic Coleman starts at US$50) and a propane-filled **fuel bottle** to operate it. Also bring a **first-aid kit, pocketknife, insect repellent,** and **waterproof matches** or a **lighter.**

WHERE TO BUY IT

The mail-order/online companies listed below offer lower prices than many retail stores. A visit to a local camping or outdoors store will give you a good sense of the look and weight of certain items.

Campmor, 28 Parkway, PO Box 700, Upper Saddle River, NJ 07458, USA (US ☎ 888-226-7667; www.campmor.com).

Discount Camping, 880 Main North Rd., Pooraka, South Australia 5095, Australia (☎ 08 8262 3399; fax 8260 6240; www.discountcamping.com.au).

Eastern Mountain Sports (EMS), 1 Vose Farm Rd., Peterborough, NH 03458, USA (☎ 888-463-6367; www.ems.com).

L.L. Bean, Freeport, ME 04033 (US and Canada ☎ 800-441-5713, UK ☎ 0800 891 297; www.llbean.com).

Mountain Designs, 51 Bishop St., Kelvin Grove, Queensland 4059, Australia (☎ 07 3856 2344; www.mountaindesigns.com).

Recreational Equipment, Inc. (REI), Sumner, WA 98352-0001, USA (US and Canada ☎ 800-426-4840, elsewhere 253-891-2500; www.rei.com).

YHA Adventure Shop, 19 High St., Staines, Middlesex, TW18 4QY, UK (☎ 1784 458625; www.yhaadventure.com).

ORGANIZED ADVENTURE TRIPS

Organized adventure tours offer another way of exploring the wild. Tours usually offer all necessary equipment and meals; always bring your own water. Activities include hiking, biking, skiing, canoeing, kayaking, rafting, climbing, photo safaris, and archaeological digs. Tourism bureaus often can suggest parks, trails, and outfitters. Organizations that specialize in camping and outdoor equipment like REI and EMS (see above) also are good sources for info.

Trips arranged in Ecuador tend to be cheaper than trips arranged abroad, but they can also be riskier. When planning any type of organized trip, verify the reputability of the company through a local tourist office or ask other travelers before you go. SAE (see p. 85) can be an invaluable resource in evaluating guides and companies; they provide trip reports that offer recommendations and warnings. The **Specialty Travel Index,** 305 San Anselmo Ave. Ste. 309, San Anselmo, CA 94960, USA (US ☎ 888-624-4030, elsewhere 415-455-1643; www. specialtytravel.com).

JUNGLE TOURS

Travelers mainly visit Ecuador rainforests to take a jungle tour through the Amazon Basin. Tours typically last from two to 25 days and include treks through rainforests, canoe rides, visits to remote indigenous communities, and overnight stays in cabaña outposts or jungle lodges. However, reaching anything even resembling untouched jungle requires lots of money and time. When arranging a trip, you should visit several different agencies and guides. Ask them to explain exactly what you will be doing and exactly how many will be going (larger groups tend to see fewer animals). Before signing, make sure you know what's included—food, speedboat transport, daytrips, and lodging are standard. Every major jungle city generally has a variety of guides who speak Spanish and English and occasionally other European languages. Finally, try bargaining—most people book these trips from home at set rates, but walk-in customers have far more leverage.

HIRING AN INDEPENDENT GUIDE. Freelance guides can offer less crowded, more adventurous, and more flexible trips than those based in lodges, and their services are often cheaper than a lodge if there's a group to split costs. However, not all guides are created equal. You might end up having an excellent time with a guide who knows what he's doing, points out interesting wildlife, and respects the land and its people—or you could go along silently as your guide tallies his profits and stares out into a jungle he doesn't know much about. Ask to see any potential guide's license and national ID card to check that the names coincide; then head to the tourist office to ask about his record. Keep in mind that the majority of guides do not have licenses because licenses cost upwards of US$1000. A license may mean that a guide is reliable, but the lack of one does not dictate that he is not.

JUNGLE LODGES. As a viable alternative to jungle tours, tourist lodges are a bit more predictable and luxurious. Many of the affordable ones sit quite close to the city and, while they offer a few trails and sometimes even a swimming pool, any sort of excursion into the jungle generally costs extra. Some lodges' trips have strict schedules while others can change to accommodate travelers' interests.

TREKKING AND HIKING

There are three ways to explore the Andes: join a tour group, hire an *arriero* (a local muleteer who acts as guide and porter), or set out alone. While each has its own distinct feel, all three ultimately tend to be similar in price.

JOINING A GROUP. Tour groups abound in the major hiking cities of Ecuador, and this may be the most practical option for solo travelers. Many agencies offer similar services at similar prices (US$40-70 per day). Ask specific questions and get all answers in writing. Some concerns include group size (more than 20 people is a bad sign); food (some agencies only supply bread and water); porters' responsibilities (most budget companies have you carry your own pack); equipment (you'll probably have to supply a sleeping bag—make sure it's a warm one); and a guide with experience and language ability.

HIRING A GUIDE. Hiring a guide may be the only option in many smaller hiking towns. *Arrieros* (US$10-15 per day) can serve as guides, porters, or both. Know in advance exactly what services your guide will provide. Some guides will only take groups of three or more people. Make arrangements with the guide at least a day or two in advance so that the guide can prepare. It is occasionally possible to hire a *burro* (US$4-5 per day), a cook (US$20 per day), and/or an emergency horse (US$4-5). Know what the *arriero* is providing so that you can make up the difference—most will provide tents but only cooks provide food. If you are not returning to the departure city, you must also pay for the *arriero's* return transportation.

GOING IT ALONE. Don't do it, especially if you're a woman. For the stubborn among you, bring a good compass and an even better map.

CLOTHING	EQUIPMENT
boots or running shoes	sleeping bag
camp shoes or flip-flops	earplugs
lots of socks (polypropylene and wool)	water bottle and water purification system
down jacket	flashlight, batteries
woolen shirt	insulated mat, if camping
shorts/skirt	backpack and daypack
long trousers	toilet paper and hand trowel
raingear and umbrella	lighter
cotton t-shirts or blouses	sunblock and lip balm
thermal underwear	towel
gloves	sewing kit with safety pins
sun hat and wool hat	small knife
snow gaiters	first-aid kit
snow goggles/sunglasses	ziploc bags

SPECIFIC CONCERNS

SUSTAINABLE TRAVEL

As the number of travelers on the road continues to rise, the detrimental effect they can have on natural environments increasingly becomes a concern. With this in mind, Let's Go promotes the philosophy of **sustainable travel**. Through a sensitivity to issues of ecology and sustainability, today's travelers can be a powerful force in preserving and restoring the places they visit.

Ecotourism, a rising trend in sustainable travel, focuses on conserving natural habitats and using them to build up the economy without exploitation or overdevelopment. Travelers can make a difference by doing advance research and supporting organizations and establishments that pay attention to their impact on their natural surroundings and strive to be environmentally-friendly. All tourism in the Oriente strives to be ecotourism. The town of Mindo (see p. 111) was one of the first in Ecuador to advocate ecotourism in the promotion of the various nearby national parks. Galápagos tours have jumped onto this bandwagon, as well.

RESPONSIBLE TRAVEL

The impact of tourist dollars on the destinations you visit should not be underestimated. The choices you make during your trip can have potent effects on local communities—for better or for worse. Travelers who care about the destinations and environments they explore should become aware of the social and cultural implications of the choices they make when they travel. **Community-based tourism** aims to channel tourist dollars into the local economy by emphasizing tours and cultural programs that are run by members of the host community and that often benefit disadvantaged groups (see p. 68). An excellent resource for information on community-based travel is *The Good Alternative Travel Guide* (UK£10), a project of **Tourism Concern** (☎ 020 7133 3330; www.tourismconcern.org.uk).

TRAVELING ALONE

There are many benefits to traveling alone, including independence and greater interaction with locals. On the other hand, any solo traveler is a more vulnerable target of harassment and street theft. As a lone traveler, try not to stand out as a tourist, look confident, and be especially careful in deserted or very crowded areas. If questioned, never admit that you are traveling alone. Maintain regular contact with someone at home who knows your itinerary. For more tips, pick up *Traveling Solo* by Eleanor Berman (Globe Pequot Press, US$18), visit www.travelaloneandloveit.com, or subscribe to **Connecting: Solo Travel Network,** 689 Park Rd., Unit 6, Gibsons, BC V0N 1V7, Canada (☎ 604-886-9099; www.cstn.org; membership US$28-45).

FEMALE TRAVELERS

Women exploring on their own inevitably face some additional safety concerns, but it's easy to be adventurous without taking undue risks. If you are concerned, consider staying in hostels that offer single rooms that lock from the inside or in religious organizations with rooms for women only. Stick to centrally located accommodations and avoid solitary late-night treks or metro rides. Always carry extra money for a phone call, bus, or taxi. **Hitchhiking is never safe.** Look as if you know where you're going and approach older women or couples for directions if you're lost or uncomfortable. Generally, the less you look like a tourist, the better off you'll be. Dress conservatively, especially in rural areas. Wearing a conspicuous **wedding band** sometimes helps to prevent unwanted overtures.

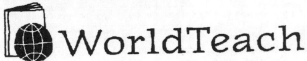

Your best answer to verbal harassment is no answer at all; feigning deafness, sitting motionless, and staring straight ahead will do a world of good that reactions usually don't achieve. The extremely persistent can sometimes be dissuaded by a firm, loud, and very public "Go away!" *(¡No me moleste!)*. Don't hesitate to seek out a police officer or passerby if you are being harassed. Memorize the emergency numbers in places you visit, and consider carrying a whistle on your keychain. A self-defense course (see p. 19) will both prepare you for a potential attack and raise your level of awareness of your surroundings. Also, be sure you are aware of the health concerns that women face when traveling (see p. 25).

GLBT TRAVELERS

GLBT (*Gay, Lesbian, Bisexual, and Transgendered*) travelers are not openly accepted in Ecuador partly due to the influence of the Catholic Church. The derogatory *"maricón"* is used more frequently than the proper *"homosexual."* However, larger cities are slowly becoming more tolerant. Listed below are contact organizations, mail-order bookstores, and publishers that offer materials addressing some specific concerns. **Out and About** (www.planetout.com) offers a bi-weekly newsletter addressing travel concerns and a comprehensive site addressing gay travel concerns. The online newspaper **365gay.com** also has a travel section (www.365gay.com/travel/travelchannel.htm). To avoid hassles at airports and border crossings, transgendered travelers should make sure that all of their travel documents are consistent with respect to the gender that they report. Many countries (including the US, the UK, Canada, Ireland, Australia, and New Zealand) will amend the passports of post-operative transsexuals to reflect their true gender, although governments are generally less sympathetic to amending documents for pre-operative transsexuals and other transgendered individuals.

Fundación Ecuatoriana de Acción y Educación para la Promoción de la Salud (FEDAEPS), Baquerizo Moreno 166 and Tamayo, Quito, Ecuador (☎02 2223 298).

Gay's the Word, 66 Marchmont St., London WC1N 1AB, UK (☎+44 20 7278 7654; www.gaystheword.co.uk), the largest gay and lesbian bookshop in the UK, with both fiction and non-fiction titles. Mail-order service available.

Giovanni's Room, 1145 Pine St., Philadelphia, PA 19107, USA (☎215-923-2960; www.queerbooks.com), an international lesbian/feminist and gay bookstore with mail-order service (carries many of the publications listed below).

International Lesbian and Gay Association (ILGA), 81 rue Marché-au-Charbon, B-1000 Brussels, Belgium (☎+32 2 502 2471; www.ilga.org), provides political information, such as homosexuality laws of individual countries.

FURTHER READING: GLBT

Spartacus 2003-2004: International Gay Guide. Bruno Gmunder Verlag (US$33).

Damron Guides (US$11-19). For info, call ☎800-462-6654 or visit www.damron.com.

Ferrari Guides' Gay Travel A to Z, Ferrari Guides' Men's Travel in Your Pocket, Ferrari Guides' Women's Travel in Your Pocket, and *Ferrari Guides' Inn Places.* Ferrari Publications (US$16-20).

The Gay Vacation Guide: The Best Trips and How to Plan Them, Mark Chesnut. Kensington Books (US$15).

TRAVELERS WITH DISABILITIES

Travelers with disabilities may find Ecuador a bit unaccommodating. More upscale hotels will generally be able to meet your needs, but public transportation systems and most hostels are ill-equipped. Those with disabilities should inform airlines and hotels of their disabilities when making reservations; some time may be needed to prepare special accommodations. Call ahead to restaurants, museums, and other facilities to find out if they are handicapped-accessible. **Guide dog owners** should inquire as to the quarantine policies of each destination country.

USEFUL ORGANIZATIONS

Access Abroad (www.umabroad.umn.edu/access), a website devoted to making study abroad available to students with disabilities. The site is maintained by Disability Services Research and Training, University of Minnesota, University Gateway, Ste. 180, 200 Oak St. SE, Minneapolis, MN 55455, USA (☎612-626-1333).

Flying Wheels, 143 W. Bridge St., PO Box 382, Owatonna, MN 55060, USA (☎507-451-5005; www.flyingwheelstravel.com), specializes in escorted trips to Europe for people with physical disabilities; plans custom accessible trips worldwide.

Mobility International USA (MIUSA), PO Box 10767, Eugene, OR 97440, USA (☎541-343-1284; www.miusa.org), provides a variety of books and other publications containing information for travelers with disabilities.

Society for Accessible Travel & Hospitality (SATH), 347 Fifth Ave., #610, New York, NY 10016, USA (☎212-447-7284; www.sath.org), an advocacy group that publishes free online travel information and the magazine *Open World* (1 year US$13, outside US US$21). Annual membership US$45, students and seniors US$30.

MINORITY TRAVELERS

Nearly all of Ecuador's population is Caucasian, indigenous, or a mixture of the two. This homogeneity means that any foreign traveler—regardless of skin color—is bound to stick out and attract substantial attention, particularly when traveling in rural or less touristed areas. In general, light-skinned travelers are viewed as wealthier and therefore are more likely to be the targets of petty crime. Travelers of African or Asian ancestry will likely attract attention from curious locals and their children, who may giggle, point, and stare. Asians are called *chinos*, while Blacks are often called *morenos* or *negros*. Usually these words are not meant to be offensive; to natives of this region they are simply descriptive terms. In many rural areas, non-Spanish speakers may be viewed as a threat.

DIETARY CONCERNS

Vegetarians are rare in Ecuador, and vegans are almost unheard of. In larger cities, vegetarians shouldn't have too much trouble; however, in smaller towns, where every restaurant seems to serve a fixed *menú*, vegetarians may have to resort to rice. Still, many restaurants can serve a vegetarian dish upon request—eggs are a popular option. When ordering, request a dish *sin carne* (without meat). Another option is to visit the local market and stock up on fruits and vegetables.

The travel section of the **The Vegetarian Resource Group** (www.vrg.org/travel) has a comprehensive list of organizations and websites that are geared toward helping vegetarians and vegans traveling abroad. Vegetarians will also find numerous resources on the web; try www.vegdining.com or www.happy-cow.net. The North American Vegetarian Society, PO Box 72, Dolgeville, NY 13329, USA (☎518-568-7970; www.navs-online.org), publishes information about vegetarian travel, including *Transformative Adventures, a Guide to Vacations and Retreats* (US$15). For more information on vegetarianism, visit your local bookstore, health food store, or library, and consult *The Vegetarian Traveler: Where to Stay if You're Vegetarian, Vegan, Environmentally Sensitive,* by Jed and Susan Civic (Larson Publications; US$16).

Travelers who keep kosher should contact synagogues in larger cities for information on kosher restaurants. Your own synagogue or college Hillel should have access to lists of Jewish institutions. If you are strict in your observance, you may have to prepare your own food on the road. A good resource is the *Jewish Travel Guide,* by Michael Zaidner (Vallentine Mitchell; US$17). Travelers looking for halal restaurants may find www.zabihah.com a useful resource.

OTHER RESOURCES

Let's Go tries to cover all aspects of budget travel, but we can't put *everything* in our guides. Listed below are books and websites that can serve as jumping-off points for your own research.

USEFUL PUBLICATIONS

Latin American Travel Advisor, PO Box 17-17-908, Quito, Ecuador (fax (32) 562 566; lata@pi.pro.ec; www.amerispan.com/lata/), publishes a quarterly newsletter on Latin America, focusing on public safety, health, weather, travel costs, politics, and economics. US$39 for 1-year subscription. Sells road, city, and topographic maps. Organizes small-group expeditions and private guides. Complete travel information service.

Specialty Travel Index, 305 San Anselmo Ave., #313, San Anselmo, CA 94960, USA (☎415-459-4900 or 800-442-4922; fax 459-4974; info@specialtytravel.com; www.specialtytravel.com), is a biannually published list of specialty travel opportunities through adventure tour operators. 1-year subscription (2 copies) US$10 (US$15 to Canada and US$20 overseas), but information is also available for free on the website.

ESSENTIALS

WORLD WIDE WEB

Almost every aspect of budget travel is accessible via the web. In 10min. at the keyboard, you can make a hostel reservation or get advice on travel hotspots from other travelers. Listed here are regional and travel-related sites to start you off; other relevant web sites are listed throughout the book. Because website turnover is high, use search engines (such as www.google.com) to strike out on your own.

 WWW.LETSGO.COM Our freshly redesigned website features extensive content from our guides; community forums where travelers can connect with each other and ask questions or advice—as well as share stories and tips; and expanded resources to help you plan your trip. Visit us soon to browse by destination, find information about ordering our titles, and sign up for our e-newsletter!

INFORMATION ON ECUADOR

CIA World Factbook: www.odci.gov/cia/publications/factbook/index.html. Tons of vital statistics on Ecuador's geography, government, economy, and people.

Geographia: www.geographia.com. Highlights, culture, and people of Ecuador.

Atevo Travel: www.atevo.com/guides/destinations. Detailed introductions, travel tips, and suggested itineraries.

World Travel Guide: www.travel-guides.com. Helpful practical info.

PlanetRider: www.planetrider.com. A subjective list of links to the "best" websites covering the culture and tourist attractions of Ecuador.

ESSENTIALS

LIFE AND TIMES

THE LAND

Travelers come to Ecuador from all over the globe to bask on Pacific beaches, scour Andean peaks, and float along Amazonian tributaries. The country's extraordinary geography has lured foreigners for centuries. The **Andes** span the western side of South America, stretching more than 4000 miles from Venezuela to the southern tip of Chile. In a classic prehistoric tale of the birds and the bees, two tectonic plates collided over 70 million years ago to produce the second-largest mountain range in the world. Wind and water have not yet worked their erosive magic on the young, rugged peaks, but the region's geology is far from static; the entire western coast of South America lies on the edge of a continental plate that is being subducted by the oceanic plate of the Pacific. Frequent earthquakes and occasional eruptions are, therefore, the norm. All along the Andes, active and extinct **volcanoes** mingle with long stretches of arable Highlands (Sierra).

The wet, cold **páramo** (high, bleak tableland) dominates the upper reaches of the Ecuadorian Andes. Seemingly bleak, this area's short, shrubby bushes burst into color from September to November. To the south, volcanoes give way to the **Highlands**, or Sierra, where two mountain ranges cradle a high, fertile valley. This arable land is cultivated with crops such as barley, wheat, and corn, resulting in the typical Andean landscape of patchwork fields dominated by snowcapped volcanoes, with an occasional sparkling lake thrown in for good measure. Coffee, bananas, and *cacao* thrive in the **Lowlands**, which were completely forested until cultivated. These fertile lands helped make Ecuador one of the first banana republics and the world's largest exporter of bananas. Swampy areas follow the coastline. The **Pacific Coast** is lined with sparsely populated, sandy beaches alongside warm waters that keep the air steamy all year. East of the central corridor formed by the Andes, the hot, humid **Amazon Rainforest** (called the **Oriente** in Ecuador) occupies much of the country's land area. Many indigenous communities (Huaorani, Siecoya, Siona, Quichua, Cofán, and Shuar) live in this region. Much of South America's world-renowned biodiversity can be found here, despite detrimental oil fields, cattle ranches, and slash-and-burn agriculture.

The **Galápagos Islands** (see p. 320) are an ecological niche all their own. Formed over the past five million years from the eruptions of underwater volcanoes, the islands began as barren lava masses. Today, they teem with animal and plant species that have crossed the water from the continent to the islands. The warm waters of El Niño and the cold ones of the Humboldt current battle to keep temperatures warm but replete with rain. The first half of the year acts as the wet season, the last half drier and cooler with temperatures below 21°C

Unfortunately, Ecuador's natural treasures haven't translated into wealth for its people. Despite the banana boom of the 50s and the oil boom of the 70s, the country's economy continues to struggle. Meanwhile, the political scene fluctuates up and down, throwing even the presidents for a loop (from 1931 to 1948, none of Ecuador's 21 presidents succeeded in completing a full term in office). Nevertheless, in the midst of adversity, the Ecuadorian people have managed to retain their energetic way of life, visible in everything from their undying enthusiasm for soccer to their lively chatter on even the most crowded of buses. Ecuador's natural wonders and personable populace will pleasantly surprise visitors.

LIFE AND TIMES

ECUADOR FACTS AND FIGURES	
CAPITAL Quito	**DECLARED INDEPENDENCE** May 24, 1822
PRESIDENT Lucio Gutiérrez	
POPULATION 13½ million	**RATIO** of foreigners to residents in the Galápagos: 3 to 1
AREA 283,560 sq. km	
INFLATION RATE 12.0%	**PRINCIPAL EXPORTS** petroleum, bananas, shrimp, coffee, cocoa, cut flowers, fish
HIGHEST POINT Chimborazo 6310m	

FLORA AND FAUNA

The breathtaking landscapes of Ecuador are home to one of the world's most diverse collections of plant and animal life. The **rainforests** of the Amazon Basin host half of the world's two million known plant and animal species. Thousands of animal species thrive beneath this thick canopy, including piranhas, dolphins, howler monkeys, bats, tapirs, jaguars, guatusa, capybaras, and three-toed sloths.

The mountainous **cloud forests** covering the upper slopes of the Andes are remarkable for their combination of cool, moist air, fairy-tale flora, and masses of endemic species. Wizened trees are covered in bright moss and colorful mushrooms. The spectacled bear, the only species of bear found in South America, resides in this Highlands Region, as does the alpaca. Ornithologists were astounded in January 1998 when a previously unknown species of bird was discovered in an area near the Parque Nacional Podocarpus (see p. 186). Mainland Ecuador alone has 1600 bird species—more than twice as many as all of North America. Home to corn, potatoes, lima beans, common beans, various peppers, and tobacco, the Highlands are also one of the few world crop-gene centers. However, like the Lowlands rainforests, these forests are quickly being destroyed. Higher up in the Andes, the less threatened *páramo* landscape takes over with colorful spring-time hues of the *tabacote*, Indian paintbrush, lupinus, and sage. Meanwhile, Andean condors and royal eagles soar above rabbits and shrews.

The Ecuadorian coast is home to the *tagua* nut (used to make buttons) and the *paja toquilla* (for the famed Panama hats), and is also home to endangered **mangrove forests.** In the Galápagos, six zones of vegetation support mangroves, cacti, ferns, orchids, coffee plants, pineapple trees, and much more. Thirty endemic species of birds, iguanas, sea lions, penguins, and the endangered giant tortoise, from which the archipelago derives its name, comprise its animal kingdom.

THE PEOPLE

The ethnic make-up of Ecuador's people has resulted from a process of continuous biological and cultural infusion, beginning with the arrival of the first inhabitants of the country's coastal regions over 12,000 years ago. No invasions by other peoples are known until the time of the **Quichua-speaking Incas,** who conquered and assimilated the natives just decades before the **Spanish.** Other ethnic groups have also been mixed into the picture—**African slaves** came to work plantations on the coast. Also, small communities of **Chinese** and **Lebanese** have immigrated here.

The majority of today's diverse population of 13½ million lives in the Highlands and coastal regions. And though the urban centers of Quito and Guayaquil each hold 2-2½ million, more and more people are moving to the sparsely populated Oriente. Issues of race and ethnicity are closely intertwined; an individual's identity as white, black, **mes-**

tizo (mixed white and indigenous), or **Indígena** (indigenous) is a combination of genetic and social factors, making it impossible to know how the population breaks down racially. The current estimate is 5% black, 15% white, 40% *mestizo*, and 40% *indígena*.

The small black population lives mostly in the northern coastal province of Esmeraldas and in the Chota Valley of the northwest. Descendants of slaves who arrived in Ecuador during the 17th and 18th centuries, black Ecuadorians maintain a distinct culture and ethnicity today. The country's white population is predominantly made up of descendants of Spanish conquistadors and colonists. Like their ancestors, they make up the majority of the country's elite and are concentrated in urban centers. *Mestizos* or *cholos* make up the bulk of Ecuador's urban population and also inhabit rural areas that sometimes overlap with indigenous communities, though Ecuador's *mestizos* are far from a culturally homogenous group.

The ancestors of the indigenous peoples lived on the land that became Ecuador when the Spaniards arrived. The largest indigenous group (numbering over two million) are the highland **Quichua,** who have many regional distinctions. They derive their name from their dialect of Peruvian Quichua. Some of the better known groups are the **Otavaleños,** who live in and around the town of Otavalo (see p. 106); the **Salasaca** (see p. 149), who live south of Ambato; and the **Saraguros** (see p. 199), who live north of Loja in southern Ecuador. In the coastal Lowlands, only a few small groups remain: the **Awa,** the **Cayapas,** and the **Colorados.** The Amazon also has its share of indigenous groups. The largest of these are the Quichua, who live in the central and southern Oriente and number over 60,000. Of the Jívaro ethnicity are the **Achuar** and the **Shuar.** Other smaller Oriente groups—some living in relative isolation—are the **Cofán,** the **Siona,** and the **Siecoya** in the Northern Oriente, and the **Huaorani** in and around Yasuní National Park.

HISTORY

THE EARLIEST ECUADORIANS

Long before the Incas arrived in 1463, **pre-Hispanic civilizations** thrived in the region. Archaeological evidence points to evidence of Ecuadorian communities on the southern coast—in the Loja area and near Quito—flourishing over 12,000 years ago. Auspicious ocean currents and winds made the coast ideal for agriculture, enabling an industrious settlement to survive for 8000 years.

The oldest extensive archaeological findings are remnants of the **Valdivians,** who lived along the coast of the Santa Elena Peninsula roughly between 3500 and 1500 BC. Early Valdivians were hunter-gatherers but later developed farming techniques. The earliest known site is **Loma Alta,** dating to 3500 BC, which features impressive pottery and female figurines. Another site, **Real Alto,** reached its peak by 1500 BC and is scattered with remnants of tens of households as well as female figurines. Such sites point to the existence of trade networks connecting the coast, Sierra, and jungle. Other cultures, such as **La Tolita,** inhabited the Pacific coast for 700 years (reaching its peak in 300 BC), producing some of the most remarkable goldwork known in Ecuador—including the famous mask of the Sun God, whose image is often replicated in Ecuadorian literature and culture. Finally, the first uses of platinum— not used in Europe until the 19th century—occurred here. Slowly, Ecuadorian cultures expanded and developed, creating a background against which later cultures would flourish.

Little is known about the different pre-Inca tribes, except that each had its own language and all frequently declared war on each other. Groups in the coastal Lowlands—the **Esmeralda, Manta, Huancavilca,** and **Puná** tribes—were hunters, fisherman, agriculturalists, and extensive traders. The sedentary and mainly agricultural Sierra tribes—the **Pasto, Cara, Panzaleo, Puruhá, Cañari,** and **Plata**—used irrigation to cultivate corn, quinoa, beans, many varieties of potatoes and squash, and fruits such as pineapples and avocados. Local chieftains raised armies, distributed communal lands, and united different villages in political confederations headed by single monarchs. Lifestyles such as these persisted in Ecuador for over 1000 years, by which time hierarchical societies had formed all over the Highlands.

THE INCA EMPIRE

At its height, the Inca Empire, controlling nearly one-third of South America and more than 10 million people, was the largest empire in the world. It all started around 1438 in a faraway land (normally referred to as **Cusco**, or Qosqo in the Inca tongue of Quichua). The origin of the first Inca is much disputed. Some say that the first Inca, Manco Cápac, arose from Lake Titicaca. Others say that he was merely a well-dressed native. Regardless, he was considered to be the son of the sun and accepted as leader of the Quechua people.

IMPERIALISM 101: HOW ECUADOR ENTERS THE SCENE. Seeking to expand their empire from its capital in Cusco (in modern-day Peru), the Inca moved into Ecuador in the late 15th century. Their conquest began in 1463 under the leadership of the warrior **Pachacuti Inca Yupanqui.** Several Ecuadorian tribes met the Inca troops with fierce resistance, and it took nearly four decades before both the Sierra and coastal populations surrendered. **Huayna Cápac,** grandson of Pachacuti Inca Yupanqui and son of a Cañari princes, became ruler of the entire Inca empire.

Though the Inca only controlled Ecuador for about 50 years before the Spanish conquest, they left a tremendous mark. Some aspects of life among the native Ecuadorian tribes, such as their traditional religious beliefs, did not change much; but nearly every other area of society was greatly influenced. The Inca introduced crops from Peru such as yucca, sweet potatoes, cacao, and peanuts. In addition, the use of llamas and irrigation also increased greatly. The biggest change involved the possession of land. All land became the property of the Inca emperor, held collectively by the **ayllu,** a kinship-based clan. Each ayllu allotted individual families land to cultivate for their own consumption, as long as it gave payments to the **kuraka,** or chieftan. Huayna Cápac grew up in Ecuador and adored his childhood homeland, naming Quito the second capital of the Inca empire. Fearful of unrest in his ever-expanding kingdom, he traveled all over the empire, quelling uprisings and strengthening alliances. These colonizations helped spread the traditionally Peruvian language of Quechua (called Quichua in Ecuador) north.

THE BEGINNING OF THE END. Huayna Cápac made one fatal mistake. Rather than leaving the empire to one heir, he split the kingdom between two sons. Cusco and the southern empire were left to **Huáscar,** a son by Huayna Cápac's sister and therefore his legitimate heir. Ecuador and the northern empire went to **Atahualpa,** borne by a lesser wife but his father's favorite. In 1532, Atahualpa decisively defeated Huáscar near Riobamba in central Ecuador, a victory that still remains a source of great national pride as one of the rare occasions when Ecuador defeated a hostile neighboring power. The Inca empire was left weakened and divided, unprepared for the arrivial of the Spanish conquistadors a few months later.

THE SPANISH ARRIVE

The Spaniards landed near Esmeraldas in northern Ecuador on September 21, 1526, but the first conquering mission, led by **Francisco Pizarro,** did not get underway until 1532. Spain's King Carlos V granted Pizarro the titles of governor and captain-general of Peru, so Pizarro set out determined to conquer the troublesome Quechua people. At a pre-arranged meeting between Atahualpa and Pizarro in the town of **Cajamarca** in northern Peru, the Inca emperor disdainfully rejected both the Spanish crown and the Christian god and was promptly attacked. The Spaniards killed thousands of Inca and held Atahualpa for ransom. As payment, Atahualpa's followers filled Atahualpa's cell once with gold and twice with silver. It turned out not to be enough. Instead of freeing Atahualpa, Pizarro put him on trial, convicting him of polygamy, worship of false gods, and offenses against the king. Atahualpa was executed on August 29, 1533.

Despite the loss of their leader, some Quechua warriors continued to defend their empire. The general **Rumiñahui,** with the help of Cañari tribesmen, was a major leader of the rebellion. In the end, **Sebastián de Benalcázar,** one of Pizarro's lieutenants, defeated Rumiñahui near Mount Chimborazo and began pushing the Inca north. In mid-1534, when Rumiñahui realized that the Spaniards would soon conquer Quito, he set it ablaze, preferring to destroy this secondary Inca capitol rather than surrender it. Rumiñahui's eventual defeat marked the final victory in the Spanish conquest. Quito was refounded by the Spaniards on **December 6, 1534,** a day that is still celebrated with parades, bullfights, and dances.

THE COLONIAL ERA

Initially part of the **Viceroyalty of Peru,** Ecuador was tightly controlled by the Spanish crown, subject to the king's administrative agencies: the **viceroy,** the **audencia** (court), and the **cabildo** (municipal council). In 1536, Ecuador gained separate status from Peru, attaining its own **Audencia de Quito**—meaning it could deal more directly with Madrid. In 1720, in an attempt to tighten Spanish control over the colonies, Ecuador became part of the **Viceroyalty of Nueva Granada,** and central authority shifted from Lima to Bogotá.

Spanish **encomenderos** (conquistadors given control of indigenous labor in exchange for Christianizing and protecting the *indígenas* living on that land) created huge plantations for themselves, which they obtained by making deals with the kurakas (local chieftans). The kurakas acquiesced to the more powerful Spaniards and agreed to hand over their ayllu's tribute payments, supposedly in exchange for the orderliness that Spanish Christianity brought to them. During the 1570s, however, Spanish officials tightened their control over the Incas, abolishing *encomiendas* (the viceroyalties given *encomenderos*) and establishing a social system known as the **repartamiento de indios,** which made the entire indigenous population vassals of the Spanish crown. It also introduced the **mita,** a system that required all men between the ages of 18 and 50 to labor for the Spanish crown for at least two months each year. Overseen by **corregidores,** new Spanish officials in charge of administering the *mita,* Ecuadorian **mitayos** (workers) labored on huge agricultureal **haciendas** or in **obrajes** (primitive textile sweatshops). The largest threat to the *indígenas*, however, was disease. **Smallpox** and **measles** brought by the colonists virtually wiped out the coastal population and drastically reduced the Sierra populations, especially during an epidemic in the 1690s.

THE INDEPENDENCE MOVEMENT

Ecuador's struggle for independence was part of a larger independence movement, sweeping Spanish America. During the 18th century, tensions escalated as the **criollos** (people of European descent born in the New World) resented their limited access to indigenous labor, high taxes of the Spanish crown, trade restrictions, and the privileges the Spanish-born **peninsulares** had in gaining political office. Tensions heightened further after Europe's Seven Years' War (1756-63), when the defeated and bankrupt Spanish kingdom passed the **Bourbon Reforms,** increasing control over the colonists and boosting tax revenue.

The first revolts against colonial rule were expressions of support for the king following France's 1808 invasion of Spain. In Guayaquil, a patriotic junta under the leadership of poet **José Joaquín Olmedo** proclaimed the city's independence in October 1820. Troops from both the independence movements of the Argentine **José San Martin** and the Venezuelan **Simón Bolívar** helped Ecuador fight in the struggle against the royalist forces. Lieutenant **Antonio José de Sucre** led a string of patriotic victories culminating in the decisive **Battle of Pichincha** on May 24, 1822. Yet independence did not mean an end to the struggle. The next year, Ecuador joined the **Confederation of Gran Colombia,** which lasted for seven years. Accompanied by Colombia and Venezuela, this alliance reflected Bolívar's grand plan to unite Latin America. Yet regional rivalries plagued this confederation causing it to split up in 1830, with a small southwestern section becoming the Republic of Ecuador.

THE EARLY REPUBLIC (1830-60)

During its tormented, early years, various rivalries plagued Ecuador, causing divisive hostilities between politicians, ideologues, and even regions. Quito and the Sierra emerged as conservative and clerical, dominated by semi-feudal estates that still relied on indigenous labor, whereas the cosmopolitan, commercial port of Guayaquil, ruled by a nouveau riche merchant class, had more exposure to the ideas of 19th-century Latin America. The liberal-conservative split made it impossible for the people of Ecuador to agree peacefully on a national leader.

The most natural leader seemed to be **General Juan José Flores,** whom Bolívar appointed governor of Ecaudor when it was part of Gran Colombia. As part of the *criollo* elite, Flores found his support among the conservative Quiteños, while **José Vicente Rocafuerte** rose as his rival in liberal Guayaquil. While Rocafuerte considered himself an enlightened despot, promoting civil liberties and developing the public school system, Flores put more effort into commanding the military and securing his power. In the end, though more successful than Rocafuerte in gaining control of Ecuador, Flores was ousted in 1845. A series of coup d'états weakened the leadership and strengthened the military. One of the more influential leaders, **General José María Urbina,** ruled from 1851 to 1856. As soon as he came into office, Urbina emancipated the nation's slaves and played a large role in ending the indigenous populations' tribute payments. But by 1859, a year known infamously as the **Terrible Year,** the country again stood in a state of near anarchy after one local caudillo stirred up anger by trying to cede some Ecuadorian territory to Peru.

THE CONSERVATIVE REGIME (1860-95)

While some hail **Gabriel García Moreno** as the father of Ecuadorian conservatism and the country's greatest nation-builder, others condemn him as its worst tyrant. During the 1840s and 50s, he watched as his country fractured along racial, regional, and class lines. His diagnosis: the nation needed cohesion. At first, he toyed with the idea of incorporation into the French empire, but when France appeared more interested in Mexico, he turned to the Roman Catholic Church.

From that point on, **Catholicism** was the magic ingredient in García Moreno's social cement. After beginning his authoritarian 15-year rule in 1860, he placed state matters such as education and social welfare within the Church's domain, hoping that religious order, hierarchy, and discipline would unify the country. An 1861 charter declared Catholicism the state religion, ties to the Vatican were strengthened in 1863, and a decade later, the republic was officially dedicated to the Sacred Heart of Jesus. In this respect, Ecuador deviated from the path of most other Latin American nations, whose military dictatorships passed anticlerical measures. Yet, despite García Moreno's ties to the Church, his accomplishments were often progressive: he constructed a railroad from Guayaquil to Quito, ending the isolation of the Sierra; built many new roads, school, and hospitals; planted Australian eucalyptus trees in the Highlands to combat erosion; and infused the cities with a greater sense of nationalism. Despite these accomplishments, García Moreno was hacked to death with a machete in 1875 by disgruntled peasants while standing on the steps of the presidential palace. Nevertheless, his brand of conservatism lingered for the next 20 years. By 1895, however, the progressive conservative leaders were plagued by scandal, and the liberals finally saw the change to make their move. Led by General José Eloy Alfaro Delgado, the **Partido Liberal Radical (PLR)** stormed Quito, emerging victorious after a brief civil war.

THE ERA OF LIBERALISM (1895-1925)

For the next 30 years, **General José Eloy Alfaro Delgado** (president 1897-1901 and 1906-11) was to liberalism what García Moreno had been to conservatism. One of his first presidential initiatives was to create a secular constitution removing many Church privileges, exiling prominent clergy, secularizing education, and ending the republic's dedication to the Sacred Heart of Jesus. Later, Alfaro created constructed ports and roads and completing the Guayaquil-Quito railroad. As it was, Alfaro's infrastructural improvements served little purpose without a profitable export to transport. The exploitation of *indígena* labor continued unchecked, and Alfaro's repression of political opponents proved just as ruthless as that of his predecessors. When he refused to step down after his second term ended in 1911, Alfaro was forced into exile in Panama. The new president died only four months later, and when Alfaro returned, a lynch mob killed him.

In the next 13 years, the government changed hands four times among liberal leaders. Executive power reduced after Alfaro's demise, a Guayaquil plutocracy of coastal agricultural and banking interests known as **La Argolla** (The Ring) started to call the shots. During World War I and the short economic boom that followed, **cocoa** (a powder made from cacao) became Ecuador's dominant export, and the country's economy briefly thrived. Disaster struck in the early 1920s when a **fungal disease** ravaged Ecuador's cacao trees and the British colonies in Africa became a major cacao-growing competitor. The resulting inflation and unemployment hit the poor and working classes especially hard. In the **July Revolution** of 1925, a group of young military officers overthrew the government in a bloodless coup. They believed they could start a new program of national regeneration and unity.

THE TURBULENT YEARS (1925-48)

Though preaching a socialist ideology, many of the leaders of the July Revolution soon discovered that army officers envisioned a new regime based more on Mussolini than Marx. The 1926-31 military dictatorship of **Isidro Ayora** seized the nation with an iron fist. Among his reforms, Ayora created the Central Bank of Ecuador, which took away the power to issue currency from private banks and devalued the (now-defunct) sucre to help Highlands exporters. One critic said that Ayora's **public cleansing** reforms meant "prohibitions on entering markets, public buildings, schools, parks, and theaters without wearing shoes—but no reforms which gave the unshod means to buy them." With the **stock market crash** of 1929, nearly every Latin American government came tumbling down—including Ayora's. Overthrown in 1931, Ayora was the first of 14 presidents to step down in the next decade. In fact, from 1931 to 1948, none of Ecuador's 21 presidents succeeded in completing one full term in office. Ecuador fared no better than the rest of the world during the **Great Depression.** The global demand for cocoa dropped drastically; the price fell by 58%; and Ecuador's exports decreased by nearly 50%. To add to the strife and instability, a four-day civil war broke out in Quito in August 1932.

The scene was perfectly set for charismatic leader **José María Velasco Ibarra,** who took on his first of five presidential stints from 1934 to 1935 (also 1944-47, 1952-56, 1960-61, and 1968-72). A master of 20th-century populist politics, Velasco later went on to create his own personal movement, **Velasquismo,** based on his charisma, a carefully cultivated image of honesty and sincerity, and fiery orations. However, the military overthrew him after less than a year for trying to assume dictatorial powers. Fiscal crises, political coups, power struggles, and fraudulent elections marked the nine years before he returned. **Carlos Alberto Arroyo del Río** claimed victory in the disputed 1940 presidential election (it was popularly believed that Velasco had been the victor). Arroyo del Río's government fell apart when a border dispute with Peru became a disastrous 1941 military defeat. Peru's occupation of Ecuador continued until January 1942, when both countries signed a treaty known as **Río Protocol,** ceding about 200,000 sq. km of Ecuadorian Oriente to Peru, and still a cause of animosity between the two countries.

Velasco returned to power in 1944 and managed to enchant the masses with his fine-tuned populist rhetoric. Yet instead of dealing with the country's pressing economic problems, Velasco obsessed over restoring Ecuador's morality and social justice. Inflation and the standard of living worsened; when he was ousted in 1947, Velasco had alienated so many of his supporters that nobody rose to defend him.

THE RISE OF THE MILITARY (1960-79)

Between 1948 and 1960, Ecuador experienced a period of political stability—for a change. Economic prosperity accompanied the country's status as the US's main banana supplier until disease ravaged the Central American crop in the late 40s. Re-elected in 1952, Velasco began referring to himself as "the National Personification." By 1960, however, lower export prices resulted in a rise in unemployment and general social discontent. The 1959 **Cuban Revolution** had profound reverberations throughout Latin America. Steering toward Communism, Velasco began including more leftists in his government and consciously antagonizing the US. The National Congress's debate over Ecuador's ideological future became so heated that gunshots were fired in the Chamber of Deputies. In 1961, Vice President **Carlos Julio Arosemena Monroy** ousted his superior and sent a goodwill mission to Washington in the hopes of renewing favorable relations. But as Ecuador grew dangerously tumultuous, the US blamed Arosemena and accused him of weakness or Communist sympathies. In July 1963, a four-man **military junta** seized power. It vowed to implement basic socioeconomic reforms and take a hard-line stance against Communism. However, after a bloody attack on the students of Central University in Quito, the military reformers stepped down.

When in doubt, Ecuadorians could always vote for Velasco, and in 1968 this master of charisma began an unprecedented fifth term. Frustrated with the gridlock caused by an uncooperative Congress, Velasco assumed dictatorial powers in June 1970. Until his overthrow in 1972, he maintained these powers with the support of the military. The 1972 military coup was not due to the army's lack of support for Velasco; rather, it was provoked by the army's fear that **Asaad Bucaram Elmhalim** might be elected after Velasco's term ran out a few months later. The leader of the populist **Concentration of Pouplar Forces (CFP)** and extremely popular two-time governor of Guayaquil, Bucaram was considered by both military and business interests to be dangerous, unpredictable, and unfit for the presidency. For the next seven years, Ecuador was ruled by military leaders determined to make structural changes in the country and encourage development. Yet they were not prepared for the 1970s **oil boom**. After joining the **Organization of Petroleum Exporting Countries (OPEC)**, the minister of natural resources tried pricing Ecuadorian oil well above the world market price. Exports fell, and combined with a lack of infrastructure reforms, the country's economic problems worsened.

The creation of a new constitution and the democratic election of a president was supposed to happen in 1976, but the process was delayed—partly to ensure that Bucaram would not be elected. He was eventually barred from running, but the second-in-command of the CFP, **Jaime Roldós Aguilera,** with his reformist platform, won a run-off election in 1979 with 68.5% of the vote. **Osvaldo Hurtado Larrea,** leader of the **Christian Democratic Party (PDC),** stood as his running mate.

A RETURN TO DEMOCRACY (1979-96)

The Roldós Hurtado regime began under auspicious circumstances. With the country's preferential treatment as part of the **Andean Common Market,** the oil boom was finally having positive repercussions for Ecuador. Unfortunately, this new wealth only increased the gap in income distribution. To make things worse, a rivalry developed between Roldós and Bucaram, and the president found himself at odds with his own party. In 1981, Roldós died in a plane crash near Loja. Ecuador's economic luck didn't last long. Oil reserves ran dry, and massive foreign borrowing led to a debt of almost US$7 billion by 1983. The warm ocean currents from **El Niño** in 1982 and 1983 brought drastic climate changes, resulting in nearly US$1 billion in infrastructure damage. Hurtado's regime responded with austerity measures to the negative economic growth and record-high 52% inflation in 1983. Unemployment skyrocketed to 13.5%, and the **United Workers Front (FUT)** launched three riotous strikes during Hurtado's term in office.

Elected in 1984, **León Febres Cordero Ribadeneyra** supported free-market economics and a pro US policy. Understandably, he was not popular in Ecuador. Oil prices continued to fall, and he continued to face troubles with the National Congress and the military. A March 1987 earthquake left 20,000 homeless and destroyed a stretch of the country's main oil pipeline, forcing the president to suspend interest payments on Ecuador's US$8.3 billion foreign debt. In 1988, the country's inflation rate and the government's austerity measures resulted in large-scale protests.

The recently elected president, **Rodrigo Borja Cevallos,** made agreements with paramilitary protest organizations, promising civil rights in exchange for demilitarization of his government. One organization, **Montoneros Patria Libre (MPL),** refused and continued with violent action. Cevallos not only faced opposition from outside the government but from within it as well. In 1989, the vice president's plans to organize a coup were exposed. Plans for another coup resulted in the 1990 impeachment of multiple members of Congress. That year also saw a rise in indigenous protests. The **National Confederation of the Indigenous Population of Ecuador (CONAIE)** planned a seven-province uprising, seizing oil wells and taking military hostages. Their demands included the return of various traditional community lands, recognition of Quichua as an official language, and compensation for environmental damage caused by petroleum companies. Though the protests ended when the government agreed to consider their demands, tensions heightened again in April 1992, when thousands of *indígenas* marched to Quito from the Oriente, demanding that their territorial rights be recognized (see p. 61).

During his 1992-96 presidency, **Sixto Durán Ballén** dealt with many of these same problems on a larger scale. Austerity measures designed to cut inflation continued to cause widespread protest and general strikes, especially with a 70% price increase in fuel in 1994. CONAIE and other indigenous movements demonstrated in mid-1994 against the **Land Development Law,** which allowed commercialization of

LIFE AND TIMES

indigenous lands for farming and resource extraction. The law was subsequently modified to protect the rights of landowners. Revelations of embezzlement by top officials led to numerous impeachments and even demands for Ballén's resignation, voiced through student demonstrations throughout 1995 and early 1996.

POLITICAL UNCERTAINTY (1996-98)

Abdala Bucaram (yet another Bucaram) of the **Partido Roldosista Ecuatoriano (PRE)** defeated **Jaime Nebot** of the **Partido Social Cristiano (PSC)** in the presidential election of July 7, 1996. Bucaram lost to Nebot in Ecuador's two biggest cities—Guayaquil (63% to 37%) and Quito (52% to 48%)—but overwhelmingly defeated him in the tiny towns in the Oriente. The conservative Nebot did not inspire enough confidence with his slogan "Primero La Gente" (First the People). On the other hand, Bucaram used the motto "Primero Los Pobres" (First the Poor), and advocated mass nationalization, insisting that the country's poor would come first when rebuilding the gubernatorial structure. After Bucaram's final 54-46% victory was confirmed, revelers from poor neighborhoods caroused all night in the city streets while disgruntled members of the bourgeoisie packed their bags.

Bucaram took office on August 10, 1996, and as his first presidential measure devalued the sucre. Not surprisingly, his popularity entered a state of rapid decline. Hikes in gas, telephone, and electricity taxes resulted in a 300% rise in utility prices. A proposal to make the sucre fully convertible against the US dollar met strong resistance in Congress, and labor reforms allowing easier dismissal of public sector employees infuriated trade unions. Surfacing reports of corruption earned the regime the nickname "Ali Abdala and the 40 thieves." By early January 1997, public discontent began to appear in the form of often violent protest, and the man of los pobres found himself abandoned by the very constituency that had put him into office. Tensions culminated on February 5 and 6, when the public sector unions, the left-wing political group **Movimiento Popular Democrático (MPD),** and the indigenous group CONAIE launched a united strike against the government.

Congress's response was swift and unprecedented. On February 6, the legislative branch ousted Abdala Bucaram from the presidency on grounds that he was mentally unfit. Bucaram barricaded himself within the presidential palace but was forced to resign when the military withdrew its support. Bucaram fled the country, insisting that a "civilian dictatorship" had been imposed and was granted political asylum in Panama. He left behind charges of misappropriating or wasting US$88 million, while taking with him paintings from the presidential palace. With military assistance, Vice President **Rosalía Arteaga** assumed control even though Congress had voted 57-2 that congressional head **Fabián Alarcón** would serve as Bucaram's successor. Arteaga's influence continues; in the summer of 1998, she launched an unsuccessful campaign to reclaim the presidential office.

DOLLARIZATION (1998-2002)

When Ecuadorians went to the polls on July 12, 1998, they elected president **Jamil Mahuad,** the Harvard-educated mayor of Quito. Mahuad inherited a severely troubled economy, and his administration took immediate and drastic measures. Nevertheless, the economy deteriorated significantly in late 1998 and early 1999. In a desperate attempt to stabilize the economy, Mahuad announced that Ecuador would replace the country's sucre with the US dollar. This announcement infuriated many Ecuadorians and ultimately caused Mahuad's demise. On January 21, 2000, a mass of Ecuadorian *indígenas*—supported by military officials and led by CONAIE—stormed Mahuad's palaces and overthrew the president in a bloodless coup. He was quickly replaced by one of the military officials, but when the US

The Transition from the Sucre to the Dollar

In his travel diary, Henri Michaux—a French poet of the early 20th century—wrote that Sucre was the "sweetest name" that someone could have given a currency. That was in 1928, during Michaux's one-year stay in Ecuador and 72 years before that "sweetness" went sour due to the most severe financial crisis in the nation's history.

Indeed, after decades of bad policy—growing indebtedness, rampant corruption, and gross misallocation of resources—Ecuador's local currency collapsed and was replaced by the US dollar. Why the switch in currency? Growing inflation (around 100% per annum) and a runaway depreciation of 525% between 1996 and 1999 destroyed confidence in the Sucre. As a result, the demand for local money sank and a speculative attack against this currency began: everyone cashed in their investments in Sucres and took out ones in dollars instead.

Thus, dollarization was accidentally imposed on the Ecuadorian economy. In March 2000, Gustavo Noboa—then president of Ecuador—made the process official by issuing an executive decree that allowed people to use the US dollar as their daily means of trade and savings. (The conversion rate was 1:25,000, which meant that each person was entitled to have one dollar for every 25,000 Sucres given up).

The US dollar's adoption was not easy at all. The eruption of this new legal tender created confusion and misapprehension, especially among the predominantly illiterate Ecuadorian rural population. Keynes would have called it "monetary illusion;" many were reluctant to exchange 50,000 Sucres for "only" two dollars. The population felt infuriated by what it considered an outrageous scam.

Despite those shortcomings—most of which have been overcome—dollarization contributed a great deal to the stabilization of the Ecuadorian economy. It permitted a substantial reduction of inflation, decreasing from 91% by the end of 2000 to 22.4% in only 12 months, without contracting the economy, as anti-inflationary policies usually do. Since then, the inflation rate has been consistently declining, reaching a level of 3% in June 2004, an historic low. On the other hand, the Ecuadorian GDP registered a 32% growth rate in 2001, one of the largest increments of the Latin American region that year. Of course, it must be considered that, in 1999 and 2000, the Ecuadorian economy decreased by 28% and 4%, respectively.

Low inflation plus low depreciation—at least for Ecuadorian standards—of the US dollar had other benefits as well: it preserved the purchasing power of local consumers. Among them, low-income families experienced that gain most dramatically. Thus, at the end of each month, Ecuadorians started to realize that they struggled less and less to make ends meet. In fact, these families discovered that they were even able to deposit a few dollars in their savings accounts, something rather extraordinary when compared with previous years.

As a result, savings slowly but steadily increased in the financial system. That not only helped to restore the credibility of local banks, but most importantly made interest rates decline. The cost of money went from a confiscating rate of 50% during the crisis years to a more affordable rate of 12% after dollarization was fully implemented. This substantial reduction in the cost of credit resulted in the expansion of investment, especially in real estate and industrial equipment, as well as in greater consumption.

Politically, dollarization contributed to the safeguarding of the country from populist economic policy. Under this regime, politicians can no longer print money at will for highly visible projects. As a result, the Ecuadorian political scene is stabilizing. However, social unrest still presents a significant threat—particularly among the country's most vulnerable populations, indigenous people and retirees. These two groups have been most affected by dollarization, and their plight has illustrated demands for a social safety net to preserve their interests.

Will dollarization survive in Ecuador? That is the key question everyone is asking. In "Crisis and Dollarization in Ecuador," a book recently published by the World Bank, experts argue that a successful dollarization experience will require the complete integration of the local financial system with international markets. Under the dollarized regime, the Central Bank no longer has the power to control the monetary supply. That role must be taken by the financial system, which has to have the capacity both to import and export capital in order to level the local monetary market.

Gonzalo Maldonado earned his MA in Government from the Harvard Extension School. He is currently an editor and regular contributor to the editorial page of Ecuador's newspaper El Comercio.

warned that a military government would not be recognized, Mahuad's vice president, **Gustavo Noboa,** took office. Noboa continued the controversial dollarization process, though Ecuador saw little immediate benefit. Continued inflation drove up prices and led to various strikes and protests. June 2001 brought a record inflation rate of 103.7%, which many Ecuadorians blamed on dollarization. Thankfully, the year closed with a 22% decrease in inflation and an overall economic growth of 5.4%. In 2002, Ecuador experienced growth, though it continued to struggle.

TODAY

In 2002, **Lucio Gutiérrez** was elected president of Ecuador. His rise to power began on January 21, 2000, when a coup of disgruntled young military officers and 5000 indigenous protesters attempted to oust President-elect Jamil Mahaud, whom they accused of corruption. Gutiérrez's role in the coup increased his popularity with the previously politically invisible indigenous populations of Ecuador. The resurgent indigenous political movement, **Pachakutik (Resurgence),** supported him through a run-off election against his rival, banana magnate Alvaro Noboa. Referred to by his supporters simply as "Lucio," Gutiérrez promised to help indigenous peoples of Ecuador gain greater equality and power within the country.

However, political instability has only worsened with his presidency. Initially a beacon of hope for *indígenas*, Gutiérrez has been criticized for abandoning his campaign promises. In mid-2004, Gutiérrez's approval ratings dropped to as low as 16%—perhaps related to the corruption scandals that have plagued his term. He recently fired his social welfare minister, one of his closest confidants, after the US placed him on a list of foreign officials suspected of corruption. Many citizens now blame Gutiérrez for the growing poverty in Ecuador exacerbated by attempts to meet the International Monetary Fund's criteria for qualifying for future financial aid. Others bemoan the millions spent on hosting the Miss Universe Pageant in 2004, claiming the money would have been better spent on social programs for the poor. Gutierrez's environmental policies are especially dubious. On February 26, 2004, when fishermen blockaded the entrance to the Charles Darwin Research Station demanding fishing rights, Gutiérrez's government relented, relaxing the preservation principles protecting the island's delicate ecosystem. A look at recent history suggests that the future for President Gutiérrez is questionable at best: no elected Ecuadorian president has finished his four-year term since 1996.

ECUADOR'S GOLD

THE BLACK KIND. Ecuador's natural ecosystems continue to be threatened by oil interests. President Noboa decided to extend the **Trans-Ecuadorian Pipeline** in order to increase oil extraction from the Oriente. The pipeline doubles Ecuador's oil transport capacity, thus supplying badly needed income. Unfortunately, the pathway cut directly through protected areas, including the beautiful Mindo Nambillo Cloud Forest Reserve, one of Ecuador's prime ecotourism destinations. The plan persisted despite outraged protesters.

THE WHITE KIND. As **Plan Colombia** (the US's billion dollar effort to eliminate coca growth and export) unfolds, Ecuador has had to take precautions to prevent the war on drugs from spilling onto its own soil. Despite its military presence near Colombia, the turmoil has crossed the border. Aerial fumigations of coca fields and increasing numbers of impoverished coca farmers have caused Colombians to flood across the border with Ecuador. Specifically, the area near Lago Agrio has been infiltrated with violence and kidnappings related to the drug trade. Disappointingly, the ills wrought by Plan Colombia have not been vindicated by its benefits. Over 500,000 acres of coca fields have been sprayed, yet the total area devoted to coca production is three times what it was five years ago.

INDIGENOUS IDENTITY

Each of Ecuador's indigenous groups has a distinct ethnic identity, and many identify more strongly with their ethnicity than with the Ecuadorian state. Until the mid-20th century, the government mainly catered to the needs of the white and *mestizo* majority of its population, and hardly at all to those of *indígenas*. As in most of Latin America, this unbalanced socio-political order is the legacy of colonial times, when indigenous peoples comprised the slave labor force in Spanish- and creole-owned haciendas, mines, and factories. Though liberal governments at the beginning of the 20th century sought to incorporate *indígenas* into the national community, the legacy of colonial exploitation remained. In the name of fighting for equality, liberals attempted to pass legislation that would free *indígenas* from ties to the church or private landholders. However, some interpreted this as an attempt by politicians to claim indigenous land and labor for themselves. Indigenous groups resisted these measures, and in 1937, two laws were enacted to reinforce indigenous rights to own land communally.

THE INDIGENOUS RESPONSE

Starting in the 1960s, indigenous and human rights organizations began to demand equality for Ecuadorian indígenas. A 1961 demonstration in Quito by 12,000 indigenous peasants demanded social change, and in 1964 an agrarian reform bill was passed that weakened the political power of the land-holding elite. Around this time, one of Ecuador's most successful and well-known indigenous groups founded the **Shuar Federation** in response to pressures from outside forces—including missionaries, colonists from the Highlands, and later, oil companies. The Shuar organized into groups of about 30 families, which hold land communally and have instituted a health care program and radio schooling system independent of the government. Although some criticize the Shuars' movement away from subsistence farming in favor of cattle ranching, this transition has helped the Shuar to prosper while maintaining their ethnic identity. Similary, the weavers of the Northern Highlands town of Otavalo (see p. 106) have preserved an ancient lifestyle—but not without catering to visitors to the famous Saturday market.

THE GOVERNMENT'S RESPONSE

More recently, the Ecuadorian government has attempted to incorporate aspects of indigenous experience and tradition into collective national identity. The **Roldós-Hurtado** administration (1979-84) expressed a desire to include formerly marginalized groups in national political life. They created the **Fund for Rural Development for Marginalized Groups (FODERUMA),** which sought to integrate peasant labor and products into the national market. However, outside administrators disagreed with indígenas on how funds should be used, prompting the common use of the nickname JODERUMA (*joder* meaning "to screw someone over"). In other cases, populations have shown more active resistance to the integration of a local, ethnic identity into a national one. A number of state-sponsored celebrations of traditional culture, aimed at fostering national identity, have received mixed responses. Many indigenous people value the attention being given to their dance and music, but more radical groups criticize them as fictionalized versions of indigenous culture. Some new celebrations are grounded in local tradition but lose their meaning in a national context. One example is Otavalo's festival of Yamor, boycotted by a group of indígenas in 1983 and 1984. Originally a celebration of the corn harvest, the tourism industry promoted it with parades and fireworks. The offended indígenas resented the use of traditional ritual to satisfy outside interests. A similar instance concerned a series of government stamps issued to celebrate Ecuador's indigenous heritage. The people of the town of Quimsa—whose culture, they said, had been incorrectly depicted—protested that the stamps implied that culture functioned like a collectible item.

THE INDIGENOUS REACTION

Irritated that the government has aimed to achieve indigenous assimilation rather than support, indígenas have developed a number of organizations to voice their desires and complaints. In 1989, these groups came together under an umbrella organization called the **Confederation of Indigenous Nationalities of Ecuador (CONAIE)**. The next year, CONAIE organized the largest indigenous uprising in Ecuador's history, paralyzing the country for a week. Their rallying cry, "500 years of resistance and survival," protested the upcoming 1992 quincentenary celebration of Columbus's landing in the Americas. Their agenda included demands to help create a satisfactory relationship between indígenas and the state, including more indigenous autonomy and a proposed constitutional amendment making Ecuador a multinational state. These demands run contrary to the state's national vision and would obstruct the government's plans for oil development. However, after the political debacle of February 1997, in which Bucaram was chased from office, the interim government joined forces with CONAIE to establish **The People's Mandate**, which presented the National Constituent Assembly as an alternative governing body. At its first meeting, 400 indigenous representatives convened to discuss various indigenous issues. In January 1998, they released a suggested new constitution for Ecuador. With demands resonant with those of the original 1990 declaration, this document has forged a strong foundation for the indigenous movement.

CULTURE

FOOD AND DRINK

Although it has yet to become a widespread international delicacy, the food of Ecuador will not leave you unsatisfied. The staples of the region are enhanced with delectable spices and careful preparation.

 EATING IN ECUADOR. Even restaurants that have a menu often have a standard *almuerzo* (lunch) and *merienda* (dinner), either of which is a two-course affair with soup before a rice-and-meat entree (sometimes juice is included). These meals are filling, fast, and usually under US$2. Even some of the fancier restaurants have a set menu for less money than the regular items.

RESTAURANTS

The most common restaurants are small, family-owned diners, referred to as **comedores.** Unequivocally the most economical way to acquire your daily sustenance and certainly the most popular way to eat out among locals is the *menú del día* (meal of the day). Sometimes referred to as *el almuerzo* (lunch) during the day, la *merienda* (snack), or *la cena* (dinner) at night, the *menú* is a set platter at a set price—usually with two courses, a drink, and various extras. If it doesn't do the trick, check out the menu for a la carte selections. To diversify your diet, you may decide to dine at three other types of restaurants. **Chifas** (Chinese restaurants), present in even the smallest of towns, are generally clean and serve tasty and filling chaufas (fried-rice dishes). **Cevicherías** serve seafood, especially *ceviche* (or *cebiche*), a popular dish made from raw seafood marinated in lemon and lime juice (whose acids partly cook the meat), with cilantro and onion. **Pollerías** serve scrumptious *pollo a la brasa* (roasted chicken). Larger and more touristed cities also offer all the fast food, international food, and vegetarian options.

COMIDA

The more adventurous might try **tronquito** (bull penis) and **yaguarlocro** (soup with blood-sprinklings)—two of Ecuador's most erotic and exotic dishes. Equally shocking to foreigners is **cuy** (guinea pig). This specialty, dating back to Inca times, gets its name from the sound the animal makes just before getting skewered and roasted: *"cuy, cuy, cuy..."* More vegetarian-friendly **llapingachos** (Andean potato and cheese pancakes) also date back centuries: the root was first cultivated in the Andes before becoming a starch staple around the world. Other veggie delights include banana and plantain dishes, which are mainstays of the *costeño* (coast-dweller) diet. **Patacones** (deep fried plantain slices) compliment the Ecuadorian favorite, *ceviche*. Other common dishes include *encebollado*, and *fritada*. The former is a soup, also known as *languriango*, made with yellow fin tuna and yuca. The latter is delectable fried pork. Breakfast *(desayuno)* is offered in most *comedores*, though it is usually light. Most common are bread, juice, coffee, eggs, and sometimes rice and beans, as well as plantain dishes such as *chirriados* in certain regions. Highly touristed areas may offer a *desayuno americano*, which includes a bit more food for the more voracious appetite. If you don't mind a light breakfast (or want a midday snack), a quick and easy way to grab a bite is to buy fruit at the local **mercado** (market) or visit a **panadería** (bakery).

BEBIDA

Fruit juices abound in Ecuador—the Oriente boasts *naranjilla* (a bitter-sweet orange-like fruit), *tomate de árbol, mora* (blackberry), *guanábana, maracuya*, and papaya juice galore. **Coffee** is not as good as it should be; it is usually served as *esencia* (boiled-down, concentrated grinds mixed with water or milk). You might also be served hot water with a can of instant coffee. **Mate de coca** (coca tea) is a good cure for altitude sickness, and a local specialty. A favorite dairy drink is **yogur,** a combination of milk and yogurt. And then there's beer. Two regional favorites are **Pilsner** and **Club.** For a sweeter buzz, try **canelazo** (or *canelito*), a combination of boiled water, sugar cane alcohol, lemon, sugar, and cinnamon. Many drinks are made from **aguardiente,** a potent sugarcane alcohol. And of course, there's the omnipresent **Chicha,** made from yucca and fermented with the saliva of the women who brew it. Look for it in houses that fly white or red flags over their doors. **Non-alcoholic chichas** (also non-saliva) come in myriad varieties throughout the region and are occasionally served straight out of a plastic bag.

Unless urgent visits to the nearest restroom are your idea of fun, **avoid drinking tap water.** Water advertised as *purificada* (purified) may have only been passed through a filter, which does not necessarily catch all diarrhea-causing demons. Water that has been boiled or treated with iodine is safe to drink; otherwise, bottled water is best. Watch out for *refrescos* and other water-based juices, and freshly-washed fruit. Also use bottled water when brushing teeth.

CUSTOMS AND ETIQUETTE

WOMEN AND MEN

Foreign visitors are often shocked by the **machismo** in some parts of Latin America. Women in bars—and foreign women in general—are often regarded as promiscuous. Females who drink and act rowdy—or even just express their opinions in a public setting—will shock men who expect and prize meekness in women. Whether you're male or female, be sensitive to rising testosterone levels. Never say anything about a man's mother, sister, wife, or girlfriend.

APPEARANCE

Personal hygiene and appearance are often difficult to maintain while traveling, but they are very important in Ecuador. Close-cropped, clean-shaven men and women who don't show much skin will receive more respect than scruffy mopheads or bra-less women. Men should remove hats while indoors.

COMMUNICATION AND BODY LANGUAGE

Latin Americans hold politeness in high esteem, both in acquaintances and strangers. When meeting someone for the first time, shake hands firmly, look the person in the eye, and say *"Mucho gusto de conocerle"* ("Pleased to meet you"). When entering a room, greet everybody, not just the person you came to see. Females often greet each other with a peck on the cheek or a quick hug. Sometimes men shake hands with women in a business situation, but the standard greeting between a man and a woman—even upon meeting for the first time—is a quick kiss on the cheek. **Salutations** are considered common courtesy in small towns. *"Buenos días"* in the morning, *"buenas tardes"* after noon, and *"buenas noches"* after dusk should be said to anyone with whom you come into contact. Another custom is saying *"buen provecho"* ("enjoy your meal") in a restaurant upon entering or leaving. When signaling for people, don't use one finger pointed upward; simply motioning with your hand in a sweeping motion is more polite. The American "OK" symbol (a circle with the thumb and forefinger) is considered vulgar and offensive. Spitting is perfectly acceptable in this region; burping is rude.

TIME

Punctuality isn't as important as it is in Europe and the US—as bus schedules will quickly confirm—but there are, of course, limits. A different perspective on time is apparent during meals, which are rarely hurried. After a big meal, enjoy the ingenious tradition of siesta, a time in the afternoon when it's just too hot to do anything but relax, have a drink, or nap; don't expect much to happen during the midafternoon, as banks and shops often shut their doors.

PHOTOGRAPHY

Be sensitive when taking photographs. If you must take pictures of locals, first ask permission—they may object strongly to being photographed.

RELIGION

Ecuador's constitution provides for religious freedom. Nonetheless, the country is predominantly **Roman Catholic.** Twentieth-century missionaries left behind a small **Protestant** population, and in recent years, **Mormon** and **Seventh Day Adventist** missionaries have been traveling to the region in ever greater numbers. In many cases, indigenous populations have merely incorporated Catholicism into earlier belief systems; the resulting **syncretized religions** intertwine the properties of indigenous gods and spirits with those of Catholic saints. Some traditions, however, have weathered the years of colonial rule. Many *indígenas* in the Andes still worship mountains where mighty spirits (or apus) that control rain and fertility reside, and in some areas **shamans** (*curanderos* in Spanish) are called upon to cure the sick.

ARTESANÍA

In the late 15th century, the Incas conquered the indigenous community of Otavalo (see 106) and forced the inhabitants to pay tribute with their textiles. A few decades later, the Spanish brought new textile technology as well as oppressive rule—forcing Otavaleños to work in poorly maintained workshops well into the 20th century. In the early 1900s, however, the people of Otavalo made their mark on the modern textile industry by producing imitations of British tweeds (called casimires). Just north of Otavalo lies Cotacachi (see p. 124), a **leatherwork** metropolis offering wallets, purses, belts, whips, and even leather underwear. The **ceramics** of the Ecuadorian Quichua Sacha Runa people, as well as those found in the **Latacunga** and **Pujilí** areas, have also become major attractions.

THE ARTS

PAINTING

Indigenismo is the movement that defines 20th-century Ecuadorian art. Among the school's most famous members is **Oswaldo Guayasamín**, known for his politically charged depictions of indigenous suffering. Among Guayasamín's most controversial work is a series of 23 panels painted in the meeting hall of the Ecuadorian Congress in 1988. The best place to see Guayasamín's work today is at his museum in Quito (see p. 96). *Indígena* **Eduardo Kingman,** who is famous for painting stylized and shadowy figures, is considered by some to be the trailblazer of the indigenismo movement. **Camilo Egas** and **Manuel Rendón** also participated in the indigenismo movement, although their styles also reveal a European influence.

Perhaps the best representations of indigenous life and struggle stem from the brushes of the tribesmen themselves. Among the most famous indigenous painters are the **artists of Tigua.** Their brightly colored paintings drawn on sheep-hide depict, in their own words, the "reality of indigenous life now and in the past—our customs, our work in the fields, our festivals, our myths and legends, our vision of nature and our dreams." **Ramiro Jácome** is the most famous painter of recent times, known for his deeply colored, abstract human figures. His and other modern Ecuadorian artists' paintings are displayed at Quito's Casa de la Cultura (see p. 97).

MUSIC

Ecuador's traditional music combines Spanish and pre-Hispanic musical styles. The most characteristic Andean instrument is the **panpipe** or *rondador*, over 2000 years old. Its relative, the **zampoña,** comes from the southern Andes but has two rows of pipes instead of one. This instrument, along with the five-note scale on which the tunes are based, gives Andean music its distinctively haunting sound. In addition to pipes, two flutes are often used—the larger **quena** and the smaller **pingullu.** The bamboo panpipes and flutes along with percussive instruments like bells, drums, and **maracas** (rattles made from gourds) are all indigenous innovations.

LITERATURE

Before the advent of writing, indigenous Ecuadorians had established an oral tradition intimately linked to their religious practices. Spanish colonialism destroyed much of this tradition and replaced it with a literature of politics. The first textual works were the writings of various 17th-century clergymen about the Spanish colony's social issues. In the 18th century, bourgeois professionals spearheaded the movement toward independence. These inventors of "the literature that did not yet have a country" were the first to explicitly focus on what was to become of Ecuadorian society. Among the many words of discontent, the writings of **Eugenio Espejo** (1747-95) stormed the scene. An advocate of social reform, he wrote on a vast array of topics including education, theology, politics, health, and the economy. He also debuted Quito's first newspaper, which lasted only three months. Ecuador's 19th-century independence from Spain cultivated a distinctive national literature, established by founding fathers **Juan León Mera** (1832-94) and **Juan Montalvo** (1832-89). Though their Romantic style was influenced by Spanish literature, the content was anti-monarchical and nationalistic. The most important work of this period is León Mera's *Cumandá*, the first Ecuadorian novel.

Since the 19th century, Ecuadorian literature has taken on a life of its own, dealing with uniquely Ecuadorian social, political, cultural, and historical topics. One of the most marked differences between the writings of the 19th and 20th centuries is the move away from a romanticization of indigenous traditions toward a more realistic portrayal of the indigenous struggle. One of the first works to mark the movement known as **Indigenismo** is **Jorge Icaza's** 1934 Huasipungo, a story of indigenous resistance to exploitation. Meanwhile, the forefather of Ecuadorian socialism, **Pablo Palacio** (1906-47), was laying the foundations of an ironic, existential, and traumatized writing style—likely influenced by his dementia. His work gained popularity in the 60s and 70s, around the same time that **Miguel Donoso Pareja** and **Pedro Jorge Vera** were voicing anti-imperialist frustration with Ecuador's dependence on foreign powers. In 1978, the first **Meeting on Ecuadorian Literature** lent legitimacy to this growing literary movement.

ARCHITECTURE

While Ecuador is home to some of the most spectacular architectural achievements in history, many of the area's ruins no longer are standing because the Spanish either destroyed or built over the ancient buildings. The new has remained intimately connected to the old; a number of important towns are built on the rubble of the Inca civilization, and in many cases, the Spaniards even reused Inca building stones. Many colonial churches are on hilltops because they were built over the foundations of Inca temples. **Colonial architecture** is a blend of the Old and New Worlds: Spaniards commissioned works in the Baroque style, but the *indígenas* who executed the works added their own distinctive cultural touches. Religious institutions have the aesthetic upper hand—churches and convents in older towns are decorated with intricately carved facades, ornate interiors sparkling with gilt, and leafy stone vines wrapping around classically styled columns. Municipal buildings and private residences are usually more modest two-story buildings with high ceilings, interior courtyards, covered verandas, and large wooden doors. The region's urban centers were built more for walking than looking, as evidenced by the blocky concrete buildings that dominate the downtown areas of most larger cities. Most of these buildings were erected in the 20th century, when architects were primarily concerned with reducing building costs.

POPULAR CULTURE

MUSIC

Despite numerous North American intruders to the Ecuadorian musical scene, traditional Andean music including **El Pasillo, El Yarabi,** and **El Pasacalle** still fills streets and restaurants. The slow, sad sound of El Pasillo is created by the guitar and rondín, a flute-like instrument. El Yarabi is the most popular, while El Pasacalle is the dance music of choice. Among those trying to sustain the musical tradition of the Andean hills is **Yarina.** Founded in 1984 by three brothers, Yarina ("Remembrance" in Quichua) strives to bring the ancient culture of Ecuador's indigenous Quichua-speaking people to the modern world. Another group fighting for cultural survival, **Capari-Cani** draws inspiration from the songs and music of the Incas. Meaning "Cry for Freedom," Capari-Cani has voiced its message in concert halls throughout the Americas. **Christina Aguilera** also released an album in Spanish in 2000 to show pride in her Ecuadorian heritage. Meanwhile, 80s pop sensation **Gerardo,** a native Ecuadorian known for singing **Rico Suave,** now resides in Guayaquil. The most popular bands are **Selva, Guarda Raya,** and **Pulpo 3.**

FILM

Still a work in progress, the Ecuadorian film industry hasn't failed to churn out its share of racy films. Try **24 Horas de Placer** (24 Hours of Pleasure), **La Lluvia Meona** (The Pissing Rain), or **SOS Conspiración Bikini.** It has also produced a few quality films in recent years. The highly acclaimed film **La Tigra** (Tigress), which debuted in 1990 and was directed by Camilo Luzuriaga, portrays Latin American magical realism beautifully through its story of a young woman confined to a life of virginity by her two older sisters. Also directed by Luzuriaga, **Entre Marx y una Mujer Desnuda** (Between Marx and a Naked Woman; 1995) draws a portrait of political activists in the 1970s. A firm believer in the future expansion and success of Ecuador's tiny film industry, producer Alfredo Marcovici personally financed the creation of **Sueños en la Mitad del Mundo** (Dreams in the Middle of the World) in 1998. The film is a compilation of three passion-filled stories that take place in modern and exotic Ecuador. With only a modest US$200,000 budget, **Ratas, ratones, rateros** (Rodents), written and directed by Sebastián Cordero, stormed the stage in 1999, winning the Trieste Latin American Film Festival. Through the lens of those at the bottom, Cordero's film touches upon the poverty and corruption that characterizes the lives of many Ecuadorians. These few famous flicks aside subtitled and dubbed versions of US blockbusters dominate.

TELEVISION

Ecuador's first television station was established in 1961 by HCJB World Radio. Since then, Ecuadorian TV has flourished—now boasting five major television networks. TV entertainment ranges from soap operas and Ecuadorian MTV to the Latin American favorite, *fútbol.* **Emergencia,** suspiciously reminiscent of the US's ER, and **De la Vida Real,** perhaps an imitation of MTV's The Real World, are also popular. Meanwhile, two comedy shows, **Ni en Vivo, Ni en Derecho,** and the classic **Haga Negocios Conmigo,** host interactive contests designed to make fools of their contestants. On the more serious side, **La TV** and **Día Día** bring Ecuadorians the most up-to-date news from around the world.

NEWSPAPERS

Ecuador publishes a wide variety of newspapers and magazines including El Comercio (www.elcomercio.com), La Hora (www.lahora.com.ec), Expreso (www.diario-expreso.com), Hoy On Line (www.hoy.com.ec), El Mercurio (www.elmercurio.com.ec), El Universo (www.eluniverso.com), and El Telégrafo (www.telegrafo.com.ec). **El Comercio** is the main newspaper in Quito while **El Universo** is read by the Guayaquil bourgeois. **El Hoy,** owned by USA Today, caters to a more intellectual crowd. Aimed at a different readership entirely, **El Extra** is Guayaquil's tabloid newspaper, featuring pictures of topless women. **El Estadio** is the sports magazine of choice.

SPORTS AND RECREATION

If you like soccer, you're in the right place. Like most of Latin America, Ecuador treats the game—known everywhere but the US as "football" or **fútbol**—as a national passion and pastime. Distant runners-up include **volleyball** and **basketball,** which have become quite popular in recent years.

If the courts don't do it for you, the slightly more adventurous can experience the thrills of the Andes. The mountain range is home to some of the best **trekking** and **mountaineering** in the world. With many peaks over 5000m high, Ecuador has become a prime destination for serious mountain climbers from across the globe. If water's your thing, there is excellent **whitewater rafting** and **kayaking** through raging rivers from the mountains to either the Pacific or the tropical Amazon Basin. Be sure to plan your trip depending on which rivers are safe during the rainy or dry seasons. Many choose to **surf** the Ecuadorian coast. For more tranquil activity, the valleys created by volcanic peaks provide perfect conditions for short- or long-distance **hikes** through pristine countryside.

Bullfighting is not just for the Spaniards. Along with Peru, Ecuador is leading the charge of Latin American bullfighting's popularity. Unlike European bullfighting, where matches are held seasonally, Latin America holds them year-round, and fans consistently fill the stadiums. In November, Quito holds the prestigious **Feria del Señor del Gran Poder.** Smaller fairs *(mini-ferias)* also take place alongside the larger ones throughout the country. International stars and local heroes paint towns red, and spectators respond—loudly.

ECOTOURISM

Ecotourism is a low-impact way to vacation, enabling travelers to learn about an environment without altering it. Better yet, ecotourism does not require the traveler to live only on berries and shrubs. Resort-style ecotourism is also possible.

COMMUNITY-BASED ECOTOURISM

Community-based ecotourism (CBE) is the recommended form of ecotourism since it provides a major source of income for indigenous communities. It is run by one of two groups: an indigenous community itself or a private company that provides jobs to the local *indígenas*.

THE GOOD

CBE offers an intimate and educational way to venture into the outdoors. Tourists stay in huts (which range from the wall-less to the resort) built by indigenous communities. These serve as base points for daily activities, which vary depending on the length of the traveler's stay. Communities recommend stays longer than three days—two weeks often being preferred. Group size can also determine what excursions are possible, and different communities prefer different sized groups. Groups of less than 10 people generally work best, though a few communities have space for very large groups. Others specialize in hosting small groups and individuals. Yet other communities have built stations used mostly for research.

Groups can pick their own daily adventures. Fit, outdoorsy groups may spend a few nights—or weeks—camping in the jungle. Hiking, trekking, and swinging from jungle vines are all part of these trips. Other groups may choose to spend more time in and around their huts. All groups will do activities that take place in the actual community—such as, listening to folklore and oral history and learning about herbal medicine. Birdwatching and animal spotting are often on the agenda.

THE BAD

For all of the benefits of ecotourism, it does come with some baggage. Travelers interested in CBE should be aware of how they will affect the community. Every kind of tourism alters the environment. In the case of CBE, no indigenous community is truly in its natural environment, for by offering to educate tourists, indigenous communities are necessarily altering the way they live.

THE CATCH-22

CBE offers communities much needed income that enables them to maintain their traditional lifestyle, for money is what keeps indigenous communities alive in the battle against government and industry encroachment. *Indígenas* have learned that their culture is a valuable commodity, and the act of selling their culture alters it. To survive, indigenous communities must become less traditional. However, most *indígenas* have been able to retain the core aspects of their cultures.

ECOTOURISM ELSEWHERE IN ECUADOR

Outside of community-based ecotourism in the Oriente, travelers ecotour in two other regions of Ecuador: the national parks and the Galápagos. In these places ecotourism takes on a slightly different flavor. The goal is simply to travel without leaving a trace—anything that you bring with you must stay with you at all times. You either take a guide, or you travel alone. By hiring a guide, you'll be sustaining a market for ecotourism that helps boost Ecuador's economy as well as save natural habitats that oil mining and other industrial practices are slowly destroying—and you'll have a better time.

ADDITIONAL READING

What follows are a few of our favorite books about (in one way or another) Ecuador—in print, available in English, and never, ever dull:

The Beak of the Finch: A Story of Evolution in Our Time, by Jonathan Weiner. About finches in the Galápagos, yet somehow engaging enough to interest non-scientists.

Living Poor: A Peace Corps Chronicle, by Moritz Thomson. An unsentimental autobiographical account of the author's stint in a coastal village in northern Ecuador.

The Voyage of the Beagle: Charles Darwin's Journal of Researches, by Charles Darwin. From 1831 to 1836, as the official naturalist of the Royal Navy Ship HMS Beagle, Darwin surveyed the coast of South America and observed phenomena that would later lead to his theories of natural selection. This fascinating book records far more than scientific observations; it reveals Darwin's personal thoughts as well.

LIFE AND TIMES

ALTERNATIVES TO TOURISM

A PHILOSOPHY FOR TRAVELERS

Let's Go believes that the connection between travelers and their destinations is an important one. Over the years, we've watched the growth of the "ignorant tourist" stereotype with dismay, knowing that many travelers care passionately about the communities and environments they explore—but also knowing that even conscientious tourists can inadvertently damage natural wonders and harm cultural environments. With this "Alternatives to Tourism" chapter, Let's Go hopes to promote a better understanding of Ecuador and enhance your experience there.

In the developing world, there are several different options for those who seek to participate in alternatives to tourism. Opportunities for volunteering abound, both with local and international organizations. Studying can also be instructive, either in the form of direct enrollment in a local university or in an independent research project. Let's Go discourages working in the developing world due to high local unemployment rates and weak economies.

As a **volunteer** in Ecuador, either on a short-term basis or as the main component of your trip, you can participate in projects ranging from teaching English to street children in Quito to helping rural communities develop environmental tourism programs. Relatively politically and economically stable compared to its neighbors Peru and Colombia, Ecuador is an ideal place to explore alternatives to tourism. As Ecuador develops, it is emphasizing the teaching of English to its children to better prepare them to enter the global community. Simultaneously, its many biological reserves welcome help in studying and preserving rapidly vanishing ecosystems. Many programs, particularly those in urban areas, offer the opportunity to volunteer, participate in a homestay, learn Spanish, or tour different areas of the nation. Other volunteerism companies offer multiple options for service, ranging from developing environmental tourism programs in rural communities to helping in orphanages. While many programs do not require fluency in Spanish, familiarity with the language is useful in Ecuador, and many volunteer organizations provide opportunities to learn, both formally and informally.

Studying at a college or language program is another option. There are many language schools in Ecuador, geared toward students of all ages. Most are flexible in terms of their period of study, ranging from several weeks in the summer to over a year. Many help coordinate further travel or volunteerism projects while in Ecuador, as well. Programs generally include a homestay. Studying in Ecuador engages the student in a world that a budget traveler might have more difficulty discovering. In addition to developing personal relationships with Ecuadorians in an academic setting, international students learn about the nation's dynamic culture.

 Start your search at ■ **www.beyondtourism.com,** Let's Go's brand-new searchable database of Alternatives to Tourism, where you can find exciting feature articles and helpful program listings divided by country, continent, and program type.

VOLUNTEERING

Ecuador, while rich in culture and history, has significant contemporary concerns in areas such as poverty, child welfare, women's rights, and environmental degredation, particularly in the rural Oriente. While volunteering in any developing nation can be dangerous for a foreigner—and Ecuador is not immune to the threats of crime and other risks—the rewards of giving your time and energy to causes that improve the nation are enormous. Volunteering opportunities in Ecuador include helping rural communities develop their economies and preserving the biodiversity of one of the most ecologically rich areas of the world.

People who volunteer in Ecuador often do so on a short-term basis, at organizations that make use of drop-in or once-a-week volunteers. Be sure to research potential programs before committing—talk to people who have participated and find out exactly what you're getting into, as living and working conditions can vary greatly. Different programs are geared toward different ages and levels of experience, so avoid taking on too much or too little. The more informed you are and the more realistic your expectations, the more enjoyable the program will be. Most participants in short term work in Ecuador choose to work in cities like Guayaquil, Cuenca, and especially Quito, where they can combine living in a major metropolitan area with community service. Others choose to head to the jungle, focusing on conservation. Much short-term volunteer work involves working on reserves in rainforest conservation or working with at-risk children in cities.

Many volunteer services charge a fee to participate. These costs can be surprisingly hefty (although they frequently cover airfare and most, if not all, living expenses). Most people choose to go through a parent organization. These are useful, particularly for first-time volunteers, because they take care of logistical details and often provide a group environment and support system.

GENERAL COMMUNITY SERVICE

These parent organizations coordinate volunteer placements in a wide variety of fields. International service groups often have programs in several nations, including Ecuador. Ecuadorian programs place international volunteers in many different types of service, without emphasizing a specific area. These are run by Ecuadorians themselves, many of whom are members of the communities that their programs serve. From planting trees to building houses, these organizations offer something for everyone.

INTERNATIONAL PROGRAMS

Amigos de las Americas, 5618 Star Lane, Houston, TX 77057, USA (☎800-231-7796; www.amigoslink.org), sends high-school and college students in groups of 2-3 to work in rural Latin American communities for up to 8 weeks. 1 year of Spanish instruction required. About US$3500, including airfare. Volunteers fund-raise half the cost.

Cross-Cultural Solutions, 47 Potter Ave., New Rochelle, NY 10801, USA (☎800-380-4777 or 914-632-0022; www.crossculturalsolutions.org), provides short- and long-term placements in health care, education, and social development. US$2100-4200.

Elderhostel, Inc., 11 Avenue de Lafayette, Boston, MA 92111-1746, USA (☎877-426-8056; www.elderhostel.org), sends volunteers 55+ world-wide to work in construction, research, teaching, and many other projects. About US$100 per day, excluding airfare.

Global Crossroad, 8772 Quarters Lake Road, Ste. 9, Baton Rouge, LA 70809, USA (☎800-413-2008; www.globalcrossroad.com), sends students to participate in many social and environmental projects in Ecuador, such as working with orphaned children, teaching English, and helping out on organic farms. Programs last 2-12 weeks. US$880-1800, excluding airfare.

Global Volunteer Network, PO Box 2231, Wellington, New Zealand (☎64 4 569 9080; www.volunteer.org.nz), has it all, facilitating volunteers' work on everything from studying tortoises on San Cristóbal in the Galápagos (see p. 340) to researching different plants in the jungle of the Lalo Lohoor dry forest.

Habitat for Humanity International, 121 Habitat St., Americus, GA 31709, USA (☎229-924-6935, ext. 2551; www.habitat.org), organizes volunteers to build houses in over 83 countries for 2 weeks-3 years. Short-term programs US$1200-4000.

Peace Corps, Office of Volunteer Recruitment and Selection, 1111 20th St., NW, Washington, D.C. 20526, USA (☎800-424-8580; www.peacecorps.gov), has programs in 70 developing nations, including Ecuador. US citizens only; 2-year commitment required.

Service Civil International Voluntary Service (SCI-IVS), SCI USA, 3213 W. Wheeler St., Seattle, WA 98199, USA (☎/fax 206-350-6585; www.sci-ivs.org), arranges placement in work camps in Ecuador for those 18+. Registration US$65-125.

Volunteers for Peace, 1034 Tiffany Rd., Belmont, VT 05730, USA (☎802-259-2759; www.vfp.org), arranges placement in work camps in Ecuador. Membership required for registration. Annual International Workcamp Directory US$20. 2-3 weeks US$200-500.

LOCAL PROGRAMS

New Horizons, 6 de Diciembre 2130 y Colón Edificio Antares, Primer piso, Of. 107, in Quito (☎/fax 2 2542 890 or 2 2541 953; www.voluntariosecuador.org), offers a variety of service programs and contributes volunteers and other resources to other NGOs throughout Ecuador, including the Galápagos. Leads and assists with many social, health, enterprise, environmental, community, and educational projects.

YOUTH AND THE COMMUNITY

Urban youth in Ecuador face many challenges, particularly in the areas of health, safety, and education. While there are many programs to help, most are critically understaffed and underfunded. Volunteers working in Ecuador have the opportunity to directly impact at-risk urban youth, often working with entire families.

INTERNATIONAL PROGRAMS

Child Family Health International, 953 Mission St., Ste. 220, San Francisco, CA 94103, USA (☎415-957-9000; www.cfhi.org), sends pre-med undergraduate and medical students to work with physicians in a mobile surgical unit in Cuenca. Focuses more on working with the community and learning about health care and less on providing medical assistance. About US$1500, excluding airfare.

Global Volunteers, 375 East Little Canada Road, St. Paul, MN 55117, USA (☎800-487-1074; www.globalvolunteers.org), works on orphanage and child care projects for disabled and impoverished children and their families in Quito. Volunteers live in a hotel. 2 weeks about US$2000, excluding airfare.

LOCAL PROGRAMS

Centro de la Niña Trabajadora (CENIT), Calle Huacho 150 y Jose Peralta, El Camal, Quito (☎2 2654 260; contact@cenitecuador.org), sends volunteers averaging 18-26 to care for at-risk girls and women for min. 1 month. Responsibilities vary. Helps coordinate housing and Spanish lessons for volunteers. Processing fee US$50.

Quito Eterno, Bolívar Oe3-18 y Guayaquil, Quito (www.quitoeterno.org). Volunteer projects include providing medical attention for low-income families, educating special-needs children, painting homes in historical Quito, and teaching English to at-risk youth.

Volunteering Ecuador, República de El Salvador 730, Quito (☎2 2430 119; www.volunteeringecuador.org), organizes and supports programs that target underprivileged urban children. For volunteers 16+. Min. stay 1 month. Registration fee US$190. Homestay fee US$360 per month. Also offers Spanish classes.

RURAL DEVELOPMENT

The rural areas of Ecuador see little of the comparative wealth found in the country's cities. For example, in the Chimborazo region, over 90% of the rural population lives in poverty. Indigenous groups, in particular, face lack of adequate education, nutrition, and access to health care. Volunteers can work in particular on children's education projects and with rural communities to help them develop their economies through sustainable agriculture.

INTERNATIONAL PROGRAMS

Global Routes, 1 Short St., Northampton MA 01060, USA (☎413-585-8895; www.globalroutes.org), offers high-school students programs focused on construction and college teaching internships throughout the world, including Ecuador; both involve homestays. US$4000, excluding airfare.

LOCAL PROGRAMS

Ecotrackers Network, Amazonas N21-217 y Roca, Quito (www.ecotrackers.com). Small groups of volunteers visit communities throughout Ecuador, spending min. 1 week in each. Volunteers can also complete projects in teaching English, environment, health, and sports. Basic Spanish required. Living expenses about US$9 per day. Registration fee US$50 plus US$2 per day of the program.

ALTERNATIVES TO TOURISM

Fundación Brethren y Unida, Granda Centeno Oe4-290 y Baron de Carondelet, 3er piso, Casilla 17-03-1487, Quito (☎2 2440 721; www.fbu.com.ec). Agro-ecological focus, aimed at improving rural people's management of environmental resources. GAP year and summer programs, as well as regular volunteer programs of min. 1 month. 1-month program US$300, including meals, accommodations, and transportation.

New Era Galápagos Foundation, (www.neweragalapagos.org), on Isla San Cristóbal, promotes sustainable development of the Galápagos through promotion of cultural and environmental activities, such as foreign languages, environmental education, and art. Spanish language familiarity expected. Min. stay 3 months.

San Miguel Eco Project, 12-27 Juan Leon Mera y Calama, Quito (☎2528 769; www.ecosanmiguel.org). Volunteer in a small Afro-Ecuadorian community, developing ecotourism, improving educational opportunities, and promoting sustainable development. About US$25 per day.

Santa Lucia Reserve (www.santa-lucia.org). Live in a tourist lodge and support community development, ecotourism, and conservation. Cost varies.

Voluntarios de Occidente, Montalvo 4-18 y Cevallos, Of. 310, Ambato (voccidente@hotmail.com), offers total immersion in rural life to volunteers 20+ for an average of 2 months. Most activities involve teaching. Functional Spanish required.

ENVIRONMENTAL CONSERVATION

Conservation is one of the most critical issues in contemporary Ecuador. Preserving the vast array of flora and fauna in this biodiversity hotspot is the goal of numerous programs. From protecting cloud forests to managing organic farms, there's an organization for every cause.

INTERNATIONAL PROGRAMS

Earthwatch, 3 Clocktower Pl., Ste. 100, Box 75, Maynard, MA 01754 (☎800-776-0188 or 978-461-0081; www.earthwatch.org), arranges 1- to 3-week programs in Ecuador to promote conservation of natural resources. Fees vary based on program location and duration. About US$1700, excluding airfare.

LOCAL PROGRAMS

Bellavista Cloud Forest Reserve, Jorge Washington E7-23 y 6 de Diciembre, Quito (☎2 223 313; www.bellavistacloudforest.com). Visitors can volunteer at the research station, where tasks include trail and fence construction and light carpentry work in exchange for reduced room rates in the hostel. Fee US$5 per day for 1st 20 days; min. stay 30 days.

The Bospas Forest Farm, (www.ecuativer.com/bospas), in El Limonal, is a 15-hectare family farm on formerly barren land on the western slope of the Andes. Owners Belgian Piet Sabbe and his wife Gabriela Olda Peralta now practice sustainable, organic farming and strive to diversify crops using agroforestry and permaculture techniques. Volunteers engage in farmwork and watershed-management.

Bosque Protector Cerro Blanco (☎2416 975; vonhorst@ecua.net.ec). Volunteers in this tropical dry forest near Guayaquil assist in trail maintenance, reforestation projects, guarding against poachers, and wildlife rescue. Current projects include saving the park's Great Green Macaws. Eric Von Horstman is the director of Fundación Pro-Bosque, which administers the park.

Centro Ecológico Cotacachi (CEC), 15-78 Peñaherrera, Morales (☎2916 525; cec@imbanet.net), has all the latest on ecological and community tourism and is connected to seven different community projects that range from well-established to novice. The center also has information on similar projects throughout the country. Volunteers work at least 4hr. per day, contribute around US$150 per month toward lodging, and provide their own food. Longer stays preferred.

Centro Intercultural de Ecoturismo (☎2889 044; www.sinchisacha.org), in Archidona. Volunteer here for US$10 per day in return for lodging and food and the opportunity to help educate local communities about environmental preservation.

Cerro Seco Reserve (☎2916 525; alight@ecuanex.net.ec), in Bahía de Caraquez. Volunteer in the dry tropical forest, either in the reserve or by helping raise funds for buying neighboring forest. Living costs about US$100 per month.

The Charles Darwin Research Center (www.galapagospark.org, www.darwinfoundation.org) focuses on the ecological welfare of the Galápagos. Check website for up-to-date info, or see **Galápagos: Isla Santa Cruz: Puerto Ayora: Sights,** p. 335.

Comité de Ecoturismo (☎3711 774 or 09 7797 327; manduryac@hotmail.com), based out of Quito is dedicated to finding more sustainable alternatives to mining and logging. Working on the construction of a small tourist information center that will also serve as a community classroom. Welcomes volunteers who can enrich the community by sharing skills in just about anything, including English, ornithology, biology, medicine, cooking, and dance. Ask for Fabián Hernandez.

Fundación Cabo San Francisco, Casilla 17-15 73B, Quito (www.cabosanfrancisco.org). Volunteers identify and classify plants and birds, as well as promote reforestation and environmental and health education in the region. US$300 per month.

Fundación Maquipucuna, Baquerizo #238 y Tamayo, Quito (☎2507 200; www.arches.uga.edu/~maqui). Spend 1-3 months working in the Maquipucuna Reserve on reforestation, organic gardening, and trail building. Volunteers live in a tourist lodge. Basic knowledge of Spanish suggested. US$12-15 per day.

Fundación Zoobreviven, 6 de Diciembre N32-36 y Whymper, Quito (☎2 252 2916; www.zoobreviven.org), helps preserve Ecuador's cloud forests through reforestation and managing the Alto Choco Reserve. Living costs US$260 per month.

Reserva Río Guaycuyacu (guaycuyacu@hotmail.com). Volunteer to be a "farm apprentice" and work farm chores at this nature reserve and family fruit farm, which promotes sustainable agriculture and conservation practices in northwestern Ecuador. Research facilities for biologists. Min. commitment 1 month. US$250 per month.

Río Muchacho (www.riomuchacho.com). Volunteer on an organic farm in the coastal rainforest. Min. stay 1 month. US$250 per month.

Rumi Wilco Ecolodge (ofalcoecolodge@yahoo.com), in Vilcabamba (see p. 194), is hidden in the Rumi Wilco Nature Reserve. Take the dirt road off Agua de Hierro, cross the stream, and follow the 1st path on the left—signs mark the way. Friendly English- and Spanish-speaking owners/biologists, Orlando and Alicia Falco, are dedicated to maintaining the recently created reserve, putting one-third of profits toward conservation. Ask about helping to process the coffee beans grown on the reserve—or about a host of other odd jobs—to get a discount on your stay.

San Miguel Eco-Project, León Mera 12-39, San Miguel (☎2528 769; www.ecosanmiguel.org), at Calama, Quito. A fledgling ecotourism project in San Miguel. As of July 2004, it was accepting applications for long-term volunteer English teachers. Volunteers prepare their own food and are given reduced-rate transportation and lodging. Ask for Carlos Donoso.

TEACHING ENGLISH

Teaching jobs abroad are rarely well paid. Volunteering as a teacher, though, is a popular option. Volunteer teachers often get a daily stipend to help with living expenses. Although salaries at Ecuadorian private schools might be low compared to the US, the low cost of living makes it much more profitable. In almost all cases, you must have at least a bachelor's degree to be a full-time teacher, although undergraduates can often get summer positions teaching or tutoring. In Quito alone, about 50 colleges and institutes offer English classes; opportunities also abound in Guayaquil and Cuenca. If you want to teach in rural areas, volunteering is the most common option, often undertaken in exchange for room and board. While teachers are formally required to have work visas, you must have this sent to you from Ecuador before your departure, which is difficult. Many travelers report that a free 90-day visitor's visa will suffice.

Many schools require teachers to have a **Teaching English as a Foreign Language (TEFL)** certificate. Not having this certification does not necessarily exclude you from finding a teaching job, but certified teachers often find higher paying jobs. Native English speakers working in private schools are most often hired for English-immersion classrooms where no Spanish is spoken. Those volunteering or teaching in public, poorer schools work more often in both English and Spanish.

Placement agencies or university fellowship programs are the best resources for finding teaching jobs. Alternatively, you can contact schools directly or just try your luck once you get there. If you are going to try the latter, the best time to look is several weeks before the start of the school year (Aug.-May). The following organizations are helpful in placing teachers in Ecuador.

NORTH AMERICAN PROGRAMS

Amity Institute, Amity Volunteer Teachers Abroad Program, 10671 Roselle St., Ste. 100, San Diego, CA 92121-1525, USA (☎858-455-6364; www.amity.org), offers both full-year and semester-long positions. Processing fee US$25-50. Placement fee US$500. For anyone with at least 2-3 years of teaching experience, AVTA also offers positions with **Teacher Workshops Abroad** (workshops@amity.org), a program that conducts pedagogical workshops for local teachers. Same fees.

International Schools Services, Educational Staffing Program, PO Box 5910, Princeton, NJ 08543, USA (☎609-452-0990; www.iss.edu), recruits staff for American and English schools in Ecuador. 2-year commitment expected. Program fee US$150.

Office of Overseas Schools, US Department of State, Room H328, SA-1, Washington, D.C. 20522, USA (☎202-261-8200; www.state.gov/www/about_state/schools/), keeps a comprehensive list of schools abroad and agencies that arrange placement for Americans to teach abroad.

World Teach, Center for International Development, 79 John F. Kennedy St., Cambridge, MA 02138, USA (☎800-483-2240 or 617-495-5527; www.worldteach.org). Teach English, math, science, and environmental education for 2-12 months in Ecuador.

LOCAL PROGRAMS

Amarongachi Tours (☎2886 372; www.amarongachi_tours.com), in Tena (see **Jungle Lodges and Tours,** p. 295). Translate native ecotourism guides' talks from Spanish to English or teach English to local community members. Volunteers get free room and board and sometimes tips. 1-2 month commitment required.

Benedict Schools of Languages, PO Box 09-01-8916, Guayaquil (☎2444 418; benecent@talconet.net). Benedict Schools in several Ecuadorian cities seek TEFL teachers for min. 4 months, although they prefer longer commitments. Salary US$2-3 per hr.

Centro de Estudios Interamericanos (CEDEI), Gran Colombia 11-02 and General Torres, Casilla 597, Cuenca (☎2839 003; www.cedei.org), offers opportunities to teach English for ESL/TEFL teachers or those with equivalent qualification. Also offers a 3-week TEFL certification course in Jan. See p. 175 for more information.

STUDYING

VISA INFORMATION

To get a student visa from the Embassy of Ecuador, you need: a valid pasport; an HIV test and doctor's certificate indicating no communicable diseases; no criminal record; 2 recent color passport-size photos; school registration or proof of admission; and a certificate from a bank indicating good economic standing with a letter from a parent/guardian indicating that he or she will support the student while in Ecuador. This visa is good for 1 school year and is not applicable to courses less than 1 year. Visa and application fees US$130.

Study abroad programs range from basic language and culture courses to college-level classes, often for credit. In order to choose a program that best fits your needs, research as much as you can before making your decision—determine costs and duration, as well as what kind of students participate in the program and what sort of accommodations are provided. In programs with large groups of students who speak English, there is a trade-off. You may feel more comfortable in the community, but you will not have the same opportunity to practice your Spanish or to befriend other international students. For accommodations, dorm life provides a better opportunity to mingle with fellow students, but there is less of a chance to experience the local scene. If you live with a family, there is a potential to build lifelong friendships with Ecuadorians and to experience day-to-day life in more depth, but conditions can vary greatly from family to family.

UNIVERSITIES

Most university-level study abroad programs are conducted in Spanish, although many programs offer classes in English and beginner-level language courses. Those relatively fluent in Spanish may find it cheaper to enroll directly in an Ecuadorian university, although getting college credit may be more difficult. Many schools accept international students. Search www.studyabroad.com for various semester-abroad programs that meet your criteria, including your desired location and focus of study. The following is a list of organizations that can help place students in university programs abroad, or have their own branch in Ecuador.

AMERICAN PROGRAMS

Boston University, Division of International Programs, 232 Bay Street Rd., Boston, MA 02215, USA (☎617-353-9888; abroad@bu.edu). Headquartered in Quito, with scheduled travel to Ecuadorian rainforests and the Galápagos. Semester- and year-long programs. Homestay. 2 years college coursework in Spanish required.

School for International Training, College Semester Abroad, Admissions, Kipling Rd., PO Box 676, Brattleboro, VT 05302, USA (☎800-257-7751 or 802-257-7751; www.sit.edu), offers programs for college students in Ecuador on culture and development and comparative ecology and conservation. Runs the **Experiment in International Living** (☎800-345-2929; www.usexperiment.org), 3- to 5-week summer programs that offer high-school students cross-cultural homestays, community service, ecological adventure, and language training in Ecuador. US$1900-5000.

University of Idaho (martin@uidaho.edu), based in Quito. Includes travel to Amazon, field trips to Valle de los Chillos, Otavalo, Cotacachi, Lake Cuicocha. Optional travel to the Galápagos. Homestay. 2½ years college coursework in Spanish required.

ALTERNATIVES TO TOURISM

ECUADOR'S PROGRAMS

Galápagos Academic Institute for the Arts & Sciences (http://192.188.53.73/ GAIAS/faculty.html). Academic and research institute collaborates with partner universities worldwide. Has programs that focus on wildlife and ecology of the Galápagos. Offers short-term and summer programs in addition to regular classes.

Universidad San Francisco de Quito, Diego de Robles y Via Interoceánica, Quito (☎2 2895 723; www.usfq.edu.ec), hosts many different exchange programs for international students, during fall, spring, and summer sessions.

LANGUAGE SCHOOLS

Language schools can either be independently run international or local organizations or divisions of foreign universities. Though they rarely offer college credit, they are a good alternative to university study if you desire a deeper focus on Spanish or a slightly lighter courseload. Such programs are also good for high school students who might not feel at ease in class with older university students.

INTERNATIONAL PROGRAMS

A2Z Languages, 5112 N. 40th St., Ste. 103, Phoenix, AZ 85018, USA (☎800-496-4596; www.a2zlanguages.com), offers 1-week to 6-month language programs for all levels in Quito. Also arranges educational and cultural tours.

American Field Service (AFS), 310 SW 4th Ave. #630, Portland, OR 97204, USA (☎800-237-4636; www.afs.org/usa), offers summer-, semester-, and year-long homestay exchange programs in Ecuador for high-school students and graduating seniors. Check the website for regional offices. Financial aid available.

AmeriSpan Unlimited, PO Box 40007, Philadelphia, PA 19106, USA (☎800-879-6640 or 215-751-1100; www.amerispan.com), offers 1-week to 6-month language immersion programs in Cuenca and Quito. Also offers educational travel programs and volunteer and internship opportunities.

International Association for the Exchange of Students for Technical Experience (IAESTE), 10400 Little Patuxent Pkwy. Ste. 250, Columbia, MD 21044-3510, USA (☎410-997-2200; www.aipt.org), offers 8- to 12-week programs in Ecuador for college students who have completed 2 years of technical study. Application fee US$25.

Languages Abroad, 413 Ontario Street, Toronto, Ontario M5A 2V9, Canada (☎800-219-9924 or 416-925-2112; www.languagesabroad.com), offers 2- to 12-week language programs for beginning to advanced students in Ecuador.

School for International Training, College Semester Abroad, Admissions, Kipling Rd., PO Box 676, Brattleboro, VT 05302, USA (☎800-336-1616 or 802-258-3267; www.sit.edu), offers semester- and year-long programs in Ecuador for US$12,150-13,100. Also runs the **Experiment In International Living** (☎800-345-2929; www.experiment.org), a 3- to 5-week summer program that offers high-school students cross-cultural homestays, community service, ecological adventure, and language instruction in Ecuador. US$4700.

LOCAL PROGRAMS

Academia de Español Quito, Marchena Oe1-30 y 10 de Agosto, Quito (☎2553 647; www.academiaquito.com.ec), is a Spanish-as-a-second-language school for executives, teens, college students, teachers, and volunteers, in the commercial core of downtown Quito. Offers cultural and tourist activities. 8 weeks with homestay about US$2500.

Instituto Superior de Español, Terán 1650, Quito (☎2223 242; www.instituto-superior.net), on 10 de Agosto, offers Spanish classes, and salsa dancing and cooking lessons. Schools located in Quito, Otavalo, and the Galápagos. Min. US$149 for 20hr.; enrollment fee US$30. SAE discounts.

DIGGING UP CULTURE
Both Ancient and Modern

Volunteering on an archaeological dig is not really about archaeology at all. Sure, it was great fun to learn how researchers study past societies by doing it myself. But what affected me most was the immersion in a totally foreign country. The dig kept me in one corner of the world long enough that I was able to form lasting relationships with local people. Had I been backpacking, I wouldn't have been able to cultivate these bonds due to my itinerant way of life.

I had been living with several other college-age volunteers in a windy attic in a small Andean village just north of Quito. We were studying pre-Inca Ecuadorian civilization before it became the northernmost region of the Inca Empire. Our goal was noble; our means for attaining our goal, often prosaic: every morning, the combination of an old bus, a jerky pick-up truck, and a 20min. scramble would dispatch us to Quitoloma. We were curious as to why the Inca had built a number of circular forts on this 3600m peak. They were not in the normal Inca style. We speculated that an unusually long war with the local Caranqui-Cayambe tribes, who after nine years finally bowed to Inca dominance, might explain their irregularities. The American professors who led our dig imagined that there had been pre-Incaic constructions on Quitoloma before the forts. Those constructions, the hypothesis went, had enabled the long resistance.

This dig was important to the local community for two apparent reasons. By discovering the secrets of an ancient people, we were helping to shed light on their ancestral past. Also, the dig brought appreciable economic stimulus to its host village. The expedition employed two cooks, a bus driver, many pick-up truck owners, and countless site workers. Moreover, there was hope that the findings might develop into a tourist site. At least, this was the hope of a local educated man and of the village priest, who doted on our expedition. But not everyone understood our motives. Our GPS devices and our digging up of pottery shards and stones gave some the impression that we were searching for gold—not quite as noble a goal.

Our project turned out to be quite an intriguing undertaking. I learned how to survey fields and dig through soil, layer by layer. Soon, an ordinary shard of obsidian,

if shaped just the right way, would excite me. Could it be evidence of a past culture? Everything, including changing soil quality, had to be plotted. Slowly the digging would descend, layer by layer, sometimes revealing interesting stratigraphies and other times resulting in nothing.

But past cultures were not all I was discovering. I found myself engaged on just as deep a level with the modern-day culture of the area. I spent a lot of time with our group's cooks, Ana and Carla. We would chat while we peeled potatoes each evening. Sometimes I would head to the Otavalo market with them, where they would amaze me with their haggling skills. Other times we would travel to the village of El Quinche, where they knelt in prayer before a statue of Madonna, a practice that scholars have connected directly back to a pre-Columbian goddess cult. The two women were functionally single mothers, since their husbands worked far away. Alone, they kept pigs and skinned *cuy* (guinea pigs) all with their youngest children tied to their backs, much like their Caranqui ancestors would have done. But for all the ancient tradition in their lives, modern technology, such as television and hi-fi stereos, also had its place.

I also formed a unique bond with Ana's daughter, Nina. Charmed by her lively personality, I began tutoring Nina in English every evening. I hoped to give her an interest in a language that could help her get a good job in the future.

Although the archaeological work continued to be intellectually stimulating, it started to feel like the most important experiences were happening in the village. The energy I had initially spent trying to understand the Caranqui-Cayambes was instead mostly devoted to understanding and befriending the villagers. It was very exciting to share a way of life so different than mine. I left with the new realization that it is perhaps more worthwhile to learn about a single place in some depth than to survey a whole area superficially, as I had done in the past. When I think of Ecuador, what comes to mind is preparing *ceviche* with Ana and Carla, or Nina sitting out in front of the house screeching the names of farm animals in English. And, yes, our dig did yield some interesting notions about the Caranqui-Cayambes.

Alexander Bevilacqua is a student at Harvard University. He participated in this achaeological dig through the Pambamarca Archaeological Project (PAP), which was organized by the University of California at Davis and directed by Professor Samuel Connel of UCLA.

La Lengua, Cólon y Juan León Mera, Quito (☎2501 271; www.la-lengua.com), offers one-on-one Spanish lessons (US$6 per hr.) with homestays and/or volunteer work in the Andes, on the Coast, and in the jungle.

Simón Bolívar, Leonidas Plaza 353, Quito (☎2236 688; www.simon-bolivar.com), offers individual Spanish classes, and salsa dancing and cooking lessons. US$7 per hr.; 5% SAE discount. AmEx/MC/V.

FOR FURTHER READING ON ALTERNATIVES TO TOURISM

Alternatives to the Peace Corps: A Directory of Third World and U.S. Volunteer Opportunities, by Joan Powell. Food First Books, 2000 (US$10).

How to Live Your Dream of Volunteering Overseas, by Collins, DeZerega, and Heckscher. Penguin Books, 2002 (US$17).

International Directory of Voluntary Work, by Whetter and Pybus. Peterson's Guides and Vacation Work, 2000 (US$16).

Invest Yourself: The Catalogue of Volunteer Opportunities, published by the Commission on Voluntary Service and Action (☎718-638-8487).

QUITO

The Pichincha massif (4794m) juts out a broad shoulder at 2800m, and there Quito (pop. 1½ million) sits, basking contentedly in thin air under blue sky. Colonial buildings, rooted to the ground and bleached white by the equatorial sun, mingle with gleaming glass structures stretching to touch the heavens. Weaving between the buildings are the Quiteños themselves, a human stew of stunning variety, noise, and energy. Part thriving modern city, part reviving colonial showcase, Quito is in every way the geographical, political, and historical center of Ecuador.

Quito's first residents were the Quitu, Cara, Shyrí, and Puruhá peoples who migrated to the area between the 6th and 10th centuries AD. The Incas conquered the city around AD 1500, making it the northern capital of their empire, but the Spanish conquistadors were hot on their heels. Francisco Pizarro's colleague Sebastián de Benalcázar invaded in 1534, and the retreating Incas razed the city to the ground. The Spanish rebuilt in their own manner, atop the ashes.

HIGHLIGHTS OF QUITO

DEFY the Sierra's *tranquilo* reputation in New Town's **nightlife** (p. 100).

CONQUER nearby **Volcán Pichincha** (p. 101), because, after all, it's there.

NAVIGATE cobblestone streets linking 400-year-old churches and plazas (p. 95).

Today, Quiteños welcome visitors to one of two areas: Old Town (*la parte colonial* or *Quito viejo*) and New Town (*Quito moderno* or *Quito nuevo*). In 1978, the United Nations declared the colonial city a World Heritage site. Partly as a result, Old Town's appearance has changed little since colonial days. Streets remain narrow, buildings retain their cool, cobblestoned inner courtyards, and daily activity still revolves around the city's many plazas. Meanwhile the capital's social and commercial engine New Town expands, filled with students, business people, and a growing number of tourists. Travelers use the area as a base from which to traipse through the Andes, battle mosquitoes in jungle lodges, and cruise around the Galápagos. Part of Quito's appeal is its eternally spring-like climate; the temperature hovers around 10-25°C (50-77°F) with little variation. Daily ups and downs are another story, as clear blue morning skies yield to huge cumulus clouds by midday and showers in the afternoon—but each day the sun returns to trace its glorious equatorial path.

◼ INTERCITY TRANSPORTATION

Airport: Aeropuerto Mariscal Sucre (☎2240 080), on Amazonas, near Florida. Taxi from US$4; set the fee before you get in. The "Aeropuerto" bus runs to the airport from Old and New Town; catch it along 12 de Octubre or Amazonas (25min., US$0.25). **Departure tax** US$25.

International and Domestic Airlines: TACA, El Salvador 1033 (☎2923 170), at Naciones Unidas. Open M-F 8:30am-5:30pm, Sa 9am-12:30pm. To: **Santiago** (6½hr., 5:15pm, US$447); **Lima** (2hr., US$350); **La Paz** (6hr., US$522); **Santa Cruz** (8hr., US$522). **TAME,** Amazonas 1354 (☎2903 909), at Colón, handles domestic flights. Open M-F 9am-6:30pm, Sa-Su 9am-noon. To: **Cuenca** (40min.; M-F 7:15am and 4:30pm, Su 4:30pm; US$63); **Galápagos** (4hr.; M-Su 7:30, 9:30am; US$333-389) via **Guayaquil** (45min.; M-F 13 per day 7am-7:45pm, Sa-Su 6-7 per day 7:30am-6:30pm; US$63); **Macas** (30min., M and Th 2pm, US$62).

New Quito

🏠 ACCOMMODATIONS
The Andes Range, **1**
La Casona de Mario, **7**

🍎 FOOD
La Ronda, **3**

🍷 NIGHTLIFE
El Pobre Diablo, **6**

🛍 SHOPPING
Centro Comercial Espiral, **4**
El Jardín Mall, **2**
Mercado Artesanal, **5**

QUITO

TO ✈ AIRPORT, (1km)
TO IMMIGRATION OFFICE (500m)
Río Coca
Río Coca
Plaza de Toros
Jipijapa
Av. de los Granados
Av. de la Prensa
Estación la Y
Juan de Ascaray
Río Amazonas
Shyris
Av. de los Granados
Los Sauces
Gaspar de Villaroel
6 de Diciembre
Eloy Alfaro
La Y
Visa
Pereira
24 de Mayo
Av. América
Naciones Unidas
Atahualpa Olympic Stadium
Naciones Unidas
TO PARQUE METROLPITANO (200m)
Av. José de Sucre
Juan de Diguja
Manosca
Av. de la República
Estadio
Río Amazonas
Marathon Sports
Shyris
Benalcázar
Portugal
Parque de La Carolina
500 meters
500 yards
Carolina
Florón
10 de Agosto
Av. Atahualpa
Av. América
Museo de Ciencias Naturales
Eloy Alfaro
TO FUNDACIÓN GUAYASMÍN (200m)
Eloy Alfaro
Bosmediano
González Suárez
Bellavista
Mariana de Jesús
Hospital Metropolitano
Ministerio de Turismo
Martín Tobar
San Martín
Casarez
Mariana de Jesús
MARIANA DE JESÚS
Rumani
Inglaterra
Italia
Alpallana
Av. de la República
6 de Diciembre
Diego de Almagro
Selva Alegre
Cuero y Calcedo
Eloy Alfaro
Alemania
Potonia
San Salvador
Ministerio de Agricultura
Mariano Aguilera
La Pradera
La Paz
González Suárez
Río Amazonas
LA PRADERA
Bello Horizonte
Andinatel
EMS (Shipping)
Berlín
TO 🍷 EL GUÁPULO (500m)
Ascázubi
Francisco de Orellana
LA COLÓN
Diego de Almagro
Yáñez Pinzón
Francisco Orellana
Colón
Santa María
Av. Colón
Luis Cordero
SEE LA MARISCAL DETAIL MAP p. 85
Av. la Gasca
Mercadillo
Páez
9 de Octubre
García
Calama
Pinta
Wilson
6 de Diciembre
12 de Octubre
Andalucía
Salazar
Santa Clara
Versailles
10 de Agosto
LA MARISCAL
Foch
Isabel la Católica
Madrid
Galavis
San Gregor
La Mariscal
Robles
Washington
Río Amazonas
Roca
Ventimilla
Tamayo
Carrión
Universidad Católica
Pérez Guerrero
18 de Septiembre
Compañía de Guías
Isabel la Católica
Toledo
Ladrón de Guevara
Albornoz
Centro Cultural Benjamín Carrión
Altamontaña
Patria
South American Explorers Club
Av. América
TO OLD QUITO (200m, see map)
Parque El Ejido
El Ejido
Casa de la Cultura & Museo del Banco Central
TO INSTITUTO GEOGRÁFICO MILITAR (600m)
Av. Universitaria

Old Quito

ACCOMMODATIONS
Grand Hotel, **9**
Hotel San Francisco de Quito, **6**
Hotel Viena Internacional, **3**
La Posada Coloniál, **8**

FOOD
Ari, **4**
Bar Restaurant Balcón Quiteño, **7**
Café Modelo, **5**
El Criollo, **1**
La Zamba Teresa, **2**

TO NEW QUITO (200m, see map)
Parque El Ejido
El Ejido
Tarqui

Panamá
Canada
Estados Unidos
Mexico
Buenos Aires
José Riofrío
Montevideo
La Habana
Haití
Luis Dávila
D. Torres
Venezuela
Julio Matovelle
Zambrano
Larrea
Larrea
Salinas
Feliciano Checa
Arenas
10 de Agosto
Boija
Antonio Ante
Alameda
Parque La Alameda

Guatemala
Condorcunga
Carchí
Bombóna
Ruben Dario
New York
Santa Prisca
Ibarra
Pedro Briceño
Gran Colombia
Espinoza
Simón Bolívar
Elizalde

Tapi
H. de Granado
Babahoya
Nicaragua
Cotopaxi
Manabí
Cuenca
Carchí
Galápagos
Venezuela
Carchí
La Basílica
Oriente
Vargas
Banco Central (southbound only)
Caldas
Hermano Miguel (northbound only)
Antepara

Esmeraldas
García Moreno
Santa Bárbara
Museo Conde de Urquijo
Museo de Arte Colonial
Olmedo
PLAZOLETA BENALCÁZAR
Plaza del Teatro (southbound only)
Teatro Nacional Sucre
Plaza del Teatro (northbound only)
Guayaquil
Montúfar
Pichincha
Esmeraldas
Vicente León
Los Ríos

TO EL TEJAR BUS STOP (100m)
La Merced
Chile
Mejía
CMT
Concepción
Andinato
Oficina Información Turista
San Agustín
La Marín
Don Bosco

Imbabura
Mideros
Palacio Presidencial
PLAZA GRANDE
Catedral
Plaza Grande (southbound only)
Espejo
PLAZA LA MARÍN
Chile
Cevallos
Calixto

Centro Cultural Metropolitano
San Francisco
La Compañía
El Sagrario
Sucre
Venezuela
Junín
Jiménez
Almeida
Inclana

Bolívar
PLAZA SAN FRANCISCO
Museo Casa de Sucre
Cine Atahualpa
Flores
Pereira
De Los Milagros
Texeira
Silva
Santa Cruz

Benalcázar
Carmen Alto
Museo de la Ciudad
Rocafuerte
PLAZA SANTO DOMINGO
Santo Domingo
Santo Domingo
Maldonado
Rocafuerte
Salvador
Rivera
Chavez

24 de Mayo
Loja
San Lázaro
Morales
24 de Mayo
Paredes
Cumandá
Poinçin
Liceo
Vasconez
Fernández Madrid
Javier Piedra

Bahía de Caráquez
Ambato
Murgueyto
Marzo
Francisco Quijano
Pascuales
Melchor Aymerich
Ramón Nava
Chongón
TO LA VIRGEN DE QUITO (50m)
Borrero
Recoleta
Terminal Terrestre
Zaldumbide
Cumandá
Santa Cruz

300 meters
300 yards

QUITO

Buses: Terminal, in Old Town, next to the highway at the end of 24 de Mayo. Take the trolley to Cumandá, and descend the stairs away from El Panecillo and la Virgen de Quito. Taxi from New Town to terminal US$2.

Esmeraldas: To **Atacames** (6½hr., every hr. 7:30am-11:40pm, US$8).

Flota Imbabura: To **Manta** (9hr., 4 per day noon-11pm, US$8).

Loja: To **Loja** (14hr., 9 per day 6am-8pm, US$14).

Occidental: To **Esmeraldas** (6hr., every hr. 6:15am-11:30pm, US$6).

Panamericana: To **Ambato** (2½hr., 3:30pm, US$2).

Pullman Carchi: To **Ibarra** (2½hr., every 30min. 3am-11pm, US$2.50).

Vencedores: To **Riobamba** (3½hr., 8 per day 4:15am-8:15pm, US$3.75).

Other Lines: To: **Baños** (3½hr., every 30min. Sa 8pm, US$3); **Cuenca** (10hr., 21 per day 6am-11:30pm, US$10-12); **Guayaquil** (9hr., very frequent 4:30am-11:20pm, US$7-9); **Latacunga** (2hr., every 30min. 10am-10:30pm, US$2); **Macas** (8hr., 2 per day, US$12); **Machala** (10hr., 12 per day 6:30am-9:30pm, US$9); **Otavalo** (2hr., every 20min., US$2.50); **Portoviejo** (9hr., US$9); **Puyo** (5hr., 3 per day, US$5); **Quevedo** (5hr., 24 per day 5am-7pm, US$4); **Santo Domingo** (3hr., 21 per day, US$6).

✈ ORIENTATION

Quito is divided into two principal areas—**New Town** is bordered by 10 de Agosto on the west, 12 de Octubre on the east, and Parque de la Carolina to the north. Its southernmost border, **Parque El Ejido**, lies between New and Old Town. Old Town is bounded by **El Ejido** to the north, **24 de Mayo** to the south, **Montufar**, to the east, and **Cuenca** to the west. The two parts of town are connected by the trolley, which runs north-south through the city along **10 de Agosto, Guayaquil,** and **Maldonado.** After exploring for the day, tourists tend to congregate in **La Mariscal,** the neighborhood surrounding **Amazonas** south of **Cordero.** The streets around Old Town can get dangerous, especially at night, though there have been recent efforts to increase police presence. Avoid El Ejido and all urban parks at night.

⊏ LOCAL TRANSPORTATION

Trolleys: The environmentally friendly *trole* system in Quito is fast, efficient, crowded, and overrun with pickpockets. You can't miss the glass-walled stops. The trolley runs along **10 de Agosto** in New Town and along **Guayaquil** and **Maldonado** in Old Town. Runs M-F 5am-10pm, Sa-Su 6am-10pm. US$0.25, children under 18 and seniors US$0.12.

Ecovía: Similar to the trolley, the cable-less *ecovía* ferries passengers on the north-south 6 de Diciembre route. Operates daily 6am-9:30pm. US$0.25, children under 18 and seniors US$0.12.

Buses: Quito's bus system is quick and efficient but complicated. All buses in the city cost US$0.25; if you are leaving the city limits, the doorman will inform you of the price. Pay after you get on, and note the signs in the front of the bus that tell the destinations. The men who hang out of the entrance as the bus approaches shout destinations as the bus slows to a halt. Quickly confirm your destination, but board quickly before the bus begins moving again. Signal that you want to disembark by walking to the door while the bus is still moving and say *"gracias"* loudly.

Taxis: Always take taxis at night (usually US$1 between sites in New Town). In general, meters are on during the day and off at night. Set the price before getting in. Legitimate taxis have blue-and-white signs with their registration numbers in the windshield. In areas with little taxi traffic, ask a local establishment's employee to call you a cab.

Car Rental: Budget Rent-a-Car, Amazonas E4-387 (☎2237 026), at Colón. Open M-F 8am-8pm, Sa 8am-2pm, Su 10am-4pm. Also at the airport (☎3300 979). Open M-Sa 7am-10pm, Su 8am-10pm. Must be over 25 to rent

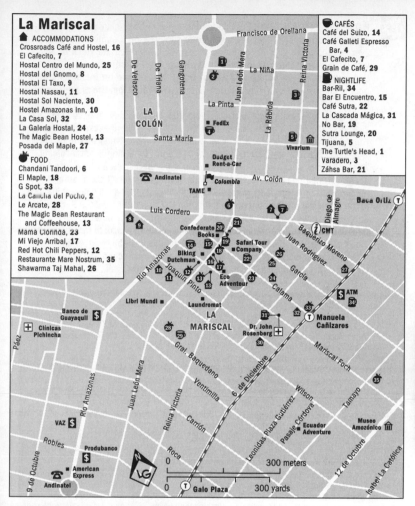

La Mariscal

▲ ACCOMMODATIONS
Crossroads Café and Hostel, **16**
El Cafecito, **7**
Hostal Centro del Mundo, **25**
Hostal del Gnomo, **8**
Hostal El Taxo, **9**
Hostal Nassau, **11**
Hostal Sol Naciente, **30**
Hostel Amazonas Inn, **10**
La Casa Sol, **32**
La Galería Hostal, **24**
The Magic Bean Hostel, **13**
Posada del Maple, **27**

● FOOD
Chandani Tandoori, **6**
El Maple, **18**
G Spot, **33**
La Cancha del Pocho, **2**
Le Arcate, **28**
The Magic Bean Restaurant
 and Coffeehouse, **13**
Mama Clorinda, **23**
Mi Viejo Arribal, **17**
Red Hot Chili Peppers, **12**
Restaurante Mare Nostrum, **35**
Shawarma Taj Mahal, **26**

● CAFÉS
Café del Suizo, **14**
Café Galleti Espresso
 Bar, **4**
El Cafecito, **7**
Grain de Café, **29**

■ NIGHTLIFE
Bar-Ril, **34**
Bar El Encuentro, **15**
Café Sutra, **22**
La Cascada Mágica, **31**
No Bar, **19**
Sutra Lounge, **20**
Tijuana, **5**
The Turtle's Head, **1**
Varadero, **3**
Záhsa Bar, **21**

Francisco de Orellana
La Niña
La Pinta
FedEx
Santa María
Vivarium
Budget
Rent-a-Car
Andinatel
Colombia
Av. Colón
TAME
Luis Cordero
Confederate Books
Safari Tour Company
Biking Dutchman
Eco Adventour
Libri Mundi
Laundromat
LA MARISCAL
Dr. John Rosenberg
Manuela Cañizares
Banco de Guayaquil
Clínicas Pichincha
Gral. Baquedano
Mariscal Foch
VAZ
Ventimilla
Museo Amazónico
Robles
Produbanco
American Express
Andinatel
Galo Plaza
LA COLÓN
Francisco de Orellana
Reina Victoria
Juan León Mera
La Rábida
Diego de Almagre
Baca Ortiz
CMT
Baquerizo Moreno
Juan Rodríguez
García
Calama
ATM
Leonidas Plaza Gutiérrez
6 de Diciembre
Wilson
Ecuador Adventure
12 de Octubre
Isabel La Católica
9 de Octubre
Páez
Reina Victoria
Carrión
Roca
Tamayo
0   300 meters
0   300 yards

QUITO

🛈 PRACTICAL INFORMATION

TOURIST AND FINANCIAL SERVICES.

Tourist Offices: From the mountains to the beaches to the jungles to the cities, Quito's tourist offices have information about all of Ecuador.

■**The South American Explorers (SAE),** Jorge Washington 311 (☎/fax 2225 228; www.saexplorers.org), at Leonidas Plaza, New Town. Canny, English-speaking staff offers honest info culled from first-hand experience. Event listings, lending library, storage, and **maps** galore. First-time visitors to Quito should peruse the recommendation sheets (US$1-1.50) that list SAE's preferred hostels and restaurants, some great alternatives to tourism (see p. 70), and first-hand reports of crime against tourists. Always looking for **volunteers.** Membership US$50, couples US$80. Open M-W and F 9:30am-5pm, Th 9:30am-8pm, Sa 9am-noon.

HOW TO SPOT A FAKE Ecuadorians are especially cautious—even para-noid—about the money they accept—and for good reason. Counterfeit cash is all over Ecuador, and if you get passed a bogus bill, chances are you'll be stuck with it. Here are some tips to make sure you don't get scammed:

Get your cash from banks and ATMs. Don't trust people on the streets who offer to change money. (If you do decide to go that route, beware of fixed calculations and other tricks.)

Pass small bills. Ask banks to change your 20s into fives right after you get your cash from the ATM or teller. The smaller the bills you have, the less bad change you are liable to receive for a 50 cent purchase. Carrying small bills in Ecuador is a good idea, anyway. Often change for 10s and 20s is simply not available.

Know the currency. Recently-minted 20s, 10s, and fives all have the faint images of their respective presidents on the far right of the "heads" side of the bill and vertical watermarks that say "USA" and spell out the bill's denomination to the left of the presidential portrait. Popular in Ecuador, the golden Sacajawea dollar-coins have a clearly visible silverish stripe around the outer edge.

Don't be afraid to return bad bills. If some unscrupulous *taxista* tries to unload a bad buck on you, demand another one. And if you have any doubts about any of the money someone is giving you, slow down the transaction and hold the bill up to the light, or you may never see it leave your hands again.

Corporation Metropolitana de Turismo (CMT) (☎2551 566), at Reina Victoria and Cordero, New Town, in the park, at the glass kiosk with blue-and-white trim. Open M-F 9am-5pm. **Branches** at the airport (☎3300 163; open daily 8am-12:30am, depending on flight schedules); in Old Town (García Moreno N12-01 and Mejía; ☎2572 566 or 2283 480; open M-Sa 9am-6pm, Su 9am-4pm); at Museo Nacional del Banco Central (open Tu-Su 9am-5pm). CMT offers **maps** and info on hotels, transportation, events, and tours throughout Ecuador.

Oficina Información Turística (☎2586 591), on Plaza Grande, Old Town. Talk to professional navy-blue-clad officers, either at the office on Pasaje Arzobispal, at the kiosk in the plaza, or on the street. English- and Spanish-speakers provide city info and run 4 tours daily (US$12, children US$4). 2 nocturnal tours provide an alternative to exploring Old Town's illuminated churches and plazas alone. Price includes admission to churches. Open daily 8:30am-5pm.

Ministerio de Turismo, Eloy Alfaro N32-300, 3rd fl. (☎2507 555; www.vivecuador.com), across from Parque la Carolina, New Town, in a state office with armed guards. The ministry provides **maps** and info on tours and lodging. Open daily 8:30am-12:30pm and 1:30-5pm.

Tours: With these Quito tour agencies, hike the mountains, kayak the rivers, and lounge on the beaches that the tourist offices above only talk about.

Ecuador Adventure, Pasaje Córdova N23-26 and Wilson (☎2223 720; www.ecuador.ec or www.galapagosadventure.com), between 12 de Octubre and 6 de Diciembre, specializes in rafting and sea kayaking trips (US$50-70 per day). Also offers 12-day multi-sport trips (US$80-120 per day), which include hiking, kayaking, climbing, and biking, all in one. 7-day Galápagos multi-sport trip US$1200-1400. Walk-in rafting daytrips every Sa, including insurance. Trips include all expenses. Open M-F 9am-7pm.

Safari, Foch E5-39 (☎2552 505; www.safari.com.ec), at León Mera, is a behemoth. Offers 25 different day tours as well as climbing and jungle tours. Specializes in climbing Cotopaxi (including acclimatization hikes) and hiking Quilotoa Lake. Will arrange jungle tours with other companies but offer no direct tours themselves. US$165-185 per person in group, US$320 for 1-on-1 service. SAE discount 10%, ISIC 5%. Open daily 9:30am-7pm.

The Biking Dutchman, Foch 714 (☎2568 323), at León Mera, offers mountain biking tours throughout central Ecuador, including Cotopaxi (1 day US$40, 2 days US$100; tours include helmets, meals, and lodging). Repair cars follow. Open M-F 9am-6pm, Sa 9:30am-1pm.

Compañía de Guías, Jorge Washington E7-424 and 6 de Diciembre (☎/fax 2504 773; www.companiadeguias.com.ec), conducts 2-day climbs to Cayambe and Cotopaxi (US$230), and Chimborazo (US$250). Also offers climbing classes. Trips available for all skill levels. Guides speak English, Spanish, French, or German. Trips include food, shelter, transportation, equipment, and an ENSA- or ASEGUIM-certified guide. Open M-F 9:30am-1:30pm and 2:30-6:30pm.

QUITO

Surtrek, Amazonas 897 (☎2231 534; www.surtrek.com), at Wilson, offers daily tours for groups of at least 2 to the Antisana Ecological Reserve. Tours include food, entrance fee, guides, and technical equipment. English- and German-speaking guides. 4-day US$390 per person; 5-day with climb of Volcán Antisana US$590 per person.

Embassies and Consulates: For Ecuadorian embassies abroad, see p. 10.

Bolivia, Eloy Alfaro 2432 (☎2244 830; fax 2244 833), at Fernando Ayarza. Open M-F 8:30am-1pm.

Canada, 6 de Diciembre 2816, 4th fl. (☎2232 040; quito@dfait.maeci.gc.ca), at Paul Rivet. Open M-Th 9am-4pm, F 9am-1pm.

Ireland, Antonio de Ulloa 2651 (☎2451 577; fax 2269 862), at Rumipamba. Open M-F 9am-1pm.

Peru, El Salvador 495 (☎2252 582), at Irlanda. Open M-F 9am-1pm and 3-5pm.

UK (☎2970 800 or 2970 801; fax 2970 807), at Naciones Unidas and República de El Salvador, 14th fl. Open M-Th 8am-noon and 2-3pm, F 8-11:30am.

US (☎2562 890; fax 2502 052), at 12 de Octubre and Patria. Open M-F 8am-12:30pm and 1:30-5pm.

Immigration Office: Jefatura de Migración (☎2247 510), at Isla Seymour and Río Coca, north of Parque la Carolina. Take a trolley to the north terminal, pass the trolley route on 10 de Agosto, turn right on Río Coca, and continue 10 blocks to Isla Seymour. Turn left on Isla Seymour to find a sign that says "Migración." Follow Isla Seymour until the park appears on your left. The building is baby blue and on your right. Tourist card extensions up to 90 days (US$1.60). Open M-F 8am-12:30pm and 3-6pm, Sa-Su 8am-noon and 3-6pm. Sa-Su, office only offers permission to leave the country.

Currency Exchange: Produbanco has 4 offices that exchange traveler's checks and currency: at Amazonas N21-64 and Robles (☎2564 500; open M-F 8:30am-6pm); at Naciones Unidas and C.C. Quicentro (☎2248 819; open M-F 10am-8pm); at Amazonas 3775 and Japón (☎2999 000; open M-F 8:30am-5pm); and at La Prensa and Homero Salas by the airport (☎2444 303; open M-F 8:30am-6pm). **VAZ,** Amazonas 477 and Roca (☎2529 212), across the street from the Hotel Alomeda Real, exchanges traveler's checks and currency. Open M-F 8:45am-5:45pm, Sa 9am-1pm. People on the street outside of VAZ also offer currency exchange. This practice is very informal; know exchange rates before partaking. **Multicambio S.A.** (☎2564 324), at Amazonas and Ventimilla, exchanges traveler's checks and foreign currency. Open M-F 8:30am-5pm.

ATMs: Many in New Town; few in Old Town. MC/V ATMs at designated **Banco de Guayaquil, Banco del Pacífico,** and BanRed machines. Expect a US$1.50 service charge.

Credit Card Offices: American Express, Amazonas 329, 5th fl. (☎2560 488; fax 2502 004), at Jorge Washington. Open M-F 8:30am-5pm, Sa 9am-1pm. **MasterCard,** Naciones Unidas 825 (☎2262 770), at Shyris. Open M-F 8:30am-5pm. **Visa,** Amazonas 4545 (☎2981 300), at Pereira. Open M-F 8am-7pm, Sa 9am-2pm.

LOCAL SERVICES

Bookstores: Confederate Books, Calama 410 (☎/fax 252 78 90; billgrok@hotmail.com), at León Mera, has a wide selection of used English-language books. Open M-Sa 10am-7pm. The **SAE** (see above) has Quito's best selection of English guidebooks, a variety of books for borrowing (deposit US$30), and a small book exchange. The highbrow **Libri Mundi** (www.librimundi.com) has 3 locations: León Mera N23-83 (☎2234 791), at Wilson; in Quicentro Shopping (☎2464 473), on Naciones Unidas and Shyris; and in Cumbayá (☎2894 894), at Pampile and Chimborazo. Not as large an English selection as Confederate books, but less pulp fiction and celebrity autobiographies and more literary reading. Books in English, Spanish, German, Italian, and French. Open M-F 8:30am-7:30pm, Sa 9am-6:30pm.

Cultural Centers: Centro Cultural Benjamín Carrión, Jorge Washington 909 (☎2221 895; fax 2223 604; ccbc@quito.gov.ec), at Páez in New Town, houses exhibits, a concert room, and a tranquil library in the restored home of writer Benjamín Carrión. Also dispenses information on city events. Open M-F 10am-6pm. **Cen-**

QUITO

tro Cultural Metropolitano (☎2950 272), at Espejo and Moreno in Old Town, houses an art museum, library, and cafe, and offers theater, music, and dance performances in its courtyard. Open Tu-Sa 9am-5pm, Su 9am-5pm. Library open M-F 8am-7pm, Sa 9am-6pm, Su 9am-1pm.

Outdoor Equipment: The Explorer, Reina Victoria E-632 (☎2550 911; www.explorerecuador.com), at Pinto. Rents and sells tons of hiking supplies. Sleeping bags US$2 per day. 3-person tents US$6 per day. Open M-F 9am-7pm, Sa 9am-2pm. SAE or ISIC discount 10%. **Altamontaña,** Jorge Washington E7-38 (☎2558 380; altamont_sec@ecuador365.com or ivanrojasb@web.de), at 6 de Diciembre, rents, sells, and buys similar, affordable equipment and arranges direct climbing, rafting, and jungle tours. Open M-F 9am-1pm and 3-7pm, Sa 9:30am-1:30pm.

Laundromats: Lavandería Calama, Calama 244 (☎2544 528), at Reina Victoria. Standard cleaning US$0.90 per kg. Open M-Sa 8am-8pm, Su 8-10am. **Opera de Jabón,** Pinto 325 (☎2543 995), at Reina Victoria. US$1 per kg. Open M-Sa 7am-7:30pm, Su 9am-5pm. Affiliated with the neighboring HI. ISIC discount US$0.11 per kg. **24hr. Laundromat,** Calama 217 (☎2225 106), at Reina Victoria. Ring the bell if you want your socks washed at 3am. 1hr. turnaround. Best prices (US$0.70 per kg).

EMERGENCY AND COMMUNICATIONS

Emergency: ☎911.

Police: ☎101. 24hr. **Criminal Investigation Office** at Cuenca and Mideros, Old Town.

24hr. Pharmacy: Farmacia Rey de Reyes, Jorge Washington E7-41 (☎2557 357), at Reina Victoria.

Hospitals: Hospital de Clínicas Pichincha, Páez N22-160 (☎2562 408), at Ventamilla, is recommended for 24hr. emergency care and pharmacy. **Hospital Vozandes,** Villalengua 267 (☎2262 142), at 10 de Agosto, on the Villaflora bus line, has American and Ecuadorian physicians and 24hr. emergency room. Consultations US$9. Open M-F 8am-4:30pm. **Hospital Metropolitano** (☎2261 520), at Mariana de Jesús and Occidental, on the Quito Sur-San Gabriel bus line. The largest, most institutional hospital in Quito, with 24hr. emergency room and M-F 9am-8pm consultations. Taxi US$2. Private medical practitioner **Dr. John Rosenberg,** Foch 476 (☎2521 104; cell 09 9739 734; pager 2227 777), at Almagro, speaks fluent English, French, German, and Hebrew.

Telephones: Quito is the easiest place in Ecuador from which to make international calls, which doesn't say much. **Andinatel,** at Amazonas and Colón, at Eloy Alfaro and 9 de Octubre, in the airport, at Benalcázar and Mejía, and at the bus station, is the best place to make calling card or collect calls. All offices open daily 8am-8pm. **Bellsouth** and **Porta** have phone booths throughout the city but require phone cards (domestic calls US$0.13 per min.). The catch is that your card only works on phones for the appropriate company. Phone booths are much cheaper but are scarce. Make sure hotels charge a reasonable flat rate for service (under US$0.50).

Internet: Everywhere along Calama, Reina Victoria, and León Mera. Expect to pay US$0.80-1 per hr. Most offer Net2Phone long-distance service (US$0.25 per min.).

Post Office: New Town Post Office, Eloy Alfaro 354 (☎2561 218), at 9 de Octubre. Mark mail "Correo Central, Eloy Alfaro Estafeta SUC#21"; otherwise it will be sent to the Old Town office. Open M-F 8am-6pm, Sa 8am-noon. **Old Town Post Office** (☎2282 175), on Espejo between Guayaquil and Venezuela, half a block toward Guayaquil from the Palacio de Gobierno. Mark mail "Correo Central Lista de Correos" to have it sent here. Open M-F 8am-6pm. **EMS** (☎2561 962), next to the post office on Eloy Alfaro. Open M-F 8am-6pm, Sa 8am-noon. **FedEx,** Amazonas 517 (☎2909 201), at Santa María. Open 8:30am-8pm, Su 10am-2pm.

■ ACCOMMODATIONS

ACCOMMODATIONS BY PRICE

Area Abbreviations: NT New Town **OT** Old Town

UNDER US$4 (❶)		The Andes Range (89)	NT
Hostal Centro del Mundo (89)	NT	The Magic Bean Hostel (90)	NT
US$4-8 (❷)		**US$8-14 (❸)**	
Crossroads Café and Hostel (91)	NT	Hostal Amazonas Inn (89)	NT
El Cafecíto (90)	NT	Hostal del Gnomo (91)	NT
Grand Hotel (91)	OT	Hotel Viena Internacional (91)	OT
Hostal El Taxo (91)	NT	🗽 Posada del Maple (89)	NT
Hostal Nassau (90)	NT		
Hostal Sol Naciente (91)	NT	**US$14-25 (❹)**	
La Casona de Mario (90)	NT	🗽 Hotel San Francisco de Quito (91)	OT
La Galería Hostal (91)	NT	La Casa Sol (90)	NT
La Posada Coloniál (92)	OT		

NEW TOWN

La Mariscal, the neighborhood between Amazonas and 6 de Diciembre, is a tourist community overflowing with hostels. Budget hotels lie slightly off main strips. Anywhere you stay, expect to pay an additional 12% IVA tax, unless otherwise stated. Accommodations rarely accept credit cards. No one has lock-outs. All hostels have hot water. Hostels usually take one of two security measures: either a guard is on 24hr. duty to buzz guests into the hostel, or guests are given individual keys to the front gate. Make it clear that you want to stay in the same room for consecutive nights; if you don't, the hotel may shuffle you around.

🗽 **Posada del Maple,** Juan Rodríguez E8-49 (☎2544 507; www.posadadelmaple.com), at 6 de Diciembre. Huge common spaces encourage mingling with new-found friends. Safe baggage room *(bodega)* upon request. Has communal kitchen. Internet and laundry service extra. Breakfast included. Reception daily 8am-9:45pm. Singles US$13.50, with bath US$16; doubles US$25/$29; triples with bath US$32.50; quads with bath US$35; quints with bath US$38. IVA included. AmEx/MC/V. ❸

Hostal Amazonas Inn, Joaquín Pinto E4-324 (☎2225 723), at Amazonas. Central, with comfortable rooms, carpets, cable TV, and private baths. The uniformed staff adds a classy atmosphere. Upstairs rooms have no windows, but some have balconies. Singles US$10; doubles US$20-22; triples US$28; quads US$36. Additional guests US$9. IVA included. Traveler's checks accepted. ❸

The Andes Range (☎3303 752; www.theandesrange.com), at Davolos and La Prensa, only a 5min. walk from the airport. Walk north on La Prensa past the Supermaxi. Turn left on Davalos. After 250m turn left at the blue guard hut. Turn left at the T and open the gate to your left. Good for much more than a 1-night stay. Aussie owner Chris Halliday sets up tours outside of Quito (about US$60 per day by minibus) and spoils visitors with 30min. free Internet per day, satellite TV, complementary chocolates, and CD stereos in every room. Laundry, breakfast, and dinner provided for an extra charge. Shuttles to the airport available. Singles US$6, with bath US$8. Ask about the off-site guest room with a view of the mountains (set to open late summer 2004). Cash only. ❷

Hostal Centro del Mundo, Lizardo García 569 (☎2229 050), at Reina Victoria. At once in the middle of the world and in the center of the tourist section of New Town, this place is a hub of backpacker social activity. Bunk beds grow more inviting after Quebecois owner Pierre hands

"IT'S WHO YOU'RE WITH"

It's around 10pm on a Friday night, the start of a wild night of partying for the guests at Hostal Centro del Mundo (see p. 89) in Quito, and the midpoint of about three straight hours of writing for me. As I struggle to block out the voices of the 20-odd 20-somethings enjoying Pierre's free vat of rum and Coke, an attractive Ecuadorian girl of about my age approaches me.

"My friend wants to meet you," she says. So I saunter over to the table in the dining room with all of the sauntering ability that is left in an exhausted body. I introduce myself to the lovely Diana (that, I learn, is her name), explain the nature of my work, and agree to reunite with her at 11:30.

11:30 rolls around, I put away my pad and paper, and join the hostel party.

"Why don't you dance?" she asks in English.

"I'm tired... I'm not drunk enough... We're not at a club..."

"Don't you know," she says, "that it's not where you are, but who you are with that matters?"

Staggered by Diana's profundity, I relent and dance until she can find another partner. She targets John.

"And why aren't you dancing?" Diana asks John, not to be persuaded from his spot leaning against the wall.

He calmly replies, "A deep river moves not but slowly."

Touché.

- Abe Kinkhopf

out free booze (M, W, F). Common room TV switches between MTV and ESPN during the evenings. The real advantage of this place, however, is the comprehensive travel guide that Pierre has posted. Advice ranges from which mountains to climb to tips on staying out of jail. Lockers available. Spanish lessons from staff (US$1.50 per hr.). Dorms US$3-5; singles US$7; doubles US$10-16. ❶

Hostal Nassau, Pinto E4-342 (☎2565 724), at Amazonas, 2 doors down from Hostal Amazonas Inn (see above). Friendly staff and cheap but large rooms make this the perfect place for the lone traveler on a tight budget. Provides safe box and space to put your own locks on the doors. Cable TV in the common room. Singles US$7, with private bath US$10; doubles US$14/$20. ❷

The Magic Bean Hostel, Foch E5-08 (☎2566 181; magic@ecuadorexplorer.com), at León Mera. This magic bean is not Jack's; it's Shel Silverstein's. Check the inside of the menu at the accompanying restaurant (see p. 92). Rooms are clean and adequate, but this hostel's connection with the downstairs restaurant is what will wake you up in the morning. Prime (though noisy) location. Safe box in office, wake up service, taxi, 24hr. guard on duty. Reception 7am-10pm. Breakfast included. Well-kept dorms US$6; singles US$25; doubles US$30; triples US$36. AmEx/MC/V. ❷

El Cafecito, Luís Cordero 1124 (☎2234 862; www.cafecito.net), at Reina Victoria. No, you're not staying in a "cafe." You're actually staying in a "little cafe." Grammar aside, El Cafecito offers comfortable rooms with colorful wall hangings, and a popular cafe where guests get a 10% discount. Canadian-owned and well-stocked with capable English-speaking staff. 2nd- and 3rd-fl. rooms equally priced. Request a 2nd-fl. room for a balcony and spectacular view. Dorms US$6; doubles US$14. AmEx/MC/V. ❷

La Casa Sol, Calama 127 (☎2230 798; www.lacasasol.com), at 6 de Diciembre. "The Andean House of Sun" certainly lives up to its name. Its brilliant orange and green exterior gives way to airy, spacious rooms and a small but cool courtyard. English-speaking staff. Lockers available. All rooms have telephones. Internet and laundry extra. Breakfast included. Singles with private bath US$23; doubles US$40. Discounts for SAE and ISIC. Call ahead to arrange stays over 15 days for a price-drop of over one third, or stay with more than 8 people for a 10% discount. ❹

La Casona de Mario, Andalucía 213 (☎2544 036 or 2230 129; www.exploringecuador.com/casona/index.html), at Galicia. Worth the walk to come home to the friendly dogs and delightful flowers. Patio, kitchen, TV lounge, laundry, and even a grill. Singles US$7; doubles US$14. 10% discount for SAE members and stays over 7 days. ❷

Crossroads Café and Hostel, Foch E5-23 (☎2234 735; www.crossroadshostal.com), at León Mera. A favorite among adventure travelers but a bit noisy at night. Perks include: 99 movies at last count, patio with fireplace, and owner Jeff's help planning trips. 24hr. cafe downstairs. Off-street parking available. Dorms US$5-6; singles US$11, with bath US$14; doubles US$16/$22; triples US$21/$30. Traveler's checks accepted. ❷

Hostal Sol Naciente, Pinto 145 (☎2229 453; hostalsolnaciente_spey@hotmail.com), at 6 de Diciembre. Cheap, informal digs. Motherly staff will fix you breakfast or lunch upon request. Neat but sparse rooms. Community kitchen, common room, access to washing machine (US$1). 2-bed dorms US$4, with TV US$5; doubles US$10. ❷

Hostal del Gnomo, Cordero E4-128 (☎2224 252; hostaldelaluna@andinanet.com), at Foch. The extra money you pay here goes toward this hostel's towering ceiling, hardwood floors, and immaculately kept garden. Communal kitchen, lockers available upon request. Note the disparity between the hotel's name and its email address; the name "Hostal del Gnomo" apparently has bad Feng Shui and is being changed. Anticipate a sign change in the near future. Reservations accepted. May 15-Sept. 15 and Nov. 15-Feb. 15 singles US$12, with bath US$16; doubles US$24/$30; triples US$30/$42; quads with bath US$50. Low season US$1-2 less per person per room. Cash only. ❸

Hostal El Taxo, Foch 909 (☎2225 593; www.hostaleltaxo.com), at Cordero. If you're into body art, you'll never want to leave. Owner Peter, proud wearer of 13 tattoos, runs a tattoo parlor in the back. Each room in this hostel is as eclectically decorated as Peter's body. Ask to see (or stay in) the pink room, just for kicks. Rooms are spacious and airy. Common area boasts a communal kitchen and a large TV with a collection of tapes and DVDs. Outdoor patio, breakfast and laundry available for an additional fee. Singles US$6, with bath US$8; doubles US$14. ❷

La Galería Hostal, Calama 23 (☎2500 307; hotallagaleria@hotmail.com), at Alamagro. Quiet and clean with a yellow motif and hardwood floors, La Galería is a laid-back and step up from its similarly priced counterparts. Lockers and *bodega* available. Internet. Cable TV coming soon. Singles US$7, with bath US$11; doubles with bath US$16. ❷

OLD TOWN

Old Town brings you close to the pulse of colonial Quito, though night offers little of interest. Be sure to take taxis after dark. Opt for nothing less than inexpensive, quality hotels with open, sun-filled patios.

▨ **Hotel San Francisco de Quito,** Sucre 217 (☎2287 758; hsfquito@andinanet.net), at Guayaquil, 1 block up from the Plaza Santo Domingo. Old Town elegance at reasonable rates in this renovated 1620 building. Comfy, carpeted rooms with bath, some with iron balconies overlooking a charming courtyard. Ask about double-tiered rooms with the iron spiral staircases leading to the beds. Rooftop terrace with great views. Breakfast and IVA included. Singles US$18; doubles US$30; triples US$36; quads US$44; mini-apartment (top floor, with stove and kitchen) US$18. ISIC discount 10%. ❹

Hotel Viena Internacional, Flores 600 (☎2954 860; vienaint@interactive.net.ec), at Chile. Just minutes from the *trole*, this is a real hotel for hostel prices. Open-air courtyard, private baths in each room, rooms open up onto courtyard. Breakfast at the restaurant below not included. Viena offers Spanish classes, massages, acupuncture, and salsa lessons to name a few. Singles US$10; doubles US$20; triples US$30. ❸

Grand Hotel, Rocafuerte 1001 (☎2280 192 or 2959 411; grandhotelquito1@hotmail.com), at Pontón. Close to the bus terminal. Internet, storage, laundry, a cafe, a common room with cable TV, and kitchen. Tourist police say to be especially cautious after dark on Rocafuerte. Singles US$4.50, with bath US$6.50; doubles US$8/$12; triples US$10.50/$16.50. IVA included. ❷

La Posada Coloniál, Paredes 188 (☎2282 859; fax 2505 240), at Rocafuerte. Nondescript but cheap and close to the Old Town bus station. Cable TV. Singles US$5; doubles with private baths US$10. Discounts for longer stays. ❷

✂ FOOD

Quito's restaurants like to tack on additional charges. There is a 12% IVA in addition to your bill and sometimes another 10% for service. Credit cards, when accepted, sometimes result in a 10-20% service charge. For cheap food, head to one of **Supermaxi** supermarkets, at the Multicentro on 6 de Diciembre and La Niña and at El Jardín shopping center. (Multicentro open M-F 9:30am-8pm, Sa 10am-8pm; Jardín open M-Sa 10am-8:30pm, Su 10am-7:30pm.)

FOOD BY TYPE

Area Abbreviations: NT New Town **OT** Old Town

COMIDA TÍPICA		Mi Viejo Arribal (94)	NT ❹
Bar Restaurant Balcón Quiteño (94)	OT ❸	The Magic Bean Restaurant and	
El Criollo (94)	OT ❷	Coffeehouse	NT ❶
La Cancha del Pocho (93)	NT ❶		
La Ronda (92)	NT ❺	INTERNATIONAL	
La Zamba Teresa (94)	OT ❷	Chandani Tandoori (93)	NT ❶
Mama Clorinda (93)	NT ❷	Red Hot Chili Peppers (93)	NT ❷
Restaurante Mare Nostrum (93)	NT ❺	Shawarma Taj Mahal (93)	NT ❶
CONTINENTAL		VEGETARIAN	
Café Modelo (94)	OT ❶	Ari (94)	OT ❶
Le Arcate (93)	NT ❷	✳ El Maple (92)	NT ❶

NEW TOWN

Pricier than those in Old Town, New Town restaurants still serve good meals on a reasonable budget. Hit the side streets off **Río Amazonas,** where **sidewalk cafes** allow for people-watching, but prepare for bombardment by beggars and vendors. **Restaurant Row,** tourist-oriented eateries in the heart of the *barrio* some refer to as **Gringolandia,** lies between León Mera and Reina Victoria, around Calama.

✳ **El Maple,** Calama 369 (☎2900 000), at León Mera. Plenty of plants and bright lighting make the atmosphere as healthy as the vegetarian food. All dishes made with organic vegetables. Coffee is to-die-for. Look for the yellow building on the corner with the words "Restaurante Vegetariano" over the entrance. Internet (US$0.90 per hr.) and Net2Phone available. *Menú* US$2-3. Open daily 7am-10pm. AmEx/MC/V. ❶

The Magic Bean Restaurant and Coffeehouse, Foch E5-08 (☎/fax 2566 181), at León Mera. With 7 varieties of pancakes, this Bean is best known for its large breakfasts, but don't count out the later meals for quality. Sit under a canopy in front of the hostel and eat to the tune of American rock music. Ample vegetarian items; all vegetables are organic. Take advantage of a well-diversified juice bar for dessert if you're not full (oh, but you will be). Entrees US$2-4. Open daily 7am-10pm. AmEx/MC/V (min. US$10). ❶

La Ronda, Bello Horizonte 400 (☎2540 459), at Diego de Almargo. This restaurant comes highly recommended as the best place for *comida típica* in Quito. Dark wood and maroon carpeting makes for a classy interior. Quiteños and tourists alike come dressed to the nines (you'll feel out of place in anything more casual than a button-down shirt and slacks). Entrees US$8-15. Open daily noon-11pm. ❺

La Cancha del Pocho (☎ 2565 293), at Amazonas and La Niña. It's wall-to-wall soccer at this little diner. Soccer on television, soccer-themed wall murals, waiters in soccer jerseys. Indifferent toward the game? The US$2 lunch specials, which include a drink, will keep you there. Open daily 10am-10pm. ❶

Shawarma Taj Mahal (☎ 09 9205 404), at Lizardo García and Reina Victoria. Sit outside under the royal blue canopy and take a load off of your wallet with some cheap Arabic food (sandwiches from US$2, plates from US$4), or go inside and smoke one of nearly 50 varieties of tobacco from a hookah (US$3). Beats the heck out of the cheap cigarettes (US$0.50 a pack) sold here. Open late. ❶

Restaurante Mare Nostrum, Foch 172 (☎ 2238 236), at Tamayo. Practice the art of fine seafood dining in a stunning 1930s mansion. Solid pewter plates, a suit of armor by the fireplace, and stained glass windows add to the Gothic castle ambience. Seafood *paella*, crab crepes, and many other fruits of the sea. Entrees US$10-20. IVA and service not included. Open daily noon-4pm and 7-10:30pm. ❺

Le Arcate, Baquedano 358 (☎ 2237 659), at León Mera. Serves melt-in-your-mouth thin-crust pizzas (US$4-9), which can feed 2 budget travelers or stuff a lone one. Formal attire recommended. Open Tu-Su 11am-3pm and 6-11pm, Sa 11am-4pm. MC/V. ❷

Mama Clorinda, Reina Victoria 1144 (☎ 2544 362), at Calama. A self-proclaimed "safe" and "typical" establishment. Serves Ecuadorian specialties like cattle tongue, roasted lamb, or figs with cheese, "just how mama prepared them." Tall travelers beware the low 2nd fl. balcony. Entrees US$4-7. Excellent *batidos* (fresh fruit blended with milk and sugar, US$1.69). Open Tu-Sa 7am-10pm, Su-M 10am-5pm. ❷

Chandani Tandoori (☎ 2221 053), at León Mera and Cordero. If you came to Ecuador to satisfy your insatiable craving for Indian food, then you came to the wrong country. But if the urge for Indian suddenly hits you, look for this modest white building with red-and-blue lettering on the outside to quell your hunger. The *menú* (US$2.50) is the way to go. When they dare you to "impress the chef" and try the "very very hot" Phall, proceed with caution. English menu. Beer available. Open M-Sa 11am-10:30pm, Su noon-3pm. ❶

Red Hot Chili Peppers, Foch E4-314 (☎ 2557 575), at León Mera. Perhaps the most eye-catching characteristic of this restaurant is the wall full of obscene messages (in both English and Spanish) directly on your right as you enter. This would be a great place to pick an argument; every inappropriate comeback is

THE HIDDEN DEAL

HITS THE SPOT

Late-night eats are a staple of the bar scene in nearly any city, and fortunately for Quito a couple of American expats have put together a burger joint that not only stays open late but also serves up burgers that may as well have come from the heart of the American Midwest. Although the name **G Spot** will undoubtedly goad your inebriated hostelmates into making repeated, and failed, attempts at sexually-charged witticisms, the real spot that this restaurant hits is the one in your stomach that craves a decent, down-home American cheeseburger.

But then again, cheeseburgers are only half the perks. Perhaps the best thing about G Spot is that it's open late. The owners take care not to leave until the last person is served, sometimes staying open until 4am. And believe me, this is a very kind act. After a few beers and a non-stop night of salsaing, a thick burger satisfies like nothing else. These late night eats won't set up your cab fare, either. Plain-Jane hamburgers start at US$0.85 and a cheeseburger only costs US$1.10. After the street vendors close, this is by far the best deal you'll get in La Mariscal after dark. Be safe and take a cab (US$1), no matter how short the walk.

José Calama 182 and Diego de Almagro. ☎ *2230 981. Open M-W 11am-11pm, Th-Sa 11am-2am, Su 1pm-10pm.*

right there in front of you. The Mexican entrees are nothing to write back to Mexico (or home) about, but the frozen margaritas (single US$2.50, pitchers from US$11) will keep anyone seated at the table (or on the floor). Open M-Sa noon-10:30pm. ❷

Mi Viejo Arribal (☎2228 538), at Juan León Mena and Foch. Big steaks done right. Relaxed atmosphere for a good price (meals start at US$7, burgers US$4, excluding 12% IVA and 10% service fee). Open daily noon-11:30pm. MC/V (min. US$15). ❹

OLD TOWN

Old Town abounds with vendors of every kind of bread, nut, and fruit. Sit down at one of its many eateries for a small lunch or snack, or make a reservation for a cheap but tasty three-course meal.

⚡ **Café Modelo,** Sucre 391 (☎2284 428), at García Moreno; a 2nd branch at Venezuela 1011 (☎2587 624), and Mejía. Businessmen, students, and tourists flock to this bright and lively hole-in-the-wall. Friendly staff. Tasty sandwiches and pastries (from around US$1) keep them coming back. Open M-Sa 8am-7:30pm, Su 8am-4pm. ❶

✈ **El Criollo,** Flores N7-31 (☎2289 828), at Olmedo. Eat like an Ecuadorian cowboy inside a pastel blue-and-peach building. Act like you know what you're doing; you may be the only non-local there. Omelettes, sandwiches, and larger Ecuadorian-style entrees (US$3-5). Open M-Sa 8am-10pm, Su 8am-6pm. ❷

✈ **La Zamba Teresa** (☎2583 826), at Chile and Venezuela, off the Plaza Grande. Cheaper cousin to the posh and expensive Cueva del Oso. High-ceilinged, very lively, very pink. Sandwiches US$1.75-3. Traditional Ecuadorian dishes US$5-9. Pastries average US$1.75. 3-course *menú* US$3. Open M-Sa 10am-7pm. ❷

✈ **Bar Restaurant Balcón Quiteño,** Bolívar 220 (☎2950 590), on the top fl. of the Hotel Real Audiencia, at Guayaquil, on the Plaza Santo Domingo. Nowhere else can you dine with such an amazing view of the colonial city. Watch Plaza Santo Domingo's street performers from a safe distance or simply sip on your cup of coffee and gaze at La Virgen as she watches over her fair city. English menu of Ecuadorian specialties. Entrees US$5. Open M-Sa 7:30am-9pm, Su 7:30-10am. AmEx/MC/V. ❸

Ari, Sucre 350 (☎2585 888), on the 2nd fl. of Galerías Sucre between Moreno and Venezuela. Pleasant Andean music accompanies vegetarian goodies. In fact, no meat is served here at all. Entrees US$2.50; fresh juices from US$1. Open daily 8am-4pm. ❶

◖ CAFES

Overflowing with trendy espresso drinks, these coffee shops are the hippest meeting places. But don't come looking for any deals—as with cafes the world over, you pay for atmosphere more than food or drink.

Grain de Café, Baquedano 332 (☎2565 975), between Reina Victoria and León Mera is casual. Pours a huge selection of imported drinks. Coffee from US$0.90. Tequila shots US$3. Happy hour daily 6-8pm. Open M-Sa noon-10pm. MC/V (min. US$8).

El Cafecito, Cordero 1124 (☎2234 862), at Reina Victoria. This cafe downstairs from the hostel serves vegetarian fare in spacious surroundings. Decent coffee drinks US$2-6. Desserts US$1-2. Guests of the attached hostel get 10% discount. Open Su-W 8am-10pm, Th 8am-11pm, F-Sa 8am-midnight.

✈ **Café del Suizo,** Foch 714 (☎2252 457), at León Mera. The self-proclaimed maker of "the best coffee in town" does indeed brew a pretty good cup. The wall to the left of the cashier's desk is well stocked with tourist maps and coupon books. Some English spoken. Coffee from US$0.80; homemade desserts US$1-2. Open daily 9am-7pm.

✈ **Café Galleti Espresso Bar,** Amazonas 1494 (☎2237 881), at Santa María. Come here for a mountain view and a quiet cup of organic coffee (from US$0.90). Burlap coffee sacks hanging from the ceiling and the Galleti coffee give this place a homey feeling.

◉ SIGHTS

OLD TOWN (LA PARTE COLONIAL)

When the United Nations declared Old Town a World Heritage Site in 1978, scores of 300-year-old plazas, churches, and government palaces were guaranteed both longevity and a high profile. Now, they're looking more or less the way they did when Ecuador was a colony. Furthermore, Quito's winning bid to host the 2004 Miss Universe pageant resulted in new signage and a concerted beautification effort, leaving Old Quito easier and more enjoyable to explore.

> ⚠ Exercise caution when exploring Old Town, even by day. Pickpockets roam the streets, particularly around the market and bus terminal. The streets get even more dangerous at night, at which time tourists are advised to stay in New Town.

LA BASÍLICA. La Basílica del Voto Nacional (1909) offers some of the most spectacular views of Quito from twin 78m towers. An elevator, a narrow spiraling staircase, and a set of ladders lead through the innards of a clock tower and a bell tower before ending in a belfry high in the sky. The view of La Virgen de Quito from any of the vantage points leading to the top is stunning. A smaller tower at the back end of the church is also accessible. The highlight of getting to this tower is traversing the creaky wooden walkway that rests on top of the ornate ceiling of the church. *(Carchí 122 and Venezuela. ☎ 2289 428. Open daily 9am-7pm. Employees warn tourists not to travel any further west on Carchí, even during daytime hours. US$2.)*

PLAZA DE LA INDEPENDENCIA. The most carefully maintained public space, Plaza de la Independencia (or Plaza Grande) is dotted with palm fronds, benches, and triumphal statuary. The plaza is the front yard of the glorious 400-year-old Palacio Presidencial, and churchyard to a cathedral nearly as ancient. Built in 1667, the cathedral contains an ornate ceiling and the tomb of Antonio José de Sucre (see p. 54), independence hero and namesake of the country's former currency. The remains of Ecuador's first president, Gabriel García Moreno, also rest here to the front and left of the cathedral at the very spot he died in August 1875. *(Open M-F 10am-4pm, Sa 10am-2pm. US$1.50, students US$1.)*

LA VIRGEN DE QUITO. Visible from most locations on the outskirts of Old Town, the majestic statue of La Virgen de Quito surveys her domain from the summit of **El Panecillo**, at the far end of Old Town. At 41m tall, the silver, serpent-stomping virgin raises her hand in benediction over Quito, uniting the city with the heavens. Pay her a visit to share the view (at least as far as Cotopaxi). The trip involves a long and dangerous walk up the stairs at the end of García Moreno—despite the efforts of La Virgen's surrounding neighborhood to solicit donations for beefed-up security, visitors are advised to take a taxi both ways. *(Round-trip, including a 20min. wait at the statue US$5-8. English-speaking guides available, US$1. Open daily 9am-5pm. Entrance into the base of the statue US$1.)*

PLAZA SAN FRANCISCO. Always well populated, the Plaza San Francisco is overshadowed by the gorgeous and gigantic Monasterio de San Francisco, constructed between 1535 and 1605. A visit to the Museo San Francisco allows visitors a close look at the church's intricate wooden choir—comprised entirely of Franciscan martyrs—as well as the cloisters decorated with 17th- and 18th-century paintings and sculptures. (Open M-Sa 9am-6pm, Su 9am-noon. Museum entrance US$2, with ISIC US$1.) Farther along the right side of García Moreno, Iglesia del Sagrario, originally the main chapel of the cathedral, features a large stone portico and bright interior. Tread lightly; Sagrario is a working church.

QUITO

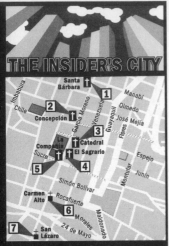

THE INSIDER'S CITY

STREET OF 7 CROSSES

La calle de las siete cruces, known as García Moreno in Old Town, is a testament to Spanish efforts to eradicate indigenous religious practices. The seven crosses trace a straight line from La Virgen de Quito to the convent of San Juan, former sites of Incan temples to the sun and moon.

1 In the Church of Santa Bárbara.

2 In the Church and Monastery of the Conception, Quito's first monastery (1575).

3 In front of La Catedral Metropolitana on Espejo.

4 On the sidewalk outside of the church of El Sagrario.

5 In front of La Campañia de Jesús, consummate example of Baroque architecture in Latin America.

6 In front of el Claustro e Iglesia del Carmen Alto, where Quito's first saint, Santa María de Jesús, once made her home.

7 At el Hospicio San Lázaro, a Jesuit home until 1767.

IGLESIA DE SAN AGUSTÍN. Down the block from the Plaza Grande, at Chile and Guayaquil, stands the **Iglesia de San Agustín,** whose adjoining convent was once dubbed the "Gold Convent" by locals for its elaborate interior, much of which stands covered in 24-karat gold leaf. Visit the adjoining museum to see the **Sala Capitulator,** where the first Act of Independence was signed in 1809, and the beautiful cloisters covered with 17th-century paintings of Miguel de Santiago. *(Open daily 7am-1pm. Free. Sala Capitulator and Gold Convent open M-F 9am-noon and 3-5:30pm, Sa 9am-noon. US$1, students US$0.50.)*

LA MERCED. Find yet another beautiful ornate church two blocks west of La Plaza Grande, on the corner of Cuenca and Chile. Hug the outer wall of the church to see a pictorial of Christ's passion. Then focus on the pillars holding up the church's towering ceiling. Watch as the Virgen at Quito presides over various scenes from Quito's history from the first event of European-indigenous contact. *(Open 6am-noon and 3-6pm.)*

IGLESIA DE LA COMPAÑÍA. A short walk down Sucre from La Plaza San Francisco at García Moreno and Sucre, this Jesuit masterpiece of Ecuadorian Baroque, Arabic, and indigenous decor has been beset by disasters. In 1868 an earthquake destroyed the church's bell tower—once the highest in Quito—which has yet to be rebuilt. An earthquake in 1987 and a fire in 1996 also did serious damage. The remains of Santa Mariana Paredes y Flores, who was consecrated by Pope Pius XII in 1950, lie at the altar of La Compañía. *(Open M-F 10am-5pm, Sa 10am-4pm. US$2, students US$1.)*

TEATRO NACIONAL SUCRE. This theater, built in 1886, has recently re-opened after more than two years of renovations. The theater hosts events as disparate as Mozart recitals, Polish dance shows, mime shows, and a cappella groups. Find it in the **Plaza del Teatro,** three blocks down Guayaquil away from San Agustín. Check ahead for show dates and ticket prices. *(Manabí N8-131, between Guayaquil and Flores. ☎ 2280 982; www.teatrosucre.com.)*

🏛 MUSEUMS

Quito's diverse array of museums exhibits nearly every kind of Ecuadorian cultural artifact—from art to armaments to achaeological relics.

NEW TOWN

CASA DE LA CULTURA AND MUSEO NACIONAL DEL BANCO CENTRAL.

This sprawling complex hosts three separate entities: La Casa de La Cultura, El Museo del Banco Central, and El Museo de la Casa de Culture. **La Casa de La Cultura** hosts exhibits of contemporary Ecuadorian art. **El Museo del Banco Central** is the consolidation of several separate Banco Central museums. The result is the most extensive museum in Quito. The winding rooms of this rust-colored, cylindrical monolith contain chronologically organized archaeological exhibits, pre-Hispanic gold, colonial paintings and religious portraits, modern art, and indigenous crafts. **El Museo de la Casa de Culture** houses contemporary Ecuadorian art exhibits and is set to re-open in the fall of 2004 after extensive renovation. The **Teatro Nacional,** on the western side of the Museo del Banco Central, hosts plays, concerts, and large events. *(All museums at Patría and 6 de Diciembre. Cultura ☎ 2920 272, ext. 320. Open M-F 9am-5pm, Sa 9am-1pm. Banco Central ☎ 2223 258. Open Tu-Su 9am-6pm. US$1.50.)*

FUNDACIÓN GUAYASAMÍN. This complex atop a hill in Bellavista highlights the magnificent work of **Oswaldo Guayasamín,** a leader of the *indigenista* movement and one of Ecuador's premier painters. His images capture the racism, poverty, political oppression, and class stratification plaguing South America (see **Painting,** p. 65). This museum also includes a spacious garden, extensive pre-Colombian artifacts, and some 18th-century colonial religious art from the Quiteña and Cusqueña schools. Spend some time relaxing on the patio before you head back down the hill. *(José Bosmediano 543. Take 6 de Diciembre north to Eloy Alfaro where Bosmediano begins, and start climbing—the museum is a 20min. walk uphill or quick US$1 taxi ride from New Town. ☎ 2446 455. Open M-F 10am-5pm. US$2, seniors US$1.50.)*

PARQUE METROPOLITANO. A nice Sunday stroll, Parque Metropolitano sprawls out over the northeastern part of Quito, attracting scores of locals on weekends to cook out and hang out. The area is well-known by hardcore birders and also boasts a herd of llamas as well as horse rides (US$1.50). Trail maps are available at the park administration office (open daily 6am-6pm). Park entry is free. To get to the park, take a bus or the Ecovía on 6 de Diciembre to el Estadio Atahualpa. From the Ecovía stop, travel east (away from Parque El Ejido and past the stadium) on Manuel M. Sanchez until you hit Carlos Arroyo Del Río and turn right. Walk uphill and turn left on Eloy Alfaro, bear right on Tola and walk until you hit Guanguiltagua, at which point a hairpin right turn will give you access to the park. From this point it is about 1km to the park office. Alternatively, taxis from La Mariscal should not cost more than US$2 and will provide more direct access.

MUSEO FRANCISCANO FRAY ANTONIO RODRIGUEZ. Situated in the valley neighborhood of El Guápalo, Guápalo's sanctuary houses a museum with excellent examples of 16th- and 17th-century Quiteño art. The self-supporting and elegantly ornamented pulpit is beautiful. If you don't want to make the steep trek into the valley, enjoy the view that the bust of Francisco de Orellana has of the valley from behind the Hotel Quito. If you do go down, don't miss the painting of La Virgen de la Nube that appeared over the valley in 1696. Plan on taking a taxi (US$2-4) back to the top or perishing on the way back up. *(Walk north away from New Town on 12 de Octubre until you reach the Hotel Quito. Hug the building around its left side. You will soon see the green iron fence surrounding the lookout that accompanies the bust of Francisco de Orellana. From there descend the stairs into El Guápulo or simply enjoy the spectacular view. ☎ 2565 652. Tours daily 9am-noon and 3-6pm, except during services. US$1.)*

INSTITUTO GEOGRÁFICO MILITAR (IGM). This institute boasts the best **maps** of Ecuador. Political, topographical, Sierra, Oriente—you name it. Many are for sale or can be copied (US$3 for a chart), but be prepared to wait. Also on display are a **planetarium,** a **geographical museum,** and phenomenal **satellite photos** of Ecuador's volcanic craters. *(On Telmo and Paz y Miño, at the hilltop. You can only reach Paz y Miño from*

Telmo, which runs along the base of the hill by a 10min. walk uphill. ☎ *2502 091 or 2520 921 for planetarium reservations; passport required to enter. Planetarium shows M-F 9, 11am, 3pm; Sa 9am. Institute and museum open M-Th 8am-4pm, Sa 8am-noon. US$1.)*

MUSEO DE CIENCIAS NATURALES. This hidden gem in the center of Parque la Carolina hosts a mind-boggling number of dead and stuffed Ecuadorian wildlife, from the impressive condors that guard the front door to the skin-crawling collection of insects that, if you're paranoid enough, seem to squirm beneath their glass encasement. *(Enter from the Shyris side of the Parque la Carolina and walk the entire length of the cobblestone driveway. The museum will be on your left.* ☎ *2449 825, ext. 10. Open M-F 8:30am-4:30pm, Sa 10am-2pm. US$1.50, children US$0.50.)*

VIVARIUM. A modest collection of Ecuador's reptilian and amphibian inhabitants that is highlighted by several impossibly large boa constrictors. Ask for a photo op with one of them. English tour books are available. *(Reina Victoria 1576 and Santa María. Planning on moving in Sept. 2004 to Amazonas 3008 and Rumipamba, near El Museo de Ciencias Naturales.* ☎ *2230 988; fherpeto@pi.pro.ec. Open Tu-F 9:30am-12:45pm and 2-5:15pm, Sa-Su 9:30am-4:15pm. US$2, children US$1.50.)*

MUSEO AMAZÓNICO. This small museum offers a brief glimpse of Ecuadorian indigenous cultures. Among the pots, pans, and spears of this museum is a shrunken head and impressive taxidermy. A short pictorial history of recent indigenous resistance to European rule dots the back wall. *(12 de Octubre 1430 and Wilson, 2nd fl.* ☎ *2236 175, ext. 133; www.upsqu.edu.ec. Open M-F 8:30am-1pm and 2-5:30pm.)*

OLD TOWN

TEMPLO DE LA PATRIA. The massive Templo de la Patria clings like a concrete spider web to the hill of Pichincha, where Ecuador's freedom fighters won independence in 1822. Its view beats all others; on a clear day, multiple snow-capped volcanoes glare like gods from the horizon. Beneath the concrete, the **Museo de las Fuerzas Armadas** displays antique firearms. An architectural masterpiece, the mausoleum-like nave of eternal flame loses some of its gravitas due to the "flame" itself: a flickering orange light bulb with a visible extension cord. Above the museum rests La Cima de la Libertad, the original monument commemorating the Battle of Pichincha. From this point it is possible to get a full view of the colorful and modern mosaic depicting Ecuador's battle for freedom. The same style of painting is employed on a smaller scale by the street painters at Parque El Ejido on the weekends. Walk past the museum to the opposite side of the parking lot and toward the light post to get a great view of the city. Romantic Quiteños often have their weddings here. *(Take a blue-and-white bus going to "Bellavista" or "La Libertad" or a red-and-white bus going to "Bellisario/Libertad" along García Moreno, and ride up the hill to the monument.* ☎ *2288 733. Open Tu-Su 10am-4pm. US$1.)*

CENTRO CULTURAL METROPOLITANO. This center showcases Ecuadorian art from the 16th century to the present. Previously a convent, university, tobacco factory, and jail, the renovated center preserves the original patios, stone stairwells, and archways, while adding an enormous patio, a skylight, hardwood floors, and brightly lighted galleries. In addition to the painting and sculpture exhibits, the center houses a **wax recreation** of the 1810 massacre that ended the *criollo* independence movement, a large municipal **library**, and the trendy El Buho Café. *(At García Moreno and Espejo, right off the Plaza Grande.* ☎ *2950 272. Library open M-F 8am-7pm, Sa 8am-5pm, Su 8am-1pm. Museum open Tu-Su 9am-5pm. US$1.50, with ISIC US$0.75.)*

MUSEO DE LA CIUDAD. The Museo de La Ciudad contains permanent exhibits on the city's history, ranging from the era of cave men to modern times. The old building has been completely restored, with beautiful wooden floors around a dual patio structure. Open-air patios allow views of the Panecillo, Pichincha, and much of Old Town. *(At García Moreno and Rocafuerte. ☎2283 882; museociu@uio.telconet.net. Open Tu-Su 9:30am-5:00pm. US$2, with ISIC US$1.)*

MUSEO CASA DE SUCRE. Yet another lovely old building wrapped around a lush courtyard, this museum celebrates Ecuador's battle for independence in the house of a key participant, **Mariscal Antonio José de Sucre.** The museum includes a free tour (Spanish only) that provides a glimpse into Sucre's personal life—or at least his chapel, bedroom, and skull. Although his actual remains rest in the cathedral on La Plaza Grande, the museum's most intriguing room details how the remains of this freedom fighter were removed and identified in 1900 after a 70-year hiatus. The deciding factor? A bullet hole in the right temple. *(Venezuela 573, at Sucre. ☎/fax 2952 860. Open Tu-Sa 8:30am-4:30pm. US$1, with ISIC US$0.25.)*

🎭 ENTERTAINMENT

SPORTS

FÚTBOL. As with the rest of the country, *fútbol* is not just a sport but a passion in Quito. Ecuador club teams and the national team play at **Estadio Atahualpa,** at 6 de Diciembre and Naciones Unidas, near Parque la Carolina. *(Take the "Estadio" bus on 6 de Diciembre, take the trolley to the Estadio stop and continue down Naciones Unidas, or take the Ecovía to the "Naciones Unidas" stop. Most games are played Sa-Su. Intra-Ecuador club games US$3-4, international games up to US$10. Purchase game-day tickets at the stadium for club games, or in advance for international matches at Marathon (☎2480 529), a sporting arena located in the mall at Amazonas and Naciones Unidas.)*

VOLLEYBALL. Volleyball is a close second in popularity to *fútbol.* Ecuador fares decently in international team competitions, but at home plays its own version called **Ecuavolley,** using a soccer ball instead of a volleyball. With only three players on a team, Ecuavolley players are allowed longer contact with the ball than in international play. Locals lay down Ecuavolley courts nearly everywhere, putting nets up on city streets, in the middle of Old Town colonial courtyards, and parks.

BULLFIGHTING. Ecuador inherited the bullfighting tradition from Spain, and partakes of it during the **Quito City Festival** in the first week of December. Contact La Plaza de Toros for more information. *(☎2246 037. Amazonas and Ascaray, at the North Terminal of the trolley. Tickets US$8.)*

THEATER

The **Teatro Nacional Sucre** (see p. 95), Ecuador's premiere showcase, has re-opened after a three-year hiatus. The **Casa de la Cultura** hosts occasional theatrical performances. In the meantime, try the **Bolívar** in Old Town. For drama and ballet, check out **El Socavón de Guápulo,** Francisco Compte 424 (☎2220 449), in nearby Guápulo. The **National Symphony** offers free weekly concerts at different sites around the city (☎2565 733). Quito's newspaper **El Comercio** and Quito's cultural centers (see **Cultural Centers,** p. 87) should have current information on these and other events.

🛍 SHOPPING

Quito's most cosmopolitan thoroughfare, New Town's **Río Amazonas,** is the most popular (though not cheapest) place to buy souvenirs and Ecuadorian handicrafts. Bargaining is rare, so if you plan to buy a lot, remember that markets in neighboring towns may offer cheaper prices. Tourist shops stock popular handmade Ecuadorian crafts: Panama hats, alpaca sweaters, colorfully handwoven rugs, leather goods, painted Tigua boxes, and handmade metal jewelry. (Most shops open M-F

10am-5pm.) **Parque El Ejido** hosts a **craft market** on weekends, offering an opportunity to hone bargaining skills and see what's out there. Pay close attention to the artists who sell their paintings on the edge of the park; you may end up taking home quite a conversation piece. (Open Sa-Su 10am-6pm.) For more handmade goods, the **Mercado Artesanal La Mariscal,** at Reina Victoria and Jorge Washington, is another option. Unless prices are marked or explicitly stated as fixed, bargaining is expected. (Open daily 9am-7pm.) The **Pialesito** market, on Cuenca near Plaza San Francisco in Old Town, is less crafty and more geared toward cheap goods— the place to go if you need a fish or a pair of bright red sweatpants. (Open daily, but more merchandise on weekends.) Hold onto your wallet or someone else will. If you forgot something at home or are just homesick for the suburban shopping experience, head to **El Jardín** mall, on Amazonas and República, where prices may just cure that homesickness. (Open M-Sa 10am-8:30pm, Su 10am-7:30pm.) Lastly, dizzy yourself at the colorful **Centro Comercial Espiral,** on Amazonas and Washington. Normal malls are all well and good, but spiral-shaped malls with nine stories' worth of small boutiques are even better. (Open M-Sa 9:30am-7:30pm.)

▓ NIGHTLIFE

After dark, curls of cigarette smoke replace bus exhaust as the real world goes to sleep and young people throughout the city let loose at Quito's wide range of bars and dance clubs. Stick to nightlife in New Town; not only is the scene hipper, but Old Town's streets are too dangerous for nocturnal merry-making. That said, New Town's not exactly a safe haven either; recent reports of robberies and assaults have put night revelers on guard. Take a taxi (usually US$1 between sites in New Town) back to your hotel, no matter how close it is.

BARS

Bar El Encuentro, León Mera 1133 (☎2509 670), at Calama. Local men and women alike stop by for booze (cocktails from US$1.50, beer US$2.50) in this bastion of machismo, wallpapered with images of naked ladies. An international crowd grooves to electronic and house music on most nights. Open M-Sa noon-3am.

Café Sutra (☎2509 106), at Calama and León Mera. Sutra wine (US$1.95) flows like a river here. Feast on shiva salad (US$4.60) and hummus (US$2.90) in the cozy loft above Restaurant Row. The menu, which features items as disparate as pizza (from US$5) and falafel (from US$5), is as eclectic as the part-postmodernist, part-Indian decor. Good people-watching at window seats. Open daily 9am-2am. AmEx/MC/V.

Bar-Ril, Lizardo García 356 (☎2226 714), at 6 de Diciembre next to La Casa de las Menestras. Quito's 1st gay bar, in a *muy* cool spot for the last 22 years. Bar in front; stage in back. Sa shows drink min. US$5. Open W-Sa 8pm-2am. AmEx/MC/V.

La Cascada Mágica, Foch E8-15 (☎2902 361), at Diego Almagro. Gaming types play pool, air hockey, foosball, and darts all for reasonable hourly rates (US$1-4). Mixed drinks US$2.50, 2-for-1 cocktails until 10pm all week. Stick to drinking; appetizers (US$5-10) are quite pricey. Open daily 4:30pm-2am. MC/V.

The Turtle's Head, La Niña 626 (☎2565 544), between Amazonas and León Mera. Quito's only brew pub. English owner Albert serves his tastiest stout and bitter (US$2.90) to a mature set who appreciate what they drink. Don't bring your dancing shoes here; grab a seat at one of the dark oak tables and talk. With great liquor and pool tables, you may stay all night. Open M-Sa 6pm-2am.

El Pobre Diablo, Isabel la Católica E12-06 (☎2235 194), at Galavis near La Casona de Mario. Quito's premier jazz bar draws sophisticated local crowds beneath artfully exposed brick and rafters with music and drinks (US$2-5). Coffee from US$1; wine starting at US$1.50. Live shows W nights (cover US$5). Open M-Sa 12:30pm-1am, Su 12:30-7pm. AmEx/MC/V.

Sutra Lounge, León Mera E5-10 (☎2906 200), at Calama. Café Sutra was so popular that they had to make another one. Hop up to the 2nd fl., slide open the glass door, and step into Quito's own technicolor dreamworld. Cool designs beneath the glass-paneled floor; choose from an array of off-beat seating arrangements to watch night-time revelers walk Quito's streets. Live music Th and Sa starts 9pm. Cocktails from US$2.50 but prices rise quickly; 2-for-1 promotions during the day. Open daily 6pm-2am.

CLUBS

Starting around 11pm, New Town's dance clubs fill with people anxious to get their groove on. **Gay** and **lesbian** travelers have options in Quito, but they are often difficult to find. Ecuadorian law only recently decriminalized homosexuality (see **Bisexual, Gay, and Lesbian Travelers,** p. 45). Check http://gayquitoec.tripod.com/ for the current scene. Late-night partiers are advised to take taxis (US$1 within La Mariscal) at all times, no matter the proximity of their next destination.

▩ No Bar, Calama 380 (☎2545 145), at León Mera, on Calama's Restaurant Row. The most traveler-friendly club in Quito smiles on multinational grinding. The dance floor often gets so crowded that patrons are forced to dance on the bar. Happy hour M-W 7-8:30pm. Cover W-Sa US$3, includes 1 drink. Open M-W 7pm-2am, Th-Sa 7pm-3am.

Zähsa Bar, at Juan León Mera and García, 2nd fl. The king of the off-night. A group of young guys rents this place out M-Th and throws small but hopping dance parties. Best known for Tu and Th hip-hop nights. Cover US$2-5 depending on promotions. Zähsa's real owners run the place F-Sa. Open M-Sa 8pm-2am.

Varadero and La Bodegaíta de Cuba, Reina Victoria 1721 (☎2542 575), at La Pinta, is packed with locals, but anyone who appreciates rhythm and style should feel welcome. Live tropical music and dancing 9:30pm-1:30am. Flat-footed guests can participate using shakers made from empty plastic spring water bottles filled with sand and rocks. If you come early, find the best place to listen to the live music. It varies from night to night. Cover Th-Sa US$4, starts at 8:30pm and includes 1 drink. Open W-Sa noon-2am.

Tijuana, at Reina Victoria and Santa María. Where the young, restless, leather-clad come to play. Plays pop mixes on a hot sound system. Drinks start at US$2. Happy hour daily 7-10pm. Cover US$3. Open M-Sa 7pm-3am.

VOLCÁN PICHINCHA

AT A GLANCE

DISTANCE: 30km	**TIME:** 10hr.
CLIMATE: May get windy and rainy at summit. Leave early to beat the clouds that settle over the crater at midday.	**ALTITUDE:** 3000-4794m
	DIFFICULTY: Difficult
FEATURES: Views of Volcán Cotopaxi	**FEES:** Refuge keeper may charge US$1 to get to summit.

🛈 PRACTICAL INFORMATION

Undoubtedly the high point of any visit to Quito is standing atop the summit of double-cratered Volcán Pichincha with the city at your feet. The younger, more active crater, Guagua Pichincha (4794m), buried the capital in 40cm of ash in 1660. Sporadic puffs and belches continue to this day, making climbs within the crater unsafe. Nevertheless, hiking up to and around Pichincha rightly remains a popular activity. Allow yourself at least an entire day to make the trip from Lloa by foot and back again. Bring warm clothes and a sleeping bag in case it becomes necessary to stay at the refuge. SAE has a key to the refuge. Contact them to be sure that it will be open in the case of

QUITO

an emergency. Try to leave early to beat the clouds to the crater. If you do make the summit, you'll be 4794m (about 15,000 ft.) high, so take it slow. The climb is long and strenuous but technically moderate; walking poles and a good pair of hiking boots are recommended. The refuge keeper may charge US$1 to get to the summit.

Transportation: Accessed the volcano from Lloa. To reach **Lloa,** take a red-and-white "Mena Dos" **bus** from the bus canopy at Américas and Colón, adjacent to the Seminario Mayor San José in Quito (35min., every 15min. 6am-7:30pm, US$0.25). Take the bus to Angamarca, the main street in Mena Dos. From there, **taxis** go to Lloa (20min., US$7-8). **Volquetas** (multicolored trucks) also run to Lloa from the junction of Venidores and Angamarca at the market and will give rides following no particular schedule (US$1). From Lloa, follow the main road up the mountain, taking the left branch at the fork in the dirt track 2km from town (by foot 5-7hr., by 4X4 1hr.), and turning when you see large, rusted metal signs for the volcano. While *Let's Go* does not recommend leaving the main track, many hikers take advantage of well-beaten shortcuts up the sides of the volcano. On the way back to Lloa, be prepared to pay a US$0.25 exit fee.

Accommodations: Stay at the **refuge** overnight (US$5). From here, the summit is a 2hr. round-trip hike.

Supplies: Bring a warm sleeping bag and food to cook in the refuge's kitchen.

 THE HIKE

Most people do Pichincha as a day-hike, but the hike can be broken up over two days by staying overnight at the refuge. The 15km path leads straight up the summit. Take the same path down. Less strenuous than some of Ecuador's other peaks, Pichincha offers dramatic views of Quito, the surrounding valley, snow-capped **Cotopaxi,** and a slew of other mountains. If it feels like you can reach out and touch the clouds, it's because you can. From the volcano's rim, watch massive cumulus clouds bouncing off the crater walls below.

Hiking down into the crater is not permitted due to recent volcanic activity. The closer crater, **Rucu,** tempts tourists to start scrambling up the hillside from the city. This is possible, but quite dangerous. **Thieves, who may be armed, occasionally lurk at the foot of the mountain.** As of this writing, recent attacks have been reported on this hike to Rucu via Cruz Loma - please exercise caution. Check with the SAE in Quito (see p. 85) for the present state of affairs. Let's Go does not recommend visiting Rucu, especially with so many equally scenic mountains nearby. **Guagua** outdoes Rucu in altitude and scenery, though one should be wary of dogs. Threatening to throw a rock usually frightens them away.

MITAD DEL MUNDO

Latitude 0°0'0". Yes, you're on the equator—Ecuador's namesake and a popular tourist destination. Both Ecuadorian and international visitors flock to this bona fide circus-style attraction, drawn partly by the geographical landmark and partly by the hoopla surrounding it. Here a yellow line bisects a 30m obelisk, capped by a 2½ ton metal globe aligned with the cardinal points of the compass. Tourists, parents, and children all sit, stand, and lie down along its length as it passes through the plaza of the neighboring tourist "village" containing restaurants and gift shops. You may want to head first to the massive Pululahua volcanic crater (see p. 114) before midday clouds obscure the fantastic views. Predictably, major **festival days** fall around March 21 and September 23 (the equinoxes), when neither monument nor tourist casts a shadow, and June 22 and December 22 (the solstices).

Flag down a green bus with a "Mitad del Mundo" sign in the window along Américas in New Town. Try the intersection at Colón. Returning buses leave from the traffic circle in front of Mitad del Mundo. Be sure to take the bus with the white sign in the front that says "Américas." (one-way 1hr., every 8min., US$0.40).

INSIDE THE COMPLEX. Walk through the gates to the globe. Bordering the path are busts of the 13 men from France, Spain, and Ecuador who explored and measured the equator from 1736 to 1744. Entering the complex costs US$1, and a single ticket (US$3, children US$1.50) gives you access to the **obelisk** and four museums. *(US$1 to park. All open M-Th 9am-6pm, F-Su 9am-7pm.)* After taking the elevator to the top of the monument, descend through the **Ethnographic Museum** that surrounds the winding staircase. The museum exhibits the clothing, food, dwellings, and customs of Ecuadorian indigenous groups. *(☎ 2395 637. Free tours in English and Spanish. Open M-Th 9am-5pm, F-Su 9am-6pm. US$1.50, children US$0.75.)* Follow the obelisk's compass southeast of the monument to the **French Museum,** which explains the history of the equator's measurement. *(Free tours in Spanish and sometimes English.)* Pop in next door to the **Ecuador Museum,** which houses stamps and drawings of the country's diverse wildlife, or the **Spain Museum,** home to a surprisingly good group of works by Guayasamín, one of Ecuador's foremost painters.

A **planetarium** waits for at least 15 tourists to arrive before beginning one of its 38min. shows. *(☎ 2395 795. Open Tu-F 9am-5pm, Sa-Su 9am-6pm. US$1, children US$0.75.)* Next door, the **Solar Culture Museum** displays ground-breaking GPS-satellite research on the astronomical significance of Ecuador's archaeological sites. *(Explanations in English and Spanish. Open M-Sa 10am-6pm.)* Nearby, toward the Mitad del Mundo entrance, **Fundación Quito Colonial** contains miniature city models of colonial Quito and downtown Guayaquil, constructed with meticulous attention to detail by Guido Falcony. *(☎ 2394 319. Open daily 9:30am-5pm. US$1, children US$0.50.)* A monument dedicated to the **Héroes del Cenepa,** near the entrance, honors the soldiers who died in the 1995 war with Peru. *(Open M-Th 9am-6pm, F-Su 9am-7pm. No separate entrance fee.)* An outside scale (US$0.25) of dubious accuracy across from the post office lures weight-watching tourists to marvel at the kilos they seem to lose on the equator (usually no more than 4kg). They haven't really slimmed down, of course; the equatorial bulge brings them farther from the center of the earth, where gravity has a weaker pull and makes everything weigh less. The **Plaza de Toros** hosts bullfights on equinoxes, solstices, and during local festivals.

OUTSIDE THE COMPLEX. The sprawling, outdoor **Museo de Sitio Inti-Ñan** ("The Path of the Sun" in Quichua) lies northeast of the obelisk. To get there, follow the equatorial line through the plaza, and continue down the hill along the path just left of the ice cream parlor. Talk to the guard at the gate if you plan on re-entering. After exiting the complex, turn left and walk uphill, keeping the wall to your left. Once inside the museum, be prepared for a startling revelation: the line-worshippers at Mitad del Mundo are deluded, because the real equator cuts a path right through the museum! To prove it, the owner will proudly pull out his handy-dandy GPS (Global Positioning Satellite) receiver and point to the string of zeros. Most convincing (though a scam) is the water demonstration. On the equator, the water drains straight down without spiraling; two feet to the south it drains clockwise; two feet to the north, counterclockwise. Along the newly-established equator are replicas of indigenous sun temples. The sites take a turn for the spooky with a "totem forest," shrunken heads, and a pickled python. Expect a much more intimate and personal experience here. *(☎ 2395 122; museo_intinan@yahoo.es or museo_intinan@hotmail.com. Tours in Spanish and English. Open daily 9:30am-6pm. US$2.)*

SANTA MARTHA ANIMAL REFUGE

On an operating dairy farm in Tambillo, the Animal Refuge houses and rehabilitates wild animals that have been confiscated by police from poachers, owners of illegal circuses, and ordinary citizens who were keeping them as pets. Some residents of the refuge, such as a 130-year-old Galápagos tortoise, whose previous owners shot bullets at his shell to demonstrate its toughness, are there permanently due to overexposure to humans or a lack of space in which to set them free. Other animals, such as monkeys, are released as soon as they are ready. Many animals die at the refuge due to maltreatment at the hands of their previous owners. Still others suffer at the refuge due to lack of funds. The refuge used to be able to afford housing animals using the profits from the dairy farm, but due to a recent drop in the price of milk, taking in more animals has become increasingly difficult. The suggested donation for visiting the refuge is US$10. **Volunteers** are welcome to help out at the refuge for US$10 per day (price includes room and board).

Contact Toby Cannon (☎09 4332 652; www.santamartha.org) to arrange a tour (in English or Spanish). Some days, such as days when new animals are being transported to the refuge, are not viable for tours. To get there, take a **bus** to **Tambillo** from the station at Old Town. From Tambillo, take one of the white **pickup trucks** (executive taxis in Tambillo; US$3) to the refuge. Ask the driver to take you to Santa Martha or Don Johnny Córdoba. Alternatively, contact Toby or SAE and find out when the next group is coming to visit and if you can join.

THE NORTHERN HIGHLANDS

North of Quito, a network of indigenous communities lives amid sparkling lakes and lush cloud forests. Locals speak Quichua on the street, wear traditional ponchos and beads, and specialize in the crafts of their ancestors. Otavalo explodes as people flock to the Saturday market to haggle over handicrafts. And in Otavalo, as well as in other towns, *indígenas* have found creative ways to maintain their traditional lifestyle in the face of Western values and technology. Relieve summit fever on the snow-capped Volcánes Cotacachi Imbabura, and trek on foot or horseback to smaller peaks, hidden falls, and high, barren *páramo*.

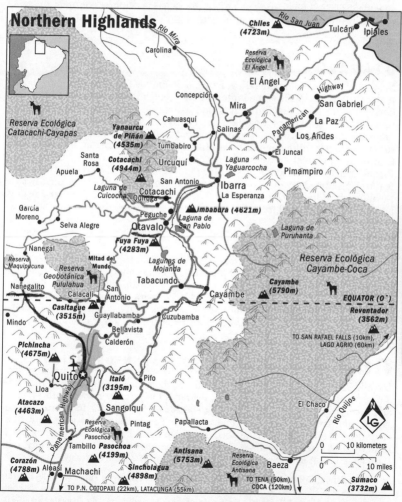

HIGHLIGHTS OF THE NORTHERN HIGHLANDS

BECOME an **ecotourist** in the national parks surrounding **Mindo** (see p. 111).

SPLURGE at **Otavalo's Saturday Market** (see p. 110). With deals this good, who can afford to be on a budget?

SUPPRESS goose bumps at the ancient pyramids of **Cochasquí** (see p. 119)

SUMMIT the towering **Volcán Cayambe** (see p. 122)

Northwest of Quito, a misty cloud forest clings to steep, Andean slopes. Here birds, butterflies, and orchids draw a binocular-wielding international crowd. Visitors can help protect the delicate ecosystems by tilling the soil in a permaculture garden or composting at one of the reserves. Others continue the success of traditional Highlands communities by completing homestays with indigenous families.

OTAVALO   ☎06

Nestled high in a mountain valley, Otavalo is famous for its indigenous goods. In the early 1980s locals gained international recognition for their weaving and music. Before then, the *indígenas* had withstood centuries of brutal conditions imposed by the first Spaniards. Recently, there has been an explosion of opportunities to learn about and appreciate the culture and history behind these products—all against a breathtaking Andean backdrop. Festivals and traditions in Otavalo date back to pre-Inca past. The largest festival, Inti Raymi, celebrates the summer solstice (June 19-24) and the corn harvest, and features costumed revelers dancing their way from house to house and town to town in return for *chicha* and *mote* (corn). The city is also a popular starting point for many regional treks.

⌐ TRANSPORTATION

Transportes Otavalo and **Transportes Lagos** leave from the Terminal Terrestre in Quito (every 20min. 5am-8pm, US$2.20). The bus terminal, on Atahuallpa and Ordoñez, sends **buses** to: **Agato** (30min., every 20min. 6am-6pm, $US0.23); **Cayambe** (45min., every 10min. 4:30am-6:30pm, US$0.75); **Ibarra** (45min., every 4min. 5am-7:30pm, US$0.43); **Peguche** (15min., every 20min. 6am-6:30pm, US$0.18); **Quito** (2½hr., every 20min. 5am-6pm, US$2). **Taxis** (☎2926 222) gather around parks, plazas, and the bus terminal, but can be scarce after about 10pm on week-nights.

◄╋ 🛈 ORIENTATION AND PRACTICAL INFORMATION

Otavalo is bordered to the east by the hill Rey Loma and to the west by the Panamerican Hwy. Within the city's grid, **Bolívar** is the primary north-south avenue, and **Sucre** (parallel to Bolívar) runs past **Plaza de los Ponchos,** the focal point of the famed Saturday market, and continues uphill to **Parque Central.** Buses usually drop visitors off at the terminal at the northern end of town, or occasionally along Roca or in front of Plaza Copacabana. If you get a bus that only drives by the city, not through it, get off at Atahuallpa and walk into town from the highway.

Tourist Office: Gobierno Municipal de Otavalo Subdirección de Turismo, Calle Bolívar 8-38 (☎2921 313; www.otavalo.gov.ec), at Juan Montalvo. Open daily 8am-5pm but often unattended. **UNAIMCO (Unión de Artesanos Indígenas de Otavalo)** (☎2920

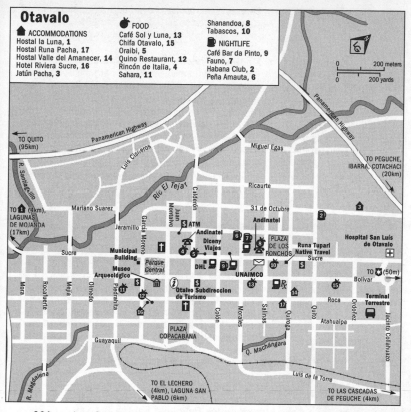

Otavalo

▲ **ACCOMMODATIONS**
Hostal la Luna, 1
Hostal Runa Pacha, 17
Hostal Valle del Amanecer, 14
Hotel Riviera Sucre, 16
Jatún Pacha, 3

🌶 **FOOD**
Café Sol y Luna, 13
Chifa Otavalo, 15
Oraibi, 5
Quino Restaurant, 12
Rincón de Italia, 4
Sahara, 11

Shanandoa, 8
Tabascos, 10

🍸 **NIGHTLIFE**
Café Bar da Pinto, 9
Fauno, 7
Habana Club, 2
Peña Amauta, 6

964; unaimco@yahoo.com), at Salinas and Sucre, 3rd fl., above the post office, organizes the summer solstice and harvest celebration called "Inti Raymi," and has other
limited tourist information. Open M-F 8am-12:30pm and 2-5pm, Sa 8am-noon.

Tours: 🔳 **Runa Tupari Native Travel** (☎/fax 925 985; www.runatupari.com), at Sucre
and Quiroga on the Plaza de Ponchos, has it all, from horseback riding in the Andes to
a multi-day stay in an indigenous village. The office also sells fair trade organic coffee,
jams, sponges, soaps, and bags made by artisans in the region to whom the profits are
returned directly. Open M-Sa 9am-6pm. **Diceny Viajes,** Sucre 10-11 (☎/fax 921 217;
zulayviajes@hotmail.com), at Colón, is founded and owned by Zulay, star and namesake of a 1980's documentary on *indígena* culture. Tours include trekking to volcanoes
and lakes in the area, visits to artisans in the surrounding communities, and a chance
to share daily life in nearby Quinchusqui. Open daily 8:30am- 1:30pm and 2-6pm.

Currency Exchange: Fax Cambio (☎2920 501), on Cristobal Colón and Sucre, changes
traveler's checks and charges 3% commission. Open daily 7am-7pm. **Banco del Pichincha,** Bolívar 616 (☎920 214), at García Moreno, offers V cash advances (M-F 8am-
noon) as does the **branch** (M-F 8am-2pm) on Sucre between Quiroga and Quito.

ATM: On Jaramillo between Juan Montalvo and Calderón takes MC/V.

Police: Policía Nacional (☎2920 101), on Paz Ponce de León, just beyond the end of
Bolívar. Open 24hr. for emergencies.

ily Chronicle

IN-RECENT NEWS

JAMBI HUASI MEDICAL CLINIC IN OTAVALO

The Ecuadorian health care system had frequently failed to provide for the mostly indigenous community in Otavalo until the Jambi Huasi clinic arrived.

Shut down many times since its 1974 founding, Jambi Huasi (Quichua for "Health House") got a new start in 1994 with US$340,000 from the United Nations Population Fund. Since then, it has become a huge success. By 1998, close to 10,000 people were accessing the clinic yearly.

Jambi Huasi is part of the growing trend in which Western medicine is incorporating so-called alternative healing methods. It has combined the supposedly incompatible practices of modern Western medicine and indigenous Shamanic healing beneath one roof. Its overarching goal is to find a way to bring quality, affordable medicine to the poorer areas of Ecuador. Currently, about 30 patients per day pay a subsidized fee and are allowed to choose between Western and traditional medicine.

But Jambi Huasi is not alone in its endeavors. Companies like Shaman Pharmaceuticals and Harvard, Stanford, and Columbia Universities have been researching how to establish integrated medicine programs. Perhaps their work, in conjunction with Jambi Huasi's, will someday bring more effective medicine to the world.

Pharmacy: Farmacia Lyz (☎2920 344), on Bolívar at Quiroga. Open M-Sa 8am-9pm, Su 1-8pm. There is a pharmacy next to the hospital (☎2920 444; see below).

Medical Services: Hospital San Luís de Otavalo (☎2920 444; emergency 2923 566), on Sucre at the northern edge of town, has ambulance service.

Telephones: Andinatel (☎2920 106; fax 2920 452), on Calderón between Sucre and Jaramillo. Open daily 8am-8pm. **Branch** (☎2926 226), on Salinas between Jaramillo and Sucre, faces the Plaza de los Ponchos. Open daily 6am-9pm.

Internet Access: Virtual Net (☎2923 540), on Sucre between Colón and Bolívar, has Internet and CD drives (US$1.20 per hr.) as well as Internet phones (to US, US$0.40 per min.; UK and Australia, US$0.25). Open M-Sa 8am-10pm, Su 9am-9pm. **Ca@ffé.Net** (☎2920 193), on Sucre and Colón, offers Internet access and Net2Phone. Internet US$0.80 per 30min. Open M-Sa 8am-10pm, Su 9:30am-8pm. **Branch** (☎2920 805), at Bolívar and Quiroga. Open M-Sa 8am-8pm.

Post Office: Oficina de Correos (☎/fax 923 520), at Sucre and Salinas, 2nd fl., at the corner of Plaza de los Ponchos. Open M-F 8am-5pm, Sa 8am-noon. **Intipungo** (☎2921 999), on Sucre and Calderón, offers DHL service. Open M-F 9am-1pm and 2:30pm-5:30pm, Sa 9am-1pm.

◤ ACCOMMODATIONS

Most options in Otavalo are congenial, inexpensive, and conveniently located in the triangle formed by Plaza de los Ponchos, Parque Bolívar, and Plaza Copacabana. Both hotels and restaurants offer special rates for large groups.

▨ **Hotel Riviera Sucre,** García Moreno 380 (☎2920 241; www.rivierasucre.com), at Roca. Rooms have all the character of this old Spanish Colonial building along with brightly painted walls and fresh flowers. A sitting room with fireplace, outdoor garden, and interior courtyard seal the package. Shared-bath rooms on the 2nd. fl. have the best views and the most light. Breakfast US$2-2.50. Singles US$5, with bath US$8. ❷

▨ **Hostal la Luna** (☎09 829 4913 or 09 973 7415; lalunaecuador@yahoo.co.uk), outside of Otavalo. The 4km cab ride up the road toward the Lagos de Mojanda is worth the US$3. Set in the hillside amid cows and cornfields with views toward Volcán Imbabura and Otavalo below, La Luna is peaceful but not isolated. More of a romantic getaway, double rooms have a fireplace and fresh flowers. Roja room has the best views. La Luna arranges horseback riding, tours to villages, and treks to the lakes and waterfalls. There is even a trail into town and a small cafe. Camping US$2 per person; 12-person dorms with bunks and small kitchen US$4; singles US$9-10, with private bath US$12; doubles US$14-18/US$20. Reservations recommended, especially on the weekends. ❷

Hostal Valle del Amanecer (☎/fax 292 0990), at Roca and Quiroga. Built of avocado trees and bamboo, it's a refreshing switch from the conventional plaster and cement. Rooms face a small courtyard with hammocks and fire pit and can get cold at night. Lots of tour buses deposit their frazzled passengers here. In-house medical attention. Breakfast included. Small restaurant serves lunch and dinner. Mountain bike rentals US$8 per day. Singles US$7, with hot bath US$9. ❷

Jatún Pacha/Chalet Sol (☎922 223), at 31 de Octubre. Tucked away from the center, this is the homiest of Otavalo's hostels. Small wooden rooms share a balcony onto a small yard and sitting area where hummingbirds sometimes stop to feed. Breakfast included. US$8 per person. ❸

Hostal Runa Pacha, Roca 10-02 (☎921 730), at Quiroga. Spacious rooms, some with balconies, hot water and cable TV all around. This homestead is a hidden gem. *Indígena*-owned and operated. With or without private bath US$5 per person. ❷

☐ FOOD

The best truly cheap options are any of the *pollerías* concentrated on Sucre. The higher the price of an Otavaleño restaurant, the more foreign its clientele.

Café Sol y Luna (www.cafesolyluna.com), on Bolívar between Salinas and Morales. Follow the wafting *incenseo* to the warm dining room/kitchen. The Belgian couple who own the cafe speak English. The chef updates his rotating photography exhibit when he is not busy with such delicacies as tofu, seitan, and pesto. Local musicians may play Sa afternoons. Entrees US$3.50-5. Open M-Tu 2-10pm, W-Su 9am-10pm. ❷

Quino Restaurant, Roca 740 (☎2924 994), at Montalvo between Hotel Otavalo and Riviera Sucre. Centrally located with good seafood, this place is a local favorite. Vegetarian options. Entrees US$3-5.40. Open daily 11am-11pm. ❷

Sahara (☎2922 212), on Piedrhita between Roca and Bolívar near the Parque Central, is all about Middle Eastern ambience. Most nights the cushions and straw mats on the floor accommodate backpackers enjoying *pipas de agua* (hookahs) with peach, mint, apple, or strawberry tobacco and candle-light dinners (US$2). Falafel and hummus US$1.50-2, pizza from US$3.50. Open daily 3-11pm. ❶

⚐Rincón de Italia, Sucre 919 (☎2922 555), at Calderón. Portraits of buxom nude women stare down from the walls as patrons feast on fantastic pizzas as well as some hummus and falafel. Pies from US$3.40. Delivery available for an extra US$1. Open daily 9am-11pm. Traveler's checks accepted. ❷

Chifa Otavalo, on Bolívar between Quito and Ordoñez, serves up heaping platters of Chinese food and asks for very little in return. Fried rice and a drink are just US$1.60. The spices are a welcome variation on local themes and it's a good place for a late-night snack (US$1.50-3). Open daily 10am-12pm. ❶

Shanandoa, The Pie Shop/Cafeteria, Salinas 515 (☎2921 465), on Plaza de los Ponchos. Not your grandmother's pie, but just as tasty. Fillings include apple, strawberry, chocolate, and lemon. For a more Ecuadorian flavor, try pineapple or *barbaro*. Big greasy burgers and sandwiches (US$2.50) are also served. Good for breakfast. Pie US$1, a la mode US$2. Open daily 7am-9pm. ❶

⚐Tabascos (☎2922 475), on the corner of Salinas and Sucre on Plaza de los Ponchos. The spacious 2nd-fl. patio overlooking the Plaza de Ponchos is a nice haven for weary shoppers. Pizza and Mexican fare from US$6-9, plus a full bar. The burritos are big enough to split. Open daily 7am-8:30pm. DC/MC/V. ❹

CAUGHT BETWEEN WORLDS

The weavings and handicrafts of Otavalo are known worldwide: Otavaleños sell wares from San Fransisco to Seville. The first to venture outside of Ecuador to sell traditional weavings was the father of Zulay, who currently owns and operates Diceny Viajes. Her father's travels to Colombia, Chile, and Peru allowed him to send Zulay and her two sisters to school in Quito. While at school in Quito, Zulay met a team of North American anthropologists and filmmakers who collaborated with her and her family on the film *Zulay: Facing the 21st Century.* It tells the story of Zulay's journey from her family's home in Quinchusquí near Otavalo to Los Angeles where she sells her family's crafts. In the film, an American city is seen through Zulay's eyes. comparing her modern life to her traditional one. The film shows Zulay returning from the US to find that she no longer belongs in her community; so, she decides to return to Los Angeles in hopes of finding acceptance somewhere. Ultimately, she returns home to her family, and the film ends with her still feeling apart from both cultures.

While the film has a melancholy ending, Zulay herself is now hopeful. Talking with me in the warmth of her kitchen, she expressed her desire to finish the story and make a sequel that includes the balance she has struck between her two worlds.

Oraibi (☎ 2921 221; www.dplanet.ch/users/oraibi), on Sucre and Cristóbal Colón. The vegetarian theme includes crepes, Spanish tortillas, varied salads, and pizzas. There is a large patio in the back with umbrellas and live Andean music F-Sa nights. Entrees US$4. Open W-Su 7:30am-9pm. ❷

◎ SIGHTS

THE MARKET. Otavalo's famous Saturday market (which also operates on weekdays) starts on the Plaza de los Ponchos but stretches several blocks onto the surrounding streets. Once a hotbed of intra-community trading, the market is now almost entirely geared toward souvenirs and *artesanía* for the tourists that come in droves. Local weavings are concentrated in the plaza and all along Sucre, where many *indígenas* set up booths in front of their shops. Some of the best wood carvings and leather goods are sold on Sucre and in the southeastern end of the market. Stands on Quiroga cook up market food. Jaramillo, the most eclectic area, sells everything from "genuine" Air Jordans to hand-carved pipes, with a produce market and stalls of *comida típica*. Thefts have been known to occur around Jaramillo. Bargaining is expected. *(Open daily 6:30am-6pm.)*

MUSEO ARQUEOLÓGICO. Although this one-room museum houses over 10,000 archaeological relics dating back as far as 17,000 years, its greatest treasure is the curator, César Vásquez Fuller. This knowledgeable old man brings to life a seemingly chaotic mix of shelved objects with first- and second-hand stories of their history and use. If you ask, he'll show you two jade pieces plucked from an Otavalo dirt pile in 2002 and carved with what Sr. Vásquez contends are Egyptian hieroglyphics. *(At the corner of Montalvo and Roca, 2nd fl., marked by a sign but easy to miss. Open when curator is there. US$2 donation requested.)*

◙ NIGHTLIFE

On weekends, Otavalo's bars and Peñas come alive with performances of traditional Andean music and Latin rock.

🏆**Peña Amauta** (☎ 922 435), at Morales and Jaramillo, with a fireplace and candles warming the downstairs bar wins the best atmosphere award. It also serves the mysterious and potent *guayusa*, made from fermented sugarcane. Live folkloric music F-Sa 10pm with some salsa and merengue when the musicians break. Beer US$1.50, cocktails US$2.50. Cover US$2. Open daily 8pm-late.

Habana Club (☎2920 493), on the corner of Quito and 31 de Octubre, national tourists and locals from the Otavalo area fill the dance floor when salsa, merengue, and cumbia pump F-Sa nights. 18+ except on Su afternoons when a younger crowd downs lite beer to the sounds of techno, house, and hip-hop. Karaoke upstairs and pool downstairs. Cover (US$2) includes a beer. Open F-Sa 9pm-3am, Su 3pm-5:30pm.

Café Bar da Pinto, on Colón between Bolívar and Sucre. Owner and artist William Pinto's passion for color spills off his murals onto the walls inside and out. The staple here is Andean music, but weeknights are an Otavalo alternative scene from Cuban son to a traveling puppet show. Cover US$1 when there is live music. Open daily 4pm-2am.

Fauno (☎2921 611), on Morales between Sucre and Jaramillo, has a slicker feel and sound than the other Peñas. Latin-rock fills the spacious tri-level club F-Sa. There are plenty of tables for snacking and drinking. Cover US$1. Open Tu-Su from 4pm.

MINDO ☎02

Just a few hours from Quito along a pleasant stretch of highway, tiny Mindo (pop. 2400) invites locals and foreigners alike to leave the concrete behind and escape to another world for a day, a week, or even longer. Leave the city early in the morning and by afternoon, find yourself navigating a river by inner tube or enjoying a colorful array of birds, butterflies, and orchids. Mindo was one of the first spots in Ecuador to catch on to the ecotourism craze and is now working to protect its natural assets by cultivating ecological awareness among residents and visitors. Choosing among the myriad outdoor activities will be the hardest part of your visit. Bring good hiking boots, sandals, a rain jacket, binoculars, insect repellant, and a bathing suit to keep your options open.

▐ TRANSPORTATION

Buses to Mindo from **Quito** (2½hr.; M-F 8am, 3:45pm, Sa-Su 8, 9am, 3:45pm; US$2.50) leave from the **Flor Valle Cayambe** office at Manuel Larrea and Asunción (☎2527 495), near the El Ejido trolley stop. Buses back to Quito (2hr.; M-F 6:30am, 2pm, Sa-Su 6:30am, 2, 3pm; US$2.50) leave from the office on the left side of Quito, the main road as you enter town. Since there are relatively few buses, it's best to purchase a return ticket upon arrival. Should you miss one of these buses, catch a taxi to La Y (US$5.50) and hop on one of the buses passing through to Quito every 15-30min. Although Let's Go does not recommend hitchhiking, some grab a ride with daytrippers from Quito who have extra room.

Within Mindo, a **bicycle** helps to make the most of the sights. **Bici Star,** across from the Centro de Información, rents well-worn mountain bikes for US$1 per hr.

✳ ▐ ORIENTATION AND PRACTICAL INFORMATION

The road to Mindo intersects the highway to Quito at what locals call **"La Y."** From there it's another 15min. into town. Even the locals don't know the street names, but it's small enough that navigations isn't difficult. Buses enter Mindo on the main street **La Vía Principal,** which passes the church on the left about halfway through town, the soccer field on the right, and dead-ends at the **Parque Central.** From where La Vía Principal ends, the road **Vía Mindo Gardens** heads out past Hotel El Gallo toward the waterfall trails and ends up at Hotel Mindo Gardens.

Tourist Office: Check with the **Centro de Información** (open daily 7am-6pm), on the right at the end of the main road, Quito, just before the plaza, to get the latest word on lodging, food, and guides. The Centro de Información is administered by the Asociación de Guías Naturalistas de Mindo. Almost everyone is a guide in Mindo but only a few are officially licensed by the Ministry of Tourism. Ask to see a license and note the name of your guide before heading out. Guided activities include *observación de aves* (bird-watching trips), *caminatas nocturnas* (night-hikes), tubing on Río Mindo (US$4), sport-fishing for trout, and rapelling down waterfalls. For more info on rapelling and camping nearby, contact **Mindo la Isla** (☎2765 466; www.mindolaisla.com).

Police: To the left on La Vía Principal, just before the bridge to the main part of town.

Pharmacy: The 24hr. pharmacy is located just off of the Parque Central, behind the church, and supplies basic, over-the-counter needs as well as fulfilling some prescriptions. Even if it doesn't look open, ring the bell and someone will attend.

Medical Services: The pink concrete clinic, **Subcentro de Salud Mindo** (open M-F 8am-4pm, Sa 8am-2pm), is next to the soccer field on the way to **Los Colibríes** (see p. 113).

Telephone: Some private residences offer the use of their phone (look for a sign that says teléfono), as does the **Hostal Arco Iris** on the Parque Central.

Internet Access: Don't count on being able to check email while in Mindo. **Hostal el Descanso** sometimes has service, but Mindo has very few telephone lines.

Post Office: The **Oficina de Correos**, next to the soccer field, is always open but has spotty service. It's better to send and receive mail in nearby Quito.

ACCOMMODATIONS

For inexpensive lodging, you might crash in one of any number of hostels near the plaza, though a little extra money and a bit of a walk or taxi drive buy a lot of ambience. There are plenty of choices along the road heading out of town at the end of La Vía Principal toward Vía Mindo Gardens, behind the soccer field and along the road toward Hotel El Carmelo.

Hostal El Descanso (☎2765 383; www.eldescanso.net). This 2-story house feels fresh and open. Rooms open onto a 2nd-fl. common deck with hammocks and mountain views. The dorm is an open sleeping area with no doors or lockers. Mosquito nets are available. Breakfast included. Dorms US$12, with private bath US$16. Traveler's checks accepted. ❸

Centro de Educación Ambiental (CEA), 4km outside of town at the end of Vía Mindo Gardens, a few km past Mariposas Mindo. The cabins are a 15min. walk from the parking area that includes a trip across Río Mindo by *tarabita* (hand-operated cable car). CEA helps conserve 192,000 sq. km of protected forest containing 450 species of bird and 370 species of orchid. They arrange trekking and tubing excursions, as well as trips to La Cascada del Nambillo. Cabins have no electricity. CEA is always looking for volunteers to help with conservation projects (see p. 74). Restaurant serves basic meals (US$3-4). Camping US$4 per person; dorms US$5 with own sleeping bag, US$6 without; private cabins US$10 per person. For more information on the lodge, contact the Amigos de la Naturaleza office (☎2765 463), at the end of the road after taking a left from the main road at the plaza (follow the signs). The Amigos take Wednesdays off. ❷

Mindo Gardens (☎2252 490; www.casablanca.com). At the end of Vía Mindo are 350 prime hectares of land where Mindo Gardens nature trails, cozy wooden cabins (upscale versions of the options down the road), and an elegant restaurant with outdoor seating on Río Mindo (prix fixe US$11). A *pizzería* makes beautiful thin-crust personal pies from scratch in a wood-fired oven (US$4.50-7). If foregoing the expensive rooms, still stop for a snack when returning from the steeper trail to La Cascada del Nambillo. Hot private baths. Breakfast included. Doubles US$50; triples US$75. ❺

Hostal Los Guaduales (HI), 200m before El Carmelo de Mindo, is part of Los Colibríes restaurant (see p. 113). The hostel is a 2-story wooden house with rooms that open onto a large sun-lit common area. Just outside the door is a short path through primary forest that leads to a campsite along Río Mindo. Breakfast included. Camping US$3; dorms US$7, with private bath US$10; HI members US$6/$7. ❷

☘ FOOD

To ease your rumbling belly, check out the small stores and cafes crowding around the main road. These other options outside of the town center offer a bit more atmosphere and the local specialties: *trucha* (trout) and *tilapía*.

Los Colibríes, a few km outside of town along the road to El Carmelo. Dine with the hummingbirds on a patio overlooking meticulously manicured gardens. Lunch includes a visit to the hummingbird gardens. Otherwise, a stroll around the grounds costs US$3, including a drink. Entrees US$4-6. ❸

Fuera de Babylon, just off the Parque Central toward Amigos de la Naturaleza Fuera de Babylon. This joint serves up reasonably priced *batidos* (blended fruit drinks) and snacks, including the requisite trout, in an all-wood dining room. Funky wooden sculptures and Bob Marley share wall space. Entrees US$1.50-3. ❶

☉ SIGHTS

Close to town is a spot for butterflies and orchids, the **Jardín de Mariposas y Orquídeas Nataly.** Turn right at the end of the Vía Principal and follow the signs. To the untrained eye, the orchid garden looks like a bunch of slightly mossy potted plants, but a tour by owner Santiago Herrera or another guide reveals a world of naturally tiny, intricate orchids in all their hermaphroditic glory. He returns 50% of the orchids and butterflies he cultivates to the forest. (US$3 per person, includes guide.) The Vía Mindo Gardens route to the waterfalls passes by the **Mariposas de Mindo** butterfly garden, hostel, and restaurant, 2km from the Parque Central. Spend as long as you like within the butterfly garden among the beautiful insects in various stages of metamorphosis (US$3) or among the bright butterfly souvenirs adorning the screened-in cafe. (☎ 2440 360; mariposademindo@hotmail.com.)

⚐ OUTDOOR ACTIVITIES

Hiking is a popular option, but since paths are sometimes hard to find and it's easy to trespass accidentally onto private reserves, a guide is recommended (US$25 per day). A guide knowledgeable in local fauna can also help you find the elusive, crimson **cock of the rock,** Mindo's most popular winged creature; ask at the Centro de Información or one of the hostels. A popular self-guided hike goes to **La Cascada del Nambillo** (The Waterfall of Nambillo) and **Cascadas el Santuario,** about 2½hr. from the plaza. The Centro de Información offers maps of the trails to the falls. Take a right off the main road just past the plaza and follow the signs to "Las Cascadas." There are two options for hiking to the falls. To the left is **Vía Mindo Gardens,** through which winds a gentle 4km road that can be biked or driven all the way to **Hotel Mindo Gardens** and the **Centro Educativo Ambiental (CEA).** From there, it is a steep 1km scramble up and another 1km down to the falls. Alternatively, you can cross the big metal bridge and go right up a longer, winding dirt road that then hooks up with the other trail for the final 1km descent to the waterfall. Just before the Nambillo Waterfall is the newly constructed cable car that travels 530m across the valley (round-trip US$2 or US$5 to get off on the other side and hike down to another waterfall, the **Cascadas el Santuario**). Tickets (US$5, students US$2, Ecuadorian nationals US$3) are required to enter La Cascada del Nambillo and can be purchased at the Centro de Información or along the trail. On Saturday and Sunday, you'll find food and drink at little snack stands along the way.

Tubing on Río Mindo can also be arranged through the Centro de Información, or through many hostels (US$4 per tube). **El Carmelo de Mindo** resort offers **horseback riding** (US$2 per hr.). A guide will accompany you for an additional US$10. To get there, start from the church that faces La Vía Principal about halfway through town, and follow the signs for about 30min. The butterfly garden, swimming pool, and jacuzzi are available for use by day guests (US$5).

RESERVA GEOBOTÁNICA PULULAHUA ☎02

The verdant volcanic crater Pululahua in the Reserva Geobotánica Pululahua offers stunning views of the jagged Andean landscape. Four kilometers in diameter, this is the largest volcanic crater in South America. The peaceful silence of the vistas belies their name; "Pululahua" is Safiki for "sorcery that causes big pain," likely a distant memory of the volcano's last cataclysmic eruption 2400 years ago—or perhaps a nod to the blisters and sore muscles that can result from the steep descent to the crater floor. The fertile soil at the bottom of the crater is a patchwork of small farms while the steep walls are home to a lush cloud forest micro-ecosystem teeming with creatures. Despite its ominous name, the lush vegetation and colorful birds promise more pleasure than pain.

☐ TRANSPORTATION. To get to **El Crater,** catch a bus passing through Mitad del Mundo's (see p. 102) traffic circle (15min., every 20min. 6am-7pm, US$0.20) on its way to Pululahua. Buses run back to **Mitad del Mundo,** often continuing to Quito, (same frequency 5am-6:30pm). Taxis and camionetas can run tourists to the first trailhead (US$2) and pick them up later for the same amount. Unscrupulous taxi drivers will try to charge US$4 each way and US$20 round-trip with a wait at the trailhead. Take the bus or bargain them down.

To get to **Area de Recreación Moraspungo,** jump on a bus passing through the Mitad del Mundo traffic circle headed to Calacalí (every 20min. 7am-8pm). It can drop you off at the turnoff to Moraspungo, but only if you explicitly ask the driver to stop there (US$0.25). From the turnoff, follow a dirt road 3km through corn fields and into the mist to the lip of the volcano. Cars pass infrequently on this road. Either walk it or hire a camioneta from Mitad del Mundo.

☐☑ ORIENTATION AND PRACTICAL INFORMATION. There are two choices for accessing the crater. The first is **El Crater.** Here, a privately owned piece of land with a lookout point called **Ventanilla,** El Crater restaurant, and **Templo de Arte,** the recently completed art gallery fashioned after Inca castles and proudly bearing a portrait of Atahualpa on its outer walls. From here a 3km switchback trail called **Sal si Puedes** (Leave If You Can) links the agricultural community of the crater floor to the rest of the world. Until now the Ventanilla viewpoint has been free, but in June 2004 officials were considering instituting a US$5 entrance fee. The second entrance point, 4km past the first toward Calacalí, is the **Area de Recreación Moraspungo** (entrance fee US$5), administered by the Ministry of the Environment. From Moraspungo, a 15km trail descends through cloud forest to the crater floor. A **refuge ❶** (☎2508 927), run by Guillermo Romero, is to the left of the crater's main road, just after the highway turnoff. (Bring food or dine at the on-site cafe. US$3 per person. Camping free. Tent rental US$1.50.)

☐ SIGHTS. The most rewarding way to visit Pululahua and Rumicucho (see p. 115) is with a guide. **Calima Tours** (☎2394 796 or 2394 797; calima@andinanet.net), in the main information building at Mitad del Mundo, can give visitors rides to sights along with related details and history. Guide and general manager Fernando shares scientific knowledge, local stories and remedies, and his own personal connection to the sights. Calima Tours takes visitors up a short path to a lookout near El Crater restaurant, not Moraspungo. Tours leave early to beat the afternoon clouds. Call ahead to arrange for guides in English or Spanish. (US$8-9 per person per sight. Open daily 9am-6pm.)

RUMICUCHO   ☎02

Although denizens of nearby villages plundered the rocks of Rumicucho ("stone corner" in Quichua) for years, the stones remain impressive. The rectangular foundations of the pre-Inca Quitu-Cara sun temple scrape the sky atop a hill that still feels sacred. Twice a year—on the equinoxes—Quitu-Cara priests used to capture the energy of the sun god as he smoldered directly overhead; touch the large ceremonial stone on the far end of the plateau to harness some of the sun's energy for yourself. Not coincidentally, Rumicucho lines up almost exactly to some of the greatest natural landmarks in Ecuador. To the north lies Volcán Cotacachi; to the south, Volcán Cotopaxi; to the east, Volcán Cayambe; and to the west, the pyramid-shaped Cerros de la Marca. The dramatic views of these volcanoes and the sheer drop of Cañón de Guayllabamba add at least as much to the ambience as the quarry trucks rumbling below take away. Rumicucho is at the base of the Kati-Killia ruins that look down over Mitad del Mundo from the hill to the North of Rumicucho. Kati-Killia's two large stone circles mark the exact equator and are perfectly illuminated as the sun breaks over Cayambe during the equinox.

The easiest way to reach Rumicucho is by camioneta from **Mitad del Mundo** (one-way US$3, round-trip with 30min. wait US$6). Alternatively, a 6km walk leads through hot, dusty, and not-so-picturesque neighborhoods for over 1hr. Take Equinoccial and make a left onto 13 de Junio, the principal strip of San Antonio de Pichincha, and turn right after 30-45min. at the Rumicucho sign near the large white church. Tours of Rumicucho generally run US$9, and of Kati-Killia, US$15. Contact Calima Tours (see p. 102) in Mitad del Mundo. Tours to Kati-Killia leave early and require a one-day notice. US$1 fee may or may not be collected. A small **restaurant** on site opens on weekends to serve drinks and snacks (US$1.50).

BELLAVISTA CLOUD FOREST RESERVE

Sticky cloud layers slide over the hills of Bellavista after midday, clinging to the steep slopes and giving sustenance to a wild array of bromeliads and orchids. At 1600-2500m, the reserve's eight sq. km teem with over 300 bird species, drawn to the area by the same attraction that draws humans: the ultra-diverse flora. Bellavista is a birdwatcher's mecca, but you don't have to know a Toucan Barbet from a Tanager-Finch to enjoy a stroll to one of its many waterfalls or the sun peeking through late-afternoon fog. Since 1991, British-Colombian owners Richard Parsons and Gloria Nicholls have dedicated themselves to protecting and restoring this piece of teeming but fragile Choco-Andean rainforest. A leader in Ecuador's growing ecotourism industry, Bellavista welcomes visits from local school groups and is constantly working on creative ways to minimize impact on the environment and involve nearby communities. Come equipped with binoculars, good hiking shoes, and rain gear to maximize your time here. An extensive network of 18 well maintained and easy-to-follow trails are carved out of the steep slopes with benches and sheltered viewpoints along the way. The trails range from a gentle self-guided tour from the main lodge to the most adventurous "S" trail with a waterfall at the end. Rubber boots are supplied upon request when it rains and gets slippery. It is possible to contact the reserve directly (☎/fax 2116 323).

Ⅲ TRANSPORTATION. The new highway that winds northwest out of Quito toward Mindo crosses the equator four times on its way to Bellavista. Buses stop at the nearby town of **Nanegalito,** which also serves as a jumping-off point for getting to La Reserva Maquipucuna. Contact the Bellavista office in Quito to make a reservation or for the latest information on transportation. (☎2232 313 or 09 9490 891; www.bellavistacloudforest.com.) **Transportes Flor Del Valle** (☎2527 495), **Man-**

uel Larrea, and **Asunción** send buses from Quito to **Los Bancos** and **Mindo** via **Nane-galito** (2hr.; M-F 5:45, 8am, 2:45, 3:45pm, Sa-Su 5:45, 7, 8, 9am, 2:45pm; US$2). Nanegalito is the town closest to the reserve. Be careful not to board a bus going north to Cayambe. Buses marked Amazonas, Kennedy, and Aloag pass through Nanegalito on their way to Mindo, Pacto, or Puerto Quito. Buses leave everyday 8-11am and after 3pm. Have the driver drop you off 3km before Nanegalito on the road to Tandayapa where there is a small sign to Bellavista. Follow the road for 12km past a few trout hatcheries and through the village of Tandayapa to reach the lodge. Allow 3hr. for the trip back downhill to catch a bus (last bus 7pm) returning to Quito. If the walk is too much for you, jump off the bus in Nanegalito, and ask at Viveres Paty for anyone with a camioneta to take you uphill to the reserve (1hr.; about US$15 per truckload to the main lodge, all the way to the Est-ación Científica 45min. US$20). Deeper pockets should check out the Bellavista Office in Quito, Jorge Washington E7-23 and 6 de Diciembre, which offers a day-trip package (US$89 per person).

⃢ PRACTICAL INFORMATION. With prior notice, the staff at Bellavista can arrange trips to Mindo, white-water rafting excursions, mountain-biking adventures, and horseback rides. Within the reserve itself, highly knowledgeable English- and Spanish-speaking guides are available. (US$10 per person for a shared guide, cheaper rates negotiable.) ⃢**Volunteers** are usually expected to stay for at least a month (US$150 per month; includes lodging and food in the Estación Científica), where tasks include building trails, making signs, and running the lodge in exchange for reduced room rates in the hostel. (see p. 74)

⃢⃟ ACCOMMODATIONS AND FOOD. At **La Estación Científica ❸,** 3km above the lodge along a four-wheel-drive road, backpackers and volunteers share cheaper, more spartan accommodations in a dorm-style hostel with sheets and blankets. Meals are available at the lodge, but it's cheaper to pick up groceries in Nanegalito and make use of the kitchen. As soon as mist and darkness descend, you'll want a head lamp or candles (electricity can be spotty) and plenty of warm layers. (Dorms US$10.) **Bellavista Lodge and Restaurant ❹** looks as if it sprouted from the forest floor. The four-story thatch and bamboo geodesic dome *(el domo)* is a bubble of civilization in the midst of the surrounding wilderness, with an international wine list and breathtaking 360-degree windows that afford quite a *bella vista* of the gaping Tandayapa Valley below. Visitors can take splendid meals, both vegetarian and non-vegetarian, in the first-floor dining area, to the tune of countless hummingbirds feeding just outside the windows. (Meal package US$25 per day. Breakfast US$6, lunch and dinner US$13.) On the second floor, rooms have balconies, hot baths, and sitting areas. The penthouse is one cozy dorm with a communal bath and balcony. (Dorms US$17, with meals US$39; singles with private bath US$43/$68; doubles US$33/$58; triples US$31/$56. Children 12-and-under half-price. Package deals available.) Near the geodesic dome are more conventional two-story **cabins.** A few kilometers below the lodge is the large cabin Casa de Davíd, with accommodations for eight people, and a kitchen. The same rates as the lodge apply. (Camping on the reserve US$6 per person. Tents US$5 per night.)

RESERVA MAQUIPUCUNA   ☎02

Reserva Maquipucuna protects an ecological gem. Its borders contain 600 sq. km of land, 80% of which is primary cloud forest. Researchers have swarmed to the reserve throughout its 15 years of existence, and their work has uncovered astounding numbers: over 2000 species of plants, 45 species of mammals, 325 species of birds, and 250 species of butterflies. Warm-blooded creatures include pumas, bears, bats, agoutis, peccaries, tapir, deer, and a growing number of visitors who come for the hiking, bird-watching, and swimming in Río Umachaca. The various projects in community development and sustainability that the Fundación Maquipucuna coordinates keep volunteers busy. From the lodge, eight well-maintained paths (ranging 20min.-10hr.) can be hiked with or without a guide and wind through pastures and secondary forest to primary forest. The reserve provides simple topographic maps and detailed trail descriptions in English and Spanish. Some trails follow parts of the Inca trail that once stretched from the Highlands to the coast but has since been lost. You'll know you're on these ancient pathways by the *culuncos*: ancient three-quarter tunnels carved out of stone.

TRANSPORTATION. To get to Maquipucuna you must go through Nanegalito, Nanegal, and Marianitas, 4km from the reserve's entrance. **Transporte Minas** (☎2586 316) runs buses from San Blas in Quito (Anteparra at Pedro Fermín Cevallos) to **Nanegal** via **Nanegalito** (2½hr.; M-F 6.45am, 1, 4pm, Sa 7, 10am, 1·45, 4pm, Su 9am, 1:45, 4pm; US$1.60). Locals report that you can catch a ride in a passing camioneta bringing milk, produce, and *campesinos* from Nanegalito to Nanegal if you are willing to wait patiently under the large Maquipucuna sign just past the kiosks on the highway. From Nanegal, catch a camioneta to the **reserve** (30min., US$8-10 per truckload). To hike into the reserve, get off the bus 2km before Nanegal, at the big white house marking the La Delicia crossing, about 45min. beyond Nanegalito. From here it's a 3km hike to Marianitas and another 4km to Maquipucuna. The reserve can get you a camioneta back to Nanegal (30min., US$8-10) for a Transporte Minas bus to **Quito** (2½hr.; M-F 6:30, 9:15am, 3pm, Sa 6:30am, 12:30pm, Su 6:30am, 12:30, 2:30pm; US$1.60).

ORIENTATION AND PRACTICAL INFORMATION. From Nanegalito, head north toward Nanegal and turn right at **Hacienda la Delicia,** continue past trout hatcheries to **Marianitas** and then down to the lodge. The lodge is at the northernmost part of the reserve within earshot of Río Umachaca. Most of the paths wind up into the hillsides to the south of the lodge. (Reserve open daily 7am-6pm. Entrance fee US$5, children under 12 free.) The lodge and reserve are just part of the Fundación Maquipucuna's broader goals—a good education and a sustainable economy for the communities in the wilderness corridor stretching from the cloud forests to the border of Colombia. The reserve is also a research site for the University of Georgia's Institute of Ecology, and there are usually three or four researchers on the reserve year-round. The Maquipucuna Foundation accepts donations. Contact the foundation at Maquipucuna Foundation Inc., 240-1 Parthenon Ln., Athens, GA 30605, USA (☎/fax 706-542-2923; www.maqui.org).

Many companies arrange **tours.** The Maquipucuna Foundation arranges a one-day tour from Quito, including transportation, food, entrance into the reserve, and a guide (US$70 per person). Spanish-speaking guides are available through the Ecotourist Center (US$10 per day). Call ahead for English-speaking guides. To make a reservation, contact the Fundación Maquipucuna, Baquerizo E9-153 at Tamayó, PO Box 17-12-167, Quito, Ecuador (☎2507 203, 2507 200 or 2507 202; root@maquipucuna.net or ecotourism@maquipucuna.net).

Local communities practice conservation and sustainable living through organic gardening and artisan shops. At the **Horongo** plantation, a group produces shade-grown organic coffee. In Marianitas, women of Marianitas and Yunguilla work in small cheese, jelly, and jewelry workshops. **Volunteers** can help out with any one of these ventures, as well as with trail maintenance and sign-making on the reserve itself. Projects are often loosely coordinated, so there is lots of room for personal creativity and initiative. Contact Andrea Almeida in Quito for more information (see above). Volunteers donate US$15 per day, which includes three meals at the lodge and accommodations at the **Estación Científica**, with a family in Horongo, or in dorms at the shiny new **Centro de Capacitación** overlooking Marianitas.

🔓 ACCOMMODATIONS. Just a short talk from the main lodge is **Casa Familiar** ❺, a secluded, newly constructed private house. It has one bedroom with a double bed and another with two twins plus a porch with the requisite hammock, ideal for a family. (US$65 per person, includes 3 meals at Umachaca Lodge.) **Umachaca Lodge** ❸, a two-story bamboo ecotourist oasis, offers hot baths and a large hammock-slung deck for relaxing to the sounds of the forest and Río Umachaca. Prices include three meals per day, with vegetarian options. (4-person dorms US$45, with private bath US$65. Traveler's checks accepted. Check with offices in Quito for prices and to make a reservation.) Overlooking the community of Marianitas is **Centro de Capacitación** ❸, a new building constructed by the Maquipucuna Foundation that houses offices, an orchid laboratory, a jelly-making workshop, and volunteers. (US$15 per day, including meals for volunteers.) **Estación Científica** ❹ hosts scientists conducting research and volunteers working on the trails. Guests stay in the wooden bunkhouse a short walk from the main lodge past the orchid garden. Tourists and volunteers contribute US$15 per day and scientists US$25 per day in return for lodging and meals. Bring a mosquito net. A **campsite** ❶ is available on the reserve for those on a tighter budget. (US$2 per night.)

RESERVA LOS CEDROS   ☎ 02

The most remote among these Cloud Forest reserves, Los Cedros is a 14km walk or mule ride from the handful of buildings that make up the nearby community of Chontal. The reserve itself has comfortable accommodations, including a honeymoon suite, for 15-16 people in an all-wood lodge with excellent views of the reserve. From there, marked trails tracked by puma and spectacled bears wind through primary forest to hidden springs and waterfalls. Like to walk? Take off for Los Cedros in the morning and have the mules bring up your bags later. **Volunteers** can stay at the reserve for US$300 per month including meals and usually work on maintaining trails (see p. 74). Be sure to contact the reserve from Quito to arrange a visit as Chontal's one telephone is often broken. José DeCoux, who speaks English and administers the reserve, also knows about volunteer opportunities in the community of Chontal. To arrange a visit, contact José directly on the reserve (☎ 2865 176). For more information, visit www.reservaloscedros.org, or contact the administrative offices in Quito at Alemania and Eloy Alfaro (☎ 2540 346). The reserve is most easily accessed August to December when trails dry out.

If grassroots eco-activism is your style, check out the newly-formed Comité de Ecoturismo (Ecotourism Committee). One of 13 community-based associations in the Manduriacos zone, the Committee is dedicated to finding more sustainable alternatives to mining and logging. It is working on the construction of a small tourist information center at the edge of town that also serves as a community classroom, and welcomes **volunteers** who can teach anything from English to medicine to cooking. Contact Fabián Hernandez (☎ 3711 774; manduryac@hotmail.com) or Jimena Mina (☎ 2866 655; cuma5_5@hotmail.com).

Transporte Minas (☎ 2586 316) runs **buses** from Quito to Chontal. The ride is 1½hr. on paved road to Nanegalito. From Nanegalito it's another 1½- 2hr. on a one-lane dirt road. If you don't mind teetering along a knife-edge ridge, get a window seat and take in the clouds and peaks stretching out below. Buses leave from San Blas in **Quito** at Anteparra and León about a block below the Iglesia San Blas (M-F 6:15, 9:30, 11am, 3pm; Sa-Su 6, 11am, 3pm) and return from Chontal (M-F 5, 6, 11am, 1:45pm; Sa 6, 11am, 1:45pm; Su 8:30am, noon, 2:30pm; US$2.50). Trying to make the trip in one day can be difficult, but should you succeed, the **Hotel San Fernando ❶**, on the left as you enter Chontal, offers basic accommodations. The little unfinished wooden rooms share a bathroom to the side of the house and the family who runs the place is kind and willing to look after anything you don't want to haul up to the reserve with you. (Vegetarian-friendly. Meals US$2. Rooms US$4.) Or stay on the reserve itself. (US$30 a day per person, including 3 meals prepared from organic produce in the large kitchen as well as round-trip mule transport.)

COCHASQUÍ ARCHAEOLOGICAL PARK

For physical grandeur, nothing in Quito's backyard compares with Cochasquí Archaeological Park. Fifteen truncated pyramids and 20 tombs spill down the mountain slopes, whose vistas extend to Quito, Cotopaxi, and beyond. The ruins, protected from the elements by a meter or more of earth and stubby grass, are disturbed only by the occasional grazing llama. The structures give silent testament to the thriving Quitu-Cara people who built these monuments between AD 500 and 1500 when the Incas invaded the area followed shortly by the conquistadors. Archaeologists have hypothesized that the pyramids served as a strategic military outpost or ceremonial site, that they were inhabited by the upperclasses, or that they formed part of an astronomical center for festival and agricultural purposes. This last hypothesis has received greater emphasis in recent years with the discovery of additional archaeological sites in the region aligning perfectly with the sun during equinoxes and solstices. Regardless of its exact function, Cochasquí's location was strategically chosen for its long, unobstructed views which, luckily, you don't have to be an archaeologist to enjoy. Spanish- and (sometimes) English-speaking guides lead a mandatory (but fascinating) 1½hr. tour of the site. (Park open daily 8:30am-4:30pm. US$3, children US$1.50.) In addition to the ruins, the tour features a garden of traditional Andean agriculture and two dwellings. The artifacts in the dwellings were donated by nearby communities. While they are not "archaeological," some are hundreds of years old. A small museum contains artifacts found at Quitu-Cara archaeological sites throughout northern Ecuador. Bring lunch, as there are no dining options nearby. (Open daily 8:30am-4:30pm.)

The best way to reach Cochasquí is via **bus** going to Otavalo from the main Quito terminal (every 10min. 6am-8:40pm). Make sure the bus is going through Tabacundo and ask the driver to let you off before Tabacundo at the turnoff to the Cochasquí ruins (1½hr., US$1), just past the toll booth. The ruins are an 8km (2hr.) scenic hike up a dirt road. Site workers driving up 8:45-9:30am can give you a lift, but if you miss them, fear not—the hike is spectacular enough to justify the trip, provided you bring enough water. Prepare for strong winds June to August and the possibility of rain during the rest of the year. Flag down a returning bus (with a Quito sign in the window) back on the highway (every 10min. until 7pm, US$1).

LAGUNAS DE MOJANDA AND FUYA FUYA

The three Lagunas de Mojanda are tucked away between the extinct volcano Fuya Fuya and a range of smaller rolling mountains 16km south of Otavalo. The trail starts at the first and largest lake, trout-filled Caricocha, situated 3700m above sea level. It continues along the cobblestone road, then diverges at the far end of the lake into an oft-used dirt trail and a lesser-used path through the grass. The former cuts to the left and winds around the back of Montaña Pequeña, leading to an amazing view of Yanacocha (Black Lake), named in response to the surrounding cliffs that keep the waters eternally shadowed. The path to the right goes up a steep bank and leads to another dirt trail. This trail winds to a view of the less spectacular Huarmicocha (Woman Lake) and provides glimpses of the misty mountaintops of Fuya Fuya and Montaña Pequeña (45min. one-way). From there, the road forks a second time. Both paths go up Montaña Pequeña to Laguna Grande, but the right-hand one, though slightly longer, is less muddy.

The 1500m climb to the top of Fuya Fuya starts at Caricocha. From the top at 4270m, **Otavalo, San Pablo,** and **Quito** stretch out below while volcanoes **Ibarra, Cotopaxi, Cayambe,** and **Cotacachi** flirt with the clouds. On a clear day the vista stretches to Achiles and Cumbo in Colombia. When the lake first comes into view, a dirt road goes up and to the left of the cobbled road. About 50m along the road, a small path starts off through the grass to the right and continues southwest straight up to the small summit. From the summit it is possible to continue along a loop back down to the lake. The trail is steep but non-technical. On a clear day it is possible to navigate to the top and back down. Under a darker sky, the various cow paths going through the grass can be confusing.

To walk to Mojanda, follow Sucre west to the outskirts of the city and cross the Panamerican Hwy. At the Y-junction, go left onto the cobbled, pre-Panamerican road toward Quito. **Taxis** (round-trip US$16) will wait up to 1½hr. at the lakes. A cheaper option is to take a cab there and hike back (3½hr.). **Runa Tupari, Diceny Viajes,** and **Hostal La Luna** can arrange half-day trekking tours (US$20 per day) to Caricocha and up Fuya Fuya, but don't allow time for walking around the lagoons. Be advised that there have been several muggings in recent years at Mojanda— **don't visit the lagoons alone.** Hostal la Luna (4km up the road toward the lakes) may have up-to-date information on hiking around the lakes.

PEGUCHE   ☎06

A few kilometers north along the old railroad from Otavalo, Peguche's mechanical looms clack away in anticipation of the Saturday market at the Plaza de Ponchos. Nearly every household along the cobbled roads of the village is dedicated to artisanship—at least when tour groups come through. Craftsmen and women open their workshops giving shoppers a chance to appreciate the process and buy goods directly from the hands that make them.

The workshop and store of **José Cotacachi** are behind the church on Peguche's Plaza Central. José is there every day working on rugs and tapestries. (☎2922 671; tejidasjosec@yahoo.com.) On the Plaza facing the church, **Artesanía el Gran Condor** sells a mix of machine-made wares and hand-crafted pieces. Some include large weavings done on the pre-Colombian-style backstrap loom, a "cajua" in Quichua. (☎2922 661.) The road at the bottom of the plaza continues to the left toward Peguche. Just past the traffic circle it bends left and heads downhill. On the left is **Taller de Instrumentos Andinos Ñanda Mañachi,** where the creators of bamboo wind instruments, such as pan pipes and flutes, give demonstrations and performances. (☎09 2189 262 or 09 9818 533; talleriandamaniachi@hotmail.com.) On the way, the hacienda-style restaurant **Sumac Micuy** caters to large tour groups of 10-100 with reservations. The restaurant prepares traditional meals in a wood-burning stove and oven. (☎2922 749. US$5 per person, with live music US$15, with music and dance US$25.) Farther from town, between sheep pastures and groves of *tomate del árbol,* the Tontaquimba family gives weaving presentations and has a small *artesanía* shop at **Inti Chumbi Taller de Mis Abuelos.** Call ahead to be served a traditional meal (US$15 per person). To get to this taller, go back uphill from the Taller de Música Andina and make a sharp left at the irrigation ditch. The soccer field and basketball court is on the right as you walk away from Peguche toward Ilumán. After about 10min., a sign points to the **Inti Chumbi** workshop (☎ 09 9189 216). Around lunchtime in Peguche's main square, smell the aroma of fries, chicken, and hot dogs freshly pulled from the deep-fryer.

Buses to Peguche leave from Otavalo (see **Transportation**, p. 120) and deposit visitors near town-center or along the Panamerican Hwy. where a cobbled road leads straight into town. It is also possible to walk to Peguche from Otavalo along the abandoned railroad tracks. These tracks intersect Peguche at the Dutch-Ecuadorian-owned **Hostal Aya Huma ❹**. Signs point toward the hostal along the cobblestone road leading into Peguche. The main building clings to the side of a small ravine where rooms with private bath open onto a common area with hammocks. (Singles US$14; doubles US$20.) Down the road, a **house ❷** offers a kitchen, a welcoming sitting area with a fireplace, dark dorms with shared baths, and a courtyard. (US$7 per person.) The hostel-owner can help you decide where to go for local weavings and the hostel itself has an in-house loom with cloth for sale. Knowledgeable staff can give maps and details about nearby hikes, arrange activities including horseback riding to artisan workshops and the springs, or schedule a *curación* (healing) by a shaman from the community. (☎ 2922 663; www.ayahuma.com. Laundry service. Open 7am-10pm. MC/V. Traveler's checks accepted.) The house (see above) down the street from Hostal Aya Huma has a **restaurant ❷** across the railroad tracks. It serves expensive international entrees, generous salads, and vegetarian options on locally woven tablecloths. A fireplace and candles illuminate the antique instruments, tools, and local costumes that adorn the high walls. Entrees US$4.50-6. **Aya Huma** and **Peguche Tío** provide diverse and pricey lunch options. Mountain bikes are a good way to get around the cobbled roads and are available for rent on the road into town just a few meters from the Panamerican Hwy. at **Ciclo Orimaxi**. (US$1 per hr. Open M-Sa 7am-7pm.) An **Internet** cafe is just up the road. (☎ 2924 374. US$1.20 per minute. Open M-F 9am-6:30pm.)

LAS CASCADAS DE PEGUCHE   ☎ 06

Tucked into the mountainside above Peguche and Otavalo, Las Cascadas de Peguche serve more as a pleasant place to picnic than as a hard-core place to trek. During the week the grounds can be quiet, but weekends bring couples, birthday parties, and vendors, right up to the falls themselves. To reach Las Cascadas from Peguche, face the church in the Plaza Central, and take the road to the right out of town. Follow signs to the waterfall (15min.). Buses passing through the center of Peguche in the direction of the falls can make a stop at the entrance. Some buses leaving Otavalo are marked "Cascadas" and pass by the entrance to the waterfalls en route to **Peguche** (every 20min. from the main terminal in Otavalo; US$0.18). From Otavalo, follow the main railroad tracks (a road after 4km) out of town. A trail goes uphill to the right as you pass the river (40min.). From the forest entrance, walk 5min., until the waterfall emerges through the misty air. Though there are beautiful trails through much of the woods, **be extremely cautious. Thieves have been known to lurk in the forest.**

For the more ambitious, Las Cascadas de Peguche can be incorporated into a 4hr. hike including **El Lechero, Laguna San Pablo,** and **Peguche.** Instead of taking the trail off of the train tracks between Otavalo and Peguche all the way to the waterfall, follow a side-path up the steep slope to the right and climb through the eucalyptus forest to the top. The forest thins near the summit. Beyond it, standing alone, is the famed **El Lechero,** an ancient tree spoken of in indigenous mythology (1hr.). The tree is not visible from the forest, and there is no obvious path to it; ask a passing *indígena* for help. Continuing on the dirt road, now passing through open fields, brings you to the very crest of **Rey Loma**, where you can see Laguna San Pablo down below. After 20min., at a T intersection, go right, and follow the road downhill to a village. Continue until you reach the asphalt road by the lake (20min.), and turn left. Follow the road around the lake and across the little river, then turn left just past the cinder-block wall (30min.). As this road winds downward, it parallels the little river, which rapidly drops away to become the falls. Pass through the forest, and when you reach a four-way intersection with wooden signs, turn left and go through two consecutive arches. Pass a collection of rocks (thought to be an ancient astronomical instrument) and follow signs to the waterfall (15min. to the bottom, 45min. to the top). Go back to the Plaza Central of Peguche through the arches and along the road (15min.). Hostal Aya Huma (see above) has hand-drawn maps and advice about this and other nearby hikes.

ILUMÁN ☎ 06

Farther up the tracks from Peguche is the less-visited town of hats and healers. **Buses** pass through Peguche going to Ilumán (see **Otavalo: Transportation,** p. 106) and return to the Peguche turn-off along the Panamerican Hwy. The main street **Bolívar** is lined with the offices of yachacs practicing traditional medicine and *sombrería* workshops. Most of the workshops display reasonably priced hats to suit international fashion trends and work with ready-made felted wool from Quito. The six sisters of the Picuasi family and their mother are carrying on their father's business of making **traditional hats** entirely by hand. They clean the raw wool and give a final pumice-stone polish to the wool hats (Natabuela in Ibarra and Pilaguines in Otavalo). To get to the **Picuasi workshop,** go uphill from the main square and left on Luis Mejía. Their house is to the left of the sky-blue Templo Alianza Nueva Vida Ilumán. For a small tip visitors can enter and watch the intensive process unfold. The final product is sought after by the local communities for festivals and pageants and is also for sale starting at US$20 (a steal for something that takes six people an entire day to create.) Wool is carded, boiled, shaped, dried, and scraped smooth every day. Knock on the door or call ahead to arrange a visit. (☎2946 287; pbelencm@hotmail.com). A few blocks south of the Parque Central along Bolívar, Breenan Conterón works on a traditional backstrap loom creating colorful *fajas* (belts). Her shop, **Artesanías Inti Chumbi,** displays crafts from artisans similar to what is found at the Plaza de Ponchos (see **Otavalo,** p. 106). With five to six days advance notice, Inti Chumbi can arrange visits to local weavers and hat-makers and prepare a typical meal complete with *chicha* (fermented yuca juice). (☎2946 387). Artisans work every day; if the place appears closed, ring the bell. Most workshops have no signs and don't receive tourists themselves. Without a tour from Otavalo or Peguche, it takes a lot of asking around and visiting cousins and aunts to find the looms. Whatever the case, get some *papipollo* (chicken and fries) (US$1) for lunch on the Parque Central.

CAYAMBE ☎ 06

The other *mitad del mundo*, Cayambe stretches out under the cloud-obscured Volcán Cayambe at latitude 0 0' 0". This used to be a stop along the way from Quito to Otavalo, but buses now take the Tabacundo route. Despite lack of tourists, the Sunday market stalls extend for blocks past the main square and attract buyers and sellers from throughout the region. On market day (Su), Rocafuerte is clogged all the way from Bolívar to 24 de Mayo, where crowds shop at the main produce market. Walking uphill from the Parque Central through toothpaste and blue-jeans-hawkers leads to a large square where locals sell bright piles of fruits and vegetables. It doesn't take long to realize that the town's speciality is the *bizcocho*, an elongated crunchy biscuit available everywhere fresh from the oven. Cayambe is also known for its cheeses and *manjar de leche*, a kind of caramel custard.

⊟⧉ TRANSPORTATION AND PRACTICAL INFORMATION. Most **buses** arrive at and depart from the traffic circle near the bright yellow **Plaza de Toros** (bull ring) at Sucre and Natalia Jarrín. Buses leave for **Otavalo** (every 10min. 5am-6pm, US$0.75). **Transportes Flor del Valle** runs buses to **Quito. Pick-up trucks** from the **Cooperativas de Camionetas el Nevado** (☎2360 544) wait near the Plaza de Toros. Regular **taxis** can be found at the Parque Central. Volcán Cayambe rises to the east. The **Panamerican Hwy.** borders the main part of town on the west and changes its name to **Natalia Jarrín** upon entering Cayambe near the **bull ring.** The main street in town is **Rocafuerte**, which runs north-south, parallel to the Panamerican Hwy. At the **Parque Central,** Rocafuerte intersects Bolívar. The **tourist office** Terán 702 (☎2361 832 or 2361 591; gobiernomc@andinanet.net), at Sucre in the municipal building at the Parque Central, can arrange tours to nearby sites. Open M-F 8am-1pm and 2-5pm. Many Quito-based **tour** companies offer climbs to the top of Volcán Cayambe, but a few outfits can be hired in Cayambe, sometimes at a lower price. Note that **essential technical climbing equipment is not available for rent in Cayambe. Intl Explorer,** on 10 de Agosto, just off Natalia Jarrín, organizes trips to the lake; hikes up Volcán Cayambe; a 4-day trek around the volcano; daytrips to waterfalls, primary forest, Quilotoma pre-Incaic ruins; tubing; and horseback riding. (☎2360 423; cell 09 7064 403. Open Tu-F 8:30am-12:30pm and 2:30-5:30pm.) **Green Travel,** on Sucre at Rocafuerte near Parque Central, offers daytrips to Laguna Verde and 2-day trips to the summit of Volcán Cayambe. (☎2363 673; greentra@interactive.net.ec. Summit trips US$150-225; price depends on group size. Open M-F 8:30am-1pm and 3pm-6pm.) **Banco del Pichincha,** is at the corner of Bolívar and Ascázubi. **Police** (☎2360 201) are on the corner of Bolívar and Juan Montalvo. **Hospital Raul Maldonado** (24hr. emergency ☎2361 053; hospitalization 2360 072), near Hostal Mitad del Mundo at Córdova Galarza and Rocafuerte, offers services in pediatrics, gynecology, surgery, general medicine, and ambulance pick-up. **Andinatel,** is near Parque Central at Sucre and Ascázubi. (☎2360 105, only answered M-F 8am-4pm. Open daily 8am-8pm.) Find **Internet** at **DM Computación,** on Bolívar at Sucre. (☎2361 873. US$0.80 per min. Open daily 9am-7:30pm.)

⧉⧉ ACCOMMODATIONS AND FOOD. Cayambe's hotels are bland but invariably equipped with TV. More interesting options are along the Panamerican Hwy. to the north. **Hostería Mitad del Mundo ❷,** on Natalia Jarrín, boasts private baths, TVs, and large windows, and has a restaurant, swimming pool, and sauna (pool and sauna open only on the weekends; US$3 for guests or public). It can be noisy at night. (US$9 per person.) **Hostería Imperial ❸,** Ascázubi NO-62, at Libertad. Cement rooms are small; some have windows. (☎2364 417. Hot private baths and TVs. Singles US$8; doubles US$16; triples US$24.) Cayambe's best restaurants are strung along the Panamerican Highway (Natalia Jarrín in town). There are also a few worthy spots in the center of town. **Café Aroma ❷,** on Bolívar and Rocafuerte, serves typical food in a fresh and inviting atmosphere. (☎2361 773. Set-menu lunches US$3.50-4.50. Open M-T and Th-Sa 7am-9pm, Su 7am-5pm.) **Restaurante Los Andes ❶,** at Natalia Jarrín and Calderón, has a spotless dining room. (☎2360 187. Set-menu lunches US$1.40, *menú* US$1.20-2.50. Open daily 7am-10pm.)

◙ SIGHTS. In the municipal building a small museum displays archaeological information about the area. South of the city near Cangahua are the ruins of **Quito Loma,** where as many as 4000 people once lived. Both the tourism office and Inti

Explorer have information on the ruins and offer tours (US$25-30). See, smell, and taste the local specialty fresh from a wood-fired oven at the **Horno de Bizcochos San Pedro**, on Olmedo between Bolívar and Sucre near the cemetery. From the Mitad del Mundo monument a short path leads up to the Castillo Guachalá, once the residence of ex-president Neptolivo Nifáz. On the first of Aug. each year, a competition called the **Ruta del Hielo** draws attention to the ancient practice of portaging huge blocks of ice from Volcán Cayambe to town (still a source of income for some). Competitors are judged based on how fast they descend and how much ice they carry. The main attraction, **Volcán Cayambe**, within the **Reserva Ecológica Cayambe-Coca**, is a nearby presence, mostly invisible above the clouds. Lots of tours go straight from Quito to the Volcano but it is also possible to arrange for a guide to the summit from Cayambe through Green Travel and Inti Explorer (see p. 122). Access a nearby refuge (3800m) by four-wheel-drive; then head for the summit. The climb (7hr.) requires technical equipment, such as a helmet, climbing equipment, etc. Make sure to acclimatize for a week before making a bid for the summit. Then trek down to Papallacta to ease those sore muscles, or hop on a bus travelling along the Panamerican Hwy. from Cayambe (see p. 122).

COTACACHI ☎ 06

Planted 12km northwest of Otavalo under the watchful eye of Volcán Cotacachi (4939m), this town is renowned as Ecuador's leatherwork capital. The stores that line 10 de Agosto promise more leatherwork than a sadomasochist's kinkiest dream. Cotacachi still has a bit of colonial architecture, and is a good starting point for getting involved in nearby ecological and community-based tourism.

⌐⑫ TRANSPORTATION AND PRACTICAL INFORMATION. Buses to Otavalo leave from the corner of Salinas and 10 de Agosto, or on Peña Herrera near the park (30min., every 15min. until 6pm, US$0.25). Buses to Ibarra leave from the Parque Central and the bus station (every 15min., 5:30am-7pm). Buses enter town from the Panamerican Hwy. on **10 de Agosto** (where most leather stores are found). 10 de Agosto is the main street running east-west and **Bolívar** intersects it running north-south. Follow Bolívar toward the large cathedral to reach **Parque Central.** Inside the Casa de la Cultura on Bolívar and 9 de Octubre, the **tourist office** can help with visa renewal and similar complaints, as well as provide information about sights and trail systems still under development. (☎ 2915 140; www.cotacachi.gov.ec.) **Banco del Pichincha**, at Roca and Imbabura, has 24hr. Cirrus **ATM** and offers V cash advances. (☎ 2915 456; open M-F 9am-4pm.) **Police** (☎ 2915 101), are on Rocafuerte between Montalvo and Bolívar. The **pharmacy** is on 10 de Agosto and Bolívar. (☎ 2915 446; open daily 7:30am-8pm.) The **hospital** is south of the main part of town on Moncayo between Moreno and Eloy Alfaro. (☎ 2915 118 or 2915 506. Ambulance services. Open 8am-1pm, 1:45-4:45pm.) **Andinatel** is behind the church on Sucre between Peñaherrera and Moreno (☎ 2915 104).

⌐⑬ ACCOMMODATIONS AND FOOD. Cotacachi's cheap lodgings are adequate but uninspiring. It is possible to stay in a family home in the indigenous communities near Cotacachi (see **Runa Tupari,** p. 106). **Hostal Sumac Huasi ❶,** Juan Montalvo 1109, at Pedro Moncayo, is *indígena*-owned, and decorated with exquisite tapestries and rugs. All rooms have private baths and TVs. (☎ 2915 873. Breakfast included. Singles US$18; doubles US$25; triples US$35. Traveler's checks accepted.) **Hostal Bachita ❶,** on Sucre between Peñaherrera and 24 de Mayo. The cheapest option has the best views. Rooms 7, 8, 9 share a cold bath, while Room 10 has a hot private bath. (☎ 2915 063. Singles and doubles US$4 per person, with private bath US$5.) Cotacachi's speciality *carne colorada* (literally red meat) is advertised on every block. It's not t-bones or flank-steak, but pork seasoned with the local spice *achiote*. This and other *comida típica*, including seafood, comprises the town's culinary offerings. **El Mesón de las Flores ❸** (☎ 2915 264; fax 2915 828), on Moreno and Bolívar, serves standard fare (US$5-6) in an unbeatable interior patio atmosphere. Open 7am-9pm. **Centro Ecológico Café**, Peñaherrera 15-78, at Morales. The coffee shop atmosphere hasn't caught on with the locals yet, but the organic chocolates, shade-grown coffee, tea-selection, and loft sitting area are popular with foreigners. The main attraction isn't the fare but a chance to meet other volunteers and travelers and to pick up pamphlets about eco-opportunities all over Ecuador. (☎ 2916 525 or 2916 465. Open Th-Su 11am-6pm.) **La Marqueza ❶**, on 10 de Agosto and Bolívar. This imposing dark-wood dining room serves *comida típica* and seafood. (☎ 2915 488. Entrees US$3-5.50. Open daily 7:30am-9:30pm. DC/MC/V.)

◪ SIGHTS. One of the access points to **Reserva Ecológica Cotacachi-Cayapas: Zona Alta** is at **Laguna de Cuicocha**. Here, near-vertical walls of a volcanic crater plummet to the deep waters of the lake; two islands jut up from the middle. A **5km path** follows the crater cliff with views of the water and surrounding peaks. The **official path** begins counter-clockwise just inside the entrance to the park, and takes 4-5hr. to complete. It climbs for the first third of the hike to a lookout point called **El Mirador** and then begins to descend. About two-thirds of the way around the lake, the path descends into vegetation and is slightly harder to follow (keep the lake on the left) until it emerges onto the ridge again and meets up with a dirt road that comes back around past the restaurant El Mirador and ends up just past the entrance point. Trucks from Cotacachi will drive the 13km to the lake (one-way US$5; round-trip US$10 may include the time they wait for you). Taxi drivers may agree to return later in the day if you plan to hike the entire rim. Settle on a price before getting in the cab. A boat makes trips around the lake (US$1.50 per person). Two hostels with restaurants—both called **El Mirador**—have set up camp by the lake. The government runs the lower, fancier one. It has an oversized dining room with windows that overlook the lake and Otavalo weavings on the walls.

From the lake, an ascent of Volcán Cotacachi begins from the antennas usually visible on the steep slope above Laguna de Cuicocha. The antennas can be accessed by a four-wheel-drive vehicle. From there it's about 3hr. (2hr. to descend) to the summit. The path is best when there is snow to anchor the loose rock, but always wear a helmet and seek shelter while resting. The path goes up about 1km before reaching a fork. The path to the right is shorter but requires technical equipment. Most hikers go to the left and follow the cairns. The trail climbs until a brief 300m flat stretch before climbing again. For the easiest path, continue around the back of the rock. Those who choose to summit without a guide must be cautious, as **hikers have gotten lost on this peak.** Camionetas charge US$40 (one-way) to the antennas and don't always make it. **Ernesto Cevillanos** of the smaller El Mirador restaurant farther up the hill has 30 years of experience climbing the mountain. He can serve as a guide or give a guaranteed ride (one-way US$50) to the antennas. Cevillanos will also guide treks from Cuicocha across the remote *páramo* of Cotacachi-Cayapas to the **Lagos de Piñán**. (☎ 06 248 039; cell 09 9908 757.)

▨ INTAG CLOUD FOREST   ☎ 06

Situated on the verdant western slopes of the Andes, this privately owned reserve protects a small portion of Ecuador's endangered cloud forests. To combat deforestation, proprietors Carlos and Sandy Zorilla have purchased as much of the land as possible. With elevations ranging 1750-2800m and temperatures ranging 12-

27°C (55-80°F), Intag's dynamism is reflected in its cloud variations, constant humidity, and incredible variety of flora and fauna. The forest is heaven for bird-watchers—about 200 different species have been identified. A stay on the **reserve** ❺ includes lodging, vegetarian meals, and a bilingual guide. Wood cabin rooms have thick blankets, and solar-heated water flows from rustic outdoor showers. (US$45 per person per night; min. 2 nights.) The Zorillas require reservations and only accept groups of eight or more; they can arrange a group for you. Call a few months in advance ☎2648 509, or email intagcloud@yahoo.com.

LA ESPERANZA   ☎06

The tiny, tranquil town of La Esperanza, on the slopes of **Volcán Imbabura** (4621m), is so small it only has one road—an ancient Inca trail since covered with cobblestones. It has a few master leatherworkers, but it is mostly known as a popular base for hiking Imbabura. To arrive at the volcano, head toward **Loma Cubilche** (3826m) and turn right on the street before the bridge. This road goes most of the way up, and various paths lead to the top. A 3hr. ascent of Imbabura is also possible after a taxi or camioneta ride (US$6) to the end of the road. **Casa Aída** has resident guides available for this hike (US$12 per person). For a good day-hike, try climbing Loma Cubilche (3hr. up, 2hr. return) to see the small **lake** on top and the amazing views back toward Ibarra and off toward San Pablo. **Buses** from Ibarra to La Esperanza (30min., every 30min., US$0.22) leave from Parque Grijalva or on the corner of de la Torre and Retorno. Taxis cost US$5. If you prefer to walk, the hike to La Esperanza is along Retorno, which turns into La Esperanza's main road (2hr., 7km). La Esperanza's only road, **Galo Plaza,** runs toward Imbabura. ▧**Hostal Casa Aída** ❷, the green-and-yellow building on the right, far up the hill from Ibarra, is a converted 300-year-old brick factory. The complex contains psychedelically painted dorms and a five-person straw hut with two loft beds accessible only by step ladder. Thick brick walls provide plenty of warmth on frigid nights. (☎2642 020. Hot shared baths. US$6 per person.) Casa Aída also boasts a fabulous **restaurant** ❶. Outdoor dining in the vegetable garden provides a view of Imbabura. Try the cornmeal pancakes with berry sauce and Aída's vegetarian dishes (US$2.50).

IBARRA   ☎06

Amidst colonial-style homes and monumental churches, Ibarra's professionals race around in taxis, buses, and Mercedes Benzes. Public parks in the northern part of the city provide a respite from the fast-paced provincial capital. Although it's not much of a tourist city, Ibarra is home to gorgeous—and underrated—churches, plazas, and public buildings. The city also serves as a good base for trips to San Antonio, Valle del Chota, La Esperanza, and Volcán Imbabura.

▐ TRANSPORTATION

Buses: Ibarra's many bus lines serve most of the Northern Highlands and the Ecuadorian coast. Most buses arrive at and depart from Ibarra's shiny new **Terminal Terrestre** on Tobar y Tobar and Eugenio Espejo southwest of the obelisk. To: **Quito** (3hr., every hr. 2:35am-9pm, US$2.50); **Esmeraldas** (9hr, US$8); **San Lorenzo** (2½hr.; 4, 5, 6, 8, 10, 11:30am, noon, 2:30, 6pm; US$4); **Santo Domingo** (4hr., every 15min., US$4); **Tulcán** (2¼hr.; 5, 5:45, 9:15am, 12:45, 1:45, 4, 6pm; US$2.50); **Otavalo** (45min., every 20min. 5am-9pm, US$0.45).

Taxis: In parks and near bus stations find **Cooperativa de Taxis Lagos** (☎2955 150) and **CIA Radio Taxi** (☎2641 777; operates 24hr.).

Ibarra

🏠 ACCOMMODATIONS
Hostal el Ejecutivo, 10
Hotel Imbabura, 3
Hotel La Nueva Estancia, 1

🍎 FOOD
Café Arte, 2
Chifa Muy Buena, 5
Frutitas, 4
El Alpargate, 11
El Charrito, 7
Restaurante Casa Blanca, 8

🍷 NIGHTLIFE
Café Arte, 2
El Encuentro, 9
Gasoline Bar, 6
Mi Viejo, 12

⚡🔲 ORIENTATION AND PRACTICAL INFORMATION

The white **obelisk** towering in the city's southeast corner serves as a good landmark. Facing the obelisk from the train station, **Mariano Acosta,** which becomes **Velasco,** intersects **Olmedo, Bolívar,** and **Sucre,** the street for hotels and restaurants.

Tourist Office: Ministerio de Turismo (☎ 2608 489; mibarratourism@hotmail.com). The new government-run tourism office has information on Ibarra and some pamphlets about attractions in the rest of Imbabura.

Banks: Banco del Pacífico (☎ 2957 714), at Olmedo and Moncayo, changes AmEx traveler's checks. 24hr. MC **ATM.** Open M-F 8:30am-4pm, Sa 9:30am-2pm.

Laundry Service: Lavafacil, Sucre 03-51 (☎ 2950 850 or 2955 764), at Grijalva. Washes and dries for US$1.20 per kg. Open M-Sa 8:30am-7:30pm.

Emergency: ☎ 101 or 911.

Police: Policía Nacional (☎ 2954 444), on Jaime Roldós near Sanchez and Cifuentes.

Pharmacy: Farmacia La Merced, Sanchez y Cifuentes 7-15 and García Moreno on the corner of Parque la Merced. Open M-Sa 8am-9pm, Su 8am-1:30pm, 4pm-9pm.

Medical Services: Hospital San Vicente de Paul, Luís Vargas Torres 1-156 (☎ 2972 272). Doctors see new patients M-F 10am-noon. Patients arrive at 7am to wait in line for medical attention. **Clínica Mariano Acosta,** Mariano Acosta 1127 (☎/fax 2642 211), is a 24hr. emergency clinic and pharmacy.

Telephones: Andinatel, at Sucre 4-48 and Moreno. Open daily 8am-10pm. **Branch** (☎2959 104), at Sánchez and Velasco. Open daily 8am-10pm.

Internet Access: Internet el Ejecutivo, Bolívar 969, between Colón and Velasco, in the lobby of Hostal el Ejecutivo (☎2956 575). US$0.90 per hr. Open daily 8am-10pm.

Post Office: Salinas 664 (☎2643 135; fax 2958 038), at Oviedo. Open M-F 8am-7pm, Sa 8am-1pm. **DHL** (☎2957 766; fax 2955 270), at Rocafuerte and Flores, in the Intipungo offices. Open M-F 9am-1pm, 2:30-6:30pm; Sa 9am-1pm.

ACCOMMODATIONS

While there is certainly no shortage of rooms in Ibarra, high-quality rooms at moderate prices can be hard to find. Budget accommodations gather along Olmedo.

Hotel Imbabura, Oviedo 9-33 (☎2950 155; fax 2958 521), between Narváez and Cifuentes, 1½ blocks from Parque La Merced. Ask for a room with windows. A lovely inner courtyard with indigenous musical instrument decorations and a goldfish pond compensate for a lack of modern amenities. The owners have plenty of information about sights and offer Spanish lessons. Ask about the artifact collection. Shared baths. US$5. ❶

Hostal la Nueva Estancia, García Moreno 7-58 (☎2951 444), at Sánchez y Cifuentes on Parque La Merced. If you've had enough funk, spunk and character a bit of splurge means color-coordinated carpet, bedspread, wallpaper, drapes, and furniture—all in aquamarine and matching dark-wood furniture. Rooms 209, 210, 309, and 310 have balconies overlooking the park; interior rooms aren't worth the price. US$12. ❸

Hostal el Ejecutivo, Bolívar 969 (☎2956 577), between Colón and Velasco. Cable TVs, Internet cafe, phones, and private baths make up for lack of courtyard ambience and shabby rooms. US$5. ❷

FOOD

Most places cater to working people on lunch breaks. So do as the locals do, and pick the eatery nearest you. Munch on international fare (shawarma, burritos, and burgers) along Oviedo, near Olmedo and Bolívar. Find food stands selling the local specialty sweets, *nogadas* (walnut nougat) and *arrope de mora* (blackberry syrup), along Parque la Merced. The same kiosks offer late-night snacks F-Sa.

Restaurante Casa Blanca, Bolívar 783 (☎2952 124), at Pedro Moncayo. Locals fill tables surrounding a small courtyard to devour cheap *empanadas, humitas,* and quilombitos (typical snacks) and drink tea and coffee. The set-menu lunch is a deal: soup, entree, dessert, and juice US$1.40. Open daily 8:30am-8pm. ❶

El Alpargate, Barrio el Alpargate 1-59/1-113 (☎2644 062). This is the dressed up version of Ibarra street food: *mote* (corn), cheese, avocado, *empanada, fritada* (fried meat), and potatoes. Huge set-menu lunch US$4.50. Open daily noon-6pm. ❷

Café Arte, Salinas 5-43 (☎2950 806), at Flores, is a cafe and gallery. Features a unique combination of coffees, Mexican specialties, and cocktails (US$2-4). Cultural films and concerts F-Sa 9pm. Open daily 9am-midnight. Knock during slow hours. ❷

Frutitas, Flores 671 (☎2950 430), at Bolívar, has breakfasts, espresso drinks, healthy fruit salads and sandwiches, and not-so-healthy ice cream sundaes (from US$1.50). People-watch from outdoor tables. Open daily 7:30am-7:30pm. ❶

Chifa Muy Buena, Olmedo 7-25 (☎2955 875), at Flores, serves big plates of fried rice and noodles any time, night or day.

El Charrito (☎2952 152), at Oviedo and Olmedo. A shotgun saloon that serves big juicy burgers (US$2-3) and beer. Open M-Th and Su noon-11pm; F-Sa noon-3am. V.

Helados de Paila Rosalía Suárez, Oviedo 7-82 (☎ 2958 778), at Olmedo. A wooden Mickey Mouse welcomes you to this ice cream shop, where the homemade flavors are sure to delight. The owner, grandson of Rosalía herself, has become an icon by perpetuating the 107-year-old recipe. Cone US$0.50, cup US$0.60. Open daily 7am-7pm. ❶

Pizza Pepperoni, Guerrero 5-64 (☎2952 512), at Bolívar. Fresh pizzas served up under posters of American pop stars and blaring TV or in the comfort of your own room. Personal pies US$4.50, large pizzas US$8.70. Open daily 4-10:30pm. ❷

SIGHTS

Ibarra offers a few landmarks of interest if you're out for a stroll. Rising more than 30m high, the big white **obelisk** at Narváez and Velasco honors Miguel de Ibarra, who founded this Spanish colony in 1606. **Parque La Merced,** on Flores between Cifuentes and Olmedo, is particularly beautiful. On the west side of the park, the **Basílica la Merced** supports a portrayal of the Virgin Mary adorned with a silver crown (only open to the public sporadically). The eclectic **Parque Moncayo,** on Flores between Bolívar and Sucre, boasts exceptional architecture, especially that of the **cathedral** and the municipal building. While the cathedral's golden altar outshines everything else, the building also houses huge portraits of all 12 apostles, painted by local artist Rafael Troya. The spotless lawns and benches of the parks invite city-dwellers to slow down for an ice cream or *nogada* in the shade.

ⓡ NIGHTLIFE

Bars and discos come to life F-Sa. Many options are along Oviedo and Torreon.

Gasoline Bar, at Olmedo and Oviedo, is a bit like a mechanic's shop with plenty of metal and pictures of girls stuck to the walls. Dance to techno, reggae, salsa, and hip-hop blasted from numerous speakers on the spacious dance floor. Open F-Sa 9:30pm-late.

El Encuentro, Olmedo 959 (☎2951 516). Its unassuming doorway opens onto a leafy courtyard. Find the intimate bar on the other side. Quirky antiques and murals decorate the walls. Great drink selection. The owners run a *pizzería* upstairs. Open M-Sa 5-11pm.

Mi Viejo, Tedoro Gómez 9-48 (☎2956 885 or 2609 798), at Sanchez y Cifuentes. Groove to live music (salsa to folkloric) within an intimate, all-wood setting F-Sa. Try hervida, the local concoction. Open M-Th 4:30-11pm; F-Sa 4:30pm-2am.

SAN ANTONIO DE IBARRA   ☎06

With its economy firmly rooted in woodcarving, San Antonio de Ibarra caters to tourists with a hankering for carved chess sets or exquisite wooden figurines. The town offers little else, but the work is of such high quality that San Antonio has secured a place for itself among the South American *artesanía* elite. Every other door around the Parque Calderón or along 27 de Noviembre, which runs alongside the park, sells variations on a few themes. Particularly popular are horses, religious icons, nudes, and Don Quixote. The **Unión Artesanal de San Antonio de Ibarra,** beside Parque Calderón, is a set of 11 woodcarving cooperatives that sell pieces straight from the tables they're made on. (Open daily 9am-6pm. V.)

Travel down 27 de Noviembre about a little more than a block from the park for **Internet access.** Lunch at **My Bryan** on Parque Calderón for *comida típica.* (☎2932 731. Set-menu lunch US$1.50.) Walk 15min. from San Antonio de Ibarra to wind up at the house of eccentric sculptor and poet **Carlos Moreta.** Carlos is gradually making his home into a bar-gallery-hostal, with exceptional views of

BORDER CROSSING: INTO COLOMBIA
Crossing the border *(frontera)* between Ecuador and Colombia at the Rumichaca Bridge is usually straightforward. Tourists are required to present a valid **passport** to be stamped at the immigration office of each country, and to turn in and/or receive a 90-day tourist card. Officials are very strict about only accepting passports as identification. However, a **provisional passport** may be acceptable. Very few nationalities need a visa to enter Colombia. Occasionally, backpackers will be asked to prove that they have sufficient funds (US$20, students US$10) for each day they plan to stay in Ecuador or Colombia. Officials may also ask to see a round-trip ticket proving that a visitor intends to leave the country within 90 days, the maximum amount of time a traveler can spend in either country in a one-year period. To stay longer, you'll need to obtain a **visa** (see **Visas and Work Permits,** p. 12). Tulcán's border and the **Ecuadorian Immigration Office** (☎/fax 2980 704) is open 24hr. Ecuador charges a US$4 **exit tax.** (The immigration office in San Lorenzo does not charge an exit tax.) If crossing from Colombia into Ecuador, be sure to get your passport stamped inside the Colombian immigration office, as thieves often pretend to be border officers. Even if you have days left on your Ecuadorian visa, you lose those days as soon as you enter Colombia and upon returning get an entirely new visa. **Check the current political situation in Colombia before entering the country as crime and civil unrest can prove dangerous to tourists. As of August 2004, Let's Go does not recommend travel in Colombia or the northern Ecuadorian provinces of Carchí, Sucumbíos, or Orellana.**

the volcano above and city below. As of summer 2004, Carlos may offer the self-proclaimed last true backpacker accommodations—bring your own sleeping bag. Check with Carlos to find out about the state of accommodations. (larvauniversal@hotmail.com. Full kitchen access. Rooms US$4.) Cooperativo 28 de Septiembre and San Miguel de Ibarra labeled "San Antonio" both go to San Antonio's Parque Calderón and can be caught at the obelisk, near the corner of Acosta and Chica Narváez in Ibarra (15min., every 10min., US$0.18). A taxi costs US$2.

THE CENTRAL HIGHLANDS

For many, central Ecuador is Ecuador. Encompassing the towering Andes that divide the country in two, this area is home to almost half of the country's population. At this high altitude, life is defined by the terrain. Locals are plagued by the constant threat of towering volcanoes but reap the fruits of the fertile land. The mountains, folded appendages of the earth jutting into the stratosphere, have the power to awe and astonish. All along the Panamerican Hwy., networks of indigenous communities live amid sparkling lakes and lush cloud forests. Locals speak Quichua on the street, wear traditional pouches and fedoras, and specialize in the crafts of their ancestors The most popular (and touristed) region in mainland Ecuador lies in the series of valleys south of Quito. In 1802, German explorer Alexander Humboldt named this seismically active zone between Quito and Riobamba the "avenue of the volcanoes." Monoliths such as Cotopaxi, Tunguarahua, Chimborazo, and Sangay line the path, luring adventurers with their breathtaking views and oxygen-starved ascents. Perceptive travelers will notice that almost every sizable city between Quito and Cuenca has been destroyed at one time or another at the whim of the tectonic plates that slide beneath them. At the base of the mountains, flora-filled parks and pleasant highland cities beg for exploration.

HIGHLIGHTS OF THE CENTRAL HIGHLANDS

ASCEND to the farthest point from Earth's core on **Volcán Chimborazo** (p. 162).

SOAK in the soothing hot spring baths at **Baños** (p. 150) after an invigorating hike.

FORGET the rest of your vacation and lounge about the **Latacunga Loop** (see p. 142).

MACHACHI AND ALOASÍ   ☎02

About 35km (and a 1hr. bus ride) south of Quito, the twin towns of Machachi (pop. 23,900) and Aloasí (pop. 6700) provide travelers with a quaint jumping-off point for excursions to several good acclimatization hikes to the volcanoes Corazón and Rumiñahui and do so with sufficient small-town charm, provided one looks in the right places. Try to be in Machachi in July, when the festival of La Chagra attracts people from all over to enjoy good food, parades, and horse races on the town's back roads. Machachi is by far the dominant of the two towns, providing Aloasí with everything from bank service to good restaurants to, well, everything. Although the central plaza and the adjacent church comprise Machachi's center, most of the action in this small town takes place between the square and the Panamerican Hwy. Aloasí depends on Machachi for everything but quiet and calm; it has enough of those to cover all of the southern Highlands. Orientation in Aloasí begins once you have been dropped off in front of the school near a small park by either a camioneta or the bus from Machachi. Don't worry if this sounds vague; there are only a few places to go from here.

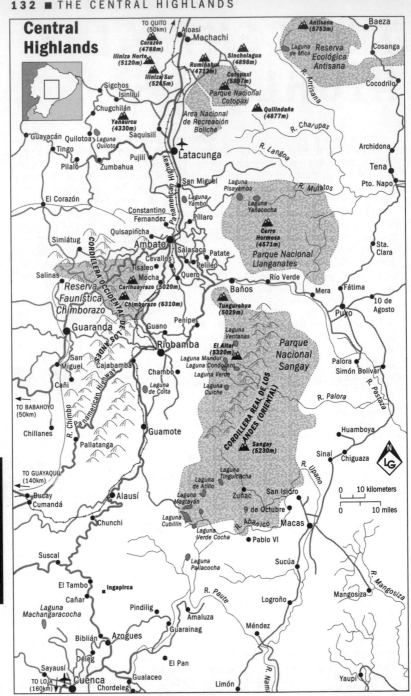

Central Highlands

⊏ TRANSPORTATION. Machachi is accessible by any **bus** running north or south on the Panamerican Hwy. From the highway, walk into town toward the statue of Mariscal Sucre on horseback. From **Quito**, catch the "Mejía" bus behind Terminal Terrestre, with "Machachi" in the window (US$0.75). In Machachi, face the church on Amazonas; turn right; and walk three blocks. Blue buses from the bus company Cooperativa La Dolorosa line up here along Amazonas and leave for **Aloasí** frequently (US$0.18). Alternatively, **camionetas** (white pickup trucks) can shuttle you to Aloasí for US$1. Don't accept anything higher. Camionetas taking groups over to Aloasí should not run more than US$0.50.

⚠ PRACTICAL INFORMATION. In Machachi, **Banco de Guayaquil** (☎2314 736), at Amazonas and Benitez, right next to Steakhouse El Rincón del Valle, has an **ATM** with credit card–cash advances. **Prado Banco,** on Pareja and Bolívar, exchanges traveler's checks and foreign currency. (☎2316 192. Open M-F 8am-6pm, Sa-Su 8am-1pm.) Contact **Destacamiento de Machachi** (☎2315 345) 24hr. for emergencies. **Policía Nacional** (☎2314 736), at Amazonas and Antonio Benitez, is available 24hr. **Hospital Cantonal Machachi** (☎2315 957), has a 24hr. emergency room. From the church, walk 3 blocks on Colón and turn left on Pareja. It's a white building with a baby blue metal gate. **Andinatel** and **BellSouth** branches along Amazonas west of the square (to the right as one stands facing the church) have telephones. **Internet** is available in a few places west of the square on Amazonas. In Aloasí, find police services at **Tenencia Política,** on Simon Bolívar, between José Ignacio al Baja and Victor Velasco. Turn away from the school and walk to the far left corner of the park, cross the street and enter through the door facing the street corner. (☎2309 058; open M-F 8am-noon and 2-6pm.) The hospital is **Subcentro de Salúd.** From the school, walk to the right. After the first left turn at Coliseo Carlos Alfredo Mosquera, take a cobblestone road on your left. (☎2309 480; open M-F 8am-4pm.)

⌂⌂ FOOD AND ACCOMMODATIONS. Amazonas in Machachi is filled with street vendors, bakeries, and small restaurants offering *almuerzos* (2-3 course lunches) for US$1-1.50. Most accommodations in Machachi are a few blocks to the south of this main strip. ▧**Hospedería Chiguac ❷**, at Los Caras and Colón. From Amazonas walk 5 blocks south of the church on Colón (the street directly to the left of the church and bordering the square) and turn right at the intersection with 3 white fences and 1 brick fence. A llama in the front yard and several small but vigilant dogs will welcome you to Machachi's best deal. The whitewashed walls and wooded rafters lend a cozy, lodge-like feel to the living room, where the owners will shower you with attention. (☎2310 396; germanimor@punto.net.ec Doubles US$30.) **Hotel La Estancia Real ❸** is two blocks to the right from the church. Turn left and walk until you hit Barriga, where the hotel is 1 block to the left of a large, partly-canopied field. All rooms have TV and private baths. (☎2315 760. Breakfast included. Singles US$10; matrimonial US$12; doubles US$16.) Aloasí offers few places to stay, but is worth checking out if you want to hear just how quiet the Andean countryside can be.

For food in Machachi, try **Casablanca ❶**, at Amazonas and Luis Cordero, has *comida típica* as well as chicken and burgers. (☎2236 316. *Almuerzos* US$1.30; ¼ chicken with rice US$2. Open 9am-10pm). **Steakhouse El Rincón de Valle ❷**, Amazonas 413 (☎2314 186), at Benitez, right next to Banco de Guayaquil, 3 blocks right of the church, gets you your meat fix for the day. Huge dinners including beef and chicken done up in multiple styles US$8. Steak, fries, and a salad around US$3.

◩ SIGHTS. Fuentes Tesalia is the only tourist attraction in Machachi or Aloasí that doesn't include traipsing up and down a mountain is a visit to the Fuentes Tesalia, the factory where the omnipresent bottled waters Güitig (carbonated, or *con gas*) and Tesalia (uncarbonated, or *sin gas*) are produced. You'll know you're close when you're in Machachi—Güitig has its brand name stamped on everything from storefronts to park benches. For US$0.50, visitors can lounge around in a well maintained park with a snack bar, volleyball courts, and a soccer field and even take a dip in one of two pools filled with the very same Güitig *(con gas)* that is sold in stores! The pools are advertised to have therapeutic qualities; you can be the judge of that. To get there, hire a camioneta to take you to "Fuentes Tesalia" (US$2). Camionetas should be waiting to take you back. If you're lucky you'll be able to hop onto one of the buses that carries factory workers back to Machachi.

VOLCÁN RUMIÑAHUI

Rumiñahui (4712m) means "face of stone" in Quichua, named after the Inca general who destroyed Quito in 1534 rather than cede it intact to the Spaniards. The three peaks, when not shrouded in clouds, provide views of Cotopaxi, Sincholagua, the Ilinizas, and much of the Avenue of the Volcanoes. In addition, this moderately difficult **hike** is the perfect way to acclimatize before contemplating an assault on Cotopaxi.

From the Limpiopungo parking lot (see below), follow the clearly trodden trail on the right side past the end of the boggy section of the lake. Turn left and walk across the field to the valley on the other side. The trail begins just to the left of a small stream at the entrance to the valley. Continue on the trail with the stream on your right until the trail disappears; continue with the stream on the right. For the central (and least technically challenging) peak, ascend the ridge you see to the right as you face the peaks. When you've ascended halfway up the peak, start cutting left across the ridge toward the central peak. If you go too high or low, you won't be able to cut across for the ascent due to dramatic drop-offs. Continue the ascent under the central peak; trails here and on the edge are not marked. At the top, some rock-climbing skills may be required to reach the summit, but a less challenging finish at the ridges between the peaks offers excellent views of either side of the mountain. The easiest way to descend is to retrace your steps, beginning the sideways traversal at the correct height to avoid drop-offs. Bring along cold- and wet-weather gear, as the climate can change rapidly. (Round-trip from lake 5-6hr.) For those short on time or lung capacity, the hike to the boggy area at the base of Rumiñahui is another great way to explore the park (round-trip 3hr.).

Those in need of a mellower hike should stick by the base and take a stroll around Lake Limpiopungo. Three different tributaries flowing down Rumuñahui's flanks fill this lake, but only to 60cm at its deepest point. On a clear day, the volcano is reflected perfectly in the calm waters. To get here from the museum, continue down the main park road past two campground signs, bearing left at the sign for the lake and arriving at the parking lot (1hr. walk). The lake is 24km from the park entrance at the Panamerican Hwy. (US$25-30 round-trip in a rented 4x4). Facing the lake, begin the hike on the far right side, following the trail around both the lake and boggy area beyond (1hr.). Refrain from taking shortcuts across shallow sections, since there are quicksand-like conditions.

PARQUE NACIONAL COTOPAXI ☎03

Cotopaxi, derived from Quichua, means "neck of the moon," probably referring to the certain times of the year when the moon appears to rest on the summit of Volcán Cotopaxi (5897m), the park's centerpiece. *Indígenas*, mountaineers, and seekers of beauty have worshiped the volcano for years, despite (or perhaps because of) its historically destructive tendencies. Cotopaxi last blew its top in

1877 and has done so every 130 or so years. So the time is ripe. Since 2001, the volcano's temperature has risen from 8°C to 40°C. Scientists predict that when Cotopaxi does erupt, its innards will form a 40-80m high wall of lava-and-everything-that-lava-picks-up, and that it will travel at roughly 60km per hr., reaching Quito in 30min., easily beating rush-hour traffic.

While many visitors come to scale the lava rock, the park offers subtler pleasures as well. The flower-filled and windswept *páramo* surrounding the peak teems with animals, and the Ministerio del Ambiente, Ecuador's park and forest service, has undertaken efforts to nurture and preserve many of them. Today, the park is hopping with white-tailed deer, which have made an impressive comeback under the watchful eyes of park management. Hot on their tails are Andean pumas, whose numbers have slowly but steadily climbed since the mid-1970s. Other mammals are seldom seen, but include the Andean fox, Andean spectacled bear, and wild horses. The park has received much attention as the last refuge of the endangered Andean condor (fewer than 100 remain in the world, and seven live here), but also boasts such regional rarities as the hillstar, the lapwing, the gull, and the tongue-twisting carunculated caracara.

AT A GLANCE

AREA: 334 sq. km

CLIMATE: June and July have high winds but are still the best visiting months. Nights are cold.

HIGHLIGHTS: Volcán Cotopaxi, Volcán Rumiñahui, Inca ruins, Lake Limpiopungo

GATEWAYS: Quito (p. 81) and Latacunga (p. 138)

CAMPING: Included in entrance fee

FEES AND HOURS: Entrance US$10, children US$5. Open daily 8am-5pm, last entry 3pm.

⌐ TRANSPORTATION

Four-by-four transportation is recommended to access the park, since the hike from the nearest bus stop is not particularly scenic (2hr. to the park entrance, 4hr. to the lake). **Buses** going between Quito and Latacunga can drop passengers at the park's southern access road, at Santa Rita. (From Latacunga: 30min., every 10min., US$0.30; from Quito: 1½hr., every 10min., US$1.50.) Those who risk hitchhiking say that it is fairly easy on weekends to catch a ride from the intersection of the southern access road and the Panamerican Hwy. However, *Let's Go* does not recommend hitchhiking. From Santa Rita, **taxis** and **trucks** take passengers to the park refuge (US$18) or the lake (US$15-25). Most hotels and hostels in the area can arrange group tours and transportation to the park.

⁊ PRACTICAL INFORMATION

Park Information: The park police manning the **entrance gate (el control)** can answer questions. A tiny **museum** on the path up to the campgrounds is a tribute to the national park and is furnished with stuffed wildlife, a 3-D representation of the park, and wall-to-wall info on Cotopaxi's history. Outside the museum is a helpful **map** of the park, which shows trails leading to the base of Rumiñahui. Museum open daily 8am-noon and 1-5pm.

Supplies: Supplies are available in both Quito (see p. 88) and Latacunga (see **Tours,** p. 139). For info on what to bring, see **Camping and Hiking Equipment,** p. 40.

Maps: The best place to buy a park **map** is in **Instituto Geográfico Militar** (see **Quito: Sights,** p. 95) or one of the outdoor stores in the Mariscal region of New Quito.

Tours: Quito is known to have more reputable guides than Latacunga, although both cities offer a wide variety of options (see **Latacunga: Tours,** p. 139, and **Quito: Tours,** p. 86). Local hotels and hostels also arrange tours. Hostal PapaGayo (see p. 137) offers especially well organized tours that vary in difficulty and length.

🏠 ACCOMMODATIONS AND CAMPING

There are several nice (though expensive) places to stay in the area near Cotopaxi National Park.

Hotel Cuella de Luna (☎2381 666; reservas@cuellodeluna.com), a 20min. walk from the entrance to the park (starting from across the Panamerican Hwy.; the route is well-marked). Offers a rustic lodge atmosphere without any of the inconveniences of a rustic lodge. All rooms have working fireplaces. Dorm in lodge's finished attic, complete with slanted roof. Other rooms have private baths. Dorms US$12; singles US$26; doubles US$38; triples US$48; quads US$58. ❸

Cabañas Los Volcanes (☎2719 112 or 2719 524), 10min. by bus south of the park entrance, in the tiny town of Lasso. Get off any bus on the Panamerican Hwy. at the Lasso gasolinera, turn to the right and begin walking. The turnoff to the left is only 2min. away and well-signed. Offers budget accommodations in cute little cabins named after the region's natural landmarks. Beds with private bath US$8; singles US$9. ❸

Tambopaxi (☎2220 241 or 09 9448 223; www.tambopaxi.com), inside Cotopaxi National Park, at the northern end. From the museum, walk 1hr. up the main road, passing Lake Limpiopungo on your left. At a fork in the road, bear left toward Control Norte and walk for another 3km. Luxury accommodations and gourmet food. 3 years old, Tambopaxi offers dorm-style rooms and camping—both provide gas-heated showers and clean bathrooms. Wheelchair-accessible. Dorms US$6; camping US$8. ❷

Campgrounds, a 30min. walk up the road from the museum, on the left, include a cabin with a fireplace, outhouse, and hose with cold water. 15min. farther up the road on the right is another campground with 2 exposed brick fireplaces and no shelter; bring your own tent. A 3rd campground, at Lake Limpiopungo, features a cabin with running water.

🍴 FOOD

The only **restaurant** ❺ is part of Tambopaxi (see above; dinner from US$9.20).

🌄 🥾 SIGHTS AND HIKES

While the snow-capped volcano is the main draw, the park offers several fantastic hiking opportunities. In addition to wandering around lava fields and *páramo,* try the following hikes.

VOLCÁN COTOPAXI. The first climbers to reach Cotopaxi's rim were the energetic German Wilhelm Reiss and Colombian Ángel Escobar in 1872; the famed volcano tamer Eduard Whymper followed in 1880. Since then, hundreds of world-class mountaineers and thousands of amateurs have completed the icy ascent to the summit. The climb is strenuous and requires ice-climbing gear but isn't technically difficult. Nevertheless, climbers of all abilities should hire a properly qualified (Ministerio del Ambiente or ASEGUIM) guide who knows the peculiarities of the ascent, especially the perilous crevasses that await unsuspecting climbers on the icy ascent. (Guides hired in Quito or Latacunga should run US$150-180 including transportation, park entrance, gear, food, and lodging at the refuge; see **Quito: Tours,** p. 86, or **Latacunga: Tours,** p. 139.) Expeditions begin from the **José Ribas refuge** (4800m) at around midnight to ensure hard-packed snow and safer conditions.

It usually takes 6-7hr. to reach the summit (5897m), but only about 2-3hr. to return. The early start makes it necessary to stay in the refuge the night before. The **shelter** ❶ for 60 people has bunk beds, cold water, electricity, kitchen facilities, and a gas oven, but lacks food (beds US$17 per person). Visitors must bring warm clothes, heavy sleeping bags, and food. It is imperative to acclimatize before attempting the hike (see **Environmental Hazards,** p. 22). A tough climb from the refuge to the glacier (under 1hr.; 5000m) probes the volcano without scaling its loftier heights. Ask at the refuge for the latest conditions before heading out. For a daytrip throughout the park, transportation from the entrance (to the museum, Limpiopango and Rumiñahui, and the parking lot below the refuge) should cost between US$35-40, including a wait.

HIKE	ALTITUDE	TIME	DIFFICULTY
Cotopaxi Rim	5897m	8-10hr.	Medium-Difficult
Glacier hike	5000m	30-60min.	Medium

> Recent glacial movement has opened up a sizable crevasse in the old route up Cotopaxi, forcing guides to compensate and use a more circuitous route to the peak. Would-be Cotopaxi conquerors should take note that the new route to the summit is considered by many to be more technically challenging and should consult a reputable guide company or with SAE before attempting the climb.

MUSEO NACIONAL MARISCAL SUCRE. Located at an altitude of 3080m, 1km before Lake Limpiopungo, the museum has a few maps of the park, including one in relief, and stuffed versions of many of the park's wild inhabitants, including the gigantic Andean Condor. *(Open daily 8am-4pm.)*

INCA RUINS. Long before it was a national park, the land surrounding Cotopaxi was home to the Incas. They used **Ingapirca** as a llama breeding area. The **Pukora El Salitre** was used as a fortress, strategically placed to look out upon the intersecting passes. The **Laguna de las Patos** (Lake of the Ducks) provides another opportunity to see the park's biodiversity up close. *(Follow the main road past the turnoffs for the lake and the Refugio Ribas. 20min. past the refuge turnoff, bear right at the fork toward Sitio Arqueológico. Continue 15min.; Ingapirca sits atop one of the last green mounds on the right. Continue on this road to an unmarked fork; bear right. Continue until you reach a small stream. Ford the stream and walk across the rocky plain until you reach the Pukora El Salitre on top of a grassy hill (1hr. from Ingapirca). Continue 30min. past the pyramid-shaped hills to reach Laguna de Las Patas. From Tambopaxi, Pukora El Salitre is a 15min. straight shot across the páramo.)*

THE ILINIZAS   ☎03

A pair of twin peaks separated by a saddle in the middle, the Ilinizas each provide travelers with something different: Iliniza Norte (5130m), the smaller of the two peaks, gives beginning and intermediate voyageurs the opportunity to acclimatize before going all-out on the nearby Volcán Cotopaxi; Iliniza Sur (5230m), on the other hand, presents a technically challenging climb for all who attempt it.

The Ilinizas are best accessed via the small town of El Chaupi (pop. 1640), which sits at the foot of the two peaks about 6km off the Panamerican Hwy. and 7km south of Machachi (see p. 131). Several excellent hostels dot this area. **Hostería PapaGayo ❷,** about 3km north of the El Chaupi turn-off on Hacienda La Bolivia, is a cheap and enjoyable place from which to branch out to the Ilinizas or any of the mountains in the area. Ask bus drivers on the Panamerican Hwy. to let you off at the entrance to Hacienda La Bolívia, just south of the *peaje* (toll booth) and follow the signs 500m to the hostel. This Israeli-run establishment boasts a busy **restaurant ❷** (entrees US$3-5), a disco, space for a bonfire, and a veritable petting zoo out back. (☎2310 002; cell 09 9903 524; www.hosteria-papagayo.com. Beds US$5-8 per person, with private bath US$9.) **Hostería San José ❸**, about 1½km from El Chaupi's city center, offers bunks in rustic thatched-roof cabins eclectically named "Pink Floyd" and "Wild West." Rooms are also available inside. Beds are nestled among black-light posters. Check out the huge peace sign outside. (☎2891 547; cell 09 9737 896. Beds US$10 per person.) The accommodations closest to the Ilinizas, **Llovizna Mist Hostal ❸**, is owned by Bladimir Gallo, who also runs the **refuge ❸** at 4700m. Don't worry; he's not charging Park Place prices. (☎09 9699 068; www.ecuador-iliniza.com. Refuge sleeps 15-20. Bring a sleeping bag and provisions for however long you plan to stay. US$10 per bed in hostel and refuge.) To get to El Chaupi, take the "El Chaupi" **bus** from **Machachi** to the end of the line (every 30min. 7am-7:40pm, US$0.36; Machachi-Chaupi until 6pm; Chaupi-Machachi bus also picks up passengers from the entrance to La Bolivia). To get to the Ilinizas, backtrack one block from the bus stop and turn left at the park. Llovizna is 200m down the road on the left. The walk to the parking lot at the base of the mountains, known locally as "La Virgen" due to the small shrine to the Virgin Mary located there, is 5km (3hr.). The normal price for a ride to La Virgen from El Chaupi is US$10-15. From La Virgen, the refuge is a 2-2½hr. walk along a well-worn trail, ascending from 3700m to 4700m.

If you're skittish about taking the route alone, drop by Llovizna on a Monday morning and arrange to make the trek up with the refuge keeper, who stays there on weekdays. From the refuge, Iliniza Norte is s 3½hr. round-trip hike (2hr. up, 1½hr. down) and Iliniza Sur is roughly a 6hr. round-trip hike (4hr. up, 2hr. down). Guides that know the mountain are recommended, especially for cloudy days when the summits are not immediately visible. s

While climbing the Ilinizas you may encounter bulls grazing on the side of the mountain. These babies are bred for the bullring and can be quite territorial; move slowly, and don't make any threatening motions while letting the bulls do their thing. By all means, resist the temptation to say "Olé" or wave a red cape.

LATACUNGA ☎03

Latacunga (pop. 54,000; 2800m) serves as a rest stop between Quito and Ambato, a departure point for scenic points to the west, and a bastion of laid-back, Andean city life. Without a doubt, it is one of the more resilient cities of the central Highlands. Between 1532 and 1904, Volcán Cotopaxi, the highest active volcano in the world, erupted three times, devastating this provincial capital each time. Each time the locals dutifully rebuilt their homes, leading one to wonder why they kept going back. Maybe it was the fruit, coffee, sugar, cocoa, rubber, and herds of cattle that are sustained by the rich, volcanic soil. Then again, perhaps it was simply Cotopaxi, its white cone towering on the northeastern horizon. Whatever the reasons, Latacunga today stands poised to once again weather Cotopaxi's godlike wrath, with little but the benediction of La Virgen de las Mercedes rising above the city from the east to protect it.

▮ TRANSPORTATION

Buses: Terminal Terrestre, across the river from the main city at 5 de Junio and the Pan-american Hwy. Buses go to: **Ambato** (1hr., every 10min. 5am-7pm, US$1); **Chugchilán** (4hr.; daily 11am and Tu and F-Sa 8:30am; US$3.50); **La Maná** (4hr., every hr., US$6); **Pilaló** (3hr., M and F-Sa 8:30am, US$2.50); **Pujilí** (20min., every 5min. 7am-

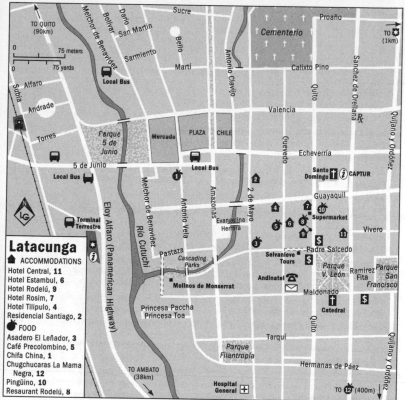

Latacunga

▲ ACCOMMODATIONS
Hotel Central, **11**
Hotel Estambul, **6**
Hotel Rodelú, **9**
Hotel Rosim, **7**
Hotel Tilipulo, **4**
Residencial Santiago, **2**

● FOOD
Asadero El Leñador, **3**
Café Precolombino, **5**
Chifa China, **1**
Chugchucaras La Mama
  Negra, **12**
Pingüino, **10**
Resaurant Rodelú, **8**

9pm, US$0.25); **Quevedo** (5½hr., every 1½hr. 5am-7pm, US$8); **Quito** (2hr., every 10min. 5am-7pm, US$2); **Saquisilí** (20min., every 5min. 6:30am-7pm, US$0.30); **Sigchos** (2hr., 5 per day 10am-5pm, US$1.50); **Zumbahua** (2hr., every hr. 7am-7pm, US$1.25). On Th, buses to Chugchilán and Sigchos leave from Saquisilí.

ORIENTATION AND PRACTICAL INFORMATION

The first glimpse most visitors catch of Latacunga is from the **Panamerican Hwy.,** which briefly runs parallel to **Río Cutuchi.** Across the river lies the city center, sloping gently uphill in a grid-like fashion. Shops line the main drag, **Amazonas,** while the municipal and tourist services are near **Parque Vicente León** on **Quito** and on **Quevedo.** Take a bus across the river or walk 10min. to get to the *centro.*

Tourist Offices: CAPTUR (☎2814 968), on Sanchez de Orellana and Guayaquil to the right of Iglesia Santo Domingo, offers tourist brochures, maps, and friendly assistance, albeit only in Spanish. Open M-F 9am-6pm, Sa 9am-1pm. There is also a **tourist office** on the 2nd fl. of the bus terminal, room 14-D, which provides information on sights, restaurants, hotels, and tours. Spanish only. Open daily 9am-6pm.

Tours: Selvanieve Tours (☎2802 529), on Saliedo between Quito and Quevedo, leads a 1-day trek into Parque Nacional Cotopaxi (US$30 per person, min. 2 people). Also rents equipment (complete outfit US$25 for 2 days). English- and German-speaking guides available. Open daily 9am-7pm.

A recent crackdown on unlicensed tour agencies has led to many unofficial tours of Parque Nacional Cotopaxi originating in Latacunga being stopped at park control. To be sure that your tour operator is legit, demand to see its "Patente de Operación Turística" from the "Ministerio del Ambiente" and confirm that everything is up to date.

Currency Exchange: Exchange your money in Ambato or Riobamba before arriving in Latacunga. **Banco de Guayaquil** (☎2813 900), at Sánchez de Orellana and Maldonado, exchanges traveler's checks. MC/V **ATM.** Open M-F 8:30am-4pm.

Market: The **mercado,** between 5 de Junio and Valencia, is a tribute to random, cheap stuff. Open daily 7am-6pm, but the best time to go is before noon.

Emergency: ☎101.

Police: ☎2812 616 or 2811 101. On General Proaño, 1km from the center; also on the bottom floor of the bus station. Open 24hr.

Pharmacy: Pharmacies dot the landscape around Parque Vicente León, but **Farmacia La Merced** (☎2813 338), at Valencia and Orellana, is the biggest and the best. Open M-Sa 7am-9pm.

Hospital: Hospital General (☎2800 331 or 2800 332), at Hmas. Paez and 2 de Mayo, has ambulance service. Open 24hr. Consultations M-F 7:30am-4pm.

Telephones: Andinatel, at Maldonado and Quevedo, allows collect and calling card calls. Open daily 8am-1pm and 2-10pm. Andinatel, BellSouth, and Porta all have phones scattered throughout the city center as well.

Internet Access: Several Internet cafes line the Salcedo walkway and the surrounding blocks. US$1 per hr. All closed Su.

Post Office: Correos del Ecuador (☎2811 394), at Quevedo and Maldonado, next to Andinatel. Open M-F 8am-6pm, Sa 8am-1pm.

■ ACCOMMODATIONS

Although Latacunga is not swamped with tourists because of its proximity to so many smaller, quieter tourist destinations, it does have its fair share of hotels. Most fill up the night before Saquisilí's Thursday market.

Hotel Tilipulo (☎2810 611; hoteltilipalo@hotmail.com), at Guayaquil and Quevedo. Latacunga's best hotel deserves its high praise from travelers. Affable owner Doña Lucila gives colorful names like "the illusions" or "the sunflowers" to homey rooms. Cable TV; private baths; balconies. Singles US$8; doubles US$16. Excludes IVA. ❸

Hotel Rosim, Quito 16-49 (☎2802 1872; hotelrosim@hotmail.com), at Padre Salcedo. Attractive woodwork and general cleanliness lend a touch of elegance. Owner Gustavo Rocha takes great pride in the cleanliness of his rooms and his staff's dedication to service. TV in rooms. Singles US$8; doubles US$16; triples US$24. Excludes IVA. ❸

Hotel Rodelú, Quito 1631 (☎2811 264; www.rodelu.com.ec), at Salcedo. Rodelú offers the most elegant digs in town; spacious rooms and a skylit staircase which leads downstairs to a quality restaurant. Doubles US$18-26; 2-room suites for 1 person US$33, for 2 people US$45. ❸

Residencial Santiago (☎2800 899), at 2 de Mayo and Guayaquil. Cheap and clean—a backpacker's only requirements. Breakfast US$1.20. Dorms US$5; singles with private bath US$6; doubles US$12. ❷

Hotel Estambul, Quevedo 6-44 (☎2800 354), between Salcedo and Guayaquil, offers spacious rooms with shared or hot private baths. Enjoy the evening air on the concrete rooftop terrace. Laundry tub available. And, if you're curious, the only thing Turkish about Hostel Estambul is one of the owner's close friends. Singles US$7; doubles US$15; triples US$22.50. Excludes IVA. ❷

Hotel Central (☎2802 912), at Orellana and Salcedo, overlooking Parque Vicente de León. The rooms here are *sencillas* (simple), with firm beds and shared bathrooms. Some rooms have views of Parque Vicente de León. US$8. ❸

◫ FOOD

Latacunga's narrow streets are crammed with scores of restaurants offering the standard lunch (US$1.25-1.50). Even cheaper meals can be found in the market. The **supermarket,** next to Restaurante Rodelú, has general food supplies. (☎2801 517. Open M-F 8am-9:30pm, Sa 8am-7pm.)

Restaurant Rodolú (☎2800 956), on Quito, between Salcedo and Guayaquil, under Hotel Rodelú. Set back from street traffic in a quiet, dignified setting. Devour a divine slice of pizza (US$1.30-2.10) or sandwich (from US$2.90). Open M-Sa 7am-10pm. ❶

Asadero El Leñador (☎2802 580), at 2 de Mayo and Salcedo. Gargantuan meals centered around huge portions of grilled meats, all under US$4. Known in Latacunga for its *trucha* (trout). *Almuerzos* US$1.40. Open M-Sa 10am-10pm. ❷

Café Precolombino, on Quevedo, between Salcedo and Guayaquil. Dine like an Inca among *indígena* tapestries. A recent change in ownership has changed this restaurant's focus from granola-type items to quick sandwiches and Mexican food, but quality still prevails. Breakfast from US$1.40, coffee from US$0.35. ❷

Chugchucaras La Mama Negra, Quijano y Ordoñez I-61 (☎2805 401), at Rumiñahui. If the bus ride to Latacunga on the Panamerican Hwy. didn't stop your heart, one of Latacunga's famous *chugchucaras* will show the ol' ticker who's boss once and for all. Fried corn, popcorn, pan-fried potatoes, *maduros, fritada* (fried pork) and a carefully prepared and fried pork skin, all for US$3.90. Yummy. ❸

Pingüino, on Quito between Guayaquil and Salcedo. Take a break from NesCafé and milk and have a cup of fresh-ground coffee (US$0.35) for once. Ice-cream parlor in front. Open daily 9am-7pm. ❶

Chifa China (☎2813 175), at 5 de Junio and Antonio Vela. The town's most popular chifa specializes in fried rice and chop suey. Speedy service will have you chowing down in the blink of an eye. Entrees US$2-3. Open daily 10am-10pm. ❷

◉ ♫ SIGHTS AND ENTERTAINMENT

The **Molinos de Monserrat,** next to the waterfall at Vela near Maldonado, rambles down the riverbank like the rocks themselves. Built by the Jesuits as a granary in 1756, the colonial structure now pays homage to the regional culture, housing a gallery of local artwork, a museum of ethnology, a small library, and a riverside amphitheater. *(Open Tu-F 8am-noon and 2-6pm. US$0.50, students US$0.10.)* The **market** is impossible to miss. Its mammoth offerings take up several blocks from the river to Amazonas; Saturday is the most popular day. *(Open daily 7am-6pm, but locals say to be there before noon.)* On September 24, *indígena* men don their (women's) finest for the traditional fiesta of **La Virgen de Las Mercedes,** a 180-year-old ceremony that involves men dressed in women's clothing squirting perfumed milk on bystanders. As if that weren't enough to do the Virgin proud, November 7 marks the 150-year-old **Mama Negra Festival,** which reenacts the story of Mama Negra, an African brought to Ecuador by the Spanish during the colonial period. Legend has it that she prayed to the Virgen de las Mercedes for her freedom, which was granted by the normally merciless Spaniards a few days later. Mama Negra proceeded to ride through the streets while proclaiming her thanks to the Virgin. Today, men parade through the streets carrying multicolored liberty flags, while other men, representing the Spanish conquistadors, pursue. But the men playing Mama Negra herself steal all the attention. The festival spills over into the parades, fairs, and bullfights of **Latacunga's Independence Day.** Yet despite these periodic activities, Latacunga remains a quintessentially provincial Andean town, ideal for relaxation. Three locales are ideal for this *tranquilo* pastime: **Parque Vicente León** and **Parque San Francisco,** on either side of the municipal building, and the **cascading parks** on either side of the waterfall behind the Molinos de Monserrat. Vicente León and Bolívar have palms, manicured bushes, and plenty of benches, while the waterfall parks allow a cool respite from the heat.

LATACUNGA LOOP ☎03

West of Latacunga, narrow streets are replaced by fields of hay, and the sheep outnumber the humans. Pastures and fields of grain abound at all elevations, supporting an indigenous population that largely eschews technology. Visiting the *indígenas* is an excellent way to submerge yourself in a foreign world, but expect to be a pioneer of sorts in finding your way. Hiking is usually necessary to reach more remote places not accessible by bus. Service to Saquisilí and Pujilí is the exception. Several of the hostels listed below offer excellent hiking routes and maps of the area. While the southern half of the loop (Zumbahua and Pujilí) offers more urban surroundings and passing buses, the northern portion, starting at Quilotoa and heading toward Chugchilán and Isinliví, has quieter rural environs. Travelers with some time on their hands might want to spend Saturday and Sunday checking out the markets in Zumbahua and Pujilí, respectively, then stay a few days in Chugchilán, branch out to Quilotoa from there, take the hike to Isinliví, and arrive in Saquisilí just in time for the Thursday morning market.

PUJILÍ ☎03

About 30min. by bus to the west of Latacunga lies Pujilí, a small city not quite far enough removed from Latacunga to have developed its own tourism industry. In fact, its main avenue, lined with blue lamp posts holding potted plants, is the Panamerican Hwy. Nonetheless, Pujilí does have some charm and is worth dropping by, if only for half a day. Sunday's the biggest market day. Pujilí is nothing if not colorful. To the north and the south of the city on the Panamerican Hwy. are two brightly colored parks that contain statues depicting the indigenous lifestyle (the only exception being the white bust of Luis Maldonado Tamayo). On a hill to the north of town lie ruins of the modern variety: Sinchahucesín, a colorful staircase bordering a large provincial crest and leading to a large cross, was supposed to lead to a municipally-run hostel at the top of the hill. The hostel remains half-built, and residents of Pujilí know little of any plans to continue construction.

Given Pujilí's proximity to Latacunga, it is best to stay in Latacunga for the night or move onto Zumbahua. However, if you simply must stay in Pujilí for the night, **Residencial Pujilí ❶** (☎2723 642) at Rocafuerte and Quevedo, a few blocks south of the market, has some grimy rooms with private baths (only 2 with hot showers; US$3 per person). Otherwise, get out while the getting is good. **Buses** run up and down the Panamerican Hwy. at almost all hours of the night. To get back to **Latacunga,** hop on a bus for US$0.30 (every 20min. but more frequent on Su, 7am-9pm).

ZUMBAHUA ☎03

As Latacunga fades into the distance en route to Zumbahua (pop. 1200; 3600m) the cloud ceiling drops and the road rises to meet the sky. The descent from these heavenly heights to Zumbahua reveals a cinder-block village with rubble in the streets. Before you high-tail it out of there, though, realize Zumbahua offers the only reasonable hostels between Latacunga and Quilotoa. **Hostal Cóndor Matzi ❶**

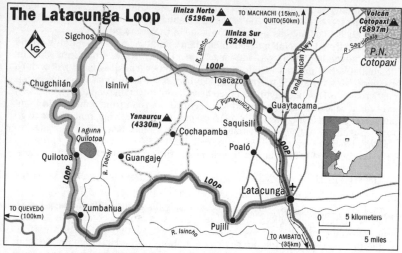

The Latacunga Loop

Illniza Norte ▲ (5196m)

TO MACHACHI (15km), QUITO(50km)

Volcán Cotopaxi ▲ (5897m)

Sigchos

R. Blanco

Illniza Sur (5248m)

R. Saquimala

P.N. Cotopaxi

Chugchilán Isinlivi

LOOP

Toacazo

Panamerican Hwy.

R. Pumacunchi

Guaytacama

Yanaurcu ▲ (4330m)

Cochapamba

Saquisilí

Laguna Quilotoa

Poaló

Quilotoa Guangaje

R. Toachi

LOOP

LOOP

Latacunga ✚

TO QUEVEDO (100km) Zumbahua

LOOP

R. Isincho Pujilí

TO AMBATO (35km)

0   5 kilometers

0   5 miles

(☎2814 611), on the market plaza, provides bright rooms with neat beds, hot shared baths, and a wood stove. (Dorms US$3.) Cóndor can arrange guided tour to Quilotoa and other nearby sites. Just around the corner from Cóndor Matzi is **Hotel Restaurant Oro Verde ❶** (☎2814 605), which offers similarly priced rooms and has a restaurant on the first floor that offers breakfast, lunch, and dinner from US$1.50. (Beds US$3.) Oro Verde also provides transport to Quilotoa for an extra fee. Reach the base of **Cerro Tacacza**, the needlepoint to the south of town, by climbing the sunken dirt road above where the bus stops. Zumbahua hosts a large **Sunday market** with livestock and local *artesanía*, such as colorful sheepskin paintings. **Buses** to Chugchilán from Latacunga (4hr., 11:30am, US$2) pass Zumbahua (2pm). To return to Latacunga from Zumbahua, flag down the Quevedo-Latacunga bus on the Panamerican Hwy. above Zumbahua (2hr., every hr. until 8pm, US$1.25).

LAGUNA QUILOTOA

With its blue-green water and sun-baked sand, **Laguna Quilotoa** looks like the Caribbean Sea at 3500m. The awe-inspiring lagoon lies in an enormous crater (rim 3854m) that was once the colossal Volcán Quilotoa. One glance will justify the arduous journey. There are well marked paths from the rim down to the water, but **hiking around the crater's edge is dangerous**—the ground can crumble easily, sending unwary hikers plummeting down the precipice.

Near the access road, the town of Quilotoa is home to several family-run "hotels" that compete for the scant overnight crowd. These accommodations may test even the hardiest budget traveler's standards. The primary concern is warmth, as temperatures plummet after sunset. That said, **Cabañas Quilotoa ❷** has common rooms with heavy wool blankets and a wood stove. The owner, a locally well-known Tigua box painter, can start travelers on their way along the tough off-road hike to Chugchilán (5hr.). The combined efforts of The Black Sheep Inn (see **Chugchilán,** p. 144), Mamá Hilda's, the Cloud Forest Hostel, and the town Chugchilán itself to line the hike with metal signs has made the hike much more navigable. (Meals US$1.50-3. Dorms US$4; private rooms US$5.) Travelers wishing to spend a rough night in the crater can now check out **Princesa Toa ❶**, an L-shaped set of rooms visible from the ridge of the crater. The rooms (US$3 per person,

US$7 including dinner and breakfast) are simple and well stocked with wool blankets. At the top of the crater, the as-yet unfinished main building at Princesa Toa looks to challenge Cabañas Quilotoa for some of the area's business.

Buses run from Chugchilán to Quilotoa (4am), and they pass by Quilotoa on the way to Chugchilán (3pm) via Latacunga (1hr., US$1). **Trucks** from Zumbahua or Chugchilán take tourists to Quilotoa (1hr., US$10 per truckload) and will wait to bring you back for a little more money. To hike from Zumbahua to Quilotoa you must cross Río Toachi Canyon and then head along the main road (5hr.), although grabbing a **camioneta** is quick and easy because the road from Quilotoa to Zumbahua has been recently paved. Bring warm cloths. Alternatively, rent a **horse** to go from Chugchilán to Quilotoa (round-trip 6-8hr., US$60). **Mules** can be rented to take you from the crater rim down to the lake (US$5). Be aware that entry into Quilotoa costs US$1. This money contributes to the crater and city's maintenence.

CHUGCHILÁN   ☎03

The tiny town of Chugchilán has seen more than its share of visitors in recent years. Part of this may be due to its oasis of idealism: the ▨**Black Sheep Inn** ❾, about 500m past Chugchilán on the road from Quilotoa. A completely organic mountainside complex conceived and constructed by a young North American couple in the mid-1990s, the inn seems to be more of the land than on the land. Ducks, llamas, and even black sheep roam the grounds, which include an organic garden, composting toilets, a sauna, a zip line, and hot showers with windows that provide soap-dropping views of the Andean countryside. The price includes two home-cooked vegetarian meals, tea, coffee, and potable water. (☎2814 587; www.blacksheepinn.com. Internet US$1.50 per 15min. July-Aug. and Dec.-Jan. dorms US$20, low season US$18; singles US$38/$36; doubles US$48/$44; triples US$69/$63; quads US$88/$80. ISIC and SAE discount 10%; for stays of 4 or more nights discount 15%. No discounts for 1-night stays.)

Because of its immense popularity, The Black Sheep Inn is currently expanding; and perhaps also because of the success of the Black Sheep Inn, the other two hostels in Chugchilán are adding rooms as well. **Mamá Hilda's** ❸, a little closer to town and run by Mamá Hilda herself, offers bar service and friendly company, although only in Spanish. (☎2814 814. Dorms US$8; private rooms US$10 per person, includes dinner and breakfast.) **Hostal Cloud Forest** ❷, next door to Mamá Hilda's, offers the cheapest rooms in town and the added security of two wary guard dogs—be careful! (☎2814 808. With dinner US$5, with dinner and breakfast US$6, with private bath US$10.)

Because of the isolation of Chugchilán's beauty, a multi-night stay may be worthwhile. If you stay at the Black Sheep Inn, the owners can suggest excellent excursions in the vicinity that vary in difficulty. Quilotoa is close, and **Río Toachi Canyon** (4-5½hr. loop) is even closer. Following your nose in the other direction will lead to a **European cheese factory** (4hr. loop), established decades ago by a Swiss entrepreneur and now run by local Ecuadorians. Mysterious **Inca ruins** of the UFO variety lie 3hr. away by foot. For avid hikers, a one- to two-day descent leads into an awe-inspiring **cloud forest** on the western slopes of the Andes. **Trucks** (US$20 per truckload) and **horses** (US$10-12 per day) are easily arranged with hotel owners. To get to Chugchilán, **buses** leave Latacunga at 11:30am (4hr., US$2.25), via Sigchos (2pm). Another bus leaves Latacunga at noon in the other direction, passing through Zumbahua at 1:30 or 2pm and arriving in Chugchilán at around 4pm. On Sunday, buses from Latacunga leave at 10:30am and 2pm, and, on Thursday, all service to Chugchilán departs from Saquisilí (see p. 145). Buses to Latacunga stop at the Black Sheep Inn (4hr.; M-Sa 3am via Sigchos, 4am via Zumbahua).

HIKE FROM ISINLIVÍ TO CHUGCHILÁN

The trail begins on a path that leads past Llumu Llama, and the route to Chugchilán goes straight while smaller trails peel off to the left and right. Thirty meters before a log bridge that crosses a stream, the trail turns around a boulder and further downstream. After traversing left over the next (smaller) log bridge, the trail ascends the opposite bank, where it winds left onto a small farm. From here, the way becomes less clear; the path cuts a line through the farmland. At the meadow's end, the path leads right. Here, some hikers are tempted to cross the stream directly on the right, but the route to Chugchilán continues straight and crosses the stream at a later point continuing right into Chillagua, a village that consists only of a couple of buildings. Just past the village, the trail bends left and descends to a stream that runs through a lush meadow. The path then follows the stream's rushing water down to the Taochi River. At the junction, the path turns to follow this river upstream, past a log bridge to a more sturdy-looking suspension bridge. Beyond that, the town of Itualo and its blue-and white church lie at the end of a narrow path. From here, the route leads out of the valley to a road. There are signs for Chugchilán, which is off to the left. In all, it's a 4-5hr. hike. Get more detailed directions before you depart. (Source: Nancy Wiltnik)

ISINLIVÍ ☎03

A spectacular ride on the steep, dusty mountain roads via Sigchos or direct from Latacunga will lead you to the tiny mountain village of Isinliví (pop. 250; 3000m), a quintessential come-for-a-day, stay-for-a-week stop on the Latacunga Loop. Since 1989 Isinliví has been home to an Italian-run mission, which introduced the trade of woodworking to the area. In addition to carving every piece in the town's eight-year-old church, the mission trains young locals in the art of woodworking. Woodwork from Isinliví is sold throughout Ecuador. The only place to stay in Isinliví is ⬛**Hostal Llullu Llama ❸** (☎2814 570 or 2814 790; isinliui@andinatel.net). All of the townspeople know where it is, not only because of Isinliví's diminutive size, but also because of hostel owner Jean Brown's (a co-founder of Quito's SAE branch) commitment to making Llullu Llama an organic part of the community. Guests can either eat dinner in-house (US$5) or request to dine in a home of one of the locals (about US$1.50). Children often stop by on their way home from classes to partake of the free tea and brownies that the hostel offers its guests. In addition, the hostel provides a book of detailed hikes around the Isinliví area, including the ever-so-important 5hr. route to Chugchilán. **Bus** service to Chugchilán is only available via Sigchos at 3am during the week and on Sunday afternoons. (Loft dorms US$5; semi-private loft rooms US$6; private rooms US$10.) Buses to Isinliví leave from Latacunga (M-W and F 11:20am via Sigchos and 1pm direct, US$2), and from Saquisilí (Th 11 and 11:15am, US$2).

SAQUISILÍ ☎03

Perhaps the most important event of the week for the residents of the province of Latacunga is the Thursday market in Saquisilí. Considered by many to be the most authentic indigenous market in Ecuador, this weekly event is a masterpiece of organized chaos. Campesinos (country dwellers) and city-folk alike fill five different squares with just about everything that makes the world go 'round: animals, produce, meat, textiles, grain, clothes, pots and pans. By far

CENTRAL HIGHLANDS

the most intriguing of Saquisilí's five squares is the animal market, about 1km north of the city center. For those travelers who have never heard a 300 lb. pig squeal as it is being lifted up onto a truck by its collar and its tail as well as those who have never contemplated the weight-bearing capability of pig tails before, the animal market is a sight to see. Expect to be completely ignored here; the animal market is a place of gravely important business. It is best to visit the animal market in the morning as early as 7am, when business is just getting started. Cheap meals starting at under US$1 are available in any of the market's squares. Buses to Saquisilí leave from **Latacunga's** Terminal Terrestre about every 20min. for the duration of the market (one-way US$0.30). Thursdays, service to Isinliví moves to Saquisilí (2hr., US$2).

AMBATO   ☎03

Located 128km south of Quito, the mountain metropolis of Ambato (pop. 175,000; 2600m), Ecuador's fourth-largest city, boasts more than just volcanoes and snowy peaks. Completely destroyed by Volcán Tungurahua's 1949 temper tantrum, the city responded first by holding a fiesta in honor of the area's flowers and fruit and second by rebuilding the city piece by piece. This creative energy has deep roots: called "the land of the three Juans," Ambato was home to novelists Juan Montalvo, Juan Benigno Vela, and Juan León Mera, as well as several other intellectual figures whose names now meet at the city's street corners and in its museums.

▐ TRANSPORTATION

Buses: The **terminal** is in the northern end of the city, about 2km down 12 de Noviembre from the *centro*. From here, buses go to: **Baños** (1hr., every 10min. 6am-7pm, US$0.60); **Guayaquil** (6hr., every 30min., US$5); **Quevedo** (6hr., 5 per day 7:30am-5pm, US$6); **Quito** (3hr., every 5min. 4am-6:30pm, US$2.50); **Santo Domingo** (4hr., 6 per day 6:45am-6:30pm, US$4); **Tena** (6hr., 6 per day 6:30am-8pm, US$6). Long-distance buses bound for Baños also stop here. Buses to **Píllaro** depart from Colón and Unidad Nacional across from the firehouse (35min., every 15min. 8am-7pm, US$0.40).

Taxis: Easily hailed on the street. Set the price before you get in. Trip across town US$1.

⚔ ▐ ORIENTATION AND PRACTICAL INFORMATION

To reach the town center from the bus terminal, turn right on the street in front of the terminal and walk uphill about 200m. At the first major intersection, catch the bus to the *centro* (US$0.18). The downtown area is contained within a five-by-five block area. Two important downtown parks are **Parque Juan Montalvo** (the government center) and **Parque Cevallos** (the departure spot for many local buses). Budget hotels border **Parque 12 de Noviembre,** but this area is dangerous at night.

Tourist Office: Ministerio de Turismo (☎2821 800), at Guayaquil and Rocafuerte, offers long lists of lodgings and festivals. Open M-F 8:30am-1pm and 1:30-5:30pm.

Tours: Clantour, Cevallos 18-57 (☎2422 455), at Castillo, arranges flights.

Currency Exchange: Produbanco, Montalvo 527 (☎2424 840), at Sucre, exchanges both traveler's checks and cash. MC/V **ATM** inside. Open M-F 8:30am-3:30pm. **Banco del Pacífico,** Ceballos 10-14 (☎2422 606 or 2422 870), at Lalama, also exchanges traveler's checks and Euros. 24hr. MC/V **ATM.** Open M-F 8:30am-4pm, Sa 9am-2pm.

ATMs: Banco del Pacífico MC **ATM** at Sucre and Montalvo. **BanRed** V **ATMs** line Sucre.

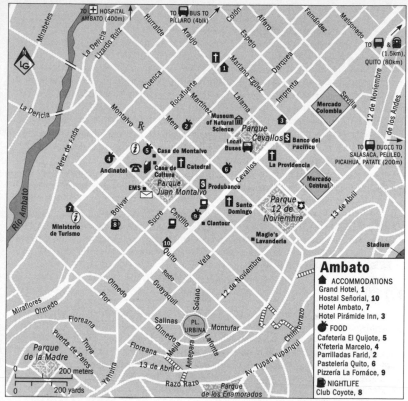

Ambato

🏠 ACCOMMODATIONS
Grand Hotel, **1**
Hostal Señorial, **10**
Hotel Ambato, **7**
Hotel Pirámide Inn, **3**

🍴 FOOD
Cafetería El Quijote, **5**
K'feteria Marcelo, **4**
Parrilladas Farid, **2**
Pastelería Quito, **6**
Pizzería La Fornáce, **9**

🎵 NIGHTLIFE
Club Coyote, **8**

Market: Partly indoors on 12 de Noviembre, between Martínez and Egüez, and a block up Vela in **Mercado Colombia.** Sells mostly local produce and household items. On M it becomes one of the largest markets in Ecuador. Open daily 8am-6pm. The Plaza Urbina, a covered circular area at 12 de Noviembre and Guayaquil, also sells produce and some clothing items. Open 8am-5pm.

Laundromat: Magie's, Montalvo 07-21 (☎2820 724), at Vela. US$0.80 per lb. Open M-F 8am-7:30pm, Sa 9am-1:30pm.

Police: Atahualpa 568 (☎2863 656). Open 24hr. More convenient destacamiento (☎2843 656) on 12 de Noviembre and Martinez across from Parque 12 de Noviembre. Open 24hr.

Pharmacy: Pharmacies abound in Ambato's city center. **Farmacia La Merced** (☎2826 517), Rocafuerte and Montalvo. Open M-Sa 7:30am-10pm, Su 5:30pm-9:30pm.

Hospital: Hospital Regional Ambato (☎2821 059, emergency 2822 099), at Pasteur and Unidad Nacional. Ambulance service. 24hr. emergency room.

Telephones: Andinatel (☎2820 301), a block away from the post office along Castillo toward Rocafuerte. Allows collect calls but not calling cards. Open daily 8am-10pm.

Internet Access: On Cevallos, Sucre, and Bolívar near Parques Juan Montalvo and Cevallos. US$1-1.50 per hr. Net2Phone available at Internet cafe at Montalvo and Cevallos.

Post Office: Correos Ecuador (☎2829 705), at Castillo and Bolívar. Open M-F 8am-2:30pm and 3:30-6pm, Sa 8am-noon. **EMS** (☎2823 332), next to the Correos. Open M-F 8am-1:30pm and 3:30-6pm.

ACCOMMODATIONS

Hotel Ambato, Guayaquil 01-08 (☎2421 791), at Rocafuerte. Follow the bellboy to a world of comfort: shining rooms with Internet access, soap, shampoo, bottled water, and cable TVs. Out back is a great view of Ambato. Singles US$42.70; doubles US$56.12. IVA not included. AmEx/MC/V and traveler's checks accepted. ❺

Grand Hotel (☎2825 915), at Rocafuerte and Lalama. Cable TVs and hot baths in every room. Karaoke downstairs for the aspiring Célia Cruz. Singles US$14; doubles US$22; triples US$28. IVA included. AmEx/MC/V. ❹

Hostal Señorial, Cevallos 449 (☎2825 124), at Quito. Escape from busy Ambato into rooms with TVs, mini-bars, and spotless private baths. The pastel color scheme will have you thinking it's Easter. Luggage storage and laundry service. Singles US$12; doubles US$24; triples US$36. IVA not included. AmEx/MC/V. ❸

Hotel Pirámide Inn (☎2421 920), at Cevallos and Egüez, above the *pollería*. Enjoy the tidy, carpeted rooms, private and temperamentally hot baths equipped with soap and shampoo, and cable TVs. American breakfast included. Singles US$12; doubles US$22; triples US$30.50. ❸

FOOD

Parrilladas Farid, Bolívar 16-74 (☎2824 664), at Mera. A local favorite for great steak, peppered pork loins, or chicken in mushroom sauce (US$4-7). The walls are festooned with wine, so pull down a bottle. Open M-Th 11am-11pm, F-Sa 11am-midnight, Su 11am-9pm. AmEx/MC/V. ❷

Pizzería La Fornáce, Cevallos 10-28 (☎2823 244), at Montalvo. Everything about this place looks, tastes, and feels wonderful. A blast of heat from the brick oven and the smell of pizzas (US$2-3) greet guests. Take-out available. Open Su-Th 11am-10pm, F-Sa 11am-11pm. ❶

K'feteria Marcelo (☎2828 208), at Castillo and Rocafuerte. A family place that's always hopping. Enjoy a gargantuan dish of ice cream for around US$1.50. Glass tables and fancy bar outclass the affordable prices. Specialty sandwiches US$1-2. Cappuccinos US$0.60. Open M-Sa 9am-10:30pm, Su 10am-9pm. ❶

Pastelería Quito, Mera 514 (☎2822 549), at Cevallos. Pasteles and a load of more wholesome goodies in an uncommonly large sitting space for a bakery. Buns and pastries US$0.10-0.20. Open daily 7:30am-9pm. ❶

Cafetería El Quijote (☎2422 424), at Montalvo and Bolívar. Airy elegance and sketches from the life of the namesake penciled onto walls. Lunch *menú* (soup, meat, juice, dessert) US$1.95. Open M-Sa 9:30am-8:30pm. ❶

SIGHTS

INSTITUTO TÉCNICO SUPERIOR BOLÍVAR (ITSB). The institute houses the **Museum of Natural Science,** which is by far the most arresting sight in Ambato. A walk through the collection starts slowly, with black-and-white photos of the Sierra at the turn of the century and some coins from around the world, including New York City subway tokens. The momentum builds with hallways full of preserved animals, including the world's largest insect species, the elephant beetle. Jaguars, tarantulas, a condor, and a pit bull all retain their final poses. The exhibit climaxes with the stuff bad dreams are made of—**freak animals,** such as two-headed goats and cyclops dogs. A dubious addition to the museum is a slice of the trunk of the first eucalyptus tree planted in Ecuador in 1865. The eucalyptus grows like a weed and threatens the natural habitats of many indigenous species of trees. *(Sucre 04-38, on Parque Cevallos, between Lalama and Martínez. ☎ 2827 395. Open M-F 8:30am-12:30pm and 2:30-6:30pm, Sa 9am-5pm. US$1.)*

MONTALVO-LAND. Ambato finds endless ways to worship its literary hero, **Juan Montalvo** (see **Literature,** p. 65), known in these parts as "The Cervantes of America." A **park** bears his name, and is bounded by a similarly named street, and on the corner of Bolívar and Montalvo, the hero's birthplace and lifelong home—the **Casa de Montalvo**—contains many of his books, including original manuscripts. The massive chapel houses his tomb. After pondering renditions, sculptures, pictures, clothes, the places he knew best, and even his manuscripts, you'll feel like you've met the man. *(☎ 2824 248. Open M-F 9am-noon and 2-6pm, Sa 10am-1pm. US$1.)* Lastly, 2km from the *centro* in the suburb of **Ficoa** lies the **Quinta de Montalvo,** Juan's country residence—a small hacienda with some personal effects, a flower garden, and a view of Ambato across the valley. *(Take the Ficoa bus from Parque Cevallos (10min., every 15min.). Open Tu-Su 9am-5pm. US$0.18.)*

PARQUE DE LOS ENAMORADOS. This small garden up the hill from Ambato's *centro* has hedge sculptures that would make Edward Scissorhands jealous. Mickey Mouse, Humpty Dumpty, a full band with dancers, and a heart pierced by a sword adorn the maze of horti-sculpture. *(From the Plaza Urbina on 12 de Noviembre and Guayaquil, walk away from the centro on Antepara and climb the stairs up to Calle Razo. The hedges lining the outside of the park are clearly visible from here.)*

🎵 ENTERTAINMENT

Ambato isn't a true party town, but it does offer windows of opportunity to let loose. The **Casa de Cultura,** Bolívar 555, 2nd fl., at Montalvo, sometimes sponsors films and concerts. *(☎ 2820 338. Open M-F 9am-1pm and 3-7pm.)* **Club Coyote,** Bolívar 2057 at Guayaquil, serves cool cerveza (US$0.80) and features live music on weekends. *(☎ 2827 886. Open Tu-Sa 4pm-3am.)* The coyote in question is indeed Wile E. Coyote of Looney Tunes fame; you probably won't find his likeness on a stained glass window elsewhere in Ecuador. There are many *discotecas* around Parque 12 de Noviembre, but tourist agencies report numerous muggings and stabbings in the area. Ambato throws the largest Carnival in all of Ecuador, climaxing in the **Fiesta de Las Flores y Las Frutas** in mid-February.

SALASACA ☎ 03

Salasaca, 14km away from Ambato on the way to Baños, consists largely of a thriving commercial strip—there's a lot of business for a don't-blink-or-you'll-miss-it village, mostly in the form of *artesanía* shops. The Quichua, who live in Salasaca and are descendants of Bolivians relocated by the Incas long ago, weave ponchos and tapestries. They sell them from their homes and at different nearby markets. Buy them here, since the same goods cost less than at the Otavalo market (see p. 106). The hostel **Runa Huasi ❷** showcases village life, with thatched roofs, sheep in the garden, and a patio with views of the valley. To get there, find the mural to the left of the Colegio los Salasacas on the main strip, and take the cobblestone road to its left (10min.). Turn left onto the dirt road at the sign. (Call Alonso Pilla ☎ 09 9840 125. Common hot baths. Spanish tours of the valley US$3 per hr. Dorms

US$7.) **Buses** to Salasaca leave from Carihuayruzo and Ilinizas in **Ambato** (30min., every 10min., US$0.50). **Baños**-bound buses leaving from Ambato's bus terminal also stop in Salasaca. All buses continue on to **Pelileo.**

PELILEO   ☎03

Pelileo, a significantly larger town with a rather turbulent history, is 10min. east of Salasaca, on the road to Baños. Destroyed five times by earthquakes, it now rests several kilometers from its original location. After Ambato, it holds the most important market in the province (Sa 8am-6pm). The road to Pelileo becomes a deep blue sea of denim—you've entered the blue jean capital of Ecuador. Despite its name, locals flock to La Moya Tourist Complex to use its indoor pool (US$2 for foreigners, US$1 for children), barbecue at the outdoor gazebos, use the paddle-boats in the complex's lake, and take advantage of the sauna and massage services (available F-Sa; pool open Tu-Sa 9am-6pm). Farther into the valley are the ruins of the old church that was destroyed in the 1949 earthquake. (To get to La Moya, walk 20min. on the road to Baños or hire a camioneta for US$1. The complex is at the beginning of the valley to the right of the road. Some ruins are a 20min. walk farther into the valley. Walk toward the blue-and-white dome of the new church into the valley.) To get to Pelileo, take the **buses** to Salasaca for US$0.10 more.

PATATE   ☎03

Across the valley from Salasaca and Pelileo lies Patate, a small town with very little to offer, with the exception of luxury hotels. Patate's location deep inside the valley shields it from the elements and makes its perpetually warm weather the envy of neighboring towns. The best place to enjoy this weather is **Hostería Viña del Mar ❹**, set right next to Río Patate. With a pool, a hot tub, horses, basketball, and tennis courts, miniature golf, and even a small chapel for marriages, the whole place takes on a Dis-neyland feel, but an integral part of that feel is its location in the valley, which Michael Eisner and his boys couldn't reproduce if they tried. To get to Viña del Rio, take the turn-off into the valley at the soccer stadium before you arrive in Patate proper. (☎2870 139. Cabins US$23.50 per person. Meals US$7.50. IVA included. MC/V.) On the other side of the mountain further into the valley is **Hacienda Los Llanganates ❺**, another group of cabins located on what used to be a 400 ha. hacienda. The rooms all have fireplaces and are absolutely gigantic. Make the most of your space, because you're paying for it. (☎2859 331 or 2859 330. US$40 per person, includes dinner and breakfast. Excludes IVA. AmEx/MC/V.) The turn-off for Llanganates comes shortly after the turn for Viña del Mar. The walk to Llanganates is 2hr. on a cobblestone road, but if you're paying for that room, you might as well shell out US$4 for a camioneta. **Buses** to Patate leave from Salasaca and Pelileo every 7min. and cost US$0.40.

BAÑOS   ☎03

Baños (pop. 20,000; 1800m) straddles the fence, one leg in the mountains, one leg in the jungle. Its proximity to Cotopaxi, Chimborazo, and the most remote regions of the Amazon is one reason this town crawls with tourists; the other is the baños themselves, geothermally heated by the same fiery god who created the nearby Volcán Tungurahua. Meanwhile, neighboring mountains provide opportunities for everything from pastoral strolls to vigorous hikes. In addition to being a traveler's haven in the general sense, Baños is one of the most handicapped-friendly cities in all of Ecuador, with ramps at all street corners in the city center and wheelchair access to several of the thermal baths. Baños has recovered from the 1999 Tun-gurahua eruption but the smoking volcano and periodic evacuation drills serve as constant reminders that the town's fate lies in nature's hands.

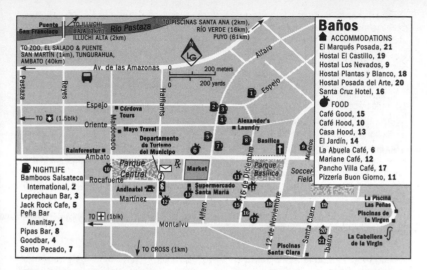

Puente San Francisco | TO ILLUCHI BAJA (1km), ILLUCHI ALTA (2km) | Río Pastaza | TO PISCINAS SANTA ANA (2km), RÍO VERDE (16km), PUYO (61km)

TO ZOO, EL SALADO & PUENTE SAN MARTÍN (1km), TUNGURAHUA, AMBATO (40km)

Av. de las Amazonas

Baños

▲ ACCOMMODATIONS
El Marqués Posada, **21**
Hostal El Castillo, **19**
Hostal Los Nevados, **9**
Hostal Plantas y Blanco, **18**
Hostal Posada del Arte, **20**
Santa Cruz Hotel, **16**

🍴 FOOD
Café Good, **15**
Café Hood, **10**
Casa Hood, **13**
El Jardín, **14**
La Abuela Café, **6**
Mariane Café, **12**
Pancho Villa Café, **17**
Pizzería Buon Giorno, **11**

🌙 NIGHTLIFE
Bamboos Salsateca International, **2**
Leprechaun Bar, **3**
Jack Rock Cafe, **5**
Peña Bar Ananitay, **1**
Pipas Bar, **8**
Goodbar, **4**
Santo Pecado, **7**

⌐ TRANSPORTATION

Buses: The **terminal** is between Maldonado and the main road to Ambato. Buses travel to: **Ambato** (1hr., every 10min. 4am-7pm, US$0.80); **Guayaquil** (7hr., 7:30pm, US$7); **Puyo** (1½hr., every 15min. 6:30am-10pm, US$2); **Quito** (3½hr., every 30min. 4:15am-6:20pm, US$3.40); **Riobamba** (2hr., every hr. 5:30am-7:30pm, US$2); **Tena** (4hr., every hr., US$4).

Taxis: ☎2740 416. On 16 de Diciembre, and clustering at the parks. Baños is small and easily navigable by foot. Taxis are best used for transportation to outlying areas.

★ ⁊ ORIENTATION AND PRACTICAL INFORMATION

The layout of Baños is simple. The tourist area clusters on **Ambato** between **Maldonado** and **12 de Noviembre**, while good restaurants and quieter hostels are south of the Ambato strip between **Halflants** and **Ibarra.** Thermal pools lie in the southeastern corner of town.

Tourist Office: Departamento de Turismo del Municipio, (☎2740 483), on Halflants and Rocafuerte next door to the post office (see below). Open daily 8am-5:30pm. **Ministerio de Ambiente,** in the bus terminal, specializes in information on **Parque Nacional Llanganates** (see p. 160) and in not being open.

Tours: Guides make Baños adventures all the more fun. Because the town is conveniently located between the mountains and the jungle, dozens of tour agencies pack the streets—although relatively few are legitimately registered. Before paying, ask for a guide's Ministerio de Turismo or Ministerio de Ambiente certification or the company's license to operate in national parks. For complete info about guided tours, see **Organized Adventure Trips,** p. 41.

Rainforestur (☎/fax 2740 743 or 2740 046; rainfor@interactive.net.ec), off Parque Central, on Ambato and Maldonado, is the most reputable agency in town. General Manager Santiago Herrera speaks good English and organizes trips to the mountains (Tungurahua, Cotopaxi, or Chimborazo) and the Oriente. US$70 per person per day for 3-4 days. "Extreme" multisport tours also available (2 nights, 3 days; US$45 per day). Open daily 8am-8pm.

Córdova Tours (☎2740 923; ojosvolcan@hotmail.com), at the corner of Maldonado and Espejo, offers a unique look at the Baños area aboard the Chiva Mocambo (an open-air bus). 3 tours per day: to the cascades between Baños and Río Verde (5hr., 9am, US$8); to bridges and miradores around Baños (2hr., 2 and 4pm, US$5); and to a nighttime look at the active Volcán Tungurahua and a bird's-eye view of Baños (2hr., 9pm, US$3). English-speaking guides available. Open daily 8am-7pm.

Mayo Travel (☎2740 803; mayotravel@yahoo.com), at Maldonado and Oriente, offers English-, French-, or Spanish-speaking guides to Parques Nacionales Cotopaxi and Sangay as well as canyoning, trekking, and jungle tours. For US$10, you can head over to a nearby bridge with Mayo and try swing jumping, a modified (and tamer) form of bungee jumping. Open daily 8am-8pm.

Currency Exchange: Banco del Pacífico (☎2740 336), on Halflants and Rocafuerte, exchanges traveler's checks and Euros. MC **ATM**. Open M-F 8:30am-4pm.

Market: Boxed in by Rocafuerte, Ambato, Alfaro, and Halflants. Open daily 7am-6pm. Su is the biggest day. An **open-air market** specializing in produce is on Ambato and Mera, on the western edge of town.

Laundromat: Alexander's Laundry, on Oriente and Alfaro. US$0.80 per kg. Open daily 8am-7pm.

Emergency: ☎2740 101 for immediate assistance. ☎101 contacts the provincial headquarters in Ambato.

Police: ☎2740 101. On Oriente, 3½ blocks west of Parque Central. Open 24hr.

Pharmacy: Farmacia Agua Santa (☎2740 385), on Ambato between Alfaro and Halflants. Open daily 8:30am-8:30pm.

Hospital: Hospital de Baños (☎2740 367), at Pastaza and Montalvo. Open 24hr.

Telephones: Andinatel (☎2740 104), at Rocafuerte and Halflants on Parque Central. Accepts calling cards and collect calls. Open daily 8am-10pm.

Internet Access: All over town. US$2 per hr.

Post Office: Correos Central (☎2740 901), on Halflants between Ambato and Rocafuerte, near Parque Central. Open M-F 8am-noon and 2-6pm.

ACCOMMODATIONS

Hostal Plantas y Blanco (☎2740 044), at Martínez and 12 de Noviembre, 1 block off Parque Basílica. This phenomenon of comfort and cleanliness has a terrace with some of the best views in Baños. The abundant plants within the white-walled rooms justify the name. Laundry, phones, rooftop restaurant. Morning steam baths US$3. American movies US$0.75-1. Singles US$5, with bath US$7; doubles US$10/$14. ❷

Santa Cruz Hotel (☎2740 648), at 16 de Diciembre and Martínez, 2 blocks south of the Parque Basílica. The light coming through big windows shows off spacious and colorful rooms. Also has private baths, a cafeteria, and a fireplace-heated patio. Video rental US$1. US$5-6 per person. IVA included. ❷

Hostal Posada del Arte (☎2740 083), at Montalvo and Ibarra. Luxurious rooms in a colorful space include balconies, fireplaces, orthopedic mattresses, and large private baths. New owner "Don Jaime" is putting in a rooftop terrace to augment the already stunning balcony views of La Cabilleru de la Virgen. No breakfast knocks US$4 off of the price, but the staff insists you'll regret it. Singles US$15-20; doubles US$24-30. ❸

El Marqués Posada (☎2740 053; posada_marques@yahoo.com), at Montalvo and Ibarra, a few blocks from the *centro*. Owned by the family that sold Posada del Arte to Don Jaime. The same family also owns a local art gallery; the paintings on the wall, by local artist Alvando Villiegas, are for sale. The large collection of ancient sculpture and pottery is not. Clean, airy rooms with private baths. Some with hammocks and a balcony. Singles US$8; doubles US$16; triples US$24. ❸

Hostal Los Nevados (☎2740 673), on Maderos by Parque Basílica. From Ambato, take the 1st left past 12 de Noviembre. Large, sparse rooms and private baths are spotless. Laundry, message board, 24hr. security. Singles US$5; doubles US$10; triples US$15. Rooms with cable TV extra. ❷

Hostal El Castillo (☎2740 285), at Martínez and Santa Clara. A caged monkey greets visitors. The castle theme falls short on the grounds that most castles weren't painted orange and black. Simple rooms, private baths, cable TV, and a pleasant courtyard. Singles US$6; doubles US$12. ❷

☐ FOOD

Locals flock to the cheap restaurants surrounding the bus station, while foreigners stick to international cuisine around the town center. To replenish your own stash, head to **Supermercado Santa María.** (On Rocafuerte, between Halflants and Alfaro. Open M-Sa 8:30am-8pm, Su 8:30am-6pm.)

▨ **Casa Hood** (☎2741 786), at Martínez between Halfants and Alfaro. A place for being, not just eating. Tasty breakfasts (US$1.50), vegetarian entrees (US$2-3), and a friendly atmosphere. Unlike most Ecuadorian restaurants, patrons are encouraged to tip. Book rental/exchange and nightly movie screenings. Open M and W-Su 8am-10:15pm. ❶

▨ **Pizzería Buon Giorno** (☎2741 724), at Rocafuerte and 16 de Diciembre. Exalted by visitors and expats alike for the first-rate, imported ingredients. Translation: a good piece of pie. Personal pizzas US$3. Open daily 12:30pm-1am. ❶

Mariane Café/Restaurant (☎2740 911), at Halflants and Rocafuerte. Provence-style French food in the middle of Ecuador. Try the filet mignon in a peppered cream sauce with vegetables. Entrees US$2.50-4.50. Chocolate crepes (US$1.50) and 0.5L of Chilean wine (US$5) provide post-meal euphoria. Open daily 4-10pm. ❶

Café Hood (☎2741 609), at Maldonado and Ambato, on Parque Central. The split of the Hood family (see above) has gifted upon Baños 2 equally friendly, equally relaxed, and equally vegetarian restaurants. Enjoy the same amenities here as in Casa Hood. Breakfast *menú* US$1.20. International entrees US$1.30-3.90. Open daily 8am-9pm. ❶

Pancho Villa Café, at Montalvo and 16 de Diciembre. Che Guevara may grace the walls, but the tasty fajitas, tacos, and burritos (US$2.50-3.50) are definitely Mexican. Top it off with a margarita or cerveza and you have a fiesta. Open M-Sa 12:30-9:30pm. ❶

La Abuela Café (☎2740 923), on Ambato across from the market. This small, dark cafe is often full—and for good reason. Homemade pies (US$2), an extensive drink list (US$2-3), and sandwiches (US$2-3) satisfy everyone. Live music to serenade diners on weekend evenings. Open daily 7:30am-11pm. ❶

Café Good (☎2740 592), at 16 de Diciembre and Martinez. No relation to the Restaurants Hood, unless you count the vegetarian menu (entrees US$2.50-4), the nightly movies, or the book exchange. The difference here is that you are supporting an Ecuadorian-owned business. Open daily 8am-10pm. ❶

El Jardín (☎09 4183 069), at Rocafuerte and 16 de Diciembre. Lilies and art prints festoon the space. Choose to sit inside or in the garden. Filling, greasy, meat-replete dishes US$4-6. Open M 6-10pm, Tu-Su noon-10pm. ❷

☉ SIGHTS

Baños is one formidable attraction, beginning at the hot-spring pools and radiating outward to the volcanoes, the Oriente, and beyond.

THE BAÑOS. Locals spill down from the mountainsides to soak themselves in the springs at sunrise; tourists who take a dip later miss the calm, clean water and the wonder of daybreak over the Andes. The pools are quietest early in the week and froth with humanity on Fridays, Saturdays, and Sundays. The most heavily trafficked are the **Piscinas de la Virgen,** at the eastern end of Montalvo. A waterfall cascades down the mountain into this pool, the only one open at night. Several murky mineral-water pools, reputedly cleaned daily, are filled with the legendary healing waters. Locally produced brochures claim that the waters "eliminate the toxins and residual products of transpiration," but rather than firing their general practitioners, most visitors prefer to think of their baths as giant hot tubs. (☎ 2740 462. Open daily 4:30am-5pm and 6-10pm.) Next door, **La Piscina Las Peñas** has a slide and specializes in screaming children and water fights. (Open F-Su 8am-5pm. US$1.) The relatively calm **Piscinas Santa Clara** are at the end of the street with the same name. (Open F-Su 8am-5pm. US$2.) Two other pools, visited mostly by locals, lie outside of town. **El Salado** is a 30min. walk or a 5min. ride (take any local bus marked "Salado;" US$0.20) from the *centro.* Head west on the road to Ambato, then turn left at the sign to El Salado. Follow the road uphill until it ends. Cleaned each day, the six pools range in temperature from cold to scalding. (☎ 2740 493. Open daily 4:30am-5pm.) The **Piscinas Santa Ana** are a 20min. walk or a 5min. bus ride on the road to Puyo. A sign on the right points the way to the tree-enclosed pools just off the roadway. (Open F-Su 8am-5pm.) If the carnival-like atmosphere of the *baños* turns you off, you're not alone. Many well-traveled people prefer the thermal baths in Papallacta (see p. 293) to those in Baños. Besides, there's plenty more to do here than listening to a four-year-old in waterwings screaming in your ear.

ECOZOOLÓGICO SAN MARTÍN. If you didn't see any animals on your trips to the Oriente and Sangay, that may be because they're all here, lounging about in bowl-shaped, metal-net-covered depressions that tumble down the slopes to Río Pastaza. In addition to housing the world's largest bird species (the Andean Condor) and the world's largest rodent species (the Capybara), the zoo also features a boisterous community of monkeys, jaguars, tapirs, and birds of prey native to the jungle and Sierra. If you're not a fan of zoos for ethical reasons, take heart: one of Baños's most widely-circulated tourist maps snidely labels the zoo "Animal Prison" in its rendition of the city. (Take a local bus from Baños's center (US$0.20) or hike up the road to Ambato (30min.), veering right at the fork by the blue-and-white shrine and continuing 300m over the bridge. Open daily 8am-6pm. Multilingual guides available. Map US$1. Admission US$1.50.)

THE BASÍLICA. The stone basilica serves as a throne to the **Virgen de Agua Santa,** who stands within in all her neon-lit glory. Legend has it that during a religious procession in 1773, Volcán Tungurahua suddenly threatened to blow its top. In a fervor the people of Baños prostrated themselves before the Virgin's image. The eruption came to a sudden halt, and the rest is history. Murals illustrate miracles that the Virgin has since performed. The church's **museum** is the place to go for Christ statues, bridal robes, pickled pythons, a collection of local soccer trophies dating back to the early 1980s, and hilariously stuffed dead animals. The Virgin was powerless to stop the taxidermist from inserting two large marbles in the eye sockets of a now dishonored, and very dead, ram. (At the corner of Ambato and 12 de Noviembre. Open daily 8am-5pm. US$0.50.)

🎵 🎬 ENTERTAINMENT AND NIGHTLIFE

Baños has some of the wildest nightlife in Ecuador, centered around Alfaro, between Ambato and Espejo. Tranquil guests may prefer to relax with a movie at **Casa Hood's** nightly 8pm showing (see **Food,** p. 153). Baños may be the one place in Ecuador where you should not ignore people handing out flyers; pay enough attention and you may find yourself enjoying happy hours from noon to midnight. Just make sure you know what to do in the event of "altitude sickness."

Leprechaun Bar, on Alfaro at Oriente. All the rage: sweaty, crowded, and full of thirsty backpackers spilling out onto the street. The last stop for many late-night revelers. Happy hour 9-11pm. Open daily 9pm-3am.

Santo Pecado (☎2740 703), on Alfaro between Oriente and Ambato. Sin like a saint while music blasts from above. Ample space to move around or sit without feeling like you're alone. Beer US$1.25. Happy hour 8pm-midnight. Open daily 5pm-2:30am.

Jack Rock Café, at Alfaro between Ambato and Oriente. The beer flows freely here, and the friendly staff will whip you good at the foosball table. Open daily 7pm-2:30am.

Goodbar (☎2740 807), at Alfaro and Oriente. The playlist is what sets this tiny bar apart: hip-hop and Bob Marley are sounds for sore ears unused to the constant barrage of salsa and reggetón pumped through the loudspeakers in neighboring clubs. Top-of-the-line caipirinhas. Open daily 8pm-3am.

Pipas Bar, at 16 de Diciembre and Ambato, is breaking into the Baños bar scene with constant food, booze, and classic tunes. Open daily 6pm-2am.

Bamboos Salsateca Internacional, at Alfaro and Espejo. Jungle decor does little to reduce the sense of imminent wildness in the classic, and best, Baños club. DJs spin everything from punk to salsa. Mixed drinks US$2-3. Cover Th-Sa men US$2, women US$1. Open M-Sa 8pm-3am.

Peña Bar Ananitay (☎2741 713), at 16 de Diciembre and Espejo, features live folk music every night. Tourists and locals flock to Baños's oldest bar to enjoy Andean tunes and salsa dancing. Mixed drinks US$1.50-2.50. Cover US$1. Open daily 9pm-3am.

OUTDOOR ACTIVITIES

Given its privileged geography, Baños is a base camp for all manner of outdoor diversion. Explore the nearby volcanic peaks, cloud forest, or jungle from here and still be back in time for a gourmet meal and an evening soak in the hot springs. Bikes of varying quality are easy to come by (US$1 per hr., US$5 per day). Check the tires for wear and inflation, and make sure that the chain is well lubricated and the gears shift smoothly before leaving. A popular trip goes 16km down the road toward Puyo to the town of Río Verde (see p. 156). The mostly downhill ride passes countless waterfalls and an unlit tunnel (bring a flashlight). To return from Río Verde, hop on a Baños-bound bus and put your bike on the roof (US$0.40).

If nearby trails look too steep and strenuous for hiking, consider letting a four-legged friend do the work (US$5 per hr.). Equine outfitters fill the *centro*. Or hop on a boat. Although many Baños tour agencies offer rafting trips, bear in mind that these rivers flow through urban areas prior to reaching the town. Clearer, more exciting rafting opportunities exist in other parts of Ecuador on **Río Toachi,** the river leading to Esmeraldas and deeper into the Oriente.

For the crazies who crave an alternative to alternative transport, there are a couple of options. **Canyoning,** the rappelled descent from the top of a waterfall, can be arranged through **Córdova Tours** in Baños (see **Tours,** p. 152). Córdova will also help if you want to play road warrior—with a **motorbike** (US$12 per hr.). All-terrain vehicles (ATVs) line the curbs and tear through the streets (US$8-10 per hr.). Just don't forget your helmet, or those rain-slicked roads could be a real drag.

HIKING

HIKE	TIME	DISTANCE	ALTITUDE	DIFFICULTY
La Cruz	3hr.	4km	1800-2200m	Easy-Medium
San Martín Bridge	4hr.	10km	1800-2800m	Medium-Difficult
El Salado Tobaganes	1hr.	3km	2000-2200m	Medium
Tungurahua	6hr.	15km	2000-5000m	Difficult

The steep, green hills surrounding Baños beckon hordes of hikers. Hiking trails abound, but maps of them do not. Chatting up an employee at a reputable tour agency before you go is a good idea.

LA CRUZ. To do the most popular Baños hike, follow Maldonado toward the mountains. At the end of the road a path leads to the illuminated cross on top of the hill (45min.). Continue past the cross on the wooded trail doubling back to the right. After rising to the village of **Runtun,** the trail loops back to Baños.

SAN MARTÍN BRIDGE. To get an up-close view of some precipices, cross the main highway at the bus terminal and head down toward **Río Pastaza,** where the shaky San Francisco bridge crosses a churning gorge. From the other side, a path leads up the steep mountainside to the twin villages of **Illuchi Baja** and **Illuchi Alta,** eventually reaching the summit overlooking Baños (1½hr.). The trail descends to the cement San Martín bridge, which spans another gorge that funnels into Río Pastaza 50m below. From there, make the simple return to town. Alternatively, you can arrive at the San Martín bridge directly via the main road to Ambato. The road forks about 20min. from Baños; bear right at the blue-and-white religious shrine and continue downhill. A few hundred meters beyond the bridge and the zoo lies a trail on the right leading down to a view of the **Cascada Ines María.**

EL SALADO TOBAGANES. For an escape from the tourist scene, take the dirt road on the right just before entering El Salado (see **Baños,** p. 150). Follow the path beside the river, which has views of forest and farms.

TUNGURAHUA. The hardcore hiker won't be disappointed by the trek up the slopes of mighty Tungurahua. This 10th-highest peak in Ecuador is currently off-limits due to its recent eruption; proceeding beyond the abandoned refuge (at 4000m) is not advisable. Still, the 2000m climb from Baños should satisfy. Take the road toward Ambato past the fork to the San Martín bridge and turn left at the green Tungurahua sign (20min.). The path soon becomes a steep, dirt trail that continues up to the refuge (6hr.). As of this writing, the US$10 park fee was not currently being collected at the unmanned Pondoa ranger station. A tour guide is an absolute must, as falling rocks, ashfall, and an increasingly unused and disappearing trail all pose real dangers. Some Baños companies provide guides (US$30; see **Tours,** p. 151).

RÍO VERDE ☎ 03

A little less than halfway between Baños in the Highlands and Puyo in the jungle, the strip called Río Verde embodies the best of both worlds. A convergence of tropical weather and rugged terrain has made its surroundings a breeding ground for waterfalls: there are over 20 of them in the area, ranging from serpentine trickles to booming cataracts. As an added perk, a number of quality cabins provide bases from which to enjoy the watery landscape.

Río Verde proper is nothing more than a few convenience stores along the highway; the real attractions lie outside, or rather, below the strip. First, **Río Verde** begins its plunge, gushing over smooth black volcanic rock at the **Cascadas San Miguel**, 250m from the highway. The path to these first falls begins directly past the bridge as you walk toward Puyo. The second falls are lower down the canyon, but higher in stature, and exponentially more terrifying (in an idyllic sort of way). Showering you with mist and humility is the **Pailón del Diablo (Devil's Cauldron)**, where Río Verde roars off a cliff to join Río Pastaza on its path toward the Amazon. Six separate demonic faces can be seen lurking in the rocks above the cauldron; some are easier to spot than others. The 1km trail down to the falls begins 50m past the path to San Miguel. At the falls, **Restaurant Bar Café El Pailón ❶** serves drinks (US$0.50-1) and requests an admission fee to help conserve the trails leading to the falls. (☎2884 204. Open daily 8am-5:30pm. US$0.50, children US$0.25.) A shaky suspension bridge farther down the trail provides another vantage point from which to admire the ferocious flume. As you stand on the bridge dangling high over the river, take heart in the fact that if the huge warning signs on either side of the bridge tell you that any more than five people at a time is gravely dangerous, then you and the four people on the bridge with you should be perfectly safe. On the other side of the bridge you'll find **El Otro Lado ❺**, comprising several immaculate cabins at the base of a forested mountain. (☎2884 193. Meals US$5. US$30 per person, including hot tub access.) Five kilometers from Río Verde on the road to Baños lies an implausible contraption, advertised as "the longest cable car in Ecuador," which ferries fearless passengers across the river canyon with a car motor. Locals use it for transport, but tourists can ride for US$1. To get to Río Verde from Baños, take one of the Baños-Puyo **buses** (30min., every 15min., US$0.40), and ask the driver to let you off at Río Verde.

PARQUE NACIONAL SANGAY

Founded in 1979, Parque Nacional Sangay serves more as a protected natural area than a tourist attraction, catering to hikers with a serious wanderlust. The park spans four provinces, contains three of Ecuador's 10 highest peaks (including two active volcanoes), and shelters a diverse selection of flora and fauna—including such rare species as the endangered Andean tapir, found nowhere else in the world. Meanwhile the park's geography ranges from high Andean peaks to lowland rainforests. Excursions to the park are less commercialized than those to Chimborazo or Cotopaxi but inaccessibility, combined with the park's objective (to protect and conserve), bars visitors from seeing Sangay's more remote areas.

AT A GLANCE	
AREA: 5178 sq. km.	**GATEWAYS:** Riobamba (p. 163), Macas (p. 310), and Baños (p. 150).
CLIMATE: Subtropical to temperate. Varies more by altitude than by season. During the wet season (Nov.-Feb. and Apr.-Oct.) more rain falls on the east side.	**CAMPING:** Campgrounds throughout the park, but none have facilities or running water.
HIGHLIGHTS: Volcán Tungurahua, El Altar and its collapsed crater, hiking El Crater, Volcán Sangay.	**FEES AND RESERVATIONS:** US$10, collected at Ministerio del Ambiente stations.

CENTRAL HIGHLANDS

◀◆ ORIENTATION

The park is divided into two sections: the **zona alta (high zone)** in the Sierra (1500-5319m) and the **zona baja (low zone)** in the Oriente (900-1500m). The zona alta contains Sangay's main attractions; its entrance points are easily accessible from Baños or Riobamba. The four main attractions in the zona alta are the relaxing **El Placer** hike, the towering fire-spewers **Volcán Tungurahua** (5016m) and **Volcán Altar** (5319m), and the remote namesake, **Volcán Sangay** (5230m). Additional hiking opportunities exist in the southwestern areas of the park.

▆ TRANSPORTATION

The road to **Pondoa** and **Volcán Tungurahua** begins 1km from Baños on the left side of the highway to Ambato. Different **buses** run to each park entrance.

Candelaria/El Releche: take a bus from Riobamba to **Penipe** (40min., 10 per day 6:30am-6:30pm, US$0.30) and hire a **camioneta** to drive the 16km to the entrance (US$10).

Alao: Buses leave from Primera Constituyente and Alvarado in Riobamba (M-Sa noon and 3pm, US$0.80

Atillo: Buses leave from 10 de Agosto and Benalcázar and go to **Cuerpo de Ingenieros del Ejército** (3½hr., M-Sa 3pm, US$2), from which it's a 1hr. hike to the entrance.

Zona Baja: Enter from Macas (see p. 313). The park has no roads or transportation.

Cañar: The Southern office, off the Panamerican Hwy. and can be reached by a Cuenca-bound bus from the north.

◤ PRACTICAL INFORMATION

Park Information: The Ministerio del Ambiente, Ecuador's national park service, provides information and guide advice in Spanish. Pay the park admission (US$10) at their offices in Candelaria, Alao, Atillo, or Cañar. Contact their Riobamba office for more information (see **Riobamba: Tourist Offices,** p. 163, or **Macas: Tours Offices,** p. 310, for zona baja information). For more trip-specific information in English, consult the South American Explorers in Quito (see **Quito: Tourist Offices,** p. 85).

Accommodations and Camping: 2 park-owned refuges without facilities in El Placer, and 1 privately run refuge near the rim of El Altar. Campgrounds exist throughout the rest of the park, but "campground" may be roughly translated as "place where people have put up tents." They have no shelter, running water, or facilities of any kind.

Supplies: Ice-climbing gear may be necessary for the upper areas of Tungurahua and is definitely necessary to climb El Altar or Sangay. Supply rental is available at Alta Montaña in Riobamba (see **Riobamba: Tours,** p. 163).

Tours: Unguided exploration is possible, but it may be preferable to go with a guided group. The park is huge and getting lost is a real danger. Guides are available in Riobamba (see p. 163), Baños (see p. 150), and occasionally at the Ministerio del Ambiente stations.

◉ ▨ SIGHTS AND HIKING

Whether climbing a volcano or fishing in a mountain lake, outdoors-lovers can find endless amusement. For more hiking information, see **Trekking and Hiking,** p. 42.

VOLCÁN TUNGURAHUA. The most popular hike up Tungurahua is accessible from Baños (see p. 156). From Pondoa, take 3hr. hike to a simple refuge. *Let's Go* does not recommend climbing higher than 4500m because the volcano is currently active (you can see and hear evidence of this on many Baños-area hikes). Many tour operators rent bikes to coast back to town from Pondoa. However, Tungurahua's other side is full of plummeting **waterfalls** that can be reached from Riobamba. The hike up the southern foothills of the volcano traverses cloud forest en route to the waterfalls, some as high as 100m. *(From Riobamba, take a bus to Penipe (see* **Transportation,** *p. 163). Park rangers at the Candelaria station can help arrange a guide.)*

EL ALTAR (LOS ALTARES). The highest mountain in the park, El Altar (5320m), collapsed in 1460 and is now partially covered by glaciers. **The summit is the most technical climb in Ecuador** and defied mountaineers' repeated efforts to scale it until 1963. However, the 8hr. climb through woodlands and plains to the spectacular **crater rim** (4200m) is more manageable. Begin from the Candelaria. *(Ministerio del Ambiente officials in Candelaria can assist you in finding a guide (US$30 per day), or failing that, will guide you themselves. Equipment is needed for the highly technical ascents of El Altar's craggy peaks, but not for the climb to the crater. Sturdy boots are recommended for all hikes. A rustic refugio near the crater rim is run by Osualdo Sedeño, the owner of the Hacienda Releche near Candelaria. In Releche, he can provide trip assistance and detailed directions to the refugio. Camping is also possible in a cave near the crater.)*

VOLCÁN SANGAY. One of the most active volcanoes in the world, Sangay constantly spews ash and smoke to signal its presence. This lava-dripping monster has three deep craters at its summit that have been known to toss out massive, red-hot boulders. If that doesn't faze you, the park's mammoth namesake requires two to nine days to conquer, depending on whether you take the longer or the shorter route. *(Begin the hike up Sangay from the entrance at Alao, on the western side of the park. A guide is a must, since both routes can be difficult to navigate. In Alao, you can find a guide (US$20 per day) and a mule (US$10 per day; only feasible on the initial portion of the shorter route). Be cautious climbing all the way to Sangay's fiery crater; you risk being caught in a lava flow. Experience is another must, and visitors should only climb as far as guides recommend. A helmet for tumbling rocks and sturdy gloves for climbing across jagged rock will come in handy toward the summit. Take a bus (see p. 163) from Riobamba to Aloasí.)*

EL PLACER. El Placer is a multi-day hike through a low, swampy area with thermal baths, trout-filled lakes, and abundant wildlife. Watch for colorful birds, jaguars, spectacled bears, and the elusive Andean tapir. *(Park employees can provide more information and arrange a guide. A tent is unnecessary since there are refugios on the hike to El Placer and at the site. Buses (see p. 163) run from Riobamba to Alaosí.)*

ATILLO AREA. Atillo is the gateway to the southern zone of El Placer. Featuring typical vegetation and wildlife (if anything in Sangay can be called typical), it is the jumping-off point for some amazing treks around 52 lakes and through several climates. To the detriment of the wildlife, a road between Atillo and Macas is currently under construction, but for the backpacker, this unfinished road is a clearly marked trail for a spectacular two- to three-day hike from the central Highlands to the steaming jungle. Along the way you'll cross bleak *páramo*, mountain lakes, and gradually thickening vegetation. Be prepared for mud due to the seemingly perpetual rainy season. Although most hikers begin Ecuador's Inca trail from Achupallas, Alta Montaña in Riobamba (see p. 163) organizes a four-day trek from Atillo to the Ingapirca ruins (see p. 179). Alta Montaña also offers one- to four-day treks around the Atillo area (both trips from US$35 per day). *(Ministerio del Ambiente staff at the Atillo entrance can provide a place to stay before setting out, directions to the trailhead, and tips on where to camp. Buses at the end of the trail in 9 de Octubre can take you back to Macas and from there the Highlands.)*

LAGO OZOGOCHE. Just past Guamote is a small sign pointing curious travelers toward Lago Ozogoche, the giant lake in the Atillo area into which thousands of migrant birds plummet to their deaths every late August and early September. These suicide birds of Ozogoche, known as cuvivis to the locals, are thought to be migrant North American birds that simply tire out and give up on their way down south. They are as much a part of the local legend as they are of scientific mystery: limited studies have found that the cuvivi feathers are well suited to the Andean weather, and the dead birds are meaty enough for the locals to gather and eat. Whatever the case, this is a sight that many tourists must see with their own eyes; on one day in September of 2003, nine buses took over 500 tourists directly to the lake to see the morbid show. *(To get to Lago Ozogoche from Riobamba, board a Cuenca-bound bus on the Panamerican Hwy. and get off just past Guamote (US$0.50) at the sign for the lake and wait for a camioneta to take you the next 1-1½hr. to the lake (US$10). In late Aug. or early Sept., inquire at the office of the Ministerio de Ambiente in Riobamba (see p. 163) for information on group tours. Pro-Bici in Riobamba (see p. 165) organizes day-long bike trips to Lago Ozogoche.)*

PARQUE NACIONAL LLANGANATES

Whether because of the largely inaccessible mountains it contains or its lack of an impressive volcanic namesake, Llangantes National Park is one of the lesser-known protected areas in Ecuador. After a five-week tour in the early 20th century, celebrated Ecuadorian explorer Luciano Andrade Marín wanted the land marked "Uninhabitable Forever" on all maps. Extremely difficult to access, much of the 219,707 hectares of this park, founded in 1996, remain unexplored by travelers. The terrain ranges from 1200m above sea level to the peak of Cerro Hermos (4571m), with countless valleys, lagoons, and small waterfalls. Many rivers—great for rafting and kayaking—flow around Tena from Llanganates. Rumor has it that gold may even be hidden within this park, but unwelcoming terrain protects it.

Park access is mostly from the Baños side. In Baños, the **Ministerio del Ambiente** (see p. 151) has information about visiting the park. Weather is notoriously wet, and vegetation is famously dense; be prepared if you plan on camping in the park. December through February is the driest season to visit, but even then it is advisable to bring waterproof clothing and to hire a local guide who is familiar with the difficult land and ever-changing climate.

THE INCA TRAIL (ECUADOR-STYLE)

Hardcore trekkers can make the difficult journey between Achupallas and Ingapirca along the Ecuadorian Inca Trail, which traverses Parque Nacional Sangay. The trail is roughly 35km long and can be tackled in as little as two days and one night (some of TerraDiversa's guides have done it in 10hr!), but many travelers opt to take three days to finish the route. The trail peaks at 4420m and never drops below 3160m, so be sure to acclimatize sufficiently. The only fees on the trail are the US$6 required to enter the ruins at Ingapirca, but only the most experienced hikers should go without a guide.

TRANSPORTATION AND PRACTICAL INFORMATION. Take a bus or car from **Riobamba, Cuenca,** or **Alausí** to Achupallas. The trail starts south of town, past the cemetery, by Río Cadrul. The route is not a circle; to get back take a bus from Ingapirca to wherever it is you want to go next. Camping along the route is possible, though there are no campgrounds. The closest place to rent equipment is Riobamba (see Equipment Rental, p. 165) or Cuenca (see p. 174). No special supplies are necessary. Guides are available in Riobamba, Alausí, or Cuenca. Groups can be assembled in Riobamba or Cuenca, but tours are infrequent.

⚑ THE HIKE. Day 1 starts in Achupallas; follow Río Cadrul and climb a peak through nearby mountains. Pass the Inca ruins and camp at **Laguna Tres Cruces** (3910m). A side trip ascends **Cerro Callana Pucará** (4190m), which offers views of Chimborazo. **Day 2** brings yet another high pass, Cuchilla Tres Cruces (4420m), then a descent to the Valle Espindola where you pick up the old Inca trail. Camp by the Inca ruins of Paredores. **Day 3** continues along the same trail and up Puyal pass (4000m), where you hike through *páramo* the ruins of Ingapirca.

RESERVA FAUNÍSTICA CHIMBORAZO

One of only two nature reserves in Ecuador, La Reserva Faunística Chimborazo is most famous for the 6310m behemoth that bears the park's name. But Volcán Chimborazo is not the only attraction of the reserve. Nearly 2000 vicuñas, relatives of the llama that were nearly wiped off of Ecuador's map 10 years ago, live nowhere else in the country. The *curlquwingue* (Carunculated Caracara) also lives in the reserve. But as for Volcán Chimborazo, most eager *andinistas* attack it in June and July, when visibility is at its best but winds are high. From October to January it is more dangerous to climb the mountain due to avalanches.

🛈 PRACTICAL INFORMATION

Tours: Guided tours are available in Riobamba (see **Tours,** p. 165). Novices should not wander past the 2nd refuge—only extremely experienced alpinists should attempt to reach the summit without a guide. The **Centro de Información "Waman Way"** in Pulinguí San Pablo, more commonly known as **Casa Condor** (☎ 09 7580 033 or 09 7580 030; casacondor@yahoo.es), an ecotourist project run by certified guides from nearby indigenous communities, offers guided daytrips (mostly in Spanish) to: **Templo Machay,** the oldest sacred spot in the province of Chimborazo (US$35); the enormous **Árbol Solitario,** a lovely tree growing at 400m amid the *páramo* (US$35); **Bosque Mágico de Polilepis,** an ancient forest of aromatic, twisting trees defying *páramo* flora logic at 4200m (US$35); **La Chorrera Canyon,** a winding gorge near the base of the volcano that offers some of the most diverse rock climbing in Ecuador, from easy climbs to sheer 90° walls that require the utmost expertise (half-day US$20); and the **Aguas Termales,** Chimborazo-heated thermal pools in a natural setting (3- to 4-day trek US$45 per day). Many of these hikes can also be arranged as horseback rides (US$20 per day, before guide fees). A 3rd possibility is the 5020m, snow-capped **Volcán Carihuayrazo,** another challenge for experienced mountaineers. Arrange trips to Carihuayrazo with Alta Montaña (see p. 165).

Maps: It is sometimes possible to get a map (US$2) at **IGM** in Quito (see p. 97).

Supplies: If planning to reach the summit, you must have a guide, crampons, ropes, and other standard equipment. Both refuges on the mountain have basic food items, coffee, and tourist souvenirs, but almost everything else (including guides) is available at **Alta Montaña** in Riobamba (see **Tours,** p. 165). Park admission US$10, ISIC US$5.

⌷ TRANSPORTATION

Those up for a challenging hike can take a Flota Bolívar or 10 de Noviembre bus from Riobamba toward **Guaranda** along the El Arenal route and ask to be dropped off at the turnoff to the **refuges** (1¼hr., US$1.20). From the drop-off point, it's an 8km hike up a dirt road to the first refuge (4800m). 4WD vehicles travel this road, and some travelers report hitching a ride. (*Let's Go* does not recommend hitchhiking.) On the way back, hop on a bus going from Guaranda to Riobamba. A relatively painless way to reach the second refuge is through

CENTRAL HIGHLANDS

the Hotel Imperial in Riobamba (see p. 166). Tell them the night before, and they'll arrange a driver who can take you to the lower refuge (1½hr., around 8am, US$25-30). **Pico-Bici** (see p. 165), in Riobamba, runs an excellent bicycle tour that begins at Chimborazo's first refuge and ends 44km later in the town of Calpi, 12km from Riobamba. The driver will wait while you hike. The drive to Chimborazo can also be done by any 4x4 taxi from Riobamba or arranged by guides in town (round-trip US$25).

ACCOMMODATIONS

Both **refuges ❸**, owned and operated by Alta Montaña in Riobamba, offer bunk beds, cooking facilities, and a fireplace (US$10 per person, IVA not included), but you must bring your own sleeping bag. **Casa Condor ❷** (see above), in Pulinguí San Pablo, offers basic bunks for US$6 per person and private cabins for US$8 per person, as well as transportation and food services.

VOLCÁN CHIMBORAZO

If Riobamba is the Sultan of the Andes, Volcán Chimborazo (6310m) is the king of volcanoes. In fact, indigenous legend considers Chimborazo *el varón* (the man) and nearby Tungurahua *la mujer* (the woman). Although Chimborazo no longer holds the title of highest mountain in the world, its summit remains the farthest from the center of the earth, peeking above the clouds into the silence of space. While summitting the volcano is best left to experienced climbers, Chimborazo's second refuge, Whymper (5000m), offers stunning views, and can be reached in half a day without any climbing experience, equipment, or extreme expense.

AT A GLANCE

DISTANCE: 10km.	**FEES:** Admission fee US$10, collected irregularly from a post just off the highway—some unscrupulous guides have taken advantage of the situation to collect the fee from tourists, then pocket it.
CLIMATE: June-July is generally the clearest time, but windy. High winds and snow storms are a threat year-round.	
TIME: 2 days.	

CLIMBING CHIMBORAZO

The climb begins with a drive to the first refuge (4800m), an ideal location for acclimatization hikes. From there it is a 200m climb (1km, 30min.) to the second refuge (5000m), where guides take you up to a **glacier** in the afternoon to get used to the equipment. Later, settle into the refuge and try to get a few hours of sleep before the midnight ascent. Leaving the refuge, the route goes to the left of a glacier and ascends to a snowy area referred to as **El Corredor.** From there, weave around the rock formation called **El Castillo,** before the long, snowy ascent up to the summit (6310m; 8-10hr.). The majority of the hike up will be done in the dark, but daylight brings unbeatable views of Ecuador if the clouds aren't too thick. Descend via the same route (3-4hr.), then drive back to Riobamba from the lower refuge. True *andinistas* might attempt **La Integral de Chimborazo,** a two-day trip that takes down all five of Chimborazo's peaks—Nicolas Martinez, Politécnica, Central, Whymper, and Veintimilla—before returning to the second refuge. This feat is incredibly rare and should not be attempted by anyone but a true expert.

RIOBAMBA ☎ 03

This self-proclaimed "Sultan of the Andes" (pop. 122,000; 2750m) is a worthy destination in itself, though it is known primarily for nearby indigenous villages, daytrips to Chimborazo, and Parque Nacional Sangay—and, of course, as the first step on the pricey yet heavily touristed train to La Nariz del Diablo near Alausí. Cobblestone streets criss-cross plazas and parks that have views of snow-capped Volcanoes Chimborazo and Tungurahua. After a devastating earthquake in 1797, the entire city moved to its present site on a highland valley plain. As a result, the city's oldest architecture is Neoclassical, with one notable exception: the cathedral on Veloz and 5 de Junio was transported stone by stone from its pre-quake location.

▐ TRANSPORTATION

Buses: Many buses travelling between Quito and Loja stop in Riobamba; to catch one, wait outside the station.

Terminal Terrestre, on León Borja (the western part of 10 de Agosto) and Av. de la Prensa, 1km northwest of the center. Buses head to: **Ambato** (1hr., every 10min. 4am-7pm, US$1); **Cuenca** (6½hr., 7 per day 5:30am-7:30pm, US$6.10); **Guayaquil** (5hr., every 30min. 2:30am-8:30pm, US$4.50); **Quito** (4hr., every 15min. 2:15am-9pm, US$3.85). To reach the center, leave the terminal, turn right twice, and walk 1km on León Borja, which turns into 10 de Agosto at Caraboro, or simply hop on one of the passing city buses.

Terminal Oriental (☎2960 766), on Espejo and Elisa Borja, northeast of town, sends buses to: Baños (2hr., every hr. 4:30am-6:20pm, US$2); **Puyo** (4hr., 9 per day 6am-6:45pm, US$3.75); **Tena** (6½hr., 6 per day 4am-3pm, US$6.25). **Bayushig** provides service to **Penipe** (40min., 10 per day 6:30am-6:30pm, US$0.40), 15km away from the Candelaria entrance to Parque Sangay. **As of August 2004, the Baños road was closed due to rockslides on Tungarahua and all buses went through Ambato (1hr., US$1).**

Guano Terminal, on Rocafuerte and Nueva York, sends buses to **Guano** (20min., every 15min., US$0.20) and **Santa Teresita** (35min., every 30min., US$0.35).

Guamote Transports, 3 blocks southeast of the Terminal Terrestre at Unidad Nacional and La Prensa, sends buses to **Guamote** (1hr., US$0.60) via **Cajabamba** (30min., US$0.35) and **Laguna de Colta** (35min., US$0.40). Buses to **San Juan** leave from Unidad Nacional and Bolivia (30min., every 30min. 6am-6:45pm, US$0.40).

Trains: The **train station** (☎2961 909) is at 10 de Agosto and Carabobo, in the town center. Open daily 8am-7pm, departure days 6am-7pm. The magnificent **Riobamba-Guayaquil** route was reopened in 1999, with limited service from Riobamba to Alausí and over the famed **Nariz del Diablo** pass (round-trip 10hr.; W, F, Su 7am; US$11). Ticket window opens 4pm on days before the railroad runs; lines begin to form 3:30pm. Purchase tickets the night before, and bring your passport or a copy of your passport to purchase your ticket. Schedules change often. Arrange private rail tours on a luxurious converted monobus through **Metropolitan Tours** (US$35; see below).

Taxis: US$1 within the city.

✦ 🛈 ORIENTATION AND PRACTICAL INFORMATION

Riobamba stretches out in a grid. **Olmedo** and **Junín** form the borders of the markets and parks, running perpendicular to **5 de Junio** and **Diego de Ibarra**. **Primera Constituyente** and **10 de Agosto** are the main thoroughfares.

Tourist Offices: Ministerio de Turismo (☎/fax 2941 213), at Borja and Pasaje, amiably distributes **maps** and brochures on all provinces in the central Sierra. English spoken. Open M-F 8:30am-1pm and 2:30-6pm. In the same complex, the **Unidad de Turismo** (☎2947 389) has a more local focus. Open M-F 8am-12:30pm and 2:30-6pm. In the terminal terrestre, **Información Municipal** (☎9620 050) can help deci-

TO GUAMOTE (1km)

Parque Guayaquil

TO ⓘ (2blk),
TERMINAL TERRESTRE (1km)

Teniente Latus

Av. Gonzalo Dávalos

*Ministerio de Turismo
Unidad de Turismo*

Brasil

Riobamba

🏠 ACCOMMODATIONS
Hostel Oasis, 13
Hotel Imperial, 7
Hotel Los Shyris, 10
Hotel Riobamba Inn, 9
Tren Dorado, 5

🍴 FOOD
Chifa Joysing, 3
El Caldero, 4
El Delirio, 8
Londres Cafetería, 12
Marisquería Esmeraldas, 6
Pizzería San Valentín, 2
Restaurant and Cafetería
Sierra Nevada, 11

🍸 NIGHTLIFE
Gens Chop, 1

Uruguay

Alta Montaña ■

Diego de Ibarra

San Juan

PLAZA
DE TOROS

León

Francia

Banco MM
Jaramillo
Arteaga

Metropolitan
Touring
V. Torres

Parque
21 de
Abril

2

Primera Constituyente

Veloz

Olmedo

Unidad Nacional

D. León Borja

Lavalle

San Antonio
de Padua

Lavalle

Lavalle

El
Espectador

Juan Montalvo

6

Carabobo

5

Museo y Centro Cultural
Banco Central de Ecuador

Dávalos

9

TO GUANO
TERMINAL (3blk)

Rocafuerte

7   8

10

11

Pichincha

García Moreno

Banco de
Guayaquil

12

España

Larrea

Parque
Sucre

Museo del
Colegio
Maldonado

Museo de Arte
Religioso

Larrea

Colón

Supermercado
Akí

Mercado
La Merced

Pro-Bici ■

Parque La
Concepción

La Concepción

Espejo

Supermercado
Camari

La Merced

Parque
Maldonado

La Catedral

TO TERMINAL
ORIENTAL (6blk)

5 de Junio

Colombia

Chile

Villarroel

Olmedo

Guayaquil

10 de Agosto

Primera Constituyente

Veloz

Orozco

Argentinos

Junín

Ayacucho

Mercado
San
Alfonso

Tarquí

Andinatel

Velasco

Casa ■
Indígena

PLAZA
SAN
FRANCISCO

Benalcázar

Parque
La Libertad

La Basílica

Mariana de Jesus

Alvarado

0   150 meters

0   150 yards

TO HOSPITAL
(6blk) Almagro

13

pher bus schedules and arrange accommodations. Open daily 7am-8pm. **Ministerio de Ambiente** (☎2963 779), on 9 de Octubre near Duchicela, in the western corner of town, at the **Ministerio de Agricultura y Ganadería (MAG),** has helpful staff who can help with excursions to Chimborazo and Sangay. Some English Spoken. Open M-F 8am-1pm and 2-4:30pm. **Casa Indígena** (☎2941 728; cell 09 7279 202; jkawuay@yahoo.es), on Velasco and Guayaquil, connects tourists with certified naturalist guides native to the areas in which they work. Arranges food, shelter, and guides in most any village within Parque Nacional Sangay. Hector Silva, president of the organization, is available M and F 9am-5pm.

Tours: Alta Montaña (☎2942 215), at Borja and Ibarra, is the most experienced climbing and trekking company in town, offering trips to **Chimborazo, Cotopaxi** (US$180), and **El Altar** (US$180-200) as well as multi-day treks through **Parque Nacional Sangay** and the **Chimborazo Reserve** (US$80 per day). All guides know English mountain-climbing vocabulary. Open M-Sa 9am-7pm. **Metropolitan Touring-Riobamba,** on Primera Constituyente, between León and Torres (☎2969 600; mtriobamba@andinanet.net), offers numerous daytrips in the Riobamba area including one in their own private railroad car, which traverses **La Nariz del Diablo** (US$35). English-speaking guides available. Open M-F 8:30am-1pm and 2:30-7pm, Sa 10am-1pm. **Pro-Bici,** Primera Constituyente 23-51 (☎2941 880 or 2941 759; www.probici.com), at Larrea, earns high praise for its guided bicycle trips (US$25-40) into the surrounding countryside. Radio communication with guides at all times. Bike rental plus detailed maps with altitude profiles US$8-20. English spoken. Open M-F 8:30am-1:30pm and 2:30pm-8pm, Sa 8:30am-8pm. If the door is locked, go across the street to the textile shop and ask for owner Galo Brito.

Currency Exchange: Banco de Guayaquil (☎2966 129), on Primera Constituyente between García Moreno and Pichincha. Exchanges traveler's checks M-F 8:30am-1pm. MC/V **ATM.** Open M-F 8:30am-5pm. **Banco MM Jaramillo Arteaga** (☎9402 669), at Borja and León, has **Western Union** service. Open M-F 9am-5pm, Sa 9am-1pm.

Outdoor Equipment: Alta Montaña (☎2942 215), at Borja and Ibarra, rents quality tents, sleeping bags, and other outdoor supplies. Open daily 9am-7pm.

Emergency: ☎101.

Police: Primero Constituyente 70-38 (☎2961 913), at 5 de Junio. Open 24hr.

Pharmacy: Farmacia Alemana, Primera Constituyente 28-74 (☎2964 132), at Carabobo. Open daily 8:30am-9pm.

Hospital: Policlínico (☎2948 790), at Proaño and Chile. Open 24hr.

Telephones: Andinatel (☎2943 036), at Tarqui and Veloz. Calling card and collect calls. Open daily 8am-10pm.

Internet Access: Throughout the *centro.* US$0.70-1 per hr. A veritable silicon valley lies between Guayaquil and 10 de Agosto on Rocafuerte.

Post Office: ☎2966 006. At 10 de Agosto and Espejo. Open M-F 8am-12:30pm and 2:30-6pm, Sa 8am-12:30pm.

ACCOMMODATIONS

Riobamba's hotels vary greatly in quality. A small increase in price can signify a huge leap in features. Saving those extra pennies may not be worthwhile.

Tren Dorado (☎/fax 2964 840), at Carabobo and 10 de Agosto. Comfortable rooms named after Zodiac signs have flowered decor, wooden dressers with mirrors, hot private baths, and sometimes cable TV. Rooftop terraces have amazing views. Restaurant. Breakfast US$2. Singles US$8-10; doubles US$16; triples US$24. ❸

Hostel Oasis (☎2961 210), at Veloz and Almagro. Across town from most of Riobamba's traditional hotels. One of the only true hostels in Riobamba, Oasis has a nice courtyard with an unnervingly friendly llama. Oasis's only real drawback is its thin, lumpy mattresses, but the atmosphere may convince you to stay anyway. Cable TV. Rooms with private bath US$7. ❷

Hotel Riobamba Inn, Carabobo 23-20 (☎2961 696), at Primera Constituyente, across from the Banco Central, boasts hot private baths, spotless bedrooms, comfy beds, and TVs in every room. The tiled floor in the hallway shines so much you might want to skate on it. Singles US$11; doubles US$21; triples US$30. ❸

Hotel Los Shyris, Rocafuerte 21-60 (☎2960 323), at 10 de Agosto. Clean rooms with TVs, phones, and shampoo and soap for the cubicle bathrooms. Dark, wood-paneled interior. Common area with Internet access (US$1 per hr.). Singles US$5, with bath US$8; doubles US$10/$14; triples with bath US$18. ❷

Hotel Imperial, Rocafuerte 22-15 (☎2960 429), at 10 de Agosto, in the heart of Riobamba. Balconies provide excellent views of Riobamba. Rooftop terrace is not optimal for lounging, but guests have access nonetheless. Arranges Chimborazo excursions. Singles US$6; doubles US$12; triples US$18. Discounts for large groups. ❷

🅲 FOOD

Riobamba has lots of budget lunch stops but little to excite the palates of passing travelers. Come dinnertime, locals crowd around outdoor stands that offer various traditional dishes. **Supermercado Aki** is at Colón and Olmedo. (☎2946 150. Open M-F 9am-8pm.) One block south, on Espejo and Olmedo, **Supermercado Camari** is open weekends. (☎2969 874. Open M-F 9am-10pm, Sa 8am-10pm, Su 8am-2pm.)

Londres Cafetería (☎2953 378), on García Moreno between 10 de Agosto and Primera Constituyente. Gorgeous pastries that look so good you won't want to eat them. Restaurant in back serves cheap *almuerzos* (US$1.50). Open daily 8am-8pm. ❶

Pizzería San Valentín (☎2963 137), at Borja and Torres. Correctly touted by some expats as the best food in town. Mexican food and sports on a large TV. The perfect place to watch the big soccer match. Entrees US$1.50-3. Open Tu-Sa 5pm-midnight. ❶

El Caldero, Unidad Nacional 29-15 (☎2955 226), at Carabobo. Tasteful decor and tasty food. Baby blue color scheme will keep you coming back on dreary Andean days. Filet mignon US$4. Open M-Sa noon-9:30pm, Su 11am-4pm. ❸

Restaurant and Cafetería Sierra Nevada (☎2951 542), on Primera Constituyente and Rocafuerte. Eat lunch in elegant, brightly colored rooms. Riobamba's upper crust comes here (entrees US$2-4). *Almuerzos* US$1.80. Open daily 8am-10:30pm.

El Delirio (☎2966 441; eldelirio1824@hotmail.com), at Primera Constituyente and Rocafuerte. Simón Bolívar once lived here. Fireplace inside and charcoal grill outside in the courtyard waft a sweet and light fragrance. Drinks US$1.50-3.50. *Comida típica* US$5-9. Open daily 11:30am-10pm. IVA and service not included. AmEx/MC/V. ❸

Marisquería Esmeraldas (☎2944 586), on Montalvo and Veloz. The concrete floor and plastic tables don't keep the locals away and shouldn't keep you away either. F-Su seafood *almuerzos* US$1.50. Entrees US$3-4. Open daily 8am-4pm.

Chifa Joysing, Unidad Nacional 29-23 (☎2961 285), at Carabobo. The huge portions of savory cuisine at this typical *chifa* will have you singing with joy. Remarkably clean. Vegetarian dishes available. Entrees US$2-4. Open daily 10am-midnight. ❶

🅶 SIGHTS

PARKS. Riobamba's scenic parks cry out for a stroll. One of the most colorful pleas comes from **Parque 21 de Abril,** also known as **La Loma de Quito,** perched above the rest of Riobamba. Couples come up for the views but often keep their gazes—and lips—locked on each other. The park also houses a church, **San Antonio de Padua.** (Church open Tu-Sa 8am-noon and 2-5pm, Su 8am-noon.) **Parque Sucre,** at España and Primera Constituyente, in the town center, graces the city with a bronze fountain and statue of Neptune installed in 1913 to commemorate the introduction of potable water to the city. Locals gather on the palm-tree-shaded benches to socialize and people-watch. The engaging **Parque Maldonado,** at Primera Constituyente and Espejo, displays a monument to its namesake, Pedro Vicente Maldonado, a local historian and cartographer who drew the first political map of Ecuador. **Parque Guayaquil,** at Unidad Nacional and León Borja, near the soccer stadium, teems with life on paths encircling a reflecting pool.

CHURCHES. La Basílica, at Veloz and Benalcázar, gained fame as the only round church in Ecuador. The main **cathedral,** at Veloz and 5 de Junio, near Parque Maldonado, is the town's oldest building and the sole remnant of Riobamba's pre-earthquake site, transported, stone by stone, in 1797.

MUSEUMS. La Concepción (or the **Museo de Arte Religioso**), at Argentinos and Larrea, displays devotional art and artifacts from the 17th to 19th centuries, housed in the tranquil, breezy rooms of an 18th-century convent. Don't let the treasure room tempt your inner thief. (**☎** 2965 212. Open Tu-Sa 9am-noon and 3-6pm. US$4, students US$2.) The **Museo del Colegio Maldonado** (also known as the **Museo de Ciencias Naturales**) is a tiny natural history and science exhibit inside the schoolhouse at Parque Sucre. It's any taxidermist's delight. (**☎** 2960 265. Open M-F 8am-1pm. US$0.25.)

MARKETS. The **Saturday market** is a huge affair. The entire length of all streets boxed in by España, 5 de Junio, Guayaquil, and Argentinos fills with vendors and shoppers. On Fridays, the market at La Valle and Esmeraldas amazes with the sheer quantity of plant material occupying its stands.

🎵 🎭 **ENTERTAINMENT AND NIGHTLIFE**

Riobamba's biggest festival, **El Veintiuno de Abril,** celebrates the city's founding. The actual holiday falls on April 21, but locals get a head start on the 20th and party until the 22nd; fairs, bullfights, and parades swamp the streets. Another fiesta occurs on June 29 to honor Saint Peter and Saint Paul. Locals light eucalyptus bonfires throughout the streets as rock bands croon till midnight. **Cockfights** take place on Saturdays in April in a house at Almagro and Olmedo. Partying happens on the weekends in Riobamba. Most **discos** cluster on León Borja between the terminal and Hotel Zeus at Duchicela. Try **Gens Chop** (**☎** 2960 707; open daily 3:30pm-2:30am), at Borja and Duchicela.

🏃 **DAYTRIPS FROM RIOBAMBA**

THE RIOBAMBA-ALAUSÍ-LA NARIZ DEL DIABLO

Arrive early at the train station in Riobamba to get a seat on the roof. The right side of the train (or autoferro) offers the best views. Don't get stuck underneath; some drivers require roof-riding passengers to switch with those who were in the cab for the way back. Others let passengers duke it out themselves. (Tickets from Riobamba US$11, Alausí US$7.80.)

This railway serves as a source of Ecuadorian pride and a feather in the cap of railroad engineers everywhere. Previously a fully operational railroad that ran from Quito to Guayaquil, El Niño's 1997-98 assault has turned this once magnificent railway into a highly priced and only slightly magnificent tourist attraction. The 3-4hr. ride from Riobamba to Alausí is not particularly breathtaking. Just after Alausí, **La Nariz del Diablo** (the Devil's Nose) is technically impressive but hardly the hair-raising experience that some travel guides make it out to be; anyone who has ridden on a bus around the northern part of the Latacunga Loop and witnessed a driver navigate a treacherous hairpin turn while simultaneously changing the radio station will most likely find the presence of tracks quite comforting. The train mounts a perpendicular cliff by means of three switchbacks in which the train actually descends caboose first—quite a feat of railroad acrobatics. In under 30km, the line descends from 2347m to 1255m. The train departs several times a week along the old tracks, which run parallel to the Panamerican Hwy. until the town of Alausí. Then, it slows to a snail's pace and cautiously descends La Nariz del Diablo.

GUANO

Catch the bus from Rocafuerte and Nueva York (15min., every 15min. 5am-7pm, US$0.20).

A short hop away, the tiny, half-asleep village of Guano makes even tranquil Riobamba seem bustling. A smattering of *artesanía* shops peddles monstrous rugs, leather goods, and hemp items; many will custom-make any design you can communicate to them with pictures or broken Spanish. **Alfombras la Ecuatoriana,** at Garcia Moreno and Colón, just off the square, does exceptional work and allows you to watch the action. (☎ 2900 237. 1x1½m rug US$70. Open daily 8am-5pm.)

SANTIAGO DE QUITO AND LAGUNA DE COLTA

The easiest way to reach Santiago de Quito and Laguna de Colta is to take a Guamote-bound bus from Unidad Nacional (3 blocks from the Terminal Terrestre) in Riobamba (35min., every 30min., US$0.40). Ask to be let off at the "Laguna," or at "La Balbanera." To return, flag down any bus on the highway with a Riobamba sign in the window.

Some 19km from Riobamba, Santiago de Quito, the original capital of Ecuador, has two major sites: **La Balbanera church** and the **Laguna de Colta.** Built in 1534 by the Spanish, La Balbanera was the first church in Ecuador—now a boxy little stone chapel beside the highway. Only a small fraction of the church's original stonework still stands unsupported by newer whitewall. Beyond La Balbanera and across the road to the left sits the large Laguna de Colta. While the lagoon is visible from the highway, there's also a road through several beautifully framed rural villages to the back of the lake. The route (2hr.) reveals rural settlements with indigenous farmers working fields on the slopes of picturesque hills.

GUARANDA   ☎ 03

Some 60km west of Riobamba lies Guaranda (pop. 20,000; elevation 2070m), the self-appointed "Rome of the Andes." Although Guaranda isn't exactly Rome, it does sit amid seven hills, which has earned it the apt nickname "The City of Seven Hills." Though it is the capitol of the province of Bolívar, Guaranda has managed to maintain an air of calmness and relaxation that other provincial capitols often lack. Visitors to Guaranda come to slow down; to check out the chocolate, cheese, and *artesanía* in nearby Salinas; to celebrate one of Ecuador's most popular *carnavales* (in February); and to take a quick detour from the well-worn tourist trail.

⌷ TRANSPORTATION. Terminal Terrestre, off of E de Caraval, is a 15min. walk from town. **Buses** head to: **Guayaquil** (4hr., every 15min. 2:45am-4:45pm, US$4); **Quito** (4½hr., every 30min. 3am-5pm, US$4.50); **Quevedo** (6hr., 10:30am, US$5); **Riobamba** (2hr., 10 per day 6am-4pm, US$2.25); **San Luis** (5hr., 5 per day 6:45am-2:15pm, US$5); **Santo Domingo** (6hr.; 5:45, 9:15am; US$6). Buses to **Salinas** (1½hr.; M-F 6, 6:30, 7am, 1pm, Sa 6am, 1, 2:30pm, Su 6, 7am; US$1) leave daily from Eloy Alfaro and Candido Ruda. **Taxis** run US$1 within the city.

◼◪ ORIENTATION AND PRACTICAL INFORMATION. Activity   centers around **Parque Simón Bolívar** at **Garcia Moreno** and Convención de 1884 and around the **Plaza Roja**, which divides **General Enriquez** from **Cañizares** to **10 de Agosto.** On Wednesdays and Saturdays, the focus of the city shifts to the **Plaza 15 de Mayo** to the north and **Mercado 10 de Noviembre** to the south. **Banco Sudamerica,** on Sucre across from Parque Simón Bolívar, has **Western Union** service. (☎2980 641. Open M-F 8:30am-5pm.) **Banco del Pichincha,** on Azuay and 7 de Mayo, has a 24hr. Cirrus **ATM.** Call ☎101 in **emergencies. Policía Nacional,** are a 15min. walk from the stairway connecting Guayaquil and Candido Rada. (☎2980 046 or 2980 022. Open 24hr.) **Farmacia La Economía,** is on Espejo between Pichincha and Sucre. (☎2983 824 or 2981 742. Open M-Sa 8am-8pm, Su 9am-4pm.) **Hospital Alfredo Naboa Montaego** is on Cisneros, north of Selva Alegre. (☎2980 230. 24hr. emergency room.) **Andinatel,** on Rocafuerte and Sucre, allows calling card and collect calls. (☎2980 357. Open daily 8am-10pm.) **Compamás,** at 10 de Agosto and 7 de Mayo, offers **Internet** access. (☎2980 357. US$1 per hr. Open M-Sa 9am-7pm, Su 2-7pm.) **Correos del Ecuador** is at Azuay and Pichincha. (☎2980 138. Open M-F 8am-noon and 2-6pm.)

⌐ ACCOMMODATIONS. Hostal de las Flores ❸ is at Pichincha and Rocafuerte. Its flowery interior, a bright courtyard, huge rooms, and a blue-and-yellow motif make this Guaranda's top choice for bang-for-the-buck. (☎2984 396 or 2983 256 Cable TV. Breakfast for groups of 5 or more US$1.50. Singles US$10; doubles US$14; triples US$24.) **Hotel Bolívar ❸,** at Sucre and Olmedo, offers clean rooms with private baths centered around an open courtyard that hosts a talkative parrot. (☎2980 547. Cable TV. Restaurant downstairs. Rooms with private bath US$8.)

❏ FOOD. Do-it-yourselfers can pick up food at either of the markets or at **"Su Tienda" Comisaristo,** on Convención de 1884 at Rocafuerte. (☎2982 368. Open M-F 9am-1pm and 2:30-8p, Sa 8:30am-8pm, Su 8:30am-1pm.) **Los 7 Santos ❶,** at Convención de 1884 and 10 de Agosto, has worked hard on its theme. Amid an Eden-like setting complete with flowers and greenery, have the lomo de mártir or some "chocolate santificado." Perhaps the most heaven-sent of this restaurant's perks: fresh ground coffee. (☎2980 612; los7santos@hotmail.com. Sandwiches US$0.80-1.10; platos fuertes US$2.50-3. Open daily 9am-10pm.) **Pizzeria Buon Giornio ❶,** on E de Carvajal and M Carvajal, serves pizzas and pastas that compete with the Sierra's best Italian eateries in a plain wooden interior with a foosball table. ☎2983 603. Personal pizzas from US$3.60. Pastas from US$3. Open Tu-Sa noon-10pm.

SALINAS DE GUARANDA ☎03

Tucked neatly into the countryside on the opposite side of Volcán Chimborzo from the Panamerican Hwy., Salinas de Guaranda (pop. 1200; 3550m), known simply as Salinas to the locals, is an example of a town that really has its act together. The town's economy revolves around 98 factories (as of July 2004) and cooperatives that produce the chocolates, cheeses, and hand-knit sweaters that have made the Salerinito name famous in many of Quito's upscale delis and markets.

All tours start at the **Oficina de Turismo** on the main plaza. (☎2390 024; turismo@salinerito.com. Open M-F 8am-1pm and 2-6pm, Sa-Su 9am-1pm.) Tourists must register here in order to take a tour of the factories and sample the delicious cheeses and chocolates. (Tours US$8 per person, to enter each factory US$1; large groups can try to bargain down.) The office also arranges trips to: **Chasojuan,** the start of the subtropical region (truck US$30, guide US$20); to a nearby volcanic crater (US$10 per person plus US$10 for the guide); **El Cañon Perdido,** a secluded canyon (US$10/$10); surrounding indigenous villages (US$12/$12); and more.

For accommodations, the tourist office will probably send you to **El Refugio ❷** (☎2390 022; US$6 per person, with private bath US$8; IVA and service not included; meals US$2-2.50), that has big bay windows with views of the valley, or **Hostal Samilagua ❷** (☎2847 075; US$4 per person), a new, cheaper, but quality hotel across the street from El Refugio. Expect great service at both. Eat at **La**

Minga, a new place on the square that sells great coffee, cheese sandwiches, and much of Salinas's locally made foods. (☎2390 042; lamingacafe@hotmail.com. Open daily 8am-10pm.) Access Salinas from **Guaranda**, at the corner of Candido Ruda and Eloy Alfaro (M-F 7:30, 8:30, 11:30am, 1pm; Sa 7:30, 8:30am; Su 8:30am, 1, 3pm; additional bus Tu, W, F 4pm). **Buses** return to Guaranda from Salinas's town square (M-F 6, 6:30, 7am, 1pm; Sa 6am, 1, 2:30pm; Su 6, 7am).

ALAUSÍ   ☎03

Complete with one of Ecuador's only working trains, boxy, colorful buildings, and a vibrant town square station, Alausí (pop. 20,000, 2600m) pulls off the cowboytown look quite well. **Hotel Americano ❷**, Moreno 51 and Ricaurte, is above the Farmacia Americano. Clean, quiet, and cozy rooms have wooden floors, street views, and baths. (☎2930 159. US$5 per person.) **Hotel Gampala ❷**, 5 de Junio 122 and Pedro de Loza, has carpeted rooms, private baths, and bright bed covers. Quaint street views available from the terrace. They also provide information and guides for the three-day hike along the Inca trail from Achupallas to Ingapirca. (☎2930 138. Singles US$6-8; doubles US$12; triples US$18.) **Plaza Bolívar** and the **train station** are at the base of the *centro*, near Sucre and **5 de Junio**, the main town thoroughfare. **Banco de Guayaquil**, 5 de Junio and Ricaurte, exchanges traveler's checks until 4pm. (☎2930 160. Open M-F 8:30am-4:30pm, Sa 9:30am-2:30pm.) Make calling-card calls from the **Andinatel**, near the train station on Guatemala and Pedro de Loza. (☎2930 104. Open M-F 8am-7pm, Sa 8am-noon, Su 8am-2pm.) The **post office** is at the corner of 9 de Octubre and Moreno. (Open M-F 8:30am-7pm.) **Buses** leave from the corner of 9 de Octubre and 5 de Junio. **Cooperativa Patria** (☎2930 189) goes to: Cuenca (4hr., 7 per day 7:30am-5:30pm, US$4); Guayaquil (5hr., 1pm, US$5); Quito (5½hr., 7 per day 5:30am-9:30pm, US$5) via Riobamba (2hr., US$1.50) and Ambato (3hr., US$2.50). **Cooperativa Alausí** has service to Riobamba (2hr., every 30min. 4am-5pm, US$1.50) and Guayaquil (5hr., 9am, US$5). Buses traveling the Quito-Cuenca route run 24hr. along the Panamerican Hwy. Transportation may also be arranged to Achupallas (1hr.).

THE SOUTHERN HIGHLANDS

As the Andes march through southern Ecuador toward Peru, breathtaking views are endless. Around every bend of the road are strings of peaks separated by vast valleys stretching off to the horizon. The Southern Highlands boast incredible climatic diversity—and the biodiversity that goes with it. Outdoor activities abound in places like Cajas and Podocarpus National Parks: in one day, go from *páramo* to cloud forest and even to desert. Far from the better-known destinations, this whole area has stayed much more relaxed than its heavily visited counterparts. Perhaps the most tranquil place in Ecuador is the luxurious town of Vilcabamba, called the "Sacred Valley" or the "Valley of Eternal Youth." Not just rural or resort-like, the Southern Highlands bustle at the cultural hubs Cuenca and Loja.

HIGHLIGHTS OF THE SOUTHERN HIGHLANDS

EXPLORE Ecuador's most famous ruins at **Ingapirca** (see p. 179).

DRINK from the fountain of youth at **Vilcabamba** (see p. 194).

BUY famous and colorful fabric in the town of **Saraguro** (see p. 199).

CUENCA
☎ 07

A bustling city by day and a laid-back getaway by night, Cuenca (pop. 350,000; 2530m) is a traveler's playground with a bevy of restaurants, accommodations, and parks. The third largest city in Ecuador, Cuenca is first when it comes to expense; prices have soared over the past two years. Despite the high costs, budget travelers still flock here to see the beautiful architecture, visit the nearby *artesanía* meccas of Gualaceo and Chordeleg, and explore Parque Nacional Cajas (see p. 182) and Ingapirca (see p. 179). Cuenca was built on the ruins of Tomebamba, a Cañari city destroyed and deserted by the Incas in their northern conquests. Today, Cuenca's graceful plazas and parks are anything but deserted.

◰ TRANSPORTATION

Flights: Aeropuerto Mariscal Lamar (☎2862 203), on España and Elia Liut, a 5min. walk from the bus terminal; 10min. by taxi from the center (US$1.50) or bus (US$0.20). Open daily 6am-8pm. **TAME,** on Florencia Astudillo 2-22 (☎2889 681 or 2889 097) and at the airport (☎2866 400). Open M-F 8:30am-1pm and 2:30-6pm. To **Quito** (45min.; M, W, F 8am; Tu, Th, Sa 9am; M-F and Su 6:15pm; US$48) and **Guayaquil** (30min.; M-F 8:30am, 5:45pm; Sa 8:30am; Su 5:45pm; US$62). **Icaro,** (☎2802 700 or 2866 921; open M-F 7am-9pm), also at the airport, flies to **Quito** (daily 7:35am, 1:15, 5:10pm; US$63; 7:40pm, US$49). **AeroGal,** España 10-89 (☎2904 444 or 2861 041; open M-F 9am-5pm), next to the airport on the 2nd fl., flies to **Quito** (M-F 8:15am, 6:15pm, Sa 10:15am, Su 6:15pm; round-trip US$100).

Southern Highlands

Suscal

Laguna
Pailacocha

Reserva
Ecológica
Manglares
Churute

El Tambo

■ Ingapirca

Caña

Río Cañar

Pindilig

Amaluza
Guarainag

Naranjal

Laguna
Machangaracocha

Biblián

Paute

Azogues

Sayaus

Gualaceo

Parque
Nacional
El Cajas

Cuenca

Chordeleg

Limón

Golfo
de
Guayaquil

Balao

Río Balao

Soldados
(4137m)

San Juan

Río Gala

Tarqui

Barmejos
(3963m)

Sígsig

San Juan
Bosco

Río Tenguel

Girón

Churuco Norte
(3419m)

Río Pagua

San
Fernando

Río Cuchipamba

El Guabo

Pucará

Machala

Río Jubones

Santa
Isabel

Nabón

Gualaquiza

Pasaje

Oña

Río Cuyes

Santa Rosa

R. Santa Rosa

Paccha

Fierro Urcu
(3788m)

El
Pangui

Río Machinaza

Piñas

Saraguro

28 de
Mayo

Río Zamora

Saracay

Zaruma

Balsás

Portovelo

El Cisne

Río Guayel

Río Zamora

Yantzaza

Marcabelí

R. Puyango

Zumbi

Olmedo

Catamayo

Loja

Timbara

Río Nanĝaritza

Celica

Catacocha

Zamora

Río Catamayo

Parque
Nacional
Podocarpus

Río Chumbiriaza

Vilcabamba

Cuco
(3609m)

Sozoranga

Cariamanga

Río Numbalá

Macará

Río Numpatakaime

Río Achuime

Río Macará

Amaluza

Yola
(2874m)

PERU

Río Jibaro

Río Vergel

Palanda

Río Mayo

Río Isimanchi

Río Chinnos

Río Numpatakai

Zumba

N

0   20 kilometers

0   20 miles

Cuenca

♦ ACCOMMODATIONS
El Cafecito, 15
Hostal Casa del Barranco, 11
Hostal Macondo, 1
Hostal Milan, 9
Hostal Paredes, 2
Hostal Siberia, 13
Posada Todos Santos, 22

● FOOD
Café Eucalyptus, 4
The English Café & Bookshop, 19
Gourda Vegetarian Restaurant, 10
Heladería Holanda, 5
Monday Blue Café-Bar, 12
New York Pizza Restaurant, 3
Raymipampa Café-Restaurante, 7
Restaurant Moliendo Café, 16
Restaurant Vegetariano
La Primavera, 18

🍸 NIGHTLIFE
Blue Martini, 8
El Cafecito, 14
KAOS, 17
La Mesa, 6
Pop Bar, 23
Tinku Bar-Café, 21
Wunderbar, 20

Buses: The **terminal** (☎ 2827 061) is on España, a 20min. walk northeast of the center. Taxi US$1.50. Buses depart to: **Ambato** (7hr., more than 30 per day, 4:30am-11:30pm, US$7); **Gualaceo** (45min., every 15min. 6am-10pm, US$0.60); **Guayaquil** (4-5hr., over 40 per day 2am-midnight, US$8). If getting off before Guayaquil, make sure to find out whether your bus is taking the Cañar/Troncal route or the Cajas/Puertoinca route. To: **Huaquillas** (5hr., 9 per day, US$8); **Ingapirca** (2hr.; 9am, noon, 1, 2pm; US$2.50); **Loja** (5hr., 14 per day 5am-midnight, US$7.50); **Machala** (4hr., 9 per day, US$6); **Quito** (10hr., 35 per day 4:15am-midnight, US$12) via **Riobamba** (5hr., US$5); **Zarama** (5hr., 4:40pm, US$5.70). The **Centro de Información** inside the terminal (see below) provides bus schedules for US$0.50. TerraDiversa, on Miguel at Larga (see below) posts bus timetables on its office wall.

Local Transportation: City buses traverse all city districts (US$0.20). **Bus #40** (US$0.20) makes the journey between the terminal and the *centro*.

Car Rental: International Rent-a-Car, España 10-50 (☎ 2801 892; fax 2806 688), across the street from the airport. US$52-110 per day. Must be over 18. Open M-F 7:15am-6:30pm, Sa 7:15am-1pm. **Localiza Rent-a-Car,** España 10-28 (☎ 2803 198; localiza@cue.satnet.net), in the airport. US$48-121 per day. 21 and over. Open M-F 7am-6:30pm, Sa 7:30am-12:30pm.

■✦🛈 ORIENTATION AND PRACTICAL INFORMATION

Most activity occurs in the 42-block area framed by **Mariscal Lamar, Tarqui, Mariano Cueva,** and **Río Tomebamba. Gran Colombia** serves as the high-end commercial drag while **Larga,** with the market, offers cheaper shopping options. Grassy-banked **Río Tomebamba** flows through town south of the *centro*, parallel to Larga. Less congested, suburban dwellings across the river provide refuge for the local elite. Another respite from everything urban, **Parque Calderón** lies at the heart of the colonial center, flanked by the cathedrals.

TOURIST AND FINANCIAL SERVICES

Tourist Office: The **Cumarca de Turismo del Azuay** (☎ 2868 482 or 2846 762), in the Bus Terminal, has a plethora of maps and pamphlets and will recommend a hostel to fit your budget. Open M-Sa 8am-8pm, Su 8am-noon. The **Centro de Información Turística** (☎ 2850 521), on Sucre between Malo and Cordero, off Parque Calderón, provides local and national tourist information. English spoken. Open M-F 9am-1pm and 2:30-5pm. The **Ministerio de Turismo** (☎ 2822 058), at Córdova and B. Malo, on the 2nd fl. of the San Agustín building, supplies **maps** and brochures. Open M-F 8:30am-5pm. **Librería Siglo XX,** Cordero 6-85 (☎ 2823 689), at Córdova, stocks convenient pocket road atlases of Ecuador (US$4). Open M-F 9am-1pm and 3-7pm. Sa 9am-1pm.

Tours: Various agencies and hostels around the *centro* advertise guided trips (US$30-45 per person) to **Cajas, Girón, Gualaceo,** and **Ingapirca.**

■ **TerraDiversa: The Travel Center,** Miguel 4-46 (☎ 2823 782; www.terradiversa.com; after hours cell ☎ 09 920 4382), at Larga. Arranges everything from standard daytrips to kayaking-, rafting-, and mountain-biking excursions. Books airline tickets. Stop here before the tourist office. Multilingual staff. Open M-Sa 9am-7pm, June-Sept. also Su 4-7pm.

MontaRuna (☎ 2828 593), now located in TerraDiversa's office on Miguel and Larga, but still operating as a separate entity, specializes in multiday horseback treks (US$50 per day). English-speaking guides. Open M-Sa 9am-7pm; June-Sept. Su 4-7pm.

Río Arriba, Miguel 7-38 (☎ 2840 031; negro@az.pro.ec), at Córdova, offers single-day and multi-day treks through Cajas, the Girón waterfalls, and the Inca trail to Ingapirca (US$100 per day). English-speaking guides. Open M-F 9am-6pm.

Currency Exchange: VAZ Corp, Gran Colombia 7-98 (☎ 2833 434; fax 2822 558), at Luis Cordero, exchanges traveler's checks and foreign currency. Open M-F 8:30am-1pm and 2:30-5:45pm, Sa 8:30am-12:30pm. **Western Union** has offices at Gran

Colombia 5-96 and Miguel; Sangurima 2-64 and Ordóñez; and Borrero 8-44. Call
☎800-937-8376 to be transferred to the Cuenca office. All open M-F 8:30am-6pm,
Sa 9am-1pm.

ATMs: Banco del Pacífico, Malo 9-75 and Gran Colombia, has a MC **ATM. Banco de
Guayaquil,** at Sucre and Borrero, has a MC/V ATM. MC/V ATM at the airport and MC
ATM outside the Museo del Banco Central on Larga. **MasterCard** (☎2883 577) has an
office at Crespo 1-777 and Estado. Open M-F 8:30am-5pm.

Consulate: Centro Cultural Abraham Lincoln, Borrero 5-18 (☎2823 808), at Vásquez,
is the designated warden of the **US Consulate** in Guayaquil and can assist US citizens.

Immigration Office: In the Edificio Astudillo on Ordoñez Lasso and Gran Colombia,
about 3km from the *centro*. Grants visa extensions of up to 90 days. Open M-F 8am-
12:30pm and 3-6:30pm.

LOCAL SERVICES

Language Schools: Centro de Estudios Interaméricos (CEDEI), Tarqui 13-24 (☎2893
003; www.cedei.org), at Río Bravo, offers semester-long group classes or individual
tutorials tailored to student's ability and interests and is always looking for recently-
graduated education majors to volunteer (see p. 76). US$6 per hr., min. 20hr. **Centro
Cultural Abraham Lincoln,** Borrero 5-18 (☎2823 898), at Vásquez, offers group and
individual classes with highly experienced staff. US$6 per hr. **Si Centro Spanish
School,** Jaramillo 7-27 (☎2846 932; spanish1@cue.satnet.net;
guido_abad@yahoo.com), at Borrero above Gourda Vegetarian Restaurant.

Markets: The **flower stalls** at Sucre and Aguirre are Cuenca's most colorful market,
while the new **Mercado 10 de Agosto** at Larga and Torres features wider aisles and
more organized shopping. **Mercado 3 de Noviembre,** on Lamar and Talbot, is a miniature city daily 9am-5pm. **Plaza Rotary,** in the Machuca and Sangurima area northeast
of the *centro,* sells everything. A smaller market in the **Plaza San Francisco,** at Córdova
and Aguirre, contains Otavalo textiles amid everyday household items.

Supermarkets: Supermercados Unidos S.A., Cordero 11-05 (☎2830 815), at Lamar.
Open M-Sa 8:30am-8:30pm, Su 9am-1pm.

Laundromats: Fast Kiln, Miguel 4-21 (☎2821 368), between Vásquez and Larga.
US$0.88 per kg. Open M-F 8am-7pm, Sa 8am-5pm.

EMERGENCY AND COMMUNICATIONS

Emergency: ☎911 or 101.

Police: Central Office, Cordero 6-62 (☎2841 319). Open 24hr.

Pharmacy: Farmacia Fybeca, on Bolívar (☎2843 200), between Aguirre and Malo.
Open daily 8:30am-9:30pm.

Hospital: Clínica Santa Ines, Toral 2-113 (☎2817 888), at Cueva on the far side of the
river, just south of 12 de Abril to the east of the University. Take Benigno Malo across
the river and turn right on Toral. Open 24hr.

Telephones: PacificTel, Malo 7-35 (☎2842 122), at Córdova, 1 block from Parque
Calderón, allows calling cards and collect calls. Internet US$1.03 per hr. Open daily
8am-10pm.

Internet Access: @lfnet Cafe (☎2850 469), at Vásquez and Borrero, offers speedy
access (US$1 per hr.) and high quality Net2Phone (to US US$0.12 per min., to Europe
US$0.20). Open daily 8:30am-10pm. **Café Y Montaña,** Malo 6-29 (☎2846 334),
between Jaramillo and Córdova, offers good connections (US$0.80 per hr., students
US$0.70). Open daily 8am-10:30pm.

Post Office: ☎2835 020. At Borrero and Gran Colombia. Offers **EMS** service (☎2838
211). Open M-F 8am-12:30pm and 2:30-6pm, Sa 9am-noon. Many central locations.

ACCOMMODATIONS

Although accommodations are on the expensive side, don't make a mad dash for the cheapest place around; quality increases drastically for a little extra cash.

■ **Posada Todos Santos,** Calle Larga 3-42 (☎2824 247), at Ordoñez. Talkative owner María worked in Cuenca's tourist office for over 25 years and will prepare you a laundry list of activities. Large, comfy rooms with private baths; showers have unparalleled water pressure. Breakfast included. Rooms US$9 per person. IVA not included. ❸

Hostal Macondo, Tarqui 11-64 (☎2840 697; macondo@cedei.org), at Lamar. One of Ecuador's best hotels, with clean, comfortable rooms, knowledgeable staff, and beautiful lawns and gardens. Kitchen access. Breakfast included. Singles US$11, with bath US$16; doubles US$17/$22; triples US$24/$28. Monthly rates available. IVA not included. HI and ISIC discount US$1. ❸

El Cafecito, Vásquez 7-36 (☎2832 337; cuenca@cafecito.net), at Cordero. Skylit cafe by day, candlelit crowd-pleaser by night. Clean, modern, colorful rooms. Full restaurant/bar (open daily 8am-midnight). Happy hour 5-7pm. Dorms US$5; singles with bath US$8; doubles with bath US$16. ❷

Hostal Tinku, Vázquez 5-66 (☎2839 845), between Hermano Miguel and Cueva. Comfortable beds, a homey feel. Offers Internet, laundry (US$0.25 per lb.), a small book exchange, and discounts at the bar down the street. Dorms US$5; private rooms US$6 per person; 1 room with private bath US$8 per person. ❷

Hostal Casa del Barranco, Larga 8-41 (☎2839 763; casadelbarranco@yahoo.com), at Cordero, features hardwood floors, private baths, TVs, and some rooms overlooking the river. Small cafe in a skylit courtyard. 6-person duplex available. Dorms US$7; singles US$10; doubles US$15; triples US$20. IVA included. ❷

Hostal Paredes, Cordero 11-29 (☎2835 674), at Lamar. Antique furnishings, a colonial interior, singing parakeets, and a veritable cloud forest of potted plants provide ample ambiance. Singles US$6; doubles US$12. ❷

Hostal Siberia, Luís Cordero 4-22 (☎2840 672), at Vásquez on the 2nd fl. Beds vary in quality. Breakfast available for large groups. US$6 per person. ❷

Hostal Milan, Córdova 9-89 (☎2835 351), at Aguirre. A bit beaten up on the outside, but the rooms are clean and the beds are firm. Most rooms have balconies overlooking Plaza San Francisco. Pool tables on the roof. Breakfast included. Singles US$6, with bath and TV US$9; doubles US$12/$18. ❷

FOOD

From traditional food to costly world-class cuisine, Cuenca satisfies even the most selective stomach. Sample traditional brick-oven bread along the "Calle de Pan," the two blocks on Mariano Cueva north of Calle Larga.

Café Eucalyptus, Gran Colombia (☎2849 157; www.cafeeucalyptus.com), at Berigno Malo. A true international cafe serving everything from pad thai to *comida típica* to buffalo wings, all done right. Unnecessarily large drink list. W is ladies night—the house fills up quickly. Open M-Th 11am-midnight, F 11am-1am, Sa 5pm-midnight, Su 5-11pm.

Raymipampa Café-Restaurante, Benigno Malo 8-59 (☎2834 159). This lively restaurant hops with gringos and hungry locals, especially around dinnertime. The view of Parque Calderón complements the casual, coffee-shop feel. Terraced seating keeps secondhand smoke where it belongs. Typical meat entrees US$3-5. Cappuccino US$0.80. Open M-F 8:30am-11pm, Sa-Su 8:30am-9pm. MC/V. IVA not included. ❷

New York Pizza Restaurant, Gran Colombia 10-43 (☎2842 792 or 2825 675), by Plaza Santo Domingo. Oversized pizza available by the slice (US$1.10, toppings US$0.35). Family-sized and Sicilian pizzas (US$6-11.50). Italian entrees US$3-4. Free delivery in the city center. Open M-F 9:30am-11pm, Sa 9:30am-2pm, Su 11am-10pm. ❷

Gourda Vegetarian Restaurant, Juan Jaramillo 7-27 (☎2846 932; guido_abad@yahoo.com), at Borrero right below the Si Centro Spanish School (see above). Tasty spaghetti (US$3), pizzas, and salads (US$2.50) amid east-meets-west decor. Uses organic vegetables only. Lunch buffet US$1.75. Open M-Sa 11am-9pm. ❶

The English Café and Bookshop, Larga 6-69 (☎2831 618), between Borrero and Miguel. Huge British breakfast US$5. Limited cooking area may delay larger groups. English newspapers and book exchange. Open daily 10am-8:30pm. ❸

Heladería Holanda, Malo 9-51 (☎2831 449), at Bolívar. Widely acknowledged as the best ice cream in town. Ample seating inside a bright, wood-paneled interior. Delicious scoops US$0.70. Open daily 8am-8pm. ❶

Restaurant Moliendo Café (☎2828 710; moliendocafe@hotmail.com), on Vásquez between Borrero and Miguel. Fresh Colombian coffee, traditional Colombian food, friendly Colombian owners. Open M-Sa 9am-9pm.

Monday Blue Café-Bar (monday6blue@yahoo.com), on the corner of Larga and Cordero. Walls are covered in beer posters. High-quality, low-cost goodies, plus the best burritos in Cuenca (US$1.50). BBQ lunch US$2.50; pizza US$3-5. Open daily 4pm-midnight. ❶

Restaurant Vegetariano La Primavera, Miguel 4-79. The humble appearance belies the magnificent meatless lunches (US$1.50). Yogurt, crepes, and fruit salads complete the meal. Open M-F 8am-9pm, Sa 8am-4pm. ❶

👁 SIGHTS

Cuenca complements its popular daytrips to Ingapirca, El Cajas, and Chordeleg with a wealth of museums, churches, parks, plazas, and chic *artesanía* boutiques (concentrated on Gran Colombia between Miguel and Borrero).

MUSEO DEL BANCO CENTRAL. This museum houses Cuenca's most extensive collection of art and artifacts. Upstairs, the ethnographic exhibit takes you through the homes, lives, and handiwork of 22 indigenous cultures. The ground floor archaeology room explains the Cañari and Inca occupation of the Tomebamba (Pumapungo) ruins and documents the nearby site's recent excavation. The museum also exibits 19th-century Ecuadorian art and a history of money in Ecuador. Visitors can wander through the ancient city of Tomebamba, which translates into "the field of knives"—Inca battles here left numerous weapons—behind the Banco Central. After conquering the area, Sapa Inca Yupanqui converted this important Cañari site into a military outpost and later, an administrative center. Traditional Inca architecture is visible over earlier Cañari constructions, and some believe that this location served as Huayna Cápac's palace. (*At Larga and Huayna Cápac. ☎2831 255. Open M-F 9:30am-6pm, Sa 9am-1pm. US$3, ISIC US$1.50. Guides are students at the State University. Tip suggested.*)

MUSEO DEL MONASTERIO DE LAS CONCEPTAS. In the same building as an active convent that houses 22 nuns, this museum lays claim to Cuenca's most impressive collection of religious art. Among the museum's 22 rooms are 64 paintings, the majority of which were painted by anonymous artists—during the 18th and 19th centuries in Ecuador, religious paintings were not considered works of art as much as teaching tools; as such, signatures on the paintings are incredibly rare. It also has over 200 sculptures, and the toys and playthings of young girls that were given to the convent along with money and jewelry as dowries upon the girls' commital to the convent. *(Miguel 6-33 and Jaramillo. ☎ 2830 625. Spanish-speaking guides. English brochures available. Open M-F 9am-5:30pm, Sa 10am-1pm. US$2.50, ISIC US$1.50.)*

MIRADOR TURI. From Turi, a treacherously high vista 4km south of the *centro*, discover a view normally reserved for high-fliers. The steep ascent pays off with a breathtaking panorama of Cuenca and the surrounding mountains. A cartographic tiled painting of the city matches the view and provides a guide to the scenery. Legend has it that an apparition of Christ appeared on the hill long ago. Locals still make pilgrimages up the hill on the last Saturday of each December, taking small handfuls of sandstone from the sight to sprinkle over their homes and loved ones for good luck. *(Take a taxi (US$2.50) or a bus (US$0.25) labeled "Turi" from the intersection of 12 de Abril and Fray Vicente Solano below the river. Or walk. 45min. to Solano from the bridge over Río Tomebamba. Follow Solano to the bridge over Río Yanuncay and walk along the various paths weaving up to the huge church on the hilltop.)*

CHURCHES. Cuenca has more churches per capita than most Ecuadorian cities, and its two most striking churches face each other across Parque Calderón. ▧**Catedral de la Inmaculada Concepción** (New Cathedral) towers over Parque Calderón and is brilliantly illuminated at night. The cathedral is one of the most famous churches in Ecuador; its ornate domes and brick facade cover a cavernous marble interior where brilliant sunlight enters through the various windows and reflects off a four-column, gold-leaf canopy. *(Open daily 7am-4pm and 8-9pm. Su Mass 8, 9:30, and 11am.)* Built in 1557 with stones from the Inca's Pumapungo Palace, the **Iglesia del Sagrario** (Old Cathedral) is currently being converted into a museum of religious art. The gorgeous **La Iglesia de la Concepta** houses a museum and still-inhabited convent. *(Open for mass Su all day.)* **San Blas**, on Vega and Bolívar, was built in 1575 in the form of a Latin cross, using stones from Tomebamba. **San Sebastián**, at Talbot and Bolívar, with its single cupola, tower, and elaborate wooden portal, stands on the edge of a beautiful plaza.

OTHER SIGHTS. Cuenca promotes national and international arts and crafts through several exhibition houses. The **Museo de Arte Moderno,** operating in the ancient House of Temperance, displays modern Ecuadorian art and hosts national and international art competitions. *(Sucre 15-27 at Talbot, on Plaza San Sebastián. ☎ 2831 027. Open M-F 8:30am-1pm and 3-6:30pm, Sa 9am-1pm. Free.)* The **Museo de Artes Populares de América (CIDAP)** has an equally impressive exhibit of Latin American sculptures, paintings, and musical instruments. *(Miguel 3-23 at Escalanata. ☎ 2840 919. Open M-F 9:30am-1pm and 2:30-6pm, Sa 10am-1pm. Free.)* For a fascinating look at what's holding Ecuador's vertebrates together check out the new **Museo Esqueletología,** where English-speaking guides explain the intricacies of the many skeletons. *(Bolívar 657 at Borrero. ☎ 2821 150. Open M-F 9:30am-1pm and 3:30-7pm, Sa 10am-2pm. US$1, students US$0.50.)* **Zoológico Amaru** has a nice collection of reptiles and fish from the Amazon and the coast. *(Malo 4-74 and Larga, right at the top of the stairs. ☎ 2826 337; www.zoologicoamaru.com. Open M-F 9am-noon and 3-6pm, Sa-Su 10am-5pm.)* The **Museo de las Culturas Aborígenes** has an impressive collection of archaeological artifacts and a nice cafe below. *(Larga 5-24 between Miguel and Cueva. ☎ 2839 181. Open M-F 8:30am-6pm, Sa 9am-1pm. US$2, students US$1.50.)* **Casa de la Mujer,** across from the market at Plaza San Francisco on General Torres. Artisans fill stalls with carefully crafted handiwork; everything from jewelry to figurines to sweaters is available here and the artisans are good enough to not have to push products in your face to notice them. *(Open M-F 9am-1pm and 2:30-6:30pm, Sa 9am-3pm.)*

ENTERTAINMENT

Fun-lovers flock to Cuenca's three most prominent festivals. The week-long **El Septenario** (Corpus Christi) celebration—in which the main plaza explodes with fireworks and dancing—begins the second Thursday in June. Cuenca stretches its November 3 **Independence Day** celebration into a four-day cultural fair. The city holds similar festivities on April 12, the day of its founding. **Multicines,** inside the Milenium Plaza on Merchán and Peralta below the river, has six screens and has run all of the smaller theaters out of town. (☎ 2888 170 or 2887 691; www.multicines.com.ec. US$4, matinees US$2.25.) Large music and drama productions are staged at the **Teatro Carlos Cueva Tamariz** (☎ 2831 688), on 12 de Abril at the Universidad Estatal campus. Additional events are held at the **Auditorio del Banco Central** (☎ 2831 255, ext. 111), at Larga and Huayna Cápac. Local newspapers *Mercurio* and *Tiempo* publish all movie and performance schedules.

NIGHTLIFE

Although Cuenca lacks the nightlife of Quito, its large tourist contingent keeps plenty of bars open throughout the week.

El Cafecito, Vásquez 7-36 (☎ 2832 337), at Cordero. Hostel by day, lively candlelit bar by night, this is the backpacker hangout. Great food and reasonably priced drinks (US$1.50-3). Happy hour 5-7pm. Open daily 8am-midnight.

Tinku Bar-Café, Larga 4-68 (☎ 2888 520), at Jerves. A good sit-down-and-have-a-drink bar to start the night. Spacious interior with a good mix of American and Latin tunes. Drinks from US$2, beer from US$1.50. Open Tu-W 6pm-midnight, Th-Sa 6pm-2am.

Wunderbar, Miguel 3-43 (☎ 2831 274), at Larga on the Escalinata. A great place to relax with a drink (US$1.50-3) and English or German newspaper. The more competitive opt for billiards, Jenga!©, or foosball. Close-quarters means things can get elbow-to-elbow pretty quickly. Open M-F 11am-1am, Sa 2pm-1am, Su 4-10pm.

KAOS, Vásquez 6-11, at Miguel. Listen to tunes while sipping a drink (US$1.50-2.50) and enjoying an Italian sandwich (US$2). Pool table and friendly staff. Happy hour 6-8pm. Open M and W 6pm-midnight, Tu and Th-Sa 6pm-1am.

Pop Bar, at Crespo and Solano. Hip youngsters of Cuenca come here to groove—and they don't mind if you join in. Pool table, mixed drinks (US$2-4), local art on the walls, and North American music. Cover US$2.50. Open W-Sa 9pm-3am.

Blue Martini, Córdova 100-14 (☎ 2842 339), at Vega. New dog, old tricks. Formerly La Bábrica, Blue Martini's sleek, steely look attracts the same dance-happy crowd as it did before. Cover US$2. Drink min. US$2. Open Th-Sa 10pm-3am.

La Mesa, Colombia 3-35 (☎ 2833 300), at Ordoñez. DJs pump out classic salsa as locals strut their stuff on the wood floor. Drink min. US$2. Open W-Sa 10pm-2am.

INGAPIRCA ☎ 07

85km north of Cuenca, Ingapirca is the most significant archaeological site in Ecuador. The Cañari used the area as a ceremonial and administrative center for thousands of years until the Incas moved in circa AD 1500 and, with master stonemasons in tow, set about constructing the marvel that remains today. The highlight of the ruins is the circular **Temple of the Sun** (37x15m), where celebrations of the annual **Inti Raymi** (New Year) festival are still carried out. The Inti Raymi celebrations take over the ruins during the third week of June. (For information contact Institución Ingapirca del Pueblo Cañari. ☎ 2215 115 or 2215 109; kurinti@cue.satnet.net.) The temple was positioned so that the solstices perfectly illuminated the altars on the eastern and western faces of the temple. Below this path lay terraced gardens for cultivating medicinal and ornamental plants, while workshops above were used for producing *chicha* (a traditional liquor). Nearby, *acllawasi* (Virgins of the Sun) resided in the monastic complex, where they performed important ceremonial rites. A 1km path marked by stone triangles leads around the site to a series of rock formations, including the face of the Inca, the face of the sun, a giant tortoise, and the Inca's chair. Some guides recommend doing the hike in reverse to get the full effect of the face. (Ruins open daily 7am-7pm. US$6, including guided tours in Spanish or English and access to the Museo del Sitio.) The **Museo del Sitio** displays the precious artifacts found during recent excavations as well as a replica of the site. (Open daily 9am-5pm.)

Lodgings can be found in the **Posada Ingapirca ❺**, near the ruins. (☎2806 023; santaana@etapa.com.ec. Singles US$35; doubles US$40.) More humble **hostels ❶** are available in the nearby town of Ingapirca (5min. walk. US$4-6 per person). None are preferable to lodging in Cuenca. **Lunch** (US$1.50) and snacks are available at the site or in town. **Restaurante El Castillo ❶**, halfway between the ruins and the town, offers slightly more expensive but high-quality food. (☎09 9983 050. *Almuerzo* US$2.50. Open daily 8am-10pm.) **Transportes Cañari** goes directly to the **ruins** from the terminal in Cuenca (2hr.; 9am , noon; return 1, 4pm; US$2). Alternatively, take a **bus** to Tambo (2hr., every 30min. 6:30am-7:30pm, US$1.50). A **local bus** from the plaza labeled "Ingapirca" or "Las Ruinas" goes the rest of the way (20min., every 30min., US$0.60). Return to Cuenca on a local bus to Tambo and then a long-distance bus to Cuenca (until 7pm).

GUALACEO ☎07

Every Sunday, the center of activity in the Cuenca area shifts eastward to the weekly market in Gualaceo, drawing bargain hunters from neighboring mountain towns and rural settlements. Local crafts are hard to come by, but heaps of fresh produce, household goods, roasted *cuy*, and underpants sell like hotcakes. On Tuesdays and Fridays the markets bustle with activity; on any other day, you can visit textile artisans in their homes for souvenirs from the source.

Facing uphill toward the bus station, the **indoor market, outdoor market,** and **main park** (in that order) lie diagonally ahead to the right. From the bus station, head up Cordero and turn right on Cuenca, or better yet, follow the herd. The **Ministerio del Turismo,** on the first floor of the Municipal building at 3 de Noviembre and Gran Colombia, provides **maps** of Gualaceo and offers tours of the nearby villages and countryside. (☎2255 131. Open M-F 8am-1pm and 2-5pm.)

Hostal Carlos Andres ❷, Gran Colombia 2-03, two blocks from the plaza (away from the market), has a marble staircase that leads to four floors of comfy rooms with baths and color TVs. (☎2255 379. Singles US$6; doubles US$10.) Close to the plaza on Gran Colombia and 9 de Octubre is **Restaurant Don "Q" ❶**. (*Almuerzo* US$2.50. Open M-F 9am-5pm, Sa 8am-6pm, Su 8am-7pm.) **Buses** for Gualaceo (40min., every 15min. 6am-10pm, US$0.55) leave from Cuenca's main terminal. Buses to Santa Barbara and Santiago de Gualaceo (40min., every 15min. 5am-7pm, US$0.55) leave from Gualaceo's terminal (☎2255 730) on the main highway to Cuenca. Buses also go to: Azogues (50min., Sa 7:15am, US$0.55); Chordeleg (15min., every 15min. 5am-7pm, US$0.20); and San Juan (40min., every 30min. 5am-7pm, US$0.30).

CHORDELEG ☎07

The market at Chordeleg has a lock on luxuries. The main plaza is absolutely studded with **jewelry** stores sparkling with good deals thanks to competition. Be wary, however, of great deals. If a jeweler won't give you a money-back guarantee and let you take your prospective buy to a neighboring store for verification, take your business elsewhere. Most jewelry merchants open their doors Tuesday through Sunday 9am-6pm but close Mondays to buy merchandise. Specialties include gold and silver necklaces, bracelets, watches, and soccer trophies. Handmade sweaters, bags, and tapestries are also sold on the main plaza, but the best *artesanía* shops, including the large and upscale **Centro de Artesanías,** are outside the town center, toward Gualaceo. They specialize in ornately painted pottery, metal sculptures, and leather goods. (Centro open Tu-Su 8am-6pm.) The newly renovated **Museo Comunidad,** on the plaza, displays *artesanía* and ethnographic material. (Open M-Sa 9am-1pm and 2-5pm.) Because it is so close to Gualaceo, there are **no accommodations** in this tiny town. **Buses** depart for Chordeleg (15min., every 30min. 5am-7pm, US$0.20) from Gualaceo's terminal. Some buses coming from Cuenca to Gualaceo continue on to Chordeleg. Buses returning to Gualaceo (US$0.20) or Cuenca (US$0.75), follow 24 de Mayo one block uphill from the plaza on Guayaquil (every 30min. 5am-7pm). The walk between Gualaceo and Chordeleg is beautiful, passing picturesque countryside and farmland. The downhill stretch from Chordeleg to Gualaceo takes about 1hr.; the return uphill 1½hr. Be careful of cars on blind curves.

SAN JUAN   ☎07

San Juan is a beautiful, relatively undiscovered village perched in the mountains across the valley from Gualaceo. The town is a day-hiker's paradise, offering varied walks in the nearby villages and hills. Hike along the tranquil, sometimes sandy **Río Santa Barbara** (4hr.); climb the majestic **Pishi mountain** (4-5hr., 2850m); walk to the indigenous **San Gabriel** community that doubles as a lookout (5hr.); trek out to the tumbling cascades of **Gupaucay and Tasqui canyons** (3hr.); check out another lookout at **Sopla Maro** (2hr.); or hike the 300m-high forest, **Bosque Aguarongo** (5hr.). Hikes are easily self-guided, but instructions, guides, and horses can be arranged at the hotel or restaurant listed below. On a mountainside farm, **Hostería San Juan ❷** provides comfortable rooms. (From the plaza turn right on Xavier Muñoz and left on Veintimilla. ☎2290 280. US$5 per person. Possible discounts for help around farm.) The **Restaurante Arco Iris ❶,** on the plaza, serves breakfast, lunch, and dinner (US$1.50 each) and can make delicious sandwiches to go. (☎2290 197. Open daily Tu-Th 7am-5pm, F-Su 9am-9pm.) **Buses** to San Juan (40min., every 30min. 5am-6pm, US$0.30) depart from the main terminal in Gualaceo. Buses depart from San Juan for Gualaceo (45min., every 30min.-1hr. 5am-7pm, US$0.30) from the plaza. Buses bound for Chordeleg (10-15min., every 30min. 5am-7pm, US$0.15) and Cuenca (US$1.25) can be flagged down from the road on the other side of the valley across the river (a pleasant 30min. hike from Xavier Muñoz).

BAÑOS   ☎07

Just a 15min. bus ride from Cuenca, this Baños doesn't have the mature touristic allure of its cousin near Ambato, but its main draw—its thermal baths—are arguably better. At the complex of baths associated with the sprawling **Complejo Turístico Durán,** hotel guests get private access to two restaurants, a bar, racquetball and tennis courts, and a gym, but share access to the baths with the paying public. Durán has three different sets of pools; admission to each mini-complex is separate and ranges from US$1.60 to US$3.05. Access to the steam rooms is included in the admission to the central set of pools. Staying at Durán costs a pretty penny, but travelers willing to splurge get the equivalent of a VIP pass to the complex in addition to comfortable rooms with cable TV. (☎2892 485. Singles US$30; doubles US$46; triples US$58. IVA and service not included.).

If you really want to make a night of it in Baños and neither Durán nor any of the cheaper **hostels ❶** at the bottom of the hill (US$4-6 per person) do the trick, the newly constructed **Complejo Turístico Agapantos ❸** might just have moved into your price range. Agapantos's sterile, brick, condominium-esque exterior yields way to clean, terraced rooms with private kitchens and TVs. The complex has its own Turkish bath but access to Baños's thermal baths is not included. (Behind Baños Merchán. ☎ 2892 015. US$12 per person.) Get to Baños from Cuenca on the #12 **bus** from the intersection of 12 de Abril and Solano (15min., every 10min., US$0.25) or get a **taxi** for US$2.50. The buses disembark at the top of a hill in front of a blue-and-white church. Walk downhill from the church, turning right at the sign for Agapantos or following the main road all the way down to Durán at the bottom of the hill. City buses out of Baños (US$0.25) are very frequent; most pass through the *centro*. Buses marked "Turismo" are the best bet.

■ PARQUE NACIONAL CAJAS

The rugged terrain and endless trails of Parque Nacional Cajas draw hikers of all skill levels for daytrips and multi-day hikes. Tiny wildflowers and vegetation thrive in the harsh, rocky landscape dotted by pristine lakes. Mountains rise to a sky-scraping 4450m and never dip below 3150m; sheer cliffs carved by glaciers cut through rolling Highlands; and from subterranean caverns, rivers rise to the surface and re-submerge into rock fissures. The park's 290 sq. km of humid, spongy *páramo* boasts more than 200 lakes (over 1000 if you count the many small lagoons that appear and disappear with the seasons) and supplies Cuenca with 60% of its potable water. El Cajas is also the only privatized national park; its control has been outsourced to ETAPA, Ecuador's main supplier of drinking water. Not to be outdone by the splendor of El Cajas's geological wonders, varied plants and flowers blanket the land with spring turf and splashes of color. Diminutive *quinua* (Polylepis) trees, the highest-altitude trees in the world, sprout their gnarled trunks from the *páramo* covering most of the park while humid virgin mountain forests cover its east and west ends. El Cajas's unique climate makes it one of the few places where the rare *cubilán, chuquiragua,* and *tushig* plants flourish. Those with a little patience (and luck) may see some of the park's standard-issue wildlife such as deer, foxes, and rabbits, as well as the more distinctive spectacled bear, llama, puma, and *tigrillo* (little tiger). Birdwatchers can marvel at Andean condors, highland toucans, and hummingbirds. Pre-Hispanic ruins lie scattered throughout, and the ancient Inca road of Ingañan stretches between Luspa Cave and Lake Mamamay in the center of the park. The best-preserved ruins are at Paredones, near Molleturo. Visit El Cajas during the end of the dry season (Aug.-Jan.). Temperatures vary dramatically, so bring warm clothes.

■ ? ORIENTATION AND PRACTICAL INFORMATION

El Cajas has two main entrances: **Soldados** in the south and **Lake Toreadora** in the north. The latter lies next to the highway that transects the park, on its way from Cuenca to Guayaquil, and is equipped with an information center and restaurant (3778m). Before entering, fishing, or camping in Cajas, visitors must notify the park wardens. (Park admission US$10, ISIC US$5.)

Transportation: Buses heading from **Cuenca** to **Guayaquil** (45min., 12 per day 5am-9pm, US$1.50) stop at the park. Ask to be let off at the "Cajas Refugio." Return buses pass by the visitors' center throughout the day. Buses to the more isolated **Soldados** entrance leave from Mercado 3 de Noviembre at Mariscal Lamar and Talbot (1½hr., 6:30am, US$2) and pass by the entrance again at around 4pm on the way back to Cuenca.

Park Information: The **office** by the northern Lake Toreadora entrance offers great **maps** (included in the entrance fee) and park information. Tourist offices in Cuenca also have maps, as well as weather and trail updates. Park office open daily 6am-5pm, ranger on duty 24hr. for emergencies.

Accommodations: The information office (see above) has a basic **refuge ❶** with electricity, cold water, kitchen access, and a place to build a fire. US$2 per person. Additional refuges are scattered throughout the park. See maps for details.

Supplies: Bring a map, compass, warm clothes, and experience to combat the fog.

Tours: Many Cuenca agencies offer tours. **TerraDiversa** offers everything from hiking to horseback riding to mountain biking to multisport trips that combine all 3. Be sure to patronize licensed tour guides that pay their taxes and are environmentally aware.

◤ OUTDOOR ACTIVITIES

HIKING. With 13 single-day trails and eight multi-day trails, Cajas is the perfect place to mix and match various routes. Travel with a guide: most trails are known only by local fishermen and guides and disappear and reappear without warning. Rangers will only allow non-expert mountaineers without a guide to hike the **loop** around **Laguna Toreadora** (trail #5; 1-2hr.), which affords great vistas of some of Cajas's 232 lakes. A longer, guided day-hike begins from the visitors' center and continues south past **Laguna Larga** and the enormous **Laguna Luspa,** before circling back. The equally large **Lago Osohuayco** makes a great two-day hike through the *páramo* with suitable **campsites** by the Inca ruins. These three lakes can be combined into one three- to four-day hike including 4km of preserved Inca highway (between Cave Luspa and Lago Mamamay). For a two-day hike through varied climate zones, enter the park from the eastern end where humid cloud forest trails lead up to **Lago Clavinco** and then to the massive **Lago Mamamay,** where there are adequate **campsites.** A four-day hike from **Miguir** down the highway toward Guayaquil passes lakes and clusters of *quinua* trees before emerging at the southern park control center at Soldados.

FISHING. Anglers flock to Cajas's trout-filled lakes, especially on weekends. Fish bite the most in the park's seldom-explored southern region, accessible via the Soldados entrance. Hike from the highway beyond Soldados to Río Chico Soldados for the best fishing, and set up camp by Lago Ventanas. Río Arriba Tours (see **Tours,** p. 174) has fishing equipment and can arrange a tour.

ROCK CLIMBING. While Cajas does not offer world-class climbing, its many exposed rock faces offer peaks amidst breathtaking scenery. The most popular scalable peak (3800m), nicknamed **Godzilla,** lies on the highway opposite Laguna Toreadora and the visitors' center. Inquire at TerraDiversa for guides.

ZAMORA ☎07

Zamora (pop. 11,000), Ecuador's city of gold, is a rustic jungle town that suddenly found itself in the center of things when Midas touched the nearby town of Nambija 20 years ago. A mining frontier culture sprouted as quickly as the Oriente vegetation, resulting in inevitable tension between entrepreneurs and locals. Zamora has adapted to these changes for better or worse: a relatively new highway winds along pristine cliffs and waterfalls through both highland cloud forests and jungle, while mining equipment and tin roofs of gold-boom houses speckle the scenic valley. The town has also become a gateway city, providing easy access to the Amazon Basin via Parque Nacional Podocarpus.

SOUTHERN HIGHLANDS

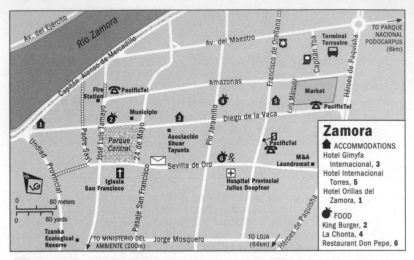

Zamora

⚓ ACCOMMODATIONS
Hotel Gimyfa
Internacional, **3**
Hotel Internacional
Torres, **5**
Hotel Orillas del
Zamora, **1**

🍴 FOOD
King Burger, **2**
La Chonta, **4**
Restaurant Don Pepe, **6**

⌨ TRANSPORTATION

Buses: Terminal, on Héroes de Paquisha (the highway), between Maestro and Amazonas. **Cooperativa de Transportes Loja** (☎2605 163) runs to: **Machala** (8hr., 8pm, US$8.50) via **Loja** (1¼hr., 6 per day 3am-6pm, US$2.40); **Quito** (16hr., 3pm, US$17); **Gualaquiza** (5hr.; 6, 10am, 2:30pm; US$3.50). **Cooperativa de Transportes Nambija** (☎2605 550) serves: **Huaquillas** (8hr., 7:45pm, US$7.50) via **Loja** (1¼hr., 16 per day 2:15am-10pm, US$1.90); and **Machala** (8hr., 8:45pm, US$7.50). **Cooperativa de Transportes Pullman Viajeros** (☎2605 614) serves **Cuenca** (7hr.; 9:45am, 6:15, 10:30pm; US$8.40).

⬛🛈 ORIENTATION AND PRACTICAL INFORMATION

Most activity takes place around the **market**, the **terminal**, and **Parque Pío Jaramillo**. The majority of tourist services lie along the busy **Amazonas** and **Diego de la Vaca**.

Tourist Offices: The **Ministerio del Ambiente** (☎2606 606), on the highway from Loja. Take the highway 200m out of town from the big green signs at the top of José Luís Tamayo; office is on the left, in a small blue trailer behind the building with the green "Dirección Prov. Agropecuaria" sign. Still commonly called INEFAN. Has info, **maps,** and tickets for Parque Nacional Podocarpus. Helps arrange trips to the Shuar communities at Nangarita. Open M-F 8am-12:30pm and 1:30-4:30pm. Travel agencies in Loja also offer guided tours (see **Loja: Tours,** p. 191). The **tourism office** (☎2605 996), on the 3rd fl. of the municipio on the plaza, has info on local waterfalls and churches, as well as Poducarpus maps. They are in the process of opening a new office closer to the bus terminal. Open M-F 7:30am-12:30pm and 2-5pm.

Currency Exchange: The **PacificTel** Office on Orellana between Diego de la Vaca and Sevilla de Oro also has a Moneygram service. Open M-F 9am-1pm and 3-5pm.

Laundromat: M&A Laundromat (☎2607 158), at Sevilla de Oro Héroes de Paquisha, across from the CACPE building, charges US$1 per dozen articles of clothing. Open whenever the owner is around. Ring the bell for service.

Emergency Numbers: Police: ☎101. **Fire:** ☎2605 102.

Police: ☎2605 101. At the corner of Orellana and Maestro.

Pharmacy: Farmacia Oriental (☎2605 322), on Sevilla de Oro, across from the hospital. Open 8am-11pm.

Hospital: Hospital Provincial Julius Doepfner (☎2605 149), on Sevilla de Oro between Jaramillo and Orellana. Open M-F 8am-12:30pm and 1:30-5pm; emergencies 24hr.

Telephones: PacificTel (☎2605 104), on Amazonas, one block from the plaza, does not allow collect calls. Open daily 8am-10pm.

Internet: SKYNet (☎2605 086), on Capitán Yoa opposite the terminal. US$1.20 per hr. Open daily 7am-11pm.

Post Office: (☎/fax 2606 002), on Sevilla de Oro near 24 de Mayo. Open M-F 8am-noon and 2-6pm.

ACCOMMODATIONS

Lodgings in Zamora may not be sweet-smelling, but they'll keep you warm and dry.

Hotel Gimyfa Internacional (☎2605 024), on Diego de la Vaca, near Pío Jaramillo, offers a respite from the heat. Scrupulously clean rooms have hot baths and cable TV. Rooftop terrace. Singles US$7; matrimonials and doubles US$13. ❷

Hotel Orillas del Zamora (☎2605 565; in Cuenca 2845 697; hotel_o_zamora@hotmail.com), on Diego de la Vaca and Alonso de Mercadillo, is a stylish and comfortable, though slightly more pricey, riverside option. Hot water, cable TV, laundry service. Singles US$12; doubles US$18. MC. ❸

Hotel Internacional Torres (☎2605 195), on Orellana between Diego de la Vaca and Amazonas, offers comfortable, carpeted rooms with lukewarm baths—and a little mildew. US$5.60 per person. ❷

FOOD

Zamora isn't famous for its cuisine, but there's a lot of it; restaurants and *picanterías* offering lunches and snacks (US$1-1.20) line Diego de la Vaca and Amazonas, especially near the bus terminal.

Restaurant Don Pepe (☎2606 358), on Sevilla de Oro, across from the hospital, was constructed by a bamboo fanatic. Plenty of *comida típica*, including the local specialty: frog (US$5). Open M-F 7am-10pm, Sa 8am-10pm, Su 9am-10pm. ❷

King Burger (☎2605 378), across from the church on the corner of de la Vaca and Tamayo, grills up burgers that overflow the bun with juicy goodness and fresh, crispy fries on the side (combos US$1-2). Open daily 8am-11:30pm. ❶

La Chonta, under the Hotel Chonta Dorado, has 3-dimensional still lifes on the walls and hearty *alumerzos* (US$1.50). Open 6am-8pm. ❶

SIGHTS

The **Tzanka Ecological Refuge** is a private, small **zoo** right in downtown Zamora. Animal-lover owners take visitors on a guided tour among parrots, turtles, a tapir, a boa constrictor, and an orchid garden. The one-room **museum** houses an eclectic collection of petrified shells, Shuar paraphernalia, the retired sucre, and old records. Enjoy a meal at the shady restaurant. To enjoy more time with the animals, **spend the night** ❸ in one of the bedrooms. Breakfast is included—as well as access to the kitchen and a terrace with foosball and a jukebox. *(Tzanka is on Tamayo, 1 block uphill from the park. US$2, children US$1. ☎2605 692; refugioecologicotzanka@yahoo.es. Lodging US$8.)*

PARQUE NACIONAL PODOCARPUS

Ecuador's southernmost national park encompasses the best of the country's various climates and presents them in all their glory to its visitors. In the *zona alta* (high zone), layer upon layer of rolling mist flows through the deep forest, and kilometers of ridge-side paths traverse the vibrant ecosystem. Meanwhile, butterflies, leafcutter ants, and all manner of other animal and plant life crowd the trails in the *zona baja* (low zone), a primary tropical rainforest along Río Bombuscaro. The San Francisco Cloud Forest in the northeastern part of the park protects an important community of grand, old Podocarpus (Romerillo) trees. The park contains an abundance of water, with numerous falls and places to swim.

AT A GLANCE

AREA: 1462 sq. km.

CLIMATE: Climate varies greatly throughout. It's best to visit during the dry season (Oct.-Dec.); otherwise it's pretty wet.

HIGHLIGHTS: Awesome views from the Sendero al Mirador, swimming in rivers, and ogling waterfalls and wildlife.

GATEWAYS: Loja (see p. 190), Zamora (see p. 183).

CAMPING: Camping is only necessary on long hikes. Cabins are better.

FEES: US$10 entrance fee. Purchase tickets at a Ministerio del Ambiente office or gateway city (see above).

▐▀ TRANSPORTATION

For the *zona alta*, the park entrance is at **Cajanuma,** an otherwise empty stretch of highway 14km from Loja on the road to Vilcabamba. A large sign marks the gate, just before a big orange-and-yellow arch. **Buses** and shared **taxis** heading to Vilcabamba from Loja will drop you off (20min., US$1)—unfortunately, this still leaves an 8½km uphill hike to the *refugio*. If you hail a passing Ministerio del Ambiente truck, it will give you a ride up. A taxi from Loja (45min.) costs US$10. To return to Loja, hike back down to the highway (1½-2hr.) to hail a passing bus.

Since there is no public transportation from **Zamora** to the *zona baja*, take a **taxi** from the terminal to the refuge. To get back, arrange a pickup with a taxi driver in advance, or try the easy 6km hike back to Zamora (1-1½ hr.).

▐ PRACTICAL INFORMATION

The park is clearly divided geographically. In the **zona alta,** accessible via Loja, mountains reach over 3600m and the climate is similar to that of the central Highlands. The lowlands **zona baja,** accessible via Zamora, is geographically and physically closer to the Oriente. The park's outskirts are highly touristed and have been impacted by illegal mining, but day hikes can lead to more rewarding areas—it takes three or four days to reach the center of Podocarpus.

Park Information: Ministerio del Ambiente offices in Loja (see **Tourist Offices,** p. 191) and Zamora (see **Tourist Offices,** p. 184) dispense information, maps, entrance tickets, and cabaña tickets (US$3 per person per night). For a list of the different plants and animals that can be seen in the park, visit the **Arco Iris Foundation,** Segundo Cueva Celi 3-15 (☎2577 449; direccion@arcoiris.org.ec), in Loja. The local non-profit conservation group has reams of information and oversees the San Francisco Cloud Forest (see p. 189). Open M-F 8am-1pm and 2-5pm.

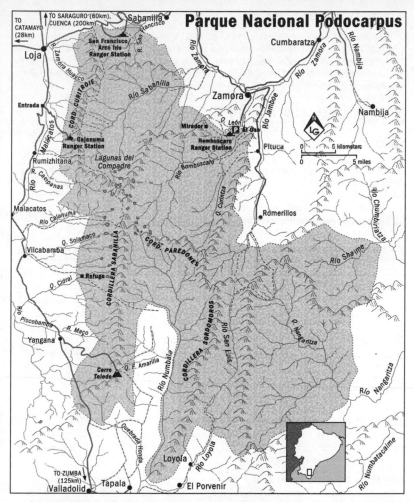

Parque Nacional Podocarpus

Accommodations: Backcountry hiking and camping is not recommended, since high altitude brings strong winds and sudden weather changes, and the vegetation is prohibitively dense. The Ministerio del Ambiente provides **cabins** ❶ throughout the park (US$3 per person per night, with bath and kitchen access US$5). Buy a ticket at a Ministerio office in Loja or Zamora. At San Francisco, the comfortable and clean—leave dirty boots outside!—lodge has a porch with views of the valley, hot showers, and a kitchen. Mattresses on the floor US$8; beds US$10.

Maps: The Ministerio del Ambiente and tourist offices in Zamora and Loja (see above) have free maps.

Supplies: Bring a waterproof outer layer, warm clothes, and sturdy hiking boots. There are no supplies available inside the park. Some tour companies in Loja will rent equipment—but only to clients. Bring your own supplies or stop in Cuenca (see p. 171).

Tours: In Loja, **Biotours Ecuador** and **Aratinga Aventuras** (see **Tours**, p. 191), have 1- to 3-day trips (min. 4-person group; US$50-150 per person per day). In Vilcabamba, **Caballos Gavilan** (see **Tours**, p. 196) offers 2- to 4-day horseback expeditions that enter the park, while **Orlando Falco** and **Jorge Mendieta** both guide walks that can include the park. **Cabañas Río Yambala** (see **Accommodations**, p. 197) offers 2-day tours to the Las Palmas Nature Reserve, which is near the new Yambura entrance and shares land with the park.

◉ ◈ SIGHTS AND HIKING

ZONA ALTA

The *zona alta* cloud forest is such a diverse ecosystem that each step is an act of discovery. Threatened **Podocarpus** (or Romerillo) trees—Ecuador's only endemic conifer—dangle from the cliffs. **Spectacled bear** and **puma** tracks can be sighted near the *refugio*. Notoriously elusive high-fliers, the **toucan de altura**, the **quetzal**, and the Andean **cock-of-the-rock** hide in the Podocarpan fog. There are four main paths through the beautiful mountain terrain, all beginning at the Cajanuma *refugio* (2750m).

HIKE	DISTANCE	TIME	DIFFICULTY
Sendero al Mirador	about 2km one-way	3-4hr.	Easy
Sendero Oso de Anteojos	400m loop	10min.	Easy
Sendero Bosque Nublado	700m loop	1hr.	Medium
Sendero las Lagunas del Compadre	15km one-way	5-6hr. or 2-3 days	Medium-Difficult

SENDERO AL MIRADOR. ◈"Path to Lookout Point" winds up through lush vegetation to provide stunning vistas through barreling fog banks. Birdwatchers can observe feathered cabarets, and lucky hikers may see a spectacled bear, mountain tapir, fox, or puma. The 3-4hr. loop, reaching 3050m, is muddy and misty in the summer, but clear and dry in the winter. Hikers can also opt out of the second part of the trail and do only the 1hr. hike to the *mirador* and back.

SENDERO OSO DE ANTEOJOS. "Spectacled Bear Path," mainly for children or families, is a short 400m loop near the entrance that features labeled plants and park trivia signs. Although this trail previews the park's natural splendor, only the paths that go onward and upward lead to the amazing views.

SENDERO BOSQUE NUBLADO. "Cloud Forest Path," a slightly tougher hike (1hr., 700m), climbs through the clouds and offers larger servings of the scenic delights below. A few posts along the trail indicate prime birdwatching locations.

SENDERO LAS LAGUNAS DEL COMPADRE. "Path to the Compatriot's Lakes," the longest *zona alta* trail (15km), winds up to 3400m on its way (5-6hr.) to 105 shimmering mountain lakes (the largest 20 ha.). Most hikers camp at the halfway point or at Laguna del Ocho (2-3day). During the rainy season (Jan.-Aug.) the trail gets nasty and can be hard to follow; park officials recommend bringing a guide.

ZONA BAJA

Multiple footpaths wind their way through dense foliage to arrive at waterfalls, *miradores*, and other hidden wonders. The most rewarding point of a long hot hike comes with a dip in the ■ **Cascada Poderosa** or in Río Bombuscaro. Botanists beeline to one site—the **Orquideario**, just past the ranger station—where highlights include nine species of orchids as well as the cascarillon tree, which produces quinine, a key ingredient in malaria remedies. Several *zona baja* trails start from the Bombuscaro ranger station.

HIKE	DISTANCE	TIME	DIFFICULTY
Los Helechos	275m	20min.	Easy
Sendero Higuerones	6km	3-4hr.	Easy-Medium
Sendero Campesino	2km	1½hr.	Easy-Medium
Sendero al Mirador	2km	2½hr.	Easy-Medium
Green Jay Trail	535m	35min.	Easy

LOS HELECHOS. This is a self-guided path so short (275m) that spending the recommended 20min. on it requires self-control. The Ministerio del Ambiente helps kill time with an instructional brochure, available in Zamora or Loja, offering 11 points of interest along the trail. From point seven on the Helechos loop, a route (335m; 35min.) has been cleared to the breathtaking **Cascada Poderosa.** Cross a tiny footbridge to sit at the base of the falls as they tumble down. Another far less impressive waterfall, **Cascada la Chismosa,** is accessible on a short path (118m; 10min.) just before reaching the *refugio* from the parking area.

SENDERO HIGUERONES. The longest *zona baja* path (6km) takes 3-4hr. roundtrip and penetrates the less disturbed reaches of the forest. Tiny streams that water thick vegetation also wreak havoc on the path during the rainy season.

SENDERO CAMPESINO. This path (2km) breaks off from Higuerones, crosses Río Bombuscaro, and follows along its far bank for 1½hr. looping back toward Zamora (ankle-deep mud at points). The trail ends with an exhilarating footbridge over Río Bombuscaro, reconnecting with the road before the El Oso parking lot.

SENDERO AL MIRADOR. This 2½hr. climb (2km) leads to a *mirador* with outstanding views. It splits from the trail to Cascada Poderosa after 5min. Toward the end the path gets steep, but the final panorama is worth it.

GREEN JAY TRAIL. Green Jay is a shorter trail (535m; 35min.) ideal for birdwatchers. Zig-zagging upward through the trees, this path gives clear views of several different layers of the forest's canopy.

SENDERO AL ÁREA DE FOTOGRAFÍA. A quick walk (150m; 5min.) down this path under overhanging greenery brings visitors to **Río Bombuscaro.**

SAN FRANCISCO CLOUD FOREST

Administered by the combined efforts of Arco Iris (see above) and the Ministerio del Ambiente (see above), San Francisco is a transitional zone between the Amazonian *zona baja* and the Andean *zona alta.* It is populated by a mix of plants and animals from both zones—including toucans, eagles, palm trees, and the namesake Podocarpus tree. The zone's longest trail leads to an ancient grove of these protected trees. Check the lodge's collection of books (for sale) about all the different species in the park. The station is on the side of the road between the two gateway cities. Take a **bus** from either **Loja** (45min., US$1) or **Zamora** (1hr., US$1.50). Ask the bus driver to stop at the San Francisco entrance to Podocarpus. This entrance has a large sign for Arco Iris and a small one for Podocarpus. Do not confuse it with the San Francisco Biological Station, which is 15min. downhill toward Zamora. Buses headed back to these two cities pass every 30min..

HIKE	DISTANCE	TIME	DIFFICULTY
Sendero Los Romerillos	about 4-5km	4hr.	Easy-Medium
Sendero Las Golondrinas	200m	5min.	Easy
Sendero Bosque Nublado	400m	15min.	Easy

SENDERO LOS ROMERILLOS. This 4hr. round-trip hike (about 4-5km) winds through the cloud forest and across Río San Francisco. The highlight of the journey is the grove of Podocarpus trees (Romerillos), some 30m tall and 4m in diameter. The most ancient are almost a millenium old.

SENDERO BOSQUE NUBLADO. Those who want to stay near the comforts of the refuge can take a quick tour of the cloud forest (400m; 15min.). Combined with **Las Golondrinas,** this trail traces a figure-eight that starts and ends at the refuge.

LOJA   ☎07

The self-proclaimed "cultural capital" of southern Ecuador (Lojanos pride themselves on speaking the best Castilian in Ecuador), Loja sits at the intersection of coastal desert, lower Andes, and Amazonian jungle—serving as a center for ecotourism in southern Ecuador. Some of the most popular spots in Ecuador lie a short bus ride away, including Vilcabamba, Zamora, Saraguro, and Parque Nacional Podocarpus. Don't forget the city itself, though: with two universities, a law school, and a music conservatory, Loja rivals its surroundings for your attention.

⌐ TRANSPORTATION

Flights: La Toma Airport, in Catamayo, is 35km from Loja. Buses go to **Catamayo** (45min., every 30min. 6:30am-7:30pm, US$0.80), and taxis (5min., US$1), from the main plaza in Catamayo, go the rest of the way. **TAME** (☎2573 030; www.tame.com.ec), at 24 de Mayo and Ortega, goes to **Guayaquil** (30min.; Tu, Th, Sa 10am; US$47.50) and **Quito** (50min.; M-Sa 7:15am; M, W, Su 5:50pm; US$59.50). Open M-F 9am-1pm and 2:30-6:30pm, Sa 9am-1pm. AmEx/DC/MC/V.

Buses: Terminal Terrestre (☎2579 592), on Cuxibamba, a 20min. walk north of the *centro* along Universitaria. **Cooperativa de Transportes Loja** (☎2579 015) sends buses to: **Huaquillas** (6hr.; 11:30am, 11:15pm; US$5); **Machala** (6hr., 7 per day 4:30am-11:30pm, US$6); **Macará** (6hr., 8 per day 7am-11pm, US$6); **Quito** (14hr., direct 12hr.; 5 per day, direct 5, 7:30pm; US$14/$17); **Zamora** (2hr., 8 per day 4am-6pm, US$2.40). **Cooperativa de Transportes Viajeros** (☎2571 626) serves **Cuenca** (5¼hr., 16 per day 4am-11:30pm, US$7.50) and **Quito** (14hr.; 3:30, 6:30pm; US$14). **Vilcabambaturis** (☎2575 196) runs to **Vilcabamba** (1¼hr., 42 per day 5:45am-10:45pm, US$1.03).

Public Transportation: Pick up **colectivos** around town (6am-10pm, US$0.20).

Taxis: Within the city US$1.

■ ⃞ ORIENTATION AND PRACTICAL INFORMATION

Cradled in a gentle valley, Loja sits at the confluence of two rivers. **Río Malacatos** runs south to north, between **Universitaria** and **Iberoamérica** through the town center; **Río Zamora** bounds the eastern side of the **centro,** which lies between the two rivers, and streets **Quito** and **Lourdes** bound the northern and southern ends. Banks and many other businesses cluster near **Parque Principal;** most hostels lie north of the market, at Rocafuerte and 18 de Noviembre.

Loja

♠ **ACCOMMODATIONS**
Central Park Hotel, 13
Hostal Londres, 8
Hotel Acapulco, 9
Hotel Chandelier, 2
Hotel Metropolitano, 5

🍎 **FOOD**
A lo Mero Mero, 6
Café Azul, 7
Cevichería las Redes, 18
Charme Encanto Francés, 15
Mar y Cuba, 14
Panifacadora Nancyta, 4
Pizzería Forni di Fango, 16
Restaurant Vegetariano "El Paraíso", 1

🍷 **NIGHTLIFE**
Beer Factory, 10
Casa Tinku, 17
La Fiesta, 12
Piano Bar Unicornio, 11
Siembra, 3

Tourist Offices: The new and well-stocked **Información Turística** center (☎2570 407, ext. 219 or 220; www.municipiodeloja.gov.ec), in the government complex on the corner of Eguiguren and Bolívar, has maps of Loja and helpful information on neighboring tourist sites. Open M-F 8am-1pm and 2-6:30pm, Sa 9am-1pm. The **Ministerio de Ambiente** (☎2585 421; podocam@easynet.net.ec), on Sucre between Imbabura and Quito, is on the 3rd fl. Open M-F 8am-12:30pm and 1-4:30pm.

Tours: Loja's proximity to natural wonders ensures many tour agencies. Here are a few:

■ **Biotours** (☎2579 387; blotours_ec@yahoo.es), on Ortega between Colón and Imbabura, between Juan José Peña and 24 de Mayo, leads excursions to: Podocarpus (*zona alta* US$120 per person, 4-person group US$48 per person; *zona baja* US$159/$58); Saraguro (US$153/$47); and the Shuar community of Nangaritza (2 days; US$391/$168); among others. Guides speak English. Trips can be tailored for birdwatching or botany. Includes food, transportation, and lodging (if necessary). Open M-F 8am-6pm.

Aratinga Aventuras, Lourdes 14-80 (☎2582 434; avearatinga@yahoo.es or aratinga@loja.telconet.net), near Sucre, specializes in birdwatching trips to Podocarpus and nearby towns. Camping equipment rental (tents US$5-10, packs US$4). Open M-F 8am-noon and 2-7pm.

Arco Iris, Segunda Cueva Celi 03-15 (☎2577 449; direccion@arcoiris.org.ec), at Clodoveo Carrión, is a foundation which focuses on conservation and educational ecotourism. Has a wealth of information on local flora and fauna and can provide guides (US$30 per day, excluding food, transportation, or equipment) for Podocarpus (see p. 186) and Manglares (see p. 281). Contact Angel Hualpa to coordinate a trip. Open M-F 8am-1pm and 2-5pm.

SOUTHERN HIGHLANDS

Immigration Office: Jefatura de Migración (☎2573 600), at Argentina and Bolivia, 2nd fl., next to the police station. Open M-F 8am-noon and 3-6pm.

Consulate: Peru, Sucre 10-64, 2nd fl. (☎2571 668). Open M-F 8:30am-1:30pm.

Currency Exchange: Banks scatter the *centro*, especially around the Parque Principal. **Banco de Guayaquil** (☎2585 025), across from the PacificTel office on José Eguiguren exchanges AmEx traveler's checks for 1% commission. 24hr. MC/V **ATM.** Open M-F 8:30am-4:30pm and Sa 9am-1pm.

Western Union: Tía (☎2577 129), a supermarket on 10 de Agosto between Sucre and Bolívar. Open M-F 9am-5:45pm, Su 8:30am-1pm.

Book Exchange: ▨ **Biotours** (see above) has a variety of English and French books.

Library: Biblioteca Municipal (☎2570 407, ext. 37), on Bolívar ½ block north of Parque Central. 7000 books for browsing but no card catalog. Ask to see the informative tourist guidebook (in Spanish) of Loja and surrounding areas. (Free to look at, US$5 to buy.) Open M-F 8am-9pm, Sa 8am-1pm.

Markets: Mercado Centro Comercial, at Rocafuerte and 18 de Noviembre. Everything from meat to the pan to fry it in. Open daily 7am-6pm.

Laundromat: Lavandería La Mágica, Rocafuerte 14-37 (☎2572 106), at Bolívar. 12 items US$4, but no undies. Open M-F 8am-1pm and 2-7pm, Sa 8am-5pm. DC/V.

Emergency: ☎101.

Police: National Police (☎2579 030), at Argentina and Bolivia. **City Police** (☎2585 606), at Imbabura and Valdivieso. Both open 24hr.

Hospitals: Hospital Isidro Ayora (☎2570 540 or 2560 159), on Manuel Agustín Aguirre, near Quito. Open M-F 8am-4pm. Emergencies only Sa-Su.

Telephones: PacificTel, at Rocafuerte and Bolívar. Open daily 7am-10pm; **branch,** on Antonio Eguiguren between Valdivieso and Olmedo, open daily 7:30am-10pm; **branch,** on Colón and 18 de Noviembre, open daily 7am-10pm.

Internet Access: Cybersat (☎2576 006), across from Plaza Santo Domingo next to PacificTel, has a fast satellite connection. US$0.80 per hr., with 10min. free for every hr. of use. Open daily 7am-10pm. **Cen@ltec** (☎2570 037), on 18 de Noviembre between Miguel Riofrio and Azuay. Also US$0.80 per hr. Has Net2phone service for US$0.25 per min. Open M-Sa 8am-9pm, Su 9am-1pm.

Post Office: Colón 15-09 (☎2571 600; fax 2582 413), at Sucre, also offers **EMS** service. Open M-F 8am-noon and 2-6pm.

▚ ACCOMMODATIONS

Loja has an over-abundance of hotels, most of which are around 10 de Agosto and 18 de Noviembre.

▨ **Hotel Metropolitano,** 18 de Noviembre 6-31 (☎2570 007; fax 2570 244), at Colón. A tribute to wood paneling. All rooms have hot baths; TVs; and big, comfy beds. Singles US$10; doubles US$20; triples US$30; quads US$40. ❸

Hotel Acapulco, Sucre 7-61 (☎2570 651), at 10 de Agosto. Luxurious rooms have TV, phone, and hot bath. Singles US$16; doubles US$26; triples US$36. V. ❹

Hotel Chandelier, Imbabura 14-82 (☎2563 061; chandelierhotel@hotmail.com), at Sucre. Carved pillars and an open, tiled courtyard create a slightly-run-down-mansion look. Some street noise penetrates, but rooms are clean, comfortable, and come with towel and soap. Singles US$5, with bath and TV US$7. ❷

Central Park Hotel, 10 de Agosto 1364 (☎2561 103), at Bolívar features rooms overlooking the Parque Principal. Phones, TVs, and hot baths. US$15 per person. ❹

Hostal Londres (☎2561 936), on Sucre just up from Hotel Acapulco. As Loja grows and prices rise, it's nice to know there is still a cheap, shared bath alternative out there. US$4 per person. ❷

◪ FOOD

Loja earns an honorable mention for two things culinary: its bread and its remarkable number of hot dogs. Bakery **Panifacadora Nancyta,** 18 de Noviembre 6-05, at Colón, diffuses savory smells throughout the city. (☎2573 169. Open M-Sa 8am-noon and 2-8pm.). **Romar,** at the corner of Eguiguren and 18 de Noviembre, is a well-stocked supermarket. (☎2576 128. Open M-Sa 8am-8pm, Su 8am-1pm. MC/V.)

▨ **Café Azul** (☎2570 230), on Eguiguren between Bolívar and Sucre. Tucked behind frosted glass, this elegant cafe lives up to its name—even the chairs are blue. Tasteful art, tasty breakfasts (US$2-2.40), and fabulous crepes (US$1.90-2.40) bring in a well-dressed business crowd. Open M-F 9am-12:30pm and 3:30-10pm, Sa 3-9pm. ❶

▨ **A lo Mero Mero,** Sucre 6-22 and Colón. A family-run restaurant that serves up tasty Mexican fare in colorful rooms sprinkled with cacti. Add a little kick to the food with the picante sauce. Tacos US$1.70-1.90; burritos US$2.30-2.70; *platos fuertes* US$3-4.50. Open M-Sa 9am-9pm. ❶

Charme Encanto Francés, Riofrío 14-55 (☎2585 819), between Sucre and Bolívar. Fancy restaurant in the front, super-chic bar in the back, this place features art on the walls and on your plate. Try the filet mignon (US$7.50) enjoyed with a glass of wine (US$2.50). Go all out with the daily *menú* (2 different meats, rice, potatoes, salad, wine; US$9.80). Open M-Sa noon-11pm. DC/MC/V. ❹

Cevichería las Redes (☎2578 787), on 18 de Noviembre, between Mercadillo and Lourdes. In a peaceful courtyard, this classy spot offers seafood (US$1.50-4.50) and *típica* fare (US$2.90-3.90). Open M-Sa 9am-9pm, Su 9am-3pm. V. ❷

Mar y Cuba, Rocafuerte 09-00 (☎2585 154), at 24 de Mayo. Waiters in jeans and bowties serve tasty *ceviche* (US$4.30), seafood, and meats (both US$4.50-4.70). Open Tu-Sa 9:30am-4:30pm and 6:30-11pm, Su 9:30am-4pm. DC/MC/V. ❷

Pizzería Forni di Fango, Bolívar 10-98 (☎2582 905), at Azuay. When the craving for Italian food hits, head to this family-style restaurant for steaming lasagna (US$3.80) or tasty pizzas (US$2.80-3.80). Delivery available. Open noon-10:30pm. DC/V. ❶

Restaurant Vegetariano "El Paraíso," Quito 14-50 (☎2576 977), at Bolívar. A place to sip delicious tea, listen to classical music, and play chess. Study the hieroglyphs on the wall while enjoying one of the many soy options on the menu. Breakfast and lunch US$1.50. Open daily 7am-9pm. ❶

◉ SIGHTS

Loja's amazing scenery makes outdoors the place to be—whether admiring the view from the Virgen de Loja statue, visiting the parks, or trekking in the hills.

▨**PARQUE JIPIRO.** Any visit to Loja would be incomplete without a sampling of the somewhat random activities at Jipiro. This expansive park amuses children with miniature reproductions of everything from the Eiffel Tower to the Kremlin to African tribal headpieces. The Chinese dock rents paddleboats (US$2 per 30min.), the "cybertren" offers Internet connections (US$0.50 per hr.), the European Castle houses a library and video room (US$0.25 per person, US$0.50 per family), and the mosque doubles as a planetarium (US$0.25, children US$0.10). Cover the 4km path to the mini-zoo on a horse (US$0.50 per 30min.; Sa-Su only) or a bike (US$2 per hr.; open daily 9am-6pm). Ask here about mountain-biking daytrips around Loja. *(Take a bus (US$0.20) north to Jipiro from Universitaria, or from the bus terminal, take Oriental de Paso (the big road going downhill from the traffic circle) to Río Zamora, and turn left as soon as you cross the bridge. Planetarium open M-Sa 9am-1pm and 3-6pm. Pool open Tu-Su 9am-9pm. US$1.20, children US$0.60.)*

■ **PARQUE UNIVERSITARIO LA ARGELIA.** This outstanding park maintains multiple hiking trails. There is a small **museum** and info center at the base of the trail, and a wooden sign outside (on the right as you enter the road) illustrates the various hikes. The trail that heads left provides a 2hr. loop through a flowered pine forest, full of tranquil mountain streams, and (especially during May) squadrons of butterflies. Those with less time shouldn't miss the spectacular city views from the *mirador*. *(Any bus headed down Iberoamérica to Vilcabamba will drop you at the gate (12min., US$0.50). Argelia-Pitas buses will drop you at the university campus (10min., US$0.20). From the campus it's a 10min. walk east across Río Malacatos and a right onto the highway. Entrance is on the left. Museum open daily 8am-noon and 2-5:30pm. Park open during daylight hours. Free. To the mirador, take the 1st right from the wooden sign, then bear left and walk 30min.)*

JARDÍN BOTÁNICO "REINALDO ESPINOSA". This beautifully landscaped, impressive botanical garden boasts 889 species of tropical plants including sections devoted especially to medicinal plants and orchids. *(In Parque Universitario la Argelia (see above), across the highway and 150m down from the museum entrance. Open M-F 9am-4pm, Sa-Su 1-6pm. US$0.60. Fundatierra (see above) can arrange tours.)*

🎵🎭 ENTERTAINMENT AND NIGHTLIFE

Weekday nightlife is scarce in Loja, but one can always go to **Cine El Dorado,** on Bernardo Valdivieso between 10 de Agosto and Rocafuerte, for the 8:15pm movie. (☎2578 466. Usually in English with subtitles. US$1.50.) On weekends many head to the *centros turísticos* in **Catamayo** (see below) for more sun and fun.

■ **Casa Tinku** (☎09 4167 046; casatinku@hotmail.com), on Mercadillo between Bolívar and Valdivieso, is a meeting place for the hip and cultured, overflowing with foreigners and locals alike. The very open, candlelit room contains a bar (beer US$0.80-1.80), live music (most Th-Sa nights), an art gallery, and the occasional theater production. Cover when live music US$2.50. Open M-Th 5pm-midnight, F-Sa 5pm-1am.

La Fiesta (☎2578 441), on 10 de Agosto between Juan José Peña and 24 de Mayo. The futuristic, mirror-covered dance floor flashes with colored lights accompanied by a rock/techno mix. Cover W-Th US$2, F-Sa US$3, including 1 drink. Open M-Th 9pm-1am, F-Sa 9pm-2am. AmEx/DC/MC/V.

Beer Factory (☎2588 986), on Bolívar at Parque Principal, has a somewhat misleading name. Loja's younger crowd packs in here for the Latin beats and thumping bass, not the cerveza. Open M-Sa 3pm-2am.

Siembra (☎2583 451), at Segundo Cueva Celi and the continuation of 24 de Mayo across Río Zamora, serves food and drink (beer US$1-1.40) to local 20- and 30-somethings under its thatched roof. Open M-Th 5pm-midnight and F-Sa 5pm-1:30am.

Piano Bar Unicornio, Bolívar 7-63 (☎2574 083), at 10 de Agosto, exudes a dark glow from the frosted lightbulbs lining the red-and-black interior. Good place to sit and nurse a cocktail; party elsewhere. Open M-Th 3pm-midnight, F-Sa 3pm-1am. DC/MC/V.

VILCABAMBA ☎07

In a nation full of quiet little towns, Vilcabamba (pop. 5000) silently holds the crown for most *tranquilo*. Warm weather and beautiful scenery have transformed this sleepy town into a unique hideaway, while numerous sprightly elders (see **Water Wonders,** p. 197) have earned the city nicknames like "Valle de la Juventud Eterna" (Valley of Eternal Youth). Until recently, however, the town was famous for another reason: fiesta-oriented foreigners flocked here to sample the hallucinogenic properties of the San Pedro, a psychotropic cactus endemic to the valley. But don't come looking to get high: local opinion and law enforcement have recently joined forces to decrease drug-related tourism; consequently, "daytrippers" attempting to procure their chemical muse will likely meet a cold reception. Luckily, the San Pedro is by no means necessary to enjoy Vilcabamba. Expats from around the world have flocked to this sacred valley for the resort atmosphere and outdoor opportunities. From spas and massage parlors to horseback rides and spectacularly scenic hikes, this town deserves to be called a paradise.

☰ TRANSPORTATION

Buses: Terminal, at Jaramillo and Eterna Juventud. **Sur Oriento** buses run to **Zumba** (6hr.; 5:30, 8am, 5:30, 9:30pm; US$5). Call their Loja office (☎2579 019; open 24hr.) for scheduling. **Cooperativa Unión de Vilcabamba Turis** (☎2673 166) sends **vans** from the terminal to **Loja** (1¼hr., every 30min. 5:45am-8:15pm, US$1). **Carla-manga** also serves Zumba.

Taxis: Leave when full from the terminal (6am-8pm). **Taxi Ruta,** Ruta 11 de Mayo at the terminal, sends **oolootivos** to **Loja** (45min., US$1.20).

Bike Rental: La Terraza, at D.V. de Vega and Bolívar, rents by the hr. (US$2) or the day (8am-8pm; US$10). Many hostels also rent to guests.

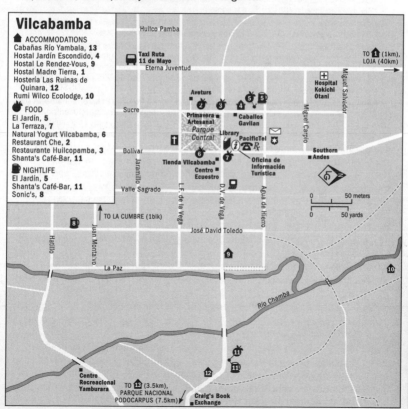

Vilcabamba

🏠 ACCOMMODATIONS
Cabañas Río Yambala, 13
Hostal Jardín Escondido, 4
Hostal Le Rendez-Vous, 9
Hostal Madre Tierra, 1
Hostería Las Ruinas de
   Quinara, 12
Rumi Wilco Ecolodge, 10

🍴 FOOD
El Jardín, 5
La Terraza, 7
Natural Yogurt Vilcabamba, 6
Restaurant Che, 2
Restaurante Huilcopamba, 3
Shanta's Café-Bar, 11

🍸 NIGHTLIFE
El Jardín, 5
Shanta's Café-Bar, 11
Sonic's, 8

Huilco Pamba
Taxi Ruta 11 de Mayo
Eterna Juventud
TO 🏠 (1km), LOJA (40km)
Hospital Kokichi Otani
Miguel Salvador
Sucre
Aveturs
Primavera Artesanal
Caballos Gavilan
Parque Central
Library
PacificTel
Miguel Carpio
Bolívar
Oficina de Información Turística
Tienda Vilcabamba
Centro Ecuestro
Southern Andes
Jaramillo
Valle Sagrado
Agua de Hierro
D.V. de Vega
L.F. de la Vega
0   50 meters
0   50 yards
8
TO LA CUMBRE (1blk)
José David Toledo
Hatillo
Juan Montavo
La Paz
9
10
Río Chamba
Centro Recreacional Yamburara
TO 13 (3.5km), PARQUE NACIONAL PODOCARPUS (7.5km)
Craig's Book Exchange
11
12
11

▄✴ 🔁 ORIENTATION AND PRACTICAL INFORMATION

Buses and taxis cruise in from Loja along **Eterna Juventud**. Most stop at the **terminal**. The **main plaza** houses a slew of restaurants, stores, and tour agencies. Hotels are scattered all over town.

Tourist Office: Oficina de Información Turística (☎2580 890), at Diego Vaca de la Vega and Bolívar, in the park opposite the church. Sells **maps** (city streets US$1.50, hiking trails US$0.50) and provides helpful information in Spanish. Open daily 8am-1pm and 3-6pm.

Tours: This small town has a lot to offer, including a diverse number of tour agencies.

> **Aveturs** (☎2580 686), in the courtyard of Hostal Valle Sagrado, 2nd fl., off Sucre by the Parque Central, is the umbrella organization for native guides. They train locals and promote self-sustaining ecotourism. 2- to 3-day trips enter Podocarpus in the Yamburara region, where there is a new communal *refugio*. Open M-F 8:30am-6pm with a lunch break.

> **Caballos Gavilan** (☎2580 281; gavilanhorse@yahoo.com), just off the park on Sucre, between Vega and Agua de Hierro, provides top-notch service. Kiwi owner Gavin Moore offers gourmet food with vegetarian options as well as bartending services and 2 nights at his cabin in the nearby cloud forests (US$35 per day). Also offers day tours (6hr.; US$30). Open daily 9am-8pm.

> **RumiWilco Ecolodge:** Bilingual Orlando Falco offers 4 different cloud forest walks (min. 4-person groups) in the southern reaches of Podocarpus. He has almost 30 years of experience as a naturalist guide in Ecuador (US$25-30 per person).

> **Centro Ecuestre** (☎2673 151; centro12@latinmail.com) offers horseback-riding tours (4hr., US$15; multi-day trips, US$25 per person per day). Open daily 9am-9pm.

> **Cabañas Rio Yambala** (see below) has a variety of offerings in Las Palmas Reserve and the neighboring areas of Podocarpus National Park. The 8hr. tree canopy tour (US$40 per person, groups of 3 or more US$35 per person) is an unconventional way to see the forest. Also offers 2- and 3-day treks on horseback (US$75-130 per person) or on foot (US$60-105 per person) that visit their *refugio* (fireplace, kitchen, and hot showers).

> **Southern Andes Mountain Trekking,** on Bolívar 2 blocks down from the Parque Central, also goes by the Spanish name Andes Sureño. Jorge Mendieta has extensive knowledge of medicinal plants and gives tours with a floral emphasis, including a 2-day trek to Las Lagunas del Compadre. (2-4hr., US$6; 6-8 hr., US$15, including lunch; longer trips, US$25 per person per day.)

Currency Exchange: Some hotels will exchange traveler's checks and cash for guests.

Work Opportunities: Ask at Rumi Wilco Ecolodge (see **Alternatives to Tourism,** p. 75) about odd jobs to be done on the reserve (coffee production, trailblazing, and more).

Language Schools: La Cumbre, Montalvo 07-36 (☎2580 283; www.cumbrevilcabamba.com), near Toledo, offers private Spanish tutoring (1-on-1 US$5 per hr., groups US$3.50 per person per hr.).

Bookstore: Craig's Book Exchange, 15min. up Vega, has numerous books (US$1.50-10; pay US$1.50 and give 1 book for 1; exchange 2 for 1). Open M-F 7:30am-6pm, Sa-Su 8:30am-6pm.

Library: Upstairs from the tourist office. Open M-F 8am-1pm and 3-6pm.

Market: Tienda Vilcabamba, in Parque Principal at Bolívar and Vega. Open daily 8am-11pm.

Outdoor Equipment: Guide agencies provide gear for clients—no renting in Vilcabamba.

Laundromat: Shanta's Café-Bar, an 8min. walk up Vega, can deliver clean clothes in 2hr. US$2.50 for 4kg. Open daily 8am-6pm.

Police: ☎2580 896. On Agua de Hierro between Sucre and Bolívar. On call 24hr.

24hr. Pharmacy: Farmacia Reina del Cisne (☎2580 289), on Bolívar 1 block down from the plaza. Open daily 7am-10pm. Emergencies 24hr. (ring the doorbell).

Hospital: Hospital Kokichi Otani (☎2673 128; fax 2673 188), 2 blocks from the plaza along Eterna Juventud. Open M-F 8am-4pm. Emergencies 24hr.

Telephones: PacificTel (☎2580 268), at Bolívar and Vega, next to the tourist office. No collect or calling card calls. Open daily 8am-9:30pm.

Internet Access: CyberSpace, on Vega at Valle Sagrado. Satellite Internet US$1.50 per hr. Open daily 9am-9:30pm.

Post Office: ☎2580 896. On Agua de Hierro. Does everything but sell stamps; get those at **Primavera Artesanal**, on Vega near Sucre by the Parque Central. Post office open M-F 7am-5pm.

ACCOMMODATIONS

Due to the steady stream of tourists, Vilcabamba has a bewildering array of excellent accommodations— everything from mountain lodges to full-service resorts.

◼ **Cabañas Río Yambala** (☎2580 299; www.vilcabamba.cwc.net). Walk 10min. from town on Vega, then 3km (1hr.) up the dirt road. Taxi from terminal US$3. Yambala, commonly known as "Charlie's," has private cabañas built high on the mountainside with balconies, hammocks, and great views. Its location in the Las Palmas Reserve assures an escape from it all. Also arranges tours (2-3 days, US$75-130 per person). Restaurant (entrees US$1-2). Breakfast and dinner included. Cabañas US$10-12, with bath US$14. V and traveler's checks accepted. ❸

◼ **Rumi Wilco Ecolodge,** hidden in the Rumi Wilco Nature Reserve. Take the dirt road off Agua de Hierro, cross the river on the slanted bridge, and follow the 1st path on the left—signs mark the way. Friendly English- and Spanish-speaking owners/biologists, Orlando and Alicia Falco, are dedicated to maintaining the reserve, and put one-third of profits toward conservation. Ask about helping to process the coffee beans grown on the reserve or about a host of other odd jobs to get a discount on your stay. All rooms have kitchens, hammocks, and drinkable water. Stay at the Pole House for privacy and the Upper House for views. Rooms with fridge and hot water US$5-10. ❷

◼ **Hostería Las Ruinas de Quinara** (☎2580 314), on Vega, a 3min. walk from the park. A whole town in 1 hotel, this resort offers a pool (with slide); jacuzzi; sauna; foosball; nightly movies; bike and horse rentals; laundry; postal service; Internet access; telephones; rooms with TVs and stereos; and basketball, volleyball, and badminton courts. Exchanges AmEx traveler's cheques for free. Resident beautician and masseuse top it off. Veggie meals and homemade bread. Arranges bus and plane travel; free transport from ter-

WATER WONDERS

Vilcabamba is unequivocally famous for its old people. Its residents regularly reach the ripe old ages of 100.

What's more, they seem to be in remarkably good health—centenarians still stroll the city streets and work in their gardens. But, as everyday as these death-eluding marvels have become, they are still held in high regard by other townsfolk. The oldest have even had streets named for them: José David Toledo and Miguel Carpio lived to 140 and 129. Husband and wife Albertano Roa Abarca and Sara Moconchi made long living a family affair. Playing the guitar for most of his life and never smoking or drinking, Albertano lived to 127, dying only one month after his wife passed away at 96.

What's their secret? Investigative medical teams have concluded that four factors lead to their longevity: the valley's mild climate, plenty of exercise, a diet low in saturated fat and high in fiber, and... the water.

Mineral-laden in general, it has particularly high levels of magnesium, which helps to break up saturated fats and prevent arteriosclerosis. Two companies, Vilcagua and Vilca Vida, have even been formed to capitalize on this "miracle" tonic. They bottle up this "fountain of youth" and sell it all over the province. So head on down to Vilcabamba and take a sip—or a tank. To your health!

minal with reservation. Breakfast included. Rooms US$7-8 per person, with bath US$9. DC/MC/V. ❷

Hostal Jardín Escondido (☎2580 281), on Sucre just off the plaza. Freshly remodeled compound in the heart of town has lush tropical plants, a pool, and a jacuzzi. Comfortable rooms with hot baths and a friendly atmosphere make this a popular destination for the backpacker crowd. Common areas have DirecTV and a selection of DVDs. Breakfast included. Rooms US$8-12 per person. ❸

Hostal Le Rendez-Vous, Vega 06-43 (rendezvousecuador@yahoo.com), at La Paz. Brand-new adobe and bamboo cabins have great beds and hot showers. Hammocks on the porch face a courtyard. Far enough from the plaza that it's quiet, but only a minute's walk to the middle of town. Trilingual owners provide great service. Breakfast with delicious homemade bread included. Singles US$10; doubles US$16; triples US$21; quads US$26. Oct. 1-Dec. 15 and Jan. 15- June 15 ask about 10% discount. ❸

Hostal Madre Tierra (☎2580 269; www.madretierra1.com), 20min. toward Loja, and 400m up a dirt road on the left. Free taxi service from the terminal. A full-service resort with all the fixings: swimming pool, gardens, spa, pool table, trampoline, and restaurant. Breakfast and dinner included. Exchanges AmEx traveler's checks (US$1 per US$20). Dorms US$12; singles with private bath US$18; matrimonials with bath US$25, with balcony US$30. MC/V. ❸

⟁ FOOD

Vilcabamba's best-kept secret is **Martha Clayton.** Whipping up bread, cookies, cakes, *bocadillas* (peanut and fudge energy bars), granola, and more, Martha distributes as far as Loja. To go straight to the source, contact her through the Carpio family, next to PacificTel in town, or ask at Cabañas Río Yambala (see above).

▨ **La Terraza,** at Vega and Bolívar, on the corner of the plaza. A popular, elegant restaurant with Thai, Italian, and Mexican cuisine. Entrees US$1.50-4. Open daily 11am-10pm. ❶

El Jardín, of Hostal Jardín Escondido (see above), serves real Mexican food (owner from Mexico City) in a lush, garden setting. Many products from local, organic farms. Homemade corn tortillas and veggie options. Entrees US$2.50-5. Open daily from 8am. ❶

Restaurante Huilcopamba (☎2580 888), at Vega and Sucre in the park, is arguably the best traditional restaurant in town. Sandwiches US$0.80-1; *desayunos* US$1-1.80; entrees US$1-2.50. Open daily 8am-9pm. ❶

Shanta's Café-Bar (see below), is best known for its nightlife, but also has fresh pizzas and spaghetti (US$2-3.50). Try its *ancas de rana* (US$4). Open daily noon-midnight. ❶

Natural Yogurt Vilcabamba, on Bolívar at the Parque Central. Small and simple, with tables out front. Veggie and organic options. Breakfast US$1.60-1.80; juices US$0.60; crepes US$0.50-2. Open daily 8am-10pm. ❶

Restaurant Che, on Sucre at the Parque Central, has appetizers (US$0.70-1.50), meat specials, pasta, and pizzas (entrees US$3-4). Sit outside and watch the foot traffic on the plaza or grab a table inside, where the walls are covered by jewelry and pictures of the restaurant's namesake. Open daily 9am-10pm. ❷

⚠ ▧ OUTDOOR ACTIVITIES AND HIKING

The countryside provides all the sights and entertainment most tourists could ask for, passing through five different climactic zones. Closer to town, **Centro Recreacional Yamburara,** a 20min. walk up the paved section of Vega, has barbeque grills, two snack bars, a swimming pool (US$0.50, children US$0.20), an impressive orchid nursery (in bloom Jan.-Mar.), and even a small zoo. (Open daily 8am-5pm. US$0.30, children US$0.20.)

HIKES. The popular hike up **Mount Mandango** (1½hr.; 2034m) to the lookout starts uphill from the bus station on Eterna Juventud and turns right just before the cemetery. The picturesque journey passes two crucifixes and some inconspicuous **Inca ruins.** A lower trek on the western side of the valley, **Camino por la Parte Baja de Valle** (Path Through the Lower Part of the Valley), is a 4hr. circuit that leaves from Madre Tierra and eventually circles back to town. Also popular is the trip to the **Agua de Hierro Springs** (1½hr.), on the other side of the valley. (Head toward the Rumi Wilco Ecolodge (see above), but don't turn left at the adobe cabins.) Just before Cabañas Río Yambala is a concrete bridge with a sign for the Sendero Oficial to Podocarpus. This leads up to a ridge with views of the valley and eventually to the park and Aventurs's refuge. Routes up the eastern side of the valley to **Mirador Cerro Yamalacapo** (round-trip 4-5hr.) and **Mirador Sucurcumine** (round-trip 3hr.) are hard to find; ask at the tourist information office (see above) for directions.

Head to the **Cabañas Río Yambala** (see above) to be in the forest. From the cabañas, trails include the **Green Trail** (1½-2hr.), a loop that climbs to a nearby ridge then back down to the road to Vilcabamba, and the **Red Trail** (5-6hr.), which climbs to Las Palmas Reserve and the cloud forests of Parque Nacional Podocarpus. Those with less time can take a 3hr. round-trip hike to the **waterfall** along the route. Other trails head to **swimming holes** and elevated **miradores** in the Las Palmas Reserve and Parque Nacional Podocarpus. Remember that Las Palmas is private land, so get permission at the cabañas first. Rumi Wilco Reserve has numerous well-marked trails with informative signs. Gully trails lead up the mountainside; other trails leads along the ridge. The US$2 entrance fee goes toward further conservation efforts and includes a map and booklet describing flora and fauna.

◤ NIGHTLIFE

Nightlife in Vilcabamba tends to be extremely erratic—some nights the party's on until the wee hours; others, the only things stirring are the crickets. Many restaurants on the plaza serve as bars and stay open until everyone goes home. On Saturday nights, **◤El Jardín** has live music. (Cover US$1.50 sometimes; band plays 10pm-late.) Bands play rock, reggae, salsa, and a little bit of everything in between. Owner Gryan Marcos often plays with one of his two bands or joins another. Don't miss him; he's played with the Wailers and opened for Bob Marley and Peter Tosh. **Shanta's Café-Bar,** on Vega has burlap and bamboo for a tropical ambience. Cowboy hats and saddles as barstools mix in a taste of the Old West. Try a shot of *el serpiente* (snake-juice; US$1.25) from the sugar cane jar on the counter. The open air bar starts bonfires when the mood is right. (☎2580 296. Open daily noon-midnight, later F-Sa.) **Sonic's,** on Toledo near Hatillo, is the only nightclub in town. The bar serves Pilsners (US$1.25) and strong mixed drinks (US$2-2.50). (☎2580 392. Occasional cover or drink min. US$4. Lively F-Sa nights. Open Tu-Sa 8pm-2am.)

SARAGURO   ☎07

Saraguro is well-known for two things: amazingly colorful cloth made by indigenous artisans and the dark clothing these artisans wear. Men wear black, calf-length pants and black ponchos; women sport long, dark dresses closed with silver *topo* pins. And both men and women have one long braid descending from a black felt hat. Legend has it that this dress originated as a way of mourning the fall of the Inca Empire. Saragurans are famously good at preserving their culture, rarely mixing even with other Quichua groups. They are also active leaders in the international Indigenous Movement. Travelers will find several stores selling Saraguran fabric and handicrafts, but the **Sunday market,** when farmers come to town, is the best time for serious shoppers. During the rest of the week, most vendors open after noon. On the corner of Vivar and El Oro, **Tienda Quizhpe** has a rainbow selection of scarfs (US$3), ponchos (US$12), and other fabrics. Owner Manuel Encarnación Quizhpe also offers tours of his fabric shop just south of town. When done perusing the handmade goods, visitors can climb Paquishapo hill, where **Iglesia Shindar** provides a pleasant overlook of the town and the perfect place for a picnic (1hr. hike; taxi US$2-3 round-trip).

Fundación Wampra, on Vivar next to Central Telefónica, serves as a tourist office, with useful info about Saraguro and its outskirts. This is a great resource for those who want to experience more than just the market in a visit. (☎2200 168; wampra@yahoo.com. Open M-F 9am-8pm.) They can help find local guides for visits to the **Bosque Protegido Washapamba,** 217 ha. of protected cloud forest only 6km from Saraguro (entrance fee for foreigners US$5). Protected and supported by a consortium of three local communities, Washapamba is home to the endangered **red-faced parrot,** the threatened **bearded guan,** and the **golden plume parakeet.** Wampra can help arrange a tour of the **Cañon Grande** by camioneta. A full-day trip in the 1000m-deep canyon goes through desert and past ruins belonging to either the Incan or Wari culture. (US$50 for the day). Another daytrip climbs **Cerro Acacana** and includes a sacred Incan pool carved into the rock. (Ask about guides in Wampra or the town of San Lucas.) Contact Rómulo Chávez at Wampra to visit **La Casa de las Antigüedades,** which serves double duty as a museum and a place to stay. The collection ranges from pre-Inca and Inca artifacts to more recent relics of *mestizo* culture. Stay there or arrange a homestay with a Saraguro family. (Antigüedades US$6 per night, meals US$2. Homestay US$20 per day, including lodging, food, and activities with the family.)

Lodgings and a few restaurants lie on or near the main square. Those wishing to stay the last week in June should make reservations in advance, as the **Fiesta de San Pedro** fills the town the week of June 29. On January 6, the last day of **Christmas** festivities, crazy characters and costumes fill the square. The stylish, new **Hostal Samana Wasi ❸,** on 10 de Marzo and the Panamerican Hwy., has bright rooms with private bath and TV and is the most luxurious hotel in town. (☎2200 315. Rooms US$8.) **Residencial Saraguro ❷,** on Loja and Luís Fernando Bravo, provides clean rooms around a beautiful garden courtyard. (☎2200 286. Common bath. Rooms US$4.) **Hostal Ñucanchik Sara Allpa ❶,** past Residencial Saraguro and left on Cartro, has large rooms at good prices. (☎2200 272. Rooms US$3, with TV US$4, with TV and bath US$5.) For some good Quichua cooking, head to El Oro. **Mama Cuchara ❶** has a large dining area with native instruments, paintings, and clothing hanging from the walls. (Meals US$1.30-1.80. Open daily 7:30am-8:30pm). For a unique atmosphere and great grilled pork (US$1.50-2), try **Cabañas Restaurant ❶.** Folkloric music plays in the background as diners enjoy a meal in private wood-and-straw cabañas. (Take Loja past CoopMego, and turn left on 18 de Noviembre. Open daily for lunch and dinner.) **Reina Del Cisne ❶,** also on El Oro, serves up all sizes of chicken dishes. (☎2200 182. Entrees US$0.80-7. Open daily 7am-10pm.)

Saraguro's main square is made up of **El Oro, Loja** (which passes in front of the Iglesia San Pedro), **10 de Marzo,** and **José María Vivar,** opposite the cathedral where buses stop. **CoopMego** sits at the corner of Loja and 10 de Marzo, but does not exchange traveler's checks. The **police** (☎101) are on 10 de Marzo. (Open M-F 8:45am-4:45pm, Su 9am-1pm.) **M@xNet,** on 18 de Noviembre past CoopMego, has satellite service. (US$1 per hr. Open daily with breaks 9am-10pm.) **Central Telefónica Saraguro** is at 10 de Marzo and Vivar. (Open 8am-10pm). **Cooperativa Viajeros Internacionales** (☎2200 165), on María Vivar, services **Cuenca** (3hr., 16 per day 5:45am-2am, US$5) and **Loja** (1¾hr., 15 per day 6:30am-1am, US$1.75). Buses can be flagged down on the Panamerican Hwy. between Cuenca and Loja.

CATAMAYO
☎ 07

Once the site of Loja itself, Catamayo has kept relatively quiet since the better-known metropolis moved 35km east in 1548. Lojanos still flock to this town on warm weekends to enjoy the *centros turísticos* (hotel/recreation centers) that line the road toward El Cisne. While there is little to do, travelers with early flights may want to spend the night here.

Lodgings in Catamayo are plain and utilitarian—cold baths are the norm. **Hotel Reina de El Cisne ❷**, on Isidro Ayora near the plaza, has breezy hallways with a few plants. (☎2677 414. US$3 per person, with private bath and TV US$6.) **Hostal Turis ❶**, at Isidro Ayora near 24 de Mayo, offers clean lodgings cheap. (☎2677 126. US$2 per person.) Next door, **Hotel Rossana ❷** has comfortable doubles with cable TVs and private baths or smaller, TV-less singles. (☎2677 006. US$4 per person, with TV US$6.) **Bachita Restaurant ❶**, at Isidro Ayora and 24 de Mayo, has two floors and makes all juices with purified water. (☎2677 836. US$1.50-4. Open 7am-10pm.)

Moneygram has an office in Cañanet, on Catamayo at the plaza. (Open M-F 2:30-5:30pm, Sa 9am-1pm.) **PacificTel** is on Isidro Ayora. (Open 7am-10pm.) **Cooperativa Catamayo,** Catamayo 3-56 (☎2677 278), near Isidro Ayora and the Parque Principal, runs **buses** to **Loja** (45min., every 30min. 6am-6:30pm, US$1). **Transportes Loja** (☎2677 151; open daily 7am-11pm) at Isidro Ayora and 18 de Noviembre, one block downhill from the park goes to Guayaquil (8hr., 8 per day 7:30am-1am, US$10), Huaquillas (5hr.; 12:30pm, midnight; US$6), Macará (5hr., 9 per day 8am-1am, US$6), Machala (5hr., 7 per day 5:30am-12:30am, US$6), Piura (8hr.; 8am, 2, 11:30pm; US$10),and Quito (16hr.; 11:30am, 2:45, 5:45, and 9pm; US$14). **Camionetas** leave when full from the corner of Isidro Ayora and 24 de Mayo to **El Cisne** (1hr., US$1.50; hard to fill M-F). Grab **taxis** to the airport (5min., US$1) or El Cisne (55min., round-trip US$15) from the plaza at 24 de Mayo and Isidro Ayara.

EL CISNE
☎ 07

The small village of El Cisne is home to a enormous cathedral that despite its bright exterior, retains a Gothic feel. Inside the cathedral, a statue of the Virgin Mary, **La Virgen del Cisne**—made for the town in 1594 by famed religious artisan Don Diego de Robles—looks down at worshippers from behind a plate of glass in her ornate, gold-encrusted home. It is this statue, not the church, town, or gorgeous mountain scenery, that draws hordes to El Cisne every year. After celebrating the last day of El Cisne's annual week-long summer festival (Aug. 20), faithful hordes descend upon the town to rush the cherished statue. Then they make the 74km trek to Loja on foot, carrying the Virgin to where she presides over Loja's annual festival, on September 8. The sanctuary is also impressive. Gargantuan in both scale and reputation, it is home to a number of ornate silver dragons and beautiful stained-glass windows. When you're done gawking at the cathedral, visit the **religious museum** in the church's catacombs; buy a ticket in the clock tower, which also houses a small bookstore and gift shop. The museum displays the Virgin's dresses as well as gifts (from several hundred toy trucks to diamond jewelry) given for her blessing. (Open daily. M-F min. group size 6. More people are likely to be around after Mass. Visitors over 6 US$1.)

Buses leave Loja's terminal for El Cisne (2hr.; M-Sa 8:30am and 5pm, Su 7:30, 8:30am; return M-Sa 12:30pm, Su 11am and 1pm; US$1.50). Or, take a bus to Catamayo (45min., every 30min. 6:30am-7:30pm, US$0.80) and then catch a **camioneta** to El Cisne (1hr., US$1.50). **Taxis** can also be hired (55min., round-trip US$15). There are **no phones** in town. Pilgrims can spend the night at the minimalist **Casa Posada El Trebol ❶**, one block downhill from the front of the cathedral on Juan Cuenca. (Rooms US$3-4; triples with private bath US$12.) **Restaurants,** mostly offering standard *menús*, line the plaza.

CATACOCHA   ☎ 07

The sun seems always to shine brilliantly on the pretty white buildings of Catacocha (pop. 4000), a small town halfway between Loja and Macará. Twenty kilometers south of the road that heads west to Machala, this area was home to the pre-
Inca civilization known as the Palta. The extensive views and pleasant, small-town
atmosphere make Catacocha an enjoyable stop on the journey south.

⬕◪ TRANSPORTATION AND PRACTICAL INFORMATION. Cooperativa Loja
(☎2683 052) has an office on Vivanco, one block downhill from the statue, and
sends **buses** to: **Machala** (4hr., 9am, US$6.25); **Macará** (3½hr., 8 per day 9:30am-
9pm, US$3.50); and **Loja** (2½hr., 9 per day 8am-6pm, US$2.30). Macará-bound
buses pass through the plaza. The **central plaza** is next to the large church, flanked
by **Guerrero** and **Vivanco. 25 de Junio** passes in front of the church. Most commercial
activity is by the statue one block down Vivanco. The **Municipio** (on the plaza)
offers helpful, tourist information and maybe even a personally guided tour. (Open
M-F 8am-noon and 2-6pm.) **Banco de Loja** is on Guerrero next to the church.
(☎2571 682. Open M-F 8am-3pm, Su 8:30am-noon.) The **police** (☎2683 101; open
24hr.) are behind the church on Guerrero. The **hospital** (☎2683 030) is open 24hr.
for emergencies. **PacificTel** is next to the police. (Open daily 8am-10pm.) **Correos,**
on Guerrero near the main plaza, sends out mail on Wednesdays. (☎2683 091.
Open M-F 9am-noon and 3-6pm, Su 9-11am.)

⬔⬓ ACCOMMODATIONS AND FOOD. New and spacious, comfortable and
pleasant, **Hotel Tambococha ❸,** in front of the church, is the best in town. Tasteful
art hangs on the walls, and rooms have TVs, tiled floors, hot private baths, and
comfortable beds with lots of pillows. Some have balconies overlooking the plaza.
(☎2683 551. Singles US$8, with breakfast US$9; doubles US$12/$14; triples US$18/
$21.) **Residencial Buena Esperanza ❷** is down Vivanco past the statue. (☎2683 031.
US$4, with private bath and TV US$6.) **Hotel Turismo ❶,** behind the church, has
bare but large rooms. (☎2683 731. Rooms with cold common baths US$3.) Most
restaurants congregate around the statue, one block down Vivanco from the central plaza. **Meson Paltense Restaurant ❶,** on Vivanco between the plaza and the
statue, stands out for its relaxing atmosphere and dark wood furniture. (☎2683
577. *Menú* US$1.50. Open daily 11am-9pm.)

◲ SIGHTS. Perched high on a ridge with views of the valleys to every side, Catacocha had strategic military importance to its ancient inhabitants, and the *centro*
still has a few great lookout points. Climb the huge boulder **Shiriculapo,** at the back
of the hospital grounds on the installed staircase. The drop to the valley floor
below is around 300m. **La Cruz del Calvario** (The Cross of the Cavalry) is a big, white
cross that overlooks the town. (5min. up 25 de Junio from the plaza.) From here,
Pisaca and **Guanghuro** are visible. These two nearby hills (in the Andean sense of
the word) make for good dayhikes. Ask for directions in the Municipio. The **Marist
Museum,** on Sucre and Lourdes in the Colegio Marista, has artifacts and information about the region's history. Near here is the **Iglesia Lourdes,** at a small plaza a
few blocks behind the main church. The walls are covered with 20 reproductions
of famous works, ranging from DaVinci to Dali, all painted by a priest.

MACARÁ   ☎ 07

The border crossing at Macará (pop. 12,500) may be one of Ecuador's best-kept
secrets. Unlike the chaotic and sometimes dangerous experience of entering or
exiting Peru at Huaquillas, going through Macará is not only painless but can even
be enjoyable. On a typical day, the gorgeous mountain backdrops shimmer and
locals nonchalantly go about their business.

Hotel Espiga de Oro ❷, on Ante, just off 10 de Agosto between the market and the plaza, offers the nicest lodgings. Hanging ferns and well-furnished lounges contribute to the pleasant atmosphere, as do the fans, phones, TVs, and baths in each room. (☎2694 405. Breakfast US$1. Singles US$6; doubles and matrimonials US$10; triples US$15; quads US$20.) If all that matters is saving cash, the **Hotel Amazonas ❶**, on Rengel near Parque Amazonas, offers dark, bare rooms with swaybacked beds and common baths. (☎2694 067. Rooms US$2.) Another comfortable option is **Hostal El Conquistador ❸**, at Bolívar and Calderón, also with phones, fans, cable TVs, and private baths. (☎2694 057. Singles US$8; doubles US$14.) **Restaurant D'Marcos's ❶**, on Calderón at Veintimilla, serves appetizing lunches and traditional dishes. (☎2694 457. Entrees US$2-3. Open 8am-midnight daily.)

The short distance between the **market** and **central plaza** is covered by **10 de Agosto**. The **Peruvian Consulate** is on Bolivar near 10 de Agosto. (☎2694 030. Open M-F 9am-1pm and 3-5pm.) **Banco de Loja**, 2½ blocks down Carlos Veintemilla from the central plaza, does not accept traveler's checks. (☎2694 246. Open M-F 8am-3pm, Sa 8:30am-1pm.) Other services include the **police** (☎2694 101; emergency 101), at Jaime Roldos and Catamayo on the other side of the airstrip, and **Hospital de Macará** (☎2694 515; open 24hr. for emergencies), on Cabo Sánchez. Find nonemergency medical consultants on the third floor of the Municipio. (☎2694 074. Open M-F 8am-noon and 2-6pm.) **PacificTel** is on the plaza. (Open daily 7am-10:30pm.) **Internet** access is available at **Compusur**, on 10 de Agosto at Bolivar. (US$1 per hr. Open daily 9am-10:30pm.) **Cooperativo Loja** (☎2694 058; open daily 7am-11pm), on Jaramillo behind the church, travels to: Guayaquil (9hr.; 8, 10pm; US$11); Loja (6hr., 7 per day 8:30am-11pm, US$6); Piura (3½hr.; 3:30am, 1, 6:30pm; US$3.50); and Quito (17hr., 2:30pm, US$17). Friendly staff on the second floor of the **Municipalidad**, on the plaza, can answer questions about tourism and provide a map. (☎2694 071. Open M-F 8am-noon and 2-6pm.)

BORDER CROSSING: INTO PERU

The bridge between Peru and Ecuador is about 2km from Macará. Taxis (6min., US$1) and colectivos (US$0.25) leave from the market area on 10 de Agosto near Bolívar (ask for "la frontera"), or you can walk (45min.) down the paved road at the end of Bolívar (follow the road through a small plaza and make a left on the main highway that leads to the border). Both the Peruvian and Ecuadorian **Immigration offices** are open 24hr. to issue or receive your tourist **T3 card** and stamp your passport. Exchange currency on the Ecuadorian side at money changers in the market on 10 de Agosto. Banks do not exchange currency. Be wary of fake bills. Exchange currency on the Peruvian side at **Banco Financiero**. Colectivos at the border run to **Suyo** (20min., s/2) or directly to **Sullana** (2hr., s/10). It is also possible to take colectivos to nearby **Piura** (35min., s/1-2).

THE NORTHERN LOWLANDS

The Northern Lowlands, from the coast to the Sierra, encompasses a motley combination of beaches, wildlife estuaries, urban centers, tropical forest (wet and dry), and some of the tallest mangroves in the world. Though weather patterns are similar down the length of the coast, changes in latitude mean

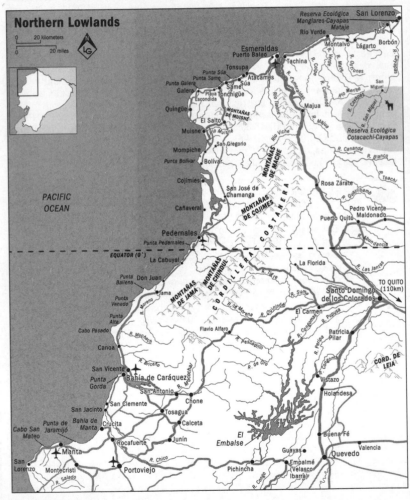

Northern Lowlands

PACIFIC
OCEAN

EQUATOR (0°)

204

changes in attitude. Those looking to party race to Atacames, where nights are spent in thatched-roof beachside bars and days are spent recovering in the sun. A mellower beach experience awaits in Playa Escondida, Same, Muisne, and Canoa, where pristine beaches stretch for miles. While the south is better known for its surf scene, the break at Mompiche is just being discovered. Blustery Manta and Crucita are the perfect places to paraglide off coastal cliffs or rip through the water kite-surfing.

HIGHLIGHTS OF THE NORTHERN LOWLANDS

MAKE FRIENDS WITH BACCHUS in party-central **Atacames** (see p. 212).

SURF the yet-undiscovered beach of **Mompiche** (see p. 220).

GET AWAY FROM IT ALL at the tranquil beach of **Playa Escondida** (see p. 218).

After El Niño, a 7.2 earthquake, and resultant mudslides, Bahía de Caráquez was reborn an "eco-city." In the far north, small towns along the coast and upriver are the birthplace of the xylophone-like Marimba instrument, and dugout canoes travel upriver into increasingly isolated pockets of Afro-Ecuadorian and Chachi (or Cayapas) civilizations. Although most of the Chachi communities have adopted western dress, they continue to speak Cha'pallachi and weave intricate baskets that are sold up and down the coast. Though now desolate, the northern coast was once home to thriving pre-Inca populations. Currently, in response to the devastating commercial logging and shrimp farming, locals have begun to find work as guides and guardians of these ecological reserves. Truly remote, newly opened paths and local guides await rubber-booted adventurers.

SAN LORENZO ☎ 06

Since mudslides dismantled the Ibarra-San Lorenzo train line, tourism in San Lorenzo has also come to a halt. Nowadays, buildings are dilapidated and boomboxes playing salsa and cumbia out-blast each other on every street corner. (Locals liken this town to García Marquez's "Macondo" from 100 Years of Solitude.) Still, the city stays busy as goods and people funnel in and out traveling to and from Colombia. It is also a point of departure to the estuaries that wind through the mangroves of Reserva Ecológica Manglares Cayapas-Mataje.

📱🚊 TRANSPORTATION AND PRACTICAL INFORMATION. Buses going to **Quito** (6hr., every hour, US$6.50) via **Ibarra** leave from the traffic circle along Imbabura, near the train station, while those going to **Esmeraldas** (every hr. 4am-6pm, US$4) via Borbón leave from 10 de Agosto, next to the park. Buses to **Guayaquil** (11hr.; 8:30am, 5:30, 6:30, and 8:30pm; US$10) leave from the park. **Boats** (lanchas), usually motorized canoes, travel to **Limones** (1½hr.; every hr. 7am-4pm; US$3), **Borbón** (1½hr.; 7am, noon, 4pm; US$3), and **La Tola** (45min., every hr. 5:30am-4:30pm, US$1.50). Almost all services are along the town's two main streets. **Imbabura** heads north from the traffic circle where buses let off. **10 de Agosto** intersects Imbabura and heads northeast past the **Parque Central** (restored with help from USAID) and down to the dock, which stretches from the train station to 10 de Agosto. Their intersection serves as a good reference point for visitors. **Foreigners should exercise caution everywhere in San Lorenzo but especially when straying from Imbabura and 10 de Agosto.**

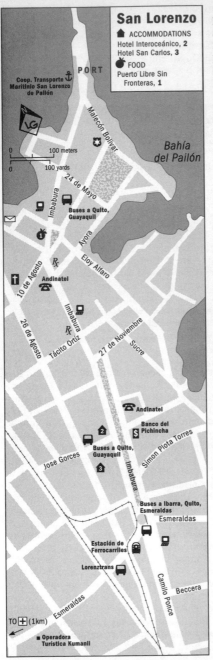

San Lorenzo

🏠 ACCOMMODATIONS
Hotel Interoceánico, 2
Hotel San Carlos, 3

🍎 FOOD
Puerto Libre Sin
Fronteras, 1

Coop. Transporte
Marítinio San Lorenzo
de Pailón

PORT

Malecón Bolívar

*Bahía
del Pailón*

0   100 meters
0   100 yards

24 de Mayo

Imbabura

Buses a Quito,
Guayaquil

Ayora

Eloy Alfaro

10 de Agosto

Andinatel

Imbabura

26 de Agosto

Tácito Ortiz

27 de Noviembre

Sucre

Andinatel

Banco del
Pichincha

Simón Plota Torres

2

Buses a Quito,
Guayaquil

3

Jose Gorces

Imbabura

Buses a Ibarra, Quito,
Esmeraldas

Esmeraldas

Estación de
Ferrocarriles

Lorenztrans

Camilo Ponce

Beccera

Esmeraldas

TO ✚ (1km)

■ Operadora
Turística Kumanli

Banco del Pichincha is on Imbabura and José Garces. (☎2780 889; open M-F 8:30am-4pm, Sa 9am-2pm.) **Police,** on 10 de Agosto by the park, can stamp your passport and provide information on border crossing. (☎2780 627. Open 24hr.) A **hospital** is about 1km down Esmeraldas toward Ibarra. Doctors attend to patients daily 8am-noon and 2-6pm—be prepared to wait in line. (☎2780 981; emergency 2780 188.) **Andinatel,** beneath the satellite tower, 100 yd. down Imbabura and on the right, allows calling card calls. (☎2780 106. Open M-Sa 8am-9pm; Su 8am-noon and 7-9pm.) **Glennet,** on Imbabura, has **Internet.** (☎2780 811. US$2.50 per hr. Open daily 7:30am-9pm.) **Correos del Ecuador,** on 26 de Agosto and Maldonado, has weekly mail delivery on Friday. (☎2780 034. Open daily 8am-noon and 2-6pm.)

🏠🍴 **ACCOMMODATIONS AND FOOD.** For San Lorenzo hotels, bigger and newer is better. The luster of these places may wear off as they go the way of the older places, but for now they still smell good. **Hotel Interoceánico ❷,** with an entrance on 26 de Agosto near Jose Garces, is San Lorenzo's newest hotel, and several bright blue stories above its neighbors. It is meticulously clean. Small rooms have TVs and fans. (Singles US$4, with private bath US$6, with A/C US$10; doubles US$12/$20.) **Hotel San Carlos ❷,** on José Garces just off Imbabura, is a big, orange version of Hotel Interoceánico (see above). Pick between slightly noisier rooms on the street and windowless interior rooms. All rooms are clean and have warm colors, mosquito nets, fans, TVs, and telephones. Rooms that share a bath are equipped with a giant roll of toilet paper on the wall above the bed. (☎2780 306; ☎/fax 2780 284. Guard out front. US$4, with private bath US$6.)

Seafood in all forms (breaded, fried, grilled, *ceviche, encocado*) rules in San Lorenzo. Check out Imbabura for good restaurants. Shacks throughout town whip up cheap fresh fruit, milk, and ice *batidos*. Unless you have an iron stomach, pass on ice. *Borojó*, a sticky Colombian food, is known as a powerful aphrodisiac. **Puerto Libre Sin Fronteras ❶**, on 10 de Agosto and Imbabura, has plenty of seafood in the open-air dining area. Entrees US$2-5. (☎2780 243. Open daily 7am-10pm.)

RESERVA ECOLÓGICA MANGLARES CAYAPAS-MATAJE

The reserve encompasses 51,300 hectares of mangrove islands home to birds, reptiles, sealife, and the occaisonal fisherman making his way through the winding estuaries in a dugout canoe. There is little infrastructure for independent visits to the reserves and guide services are only beginning to form. To the east of San Lorenzo past the stilted houses of San Antonio a narrow estuary (usually only passable at high tide) leads to the **Cascada de la Princesa Täri** (named for a princess of Épera legend who bathed in the pools above the falls). Freshwater from the jungle spills over the rock and gushes through holes to mingle with warm salt-water. Just before the falls, a few sticks mark a landing spot, and a trail leads a few meters to the top of the falls. The pools carved into the soft rock where princess Täri bathed are also said to be where indigenous women came to give birth. Be careful of the pools as some are actually drainage shafts all the way through the rock. The cascade is only accessible by private boat.

At the archaeological site **Tolita del Pailón**, visitors should do their best to tread carefully and avoid the 1500 year old pottery shards and stone implements littering the beach. Further inland are the burial mounds of the Tolita people who once inhabited the mangroves. The bits of jade and gold the mounds once contained have been looted and the bits littering the beach have been left to the tides. The appropriately named "Bird Island"—**Isla de los Pájaros**—near the Colombian border is a small pit of sand extremely popular with local birds and migrants. A variety of birds mainland Ecuadorian natives to Galápagos visitors to Canadian migrants all mingle here.

The calm, gray-sand beaches near the town of Palmarreal (a collection of shacks looking toward the Colombian side of the mangroves) are usually deserted save for a farmer checking on bananas or watermelons. South from Palmarreal is **Playa Cauchal** and further along is **Playa San Pedro**. A boat leaves San Lorenzo for **Palmarreal** daily at 7:30am and 2pm. Boats return from Palmarreal at 10am and 4pm. (US$3.) Another boat goes directly to San Pedro, leaving San Lorenzo at 7am and 2pm and returning immediately. (US$2.) Check the docks for current boat schedules. For any travel into the Reserve and especially travel north toward the border with Colombia, contact the **Policía Turística** (☎2780 832) stationed at Palmarreal for updates on the area. Notify them about where and when you plan to travel. Some public transportation goes into the reserve. Julio Moreno (☎2789 138) at Operadora Turística Kumanii has info about package tours.

The **Ministerio del Ambiente** (☎2781 174) is officially in charge of the reserve. Since there is only a trickle of tourism in this area, park rangers are dedicated to dealing with the 50 subsistence fishing communities within the reserve's boundaries. Projects include reforesting shrimp farms, community education, and charity work. Many of the rangers were born in these reserve communities. The office, near the Parque Central one block east of the basketball court, has limited information of interest to tourists. (Open M-F 8am-noon and 2-4pm.)

RESERVA ECOLÓGICA CHUCCHUBÍ

This small private reserve (700m above sea level) is developing trails to several waterfalls through teeming primary forest. Off of the highway leading to Ibarra are a few small buildings and a gate marking the entrance to the reserve. From the

A COMMUNITY'S EFFORT TO STAY AFLOAT

Though tourism has become an enormous benefit to the Ecuadorian economy, it has not aided Ecuadorians across the board. For years, local guides in San Miguel, a region containing large tracts of untouched and lush rainforest, have had to rent a private canoe in order to take tourists on visits inside the nearby Reserva Ecológica Cotacachi-Cayapas. Canoes are large purchases, usually far too expensive for a single villager to buy. One community, however, saw a way around this problem. For several months, the San Miguel Women's Committee has been saving profits from stays at the hotel to make a major purchase: a dugout canoe large enough for several visitors that can be used for free by guides taking trips inside the reserve. To buy the canoe, the women travel a few miles upriver to the Chachi village of Corriente Grande where the boats are carved by hand from a single tree-trunk. After some discussion over the price and quality of the brand-new canoe and the sharing of bananas and boiled nuts, the new canoe is lashed to an old one and motored home. The men permanently stationed near the dock ogle the new craft and debate whether the price was right and exactly how many "people" versus how many "tourists" will be able to fit. US$80 later, the community has its own canoe.

gate, a path follows along the left bank of the river. The trail crosses the river and goes over barbed wire and up through a banana farm. The trail goes on about 45min. up and down before reaching the first waterfall, **Cascada de las Mariposas** (100m). In the morning, parrots bathe en masse in the pools above, and, during June and July, orchids growing along the rocks of the falls begin to flower. Just below this first falls the trail goes to the right about 10min. to a small falls with a large, deep pool. There is a 300m waterfall about 45min. past this small pool. The trails here are unmarked and may not have been cleared recently. Owner and ornithologist Raúl Aldaz is usually around and willing to guide visitors through flora and fauna or cut a trail with his machete. Call him to arrange a visit. The reserve is about 1½hr. outside of San Lorenzo on the road to Ibarra. Buses going back to San Lorenzo pass about every hr. The last bus is at 7pm (US$2). Entrance fee US$5.

BETTER THAN BOTTLED WATER
Trying to avoid the contaminated water supply doesn't mean you always have to go with *agua sin gas, por favor* (water without carbonation, please). On the coast, *jugo de naranja natural* is usually pure orange juice, without sugar or water. On the street it sometimes has ice-cubes which may not be purified. *Agua de coco* (coconut water) or *pipas* (coconuts with a straw) are another good hydration option.

■ SAN MIGUEL   ☎ 06

Perched on a hill at the confluence of Ríos San Miguel and Cayapas, the friendly village of San Miguel (pop. 180) eagerly awaits the few tourists who venture into the beautiful *zona baja* (lowland region) of the vast Reserva Ecológica Cotacachi-Cayapas (see p. 209). Home to the only ranger station in the reserve's Lowlands, San Miguel is a necessary starting point for excursions. Transportation to San Miguel is limited to motorized **canoas** (large dugout canoes with outboard motors) that leave from the town of Borbón (3-4hr., 10am, US$8). Look for the "Ecotourism San Miguel" canoa, which returns to town early each morning (3:30am). San Miguel is located around one hill, at the top of which lies a wooden **hotel ❷**, run by the industrious San Miguel Women's Committee, offering screens and mosquito netting in simple rooms without electricity. The shared bath is clean but water must be scooped from the rainwater bucket for showers. The large deck with hammocks is a nice spot to watch Río Cayapas flow through the dense jungle. (Meals US$2.25. Rooms US$4. US$30 includes all transportation, food, lodging, guides, and entrance to the reserve.) Cristóbal Medina (the park ranger) owns the town's only store, **Despensa '4' Hermanos,** halfway up the hill from the dock. Limited supplies are available.

The residents of San Miguel are currently working on turning tourism into a venture that benefits the entire community as an alternative to logging. As part of the project, the women of the town run the hotel, while the men are trained as jungle guides. **The San Miguel Eco-Project** (☎2528 769; www.ecosanmiguel.org) is still a fledgeling operation. Before visiting, call **Carlos Donoso** at the Quito offices (León Mera 12-39 and Calama. Open M-Sa 9am-8pm.) The contact for the San Miguel Eco-Project in Borbón is Jimmy Yancz Plaza (see **Borbón,** p. 211). As of July 2004, the Eco-Project was accepting applications for long-term volunteer Englis-teachers in San Miguel. Volunteers prepare their own food and are given reduced-rate transportation and lodging (see p. 74). There is also a small **community reserve** that San Miguel has maintained in the face of logging interests that can be accessed by foot with a local guide. Trails lead through bananas and fruit trees and within a few minutes are within primary forest—along the way, snack on whatever happens to be ripe, from guava to pineapple.

RESERVA ECOLÓGICA COTACACHI-CAYAPAS

The 23,956 sq. km of the Reserva Ecológica Cotacachi-Cayapas encompasses towering mountains, gushing rivers, and pristine forest. The large rise in elevation (from 200 to 4939m) supports a splendid array of animals, including the puma, ocelot, tapir, condor, and Andean spectacled bear. A recent biodiversity survey found 500 bird species alone within the reserve's borders. To accompany this wealth of wildlife, an infinite number of rivers wind through the park, ultimately forming the great Santiago-Cayapas River.

AT A GLANCE

AREA: 23,956 sq. km.

CLIMATE: High zone 12-15°C; low zone 24-26°C. The low zone is difficult to access Dec.-Apr. because of heavy rains.

HIGHLIGHTS: Salto del Bravo, Cascada de San Miguel, Volcán Cotacachi, Lago Cuicocha.

GATEWAYS: San Miguel (p. 208), Cotacachi (p. 124).

CAMPING: Possible.

FEES: Park entrance US$5, paid to park ranger.

✈ 🛈 ORIENTATION AND PRACTICAL INFORMATION

In the northwestern corner of the Sierra between the provinces of Imbabura and Esmeraldas, the reserve is split into two major areas: the *zona baja* (low zone) and *zona alta* (high zone). The *zona baja* is composed of lush Lowlands rainforests (200m) in the province of Esmeraldas, while the *zona alta* ranges from misty cloud forests to barren *páramo* near Volcán Cotacachi (4939m).

Transportation: The *zona baja* is accessible from San Miguel (see p. 208) and Playa de Oro, though Playa has not restored the trails leading to the reserve. *Zona alta* is accessible from Cotacachi (p. 124). The park entrance lies 18km west of Cotacachi.

Park Information: There are ranger stations in San Miguel and at the park entrance near Cotacachi. The entrance fee near Cotacachi is US$1 and the fee at San Miguel is US$5.

Supplies: The park ranger and community of San Miguel can provide limited supplies, including food and rugged tents. To be safe, bring your own supplies (see p. 40).

Tours: The recommended way to visit the *zona baja* is with a guide. The park ranger in San Miguel can offer his expertise and guidance. The **San Miguel Eco-Project** (see p. 209) connects visitors with knowledgeable local guides from San Miguel. All funds benefit the entire community. The *zona alta* is more conducive to unguided exploration.

🆔 SIGHTS

The highlight of the **zona baja** is a two-day jungle trek to the waterfall **La Cascada de San Miguel** that tumbles 100m into the forest. The journey involves a motorized canoe up **Río San Miguel** to the Chachi village of **Corriente Grande**, the last bit of civilization before the untouched forest. The 11km trail into the forest starts a few more hours upriver by paddled canoe. The path to the waterfall climbs for 2hr. to the small **Río Pinupí,** where most groups stop and set up camp. The next day, another 2½hr. climb beneath the canopy emerges on a ridge just before the falls. La Cascada de San Miguel is a great place to spot large mammals and an array of birds. A shorter trail, **Sendero Río,** follows the river from the trailhead to La Cascada de San Miguel and features identification placards on the trees. Along Río Cayapas are three waterfalls of Calle Manza, whose community is working on cutting new trail to the falls. A guide is necessary for all travel in the *zona baja*. When the rivers swell from heavy rains and the trails turn to mud (Dec.-April), the *zona baja* can be difficult to visit. Be sure to bring bug repellent and wear light, loose clothing to cover up year-round.

LIMONES   ☎06

Fish, bananas, and coconuts are staples in this small town. Limones is situated on a mangrove island accessible only by boat and has few motorized vehicles on its streets. Most folks stop by Limones on the way from San Lorenzo to La Tola by boat. However, those who stick around can lounge on two beaches—mangrove and gray sand. On Nov. 3 every year, fishermen decorate their boats with flowers and images of San Martín (the patron saint of fisherman). **Boats** to from San Lorenzo depart daily (see p. 205). **Hospital Civil** (☎2789 129 or 2781 128) is at the end of Sucre, and **Farmacia Andreíta** (☎2789 236), 24hr. pharmacy, is a few houses before the hospital. The **police station** (☎2789 241) is on the water by the Capitanía. **Andinatel** is near Parque Central. (Open M-Sa 8am-noon and 3-9pm, Su 9am-noon and 7-9pm.) The hotels of Limones will do for a night but don't inspire a longer stay. **Hotel Salúd ❷**, the best bet, has all-wooden rooms with fans and firm mattresses, though some rooms are windowless. It has the convenience of an Internet connection and a pharmacy downstairs. (Rooms US$5, with private bath US$7.) The stark **Hotel Mauricio Real ❶** is near the dock. Rooms come with mosquito nets, squishy beds, one-channel TVs, and nothing else. (Rooms US$3, with private bath US$6.) **El Criollo ❶,** near the brilliant blue municipal building, has the usual shrimp, fish, and fried conch *encocado.* (☎2789 170. Breakfast US$1.50, lunch and dinner US$2, menu items US$3.) An all-bamboo bar right on the water, **El Pelícano** opens for drinks and music Friday and Saturday nights.

LA TOLA   ☎06

This small town on the mainland sees a lot of travel as buses deliver people and passengers from Borbón and areas farther inland, and boats depart for Colombia and stilt-towns on the way. La Tola has even less of a tourist scene than San

Lorenzo, and locals are a bit surprised to see tourists ambling around. **Boats** leave San Lorenzo for La Tola daily (see p. 205). **La Costeñita** and **Trasportes del Pacífico** run **buses** between Esmeraldas and La Tola daily (3hr., every 15min., US$3.50).

To explore the nearby reserve **Majagual** (off the highway, a few km from La Tola, on the way to Esmeraldas) that protects the largest mangrove trees in the world, first find a local guide. Orín Ferrín, Ali Charcopa, Katita Perca, and Ernesto Morales can either serve as guides or help locate one in the community. Ask to see a license before heading out. None of the guides speak English. If you visit Morales, he or his father are eager to intone the odes they have written to the gargantuan mangroves. There is also a nearby archaeological site, **Tolita Pampa de Oro**, which is home to **Tolita del Pailón** (see **Reserva Ecológica Manglares Cayapas-Mataje**, p. 207). **Comedor Maurita ❶** has cheap seafood, fried and *oncocado*. The kitchen opens to the dining room. (☎2786 107. *Menú* US$1.50-2, other dishes including tasty lobster-like langostino US$2.50.) A small **hotel ❶** is about a block closer to the dock from Comedor Maurita. The shared showers are just faucets. The newer second-floor rooms open onto a bare, concrete rooftop and have large windows. (☎2786 088. Rooms with fan and shared bath US$3-4, new rooms US$4-5.)

BORBÓN   ☎06

At the mouth of Río Cayapas, this town has recently seen a lot more timber than tourists passing through. The road to Borbón (home to Papá Roncón, King of Marimba) is only 15 years old but has led to rapid population growth and a new way of life for the once-isolated Afro-Ecuadorian and Chachi communities along Ríos Santiago and Cayapas that reach the sea at Borbón. Despite the timber cash flowing through town, the standard of living is low and the town has a reputation for being rough. **Locals warn "gringos" to be very careful of crime.**

Travelers will find few worthy hotels in Borbón. **Hotel Castillo ❷** (☎2786 613 or 2786 578), on 5 de Agosto and Rioverde near the buses, has tile and cement rooms that are clean and fairly new. Some rooms have big windows; some have none. (Rooms with TV, fan, and mosquito net US$6.) **Hostal Costa Norte** (☎2786 573), on 5 de Agosto and Pedro Chiriboga, has depressing but clean cement rooms with private bath, TV, and fans. (Singles US$6; doubles US$10.) To find **Restaurante El Sazón del Río Santiago ❷**, walk away from the Coliseo Municipal downhill toward the water two blocks and turn left. The restaurant is bright orange and on the right. Wholesome aromas fill this spiffy open-air dining room and waft onto the street. Most meals, including *ceviche*, are around US$3 but go up to US$7 for delicacies like lobster. The speciality is a simple steamed fish with herbs and fresh lime. (☎2786 623. Open daily 7am-10pm.) **Ballet Azul ❶**, near the buses, is a friendly place to eat. Meals (US$1.50) come with fresh bananas.

Transportes del Pacífico (☎2786 706) sends **buses** to Esmeraldas (2¾hr., every 30min. 6:20am-8pm, US$3.50) and San Lorenzo (1hr., every hr. 7am-9pm, US$1). **TransEsmeraldas** sends buses to **Guayaquil** (11hr., 10am and 8pm, US$9) and Quito (8hr., 11am and 9:30pm, US$8). There is **boat** service to Limones (1½hr.; 7:30, 10:30am, 4pm; US$3). **Chivos** (trucks with open air bench seating jury-rigged in the back) are a thrilling, uncomfortable way to travel between San Lorenzo and Borbón (1¾hr., US$1). **Buses** arrive at and depart from the front of the big cement Coliseo Municipal. From there it is a short walk or bicitaxi ride (US$1) down to the *malecón* (pier) and dock. Borbón is a tangle of streets but small enough to navigate fairly easily. The **police** are located a few blocks from the *malecón*. (☎2786 300.) The **hospital** is up the hill from the bus station. (☎2786 404; emergency 2786 542.) **Andinatel** has booths on Valdéz and Cueva de los Tallos. (☎2786 001. Open M-Sa 8am-9pm, Su 8am-noon and 7-9pm.)

ESMERALDAS   ☎06

When a throng of emerald-clad locals greeted the conquistadors arriving on Ecuador's northern coast, the Spaniards concluded that the area must be rich with the rare green gems. They were wrong, but the town's new name stuck. Today, Esmeraldas is the end of the line for Ecuador's oil pipeline and has the largest crude oil refinery in the country. Esmeraldas also shoulders a reputation as one of the country's most dangerous cities, and most newcomers press on quickly.

Esmeraldas's hotels won't be the highlight of your trip. Few places offer mosquito nets, and the ultimate choice is between grimy and expensive. The best for the budget is **Hostal Galeón ❷**, Piedrahita 3-30, has decent rooms, clean sheets, private baths, and cable TVs. (☎2723 820 or 8236 756; fax 2725 924. Singles US$7, with A/C US$10.) Restaurants are around Parque Central, especially *chifas* and grilled chicken joints. **Restaurante Vegetariano ❶**, is down Bolívar from the park with the water on your right, left on Roca, and to the left on the 2nd fl. Tasty vegetarian and health-conscious lunches including brown rice and iced tea are served in a breezy dining room. (☎2726 845. Meat options available. Entrees US$2. Open M-Sa 8am-3pm.) Buses stop either at the **bus terminal** on **Malecón** (Transportes del Pacífico at Piedrahita or Cooperativo La Costeñita at 10 de Agosto), or by **Parque Central** (Transportes Esmeraldas). Bordered by **Bolívar, Sucre, 10 de Agosto**, and **9 de Octubre**, Parque Central serves as a good reference point. From the bus stops on Malecón, head up away from the water a few blocks to Parque Central. Another block from Malecón is Olmedo, the large avenue with a tree-lined Parkway that runs parallel to Malecón and is busy with people and services during the day. **Banco Pichincha** at 9 de Octubre and Bolívar, across from Parque Central, has a 24hr. **ATM** (DC/MC/V). (☎2728 741. Open M-F 8:30am-7pm, Sa 9am-2pm.) For **emergency** call ☎101. **Police** are at Bolívar and Cañizares. (☎2700 559. Open 24hr.) Many pharmacies are around Parque Central. **Andinatel** is on Bolívar between 9 de Octubre and Piedrahita, near Parque Central. (Open daily 8am-8:30pm.) **Compunet**, down Bolívar from the Parque Central, has **Internet**. (☎2721 578; fax 2728 670. US$1.20 per hr. Open M-Sa 8:30am-7pm.) **Post Office:** ☎2726 834. At Colón between 10 de Agosto and 9 de Octubre. Open M-F 8:30am-12:30pm and 2:30-6pm, Sa 9am-12pm. **Transportes Esmeraldas** (☎2721 381), on 10 de Agosto between Sucre and Bolívar, runs luxury buses to **Quito** (6½hr.; 12:30, 12:55, 10am, 1, 11pm; US$7) and **Guayaquil** (8hr., 14 per day 5:30am-12:15am, US$7) both via **Santo Domingo** (3hr., US$3). **Cooperativa La Costeñita** (☎2723 041), at Malecón and 10 de Agosto, and **Transportes del Pacífico** (☎2713 227), at Malecón and Piedrahita, both have daily service to: **Muisne** (2¼hr., every 20min. 5:20am-9pm, US$1.60) via **Atacames** (1hr., US$0.75), **Same** (1½hr., US$1.10), and **Súa** (1¼hr., US$1); and La Tola (3hr., every 15min., US$3.50).

ATACAMES   ☎06

The most tourist-happy beach on the northern Pacific Coast, Atacames is quite the party destination. Every week, Ecuadorians pour in from northern Sierra and surrounding coastal towns, filling hostels, bars, and clubs. Construction is constantly underway to meet demand, so the skyline is composed as much of rebar and cinderblocks as thatched roofs. By day the crowds swim, tan, and shop; by night, they hit the dance floor. Come Monday, Atacames exhales; blenders whir at half-speed and revelers rest up for the next weekend. The city throws fiestas like few others in Ecuador; solitude-seekers may want to plant their beach umbrellas elsewhere.

⌐ TRANSPORTATION

Buses: From the central stop on Principal, **Parada** buses head south to **Muisne** (1½hr., every 30min. 5:30am-9pm, US$1) via **Súa** (10min., US$0.25), **Same** (25min., US$0.50), **Tonchigüe** (30min., US$0.50), and **El Saltro** (1hr., US$1.50). **Cooperativa La Costeñita** goes to **Playa Escondida** (1hr.; 6, 9am, 2, 4pm; US$1.50). **Transportes Occidentales** (☎2760 547), just across the footbridge, goes to **Guayaquil** (8hr., 11:15pm, US$8) and **Quito** (6hr.; 9:30, 11:30am, 2, 11:45pm; US$7). **Tranportes Esmeraldas** (☎2731 550), in a large, modern building a few blocks from the footbridge, goes to: **Quito** (7hr.; 10:30am, 1:30, 3:30, 11, 11:30pm; US$8); **Manta** (10hr., 9:30pm, US$9) via Portoviejo; **Guayaquil** (8hr.; 9am, 10:30pm; US$8). The green buses of **La Atacameñita** run from Tonsupa through Atacames to **Súa** (15min., every 10min. 6:30am-10pm, US$0.25). These stop at the Parada Interplayas, on Las Acacias. Others go north to **Esmeraldas** (1hr., every 30min. 6am-8:30pm, US$0.80).

Taxis: Standard taxis are scarce and expensive. The trip between Atacames and Esmeraldas costs around US$15. "Ecological tours" (bikes with carts) pedal people around town (US$0.50 per person; fixed rate in town; tips suggested).

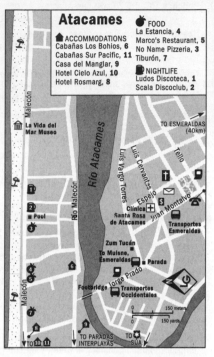

Atacames

♠ ACCOMMODATIONS
Cabañas Los Bohios, 6
Cabañas Sur Pacific, 11
Casa del Manglar, 9
Hotel Cielo Azul, 10
Hotel Rosmarg, 8

♦ FOOD
La Estancia, 4
Marco's Restaurant, 5
No Name Pizzeria, 3
Tiburón, 7

♫ NIGHTLIFE
Ludos Discoteca, 1
Scala Discoclub, 2

♦♫ ORIENTATION AND PRACTICAL INFORMATION

Buses stop along **Principal** (also called **La Carretera**); the central stop is at the sign saying "*parada.*" **Jorge Prado** leads across a footbridge over **Río Malecón**. Turn left at the big sign for Los Bohios to reach the **Malecón**, a strip of budget hotels, discos, and restaurants along the beach. Back in town, most services are around **Parque Central**. With your back to the ice cream bar near the *parada*, walk straight and make a right on **Juan Montalvo**; the park is on the next block.

Currency Exchange: Banco del Pichincha (☎2731 029 or 2731 297), at Cervantes and Montalvo. With your back to the ice cream bar near the bus stop, it's 100m up the right side of the street. Exchanges traveler's checks for a 1% commission. Offers V cash advances M-F 8:30am-2:30pm. 24hr. **ATM.** Open M-F 8:30am-5pm, Sa 9am-2pm, Su 9am-1pm. There is also an **ATM** on Malecón to the right of the footbridge.

Laundromat: Zum Tuncán (☎2731 191), on Luís Vargo Torres; sign visible from Jorge Prado. US$1.54 per kg washed and dried, US$0.88 per kg washed. Open M-F 9am-6pm, Sa 9am-2pm.

Police: ☎2731 275. On Las Acacias. Across the large bridge at the west end of town, Las Acacias runs down a hill to Malecón. Station is just a few blocks before the beach.

Hospital: Clínica Santa Rosa de Atacames (☎2731 916), on Cervantes. With your back to the ice cream bar near the bus stop, walk 100m. The clinic is on the left. 24hr. emergency care. Open 7am-7pm.

Telephones: Andinatel (☎2731 106), at Montalvo and Tello on the corner of Parque Central. Allows calling card and collect calls. Open daily 8am-1pm and 2-9:30pm. **Branch** just to the right of the footbridge facing Río Malecón on the way to the beach.

Internet Access: Principal Librería y Papelería (☎2731 441), at Montalvo and Tello, bordering the park. US$2.40 per hr. Open M-F 8:30am-noon and 2:30-6pm, Sa 9am-1pm. **Cyber Kenya** (☎2760 840), on the malecón. US$2.40 per hr. Open M-Sa 8am-9:30pm, Su 8am-2pm.

Post Office: On Espejo, just past the bank on Principal. Open M-Sa 8:30am-noon and 2:30-6pm. Knock 2 doors down if no one answers.

◤ ACCOMMODATIONS

At first, it might seem as though Atacames has too many accommodations; then the weekend arrives, hotels fill with fun-seekers, and there's hardly a vacant room. Plenty of cheap places lie between the beach and Río Malecón. Nicer places are to the left as you face the water, where Malecón leads away from the beach; these places open right onto the sand. Noise from bars and clubs can sometimes prevent a good night's sleep, especially in centrally located hotels along the beach. Prices start climbing in July and peak in August. During the low season (Oct. to mid-Dec. and Mar.) or mid-week, visitors may be able to negotiate lower prices.

Hotel Cielo Azul (☎2731 813 or 09 4662 783; www.hotelcieloazul.com). At the left end of the beach facing the water, Malecón goes inland 1 block and continues behind a few hotels with direct beach access. This luxurious, brand-new hotel features a pool, balconies, TVs, hot water, hammocks, fridges, and direct beach access in a low-key setting. Rooms have fan and mosquito net. High season US$20. Low season US$15. ❶

Hotel Rosmarg (☎2731 512 or 2760 641), on Malecón. After reaching the beach via the footbridge, take a left and look for a large blue sign. This 4-story building offers a prime party location and newer digs than most. Be sure to ask for a room with a view, lest you find yourself in one of the few cave-like dwellings without windows. US$8; singles US$12-$15; doubles with view US$20. ❷

Cabañas Sur Pacific (☎2731 248), next to Hotel Cielo Azul (see above). The least expensive option with direct beach access. 2 rows of clean cement cabins face each other across a parking lot on the way to a fenced-in swimming pool. A more rustic 6-person dorm room on the 2nd fl. of the house opens onto a big porch overlooking the beach. Restaurant downstairs. High season US$10. Low season US$6. ❷

Residencial la Casa del Manglar (☎2731 464). Go left after crossing the footbridge, walk 50m; hotel is on your left. Even though close to the beach (plan on awakening to fishy smells), this hotel's location overlooking Rio Malecón ensures a peaceful night's sleep. The hey-day of this place has passed, but there is a nice spot on the top fl. for lounging. Singles US$6, with bath US$7. ❷

Cabañas Los Bohíos (☎/fax 2731 089). Cross the footbridge going toward the beach and make a right to reach these small, tidy cabañas. No great scenery, but a few ferns and hyacinths decorate the cement walkways. Complete with TVs, clean private baths, pool, and a guard. High season US$13.50. Low season US$8. ❸

> ### ENCOCADO: A LOCAL DISH
> Fish, shrimp, conch, lobster. From the meeting of abundant sea-life with the ubiquitous coconut comes *encocado* (coconuted), an indulgent coastal speciality. The sauce ranges from a subtle coconut soup to an intensely spiced coconut curry. Be sure to pronounce it like the locals when you order: *encocao.*

FOOD

Atacames offers some international cuisine, but seafood still dominates. The competition is fierce among the handful of Italian-owned pizzerías on Malecón where street-hawkers lure passers-by to one of the equally authentic pizza/pasta places. Along Malecón, sidewalk chefs cook up shish kebabs and corn on the cob.

No Name Pizzeria (☎ 09 045 186), on Malecón, 3 blocks to the right of the footbridge, along the beach, 2nd fl. There are plenty of equally tasty and authentic pizzerías within a few blocks, but No Name boasts a warm, wooden 2nd-fl. dining room great for watching the malecón come to life below. A favorite among travelers for its delicious, monot ony-destroying cuisine. Serves large pizzas (US$10-14), salads (US$2.50), and pasta dishes (US$4-6.50). Open daily 6pm-late. ❷

Tiburón (☎ 2731 680). Murals of the restaurant's namesake (shark) and other sea creatures adorn the walls. Big portions and an attentive staff make this a good pick. Most dishes US$3.50-4.50; up to US$12. Open daily 8am-9:30pm. ❸

La Estancia (☎ 2760 296 or 2731 847; jaimeburgos@andinanet.net), on Malecón, ½ block to the right after the footbridge. You're paying for atmosphere first and food second, but it's worth it. The elegant and creatively decorated dining room is filled with woven folk art from the region. US$5-12. IVA and service 22%. Open daily noon-10pm. Peace Corps volunteers discount 10%. DC/MC/V. ❸

La Luna (☎ 09 9586 790). La Luna is downstairs from Pizzería Pavorotti with an inviting, small, open-air dining room. Serves local specialties, including *ceviche* and *encocado* (US$4-6), lobster and giant shrimp (US$10-11). Open daily 7am-10:30pm. ❸

Pizzería Pavorotti (☎ 09 9586 790), upstairs from La Luna. A mangrove-wood balcony encloses the pizzería. Individual pies from US$5, large US$10-14. Open 4pm-1am. ❸

Marco's Restaurant (☎/fax 2731 126), on Malecón, next to La Estancia (see above). Seafood any way you like it. Clean, open-air, modern dining room. Entrees US$4, up to US$11. Open daily 7:30am-9:45pm. DC/V. ❷

BEACHES

Atacames's beaches are soft, reasonably clean, and extend far in either direction. First-rate views of **Punta Esmeraldas** to the east and the jagged **Isla de los Pájaros** (Island of the Birds) to the west frame the enormous expanse. Sunbathers and soccer players coexist peacefully on the beach while **banana boats** (US$2 per person) buzz by on the south side of the beach. If you prefer lounging on a boat, try **whale-watching** (US$10, prices negotiable; be sure to condition payment on seeing whales). Boats bobbing just offshore are also eager to take tourists to see the blue-footed boobies, frigate-birds, and pelicans of Isla de los Pájaros or through the nearby mangroves (US$2-3 per person). On the east end of Malecón is **La Vida del Mar Museo y Acuario Marino,** where tanks display various forms of sea life, some living and some not. (US$0.75. Open 9am-9pm.)

Although Atacames's beaches are beautiful, they are also dangerous. The undertow is quite strong—several people get caught in it and drown each year. Take caution when exploring the waves in this area.

NIGHTLIFE

With seemingly endless grass-hut bars, a handful of discos, and pizza parlors that morph into karaoke joints by night there's something for everyone. Most places offer the same fruity mixed drinks, thatched roofs, low prices (cocktails US$1-4), and extended hours (daily 4pm-3am). Wander around to see who has the best two-for-one deal. Malecón is generally well lighted and populated, but visitors should always be cautious, even when the streets are busy. Late-night beach walks are a bad idea.

Scala Discoclub, along Malecón after reaching the beach from the footbridge; take a right and it's a few blocks up. The hottest *discoteca* around. Partiers of all ages cram together under neon lights that illuminate tributes to Elvis, Metallica, and Claudia Schiffer while enjoying the latest rock, hip hop, and merengue mixes. Beer US$2. Cover US$2. Open daily 8:30pm-3am.

El Oasis de Nagiba Bar, to the right of the footbridge, along the sand. Hanging swings replace bar stools and a small dance floor lets you groove all night. The specialty drink is the nagiba (made from fruits and rum; US$2). Happy hour daily 8:30-9:30pm.

Ludos Discoteca, along Malecón, past Scala Discoclub. Complete with fog machine, 2nd-fl. lounge, and hanging metal cage, this club plays the latest Latin American mixes. Cocktails US$2-5. Cover US$2. Open Th-Sa 8:30pm-3am.

SÚA ☎06

Atacames's closest neighbor, this small fishing village provides a more easy-going atmosphere and cheaper accommodations. The beach here is smaller and protected, but the oversized concrete malecón—built to accommodate the tour buses that pull in on the weekends—compromises the seaside charm.

▉▊ TRANSPORTATION AND PRACTICAL INFORMATION. To reach Súa from **Atacames,** take a **bus** (10min., every 15min., US$0.25) or walk south along the beach at low tide (30min.). Rent **boogie-boards** and **water-tricycles** on the beach (US$1-2 per hr.). Find an **Internet cafe** to the right along Malecón as you face the water near Hotel Chagra Ramos. (US$2.40 per hr.) **Andinatel** across the street opens sporadically on weekends, holidays, and July and August. **Boats** wait just offshore to take passengers **whale-watching** (July-Sept. US$15) or to **Isla de los Pájaros** (US$2-3). Boats pack on as many passengers as will pay; make sure there are enough lifevests to go around.

TIP **WHALE-WATCHING SAVVY.** Most whale-watching boats are run by fisherman who pack tourists in at US$15-20 a head. If you hang out on the beach and wait for a big tour group to hire a boat, the captain will be more willing to bargain down to a tag-along rate of US$8-10. Just make sure the boat isn't overloaded, as captains will pack in as many paying customers as possible.

▉▉ ACCOMMODATIONS AND FOOD. Accommodations in Súa don't cost much, although prices vary significantly by season and rise in February during the Carnival. **Hotel Chagra Ramos ❷,** on the far northern side of the beach, is a vertical cluster of tin-roof, hillside villas and cabañas built into the steep hillside. Villas have private baths. Window screens provide cool, itch-free sleep. (☎2731 006. Singles US$6; doubles US$12.) **Hotel Buganvillas ❷,** on Malecón, has rooms that overlook a couple of rooftops and a parking lot as well as the ocean. Back rooms directly facing the water are larger, with real beds—not cement platforms. (☎2731 008. Rooms with fan and private bath US$6.) Súa's *malecón* is lined with almost identical, clean, open-air restaurants with great seafood. *Ceviche* stands appear in the streets on weekends and during high season (July-Aug.). **Hotel Chagra's Restaurant ❷** (see above) serves quality renditions of local seafood recipes (US$3.50-6.50) inside or on the ocean-front patio. (Open daily 7:15am-9pm.) **Restaurant Bahía ❶,** near Hotel el Shaman (see above), is open on two sides and has the usual suspects (seafood, *ceviche*) with a few chicken and meat options. Entrees run US$2.80-3.50. Specialties like giant shrimp cost US$5. (Open daily 7am-10pm.)

⬛⬛ SIGHTS AND NIGHTLIFE. South of the bay is a hidden cove. To access it, walk away from the beach past Hotel El Shaman; go right at the end of the road across the bridge; and continue 20min. For a great view of Atacames and the less-developed coastline to the south, follow the same path but bear right and climb the large green bluff along a dirt path (about 30min.). A few open-air bars on the Malecón serve cocktails (US$3) all day long and into the night. On weekends the bars crank salsa into the night, too.

SAME ☎06

Same (SAH-may), 7km southwest of Súa, stretches almost 3km in length, although it's never more than 20m wide. Its green surf, a refreshing 25°C (75°F) year-round, is said to be the best in the area, drawing the more fortunate of Ecuadorian society to its expensive hotels and timeshare condominiums. From **Atacames,** catch a Same-bound **bus** (25min., every 15min. 5am-10pm, US$0.30).

Visitors will find that lodging is slightly nicer here than in the surrounding towns. Graced with only a few budget establishments, Same stresses quality rather than quantity. ⬛**Azuca ❷** is at the southern end of Same, on the highway. The Colombian woman who owns this hostel and restaurant (see below) recalls when the only road in Same was a muddy path crossed as often by nesting sea turtles as humans. The whole place is a labor of love, with painted walls, seashells, hanging driftwood, and small canvases. High-ceilinged rooms with mosquito nets and private baths. Though it's Same's best deal, its only two rooms are rarely vacant. (☎09 9626 443. High season quads US$20. Low season US$12.) **Casa del Sol ❷,** is a cookie-cutter youth hostel part of a chain of Argentinian hostels throughout South America. A beautiful house with dorms upstairs, two doubles downstairs. Giant fruit and cereal breakfast included. Small but completely open house: shared bedrooms, 2nd-fl. porch, sitting area, kitchen, and bathrooms. Reserve far in advance for high-season stays. (☎2733 284 or cell 09 8339 438; casadelsol3@yahoo.com. Dorms US$6; doubles US$12.)

It's worth saving up some funds for the excellent (but expensive) dining in Same. ⬛**Azuca ❷** (see above), the restaurant downstairs from the hostel, strikes the perfect balance between elegant (white tablecloths and fresh gardenias) and homey (the owner/chef/resident artist who attends the tables). Corn for *empanadas* (meat pies) and *arepas* (corn pancakes) is even ground in-house. All entrees (US$4.50-10) come with a crisp house salad. Open daily 8am-9pm. **La Terraza ❷** serves the ubiquitous fresh seafood but with the option of having it tossed in with spaghetti or sprinkled on thin-crust pizza. Serious waiters breeze past the candlelit tables overlooking the water. (☎09 4952 269. Pizza US$6; pasta US$6-8; seafood US$4-12. Open daily 11:30am-4pm and 7-10pm.)

■ RESERVA ECOLÓGICA PLAYA ESCONDIDA ☎06

Owner Judith Barrett was driving her jeep up the beach from Tonchigüe in search of an ideal spot to pitch a tent and got as far as the stretch of sand that is now part of her 100 hectares reserve, tucked between the Ecuadorian hills and the Pacific Ocean. Recent excavations for a new foundation have turned up Tolita pot shards and ceramic figurines, suggesting that the place was previously inhabited. Now, this "hidden beach" sees more sand crabs than people—and the occasional nesting sea turtle. High tide is the best time for swimming, but low tide brings tidal pools (home to all sorts of marine creatures) and stretches of firm sand that allow for long walks along the beach. Head south at low tide to discover the caves and arches carved out of the cliffs. A newly cut trail follows a river up into the tropical forest and is a great place to see early morning wildlife and a giant ebony tree. The trail starts just past the bamboo footbridge. Another path climbs for about 20min., past the cheaper lodge to a bluff with views of the coastline. **Volunteers** work 6hr. days and contribute US$8 for food and lodging. During high season, there is work housekeeping and running the kitchen. During low season, tasks focus on improvements—mainly carpentry and gardening. Playa Escondida is just south of Tonchigüe, along the dirt road that leads to Punta Galera. Playa Escondida is accessible on foot from Tonchigüe at low tide, but be ready rock-scrambling.

The more expensive **rooms ❸** are partially exposed to the elements. Hang your hat on wave-sculpted driftwood and cross a seashell-encrusted threshold into the bathroom. These rooms have their own showers. Cheaper rooms are simpler, constructed from cane and wood, and have shared showers. Composting outhouse makes for a rugged beach experience. (☎2733 106 or 09 733 368. Camping US$5 per tent.) The **restaurant ❹** at the lodge is anything but simple. Though slightly pricey, the food tastes great and looks fantastic, garnished with leaves and fresh flowers, and is served on the candlelit patio. (Entrees US$6-8.)

Any **bus** connecting Muisne and the northern beaches passes Tonchigüe. Only **Cooperativa La Costeñita** sends buses to Punta Galera, leaving Atacames (1hr.; 6, 9am, 2, 4pm; US$1.50). **Chivos** leave Esmeraldas going to El Cabo and pass by Playa Escondida and Galera (1½hr.; daily 10:30am, 1:25pm; US$1.75).

TONCHIGÜE ☎06

Most of the sea creatures that wind up on dinner plates from Atacames to Súa pass through Tonchigüe. Wooden canoes and small motorboats line up on the beach, leaving little room for sunbathing. Their cargo goes straight to the kitchens of the open-air eateries along the *malecón*. Tonchigüe is a 45min. walk along the beach from Same at low tide. In Tonchigüe, cheap hotels comprise the selection of accommodations. Those looking for a fancier place should head for the resorts along the beach coming from Same. The newly renovated **Hostal Mary ❷** is a bright orange two-story house on the *malecón*. Unadorned but clean rooms have private bath, fan, mosquito net, and tiled bathroom. Hang out on the upstairs balcony. The family that owns the hostel lives downstairs. (☎2732 057. US$5 per person.) Restaurants in Tonchigüe boast seafood that is direct "from the sea to your table" and give a view of the working fisherman who make it all possible. **La Sirenita ❷,** in the middle of the *malecón*, serves tasty *comida típica* in a sea-blue dining room furnished with wooden tables and chairs. (☎2732 123. All dishes US$3. Open daily 9am-10pm.) Further down the *malecón* are the plastic tables, chairs, and flowers of **Sol y Mar ❷.** Neon signs on the walls serve as a menu displaying what's available. (☎09 8380 693. Entrees US$2.50-3; giant shrimp $9. Open daily 7am-8pm.) **Costeñita** and **Pacifico buses** from Atacames pass by Súa and Same on the way to Tonchigüe and then continue on to Muisne (every 10min., US$0.50).

MUISNE ☎ 06

In recent years, numerous new hotels have come to speckle the beautiful, virgin beaches between Atacames and Pedernales. One of the more established, yet still quiet, stops along the coast is the car-free island of Muisne. This island conjures up images of the ideal tropical beach vacation: long, wide, palm-fringed beach and waves whispering you to sleep. Weather patterns often yield gray mornings, but hot afternoons give visitors a warm welcome.

▐▌ TRANSPORTATION AND PRACTICAL INFORMATION. Muisne-bound **buses** stop by the docks on the mainland. From there, **boats** run to the island (5min., every 5min. 4am-noon, US$0.15), where **bicitaxis** offer rides to the beach (US$1). From the mainland docks, **Transportes Pacífico** and **Transportes la Costeñita buses** go to: **Esmeraldas** (3hr., every 20min. 4:30am-9:30pm, US$2.20) via **Same** (55min., US$0.90); **Súa** (1¼hr., US$1); and **Atacames** (1hr. 20min., US$1.20). To reach **Pedernales** from Muisne, take a bus to **Salto** (20min., every 20min. 7am-7pm, US$0.50) and board a direct **camioneta** to **Chamanga**. Buses to **Pedernales** (2hr., every 30min. 6am-6:30pm, US$2) leave from Chamanga. Bici-taxis waiting near the dock are the principal form of transportation on the island and can take passengers to the beach (US$0.50-1). **Isidora Ayora,** the main street, leads inland from the docks 2km to the beach and hotels on the opposite side. There are **no ATMs** in Muisne. The **police station** (☎2480 005) is on Manabí, the street parallel to the main road, just before the central park. The **hospital** (☎2480 269), on Manabí, is a block after the park. The **Andinatel** telephone office is on the left, when coming from the docks, but it doesn't allow calling-card or collect calls. (☎2480 140. Open daily 8am-12:30pm and 2-9pm.) It may be possible to check email using the radio station **Internet** access in the home next to Pastipan. (US$2 per hr.)

▐▌ ACCOMMODATIONS AND FOOD. The few hotels in Muisne provide quality quarters and come equipped with mosquito nets (a must). There are a few concrete hotels in town and on the way to the beach, but plenty of good options are just a few meters away from the high tide mark. The English-speaking owners who run the pink ▨**Hotel Playa Paraíso ❷,** to the left as you reach the beach from the main road, treat guests like family. Relax in one of the many hammocks lining the beach, or enjoy the open-air patio as you shoot the breeze with newly made friends. The garden in back reveals more expensive cabañas with private baths and no ocean

ON THE MENU

GOING BANANAS

From the sweet, tiny *oritos* (little gold ones) to the big starchy *verdes* (green ones), Ecuador's "mega-diversity" seems to extend even to this household fruit. Myriad sizes and flavors find their ways into a variety of meals. The Chachi *chucula,* a warm cinnamon-spiced banana and coconut drink, is made with the sweet *guineo. Verdes* double-fried and smushed flat, served with rice and fish, are known as *patacones.* Ripe versions of the *verde* and hearty *plátanos* surface in soups or are boiled as a side dish with *pescado tapao* (steamed fish). Savory *bananos* are swirled into *batidos;* passed around raw as an appetizer; or thinly sliced, fried, and bagged as *chifles* for a snack-on-the-go. Also, try *bolón de verde,* a big ball of deep-fried, mashed plantains with cheese in the middle. *Empanadas de verde* are almost the same thing, but the dough is actually just mashed green plantains.

Watering mouths who'd like a quick snack might try this recipe for *Pipas,* whole coconuts with the top whacked off by machete.

Step 1. Suck out the juice, a nice way to get a clean cool drink on the street.

Step 2. Hand over the *coco* to the professionals who will fully demolish the shell so you can enjoy the meat inside.

Some of the *pipas* have a palm sprouting out of the top, which means that a spongy "heart of coconut" is waiting inside.

view. With a giant thatched-roof bar, volleyball court, pool table, and barbeque out back, the only things missing are tiki torches and body shots. (☎2480 192. Singles US$4; doubles US$8; single cabañas with private bath US$8; doubles cabañas US$14.) Next door is **Marango Spanish School ❷**. The shared kitchen and baths give this place a communal feel, and no wall lacks decoration. Marango organizes excursions, including tromping around the mangrove swamp, hiking in the tropical forest, or checking out nearby surf-spot Mompiche (see p. 220). And, of course, it gives Spanish lessons for US$5 per hr. (In Muisne ☎2480 301; in Quito 2546 157; www.marango.org. Singles US$4; doubles US$8.) **Hostal Calade ❷**, on the beach to the left of the main road, is just past Marango. Warm showers complement the warm hues on the walls. The hostel's restaurant serves salads (US$1.50-2) and chicken dinners (US$3), a welcome change for those weary of fish and shrimp. (☎2480 279. Laundry service. Singles US$5; doubles US$10.) **Cabañas San Cristóbal ❷**, on the beach to the right of the main road, is a low concrete row of spacious, tiled rooms with private bath. Past the iron bars on the windows is a view of the crashing waves of the Pacific. Rooms are nearly mosquito-proof and have fans and nets over the beds. (☎2480 264. Singles US$10; doubles US$12.) Most restaurants along the sand are quite similar; take your pick. **Restaurant El Delfín ❶** is where the main road meets the beach. (☎2480 037. Set-lunch and dinner US$2.50, a la carte US$2-4; giant shrimp US$13. Open daily 7am-8pm.)

⬛ **BEACHES.** Muisne's beach extends for more than an hour's walk in either direction, being longest at low tide. Although the town isn't especially known for its **surfing**, locals have begun to pick up the sport. High tide brings decent waves, but if you plan on hitting the surf, watch out for the small **stinging jellyfish** (prevalent July-Oct.). Most stings are mild and can be healed with a dab of vinegar, available at any local restaurant. When you tire of avoiding jellyfish, **boating** through the mangroves is a pleasant diversion, even though frequent shrimp farms break up the landscape. Rides through the mangroves sometimes have a destination, such as **Isla Bonita,** with its rolling green hills and rocky cliffs; other times, they meander aimlessly around the lush vegetation. If you plan to leave the sheltered area behind the Muisne Island, be prepared for rolling waves. Boats can be found at the port (US$12 per hr.). Having a driver wait for hours can get expensive; arrange for a pick-up later to avoid paying exorbitant fees. Make sure to pay the driver after he picks you up, as Isla Bonita is uninhabited and a sub-optimal place to get stranded. If you'd like to stick to solid land, **horseback rides** along the beach are also available (US$5 per hr.). Avoid the unlighted areas of the beach at night; Muisne has experienced some crime in recent years.

IT'S NOT JUST SAND YOU'RE WALKING ON. According to the locals in Muisne, the lengthy Playa de Coco, named for the graceful palms, will be changing its name to Playa de Coca, after 2000kg of refined coca leaves dumped offshore washed up. The police were able to recover about 700kg. As for the rest, whether buried or covered by the traffickers, the story is that "it's not just sand you're walking on."

MOMPICHE ☎06

At this little-known point break, life alternates between catching fish and catching waves. The tourism that has sprung up caters to a laid-back and low-budget set. Besides the long beach in front of the town, there are several uninhabited black-sand beaches with decent surf south of the point. To get there walk left along the beach facing the water past the Casablanca cabañas and go left along the dirt road 15-20min. On the right is an overgrown dirt road blocked to cars by wooden posts.

Follow this a few minutes down to the beach. Continue left across the rocks at low tide to find another beach. The road continues to an unfinished bridge connecting the mainland to the island of Portete, where there is also a long, empty palm-fringed beach. Ask in town about getting a small **canoe** to take you to Portete and back. Food is all típica seafood on the water, or you can go in with friends and have a do-it-yourself parrillada (barbeque) on the beach.

Facing the water, walk left to find the **Hostería Gabeal ②**, a hotel with singles, doubles, a couple of four-person cabañas on stilts—and a restaurant. Rooms have mosquito nets, private bath, and ocean views. (☎09 9696 543. High-season singles US$6; doubles US$12; 5-person cabañas US$60. Low-season 5-person cabañas US$40.) On the way is **DMCA Surf Hostal ①**, owned by an American-Argentinian couple who plan to complete renovating a dormitory, private rooms, a cabaña, and vegetarian restaurant in October 2004. Check here for surf info and board rental. (☎09 7739 874; martindmca@hotmail.com. Dorms US$2.50; private rooms US$4, with private bath US$6; 4- to 5-person cabañas US$20-25.) A little farther along is the small, luxurious **Balkonia Kingdom ④**. This hotel boasts a few newly con-structed two-bedroom apartments with a kitchen-living room overlooking the beach (☎09 7667 120. 5-person cabañas US$15 per person, min. 4 people during high season.) **Comedor Erizo ③** serves a decent catch-of-the day right on the beach and will allow camping for free and use of the bathroom and shower. (☎09 9455 498. Fish US$3; shrimp US$4. Open daily 7am-9pm.)

The fork in the highway where buses go off to Muisne is called El Salto. Muisne-bound **buses** leave Atacames and pass through **El Salto** (1hr., every 30min. 5:30am-9pm, US$1.50). From El Salto, **Transportes River Tablazo** sends buses to **Mompiche** (1hr.; 7:30am, 2, 3:40pm; US$0.50). Buses stop at the beach.

PEDERNALES ☎05

Pedernales hosts the largest market on the northern coast and serves as an impor-tant center for the shrimp industry. While locals may consider Pedernales crucial, travelers searching for the perfect beach paradise normally look elsewhere, and most visitors view the town only as a key transportation link along the coast.

⌷ TRANSPORTATION. Buses go to: **Guayaquil** (7hr., 11pm, US$8; 9:40am, 10pm; US$9); **Manta** (6hr., 12 per day 6am-6pm, US$6) via **Bahía de Caráquez** (2¾hr., US$3), **San Vicente/Canoa** (2hr., US$2.50) and **Portoviejo** (5hr., US$5); **Quito** (5hr.; 3:30, 11:40am, 1, 1:40, 3, 5, 11pm; US$9); **Santo Domingo** (3hr., every 20min. 3:15am-11pm, US$3); and **Chamanga** (1¼hr., every 30min. 6am-7pm, US$2). From Cha-manga catch buses passing every 30min. to **Esmeraldas** via **Tonchigüe, Same, Súa,** and **Atacames.**

⬛⬛ ORIENTATION AND PRACTICAL INFORMATION. Pedernales's central **plaza** sits at the intersection of the two primary streets: north-south **López Castillo** and east-west **Eloy Alfaro.** The town's lackluster port and surrounding beach are at the west end of Alfaro. The **Terminal Terrestre** (bus terminal) is across from the sta-dium on Juan Pereira between Manabí and Alfaro. Walk from the port on Alfaro, turn left one block after the church, and it's on the next block. To find the **police** (☎2681 101), walk five blocks from Parque Central, away from the water on Acosta; turn right on Tachina and left on Moreno. The hospital, **Clínica Española Ecuatoriana,** is past the stadium on Ibarra. (☎2680 159. Emergency 24hr.) **Pacifitel** is on Alfaro, ½ block from Parque Central, away from the water. (☎2681 105. Open M-Sa 8am-8:30pm, Su 8am-2pm.) Another is on Acosta, ½ block from Parque Cen-tral toward the water. (☎2680 221. Open daily 7am-10pm.) Find **Internet** access on Moreno and Castillo, 1½ blocks from Parque Central. (☎2680 149. US$1.50 per hr.)

Open daily 7:30am-9:30pm.) **Banco del Pichincha** is across the street from the Internet access point. (☎2681 240. Open M-F 8am-4:30pm, Sa 9am-1pm. Offers V cash advances M-F 8am-2pm. 24hr. MC/V **ATM**.)

⌐ ACCOMMODATIONS. Those who arrive late should probably find a place in town, rather than wonder around by the beach. Most options in town are about three blocks past the church on Alfaro. Where Alfaro meets the beach there is a small *malecón* with beach bars in the sand, seafood places along the road and budget hotels. **Hotel Playas ❷** is at Juan Pereira and Pedernales only ½ block from the bus station. It offers helpful information and maps of the area, and extremely well-scrubbed baths and rooms. (☎2681 125 or 2680 045. Rooms US$5, with private bath and color TV US$6.) The sparkling, sky-blue **Hostal Albelo ❷**, on Acosta near Malecón, prides itself on meticulous rooms and orthopedic mattresses. Spacious quarters have TVs, fans, and the name of the hotel proudly stamped on very clean sheets. Some rooms have ocean views. (☎2981 372; albelo@andinanet.net. Singles US$7; doubles US$14; triples US$21; quads US$28; quints US$35.) **Hostal Mr. John ❷**, across from Hostal Albelo on Acosta, has sterile, all-white rooms that smell freshly laundered. The owner "Mr. John" speaks English. Some rooms have balconies, but the few with direct ocean views do not. (☎2681 107. Fans, TVs. Doubles US$16; triples US$24; quads US$32.)

◻ FOOD. The *malecón* has solid seafood eateries. Go to the town center for a bit of variety. To begin with, **Chifa Chang ❶**, on Alfaro and Velasco around the block from the bus terminal serves big, cheap portions of Chinese food. Go with tallarines (noodles) for leafy greens unheard of in *comida típica*. (Good veggie options and seafood variations. Entrees US$1.50-3. Open daily 10am-10:30pm.) **Yogu Mania ❶**, on Alfaro, ½ block from the park toward the water, dishes up fresh, buttery *pan de yuca* (US$0.17). Blenders whip up homemade yogurt and fruit *batidos* (shakes; US$0.80-1.50). (☎09 7067 662. Open daily 9am-11pm.) **La Choza ❶**, on Eloy Alfaro and Malecón, has an all-bamboo interior, good service, and tasty seafood specialties. Try the filling vegetarian *bolones de verde* (big cheese-filled ball of fried plantains) for breakfast. (☎2680 130. Set-lunch US$1.50-2; *menú* US$3-5; giant shrimp US$8. Open daily 7:30am-8:30pm.)

◪ SIGHTS AND ACTIVITIES. The town is working hard to promote itself as a tourist destination and has come up with the **Cocktail Festival,** celebrated August 6th in which the handful of identical thatched-roof beach bars each invent a new cocktail. Pedernales also has the distinction of being the westernmost part of the continent through which the equator passes. A stone in the central plaza commemorates this discovery by a French and Ecuadorian geographical mission between 1736 and 1744. Pedernales hosts a national **surfing competition** in October. The surf is best when it's warmer (Nov.-Dec.) For lessons and info, contact Raúl Macias (☎09 7260 553). An international *corvina* **fishing competition** casts off on August 10. When the humpback whales swim through, (July-Sept.), tours leave from the beach to catch a glimpse.

CANOA ☎05

Travelers going up and down the Ruta del Sol wash up at this wide white-sand beach to rest up before diving into the wilder scene at Montañita (see p. 249) and Atacames (see p. 212). Canoa is lesser-known but there is no shortage of hammocks, daiquiris, and bamboo lodges. Beside surf lessons (US$5 per hr.) and boogie-boards for rent (US$1 per hr.), Canoa is near Río Muchacho Organic Farm. For information about visiting the farm check in with the Guacamayo Canoa Tours office (see below). A walk to the northern end of the beach at low tide winds up at two caves that withstood an earthquake and El Niño hurricanes.

⊟⊠ TRANSPORTATION AND PRACTICAL INFORMATION. Buses drive to **Pedernales** (2hr., every hr. 7am-7pm, US$2.50) and **San Vicente** (15min., every hr. 6am-6pm, US$0.35). **Ferries** run to Bahía de Caráquez from San Vicente. **Guacamayo** (☎2616 384 or 09 4178 459), in front of Hotel Posada de Daniel, has info on horseback riding (US$5 per hr.), hang-gliding (with several days advance notice), birdwatching in the mangroves, monkey-spotting in the tropical dry forest, and a day hike to the virgin beach of Cabo Pasado. When the waves are best (Dec.-Feb.), Guacamayo leads multi-day surf trips up and down the coast and to the Galápagos. Open daily 7am-8pm. **Pacifictel** is on the main street that runs parallel to the beach.

⌐◻ ACCOMMODATIONS AND FOOD. ⬛Hotel Bambú ❷, on the beach all the way to the right as you face the water. Has an ideal location, in the sand on the beach. Treats its international crowd to hot water, hammocks, balconies, spotless bamboo rooms, camping, and a common lounge. (☎09 9263 365. Boogieboards US$1 per hr. Camping US$2 per tent, with tent rental US$4; dorms US$4; singles US$7, with private bath and balcony US$16; doubles US$10-14/ $20-28; triples US$18/$28; quads US$36.) **Hostel Posada de Daniel ❸**, near Parque Central. Several cabañas on the grassy hillside look over the town to the beach. Features a swimming pool and nearby bar, foosball, pool, and satellite TV. Guacamayo Canoa Tours office (see above) is in the hotel. Offers doubles, triples, and 5 6-person cabañas with mosquito nets, private bath, and porch. (☎2616 384; cell 09 4718 459. Best views from cabañas #6, 9, 11, and 14. High season US$8-10 per person. Low season US$6.) **Hotel País Libre ❸**, 2 blocks from the beach on the same road as Hotel Bambú. A multi-story bamboo structure with a nice pool and bar/*discoteca* that opens F-Sa 9pm-late or for special functions. Accented with abstract paintings. (☎2616 387; cell 09 7892 885. Provides info on Spanish classes and dance lessons. Doubles with hot private bath and fan US$24; triples US$36; quads US$48.) **Hotel Palmeras Beach ❷**, near the soccer field. Tidy bamboo rooms with tiny windows; some open onto the courtyard. (☎2616 339 or 09 9785 345; www.palmerasbeach.com. Laundry service. Singles US$4, with shared bath US$7; doubles US$8/$13.) Some Ecuadorians say comida manabita (food from Manabí) is the tastiest. **Restaurant Torbellino ❶** has an open patio where seafood and meat are served *frito* (fried), *apanado* (breaded), *a la plancha* (grilled), *al ajillo* (swimming in butter and herbs), or *biche* (in a peanut and vegetable soup), in enormous portions. (From Hotel Bambú, facing the water, go left 1 block and inland 2 blocks. Set-lunch US$1.70; *menú* US$1.50-4. Open daily 7:30am-5pm.) **Surf Shak ❶**, on the beach, serves pizza, burgers, and homemade cookies. (Meals and snacks US$1.50-5. Barbeque Sa-Su. English-speaking owners also rent fiberglass surf boards (US$2 per hr.) and boogie boards (US$1 per hr.). Internet US$2 per hr. Open Tu-Su noon-11pm.) **Hotel Bambú ❶** (see above), serves pasta (US$3.50-4), breakfast crepes (US$1.50), and real coffee in addition to typical seafood offerings. (Cocktails US$1.40-2.50; set-lunch US$2; *menú* US$3.50-5. Open daily 7:30am-9:30pm.)

◧ NIGHTLIFE. After dark, the crowd bounces between cheaper drinks at **Coctelitos Bar** (☎2616 372; drinks US$1.50-2.50; open daily 9am-midnight) and a better atmosphere across the street at the two-story bar and dance floor of the **Coco-Bar Discoteca** (☎09 8471 090; drinks US$1.50-3; open daily from 4pm). When the bars close, the party usually finds its way to the beach for a bonfire.

SANTO DOMINGO DE LOS COLORADOS   ☎02

Santo Domingo is the stereotypical juxtaposition of Spanish and indigenous cultures. Christened in honor of the Catholic saint and the Colorados (also called Tsachilas), a local indigenous group, the city has escaped from its roots into the realm of congested concrete urbanity. The scant clothing and red bowl-cuts of the Colorados, commonly exploited on postcards and store signs, are the only connection this bustling hub between the coast and the Sierra keeps with its indigenous past.

▐▐ TRANSPORTATION AND PRACTICAL INFORMATION. Buses depart from the terminal (5min. outside downtown along Tsachilas) to: **Esmeraldas** (3hr., every 15min. 5am-7pm, US$3); **Guayaquil** (5hr.; every 20-40min. 1am-8:30pm; standard US$5, luxury US$6.); **Quito** (3hr., every 10min. 3am-9pm, US$2.50); **Pedernales** (3hr., every 20min. 3am-10:30pm, US$3.50); **Coca** (12hr., every 30min. 5:30am-9pm, US$10); and **Cuenca** (13hr.; 7:30am, 12:30, 7:40pm; US$12). **Parque Central** is bordered by Tulcán, Quito, and Tsachilas. Centro de Computación Copiado los Angeles de Charly on Quito and Tsachilas near Parque Central sells a decent city map(US$1.40). **Banco del Pichincha**, between Tulcán and Tsachilas, by the park, offers V cash advances 8am-2pm. 24hr. V **ATM**. (☎2751 278. Open M-F 8am-6pm, Sa 9am-1pm.) **Wash & Wear**, on Ambato and Latacunga, between Quito and Galápagos, has regular laundry service (US$1.75 per kg) and dry cleaning (US$5.10). (☎09 7072 652. Open M-Sa 8am-6:30pm.) **Police** (☎2743 916), are on 3 de Julio and Latacunga. **Farmacia Paris 2**, is at 29 de Mayo and Tsachilas. (☎2272 080. Open daily 9am-9pm.) **Hospital Dr. Gustavo Domínguez** (24hr. emergency ☎2750 333), is on Quito, at Km1. **Andinatel**, on Quito and Toachi, 3 blocks from Parque Central toward the Andes. (☎6760 256. Open daily 8am-1pm and 1:30-10pm.) **Servie-net**, at 29 de Mayo and Tsachilas, offers **Internet**. (☎2760 117. US$1 per hr. Open M-F and Su 8:30am-9pm.) **Correos de Ecuador** are on Tsachilas and Río Baba. (☎2750 303. Open M-F 8am-5:30pm, Sa 8am-noon.)

▐▐ ACCOMMODATIONS AND FOOD. There are reasonably priced hotels next to the bus station and downtown, especially near 29 de Mayo. The fancy hotels line Quito, about 1km outside of town. **Hostal Patricia ❷**, across from the bus terminal, has small, clean rooms, and cold private baths. Interior rooms are stuffy. (☎2761 906. Singles US$4, with TV US$5; doubles US$7/$10; triples with TV US$12.) **Hotel Genova ❸**, at 29 de Mayo and Ibarra, has comfortable sitting areas and tidy rooms with large windows, TVs, fans, and hot private baths. (☎2759 694. Singles US$10; doubles US$15, triples US$21.) Chifas abound in this town's dining scene, and rows of impaled chickens rotating over coals are on nearly every block. Nicer restaurants are with the nicer hotels on Quito a kilometer outside of town. **Gran Restaurant Vegetariano "Shael" ❶**, on Tsachilas near Río Baba, serves a 2-course veggie lunch. Stock up here on soy milk, tofu, and granola. (☎2753 609. Lunch US$1.50. Open daily noon-2:30pm.) **Ch'Farina ❶**, on Quito at Km1, has hearty, uninteresting pizzas. The national chain serves salads (US$2.10-4.73), personal pizzas (from US$2.25), family-size pizzas (from US$8.60), and pastas (US$3.70-5.45). (☎2763 500. Free delivery. AmEx/DC/MC/V.) **La Casa Grande ❶**, on Quito at Km1, on the way to Ch'Farina from the center of town. Specialties from the coast and Sierra, served in a dining room with A/C and tablecloths. (☎2750 587; fax 2750 133. Set-menu lunch US$2.50; *ceviche* US$6-7; pastas, meat, and seafood US$2-10. Su buffet 9am-4pm. Open M 9am-4pm, Tu-Su 9am-9pm.)

▐▐ SIGHTS AND NIGHTLIFE. The nearby **Colorados** live in hut villages on the outskirts of the city, along Quevedo. While they will let you observe their lifestyle and take pictures, they are not exempt from capitalism—they expect payment. Marcelo Aguavil's knowledge of medicinal plants growing all around the house is sought to treat maladies from rheumatism to depression. The house is just off the Km7 mark from Quevedo. From the end of the **bus** line, the house is about 1km down the paved road on the left—look for the small sign. The Colorados are accessible via **taxi** (round-trip US$10) or bus. Catch a bus marked "Vía Quevedo" outside of the bus station or as it passes through the city (round-trip US$0.25). Ask the driver if the bus goes to the end of the line (a la última parada), as certain buses only travel within city limits. The jammed market scene around Ambato and 29 de Mayo is entertaining in itself where vendors hawk wares from quail eggs to mattresses.

Open-air bars line Quito just before the traffic circle on the way out of town toward Quito. **Cleopatra** has comfy wicker chairs and a dance floor. Suck on flavored tobacco hookahs (US$2) or scarf down shwarma (US$1.50) on Friday and Saturday nights. (Open daily from 3pm.) *Discotecas* are nearby along Guayaquil, between Río Saloya and Río Mulaute. Locals prefer **Mi Tierra**, on Pallatanga just off of Guayaquil, for dancing to the latest in salsa and reggetón.

BAHÍA DE CARÁQUEZ   ☎ 05

In February 1999, Bahía declared itself an "eco-city," signaling the importance of protecting delicate ecosystems, appreciating nature, and conserving ancestral culture. The standard of living is high, and this modern peninsular city is one of the few to strive toward environmental consciousness. *Serranos* (people from the mountains), representing a good portion of Ecuador's swanky elite, spend weekends and summers residing in the sparkling white high-rises that decorate Bahía de Caráquez. Sailboats bob in the harbor, as Bahía is an increasingly popular stop for international yachters on their way to Galápagos or around the world. The higher standard of living also means greater resources for travelers of all varieties.

▐ TRANSPORTATION

Buses to **Quito, Guayaquil, Manta,** and **Santo Domingo** depart from San Vicente (just north of Bahía) and Bahía, but buses to destinations along the northern coast leave only from San Vicente, the town on the northern side of the bay. In San Vicente, **Reina del Camino, Coactur, Costa Norte,** and **El Carmen** buses depart from the station near el mercado (a short walk or **bici-taxi** ride inland from the docks) to: **Pedernales** (3hr., 2 per hr., US$3) via **Canoa** (20min., US$0.50); **Santo Domingo** (5hr., 6 per day, US$6); **Guayaquil** (6hr., 11 per day

Bahía de Caráquez

🛏 **ACCOMMODATIONS**
Bahía B&B Inn, **5**
Centro Vacacional Life, **3**
Hotel La Herradura, **1**

🍴 **FOOD**
Columbiu's, **7**
Comedor Isabela, **2**
La Terraza, **9**
Muelle Uno, **8**

★ **ENTERTAINMENT**
Cinema Bahía, **10**

▌ **NIGHTLIFE**
Gordon Blue's, **4**
Sports Bar, **6**

5:50am-4:30pm, US$6.50); **Manta** (3hr., 7 per day, US$3.50). Buses to Guayaquil and Manta pass through **Portoviejo** (2¼hr., US$2.50); **Quito** (4hr.; 10am, 9:30pm; US$7.50) via **Santo Domingo** (4hr., US$5); and **Chamanga** (3½hr., 6:30am, US$5). In Bahía, **Reina del Camino** and **Coactur** buses come and go from the terminal on Malecón, a few blocks upriver from the docks to: **Guayaquil** (6hr., every hr. 4:20am-11:30pm, US$6) via **Portoviejo** (2hr., US$2); **Manta** (3hr., every hr. 5:30am-6pm, US$2.90) via Portoviejo; and **Quito** (7-8 hr.; 4 per day; regular US$7.50, luxury US$9) via **Santo Domingo** (4 hr., US$5).

Ferries leave from the dock on Malecón and Aguilera for **San Vicente** (10min.; every 15min. 5:45am-5:45pm, US$0.29; 5:45pm-11pm, US$0.35; 11pm-5:45am, US$5). The **car ferry** leaves San Vicente from a dock about a 5min. walk toward the airport from the passenger dock and arrives next to the passenger dock in Bahía. Pedestrians go for free. The ferry leaves when it's full, usually every 20min., and the trip lasts 15min. **Caráquez Ltda.** (☎2690 536) **taxis** operate until 1am.

A TRANSPORTATION TIP Make friends with the driver's assistant. This is the guy who takes money and herds people on and off the buses. A "stop" can mean little more than slowing down to let a few passengers tumble off or clamber on. Stops are not called out and not marked. Make it clear to the driver's assistant that he should let you know when you are nearing the stop.

✦ 🛈 ORIENTATION AND PRACTICAL INFORMATION

Bahía is built on a peninsula with the Pacific Ocean on the west side and the wide mouth of Río Chone on the other. Boats from San Vicente drop visitors off at the docks along **Malecón**, the main street by the beach, near **Aguilera**. Malecón changes its name depending on where it is in the city. On the Pacific side it is called **Circunvalación**, for example. Most services and accommodations are found within the grid marked by **Malecón, Bolívar, Montufar, Morales,** and **Salinas** and the intersecting **Vinueza, Peña, Aguilera, Ante, Ascazubi, Riofrío, Arenas,** and **Checa.**

Tourist Office: Ministerio de Turismo (☎2691 044 or 2690 372), at Bolívar and Malecón Virgilio Ratti, in the blue building. Has information on Bahía's hotels and sights, but mostly directs visitors to private tours. Open M-F 8:30am-1pm and 2-5pm.

Tours: 🔲 **Guacamayo Bahíatours,** Bolívar 906 (☎2691 107; fax 2691 412), at Arenas, offers city info, maps, tour options, and information about the nearby Río Muchacho Organic Farm. Guacamayo coordinates 1-to 3-day visits to the farm to learn permaculture, chocolate-making, *tagua* carving, and cheese-making, and to explore the surrounding dry tropical forest (US$35 per day, including food). **Dolphin Bahía Tours,** on Bolívar and Ascázubi, offers trips to Isla Corazón and arranges daytrips and overnight visits to the **Chirije** archaeological site (see below). Open sporadically; if no one is on the office, check with Jacob Santos at Bahía Bed and Breakfast Inn (see below).

Bank: Banco de Guayaquil (☎2692 205 or 2692 206), on Riofrío and Bolívar. Exchanges traveler's checks. Allows cash advances. Has 24hr. DC/MC/V **ATM.** Open M-F 8:30am-4:30pm, Sa 9:30am-1:30pm. **Banco del Pichincha** (☎2692 981 or 2692 082), on Ascázubi and Bolívar. Offers V cash advances M-F 9am-2pm. Has 24hr. DC/MC/V **ATM.** Open M-F 9am-4pm, Sa 9am-1pm.

Work Opportunities: Ask **Jacob Santos** (☎2690 146; hc4js@ecua.net.ec), the owner of Bahía Bed and Breakfast Inn, who has information regarding teaching English in the community in exchange for Spanish classes.

Volunteer Opportunities: Volunteers (see p. 75) at the **Río Muchacho Organic Farm** work the gardens, make arts and crafts, tend the compost or teach in the Escuela Ambientalista (environmental school). Volunteers contribute US$28 per week to cover food and dormitory housing. The company also offers a day-long tour of the city of Bahía, including a visit to the recycled paper workshop and a stop at an organic shrimp farm (US$37), and a half-day birdwatching trip up the estuary to the mangroves of Isla Corazón (US$17). Open M-F 7:30am-6pm, Sa 9am-4pm, Su 10am-2pm.

Police: ☎2690 045 or 101. Behind the bus station on María Velasco Ibarra.

Hospital: Clínica Viteri (☎2690 429), at Riofrío and Bolívar. 24hr. medical attention.

Telephones: PacificTel (☎2690 020), at Malecón and Arenas, doesn't accept calling cards. Open daily 8am-10pm.

Internet Access: Genesis.net (☎2692 400), on Malecón, a block to the right with your back to the docks. Internet US$1.60 per hr. Internet phone calls to the US US$0.20 per min. English spoken. Open M-F 8am-8:30pm, Sa 9am-8:30pm, Su 10am-4pm.

Post Office: ☎2691 177. On Malecón across from the ferry. Open M-F 8am-4:30pm.

▟ ACCOMMODATIONS

Budget travelers should stay along Bolívar, away from the waterfront's condos.

Bahía Bed and Breakfast Inn, Ascázubi 316 (☎2690 146), at Morales, has unadorned, clean rooms with wooden floor, fan, and leaky bathroom. Painted birds and old family portraits decorate the common space, which is also accompanied by a small balcony overlooking the backyard. Creatively painted restaurant walls render an interesting atmosphere to enjoy the complimentary breakfast. Singles US$5, with bath and TV US$7; doubles US$10/$12. ❷

Centro Vacacional Life (☎2690 496), on Viteri and Dávila. On Malecón Santos, walk about 8 short blocks toward the peninsula at Dávila. 6 70s-style concrete houses in the midst of Bahía's fancy summer home scene have 2 bedrooms and a living room/kitchen. Check out the common area with pool tables, foosball, and a children's playground. US$10 per person. ❸

Hotel la Herradura (☎2690 446; fax 2690 265), on Bolívar and Hidalgo. Artwork covers the walls of this old hacienda in the city. The antique furniture has been in the family for generations. Blue-and-white rooms are small and neat. Singles ground-level with fan US$10, with private bath and A/C US$25; doubles with private bath and A/C US$35; triples US$45; quads US$50. Ask about room #306, the honeymoon suite. ❸

▟ FOOD

There is a cluster of inexpensive eateries by the docks that serve typical coastal entrees and *parilladas* (grilled meats).

Colombiu's, Bolívar 1205 (☎2690 537), at Ante. This shaded brick-patio eatery has a gazebo formed by trees in its dusty courtyard. Generous portions of meat and seafood. Some veggie options. Set-lunch and dinner US$1.30. *Menú* US$2.50-5.50; full *parillada* (US$5.50). Open daily 8am-10pm. ❶

Comedor Isabela (☎2690 446), in the Hotel Herradur. A high-ceilinged dining room proudly displays the results of generations of art and antique collecting. Large windows face the Pacific. Upscale atmosphere with reasonable prices. *Ceviche* US$3-6; seafood, chicken, and steak US$2-6. Open daily 7am-10pm. ❶

La Terraza (☎2690 787), on Malecón by the docks, has a pretty, covered terrace with a great view of passengers donning neon-orange life-vests for the trip across Río Chone. Wash down tasty seafood dishes (US$2-5) with refreshing juices. 2-course set-lunch US$1.20. Vegetarian options. Open daily 6:30am-4pm. ❶

Muelle Uno (☎2692 334), next to La Terraza (see above), offers high quality food, low prices, and prime views. House specialty is meat (US$3.50), but there are a few vegetarian options as well. Spanish and English menu. Set-lunch US$2; seafood US$3-8. Open daily 10am-noon. ❶

 BEACHES

Surfers tend to cluster on the rocky shores at the western end of Malecón; waves generally break far enough out to ensure safety. Although Bahía itself does not have much of a beach, the almost uninhabited **Punta Bellaca** is not too far away. The relatively long walk south on along the Pacific is only possible at low tide, but taxis are eager to take people there (US$3) and will set a time to pick you up. During high season the beach is packed; other times of the year, deserted.

SIGHTS

Bahía also has several islands situated just offshore. The **Islas Fragatas** and **Isla Corazón (Heart Island)** are home to large colonies of over 30 species of marine birds, including South America's largest population of the famed **frigate birds**. The best time to visit these islands is from August to December, the frigates' mating season. Guacamayo Bahíatours and Dolphin Bahía Tours lead tours to see both sites. To visit Isla Corazón on your own, cross over to San Vicente on the ferry and take a short bus ride south to Puerto Portovelo where local fisherman have been trained as guides and will take you in a dugout canoe through the mangroves (US$5). If your Spanish is good, ask them about tales of "El Duende," the elves who protect the mangroves. Nearby **Jororá** and **Punta Bellaca** contain all of Ecuador's remaining tropical dry forest. From December to May, the forests are lush and green, while during the rest of the year, they become completely arid and void of vegetation, save the cactus, *palo santo* (whose wood is burned as a bug repellent), and the striking ceiba tree that produces a cotton-like fiber that was used to stuff mattresses, pillows, and life jackets during WWII. Dolphin Bahía Tours owns and operates the ▨**Chirije** archaeological site on the beach past Punta Bellaca. Excavation has turned up layers of cultural and geological history. Once a refueling spot for drug-traffickers, the site provides cabins and a restaurant for tourists and archaeologists. Access this deserted island paradise by driving along the beach at low tide. Strolls along the beach and into the forest turn up artifacts from the **Jama Cuaque, Manteño, Chirije,** and **Bahía** cultures, as well as prehistoric fossils. There are guided daytrips to the site and museum, and horseback riding excursions and hikes into the forest. Wooden cabins at Chirije can accommodate six to eight people (breakfast included). The setting is remote but the restaurant brings in copious amounts of fresh food (US$6-9).

Back in town, the **Museo Bahía de Caráquez,** in the Banco Central del Ecuador building, is a big museum for such a small town. It exhibits artifacts of coastal Ecuador from the last 10,000 years. The museum also contains an exposition of modern Ecuadorian art and a resource library. Archaeologists-in-residence work to identify pieces from nearby excavation sites. (On Malecón, to the left of the docks. Open Tu-F 9am-5pm, Sa-Su 10am-2pm. Admission US$1, including a guided tour in English or Spanish.) For more local sights, check out **Miguelito,** the 94-year-old Galápagos turtle, at the Miguel Valverde school uphill on Ascázubi, or go to the lookout point at the top of the hill along Ascázubi to get an aerial view of the peninsula and the occasional **humpback whale** (July-Sept.).

🎵 ENTERTAINMENT

Finding the hot nightlife in Bahía isn't difficult, as the options are scarce. **Gordon Blue's** on the corner of Arenas and Morales is a dim-light courtyard bar with creative seating options from a regular bar-stool to a hanging saddle to a rope hammock. The music is all over the place: from Led Zeppelin to Ricky Martin. Dancing has been known to break out on the weekends. The owner speaks English and can arrange salsa lessons. (☎09 7284 928. Open W-Sa 6pm-3:30am.) **Sports Bar,** a rooftop bar on the water next to the passenger ferry, has cheap beer, pool tables, and live TV sports coverage. (☎09 4671 801. Imported beer US$2, pitcher of Pilsner US$2. Open M-Th 3pm-midnight, F-Sa 3pm-2am.) For a mellower night, the **Cinema Bahía** shows a film (US$1.50) in its improvised big-screen theater every Friday and Saturday at 8:30pm. (Bolívar 1418 and Vinueza. ☎2692 853.)

CRUCITA   ☎05

Only an hour's bus ride from Portoviejo, Crucita is the capital's favorite beachside getaway. Anyone arriving during high tide might wonder about its popularity, as the beach is barely visible. But when the tide ebbs, it leaves clean, firm sand bordered by calm, green-blue water. The bluffs to the south create a perfect location for hang-gliding or paragliding 340 afternoons out of the year. **Transportes Crucita** runs **buses** from the main terminal in **Portoviejo** to Crucita (1hr., every 15min. 6:20am-10pm, US$0.90). Buses also run to **Manta** from the southern end of the beach (1½hr., 1 per hr. 5:20am-4:40pm, US$1.40).

🏠 **ACCOMMODATIONS AND FOOD. Hostal Voladores ❷,** on the southern end of the beach, has cheerfully painted cement rooms with hot private baths, bamboo rooms with shared baths around a small pool, and an 8-person wooden house on the beach. Owners Raúl and Luis Tobar offer paragliding and hang-gliding, as the name Voladores ("flyers") might suggest. (☎2340 200; hvoladores@hotmail.com. Internet US$4 per hr. Breakfast included. Singles US$6, with private bath $12; doubles US$12/$24; private house US$10 per person.) **Hostería Zucasa ❸,** on the *malecón* north of Hostal Voladores. Dozens of new wooden cabañas and a few older cement ones fill the mostly barren lot. All of the rooms have a small porch with a hammock and share 2 small pools. (☎2340 133; cell 09 8151 656; munozbrio@interactive.com. 3- and 5-person cement rooms US$10; singles with fan and tiled private bath US$12; doubles US$24; triples US$6; quads US$48.)

Almost every building on Malecón sports a restaurant sign. Most serve typical seafood and *ceviche*. There are a few cheap burger-and-*batido* (shake) places. **Atlas Delta #1 ❶,** on the far southern end of the boardwalk, is a family-owned eatery that offers a great balcony view of the beach. (☎2340 337 or 2340 170. Traditional entrees US$2.50-5. Open daily 7am-9pm. MC/V.) **La Loma ❶,** at the top of the hill south of town, above the landing spot. OK seafood and burgers, but an amazing cliff-side location. Grab a beer and watch the paragliders take-off or glimpse dolphins in the water below. (Dishes US$1-3. Open daily 9am-6pm.)

🪂 **OUTDOOR ACTIVITIES.** Head to Hostal Voladores for some X-treme flying. They offer paragliding and hang-gliding. Certified flyers can rent paragliders and hang-gliders for solo soaring. Others can either fly tandem or give advanced warning and take a lesson (4-days US$250, including equipment) to be soaring solo in no time. (Tandem paraglide US$15; hang-glide US$50, weekdays best. Paragliders US$20 per day; hang-gliders US$30 per day.) Hostal Voladores also offers **horseback riding** on the beach (US$5 per hr.), **mountain biking** (US$5 per day), and **sea kayaking** (US$5 per hr.). **Motorboats** will also tow people along in banana/hot dog boats (US$1 per person).

MANTA   ☎ 05

In pre-Columbian times Manta was home to the Jocay, a community known for its maritime accomplishments. Now, the town's convenient coastal location has continued to spur population and economic growth. Dominated by an immense harbor, Manta recently surpassed Guayaquil as Ecuador's largest center of seafaring activities. While many residents are at sea by day, they filter back into bars and *discotecas* at night, often joined by soldiers from the nearby US military base.

▄ TRANSPORTATION

Flights: Eloy Alfaro Airport, 5km northeast of the town center. **TAME** (☎2622 006 or 2613 210), at Malecón and Calle 13, books flights to **Quito** (30min.; M-Sa 8am, M, W, F, Su 8:30pm; US$52), and provides direct transportation between Manta and Portoviejo for travelers going to and from Quito at no additional cost. Open 8:30am-1pm and 3-5:30pm. **I'caro** (☎2627 363, or 2627 344; www.icaro.com), at Malecón and Calle 23 in the Oro Mar tower, has flights to **Quito** (35min.; M-F 7:40am, 1:50, 6:30pm, Sa 7:40am, 4:50pm, Su 4:30, 6:30pm; US$53). Open M-F 8am-7pm, Sa-Su 10am-4pm.

Buses: Buses come in 2 forms, regular and luxury. A small terminal for Reina del Camino and Transportes Esmeraldas ejecutivo (luxury service) is toward Tarqui, 1½ blocks past the regular terminal. US$1 more gets A/C, more room, and a vendor-free direct trip. The standard-service **terminal** is along 24 de Mayo/Calle 7 just past Av. 4. All northbound buses pass through Portoviejo; some southbound buses follow the coastal "Costa Negra" route, and others take the inland route via Jipijapa. **Transportes Crucita** goes to **Crucita** (1½hr., every 45min. 7:30am-6:40pm, US$1.40); **Reina del Camino** and **Transportes Reales Tamarindo** go to **Esmeraldas** (9hr., 9 per day 3am-9:45pm, US$7-8). Reina del Camino goes to **Guayaquil** (3½hr., every hr. 2:15am-8:30pm, US$4-5). **Transportes Montecristi** goes to **Montecristi** (30min., every 5min. 6am-7pm, US$0.40). **Cooperative de Transportes Manabí** goes to **Portoviejo** (1hr., every 10min. 4:45am-10pm, US$0.90). **Turismo de Manta** and **Transportes Crucita** go to **Puerto López** (2½hr., every hr. 4am-6pm, US$3). Several companies have buses to **Quito;** the most frequent is Reina del Camino (9hr., every hr. 4am-10pm, US$7-9) via **Santo Domingo** (6hr., US$5).

Local Transportation: Buses cross the city (US$0.25), usually running along Malecón and passing the bus terminal. **Taxis** go anywhere in Manta (US$1).

▄ ▐ ORIENTATION AND PRACTICAL INFORMATION

Buses enter the city via **4 de Noviembre,** passing through **Tarquí** (the neighborhood north of the river) before crossing the foul-smelling **Río Manta** into downtown. If you plan on staying in Tarquí, save yourself a hike by getting let off at the **bridge** that crosses into central Manta. The **terminal** is just west of the **harbor,** close to the bridge over the inlet. In the town center, the streets running parallel to the coast are **avenidas,** with numbers increasing the farther one gets from the water. Streets leading uphill away from the water are **calles,** numbers beginning at Río Manta.

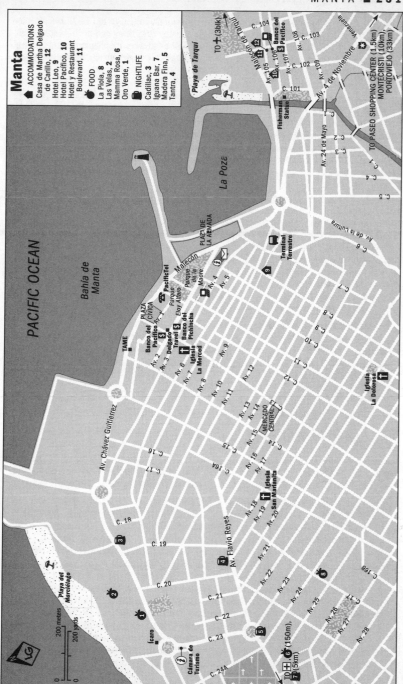

Manta

▲ ACCOMMODATIONS
Casa de Martha Delgado
de Carillo, 12
Hotel Leo, 9
Hotel Pacifico, 10
Hotel y Restaurant
Boulevard, 11

● FOOD
La Piola, 8
Las Velas, 2
Mamma Rosa, 6
Oro Verde, 1

■ NIGHTLIFE
Cadillac, 3
Iguana Bar, 7
Madera Fina, 5
Tantra, 4

PACIFIC OCEAN

Bahía de
Manta

Playa del
Murciélago

Ícaro

Cámara de
Turismo

PLAZA
CÍVICA

TAME

Banco del
Pacífico

Pacifictel

Travel

N. 3 Delgado

Banco del
Pichincha

Iglesia
La Merced

Parque
Eloy Alfaro

Parque
de la
Madre

Malecón

PLAZA DE
LA ARMADA

La Poza

Playa de Tarqui

Malecón de Tarqui

Banco del
Pacífico

Fisherman
Station

Av. 24 de Mayo

Terminal
Terrestre

Av. de la Cultura

Iglesia
San Marianita

MERCADO
CENTRAL

Iglesia
La Dolorosa

Av. Chávez Guitiérrez

Av. Flavio Reyes

Av. 4 de Noviembre

TO PASEO SHOPPING CENTER (1.5km),
MONTECRISTI (10km),
PORTOVIEJO (33km)

TO (3blk)

Venezuela

200 meters
200 yards

C. 101
C. 102
C. 103
C. 104
C. 105
C. 106
C. 107
C. 108
C. 109

Av. 105
Av. 106
Av. 107
Av. 108

C-1
C-2
C-3
C-4
C. 5
C. 6
C-7
C-8
C-9
C-10
C-11
C-12
C-13
C-14
C-15
C-16A
C-16
C. 17
C. 18
C. 19
C. 20
C. 21
C. 22
C. 23
C. 24A

Av. 2
Av. 4
Av. 5
Av. 6
Av. 7
Av. 8
Av. 9
Av. 10
Av. 11
Av. 12
Av. 13
Av. 14
Av. 15
Av. 16
Av. 17
Av. 18
Av. 19
Av. 20
Av. 21
Av. 22
Av. 23
Av. 24
Av. 25
Av. 26
Av. 27
Av. 28

C. 16B

(150m),
(5km)

Tourist Office: Cámara de Turismo, at Malecón and Calle 23, in the same building as KFC, can make recommendations on places to stay and things to do in Manta. Has maps of the coast. **Ministerio de Turismo** (☎2622 944; www.municipiodemanta.com), at Av. 4 and Calle 9 in the Municipalidad building, is less geared toward helping tourists, but they can point you in the right direction. Open M-F 8am-5pm.

Tours: Delgado Travel (☎2627 925, 2627 926, 2622 813, or 2623 671; 24hr. cell 09 8472 945; www.ecuadorpacificosur.com), on Av. 2 and between Calles 12 and 13, offers **car rental,** an international **postal service,** and tours of Manta, Montecristi, and Parque Nacional Machalilla. Open M-F 8:30am-1pm and 3-6:30pm, Sa 8:30am-1pm.

Currency Exchange: Banco del Pacífico (☎2623 212), at Av. 2 and Calle 13. Exchanges up to US$200 in traveler's checks. V cash advances until 4pm. 24hr. MC **ATM.** Open M-F 8:30am-5pm. **Branch** (☎2623 212), at Av. 107 and Calle 103 in Tarquí. Has a 24hr. MC **ATM.** Open M-F 8:30am-4pm, Sa 9am-2pm. **Banco del Pichincha** (☎2626 844, 2626 845, or 2626 846), Av. 2 and Calle 11. Offers MC/V cash advances M-F 9am-2pm. 24hr. DC/MC/V **ATM.** Open M-F 9am-5pm, Sa 9am-1pm.

Emergency: ☎101.

Police: ☎2920 900. At 4 de Noviembre and Venezuela, 2 blocks from Río Manta bridge on the Tarquí side. Open 24hr. **Servicio de Migración** (☎2921 200) renews tourist visas. Open M-F 8am-noon and 3-6pm.

Hospital: Hospital Rodríguez Zambrano de Manta (emergency ☎2625 610 or 2620 595, ext. 5068), at Calle 18 and Calle 12, Barrio Santa Marta. Take a university bus headed along Malecón all the way up (US$0.25). Open 24hr. for emergencies. Ambulance service. Across the street is the new, private Clínica Hospital del Sol (24hr. emergency ☎2612 203). The doctors at the clinic were all trained outside of Ecuador.

Telephones: PacificTel (☎2622 700), at Calle 11 and Malecón. Open daily 8am-10pm.

Internet Access: CoolWeb.ec (☎2629 831), at Av. 3 and Calle 11 along the pedestrian-only part of the street. Internet US$1 per hr. International calls to US US$0.10 per min., to UK and Australia US$0.25 per min. Open M-Sa 8:30am-9:30pm, Su 10:30am-2:30pm. **Cyber Café Tarqui.com** (☎2621 140), on Calle 103 and Av. 106. Internet US$1 per hr. Open M-Sa 8am-8pm, Su 8am-1pm.

Post Office: ☎2624 402. At Av. 4 and Calle 8 in the Municipalidad. Open M-F 8am-4:50pm, Sa 8am-noon.

ACCOMMODATIONS

Though most of the action is in downtown Manta, hotels there tend to be geared toward the wealthy. Across the river on Malecón de Tarqui there are plenty of cheaper, but still overpriced places. Be prepared to pay more for decent housing.

Casa de Martha Delgado de Carrillo (☎2620 659), at Av. 105 and Calle 103. This private home with several rooms for rent is Tarquí's hidden budget option. No sign—check in with the owners at the Carrtur Travel Agency around the corner. Basic rooms are clean with high ceilings, private baths, and sagging mattresses. Singles with fan US$6, with A/C US$8; doubles US$12/$16. Ask about deals in the restaurant downstairs. ❷

Hotel Leo (☎2623 159; cell 09 8856 736), at Av. 9 and 24 de Mayo, has vast, clean, but undecorated rooms a few steps from the bus terminal. Good for spending the night if arriving late or just passing through. Singles with fan, TV, and private bath US$10, with A/C and windows US$15; doubles US$20/$30; triples US$30/$40; quads US$40/$50. Discounts for multiple-day stays and groups. ❸

Hotel y Restaurant Boulevard (☎2625 333, 2612 650, or 2621 836; fax 2610 980), at Calle 103 and Av. 105. This is the older of the hotel's 2 locations that are within a block of one another. The older rooms all have windows onto the street, a hodge-podge of decorations and furnishings, and shockingly hard mattresses. Singles with hot private bath, TV, and an A/C unit jammed through the wall US$9; doubles US$12. ❸

Hotel Pacífico (☎2622 475 or 2623 584), at Av. 106 and Calle 101, is one of the cleanest options. The interior is like an Escher drawing. All rooms come with private baths and TVs; some have ocean views. Singles US$8, with A/C US$10; doubles US$15/$20; triples US$20/$25. ❸

◖ FOOD

Thanks to its important seaport status, Manta has a substantial number of good eateries serving fresh seafood. Restaurants cluster along **Malecón** and uphill from **Murciélago Beach**, including a Kentucky Fried Chicken and American Deli for those longing to return to their Western existences. Eateries right along Murciélago beach (identifiable by their matching green roofs and white walls) are referred to as **Malecón Escénico**—essentially a union of restaurants, all with the same menus, hours, and prices. The counterpart to Malecón Escénico along the **Playa de Tarquí** is **Parque del Marisco,** where the owners' laid-back attitudes show in the hammocks, plastic furniture, and grass huts. In Tarquí, **El Acuario** is slightly more expensive but is its own world of tangled wood, shark jaws, and giant antique glass floats. The Tarquí restaurants' claim to fame is one of the world's largest *ceviches*, made in September 1997.

La Piola (☎2610 114; cell 09 7681 112 or 09 9069 242), on Calle 17 and Av. 24. Professional staff serve expert sauces atop perfectly cooked penne, tagliatelle, risotto, and linguine in the clean, spare dining room. Compared to the lush resort restaurants, the prices are great. Despite what the menu says, there are usually only a few dishes available. Pasta US$4-6; meat and fish US$4-8; 3-course set-menus US$8-13. Open daily 9am-11pm. ❷

Las Velas (☎2629 396; cell 09 9098 167), on Malecón Escénico, all the way to the left as you face the water. This outdoor eatery stands out from similar places for its comfy chairs and attention to presentation. Seafood and *ceviche* US$2.50-4.50. The specialty is the pork, chicken, and seafood paella (US$7.50). Open daily 9am-11pm. ❶

Oro Verde (☎2629 200, ext. 849), at Malecón and Calle 23. Pricey, decadent international entrees from Garam Masala shrimp to saffron risotto. Boasts a sushi bar and outside deck with views of Playa Murciélago. Salads US$5-9; sandwiches US$5-6; entrees US$8-33. Sushi pieces US$4.50-7.50; 8-piece rolls US$5.50-13.30. Restaurant open daily 7am-11pm. Sushi bar open M-Sa 7-11pm. ❷

Mamma Rosa (☎2626 079 or 2628 682; cell 09 9852 461 or 09 9946 729; mamma-rosa@latinmail.com), on Flavio Reyes and Perimetral a block past the cemetery on Flavio Reyes. Red-checkered tablecloths fill the interior courtyard. Within walking distance of the major clubs and bars, this is a prime spot for beginning a night out in Manta. The specialty is Italian but there is *comida típica* as well. Pasta, ravioli, risotto, and lasagna US$3.70-6; pizza US$4.80-7.80; traditional seafood US$4.80-11; and *parilladas* US$4.10-10, for 2 US$12.50. Open daily noon-3am. ❷

◉◖ BEACHES AND SIGHTS

Manta has two beaches: **Playa Murciélago,** up Malecón and to your left from the terminal when facing the water, and **Playa de Tarquí,** to the right down Malecón. A 5min. drive or 20min. walk west of the center, Murciélago is a wide stretch of soft sand with a strip of good beachfront restaurants. Its proximity to the Oro Verde (see above) and other luxury hotels clinging to the bluffs means that it is better maintained than most public beaches. The surfing here is more about the wind than the waves. Look for the bright sails of kite-boarders. The guys practicing give lessons. The sport is not easy to pick up and it's best to space out inevitable frustration over a couple of days. (Contact Robert Bedoya,

Adrian Rendón, and Wladimir Paternina at ☎ 09 4871 684; ra_wind@yahoo.com, wpacalima@latinmail.com, or adrian_carter@latinmail.com. Complete 8hr. course US$195, including equipment. Lessons US$30 per hr. Rental US$10-15 per hr. Quick drag-along without the board US$5.) On the other hand, Tarquí's littered beach could not be calmer, serving as a playground for pelicans and frigate birds. The small, calm beach of **Playa Piedra Larga,** with a few restaurants and bars in the sand, is a few minutes south of town by car or bus. To get to Playa Piedra Larga, take a taxi (US$3) or catch one of the white **camionetas** going to San Mateo (every 30min. 5am-6pm, US$0.25) that leaves from the Mercado Central at Av. 22 and Calle 13. A popular daytime destination is **El Paseo Shopping,** on the highway to Portoviejo.

The **Museo del Banco Central,** at Av. 8 and Calle 7, is in the center of town near the bus terminal. It displays a permanent archaeological exhibit of ancient ceramics and a rotating exhibit of contemporary Ecuadorian art. (☎ 2622 956 or 2627 562. Open Tu-Sa 9am-5pm, Su 10am-3pm. Adults US$1, students US$0.50.)

🎵 🎭 ENTERTAINMENT AND NIGHTLIFE

The **modern mall** houses a food court and a **Supercines 8,** which shows several afternoon and evening Hollywood movies. Some are in English and some are dubbed. (Tickets M-Th US$2.80, F-Su US$4.) As befits an industrious city of this size, weekend nights in Manta radiate with energy. The **Manicentro,** centered around Flavio Reyes and Calle 24, several blocks uphill from the end of Murciélago beach (see above), is the focal point for a number of bars and clubs.

Tantra (☎ 2613 727), at Flavio Reyes and Calle 20, is the hippest club around. A younger crowd dances to the latest Latin mixes, sipping cocktails (US$4.50; beer US$2.50) under a big gold papier mache buddha. Cover US$5 includes 1st drink. Additional min. consumption US$5. Open W-Sa 9pm-3am.

Madera Fina (☎ 2610 507), at Flavio Reyes and Calle 23, offers a more romantic setting and draws more mature crowd. Dimly lighted interior is all wood, stone, and thatch. Tables (some with old porcelain toilets as seats) crowd around the dance floor. Min. consumption women US$6, men US$9, couples US$15. Open Th-Sa 9:30pm-3am.

Cadillac, on Malecón and Calle 19, is practically an annex of the US military base. English-speaking owner Max describes the place as a "classic American bar." Sells beautiful balsa-wood surfboards made by the acclaimed Moreno of Montañita. Serves spicy Cadillac Wings US2.50-4. Beer US$1. Happy hour M-F 5-8pm. Open daily 5pm-1am. Discounts for students with ID.

Iguana Bar (☎ 2628 063; cell 09 7194 688), 5km outside of Manta in Playa Piedra Larga (see above), on the road to San Mateo. Don't let the out-of-the-way location fool you. Aug. and Dec.-Feb. F-Sa this is the place to be. One of just a handful of buildings on the small beach Playa Piedra Larga, this open-air bar has a well-lighted dance floor and plays the latest local trends and even some "gringo music." Cocktails US$2.50-3.50. Meals US$3.50-6.

📷 DAYTRIP FROM MANTA: MONTECRISTI

Buses arriving in Montecristi (30min. from Manta) drop passengers off along the central plaza, bordered uphill by the streets 9 de Julio and Sucre, and the cross streets 23 de Octubre and San Andreas. Buses en route to Manta leave every 5min. Those heading to Jipijapa or Portoviejo pick up passengers along the highway at the bottom of 9 de Julio; the plaza is a 10min. walk uphill.

Between rowdy Manta and Portoviejo lounges mellow Montecristi, patiently churning out its world-famous and sadly misnamed Panama hats. Though these high-grade hats have always been made in the countryside surrounding Montecristi, most of the ears their woven brims shelter have never heard of the city, as almost every local will tell you.

Shopping in Montecristi is slow unless your visit coincides with the arrival of a giant tour group. The principal street, **9 de Julio,** presents a cluster of hat shops, all selling similar items at comparable prices. Hats start at US$6 for **gruesos** (made from the coarsest straw, usually taking 3 days per hat), US$15 for **finos** (softer, more delicate, and processed in a single month), and become expensive with the US$200 **extrafinos**—the most carefully constructed and delicate of them all. Unit prices drop steadily the more hats you buy. Along with the famed Panama hats, most of these shops sell straw handbags, baskets, dolls, and tagua-nut carvings. Few hats are made in town; town stores only finish the hats. To get the fullest view of the hat-making process, head to the countryside where hats are actually woven.

If you are interested in learning more about this art, visit the **Artesanía Franco Workshop,** at Eloy Alfaro and 23 de Octubre. Franco buys the woven hats from the weavers who work in the surrounding countryside and then shapes and finishes them according to different styles right there in the workshop. Franco's son (also Franco) is willing to take visitors to the nearby towns of **Las Pampas** and **Piles** to meet the weavers and observe the labor that goes into each hat. (☎09 105 230. Open daily 9am-9pm, or whenever you knock on the front door.) It may be possible to catch the weavers themselves in Montecristi at sunrise on Friday and Saturday, when they come to the Parque Central to sell four or five hats to the finishers. An old two-story building across from the Casa de Eloy Alfaro (see below) houses arts and crafts. Although some of the sellers are involved in the finishing process of the hats, there is no traditional weaving. Most of the craftsman are at work churning out dolls, purses, and jewelry.

PORTOVIEJO ☎05

Originally situated on the coast, Portoviejo ("Old Port") moved 40km inland to its present land-locked locale to avoid continual pirate attacks. Over the years, the distance from the coast has become cultural as well as geographic. While its maritime neighbors seem more relaxed and carefree, Portoviejo's population hurries along to the drone of its sober duties—commerce, industry, and education. Although often regarded as the stiff-necked, straight-laced capital of an informal province, Portoviejo is well-respected by coastal residents.

TRANSPORTATION. Aeropuerto Reales Tamarindo, 3km northwest of the town center, can be reached by taxi (5min., US$10). **TAME** (☎2632 429), on Chile and América, books flights from Manta to Quito and provides land transportation between Manta and Portoviejo free of charge. **Buses** go from the terminal to: **Bahía de Caráquez** (2¼hr., every 45min. 4:30am-9:40pm, US$2.50); **Guayaquil** (4hr., every 30min. 3:10am-10:30pm, US$4); **Jipijapa** (1hr., every 30min. 3:10am-10:30pm, US$1.25); **Manta** (45min., every 5min. 5am-10:30pm, US$0.90); **Pedernales** (4hr., every 30min. 4:30am-7:40pm, US$5); and **Quito** (7-8hr., every 30min. 3:45am-11:30pm, US$8) via **Santo Domingo** (6hr., US$5). The red-and-white **Cooperative Portoviejo** and pastel **Valle del Flor** buses serve the city. The **Cooperativa de Taxis "San Marcos"** (☎2930 905) has 24hr. taxi service—US$1 to most places within the city.

ORIENTATION AND PRACTICAL INFORMATION. Portoviejo seems sprawling, but everything essential is in the *centro*, the grid of streets between **Parque Alfaro** and **Parque Central.** Buses coming from the north usually enter the

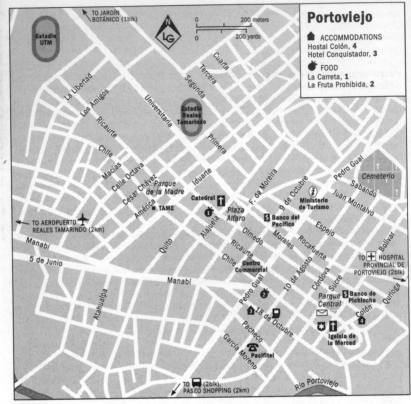

Portoviejo

▲ ACCOMMODATIONS
Hostal Colón, **4**
Hotel Conquistador, **3**

🍴 FOOD
La Carreta, **1**
La Fruta Prohibida, **2**

city along **Universitaria.** To reach the center, get off two blocks after the **stadium** (Estadio Reales Tamarindo) on the left (get out before the bus turns). Walk straight two blocks along Universitaria (don't follow the bus) toward the cathedral domes in Parque Alfaro. **Olmedo** runs from the plaza to the park. Running parallel to it are **Ricaurte** and **Chile.** The main streets running perpendicular from the plaza to the park are **9 de Octubre, Pedro Gual, 10 de Agosto,** and **Sucre. Banco del Pacífico,** at 9 de Octubre and Rocafuerte, exchanges traveler's checks and offers V cash advances M-F 8:30-2pm. It also has a 24hr. MC **ATM.** (☎2639 300. Open M-F 8:30am-4pm, Sa 9am-2pm.) The **police** (☎101 or 2631 190) are on 18 de Octubre between Sucre and Bolívar. **Hospital Provincial de Portoviejo** (emergency ☎2630 087 or 2636 520) is at Rocafuerte and 12 de Marzo. Find **Pacifictel** at 10 de Agosto and 18 de Octubre. (☎2636 021. Open daily 8am-10pm.) **Mr. Chat,** on Bolívar between Ricaurte and Chile provides **Internet.** (☎2634 373. US$1.20 per hr. Open M-F 9am-8pm, Sa 9:30am-2pm.) The **post office** is at Ricaurte 217 at Sucre on Parque Central. (☎2632 384 or 2635 198. Open M-F 8:30am-12:30pm and 1:30-5:30pm.) Find **DHL** and **Western Union** at Pedro Gual 621. (☎2638 882. Open M-F 8:30am-1pm and 3-6:30pm.)

🏠🏠 **ACCOMMODATIONS AND FOOD.** Budget lodgings are situated between the town's two parks, while more expensive accommodations are on Pedro Gual. To get to **Hostal Colón ❷,** walk down Olmedo From the plaza, past the park, to

Colón. Slightly smaller than the other budget hotels, this place is basic but kept-up. Rooms have baths, TVs, and fans. (Colón 212, at Olmedo. ☎2634 004. Singles US$6; doubles US$12.) **Hotel Conquistador ❸** is at 18 de Octubre and Pedro Gual. From the plaza, walk down Olmedo and turn right on Gual. The hotel is 3 blocks down on the left. It offers clean rooms with TVs and A/C. (☎2631 678; hotelconquistador@hotmail.com. Reservations required. Singles US$13; doubles US$26.) Portoviejo's cuisine is slightly different from that of its coastal neighbors. Although local joints offer many of the region's typical fish dishes, beef and fowl dominate. The mall **El Paseo Shopping** has a food court that includes a Fruta Prohibida (see below). Expect to wait in line with locals at the wildly popular Kentucky Fried Chicken. **La Carreta ❶,** at Olmedo across the street from the Cathedral, is one of the nicer restaurants in the *centro* and a favorite among locals. It has a second location near the bus station. (☎2652 108; branch ☎2932 123 or 2932 124. Set-lunch US$1.60; entrees US$2.50-4. Both open M-F 7am-10pm, Sa 7am-3:30pm.) **La Fruta Prohibida ❶,** at Chile between 9 de Octubre and Gual, is a fancy soda fountain good for a full meal or snack to go. The fruit might be forbidden, but it's definitely fresh. (☎2637 167. Fruit salads US$1.20-1.80; sandwiches US$1-2. Open daily 9:30am-11pm.)

◑ ◢ SIGHTS AND ENTERTAINMENT. Recently constructed churches aren't so much relics as multi-colored dreamsicles best described as Medieval-Russian-Gothic. The massive **Cathedral** on Parque Eloy Alfaro is filled with paintings depicting classic biblical scenes but with a contemporary Manabí twist. Just outside town past the university is the **Jardín Botánico** and reserve where 50 hectares of land are dedicated to preserving local forest, growing endemic plant species, and rehabilitating wildlife from parrots to spider monkeys to alligators. Admission US$1 includes a guided tour by one of the university's tourism students. (☎2632 677; cell 09 7107 108.) Portoviejo offers consumer frenzy. The **Centro Comercial** and surrounding streets as well as the slick **Paseo Shopping** are as entertaining as the movies playing at **Supercines 8.** Movie theater screens afternoon and evening shows. (☎2934 707. Tickets M-F US$2.80; Sa-Su US$4, matinee US$2. ISIC discount US$0.50.) To reach the Paseo Shopping, take a cab or catch a bus near the Fybeco sign on 9 de Octubre near Rocafuerte. If you're looking for nightlife, drive on over to Bahía de Caráquez.

THE SOUTHERN LOWLANDS

If it's beaches you're looking for, you've come to the right place. In the Southern Lowlands, you'll find coastline galore, from tranquil, secluded inlets to surfer towns where the lifestyle is governed by the mantra: surf hard by day, party harder once the sun goes down. Experience the unique natural beauty of the Southern Lowlands firsthand at the reserves, or combine seashore with skyline by visiting sunny Guayaquil, Ecuador's economic center. This big city has recently undergone a complete makeover, and now its colorful neighborhoods are a popular destination for travelers looking to experience the culture of a southern city.

HIGHLIGHTS OF THE SOUTHERN LOWLANDS

RIDE the waves in the surf-town of **Montañita** (see p. 249).

CRUISE past whales at Isla de la Plata, in **Puerto López** (see below).

IMMERSE yourself in the cultured, cosmopolitan vibe of **Guayaquil** (see p. 263).

PUERTO LÓPEZ   ☎ 05

Once just a quiet fishing village, Puerto López (pop. 15,500) has recently taken advantage of its natural treasures to become a popular coastal destination. Most come to explore nearby Parque Nacional Machalilla (see p. 243), whose tropical dry forest, cloud forest, offshore wildlife, and archaeological sites offer a unique look at coastal history and ecology. Perhaps most responsible for the town's slow but steady stream of tourists is its proximity to famed Isla de la Plata, touted by locals as the "poor man's Galápagos." Tours to these two destinations are just the beginning. Each summer (July-Oct.), the Humboldt Current brings cooler water and gray skies, creating an ideal habitat for the nearly 200 humpback whales that come to the coast to mate. The tail-smacking, high-jumping whales are every bit as spectacular as the dozens of tour agents promise. Puerto López is bound to see an explosion of tourist activity in the next few years; plans to pave more roads and clean up the *malecón* are testament to the town's inevitable transformation. But for now, the dozens of fishing boats hugging the shore and *motos* shuttling villagers around town speak to an undeniably traditional and independent way of life.

◨ TRANSPORTATION

Buses: All buses come and go from the corner of Machalilla and Córdova. To: **Guayaquil** (4hr.; 5, 7, 9am, 1, 4pm; US$6.50); **Jipijapa** (1½hr., every 30min. 6:30am-7pm, US$1.50); **Manta** (2hr.; 6:15, 10, 11:45am, 1:30pm; US$2.25); **Quito** (11hr.; 5, 6:30, 9am, 6:30, 8:30pm; US$12); **Salinas** (2½hr., every 30min. 6:30am-6:30pm, US$4) via **Salango** (10min., US$0.25), **Puerto Rico/Alandaluz** (15min., US$0.40); **Montañita** (1hr., US$1.50); **Valdivia** (1¼hr., US$1.65); **Ayangue** (1½hr., US$1.80); **Santa Elena** (2hr., US$3.50); and **La Libertad** (2¼hr., US$5).

Motos: Resemble rickshaws and make quick trips around town. US$0.50-1.

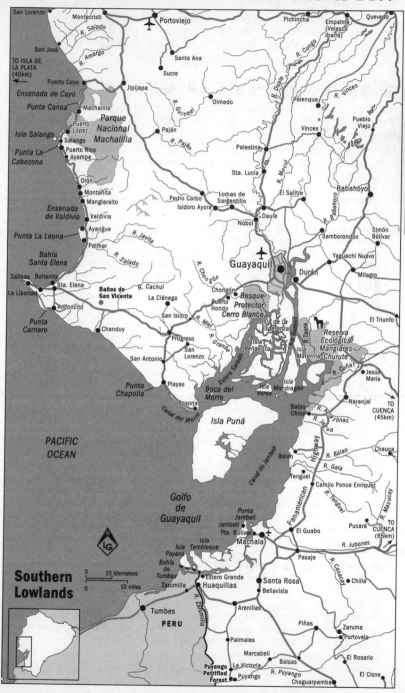

**Southern
Lowlands**

Bikes: Machalilla Tours (see **Tours,** below) and the **white house** next door to Hotel Pacifico rent bikes. US$1 per hr., US$5 per day.

Kayaks: Machalilla Kayak, a booth set up on Malecón, rents kayaks. 30min. US$2 per person, 1hr. US$3, 2hr. US$5, 4hr. US$9, 1 day US$14.

◄► 🛈 ORIENTATION AND PRACTICAL INFORMATION

The principal road in town, **Machalilla,** continues north to Jipijapa and south along the coast to La Libertad. Buses stop on the corner of **Córdova** and **Machalilla,** just north of the church and market. Four blocks west of Machalilla, Córdova intersects **Malecón,** which runs the length of the beach.

Tourist Office: Puerto López has no official tourist office, but English- and Spanish-speaking Kevin and Diane at **Whale Café** (see **Food,** p. 242) know almost everything about the town and nearby national park. The **Parque Nacional Machalilla Headquarters,** on Alfaro, just east of Machalilla and near the market, provides extensive park info via an interactive English/Spanish computer program. The office also sells park entrance tickets. Open M-Sa 8am-5pm, Su 8am-1pm.

Tours: Dozens of companies line Malecón and Córdova and offer almost identical tours to Parque Nacional Machalilla, whale-watching excursions, horseback riding trips, and more. Most guides speak Spanish only; ask if translators or English-speaking guides are available. During high season (June-Sept.), whale-watching is combined with trips to Isla de la Plata. Groups of fishermen may offer inexpensive whale-watching trips as well; be sure to see the boat and make sure it has 2 engines (in case 1 dies) and life jackets before committing. If you prefer to whale-watch only and skip the Isla de la Plata tour, agencies will let you join their boat tours and snorkel around Isla de la Plata instead of disembarking (US$20-25); bargain for a better price. Alternatively, arrange a whale-watching trip from Salinas (p. 254) or through Casa Blanca in Montañita (see p. 249). The following tour agencies are considered reputable in Puerto López. Prices listed below for trips to any part of Parque Nacional Machalilla do not include park entrance fees. Be warned that most tour agencies accept cash only.

Machalilla Tours (☎2304 206 or 2300 206; machalillatours@yahoo.com), on Malecón just north of Córdova. English- and Spanish-speaking Mayra and Fausto run a popular and friendly agency. Winston is a highly recommended Isla de la Plata guide. Horseback-riding trip from US$30, fishing/snorkeling at Isla Salango US$30, Isla de la Plata tour US$30, 2-day camping trip to Agua Blanca and San Sebastián US$70. Cash or traveler's checks accepted. Open daily 7:30am-8pm.

Mantaraya (☎2462 872 or 2300 233; www.advantageecuador.com), on Malecón just south of Córdova. Isla de la Plata tour US$30, fishing trip to Isla Salango US$35, 1-day horseback ride to Agua Blanca and San Sebastián US$45, dives from US$95. Open daily 8am-7pm.

Hotel Pacífico (☎2300 133 or 2300 147), on Malecón near Lascano, owns two boats that sail to Isla de la Plata. Nestor Machán, a guide who works for the hotel, arranges good hiking/camping trips to San Sebastián. US$30, 8-person min. AmEx/DC/MC/V.

Exploratur/Exploramar (☎2604 123; www.exploratur.com), at Malecón and Córdova, is a certified and reputable diving center. English spoken. Ask about discounts for groups. Daytrips from US$100. Open daily 8am-8pm.

Currency Exchange: Banco del Pichincha, at Córdova and Machalilla, charges a 2-3% commission to exchange traveler's checks and offers V cash advances. Get there first thing in the morning to avoid the long lines. Open M-F 9am-5pm. Jipijapa (see p. 247) has the nearest ATM.

Work/Volunteer Opportunities: Several tour agencies seek foreigners to translate for their Spanish-speaking staff and guides; English and German are in the most demand. Ask around to trade your bilingual abilities for a free or reduced-price tour.

Language Schools: La Lengua (☎2501 271; www.la-lengua.com), offers 1-on-1 Spanish lessons (US$6 per hr.) with homestays and/or volunteer work. (See p. 80.)

Laundromat: Bosque Marino, on Malecón near the post office. Up to 4kg. US$3.50.

Emergency: ☎911.

Police: ☎2604 101 . On Machalilla and Atahualpa.

Medical Services: Centro de Salud de Puerto López, at Machalilla and Lascano. Open M-F 8am-3:30pm.

Telephones: Pacifictel, at Machalilla and Alfaro. Local calls US$0.18 per min. No international calls. Open M-Sa 8am-9:30pm. A **booth** next to Farmacia Edicíta, on Machalilla, charges US$0.80 per min. for international calls. Available daily 8:30am-10pm.

Internet: Sunset Cybercafé, on Córdova, just west of Machalilla. US$1 per 30min. Open M-Sa 8:30am-10pm, Su 8:30am-9pm.

Post Office: On Malecón, just south of Córdova. Open M-F 8am-noon and 2-6pm, Sa-Su 8am-3pm.

Puerto López

♠ ACCOMMODATIONS
Hostal Sol Inn, 5
Hostal Villa Colombia, 12
Hostería Itapóa, 4
Hostería Mandála, 1
Yubarta Hostal , 2

🍴 FOOD
Arazá Restaurante
Vegetariano, 6
Bellitalia, 3
Carmita Bar
Restaurant, 9
Geo's Grill & Bar, 7

Restaurant
Spondylus, 10
Tsunami, 8
Whale Café, 15

🌙 NIGHTLIFE
Bar Aqa, 14
Clandestino Bar, 11
Resaca Bar, 13

ACCOMMODATIONS

A wide selection of cheap lodgings, most of which are on or near the beach, provides budget travelers with many good options. Be warned that "hot" showers in the cheapest places are usually tepid at best. It's best to makes reservations during the high season (July-Sept.) if you're keen on staying at a specific hostel.

Hostal Sol Inn (hostal_solinn@hotmail.com). Just few years old, Sol Inn is becoming a backpacker favorite with its reasonable rates, and laid-back atmosphere. Bamboo-lined rooms sport comfy beds, bedside lamps, and clean warm showers, although the shared baths and outdoor sinks lack privacy. Guests have access to an outdoor kitchen and social lounge area. Book exchange and laundry (US$4 per load). French and English spoken. Singles US$5, with private bath US$8; doubles US$8/$12. ❷

Yubarta Hostal (☎2604 130; enriquea61@yahoo.com or alegria_p@hotmail.com), toward the northern end of the beach on Malecón, about a 10min. walk from Córdova. Husband and wife owners are former national park guides and are restoring the mangrove area surrounding the simple but colorful bamboo cabañas. All rooms have spotless hot private showers, and guests can use the pool table and kitchen. English and French spoken. High season US$7, low season US$5. ❷

Hostería Itapóa (☎09 9843 042). Walk north along Malecón, make a right on Calderón, and take the 1st left. A few blocks removed from the main tourist strip, Itapóa offers charming cabañas around a grassy courtyard. Turkish bath, hydromassage, hot private showers, and hammocks explain why this Brazilian-owned place is popular with travelers. Low-season breakfast included. High season US$7, low season US$5. ❷

Hostal Villa Colombia (☎2604 105 or 2604 189), 1 block up Córdova, away from the beach, on the right. Colombia offers simple but clean rooms with hot private showers, kitchen use, and 2 of the friendliest owners ever. Ask about discounts for long stays and dorms for groups of 4 or more. Dorms US$4; singles US$5; doubles US$10. ❷

Hostería Mandála (☎/fax 2604 181; www.hosteriamandala.com), at the northern end of the beach on Malecón, a 15min. walk from Córdova. Enormous "whale fins of peace" greet travelers to this rustic and quiet beachfront lodge. The 21 comfortable cabañas dot a lush garden and include fans, high-ceilings, wood floors, hot private showers, and balconies. Excellent restaurant (breakfast US$2.50-3.50), relaxing music, dartboard, and lots of musical instruments available for use complete the luxuriously laid-back mood. English, German, Italian, French, and Swedish spoken. Ask for discounts in low season and for long stays. US$15. ❹

🚻 FOOD

For such a small town, Puerto López is blessed with a number of good, albeit somewhat expensive and touristy restaurants; most line the Malecón. Thrifty travelers hoping to take advantage of the guest kitchen in their hostal should bring most ingredients with them, as Puerto López has no sizable supermarket. Fresh fruits, veggies, and meats, however, are sold at the produce market on Machalilla.

🍴 **Bellitalia** (☎2771 361), 3 blocks to the right when arriving at the beach from Córdova; follow the blue arrow signs from Malecón. Though out of the way, this romantic restaurant is a diamond in the rough. Classic Italian food and fabulous homemade specialties, prepared by Italian natives, are served by candlelight in the garden's gazebo. Big salads US$2.70-3.60, pastas US$4.30-5, vegetarian lasagne or cannoli US$6, seafood dishes US$7. Open daily 6-10pm. ❸

Whale Café, left off Córdova onto Malecón and a few blocks down on the left. Fresh-baked bread, homemade pizza crust, real tomato sauce, and fresh romaine lettuce shipped all the way from Manta lend a special, wholesome touch to the salads (US$3.25-4.50), pizzas (small US$3.25-4.75, large US$6.50-9.50), and amazing sandwiches—try the avocado, tomato, and cheese combo (US$3). American owners Diane and Kevin have tons of info about the national park and also make killer breakfasts. Apple cinnamon or banana pancakes US$3, veggie omelette US$3. Book exchange. Open daily 8am-9:30pm. ❷

Carmita Bar Restaurant (☎2300 149), on Malecón just south of Córdova. One of Puerto López's first restaurants, Carmita has been serving first-class *típico* meals and seafood for over 30 years. Long-time patrons recommend the shrimp and octopus omelettes (US$4-5) and spondylus in peanut sauce (US$6). Open daily 8am-10pm. AmEx/DC/MC/V. ❷

Arazá Restaurante Vegetariano, on Córdova near Malecón. This veggie-friendly gem was inspired by the vegetarian students learning Spanish at the owners' language school. Grab 1 of the 4 wooden tables and stuff yourself with big portions of meat-free delights. Several fish and shrimp entrees (US$3-4) also available. Breaded cauliflower with broccoli and almond sauce US$3, Thai curry lentil US$3.50, samosas US$2.50, salads US$2.80-3, pastas US$3.50, crepes US$1.50. Open daily 1-10pm. ❷

Restaurant Spondylus (☎2604 128), at Córdova and Malecón. One of the town's most popular restaurants, frequented by locals and travelers alike. Try its namesake dish, regional specialty spondylus (US$6). Other entrees US$2-5. Open daily 8am-11pm. ❶

Geo's Grill and Bar, on Córdova before Malecón, next door to Arazá. The open-air grill at this touristy patio restaurant breathes aromas of grilled meat all the way to the beach. The grilled shrimp with wine and garlic (US$8) is to die for, but burgers (US$2-3), kebabs (US$1-2), and sandwiches (US$2.50-3) are a bit easier on the wallet. Veggie and avocado Geos, one of the signature plates, is a fresh and tasty meat alternative. Beer US$1.20-1.50, huge shakes US$2, cocktails US$2.5-3. Open daily 11am-3pm and 5-11pm. ❷

Tsunami, on Córdova, near Montalvo. Red walls, bamboo finishings, wooden benches, and swings create a casual romantic atmosphere. Good service and simple but well-made dishes. *Ceviche* US$2.50-4, pastas US$2.50-4.50, grilled and breaded fish US$2.50, shrimp rice US$3.50. Open Tu-Su 6pm-midnight. ❷

👁 🗔 SIGHTS AND BEACHES

Puerto López is best known as the gateway to **Parque Nacional Machalilla** (see p. 243). Multiple competing tour companies (see **Orientation and Practical Information,** p. 240) offer trips to the park—including **Isla de la Plata** (situated 40km off the coast of Puerto López), and **humpback whales** (late June-Sept.)—at standardized prices. **Exploratur** and **Mantaraya** also offer **scuba** packages (see p. 240). If you'd rather keep your feet on solid ground, visit Puerto López's own mediocre **beach** or the much more popular and picturesque **Los Frailes** (see p. 246), up the coast in Parque Nacional Machalilla. The park's most popular hike is a two-day camping or one-day horseback ride trip to **Cerro San Sebastián,** just beyond Agua Blanca (see p. 245). The only real site in town is great for anyone with a little rusty on their whale trivia—Hostería Mandála (see **Accommodations,** p. 242) has posted about 100 interesting facts about humpback whales in four languages. The wooden signs begin at the northern end of the beach near the hotel, lining the dirt path to the main road.

🔊 NIGHTLIFE

Most of Puerto López's bars are relatively new and cater unabashedly to tourists. During the low season, the town can be dull, but weekends during the high season (July-Sept.) are lively, salsa-filled occasions of endless Pilsners and caiprinhas.

Clandestino Bar, at Córdova and Montalvo. Dread-locked bartenders serve strong caiprinhas (US$2) and Pilsners (US$1) to mingling young tourists and locals before inviting them to salsa. Lively music keeps the party going late into the night on weekends. Open daily 8pm-late.

Resaca Bar, on the beach, a few blocks south of Córdova. *Resaca* means "hangover" in Spanish, and that's exactly what you'll have after a few of the meticulously prepared and deceptively strong drinks at this boat-turned-bar. Caiprinhas and piña coladas are the specialties, but the cleverly named Sex on the Boat and López Libre are good standbys. Relatively quiet most nights, but Resaca's occasional parties do not disappoint, and flaming shots keep things interesting. If you dance the night away, stick around for pancakes and crepes (US$1-2) in the morning. Cocktails US$2-3. Open daily 8am-late.

Bar Aqa, on Malecón, opposite Resaca Bar. Totally laid-back vibe, with Bob Marley paintings and packs of smokes adorning the walls. Upstairs balcony is great for shooting a rack of pool or enjoying a beer (US$1-1.25), and the owner plans on serving inexpensive pizza-by-the-slice from lunch until late into the night. Open late, but doesn't get busy until about 10pm. On weeknights, the crowd is almost exclusively foreign. Cocktails US$2-3. Open daily 7pm-2 or 3am.

PARQUE NACIONAL MACHALILLA

Parque Nacional Machalilla preserves archaeological riches, one of the most pristine cloud forests in Ecuador, and the only protected virgin dry tropical forest in South America. Although the relatively arid, often colorless tropical forest may not be the most beautiful ecosystem around, its proximity to the widely fluctuating currents of the Pacific Ocean allows for remarkable biodiversity and a few of the most unspoiled beaches in the country. Even better, the park includes **Isla de la Plata,** an island offering some of the same experiences that have made Ecuador's other islands (e.g. the Galápagos) so popular for only a fraction of the cost. From late June to October, the park is also home to a large population of **humpback whales**, who seek the warmer coastal waters to mate and nurse their young.

Those who come to Machalilla after visiting some of Ecuador's other protected areas will be pleasantly surprised by the park's infrastructure, administration, and community involvement. Park offices and ranger stations are consistently staffed by knowledgeable guides, and littering rules are strictly enforced. Perhaps most impressive is the park's commitment to long-term conservation and ecotourism. Members of several of the native *comunas* (communities) within the park work as guides and participants in environmental education. Continual research explores avenues toward sustainable development and responsible tourism.

AT A GLANCE

AREA: 555 sq. km, 50km of coast, 20,000 hectares of ocean

CLIMATE: Tropical and misty year-round, but cooler and often overcast June-Dec.

HIGHLIGHTS: South America's only protected virgin dry tropical forest, cloud forests, excellent humpback whale-watching (June-Oct.), stunning beaches

GATEWAYS: Puerto López (see p. 243)

CAMPING: Though camping is allowed at San Sebastián and Agua Blanca (US$25 per day, including food, guide, and transportation), there are no facilities.

FEES: Land and island ticket US$20. Land only US$12, Isla de la Plata only US$15. All tickets valid for 5 days.

▐ PRACTICAL INFORMATION

Transportation: Trips to the park's main attraction, Isla de la Plata, are arranged by tour agencies in Puerto López (see **Orientation and Practical Information: Tours,** p. 240). Visiting Agua Blanca and Los Frailes, however, is easy without a guide. From Puerto López, take a Jipijapa-bound bus (every 30min. 6:30am-6:30pm, US$0.25) to the park entrance of Agua Blanca (about 5km north of Puerto López) or Los Frailes (about 8km north of Puerto López). From the park offices on the highway, walk 3-5km to the sites. Alternatively, pay a truck in Puerto López to drive you to Agua Blanca (about US$5) or Los Frailes (about US$8). The truly independent traveler can easily bike to both sites; for bike rental info, see **Puerto López: Transportation,** p. 238.

Park Information: The primary source of park information and maintenance is at the **Parque Nacional Machalilla Headquarters** in Puerto López (see p. 240). Open M-Sa 8am-5pm, Su 8am-1pm.

Maps: The park **headquarters** (see above) has a large map of the park and its trails but no small maps for tourists.

Supplies: Trekkers who plan to climb Cerro San Sebastián or to hike inland into the forest will need rain gear, good hiking boots, and strong insect repellent. Guided camping tours to San Sebastián include food, water, and tents. You may also want to bring snorkeling equipment because agencies have a limited supply of varying quality.

Tours: Guides are required for trips to Isla de la Plata, San Sebastián, and the Agua Blanca ruins. Los Frailes is easily visited without a guide. Tour operators are based in Puerto López, (see **Orientation and Practical Information,** p. 240, for info).

◉ ▐ SIGHTS AND HIKING

Isla de la Plata is the most visited area of the national park, but those with limited funds can easily visit Los Frailes and Agua Blanca to see diverse landscapes within the park boundaries. Buses to Jipijapa from Puerto López can drop passengers off at the entrance to Agua Blanca and Los Frailes, where it is a 3-5km walk to the sites. A popular and more adventurous way to visit Agua Blanca and Los FraEiles is by bike (see **Puerto López: Transportation,** p. 238). If you leave Puerto López by bike by 9 or 10am, you can easily visit both sites and be back by 4 or 5pm.

AGUA BLANCA. Agua Blanca provides an interlude from wilderness education, with both an archaeological **museum** and the **ruins** of the Manteña culture (800-1532 A.D.), the last indigenous civilization prior to the Spanish Conquest. The small thatched-roof museum is run by the Agua Blanca community, distant ancestors of the ancient indigenous culture. Community guides conduct brief tours of the museum and hike (2.2km, 1½hr., Spanish only) through the ancient Indian ruins. A handful of glass displays with a few English explanations contain various Manteña artifacts, including stone seats and copper jewelery from funeral sites. The giant pottery **urns,** the first site along the trail, were only recently discovered in 1983 when an El Niño storm tore

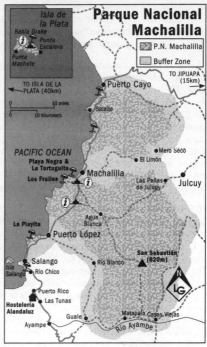

through the valley; the resulting erosion uncovered the ancient funerary urns. Unfortunately, the ruins, 30min. further along the trail, are a bit anticlimactic, since they were only basic foundations of Manteña homes and places of worship. The nondescript fragments that have been excavated, however, are almost perfectly aligned with the summer and winter solstices and reveal symbols of political and religious powers in the social hierarchy of the Manteña culture. Although the immense, green **sulfur pond** on the way back to town supposedly does wonders for soreness and clogged nasal passages, the murky waters may cause skin to smell of sewage and emit a strange green glow. Guides are required to visit the ruins. *(To visit Agua Blanca, take a Jipijapa-bound bus from Puerto López to the ranger station 5km north of town; from here it's a 5km walk down an unpaved road to the museum entrance. Alternatively, bike the relatively flat 10km or pay a camioneta or moto to take you from Puerto López (US$5). Museum US$3, including a guided tour.)*

SAN SEBASTIÁN HUMID FOREST. Hiking the trail (12km, 4-5hr.) from Agua Blanca to San Sebastián and back, traversing strikingly different climates from dry tropical to humid forest, requires two days and a guide. Many prefer to explore the cloud forest on horseback, however, which can be done in one day. The moderately difficult trail climbs through remnants of primary forest and transition zones to the 820m cloud forest summit. But what awaits at the end will make up for your sore rump—San Sebastián sports many **exotic species,** including tarantulas, giant centipedes, scorpions, coral snakes, howler monkeys, guantas (agoutis), anteaters, and numerous bird species. The forest is damp and misty year round, but May-Nov. are the wettest months. The trail can get muddy, so bring good hiking shoes, waterproof gear, and insect repellent. *(Guide required. Best guides are found in Puerto López; Nestor Machán at Hotel Pacífico and Angel Pincai at Bosque Marino (see **Puerto López:***

Orientation and Practical Information, p. 240) come highly recommended. They can provide information about the current state of the trails or guide you themselves. Rates are usually cheaper if you bring your own food and go in a group of 2 or more people. Horseback tours from US$45, 2-day hiking/camping tours from US$70.)

LAS GOTERAS. An alternate way to explore the humid forest without the time commitment and expense is to visit Las Goteras. The entire trip (4-5hr.) is relatively difficult; the path to the forest is almost all uphill, and the forest itself is a slow trek through thick, slippery mud. However, the end offers gorgeous views of the surrounding mountains and, on a clear day, the ocean below. Trees become bigger and more lush on the way up the mountain, and the humid forest hosts a variety of fascinating flora and fauna: coffee and mango trees, bright butterflies, plentiful birds, and maybe a monkey or two. *(Las Goteras trails are currently closed but may be open for trekkers soon. Inquire at the Parque Nacional Machalilla Headquarters about the current state of the trails. David at the Whale Café in Puerto López and Nestor Machán at Hotel Pacífico are also good resources for info about these trails.)*

LOS FRAILES. These secluded shores, 3km north of the entrance to Agua Blanca, add even more diversity to the national park's landscape. The excursion starts at the Los Frailes gate on the road from Puerto López. A park ranger here will ask to see your entrance ticket—be sure to bring it with you. About 100m past the gate, the road forks. The dirt road on the left continues 3km to Los Frailes (30min.). The narrower trail to the right (25min.) leads to the tiny rock cove of **Playa Negra,** a small beach layered with black sands and lapped by calm waters perfect for **snorkeling.** From December to April, sea turtles also visit to nest in the dark sandy shores. Five minutes farther along the trail lies **La Tortuguita,** a cove surrounded by curious rock configurations and soft sand. Be careful while swimming at Tortuguita because of the strong currents and low line of rocks. From there, two paths—one easy and low, the other overgrown and high—lead to the immense third beach, **Los Frailes,** one of Ecuador's cleanest and most picturesque beaches. The golden arc of sand is perfect for sunbathing and cool dips in the tranquil waters. The high road also leads to a **mirador** with spectacular views of the ocean. Guides are available in Puerto López (US$15), but are, for the most part, unnecessary. *(Take a Jipijapa-bound bus from Puerto López (about 10min., every 30min. 6:30am-6:30pm, US$0.25) to the entrance; from there, it's about a 30min. walk to the beach. Alternatively, rent a bike from Puerto López (see **Puerto Lopez: Transportation,** p. 238) and ride the relatively flat 13km to the beach. Camping is not allowed, but public toilets are available. Beaches and ranger station open daily 8:30am-4pm.)*

ISLA DE LA PLATA. The *plata* (silver) that gives this island its name refers to the legendary treasure of notorious pirate Sir Francis Drake. Supposedly, after "liberating" his booty from the Spanish galleons, Drake hid it somewhere in the sea surrounding this 12 sq. km island, which lies 40km offshore of Puerto López. Today, the island is more popular with tourists admiring its pristine natural environment and diverse wildlife than with scavengers in search of lost treasure.

 The boat journey from Puerto López to Isla de la Plata takes two solid hours, and the sea swells are often large and turbulent. Anyone even slightly susceptible to motion sickness should take appropriate precautionary measures.

Although the Galápagos Islands offer the best opportunities for booby-watching, Isla de la Plata is a close second. The boobies in question include the outlaw **masked booby,** the comical **blue-footed booby,** and the small but abundant **red-**

footed booby. In addition to boobies, La Plata has the largest colony of frigate birds in the world. During mating season, the pitch-black male frigates inflate the flashy red pouch under their skin and wait on the dry saltbush branches to attract a female. From April to November the rare **waved albatrosses** wing in for mating season, and perform spectacularly unique mating dances and beak-warring rituals. Aside from the birds, a small offshore colony of geriatric **sea lions** is occasionally spotted sunbathing, and from July to September, the waters teem with **humpback whales.** The whales, best seen on the boat ride from Puerto López, migrate here from the Antarctic to mate in warmer waters. From **Bahía Drake,** the island's only inlet and dock, two **trails** (2-3hr. with stops) head up hills, over dales, and through nesting sites. Sendero Punta Machete (3½km), the most frequently traversed trail, wanders through several colonies of blue- and red-footed boobies, while Sendero Punta Escaleras (5km) offers better chances to see the magnificent frigates. The standard daytrip package includes guide, food, and snorkeling (US$25). Sturdy shoes are recommended for either trail, although you should bring sandals or go barefoot for the wet landing on the beach. (Guide required. The only way to visit Isla de la Plata is on a tour, and most tour agencies are in Puerto López. Machalilla Tours and Mantaraya (see p. 240) are recommended. The standard daytrip tour includes a sail to the island, a light snack, a few hours' hike around the island, a brief chance to snorkel, lunch, and a sail back to Puerto López. From June-September, these trips often include whale-watching. Tours are US$30 per day.

JIPIJAPA
☎ 05

Unfortunately, most of the fun associated with Jipijapa (pop. 80,000) comes from saying its name, pronounced "heepy-hoppa." Situated 60km south of Manta, Jipijapa chiefly serves as a transportation hub for travelers shuttling back and forth to the sandy shores of communities such as Puerto López and Montañita. Other than the numerous buses that leave from its terminal and the ATM in the central plaza, Jipijapa offers little of interest to visitors.

Should you inexplicably find yourself staying overnight, try **Hostal Jipijapa ❸,** at Santistevan and Eloy Alfaro. From the central plaza with the bank on your left, walk up Sucre three blocks, turn left on Santistevan, and walk five blocks to Eloy Alfaro. The hostel provides clean, comfortable rooms with fans and hot private baths. (☎ 2601 365. Singles US$10, with A/C US$12; doubles US$14/$16.)

Most services are located around Jipijapa's central Plaza, which is squared off by Sucre, Colón, Bolívar, and 9 de Octubre. The **bus terminal** is a few kilometers west of the *centro*, near the traffic circle. To get there, take a colectivo (US$0.25) or taxi (US$1) from Bolívar. From there, **buses** leave for: Guayaquil (every 30min. 6:30am-7:30pm, US$5); Manta (1¼hr., every 30min. 6am-6pm, US$1.25); Puerto López (1½hr., every 30min. 5am-6pm, US$2) via Puerto Cayo (1hr., US$1); Quito (8hr.; 6:15, 10:15am, 8:15pm; US$8). **Banco del Pichincha,** on Sucre between Colón and 9 de Octubre, has a 24hr. Cirrus/Nexus/Plus **ATM** and offers V cash advance. (☎ 601 855. Open M-F 8:30am-3:30pm.) The **Tía Supermarket,** on Colón between Sucre and Bolívar, has a **Western Union** branch. (Open M-Sa 9am-6pm, Su 10am-2pm.) In an **emergency,** dial ☎ 101. **Fharmaton,** at Bolívar and 9 de Octubre, is a conveniently located pharmacy. (☎ 2600 510. Open daily 8am-9pm.) Make phone calls at **PacificTel,** whose main branch is at Bolívar and 9 de Octubre. (Local calls US$0.15 per min., regional and national calls from US$0.18 per min., to US and Spain US$0.25 per min., to rest of world US$0.36-0.90 per min. Open daily 8am-10pm.) Find **Internet** access at **Zona Cero Cyber,** at Santistevan and 10 de Agosto. (US$1.40 per hr. Open daily 9am-9pm.) The **post office** is behind the church. (☎ 2602 011. Open M-F 9am-1pm and 2-5pm.)

PUERTO CAYO ☎05

Just beyond the Parque Nacional Machalilla boundaries slumbers the fishing village of Puerto Cayo, a miniature and less attractive version of Puerto López, 15km south. Although Puerto Cayo has a fair number of accommodations, most travelers prefer to stay in Puerto López, from which access to the national park is much more convenient. The small town's dubious attraction is its beach, which sees more fishing boats and litter than swimmers or sunbathers.

Buses from **Puerto López** (30min., every 30min. 6:30am-7pm, US$0.50) pass through Puerto Cayo before arriving in Jipijapa (1hr., US$1). Most activity and business takes place on or near the *malecón*. The town lacks most practical amenities; stock up on cash, medicine, and snacks in Puerto López or Jipijapa if you're planning on spending some time here. **Residencial Zavala ❷**, on the *malecón*, has good budget lodgings. Rooms are small but clean and have cold private baths. A view of the ocean or a meal at the attached, inexpensive restaurant may spruce up your stay. (US$7 per person.) One of better places to stay in town is **Hostal los Frailes ❹**, at Calle 3 and Malecón. Sparkling, tiled rooms have hot private baths, TVs, A/C, and mini-bars, and most have sea views. The friendly hostel also offers tours, a guard, and a restaurant. (☎2616 014. Breakfast included. Sa-Su singles US$20; doubles US$28. M-F 10% discount.) Most of Puerto Cayo's modest *comedores* specialize in fish, much of which is brought in fresh from the sea the very morning it's served. Locals recommend **La Cabaña ❶**, a block from the beach, for slightly expensive but excellent fish, shrimp, octopus, and spondylus dishes. (Entrees US$3-8. Open M-Sa 11am-10pm, Su 5-10pm.) A handful of other less expensive restaurants along the *malecón* serve seafood and other *típico* fare.

SALANGO ☎05

The quiet and friendly fishing village of Salango rests 6km south of Puerto López, concealing a huge collection of archaeological artifacts beneath its sands. Six pre-Hispanic communities thrived here for nearly 5000 years and left behind remnants of everyday life, including jewelry, artwork, and ceramics. Although much remains to be excavated, many items now fill Salango's archaeological museum, **Museo a los Balseros del Mar del Sur,** which sits near the northern end of the beach. Glass encasements with Spanish explanations display various ancient artifacts from Salango, Isla de la Plata, Puerto López, Machalilla, Río Chico, and Agua Blanca. (Museum open daily 9am-noon and 1-5pm. US$1, students and children US$0.50).

Salango's tradition as a seafaring village is echoed in the activities it offers visitors: **scuba diving, snorkeling, fishing,** and **dining.** Several tour agencies in Puerto López (see **Puerto López: Practical Information, Tours,** p. 240) arrange daytrips to **Isla Salango,** just off the coast, where the first three of those activities are popular. After fishing or swimming amidst Salango's underwater wonders, many visitors complete the day at one of Salango's famed seafood restaurants. **El Delfín Mágico ❷**, a few blocks down the street parallel to the Malecón, near the park, is the most well-known. A mind-boggling variety of seafood, from shrimp and *dorado* (dolphin fish) to the more adventurous octopus and *perceves* (gooseneck barnacles) are prepared using the secret recipes of the restaurant's owner and local celebrity, Sr. Alfred Pincay. Locals recommend the spondylus in peanut sauce (US$6.50) and the lobster (US$12), prepared any way you like it—grilled, broiled, breaded, fried, in garlic sauce, or in lime juice. (☎2780 291. Entrees US$3-12. Open daily 8am-8pm, sometimes until 9pm.) A quieter and slightly less expensive option is the beachfront **La Isla Restaurant ❶**, on the Malecón. (☎2780 282. Fish US$2-3, spondylus *ceviche* US$7, grilled lobster US$10. Open daily 8am-10pm.) La Libertad-bound **buses** from Puerto López can pass Salango (10min., every 20min., US$0.25).

HOSTERÍA AND PUEBLO ECOLÓGICO ALANDALUZ ☎05

Designed as a garden-filled village, Pueblo Ecológico Alandaluz is a gorgeous beach resort 600m south of the tiny village of Puerto Rico, just off the road between Puerto López and Montañita. In 1998 it was rated one of the seven best socially responsible ecotourism projects in the world. Constructed of rapidly growing, locally cultivated plants like bamboo and *caña de guadúa*, Alandaluz is a temple of eco-friendliness and one of Ecuador's most successful examples of sustainable development. A 10min. walk through the well-kept gardens provides an excellent feel for the place, and the long, wide, beautiful **beaches** are amazingly relaxing. The reserve's complex also offers a children's play room, tours to Isla de la Plata, trekking information, horseback riding, mountain biking, and opportunities to participate in local environmental projects. Most popular with ecologically minded visitors is the tour to **Cantalapiedra,** a nearby **organic farm** from which Alandaluz's chefs procure their organic vegetables and aromatic coffee. (4hr.; US$18 per person, including lunch; min. 2-person.) Alandaluz is 6km south of Salango; **buses** running along the coast between La Libertad and Puerto López will drop you off. From **Puerto López,** it is a 20min. ride (US$60).

Visitors can make their contribution to preserving the environment by frequenting the *baños ecológicos* (ecological bathrooms), where waste is mixed with sawdust and dried leaves to speed up decomposition. All of the luxuriously rustic cabins have cheerful curtains, mosquito nets, bamboo bed frames, and comfortable mattresses. The **lodge ➎** also includes special suites; **Cabaña del Árbol,** the honeymoon suite, is built into a tree, while **Los Torres** has a spectacular ocean view. Most rooms have private baths, but the few common facilities are impeccably maintained and have high-pressure, hot water showers. (☎2780 686 or 2780 690; alandaluz@interactive.net.ec. Laundry, air-dry only, US$3.50 per load. Reservations recommended July-Aug. Camping US$4 per person. Singles in exterior cabins US$14, in garden with eco-toilets or in *huerta* cabins with conventional toilets US$24, on beachfront with eco-toilets or in garden cabins US$25; doubles US$23/$30/$37; triples US$32/$38/$48; quads US$43/$48/$60. Extra adult US$9, extra child US$6. Ask about ISIC discounts. AmEx/DC/MC/V.)

Relax at Alandaluz's cozy bamboo **bar** (open daily 7-11pm) or savor vegetable and seafood dishes at the first-class **restaurant ➍.** The chef uses an oven constructed of hardened fecal matter to create his pride and joy, *viudo de mariscos* (US$6.50), an enormous serving of baked seafood inside a bamboo cane; the vegetarian *viudo* (US$4.15) is equally scrumptious. (Breakfast US$2.50-4, set 4-course lunch/dinner menu US$6, house specialities US$5-12. Open daily 8am-9pm.)

MONTAÑITA ☎04

If you want to party, this is the place to get down and sandy. Montañita throbs with the wave-crashing vibes of its seasonal international surfing crowds. During the high-season (Dec.-Apr.), streets become a barefoot parade, flowing with long hair and bronzed torsos. The town calms down considerably in low-season, but a band of die-hard surfers resides here year-round. While days are spent in the surf, nights are full of beach parties, bonfires, and general seaside debauchery. Legends of this revelry are too intriguing to ignore; Montañita attracts quite a bohemian crowd. Nomadic artisans, nostalgic hippies, and trippy gringos mingle with locals, making for an unusual demographic medley.

▮ TRANSPORTATION

Buses: From the bus stop on the highway outside the *pueblo,* buses run to: **Jipijapa** (2½hr., every 20min. 6am-6pm, US$2.50) via **Puerto Rico** (45min., US$1.25), **Salango** (50min., US$1.25), and **Puerto López** (1hr., US$1.50); **La Libertad** and **Salinas** (1½hr., every 20min. 6am-6pm, US$2.20) via **Ayangue** (50min., US$1) and **Valdivia** (30min., US$0.75).

SOUTHERN
LOWLANDS

Vans: Fly to Montañita (☎ 2680 457 or cell 09 9448 408; flytomontanita@hotmail.com) offers daily direct service between Montañita and **Guayaquil** in A/C vans.

ORIENTATION AND PRACTICAL INFORMATION

Montañita is comprised of two sectors separated by a 1km walk down the beach or highway. To the south, the lively and tourist-packed **Pueblo** houses most of the town's residents, hotels, and restaurants. Here, **Rocafuerte** runs from the highway to the beach and **15 de Mayo,** perpendicular to Rocafuerte, is the last street before the sand. Few locals, however, know or use the street names. A small **plaza** and **church** on 15 de Mayo are 100m from Rocafuerte. Montañita's quieter northern sector is known as **La Punta** and has just a few tranquil accommodations. A dirt path runs from the highway to the beach, where swells are popular with surfers.

Tours: Montañita Extreme (☎ 09 9446 363) has 2 offices, one on the right side of the highway just north of the *pueblo* and the other opposite its jointly owned hostel, La Tierra Prometida (see **Accommodations,** p. 251). Offers combined whale-watching and snorkeling tours mid.-June to Sept. (3-4hr., US$25), horseback riding tours (2hr., from US$15), ATV rentals (US$10 per hr.), and ATV tours to a nearby waterfall (3-4hr., US$30-35). Cash only. **La Casa Blanca** (see **Accommodations,** p. 251) offers whale-watching tours from Salinas (US$30 includes 1 night's stay).

Currency Exchange: There are **no banks or ATMs** in Montañita; La Libertad (see p. 257), 1½hr. south, offers the closest and most comprehensive financial services. **Farmacia San José** (☎ 2901 201), next to Bell South on 15 de Mayo, occasionally exchanges traveler's checks for a 5% commission. Open daily 8am-11pm.

Supermarket: Comercial Alicia, on 15 de Mayo (open daily 6am-2am) and **Dispensa Ariana,** on Rocafuerte at 15 de Mayo (open daily 7:30am-midnight) stock the town's most comprehensive, although still limited, selection of basic foods and snacks.

Laundromat: Most hostels wash and dry laundry for US$3-4 per load. Otherwise, try **Lavandería Espumita,** on 15 de Mayo. Open M-Sa 9am-6pm; sporadic closings.

Emergency: ☎ 101.

Medical Services: Farmacia San José (☎ 2901 201), on 15 de Mayo. Open daily 8am-11pm.

Telephones: Bell South, on 15 de Mayo, near the church. Local calls US$0.18 per min.; to US, US$0.25 per min.; to Europe, from US$0.32 per min. Open M-Th and Su 8:30am-8:30pm, F-Sa 8:30am-10pm.

Internet Access: Cyber Club Montañita (☎ 2901 299), around the corner from Hostal Papaya (see **Accommodations,** p. 251). US$2 per hr. Open daily 9am-10pm. Look for upcoming Internet service at **Montañita Extreme** (see **Tours,** above) as well.

Post Office: There are **no post offices** in Montañita. Puerto López, 1hr. north, offers the closest postal services.

ACCOMMODATIONS

With so many cheap and comfortable accommodations, Montañita makes it easy to come for a night and stay for a week. Lodgings in the Pueblo are generally louder, especially on the weekends; La Punta offers more peace and quiet. Bamboo balconies, palm-thatched roofs, hammocks, hot water, and friendly surroundings are fairly standard. Prices and availability vary substantially from high to low season. Bargain for discounts if you're staying awhile, and call ahead for reservations December to April and July to September. **Beach houses** often offer rooms for rent; ask around or check the notice boards around town to see what's available.

IN THE PUEBLO

Hostal Papaya. Take the 2nd right off the main beach as you walk from the highway; the hostel is the last place on the right. Extremely friendly staff offers surfing lessons in the morning, plays movies and music all afternoon, serves drinks in the evening, and throws fantastic parties at night. Rooms are comfy with wood floors, balconies, hammocks, mosquito nets, fans, and hot private showers. 3rd-fl. patio and kitchen use are nice perks. English, Spanish, and French spoken. US$5 per person. ❷

La Tierra Prometida (☎2575 216 or 09 9446 363; hoteltierraprometida@hotmail.com), on the same street as Hostal Papaya. This backpacker magnet is the be-all and end-all of laid-back hangouts. Israeli management keeps its young clientele happy with neat rooms, eccentric paintings, a pool table, a TV room with videos, Playstation II, surfboard rental, hammocks, hot water, and an endless supply of fellow travelers. Most popular is the casual street-side cafe Hola Ola, where guests sit around, play cards, and drink beers all day. Staff also offers several tours through its travel agency, Montañita Extreme (see **Tours,** p. 250). M-F and Su US$5 per person, with private bath US$7; Sa US$8/$9. ❷

La Casa Blanca (☎2901 340; lacasablan@hotmail.com). Take the 2nd right as you walk on the main road toward the beach from the highway; it's the last place on the left opposite Hostal Papaya. This popular backpacker hangout has spacious rooms with high ceilings, balconies, fans, and hot private baths. Restaurant, TV, and multilingual owner. Surfboard rental US$2 per hr. Dorms with group of 4-6 people US$5, singles US$6-8; doubles US$10-16. ❷

El Centro del Mundo is the towering building at the end of Rocafuerte; make a right when you hit the beach, and the hostel is 50m down on the right. The laid-back sibling of the popular hostel of the same name in Quito (see p. 89). Simple rooms have wood floors and mosquito nets. Dorms consist of an open-air attic and rows of mattresses with netting. Hot baths. Beach-front patio/bar and pool table (US$1 per hr.) encourage evening socializing. Dorms US$4; rooms US$5 per person, with private bath US$6. Traveler's checks accepted. ❷

Hostal Restaurant Mauna Loa (jessiceherre@hotmail.com), just past Papaya Hostal and Casa Blanca. Cozy bamboo-lined rooms with hot private baths and individual balconies are almost identical to surrounding hostels, but the prices are usually a touch cheaper. Clean kitchen, TV room, and lots of plants to boot. High season US$5 per person; low season US$4. Discounts available for groups. ❷

OUTSIDE THE PUEBLO

La Casa del Sol (HI) (☎2901 302; www.casasol.com), in La Punta behind Kale (see **Food,** below). A bit pricey, but offers clean, spacious rooms, book exchange, surfing lessons, satellite TV, hot water, bar/restaurant, laundry, comfy hammock-filled patio, and kitchen use in a quiet, rustic setting. Breakfast included. Cabañas sleep up to 8, and an apartment is available for rent. Dorms from US$8; singles with bath US$18; doubles US$24; triples US$36. Discounts for longer stays. HI discount US$1. ❸

Kamala Hostería (☎09 9423 754; www.kamalahosteria.com), about 1km south of the *pueblo,* between Mangarato and Montañita. A funky, friendly hostel on a quiet stretch of beach and run by laid-back former backpackers who know how to have a good time. Ecuadorians and foreigners come in droves to Kamala's famous monthly, wild, full-moon parties, which feature international DJs, fire juggling, and beachside bonfires. Cozy wood and bamboo bungalows have mosquitos nets, hammocks, and hot showers. All are designed to receive maximum sunlight. Diving courses, horseback riding, surfing lessons, cable TV, volleyball net, and restaurant. Camping available. Dorms US$5 per person; private rooms from US$8 per person. ❷

Paradise South (☎2901 185; www.paradisesouthec.com). From the Pueblo, walk about 250m on the highway toward La Punta. A dirt path on the left reveals a large, grassy area surrounded by 18 neat, tiled cabañas with hot spotless baths and a rustic feel. Busy in high season, when a young, international crowd plays volleyball, pool, and ping-pong in the courtyard, or heads to the nearby beach. Satellite TV in reception area. Bar, laundry service, and some gym equipment available. Breakfast included. Check-out 1pm. High-season singles with shared bath US$8; doubles with private bath US$15, with A/C US$35. Low-season singles US$6; doubles US$12/$30. AmEx/MC. ❹

🍽 FOOD

Montañita's restaurants are sure to replenish calories lost in the waves. For vegetarians, the gentle menus are a refreshing break from *ceviche*-dodging.

■ **Chocolate Bar and Grill,** on 15 de Mayo, opposite the plaza. Montañita's warmest restaurant owners also serve some of the town's most scrumptious and filling meals. Everything from the garlic fried shrimp (US$3) and eggy fried bread (US$1.75) to the enormous veggie burger with potato wedges (US$2) hits the spot. The banana and chocolate crepes (US$2), are especially sublime. Board games, good music, and an occasional live guitar jam complete the charming mood in this small eatery. Open Tu-Su 9am-10:30pm. ❶

Kale (☎2755 717), on the beach in *La Punta*. Watch surfers rip it up on the waves as you devour burritos (US$3-4), tacos (US$2-3), monterrey jack enchiladas (US$3-4), chips and fresh guacamole (US$2) and more Tex-Mex favorites, right on the beach. Good tunes complement the ideal beachfront location. Open Tu-Su noon-10pm. Not open year-round, so call first. ❶

Magia Roja, in the *Pueblo* on Rocafuerte. With 9 different breakfast combos (US$1.50-2.80) and sweet-tooth satisfiers like pancakes with fruit and wine syrup and banana and chocolate pancakes (US$2.50), this cozy, bamboo walled cafe provides more than enough reason to scramble out of your mosquito-netted bed in the morning. But if you still feel like lounging, grab a seat on the cushions in front of the TV for breakfast in bed. Veggie or chicken burrito US$2, nachos and guacamole US$2.50, shrimp or squid in garlic sauce US$4-5. Open M and W-Su 9am-midnight. ❶

Pizzería Marea Alta, in the *Pueblo*. Take 2nd right walking on the main road toward the beach, and then take 1st left; restaurant is 50m down on the left, just past Alibabar. Argentinian chef whips up delicious, wood-oven pizzas (US$4-8) and fabulous Nutella crepes (US$2). Open daily noon-10pm, but closes occasionally in low season. ❸

Funky Monkey (☎217 5780 or 213 9613; www.funkymonkyhostal.com), in the *Pueblo* near La Tierra Prometida. Vegetarians rejoice! Tons of delicious meat-free entrees and snacks and delicious fruit-filled pancakes (US$1.50-2.50) for breakfast. Soy and lentil burgers US$1.50, burritos US$2-3. Open daily 8am-11pm. ❶

🏖 BEACHES AND OUTDOOR ACTIVITIES

Though famous for its ability to reel in party-philes worldwide, Montañita's most prized possession is its **surf;** an international surf competition is held here every March. The main beach extends for about 1km from the *Pueblo* to *La Punta*. The relatively calm beach at the *Pueblo* appeals to swimmers and sun bathers, while jagged cliffs and a strong rip at *La Punta* create one- to two-meter swells too rough for swimming but ideal for navigating on a surf board. Dozens of hostels in town offer surf lessons (2hr.; about US$15, including board rental) and rent boards (US$2 per hr. or US$10 per day). Keep in mind that at high tide, waves can swallow a good portion of the shore, and weather during the low season (June-Nov.) can be too overcast and chilly to enjoy the beach.

If the surf's *not* up, **El Muro de Escalada**, a 20m climbing wall, brings beachfront rock-climbing to Montañita. To get there, take the second right walking along the main road toward the beach, and make a left at Casa Blanca. (30min. US$1.50. Open daily 9am-9pm.) Thrill seekers can discuss **paragliding** with **Raúl** at the climbing wall about . (☎ 09 2175 296. 1 tandem fly US$20, 4-day course US$250.)

NIGHTLIFE

As night falls, surfers bring in their boards, throw on their sandals and shirts (or just the former), and get ready to party till dawn. Beach bonfires are the norm, and many hostels have been known to throw wild bashes. Kamala Hostería's (see p. 251) monthly full-moon parties lure revelers from all over the country.

Lotus (watersn@hotmail.com), in the *Pueblo*, right on the beach at the end of Rocafuerte. Canadian owner Natasha blends a hip, funky, lounge atmosphere with no-fuss food and spring break-like drinks. Huge bay windows overlooking the ocean make sunset happy hours (around 6:30pm) incredibly scenic. Popular late-night munchies include Cajun specialities and pub food like chicken fingers and burgers (US$3.50-7). BBQ ribs every Su. Shooters and jello shots US$1, martinis and piña coladas US$2. Free movies daily 8pm. Open daily 5pm-2am.

Mahalo (☎ 2913 106). Take 1st left walking along the main road toward the beach; it is just a few meters down on the right. Mahalo takes the nightlife prize. Its sandy floor, surf videos, and rock music make for a friendly, California-esque atmosphere. If you've got that competitive itch, challenge someone to a friendly game of pool—or Jenga. Mixed drinks US$2. Open daily 7pm-noon.

Alibabar (☎ 09 9674 142; maria_garcia_r@hotmail.com). Take 2nd right from the main road and a left before La Casa Blanca (see p. 251)—look for red-and-gold painted walls on the left. This bar/*discoteca* rents hookahs (US$3 per hr.), has a PacMan game at the bar, and plays groovy techno, alternative, and electronic beats. DJ on weekends. Beer US$1.50. Open daily 8pm-late.

VALDIVIA ☎ 04

This pint-sized coastal village, approximately 50km north of La Libertad, 5km north of Ayangue, and 15km south of Montañita, offers a bit of history and a small, quiet beach, frequented almost exclusively by fishermen. **Museo Valdivia**, just off the main road in the town center, is the town's only attraction. The small museum displays artifacts from the Valdivia people, who lived here from about 4200-1500 BC and were members of the oldest known American culture. To those unable to translate the Spanish signs, the numerous artifacts may appear to be nothing more than a collection of old rocks, but Spanish-speaking history and archaeology buffs may find the photographs from the excavation of the Valdivian ruins worthwhile. All visitors, however, will find the random *zapatería*, with a few pairs of high-heeled shoes, rather out of place. The museum occasionally sells locally made handicrafts. (Museum open daily 9am-6pm. US$0.80, children US$0.40.)

AYANGUE ☎ 04

Although Ayangue is just 5km south of Valdivia, a monstrous rocky point separates the two towns, making buses the only inter-village transportation (from Montañita US$0.85). From the "Welcome to Ayangue" signs where the bus will drop you off, **camionetas** (5min., US$0.25) will take you to town. Alternatively, walk 30min. westward along the same road. This road leads directly to Ayangue's **beach,** a picturesque cove surrounded by high cliffs and filled with fishing boats. The currents can get strong, but when the water is calm it's a beautiful swimming spot. During the low season, when weather elsewhere on the coast is drearily overcast, Ayangue's cove is often magically sunny. The town itself offers limited food and shelter; you're much better off staying in nearby Montañita. But if you need a break from tourist-laden beaches, spending a night or two at **Hostería Pangora ❹,** about a 50m walk up the beach from the main road, will do the trick. Unwind on the hammock-filled beachfront patio or in the TV lounge, or rent a bike, body-board, or kayak to explore the refreshing waters or nearby mountains. Each of the seven rooms has wooden floors and private baths (most with ocean views and hot water), and the friendly owners arrange four-, five-, and eight-day tours of sights and beaches along the coast. (☎2398 460 or 2916 126; www.galatravel.com.ec. Tours from US$50 per day. Rooms US$15 per person.) **Hostal Sol y Mar ❷,** on the side road right before the beach, is much cheaper but also more basic. Somewhat musty and small rooms have private cold baths and fans. (☎2916 014. US$5 per person.) You can find good, cheap food at the numerous *comedores* along the beach or at **Los Helechos ❶,** just past Hostal Sol y Mar, which serves *comida típica.* (Most plates US$1-3. Open daily 8am-10pm.)

SALINAS ☎04

At the western tip of the Santa Elena Peninsula, Salinas is the relatively posh getaway of Ecuador's wealthiest elites. While the rest of the country continues to struggle economically, Salinas brims with affluence. Packed with the luxurious vacation homes and condominiums of well-to-do Guayaquil residents, the town is hopping from December to April, when the many discos and restaurants that were asleep during low season suddenly spring to life. In addition to its cosmopolitan air, Salinas boasts fast food, a supermarket, a nearby shopping mall, Dunkin Donuts, and one of the prettiest beaches around. With a little creativity, the budget traveler can enjoy Salinas for only a pittance more than the rest of Ecuador.

▄▐ TRANSPORTATION AND PRACTICAL INFORMATION

The Salinas Yacht Club divides the beach into two sections: **Punta Chipipe** to the west and **San Lorenzo** to the east. Almost all accommodations, restaurants, and services line **Malecón** and **Gallo,** which run parallel to the beach in San Lorenzo. Salinas's streets are jumbled and poorly labeled, so ask around for directions.

Buses: La Libertad (see p. 257), Salinas's eastern neighbor, is the peninsula's transportation hub. In town, **Cooperativa Libertad Peninsular,** on Gonzalez and Las Palmeras, goes to **Guayaquil** (2¾hr., every 20min. 3:40am-8pm, US$3) via **Progreso** (1hr., US$1.50). Buses go around the clock to **Santa Elena** (25min., US$0.30) via **La Libertad** (20min., US$0.25) from Gallo. Just flag down one of the passing vehicles.

Tours: Several local companies offer tours.

Macchiavello Tours (☎2772 425), on Malecón in the Hotel Casino Calypsso, arranges daytrips to nearby museums and tourist attractions, whale-watching trips (US$25), and sportfishing tours. Guides speak Spanish, English, and German.

Guayatur Agencia de Viajes y Turismo (☎2322 441; fax 2328 661), at Gallo and Rumiñahui, can arrange whale-watching trips (US$25) and city tours. Open M-F 9am-5pm, Sa 9am-2pm. AmEx/DC/MC/V.

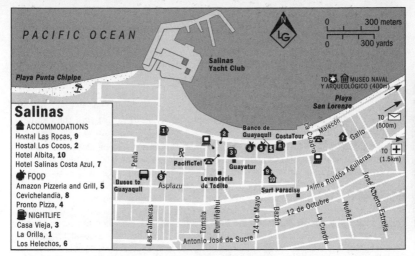

Salinas

■ ACCOMMODATIONS
Hostal Las Rocas, 9
Hostal Los Cocos, 2
Hotel Albita, 10
Hotel Salinas Costa Azul, 7
● FOOD
Amazon Pizzeria and Grill, 5
Cevichelandia, 8
Pronto Pizza, 4
◐ NIGHTLIFE
Casa Vieja, 3
La Orilla, 1
Los Helechos, 6

CostaTour (☎2770 095), on Malecón between Bazán and La Cuadra, offers tours to Baños de San Vicente, Libertad Bolívar, Farallón Dillón, and other popular sites along the coast. Also arranges snorkeling and diving trips (from US$100), sportfishing, and bird and whale-watching excursions (from US$25).

Pesca Tours (☎2772 391; www.pescatours.com.ec), on Malecón, specializes in sportfishing trips. 11hr. daytrips start at about US$375, including all fishing gear. Prices rise Sept.-Dec.

Banks: Banco del Pacífico (☎2774 137), on Gallo, between Las Palmeras and Tomala. 24hr. Cirrus/MC **ATM.** Open M-F 9am-5pm, Sa 9am-2pm. **Banco de Guayaquil** (☎772 552), on Malecón, between 24 de Mayo and Bazán. 24hr. Plus/V **ATM.** Open M-F 8:30am-4:30pm, Sa 9am-1pm.

Laundromat: Lavandería, at Gallo and Bacilio, near Café Planet. US$4. Open M-Tu and Th-Su 9:30am-6:30pm. **Lavandería de Todito,** on Rumiñahui between Gallo and Aspiazu. US$0.40 per lb. Open daily 8am-6pm.

Supermarket: Mi Comisariato, on Gallo and Bacilio. Open M-Th 9am-8pm, F-Sa 9am-9pm, Su 10am-8pm. AmEx/DC/MC/V.

Emergencies: ☎911.

Police: ☎101, at Malecón, Guayas and Quil, near the Museo Naval.

Pharmacy: Farmacia Sabano (☎2774 058), at Gallo and Calle 18. Open daily 8:30am-midnight. Another location on Malecón, 1 block east of Hotel Los Cocos.

Medical Services: Dr. José Garces Rodríguez (☎2776 017), in Ciudadela Frank Vargas Pazoz. From the Yacht Club, go down Malecón, and take a right on Las Américas; the hospital is 1½km away. 24hr. emergency room and ambulance service.

Telephones: PacificTel, at Rumiñahui and Gallo. Another location at Malecón and Tomala. Local calls US$0.16 per min., regional US$0.19 per min., national US$0.25 per min., international from US$0.25 per min. Open daily 8am-9pm. **Cyber@Cafe** (see below) charges US$0.20 per min. for calls to the US.

Internet Access: Cybermar (☎2271 355), at Gallo and Tomala. US$1.80 per hr., Net2phone US$0.20 per min. Open daily 9am-10pm. **Planet Café** (☎2775 500), on Gallo, between Gilbert and Núñez. US$0.50 per 3min. Open daily 9:30am-10pm. **Cyber@Cafe,** on Malecón near Las Palmeras. US$1 per hr. Open daily 9am-9pm.

Post Office: On Gallo near Barcelo Hotel. Open M-F 9am-1pm and 2-5pm, Sa 9am-noon.

ACCOMMODATIONS

Salinas's budget accommodations are few, but not far between. Most congregate on Gallo between Rumiñahui and Nuñez. The cheapest rooms are generally very basic; spending a couple extra dollars buys hot water and cleaner lodgings. Bargain actively during low season.

Hostal Los Cocos (☎2774 349), on Malecón at Rumiñahui, in a yellow building. One of the only budget places right on the beach, Los Cocos is small and friendly. Clean rooms have private warm shower, cable TV, and optional A/C, but vary in size. You can eat good pizza (US$3-5) and lounge in the attached restaurant all day. US$10-12. ❸

Hotel Albita (☎2773 211 or 2773 662), on Aspiaza between 24 de Mayo and Buzón. Quiet location with basic but comfortable rooms. Powerful fans, good window screens, TV, phone, and warm private showers. Ask for a room with a balcony. US$7. Discounts available for long stays. ❷

Hotel Salinas Costa Azul (☎2774 280), at Gallo and Estrella, opposite the fire station. This large hotel lacks character but makes up for it in perks. Rooms are big but simple, equipped with hot private showers, cable TV, and phones. Attached restaurant, pool, and *discoteca* make Costa Azul popular with Ecuadorian families. Breakfast included. Reception 24hr. Checkout 2pm. Singles US$15, with A/C US$30; doubles US$25/$30; triples US$35/$40; quads US$40/$50. AmEx/DC/MC/V. ❹

Hostal Las Rocas (☎2771 096 or 2773 070), on 24 de Mayo near Gallo. Cheap and spartan accommodations for travelers looking to spend time on the beach and not in ther rooms. Reception 24hr. Checkout 2pm. Singles US$4, with private bath US$10; doubles US$6/$15; quints with private bath US$25 per person. ❷

FOOD

Catering to their upscale patrons, most of Salinas's restaurants serve pricey Ecuadorian and international fare in a fancier, sit-down environment. But no-fuss travelers will find good deals on large servings of meat and seafood at the several street grills along Malecón and Gallo around dinnertime. During the low season, many restaurants open only for dinner or on the weekends.

Cevichelandia, on Las Palmeras between Gallo and Gonzalez, is a *ceviche* fan's culinary fantasy. The Salinas version of fast food, this plaza is filled with fishy stands. Prices and dishes are similar throughout, but **Don Kleber** and **Carmita** are highly recommended. **Chelita** has good juices. *Ceviche* US$3.50. Most open daily 8am-5pm, but many close in the low season. ❷

Amazon Pizzeria and Grill (☎2773 671), on Malecón and 24 de Mayo, offers some of the highest quality food in Salinas, from vegetarian items with soy substitutes (US$4-5) to pizzas cooked in an open oven (large US$5-12). Candles, stucco walls, and ivy create a romantic environment. Open daily noon-midnight. ❷

Pronto Pizza, Malecón and 24 de Mayo, dishes out cheap, fast, delicious pizzas (US$1 for a large slice and a Coke), *empanadas* (US$0.75), and more. Popular for takeout and late-night snacks. Open daily noon-2am. ❶

BEACHES AND SIGHTS

Salinas's two beaches, **Punta Chipipe** and **San Lorenzo,** are divided by a small peninsula that houses the Salinas Yacht Club. Both are flanked by beachfront development, but Punta Chipipe is wider, cleaner, and much quieter than its neighbor. San Lorenzo is narrow and palm-laden, and its sands are usually packed to capacity in the high season. The water is even more congested, teeming with every kind of watercraft imaginable: yachts, luxury sailboats, time-worn fishing dugouts, banana boats, paddle boats, and jet skis, to name a few. Join in the water diversions: **banana boat** rides (15min., US$3 per person); **paddle boats** (30min., 4 person max., US$2 per person); junior **motorboats** (30min., US$12); or evening **tour boats** (1hr., US$5-10, includes open bar). High-speed enthusiasts can get their fix on **jet skis** and **water skis** (both US$15 per 30min.), while land-lubbers can enjoy pedal-powered **bike-cars** (US$2 per 30min.). Salinas also boasts a few nearby **surf breaks;** F.A.E., Chocolatera, Punta Blanca, and Punta Carnero are the most popular. Victor Bazan at **Surf Paradise** (☎2774 924), on Aguilera between La Cuadra and Bazan, offers lessons (US$15 for 2hr.), rents boards (US$10 per day), and provides transportation to various surf spots. (Open daily 6:30am-7pm.)

During the low season, when overcast days and cooler temperatures make sunbathing and swimming less appealing, **whale-watching** is the preferred ocean activitiy. From June to September, humpback whales inhabit Ecuador's warmer coastal waters for mating and calfing before retreating to cooler offshore regions for feeding. Guayatour, CostaTour, and Macchiavello Tours (see **Tours,** p. 254) arrange whale-watching excursions (US$25 per person for 3-4hr. tour). If after viewing the whales, you want to catch some fish of their own, Salinas is one of the best places in South America to do so. About 13km offshore, the continental shelf drops over 2000m, yielding phenomenal deep-sea fishing opportunities. **Pesca Tour** (see **Tours,** p. 255) is the town's most reputable sportfishing operator.

For tight-budget travelers, the **Museo Naval y Arqueológico,** on Malecón at Guayas and Quil, a few blocks west of Hotel Barceló, is a less expensive opportunity to experience the high seas. The museum compiles a variety of artifacts, from 15th-century currency to a torpedo used by the Ecuadorian Navy. (☎2771 279. Open M-F 8am-1pm and 3-5pm, Sa-Su 10am-1pm and 3-7pm. US$2, guide included.)

◤ NIGHTLIFE

When the sun goes down, Salinas's sandy carnival moves indoors to the town's numerous bars and discos. Nightlife in Salinas means bar-hopping; just follow the crowds and teeth-rattling music. During the low season, however, many night-spots hibernate, and those that do open their doors on weekend evenings often exude a much more relaxed atmosphere. Bars open and close frequently, so ask to find out where the party's at.

La Orilla, on Malecón and Las Palmeras, only fills up around midnight on weekends, extending the party until dawn. Frequent live music. Cover US$5. Open Th-Sa 9pm-4am.

Los Helechos (☎2773 984), at Malecón and Gilbert. A mix of tourists and locals play pool and watch the party spill out the door. Beer US$1.50. Open daily 8pm-late.

Casa Vieja, on Gallo and Rumiñahui, a mellow open-air bar/cafe, plays good rock and Latin mixes. Relaxed atmosphere in early evening grows louder and more crowded around midnight. Open daily 6pm-3am.

Bar y Restaurant El Capitan, on Malecon near Estrella. Sandy floors, a tiki-sytle bar, bamboo architecture, and pool tables provide a relaxed, straight-off-the-beach atmosphere. Reggae, Latin pop, and young dancing bodies spill out of the open-air bar when the party starts late night. Open daily 9am-1am.

LA LIBERTAD   ☎04

Less glamorous than its ritzy western neighbor Salinas (see p. 254), La Libertad (pop. 50,000) is the transportation hub for the Peninsula de Santa Elena. Travelers often find themselves passing through this city in order to catch buses to

MONEY MANAGEMENT Financing your travels from the ATM can prove challenging in Ecuador, where the crisp US$20 notes fresh from the bank are not accepted for small purchases at most shops, restaurants, and hotels—even many of the most established businesses. Most banks will provide change of US$5 and US$1 notes for larger bills. Although a stack of ones is more cumbersome than a few US$20 bills, you'll be able to travel, shop, and dine much more easily with these smaller bills.

Guayaquil, the northern coast, and Quito. For residents of the smaller coastal towns along the peninsula, La Libertad's stores, banks, and sprawling market make the bustling town a convenient daytrip to stock up on supplies.

▐ TRANSPORTATION Most of the action occurs along **9 de Octubre,** one block from the water, and on the perpendicular **Guayaquil,** which ascends inland for several blocks. From the intersection of these streets, **Cooperativa Trans Esmeraldas,** on 9 de Octubre and Barrerio, sends **buses** to **Quito** (10hr.; 7:30, 8:30, 9:30pm; US$9) via **Santo Domingo.** Across the street, **Cooperativa Libertad Peninsular** (☎2786 433) and **Cooperativa Intercantonal Costa Azul** go to **Guayaquil** (2½hr., every 15min. 3:30am-9pm, US$2.50-3.40). Buses to **Baños** (8hr., 9pm) depart from the dead end near the water on Guayaquil, just past 9 de Octubre. Frequent buses to **Salinas** and **Santa Elena** run along 9 de Octubre. Red-and white-striped buses going to **Los Baños de San Vicente** (30min.; 7:30 and 9:30am daily US$0.80) leave from the market (see below) in front of the Mercado de Viveras building, but service is inconsistent. All other buses depart from the **Mini Terminal Terrestre;** walk seven blocks up Guayquil and make a right when you get to the blue and white monument where the road splits; the terminal is about 200m further. Numerous bus cooperatives send buses to: **Aconcito** (30min., every 15min. 6am-8pm, US$0.30) via **Punta Carnero** (25min); **Loma Alta** (7, 11am, 12:45, 4pm; US$4); **Manta** (5hr., every 15-30min. 4am-8pm, US$6.50) via **Ayangue** (45min., US$1.75), **Valdivia** (1hr., US$2), **Montañita** (1½hr., US$3.50), **Puerto López** (2½hr., US$5), and **Jipijapa** (3¾hr., US$5.60).

⊠ PRACTICAL INFORMATION Banco de Guayaquil, three blocks up from Guayaquil and 9 de Octubre with the ocean on the left, exchanges traveler's checks and has a Plus/V ATM. (☎2785 892. Open M-F 8:30am-5pm, Sa 9am-2pm.) **Banco del Pacífico,** near Banco de Guayaquil, has a Cirrus/MC **ATM.** (☎2784 888. Open M-F 8:30am-5pm, Sa 9am-2pm.) **Western Union** has a branch at the **Tía Supermarket** on 9 de Octubre. (Open M-Sa 9am-7pm, Su 9am-noon). Several pharmacies line the main drags, but **Farmacy Turno,** on 9 de Octubre, is one of the most comprehensive. (☎2786 515. Open 24hr.) La Libertad's immense and diverse **market** stocks everything from meat and produce to clothing and toiletries. To get here, walk six blocks up Guayquil, make a left when you see a sign saying "La Bamba Peninsular," and then walk five more blocks. (Most vendors open daily 7am-8pm.) The best **Internet** cafe in town is on 9 de Octubre, opposite Banco del Pacífico; it also has good rates for international **phone calls.** (Internet US$1 per hr. Local calls US$0.14 per min., to US US$0.15 per min., to Europe from US$0.22 per min. Open daily 8am-10pm.) A **post office** is next door to the Coopertiava Libertad Peninsular bus office on 9 de Octubre. (Open M-Sa 7am-7pm.)

▐◖ ACCOMMODATIONS AND FOOD Most travelers visit La Libertad only to catch a bus, but if you must spend a night, several basic, inexpensive lodgings line Barreiro, which intersects 9 de Octubre near the Cooperativa Libertad Peninsular bus terminal. **Residencial Turis Palm ❷,** on 9 de Octubre opposite the terminal, is centrally located with no-frills rooms. (☎2785 149. Singles US$4 per person.)

Closer to the main bus terminal is **Hotel Costa Brava,** at Av. 7 and Calle 17. To get there, walk one block from the terminal with the bus offices on the left, and turn right; it's one block ahead. Unexciting but clean rooms with private baths await. (☎2785 860. US$8 per person.) Between bus departures, **Restaurant Saavedra ❷,** on the corner of 9 de Octubre and Guayaquil, is a popular place for a quick bite to eat. Entrees range from the standard *ceviches* (US$2.50-4) and rice and beans with meat (US$2.80-3.50) to the more adventurous pork chop with pineapple. (☎2786 429. Open daily 8am-11pm.) Similar *típica* fare is served at the *patio de comidas* in the Centro Comercial Monero, on Guayaquil, four blocks from 9 de Octubre. Of the many small stands, **Comedor Normita** and **Comedor la Pinta** are among the most popular. (Most open daily 8am-9pm.)

BAÑOS DE SAN VICENTE   ☎04

Not to be confused with Baños, the central Ecuadorian city known for its water-fall- and mountain-flanked thermal springs, Los Baños de San Vicente offers a less than idyllic site for the purification of body and communion with Mother Nature. The dreary cement complex is rather small, poorly maintained, and serviced unreliably by public transportation. Nonetheless, those with time to kill who are willing to experiment with the baths' reportedly therapeutic waters will find Los Baños a relatively cheap, although by no means luxurious, getaway, just 20km east of La Libertad. Hailed as a miracle of natural healing, San Vicente's muddy volcanic crater contains a unique amalgam of 18 minerals found only in Germany, France, and Ecuador. The power of this mineral blend supposedly creates a natural panacea for ailments such as arthritis and rheumatism. Ecuadorian families and senior citizens flock to San Vicente to experience this aqua therapy and enjoy extras, including massages and steam baths. General admission to the park includes access to a mud bath, two cold pools, and a small hot pool. Park employees can recommend how long to remain in each in order to maximize benefits. **Massages** using mud or *savila*, a natural aloe, relieve tension (US$2.50-3), while **hydra-massages** (20min. of high-powered Jacuzzi jets; US$2) offer a soothing soak. The park also offers **internal purification,** which involves sweating away the evil buildup of life in an herb-scented steam bath (US$1 per 20min.). Bring your own towel.

Several inexpensive *comedores* and street vendors offer refreshment outside the complex. Should you decide to spend the night, **Hotel Florida ❷** is just behind the park. The comfortable TV lounge leads to clean rooms with screened windows, and the owner claims his showers contain the same powers as the baths. (☎2535 101 or 09 9620 018. All meals included. Singles US$15; doubles US$30.)

Public transportation to the baths exists but is notoriously unreliable. Locals claim that a **bus** leaves daily for the baths from the market in La Libertad (7:30 and 9:30am) and the tourist office in Santa Elena (11am); all return from the baths 1-1½hr. after arriving. If the bus does not seem to be coming, you can take a taxi from the tourist office in Santa Elena and have it wait for you to come back (one-way US$5-6, round-trip US$11). As a final option, you can take a Guayaquil- or Progreso-bound bus from La Libertad or Santa Elena, ask to get dropped off at the entrance the to baths, and walk another 8km down a side road. (Baths open daily 7am-7pm. US$1.50, children and seniors US$0.75.)

SANTA ELENA   ☎04

Unlike its more boisterous neighbors, Santa Elena embraces its small-town personality, most apparently in the revamped central plaza, where folks of all ages partake of the long forgotten art of conversation and school children play pick-up *fútbol*. Most foreigners traveling *La Ruta del Sol* limit their experience of Santa

Elena to glimpses through bus windows, but hard-core history buffs take a La Libertad-bound bus (US$0.25) or taxi (US$1) to the town to spend an hour visiting the small Museo de Los Amantes de Sumpa, the town's only real site of interest.

■ 🖪 ORIENTATION AND PRACTIAL INFORMATION. Most of the action in Santa Elena centers around the **plaza**, bordered by Guayaquil (the main drag), 10 de Agosto, 28 de Agosto, and Sucre. **Buses** heading to **Ballenita** (5min., every 15min., US$0.20); **Guayaquil** (2½hr., 3:50am-8pm, US$3) via **Progreso** (1¼hr., US$1.50); and **Salinas** (20min., every 10min., US$0.40) via **La Libertad** (10min., US$0.20) leave from the **Oficina de Turismo**, on Guayaquil and Fuentes, a few blocks east of the plaza. **Taxis** gather near the Oficina de Turismo and on 18 de Agosto, opposite the church. The **Oficina de Turismo** has **public toilets** and information on the entire Santa Elena Peninsula. (☎2940 375. Open M-Sa 8am-5pm.) **Banco del Pacífico**, at Guayaquil and 10 de Agosto, has a MC **ATM**. (Open daily M-F 8:30am-4:30pm, Sa 9am-1:30pm.) The **police** (☎999) are on Rocafuerte near 10 de Agosto, three blocks north of the plaza. **La Hospital Cristo Redentor** is next to the church, at the corner of the plaza. (☎2940 415. Open 24hr.) **Farmacia Lupita**, at Guayaquil and 10 de Agosto, is one of many pharmacies near the plaza. (Open M-Sa 8:30am-9:30pm, Su 9am-1pm, 6-9pm.) **Bell South** has a branch on the main road near Banco del Pacífico. (Calls to US$0.25 per min., to Europe from US$0.40 per min. Open M-Sa 8am-11pm, Su 9am-1pm and 5-10pm.) **Pacifictel** is across the street from Bell South. (Calls to US and Europe from US$0.22 per min. Open daily 8am-11pm). **Play@NET**, on 10 de Agosto next to the central plaza, has Internet access. (☎2940 787. US$1.40 per hr.)

🖪 🖸 ACCOMMODATIONS AND FOOD. Most travelers prefer to stay in nearby Salinas or farther north along the coast; nonetheless, the tiny town has a surprising number of accommodations. **Hostería el Palacio de las Sumpas ❷**, at Sucre and Montavalo, two blocks north of Guayaquil, is one of the best values in town. Wide hallways and pleasant sitting areas open up to comfortable rooms with hot water baths and TVs. (☎2940 578. Ring the bell by the black door on Sucre. Reception daily 6am-10pm. US$5 per person.) More luxurious is the recently built **Hotel el Cisne #2 ❸**, on Guayaquil near Sucre, just past the plaza. Modern rooms are plain but sparkling with TV, phone, comfortable bed, and hot showers. (☎2941 572. Breakfast US$2-2.50. Reception 24hr. Singles US$11, with A/C US$15.40; doubles US$16.40/$18). Its sibling **Hotel el Cisne #1 ❷**, around the corner on Sucre, is cramped but more economical. Three flights of stairs lead to slightly worn out rooms with TV, fans, and cold baths. (☎2941 572 or 2940 038. Singles US$6; doubles US$9; triples US$12.) Several inexpensive and standard *comedores* line Guayaquil and surround the plaza. Locals gather for lunch and snacks at the cheery **Congregal Restaurant D' Alfred ❶**, on Sucre between Guayaquil and 18 de Agosto, near the plaza. Hearty lunches (US$1.50) and *ceviches* (US$2-2.50) are served at booths with checkered tablecloths. (Open daily 9am-10pm.)

🖸 SIGHTS. The **Museo de Los Amantes de Sumpa's** exhibit on the burial rituals of the ancient Las Vegas culture (8800-4600 BC) contains Ecuador's oldest archaeological artifacts. Several ancient tombs, all of which were discovered in 1970, are displayed. The museum's most famous exhibit, an 8000-year-old tomb of a young man and woman buried in an embracing position, demonstrates the interesting funeral rituals of the Las Vegas people. Archaeologists discovered that most tombs shared striking similarities: the man was always buried with his right hand on the women's waist, the woman with her left arm over her head, and rocks placed symbolically to protect the tombs from evil spirits. In addition to the ancient tombs, the museum has well-organized exhibits on regional indigenous *artesanía*, navigation, home life, and a model of a rural home. (☎2940 826 or 09 7045 613. To get there, walk 10min. up Guayaquil with the plaza on the right, make a left at the first fork, a right at the second fork, and walk another 10min. until you see the sign for the museum on the left. Open Th-Sa 9am-4:30pm, Su 10am-3pm. US$1.)

BALLENITA   ☎04

At the epicenter of Ecuador's oceanic obsession lies Farallón Dillon, a sanctuary of seafaring, honoring centuries of oceanic exploration and history. In the tiny town of Ballenita, just a few kilometers from Santa Elena, Farallón Dillon makes a great daytrip or lunch stop for anyone with an interest in any and all things from the sea. Friendly and knowledgeable guides lead visitors through a large nautical **gallery** full of interesting antiques, from rusting anchors and colonial navigation instruments to pirate paintings and ruins from El Capitana, a Peru-bound ship that sunk in 1664 and was discovered off the coast of Ecuador near Chanduy in 1997. The complex's restaurant is similarly decorated in unique nautical artifacts—check out the 100-year-old diving suit and authentic submarine door that grants entry to the restrooms. Perhaps the most interesting piece of history is Captain Dillon himself, a charming Irish sea captain who happily sits with visitors and recounts stories from his many voyages. English-speaking manager Douglas Dillon is an excellent resource for information about travelling in the Santa Elena peninsula and along the coast. Just outside the restaurant is a lookout onto the wide **beach,** where whales are sometimes sighted from June to September.

Need more than a few hours to absorb the phenomenal views, excellent seafood (most entrees US$4-8), and marine history? Farallón Dillon offers a few cozy **rooms** complete with tennis courts and private beach with a snorkeling area. To get here, take a Ballenita-bound **bus** from Santa Elena and ask to be dropped off at the entrance road to Farallón Dillon; all drivers should know it. From where the bus drops you off, it's a 1km (15min.) walk down Carrera to the gallery and hotel—just follow the signs. (☎/fax 2953 611; www.farallondillon.com.ec. Reservations recommended for rooms. Singles US$18; doubles US$30.) ❹

PLAYAS   ☎04

As one of the area's cheapest beach resorts, and the closest to Guayaquil, Playas inevitably receives masses of city residents during sweltering weekends, both from Guayaquil and the southern Sierra region. Local tourist dollars bring their own problems, though, as frequent invasions have left the dusty village over-visited and in disrepair. Even in the low season (May-Dec.), when the weather is often dreary and many of the town's restaurants and bars close, the long beach remains streaked with dirt and litter. Nevertheless, the town suffices as an affordable city escape relatively free of foreign tourists.

▐▊ TRANSPORTATION AND PRACTICAL INFORMATION

Playas's layout is a bit confusing, streets are poorly labeled, and few locals know or use the proper street names. Playas's main street, **Guayaquil,** lies a few blocks up from the beach and houses most services. Facing away from the beach, the streets intersecting Guayaquil from left to right are **Gilbert, Garay, Paquisha,** and **Parades.** **Malecón** runs along the waterfront. Parallel to it is Aguilera. The **central plaza,** at Gilbert and Guayaquil, marks the center of town and is a good reference point.

> **Buses: Transportes Villamil,** at Gilbert and Guayaquil, and **Transportes Posorja,** near the central plaza and around the corner from the church, send buses to **Guayaquil** (2hr., every 15min. 4am-8pm, US$2.40) via **Progreso** (45min., US$1). Most buses also stop in front of Banco de Guayaquil (see below), but can be stopped anywhere.

Taxis: Taxis and camionetas line up at Gilbert and Guayaquil, near the central plaza.

Currency Exchange: Banco de Guayaquil (☎2760 040), at Guayaquil and Gilbert, has a Plus/V ATM. Open M-F 8:30am-4:30pm, Sa 9am-1:30pm.

Western Union: In the Tía supermarket, on Guayaquil between Garay and Paquisha. Open M-Sa 9am-7pm, Su 9am-noon.

Police: ☎09 7162 282. On Garay near Guayaquil.

Pharmacy: Farmacia Villamil (☎2761 607), on Guayaquil between Garay and Paquisha. Open daily 8am-10:30pm.

Medical Services: General Villamil Playas Hospital (☎2760 328), on Guayaquil, 1½km east of town.

Telephones: Cabinas Telefónicas, on Garay near Guayaquil, allows local, regional, national, and international calls. Calls to US and Europe from US$0.50 per min. Open M-Sa 9am-6:30pm, Su 9am-3pm.

Internet: Cyber Cl@di, on Paquisha, 1 block south of Guayaquil. US$1.75 per hr. Open M-Sa 8:30am-8pm, Su 8:30am-3pm. **Playas Cyber Café,** 325 Aguilera, 2 blocks east of the central plaza. US$1.80 per hr. Open M-Sa 9am-9pm, Su 9am-2pm.

Post Office: On Gilbert, around the corner from the bus office. Open M-Sa 9am-7pm, Su 9am-noon.

⌁ ACCOMMODATIONS

In general, budget accommodations line Malecón and Guayaquil, which makes them ideal for stumbling home from a long night of bar hopping. Pricier and quieter options dot the beach west of town. Note that mosquitos adore Playas; netting or window screens are essential.

Hostería el Delfín (☎2760 125), on Malecón, 1½km east of town. Spacious rooms with wooden floors, hot private baths, TV, towels, and balconies more than compensate for the long walk and extra dollars. A beachfront patio, pool table, restaurant, bar, and occasional live music create a relaxed, social atmosphere. US$10 per person; 5-person cabañas US$35. ❸

Hotel Rey David (☎2760 024), at Malecón and Calle 9, near the beach. Clean and well-lit, if plain, rooms. Fans, firm beds, and cold private baths. Ask for a room with ocean views. Reception 24hr. US$8 per person with fan, with A/C US$12. ❷

Hostería La Gaviota (☎2760 959 or 2760 646), on Malecón, 1km east of town. Quiet lodgings on a quiet beach. Rooms are clean but simple, with cold private bath and fan, but the friendly owners can take you surfing (if you have your own board) and on horseback rides along the beach (US$2 per hr.). Hammocks on the beachfront patio, a TV room, and good restaurant are perks. Reception open 24hr. US$7 per person. ❷

Hotel Brisas del Pacífico (☎2761 730), on Malecón about 1km east of town in a large yellow building. Beach breezes cool the spotless and comfortable rooms, which have TVs, hot private baths, telephones, and fans. Chairs and hammocks grace the social, beachfront patio. US$15 per person. ❹

◘ FOOD

Playas is every seafood-lover's dream. Dozens of inexpensive and remarkably identical *cevicherías* and *comedores* line the beach, serving lobster, shrimp, crab, octopus, and fried fish. Many close in the low season, especially on weekdays, but enough remain open to provide a decent and effortless selection.

Sabory Yogurt, on Gilbert and Guayaquil, opposite the bank. Huge, warm subs (US$0.80-1.50), yogurt (US$0.70-1.00), and fresh fruit salads (US$0.80) offer a welcome break from *ceviche*. Vegetarians can request a special meatless sub or sandwich. Open M-Sa 8am-10pm, Su 9am-8pm. ❶

Restaurant Jalisco, Av. 7 and Paquisha, 1 block south of Guayaquil. Appears strikingly standard at first, but locals swear that the *almuerzos* (US$1.50) and other Ecuadorian fare is the best bang for your buck in Playas. Open daily 10am-10pm, but closes most weekdays in the low season. ❶

BEACHES AND NIGHTLIFE

As the town's name implies, flocks of Ecuadorian tourists come here for the beach. Far from picturesque, however, the vast, litter-sprinkled sands of Playas are popular more for their convenience and size than their beauty. During the low season, both the beach and the town's dozens of bars are all but deserted. But nights are alive and swinging in the high season, when many discos party until dawn. The several bars in the central plaza are a good place to festivities.

Oh Sole Mío, on Calle 9 between Malecón and Aguilera, near Hotel Rey Davíd. Huge, open-air bar and disco, where old and young alike show off their Latin dance moves. Occasional live music, especially on weekends during the high season. Beer US$1-1.50. Cover US$1. Open daily 8am-late.

La Pena, on Aguilera near Hotel Rey Davíd. This popular disco picks up with loud music and a younger crowd around midnight. Cocktails from US$2. Open Tu-Sa 7pm-late.

El Pescador, across from Hotel Rey Davíd. Casual music in a marine-themed bar and lounge. More relaxed than most of Playas's crowded discos. Beer US$1-2. Open Su-Th noon-midnight, F-Sa noon-late.

GUAYAQUIL ☎04

Up until recently, tourists knew Guayaquil (pop. 2.2 million) as little more than an inconvenient stop en route to the Galápagos. The bustling port city had a reputation for crime, clutter, and commerce. Eager to change the city's image, however, the government has given Guayaquil a complete facelift, and the result marks one of the most extensive urban restoration projects in the continent's history. The result of Guayaquil's makeover has been a gradual conversion from its former beleaguered reputation to a city now well known for its history, culture, and newfound modernity. From the sparkling new Malecón 2000 to the recently refurbished Cerro Santa Ana neighborhood, the modern Guayaquil is eager to share its attractions and improved infrastructure with any visitor who gives it a chance.

The city's first inhabitants arrived 5000 years ago, bearing South America's first ceramics. Guayaquil remained an indigenous community for nearly 4500 years, until Spanish *conquistador* Francisco de Orellana arrived at the Santa Ana hills in 1537. Legend has it that a native chief named Guayas and his wife Quil committed suicide before surrendering their beloved home to the Spaniards. Their martyrdom inspired the name of what is now the most populous city in Ecuador. Today Guayaquileños are just as proud of the city's heritage as their Indian ancestors and eager to show it off. First-class restaurants, bumping clubs, shopping malls, and markets intermingle with museums and colorful neighborhoods, making Guayaquil a mix of commerce, class, and culture.

 Guayaquil is a site for frequent public demonstrations. *Let's Go* recommends steering clear of any rallies, as police may use tear gas.

■ INTERCITY TRANSPORTATION

FLIGHTS

Simón Bolívar International Airport (☎282 100; fax 290 018), on Av. de las Américas, 5km north of the city. Taxi from the airport to Guayaquil Centro US$3-4. Several buses (US$0.25), including *líneas* #2, 74, and 143, also pass by the airport on Av. de las Américas heading to downtown Guayaquil. The recently renovated airport features an architecturally stylish metallic structure enclosing its arrivals, departures, and ticketing areas. All international and most domestic flights arrive and depart from the 2 adjacent terminals on the main road, while smaller domestic flights take off from the smaller *Terminal de Avionetas*, 1km south. **International departure tax** US$10 (cash only).

INTERNATIONAL AIRLINES

Aerolinas Argentinas, Quisuis 1502 (☎2690 012), in Tulcán. **Air Canada,** S. Jorge 208, 3 etapa (☎2690 539). **Air France,** Miguel H. Alcivar, Manzana 506, Of. 701 (☎2687 149), in the Edificio Torres del Norte B. **Alitalia,** Icaza 407 (☎2302 050), at Cordova. **American Airlines,** Aguirre 116 (☎2327 082), at Pichincha. **Continental Airlines,** 9 de Octubre 100, 29th fl. (☎2288 987), on the Malecón. **Copa,** 9 de Octubre 100, 25th fl. (☎2303 227 or 2303 239), on the Malecón. **Iberia,** 9 de Octubre 101 (☎2329 558 or 2284 151), on the Malecón. **KLM** (☎2692 876), in the Hilton Colón Hotel in Kennedy Norte. **Lufthansa,** Malecón 1401 (☎2324 360), at Illingworth. **Taca,** 9 de Octubre 100, 25th fl. (☎2562 950 or 2293 880), on the Malecón. **United Airlines** (☎2690 318), at Justino Cornejo and Luis Orrantia in the Edificio Torres Altas.

DOMESTIC AIRLINES

Aerogal (☎2284 218 or 2287 710; www.aerogal.com.ec), in the domestic terminal at the airport. To: **Isla Baltra** (2½hr., Tu-W and F 9:30am, US$344) via **San Cristóbal** (Th 9:30am, Su 10:15am; US$344); **Quito** (45min.; M-F 7:05, 8:30am, 1:55, 6:35pm, Sa 9:40am, 1:55pm, Su 1:55, 3:30, 6:35pm; US$50); **San Cristóbal** (30min.; M-Th, Su 9:30am; US$344).

Austro Aereo (☎2296 685, 2286 687, or 2284 084), in the domestic terminal at the airport. To: **Cuenca** (US$40).

Icaro (☎2294 265 or 239 34 08; www.icaro.com.ec), in the domestic terminal at the airport. To: **Cuenca** (30min.; M-F and Su 5:05pm, Sa 8:35am); **Quito** (45min.; M-Th 8, 10:15am, 2:40, 5:50, 8:05pm, F 8, 10:15am, 12:20, 2:40, 5:50, 8:05pm, Sa 10:15am, 2:40, 4:15pm; Su 12:20, 5:50, 8:05pm).

TAME, 9 de Octubre 424 (☎231 0305; www.tame.com.ec), at Icaza, in the Gran Pasaje Building. Another office in the airport. Open M-F 9am-6pm, Sa 9am-1pm. To: **Isla Baltra** (1½hr.; daily 11am; US$304-344, ISIC discount 15%); **Coca** (2¼hr.; M-Sa 7am, Tu-F 3pm, Su 9am); **Cuenca** (30min.; M-Sa 7pm, M-F and Su 5pm; US$44); **Esmeraldas** (2¾hr.; Tu, Th-F, Su 1:45pm; US$63); **Lago Agrio** (2hr.; M and F 9am and 3pm, Tu-Th 9am, Sa 7:45am); **Loja** (30min.; Tu, Th, Sa; US$61); **Machala** (25min.; M, W, F 9am; US$54); **Quito** (45min.; 12 per day M-F 7am-7:45pm, 7 per day Sa 7am-5pm, 5 per day Su 9am-6:30pm; US$107); **San Cristóbal** (1½hr.; M, W, Sa noon; US$304-344); **Tulcán** (2½hr.; M, W, F 9am).

Trains: Train service from Guayaquil is unavailable. In order to catch the express train to **Nariz del Diablo,** take a bus from the terminal to **Alausí** (4hr.).

Buses: Jaime Roldós Aguilera Terminal Terrestre Américas (☎9306 117), north of the airport. Taxi from Guayaquil Centro US$3-4; bus US$0.25. Purchase your ticket from the more than 50 bus company windows and proceed outside or upstairs to board your bus (US$0.10 to enter boarding area). For the cheapest ticket, compare several companies' prices, as nicer coaches with A/C, TV, and bathroom charge more. Most cities are serviced at least once, if not several times, per hour at all times of day. The follow-

**Guayaquil
Centro**

🏠 **ACCOMMODATIONS**
Hostal D'La Rosa, **7**
Hotel Alexander, **2**
Hotel Caprí, **1**
Hotel Ecuador, **6**
Hotel Sander, **3**
Hotel Vélez, **4**
Rizzo Hotel, **12**

🍎 **FOOD**
Aroma Café, **18**
Casa Baska, **10**
El Galeon de Artur's, **15**
FrutaBar, **14**
La Canoa, **11**
La Pepa de Oro, **9**

⭐ **ENTERTAINMENT**
Supercines, **8**

🎭 **NIGHTLIFE**
Resaca Bar & Rest., **17**

🏛 **MUSEUMS**
Casa de la Cultura /
  Museo de Arte
  Prehistórico, **5**
Museo del Banco
  del Pacífico, **16**
Museo Municipal, **13**

TO POLICENTRO (1.5km),
URDESA (4km)

TO 🏥 (2.5km), ✚,
🚌 (5km),
MALL DEL SOL (4km),
KENNEDY NORTE,
KENNEDY MALL,
🚌 (5km)

Libertador
Kennedy
Gual
Coronel Dasriel
Los Ríos

American ■
Express
Esmeraldas
José Mascote
José Mascote
1 de Mayo
Pedro Solano
Alej. Lascano
Vicente de Piedrahita

Banco del
Pacífico 🏦
Av. del Ejército
Chasquitur ■
García Morena
Quisquis
Urdaneta
Manuel Galecio

Av. del Ejército
García Moreno
José de Antepara

US 📮

José de Anteparra
Velez
Hurtado
9 de Octubre

TO 🚌 CHONGÓN,
CERRO BLANCO
(.5blk)

Aguirre
Luque
Machala
Quito

Parque
Victoria
Pedro Moncayo
Montufar
6 de Marzo
10 de Agosto

🏛 5

Manuel Galecio
Machala
Quito

Parque
Centenario

Pedro Moncayo

Julián Coronel

Cementerio
La Ciudad
Blanca

Juan Pablo Arenas
Manuel Galecio
Vicente de Piedrahita

Lorenzo de Garaycoa
💻
José A. Campos
Manuel Rendón
Junín
Urdaneta
Padre Solano
Rumichaca
Riobamba
Lascano

Rumichaca
R̃x
⭐ 8

García Avilés
Clemente Ballén
Aguirre
Luque
Velez
MI ■
Comisariato
Icaza
9 de Octubre

Ximena
Boyacá

10 de Agosto
💻 9
Boyacá
Escobedo
Escobedo
G. Escobedo

Baquerizo Moreno

Juan Montalvo
Loja

Metropolitan
Cathedral ✝
Chimborazo

Iguana
Park
Unicentro 🏛 10
Mall
Chile

🏛 11
🏛 12
PacificTel ✉
Sucre
Pedro Carbo

Gran
Pasaje
Building

San ✝
Francisco
14

Centro
■ Viajero
Galasam
Tours
Western Union/
■ DHL

Canada,
Colombia
Pedro
Carbo
La Merced ✝
Rocafuerte

Córdoba
UK 📮

Menicburo
Tomás Martínez
Padre Aguirre

Mercado de
Artesanía
TO IGLESIA SANTO
DOMINGO (4blk),
🏛 15 (6blk),
LAS PEÑAS

🏛 13
Guayaquil
Biblioteca
Municipal

Municipalidad ℹ
de Turismo ■
Tours
Palacio
Municipal
Palacio del
Gobernación

Ministry of ℹ
Tourism
Pichincha
National ■
Tours

🏛 16
Banco de 🏦
Guayaquil

Banco del 🏦
Pacífico

Galapagos
Sub-Aqua

Roca
Rocafuerte
Oriana
Imbabura

Rocafuerte
Panamá

Clocktower
Fountain
Mirador
(lookout)

La
Rotonda
Malecón 2000
Malecón 2000

17

18

🗺

**Río
Guayas**

0 _____ 150 meters

0 _____ 150 yards

ing is an approximate timetable of bus departures: To: **Ambato** (5½hr., over 50 per day 24hr., US$4-5) via **Riobamba; Babahoyo** (1hr., every 5min. 5am-10:30pm, US$1); **Cuenca** (4hr., 23 per day 3:30am-midnight, US$7); **Daule** (1hr., every 5min. 8am-1pm and 3-5pm, US$0.80); **Esmeraldas** (8hr., 22 per day 7am-11:30pm, US$10); **Huaquillas** (4½hr., every 30min. 24hr., US$4.40); **Ibarra** (11½hr., 20 per day 24hr., US$10); **Jipijapa** (3hr., every 40min. 4am-8:20pm, US$3); **Lago Agrio** (16hr.; 3:50, 4:05am, 1, 1:45, 4pm; US$11); **Latacunga** (6½hr., 10 per day 5:30am-7:30pm, US$8); **Machala** (3hr., every 30min. 24hr. US$3); **Manta** (3¾hr., every 40min. 4am-8:20pm, US$3); **Montañita** (4hr.; 5:30am, 1, 4:30pm; US$4); **Playas** (2hr., every 10min. 4am-8:30pm, US$2.40); **Puerto Lopez** (2½hr., every 30min. 6:15am-8:15pm, US$2.80); **Quito** (8hr., over 50 per day, US$9); **Salinas** (3hr., every 10min. 3:30am-10:30pm, US$2.70) via **La Libertad; Santo Domingo** (5hr., every 30min. 3am-8:15pm, US$5); **Tulcán** (13hr., 20 per day 24hr., US$12).

■ ORIENTATION

Guayaquil sprawls to the north and south, but the two sq. km that comprise the Centro west of the Rio Guayas are easily navigated. Organized in a rough grid system, *avenidas* (avenues) run north-south, and *calles* (streets) go east-west.

The recently refurbished **9 de Octubre,** which runs southeast-northwest through Guayaquil Centro, is the city's main thoroughfare and the site of many upscale hotels, shops, and fast-food chains. At its easternmost point, 9 de Octubre (named for Ecuador's independence day) intersects with **Malecón Simón Bolívar** at **La Rotunda,** a monument honoring Simón Bolívar and José de San Martín, who freed ten South American countries, including Ecuador, from Spanish rule. La Rotunda also marks the mid-point of the beautiful **Malecón 2000** (see **Sights,** p. 274), a 2½km riverfront walkway flanked by the **Mercado Artesanal** (see **Shopping,** p. 278) at its southwesternmost point, and the fascinating **Las Peñas** neighborhood (see **Sights,** p. 275) and **Cerro Santa Ana** (see **Sights,** p. 274) to its north. Although the city has become significantly more tourist-friendly over the past three years, exercise caution after dark, especially in the blocks surrounding Parque Victoria.

Just north of Guayaquil Centro lie several quieter *ciudadelas* (neighborhoods). The relatively wealthy areas of **Alborada, Kennedy, La Garzota, Los Sauces,** and **Urdesa** don't offer much history but are replete with expensive, albeit excellent, restaurants, shopping malls, and neuron-jolting nightlife.

⃞ LOCAL TRANSPORTATION

Buses: City buses (US$0.25), often referred to as *carros,* travel throughout the Centro and to outlying neighborhoods such as Alborada, Durán, Kennedy, Urdesa, Garzota, and Los Sauces. Nearly all city buses belong to cooperatives, identified by the "Coop" on the front window; don't confuse the name of the bus cooperative with the destination of the bus, as they frequently differ. *Líneas* (route numbers) and destinations are displayed on the front windows. Guayaquil's dozens of bus lines cover almost every city street, but it's easiest to flag one down on the Malecón, 9 de Octubre, Rumichaca, Quito, and 10 de Agosto. Travelers unfamiliar with Guayaquil's layout may find the bus system confusing, especially since there is no central stop or terminal in the city center, and several different bus routes complete the trip to and from most destinations. Confirm that the bus stops exactly where you want to go before you board, and be prepared to jump on and off quickly since buses rarely make complete stops. While there is no specific schedule, you can catch most buses daily 6am-midnight. It is best to have exact or small change on hand.

Taxis: Guayaquil's many taxi drivers are notorious for taking advantage of travelers, especially those who don't speak Spanish. Most will quote you a fixed price to your destination instead of using a meter to determine the exact price. Suggest a price before you get in, and leave if the driver doesn't agree. As you walk away, chances are he will either turn on his meter or agree to your price. Taxis within the Centro should cost US$0.50-$1 and between the Centro and the airport or outlying neighborhoods US$2-4. Hiring a taxi by the hour costs US$10-20, depending on the company. Drivers may charge more at night, when it's often considered safer to take taxis than to walk or take buses. Most hostel owners are more than happy to call a taxi for their patrons. Many drivers either don't carry change or won't admit they do, so carry exact change whenever possible. Taxi companies: **Carrousel** (☎2110 610), **Flash Car** (☎2245 070), **Taxi del Guayas** (☎2301 393), **Taxi Paraíso** (☎2201 877).

Ferries: The Municipalidad de Guayaquil is planning a regular ferry service to Durán and El Parque Histórico Guayaquil (see **Sights**, p. 277) from the dock on the Malecón 2000 near Sucre. As of June 2004, the Huancavilla boat (☎2561 957 or 2561 925; every 1½hr. Sa-Su 1-7:30pm; US$3, children and seniors US$1.50, under 4 free) left the dock for El Parque Histórico Guayaquil only during high tide; call in advance to check on conditions.

Car Rental: Renting a car in Guayaquil is not recommended, not only because it is very expensive, but also because Guayaquil's drivers are fast and aggressive, and most roads lack clearly marked lanes. If you prefer the convenience of a private car, **Centro Viajero Travel Agency** (see **Practical Information: Tours**, below) as well as **Ejecutivo's Car** (☎2210 306, cell 09 9894 221) can arrange a car and driver. If car rental is absolutely necessary, try: **Avis** (☎2395 554 or 2287 906), at the airport and in the Hilton Colón Hotel; **Budget** (☎2288 510 or 2284 559), at the airport and on Garcia Moreno and Hurtado; **CarMax,** Juan Pablo Arenas 302 (☎2300 973 or 2301 339), at Alejo Lascano; **Ecuacars** (☎2285 533 or 2283 247), at the airport; **Hertz** (☎2293 011), at the airport outside the international departures entrance. Be sure that insurance and mileage are included in the rental package. Most rent to drivers 25 and up. US$26-115 per day, excluding tax. See **Essentials**, p. 30.

▸ PRACTICAL INFORMATION

TOURIST AND FINANCIAL SERVICES

Tourist Offices: Ministry of Tourism (☎2568 764; fax 2562 544), at Pichincha and Icaza, 6th fl., across from Banco del Pacífico in the large tan building adorned with paintings. Excellent maps of Guayaquil Centro, the northern suburbs, and Ecuador. Open M-F 9am-5pm. **Dirección Municipalidad de Turísmo** (☎2524 100, ext. 3477; www.guayaquil.gov.ec), at Malecón and 9 de Octubre in the Municipal building, has general information about sights, festivals, cultural events, and museums in Guayaquil. Some English spoken. Open M-F 9am-5pm.

Tours: Most travel agencies in Guayaquil cluster on or around 9 de Octubre near the Malecón. Many cater mostly to Ecuadorian or other South American tourists and therefore speak mostly Spanish.

Agencia de Viajes Galasam, 9 de Octubre 424 (☎2304 488; www.galapagos-islands.com), on the ground floor of the Gran Pasaje Building between Baquerizo Moreno and Cordova. Runs city tours (3hr., US$15), but specializes in last-minute budget Galápagos tours; English-speaking manager Christian suggests calling approximately 1 week before your preferred departure date for the best deal. Unlike many other travel agencies, Galasam owns and operates its own boats, which range in quality from tourist class to luxury. All boats include snorkeling and a level 3 or 3-plus naturalist guide. Ask about getting a free night's stay at Galasam's hostel, Villa 97 (see **Accommodations,** below), if you book a Galápagos tour. Open M-F 9am-6pm, Sa 10am-1pm. AmEx/MC/V. Cash or traveler's checks preferred.

Centro Viajero Travel Agency, 1119 Baquerizo Moreno (☎2564 064 or 2301 283, 24hr. cell 09 9752 433; centrovi@telconet.net), on the 8th fl. of the Edificio Plaza, just off 9 de Octubre. Owner Karen Boley de Chang moved to Ecuador from the US 22 years ago and is an great resource for advice and information about Galápagos tours. Specializes in last-minute deals on 3 day/4 night, 4 day/5 night, and 7 day/8 night Galápagos tours. In high-season Galápagos travel (Jun.-Aug. and Dec. to mid-Jan.), Karen recommends inquiring by phone or email up to 3 weeks in advance for last-minute deals. Centro Viajero can also organize customized tours for groups and hire a car and driver. English, Spanish, and French spoken. Open daily 9am-7:30pm. AmEx/D/MC/V.

Chasquitur, Urdanetta 1418 (☎2281 084 or 2281 085), at Av. del Ejército in Urdesa, organizes tours to Reserva Ecológica Manglares Churute and other daytrips. Open M-F 9am-5pm.

Dreamkapture Travel, Alborada 12a etapa (☎2242 909; www.dreamkapture.com), Benjamin Carrion and Francisco de Orellana. Friendly English-speaking staff can arrange economical Galápagos tours (tourist-class from US$290, superior-class from US$540), scuba-diving trips (daytrips from US$110, multi-day trips from US$470), and more.

Galápagos Sub-Aqua, Orellana 211, Oficina 402 (☎2305 514 or 2305 507; www.galapagos-sub-aqua.com), at Panama. A well-known and experienced operator of diving tours in the Galápagos. All tours leave from Puerto Ayora and can accommodate beginner, intermediate, and advanced divers. Daytrips from US$100. Multi-day trips and week-long hotel packages also available.

Metropolitan Touring, Antepara 915 (☎2320 300; www.metropolitan-touring.com); also at 9 de Octubre and in the Hotel Hilton Colón (☎2692 917). 50 years of experience offering tours of Guayaquil, Bosque Protector Cerro Blanco, Puerto Honda mangroves, Reserva Ecológica Manglares Churute, Parque Nacional Machalilla, Manta, and more.

Municipalidad de Guayaquil (☎2531 691 or 2524 200, ext. 7402 or 7403, ask for Señorita Loira Delgado or Señor Gabriel Castro) frequently offers **free city tours** of Guayaquil's historic sites.

National Tours (☎2321 705), on Aguirre between Malecón and Pichincha, tours the Galápagos, Sierra, and Oriente. Open M-F 10am-pm, Sa 10am-noon.

Consulates: Canada, Córdova 812, 21st fl., Of. 4 (☎2563 580; fax 2314 562), off Manuel Rendón. Open M-F 9am-noon. **Germany** (☎2206 867), at Las Monjas and Carlos J. Arosemena. **Sweden** (☎2254 111; fax 2254 159), at Via Daule Km6½. **UK,** Córdova 623 (☎2560 400 or 2563 850, Sa-Su emergency cell 09 9429 107; fax 2562 641), in the Edificio de Agripac at Padre Solano. Open M-F 8am-6pm. **US** (☎2323 570, 24hr. emergency cell 02 9321 152; www.usembassy.org.ec), at 9 de Octubre and García Moreno. Open M-F 7:30am-4:30pm.

Immigration Office: ☎2297 004. On Río Daule, close to the bus terminal.

Currency Exchange: Casa de Cambios Delgado, 9 de Octubre 413 (☎2511 605), at Chile. Wander Cambios (☎2399 093), at Kennedy and Av. de las Americas; 2nd location at the airport.

ATMs: Several banks occupy the corners near 9 de Octubre and Pichincha. **Banco del Pacífico** (☎2566 010), at Pichincha and Icaza near the Malecón and also in the Unicentro Mall, has 24hr. Cirrus/MC ATMs. **Banco de Guayaquil** (☎2517 100), across from Banco del Pacífico, has 24hr. Cirrus/MC/Plus/V ATMs. All exchange money and offer cash advances on credit cards. Most banks open M-F 9am-5pm, Sa 9am-1pm.

Western Union: There are numerous operators on 9 de Octubre between Chile and Malecón, including a **24hr. office** at Guillermo Pareja Rolando 565 (☎180 0937 837), in Alborada in the Edificio de Bronce. Also in the Centro Comercial Malecón, on the Malecón 2000. Offices open M-F 8am-7pm, Sa 9am-5pm, Su and holidays 9am-1pm.

Credit Card Offices: American Express, 9 de Octubre 1900, 2nd fl. (☎2394 984 or 2286 900), at Esmeraldas. English spoken. Open M-F 9am-1pm and 2-6pm. **Citibank,** 9 de Octubre 416 (☎2564 780 or 2564 650), at Chile. **Mastercard** (☎2561 730 or 2511 500), at Córdova and 9 de Octubre in Edificio San Francisco, Of. 300.

LOCAL SERVICES

Cultural Center: Casa de la Cultura, on 9 de Octubre at Moncayo, just west of the Parque Centenario, has frequent plays, concerts, art exhibits, and art shows (all in Spanish). Monthly schedules of events available.

Supermarket: Mi Comisariato, entrances on Vélez and 9 de Octubre, between Bocayo and Avilez. Stocks a wide variety of groceries and snacks. Open daily 9am-8pm. MC/V.

Laundromat: Few and far between in Guayaquil Centro, and almost all specialize in dry cleaning. **Lavandería Espumita** and **Lavandería Pato**, on Isidrio in Los Sauces, Sauce 1, offers wash and dry for US$2.60 per load. Open M-F 9am-7pm, Sa 9am-4pm.

Public Toilets: Several clean, well-maintained public restrooms along Malecón. Find toilet paper In dispensers outside the stalls. Open 7am-midnight.

EMERGENCY AND COMMUNICATIONS

Emergency: ☎911.

Police: ☎101 or 2392 221. Where Cordero meets Américas, 3km from the airport. Officers also line Malecón.

Fire: ☎102.

Information: ☎104.

24hr. Pharmacy: Fybeca, 9 de Octubre 827 (☎2322 614), at Rumichaca. Other **branches** at Luque and Chimborazo (☎2328 838), Moncayo and Vélez (☎2510 584), Rendón and Moreno (☎2310 532), and Gomez and 6 de Marzo (☎2410 644). Most open M-Sa 8am-10pm. AmEx/MC/V. **Farmacia Victoria** (☎1 800 VICTORIA/8428 6742 or 2518 347), at 6 de Marco and Vélez, next to Parque Centenario. Open daily 9am-10pm. AmEx/MC/V.

Medical Services: Hospital Clínica Kennedy (☎2289 666, emergency ext. 100; ambulance 2289 010 or 2292 770), in Alborada, across from the Policentro mall, has the best service. **Red Cross** ambulance service (☎2560 674 or 2560 675). **Roberto Gilbert-Elizalde Children's Hospital,** Roberto Gilbert-Elizalde and Nicasio Safadi (☎2287 310, ext. 281 or 314), in Atarazana, specializes in pediatrics and burn intensive care.

Telephones: PacificTel branches all over town. Main office at Ballén and Pedro Carbo; enter from Ballén. Local calls US$0.13 per min.; to Europe US$0.22-0.35 per min., to the US, US$0.22 per min. Open daily 8am-10pm. **Cyber Pas@je Net,** in the Gran Pasaje Building on 9 de Octubre between Baquerizo Moreno and Córdova, and **Cyber** (see **Internet Access,** below) offer cheaper rates. To Europe US$0.15 and up per min., to the US, US$0.10 per min. Open daily 9am-8pm. Purchase **pre-paid phone cards** for BellSouth and Porta pay phones from various pharmacies and stationers around town.

Internet Access: Internet available on almost every block along 9 de Octubre. Most charge US$1 per hr. Some of the cheapest Internet cafes are on Rumichaca near 9 de Octubre. **Online Cyber,** on Rumichaca between 9 de Octubre and Rendón, has slower but cheaper service. US$0.50 per hr. Open M-Sa 9am-10pm, Su 10am-6pm. A bit further from the main street is **Cyber,** on Aguirre between Garacoya and Rumichaca. US$0.60 per hr. Open M-F 7am-7pm, Sa 7am-5pm.

Post Office: On the western side of Pedro Carbo between Aguirre and Ballén. Open M-F 9am-7pm, Sa 9am-noon. Additional locations at the bus terminal, at Estrada and Las Lomas in Urdesa, in Policentro Mall, and in the airport. **DHL** has several offices, including the Mall de Sol, near Policentro Mall, and 9 de Octubre 404 (☎2301 353). All open M-F 9am-1pm and 2-6pm. **FedEx,** Av. de las Americas 920 (☎2690 180; fax 2292 028), at Av. C. L. Dañin. **Postal code:** 10595.

☷ ACCOMMODATIONS

Budget travelers will be sorely disappointed with Guayaquil's lack of inexpensive, quality accommodations. The classier hotels in the busiest part of the Centro are bursting with amenities but don't come cheaply, as they target business travelers. Visitors to Guayaquil who don't mind the short bus or taxi ride to the Centro or are just staying for a night before catching a bus or plane may prefer the simple but affordable options in the more peaceful northern suburbs.

THE CENTRO

Hotel Alexander, Luque 1107 (☎2532 000; hotelalexander@hotmail.com), between Quito and Moncayo. Tastefully decorated with a wealth of paintings. Carpeted rooms have A/C, TVs, phone, hot baths, and lock box. 24hr. restaurant with inexpensive meals. Reservations recommended. Singles US$20; matrimonials US$23.50; doubles US$26; triples US$35. ❹

Hotel Sander, Luque 1101 (☎2320 030), at Moncayo. Larger than most of its budget-minded counterparts, Sandler is a decent value for the shoestring traveler and hard to beat for groups of 2 or 3. Rooms are small but clean and come with fans, color TV, private cold baths, desks, and chairs. Attached restaurant serves good, cheap meals. Reception 24hr. Check-out 24hr. after arrival or 2pm. Singles and doubles with fan US$9, with A/C US$11; triples US$13; family room with A/C US$16. ❸

Hostal D'La Rosa, Luque 1000 (☎2326 880), at 6 de Marzo. Dark wood flooring and romantic stained glass windows add character to D'La Rosa's reception area. The rooms, however, are small and simple but clean, with TV, fan, and cold bath. Breakfast included. Singles with fan US$10, with A/C US$14; doubles US$14/$17. ❸

Hotel Vélez, Vélez 1021 (☎2530 292 or 2530 311), between Quito and Pedro Moncayo. 6 stories of small, clean rooms with firm beds, cold baths, TVs, and daily cleaning service. 24hr. restaurant attached. Reception 24hr. Check-out 24hr. after arrival or 2pm. Singles and doubles US$10, with A/C US$11; triples US$13.70/$17.70. ❸

Rizzo Hotel, Ballén 319 (☎2325 210; hrizzo@gye.satnet.net), at Chile. 5 floors of clean, spacious tiled rooms with private baths. Towels, soap, TV, fridge, and chair in every room. Breakfast included. Reception 24hr. Check-out 1pm. Singles and doubles US$36; triples US$45; quads US$60. Discounts available for longer stays. ❺

Hotel Caprí (☎2530 095; fax 2321 216), at Machala and Luque, provides plain but comfortable rooms. Marble bed frames and spotless showers add pizzazz. Hallways are dimly lit but clean. All rooms have A/C, TV, hot bath, and refrigerator. Singles and doubles US$15; quads US$25. AmEx/D/MC/V. ❹

Hotel Ecuador (☎2321 460), on Moncayo between Luque and Aguirre. What the well-used rooms lack in character, they make up for in perks, like a TV, phone, and private bath. Restaurant (breakfast US$1) open 7am-9pm. Reception 24hr. Check-out 24hr. after arrival or 2pm. Singles and doubles with fan US$8.70, with A/C US$10.40; triples and quads with fan US$16. ❸

NORTH OF THE CENTRO

Some travelers prefer to stay in Guayaquil's quieter northern suburbs, which are closer to the airport and bus terminal. Reservations are highly recommended for the following accommodations. A taxi from the suburbs to the Centro should cost no more than US$3-4; double-check at your hostel. Additionally, several buses (US$0.25) run to and from the city and suburbs.

Dreamkapture Hostal, Alborada 12a etapa, Manzana 2, Villa 2 (☎2242 909), in a small alleyway next to a pink building. There is no sign, so give your taxi driver the address, walk down the alley, and look for the building with the large paintings on its exterior walls. Guayaquil's small but steady stream of backpackers flock here for the relaxing and friendly atmosphere, TV lounge, abundance of tourist info, and pleasant, clean rooms. Also arranges Galápagos tours, 1- and 5-day diving tours, and more. English spoken. Breakfast included. Airport transfer US$5. Reservations recommended. Singles US$12; doubles US$20; triples US$37; quads US$32. Private bath US$3. ❸

Ecuahogar (HI), Avenida Isidrio Ayora, Manzana F-31, Villa 20, Los Sauces 1 (☎2248 357 or 2732 281; www.ecuahostelling.net). This friendly hostel has reasonable rates, decent rooms, and a friendly staff. Clean rooms have comfortable beds, towels, private or shared cold baths, and powerful fans. The bright reception area has a TV, phone, fax, safe deposit box, mini-market, and some tourist information. Guests often relax in the 3rd-fl. lounge or rooftop patio. Conveniently located near the airport and bus terminal. Breakfast Included. Reservations suggested, especially July-Aug. Singles US$12, with A/C US$15, with private bath US$14; doubles US$18/$22/$25; triples US$24/$30/$20; quads US$32/$40/$40. HI discount 10%. Cash only. ❸

� FOOD

THE CENTRO

Along the sidewalks of the Centro, locals frequent the numerous, one-room restaurants whose tables spill out into the streets. These homogenous *comedores* serve cheap lunches and snacks (US$1-2.50). Note that price tags do not necessarily reflect food quality. Although many of the pricey hotels in the Centro have fine international dining, don't overlook the cheap local lunch stops for quick and hearty traditional meals. Also, dozens of fast-food chains line the Malecón 2000.

�● **Aroma Café,** on the Malecón just past the botanical gardens, where Tomás Martínez intersects with the Malecón. Excellent *típico* fare with romantic, tranquil ambience. Covered outdoor seating area overlooks a well-maintained garden, pond, and waterfall. One of the few restaurants where even vegetarians can enjoy a traditional Ecuadorian meal. English/Spanish menu. Lunch special (3 selections with fried plantains and drink), US$3.60. Traditional baked corn soufflé US$2.30, fried pork stew with homemade fried plantains US$6, grilled sea bass US$6.50. Open daily noon-midnight. ❷

�● **Casa Baska,** Ballén 422 (☎2534 599), at Chimborazo near Parque Bolívar. Even the most die-hard Spaniards swear Casa Baska's sensual Spanish cuisine is the best ever. A loyal clientele of affluent locals, businessmen, and foreigners enjoy precariously prepared delights like grilled prawns, marinated shrimp, and seafood paella in a traditional, romantic ambience. Reservations recommended on weekends, especially for large groups. Most entrees US$7-15. Open M-Sa noon-11pm. AmEx/DC/MC/V. ❹

El Galeon de Artur's, Diego Noboa 110 (☎231 2230 or 230 53 47), at step #52 on Cerro Santa Ana. 2 floors of the some of Guayaquil's best and more well known *comida típica*. Friendly waiters and occasional karaoke make for a casual, homey meal. Most entrees US$3-8. Open daily 6:30pm-late. ❷

La Canoa (☎2329 270, ext. 227 or 228), on Chile between Ballén and 10 de Agosto, next to Hotel Continental. This long-time staple of simple but tasty Eucadorian meals hasn't closed for a single day in over 30 years. Great service and a casual atmosphere make La Canoa a great stop for lunch or coffee. Salads US$1.50, sandwiches US$3-5, *típico* meat and chicken entrees US$3-6. Breakfast buffet US$8. Open 24hr. MC. ❷

Sofieri Cafe (☎2511 282 or 2512 256), on the Malecón at Villamil. Floor-to-ceiling windows give splendid views of Río Guayas, especially charming after dark. Extensive Spanish menu of tasty Ecuadorian and international entrees. Outdoor seating available. *Ceviche* US$5-7, pastas US$5-7, *típico* meals US$2.50-6, seafood US$5-17. Happy hour daily 4-8pm. Open daily noon-midnight. AmEx/DC/MC/V. ❷

La Pepa de Oro (☎2329 690), in Hotel Gran Guayaquil, at Boyacá and 10 de Agosto. Quality food with a pleasant view of the hotel's cascading waterfall and colonial artwork. Specializes in creative meat and seafood dishes like tropical smoked pork with mango sauce (US$5) and beer-battered fried tilapia (US$6). Standard pasta, pizza, and fajita dishes also available. Spanish/English menu. *Típico* Ecuadorian meal of beef tenderloin or smoked pork chop with rice, lentils, farm cheese, and plantains US$4.75. Sunday buffet US$9.35, children US$7.75. Open 24hr. ❷

FrutaBar, 9 de Octubre, 2nd fl. (☎2302 806), at Chile. Another location in Urdesa at Estrada 608 (☎2880 255), between Las Monjas and Ficus. FrutaBar transports a laid-back beach vibe to the busy streets of Guayaquil. Sip a tropical concoction of blended fruits from a surfboard table inside, or people-watch from the outdoor balcony overlooking 9 de Octubre. Fresh juices and shakes served in large glasses US$1.70-2.50, excellent warmed sandwiches US$2.60-3.50. 9 de Octubre location open M-Sa 8am-10:30pm; Urdesa location open M-Sa 8am-midnight. ❶

URDESA

The eateries on Victor Emilio Estrada in Urdesa are generally more expensive than many Centro options, but several offer delicious food at reasonable prices, and the pricier ones are worth the splurge.

■ **La Parrillada del Ñato,** Estrada 1219 (☎2387 098). You can't miss the gigantic sign or the smell of meat grilling on an open stove. Unearthly portions of fabulous beef make this restaurant popular with suburban locals, many of whom have been dining here for years. The menu is full of good choices, and the house specialty steak (US$15) can easily serve 3 people. AmEx/DC/MC/V. ❺

■ **Melting Pot,** at the corner of Ficus and Estrada. A surefire cure for any homesick traveler. With hand-written menus, ingredients on display, decorative artwork, and a small outdoor garden with seating, this small French cafe feels more like a family kitchen than a restaurant. Although the menu changes occasionally, elegantly prepared entrees like beef with almonds and potatos (US$7), savory crepes (US$1.60-4.50), homemade quiche (US$3), and marinated peppers (US$2.50) are standouts. Dessert crepes stuffed with nutella, caramel and rum, tiramisu, apple, or chantilly (US$2.30-3.50, US$0.70 extra for ice cream) will satisfy any weary traveler's tastebuds. Spanish menu. French spoken. Open M-Sa noon-10pm. ❷

■ **La Tratteria de Enrico,** Balsamos 504 (☎2387 079 or 2388 924), between Ebanos and Las Monjas. Nowhere but Enrico's are all the senses satisfied at once. Watch fish swim around the aquarium in the ceiling, hear lively Napoli music, smell fresh garlic and marjoram from the kitchen, savor tantalizing Italian entrees, and feel pleasantly tipsy after a few glasses of house *sangría* (US$3/cup, US$10.50/L). Enrico's is certainly not cheap, but locals affirm its status as one of Ecuador's best Italian restaurants. Complimentary bread, olives, and dessert square make it easier to swallow the bill. Various pastas US$6-13; grilled sea bass US$10; ravioli stuffed with crab, shrimp, and lobster US$12; mussels with tomato and white wine US$13; lobster stuffed with cream, mushrooms, and white wine US$28. Spanish/English menu. Reservervations recommended for large groups. Open daily 7pm-midnight. AmEx/DC/MC. ❺

Tsuji de Japón, Estrada 813 (☎2881 183 or 2882 641), between Guayacanes and Higueras. Cross the red-banister bridge to this classy Japanese restaurant. Try traditional dishes (US$12) grilled right at your table, or head over to the sushi bar. Open daily noon-3pm and 7-11pm. ❺

El Hornero (☎2384 788 or 2882 367), at the corner of Estrada and Higueras, across the street from Lo Nuestro. Serves mouth-watering, brick-oven pizzas (US$1-3 for personal, US$3-6 for 2 people, US$5-11 for 3 people, US$6-15 for 4 people) and calzones (US$3). Open daily noon-midnight. DC/MC/V. ❶

URDESA NORTE

0   200 meters
0   200 yards

Centro Comercial

Urdesa

🍴 FOOD
El Hornero, **3**
La Parrillada del Ñato, **1**
La Tratteria de Enrico, **9**
Lo Nuestro, **2**
Melting Pot, **5**
Restaurante Anderson, **8**
Tsuji de Japón, **4**

🍸 NIGHTLIFE
Chappuc's Bar, **6**
El Manantial, **7**

Plaza Tríangulo

URDESA CENTRAL

TO GUAYAQUIL CENTRO(4km)

Lo Nuestro, Estrada 903 (☎2386 398 or 2336 898), at Higueras. If the picturesque colonial archictecure, pink wooden shutters, and century-old framed newspapers don't lure you into Lo Nuestro, the elegant dining surely will. A diverse menu features such entrees as *pollo* tutti frutti, Spanish beef, shrimp ravioli, and oven-baked salmon (US$5-15). Open M-Th noon-3pm and 7pm-midnight, F-Su noon-midnight. ❺

Restaurante Anderson, Estrada 505 (☎2880 690 or 2389 766), between Ebanos and Mojas. Live like a king but don't pay like one during the cafe hours (M-Sa 3-8pm), when this upscale French continental restaurant serves delicious sweet and savory crepes and sandwiches at unbeatable prices (US$2-5). Most seafood and meat entrees US$7-30. 2-for-1 cocktails 4:30-8pm. Open M-Sa noon-midnight. AmEx/D/MC/V. ❷

🔲 SIGHTS

Thanks to the government's extensive efforts to clean up the city's image, improve its infrastructure, and restore many historic sites, Guayaquil is finding its way onto an increasing number of tourist itineraries. The Centro itself merits a day or two of exploring its museums, monuments, markets, and the Malecón. A few more days are well-spent hiking the nearby ecological reserves (see **Daytrips**, below).

EL CENTRO

■ **CERRO SANTA ANA.** Cerro Santa Ana is a small hill that was once the site of one of Guayaquil's oldest, and at times poorest, neighborhoods. Thanks to the Municipalidad de Guayaquil, which began reconstructing the area in 2001, Cerro Santa Ana is now one of the Guayaquil's most frequently visted attractions. Tourists and Guayaquileños alike climb Santa Ana's 444 numbered stairs, which ascend through a beautifuly restored, although rather touristy, collection of colorful colonial houses, shops, and cafes. Weekend afternoons and evening are the busiest times; many shops and restaurants remain closed on weekdays, especially in the daytime. To grasp the extensiveness of the restoration project, take a look at the photographs of the area before it was refurbished, displayed along the ascent. The most notable results of the renovation are improved potable water supplies, repaired and restored houses, new gardens and walkways, and the construction of a number of interesting historic monuments. **El Fortín de Santa Ana** and a small, outdoor **museum** await weary climbers at step 385. The large pirate ship, dozens of navigation instruments, and various weaponry, some dating to the 16th century, mark the site from which Guayaquileños defeated pirates in 1624. At the summit of the hill, 59 steps further, sits the tiny **Capilla Santa Ana Church,** which occupies the space where Guayaquil's first church was built in 1590. Opposite it is a stunning ■**lighthouse** (referred to as *el faro* by locals). Visitors can climb the lighthouse for unbeatable views of Ríos Babahoyo and Daule to the north, downtown Guayaquil to the South, Isla Santa and Durán to the east, and Cerro del Carmen and the rest of the city to the west. *(Walk north along the Malecón and exit to the street through the gates opposite the MAAC Cíne. The entrance to Cerro Santa Ana is about 50m to the left. Weekends are busiest; many shops and restaurants remain closed on weekdays, especially during the daytime. Open daily 10am-10pm. Free.)*

MALECÓN 2000. Spanning 2½km along Río Guayas, the grand-scale urban regeneration project known as the Malecón 2000 is Guayaquil's new and strinkingly modern main attraction Completed in 2003, the wide, well-lit, meticulously maintained, and heavily guarded riverfront walkway is a welcome respite form the bustle of Guayaquil Centro. At its southern-most end is the Mercado Artesanal (Artisan's Market; see Shopping: Markets, below), a collection of vendors selling traditional handicrafts. Just slightly north is the immense steel and glass Mercado Sur (South Market), orginally built in 1907 by famous French engineer Gustave Eiffel. In the early decades of the 1900s, Mercado Sur was Guayaquil's busiest marketplace. Recently restored, the market is slowly reestablishing itself as a center of business for the city's vendors. Continuing north along the Malecón, the Monumento Olmedo commemorates José Joaquin de Olmedo (1780-1847), a famous poet, Guayaquil's first *alcalde* (mayor), and Ecuador's first vice-president following the famous revolution of October 9, 1820. A brief stroll past the Centro Comercial Malecón (Malecón Shopping Mall) is a large Moorish clocktower. Though restored many times, the 22m structure dates back to the 18th century and was traditionally used to call locals to prayer. First inaugurated in 1842 after a epidemic of yellow fever swept Guayaquil, the clock was moved and restructured four times before arriving on the Malecón. Visitors can climb the winding staircase inside for spectacular views of Guayaquil. Halfway down the Malecón at the intersection of 9 de Octubre is La Rotunda, a semicircle of 10 columns commemorating the annexation of Guayaquil to the Gran Columbia. Each column bears the seal and flag of the 10 countries that famous revolutionaries Simón Bolívar and José de San Martín helped liberate from Spanish rule. Along the southern half of the Malecón are an exercise area, beautiful botanical gardens, the brand new Muséo Antropológico y de Arte Contemporaneo (see below), and South America's first IMAX theater (see below).

LAS PEÑAS. Past the MAAC Cine and IMAX at the northern end of the Malecón is the Las Peñas neighborhood, the site of old Guayaquil in 1537. Although the great fire of 1896 devastated much of the original colonial architecture, Las Peñas still contains some of Guayaquil's oldest houses. In October 2003, the World Monument Watch added Las Peñas to its list of 100 Historic, Architectural, or Cultural Monuments most deserving of protection. A single cobblestone street, Numa Pompilio Llona, named for the illustrious Ecuadorian poet, diplomat, and patriot of the same name (1832-1907), winds up a small hill through Las Peñas. It begins just beyond the gates of the Malecón, to the right of the stairs leading to Cerro Santa Ana. Testament to the many famed national artists who were born in this neighborhood, several **art galleries** line the narrow road through Las Peñas. *(Walk north along the Malecón and exit to the street through the gates opposite the MAAC Cine. The narrow Numa Pompilio Llona begins about 50m to the left, just before Cerro Santa Ana.)*

THE CEMETERY (LA CIUDAD BLANCA). West of Las Peñas, Guayaquil's hillside cemetery begins near Coronel and Riobamba and wraps around the mountain. The site of over 630,000 graves, the cemetery is easily the city's largest burial grounds. **Mausoleums** and **elaborate tombs** containing the remains of the wealthy occupy the lower parts of the hill, while poorer Guayaquileños generally have smaller graves higher on the slopes. Winding paths traverse the resting sites, the most famous of which leads to the ornate grave of former President Vincente Rocafuerte. A statue of the Virgin Mary overlooks the cemetery near the top of the hill; people say the city has grown more rapidly to the south because locals prefer to live with the statue of the Virgin looking down on them rather than with her back to them. The cemetery is considered one of the most beautiful in South America because of its more than 200 statues of Italian white marble. *(Take bus #74 from Rumichaca and 9 de Octubre to the "Cementario" (US$0.25) or catch a taxi (US$1). The Tourism Office recommends visiting M-Sa in the daytime or Su for safety reasons. Open daily dawn-dusk. Free.)*

IGUANA PARK. With the alternate aliases of **Parque Bolívar** and **Parque Seminario,** this attraction is commonly known by what it contains—loads of iguanas. Some up to 1½m long, the scaled reptiles pace the walkways, climb the trees, gobble vegetation and bananas kindly provided by fascinated children, and pose for the cameras. While these bad boys are fun to watch in their slow and methodical movements, they are notorious for spontaneously ejecting streams of liquid excrement from their tree-top hide-outs. Visitors aren't pooped and peed on regularly, but it's wise to keep an eye out for **flying bowel-pellets.** When not dodging such projectiles, visitors can appreciate the 43 species of flora and fauna, small pond of multi-colored tilapia fish, massive **cathedral** across the street (see **Churches,** below), and statue of Simón Bolívar. *(Bounded by Chile, Chimborazo, Ballén, and 10 de Agosto; opposite Unicentro Mall. Open dawn to dusk. Free.)*

PARQUE CENTENARIO. Guayaquil's largest park is also its most pleasant, with dozens of benches, shady trees, and ornamental plants in an area the size of four city blocks. Testament to the relaxing ambience of the park are the dozens of Guayaquileños who doze here daily. The plaza's most notable monument, a large column in the center, honors *los padres de la patria* (fathers of liberty) Simón Bolívar and José de San Martín. *(Bounded by Rendón, Veléz, Moncayo, and Garacoya; walk west, away from the Malecón down 9 de Octubre, and you'll run into it. Open dawn-dusk. Free.)*

CHURCHES. Some of Guayaquil's most beautiful buildings are its old Catholic churches, characterized by beautiful stained-glass windows, Gothic architecture, and gold-covered altars. Overlooking Iguana Park, the **Metropolitan Cathedral,** on Chimborazo between Ballén and 10 de Agosto, draws reverence from even the most skeptical viewers, with a striking gray-and-white interior and

IN-RECENT NEWS

WHO'S STEALING ALL THE ORCHIDS?

Want a sea cucumber? Check the Ecuadorian black market. The aphrodisiac, found off of the Galápagos and Ecuadorian mainland coast, is one of the world's most coveted species. Got a hankering for shark fins? Monkeys? Parrots? Orchids? Species of orchids nearing extinction can fetch up to US$10,000.

Of course, removing a near-extinct species from its natural habitat does little to ensure its survival. Such is the problem that Ecuador faces today. Ecuador's diminutive size makes the imperative to conserve its natural resources all the more urgent, but some Ecuadorians are more interested in the prospect of making a quick buck than preserving the country's delicate and world-renowned ecosystem.

The detrimental effects of this illegal plucking are worsened by constant deforestation in the form of city expansion and illegal logging. A smaller habitat translates to a less diverse gene pool. As the population dwindles it weakens.

Right now, Ecuador suffers from a lack of a well delineated and strictly enforced law to regulate harvesting and transport of animals and plants. Until changes are made, hunters will continue to harvest not only those species that are plentiful, but also those species whose presence will be missed only after they have disappeared completely from the face of the earth.

spectacular stained glass. For something with a little more history, try the **Iglesia de Santo Domingo,** at the northern end of Rocafuerte and Coromél. First built in the 16th century, Santo Domingo is Guayaquil's oldest church. Its 1938 restoration includes several of famous works of Ecuadorian painter Salas. (Visiting hours daily 8am-noon and 3-6pm.) To see some incredibly ornate gold work, head to Gothic **La Merced,** on Rocafuerte and Rendón. Where Rocafuerte becomes Pedro Carbo at 9 de Octubre, the Centro opens up to a plaza dominated by the facade of the **Iglesia de San Francisco,** which houses an elborate golden altar.

🏛 MUSEUMS

MUSEO MUNICIPAL. For those comfortable with Spanish, the Museo Municipal provides an excellent overview of Ecuadorian history and culture. It begins with an explanation of the transition from nomadic to sedentary pre-Hispanic civilizations and traces the development of the Ecuadorian identity through Spanish colonization, independence, and modern life and politics. The museum also has a permanent exhibition of paintings of all of Ecuador's presidents, an archaeological exhibit, and temporary exhibits ranging from colonial to contemporary art. Be sure to check out the shrunken heads on display. *(On Sucre, between Chile and Pedro Carbo.* ☎ *2531 691. Photo I.D. required to enter. Open M-F 9am-5pm, Sa 9am-2pm. Free.)*

OUTSIDE EL CENTRO

BOTANICAL GARDENS. Guayaquil's large and well-maintained gardens are about 15km from the Centro at Cerro Colorado, in northern Guayaquil near the Las Orquídeas housing development. These gardens have 324 botanic species, all of which are grown in their native habitats. Also not to be missed are the 73 kinds of birds and 60 butterfly species hiding amid the vegetation. The gardens consist of three main areas. The first contains a wide variety of orchids as well as an auditorium in which local artists often hold conservation-related programs. In the second section, visitors can view artwork from Guayaquil's first inhabitants, the Valdivians, and learn about traditional Ecuadorian cash crops. The final sections contain aboriginal nature drawings and a beautiful butterfly garden. Long pants, closed-toe shoes, and insect repellent are recommended. *(From the bus terminal, take bus #63 to Orquídeas and tell the driver to let you off near the gardens.* ☎ *2417 004 or 2416 975; jbotanic@interactive.net.ec. Open M-F 9am-5pm. US$5, guide US$2.)*

EL PARQUE HISTÓRICO GUAYAQUIL. Just 15min. from downtown, across the Daule bridge, sits one of Guayaquil's most interesting sites, a 20-acre park honoring the city's history, environment, traditions, and culture. Visitors can explore many different zones in the park. The wildlife zone is a well maintained outdoor zoo of many native plant and animal species, many of which are endangered. Beyond the zoo is a reconstruction of the Malecón in old Guayaquil, which fuses the impressive colonial architecture of the early 1900s with pleasant views of Río Guayas. In the traditions zone, an authentic *hacienda* and farm, complete with chickens and roosters, bring the Ecuadorian experience in *el campo* (the countryside) to life. *Campesinos* (peasants) dressed in traditional garments often sing and dance for groups of visitors. Adjacent to the traditions zone is a small garden of endemic plants and important fruits and vegetables; park staff sometimes perform puppet shows here to teach children about the environment and Ecuador's many endangered species. The third zone of urban architecture uses original remains of Guayaquil's antique buildings, which were destroyed by a number of earthquakes over the past two centuries. A small cafe, restrooms, potable water, and (Spanish) guides are available. *(From the bus terminal, take a Cooperativa Intercantonales de Santa Ana (C.I.S.A.) bus; the ticket window is toward the far right-hand side of the ground floor. Get off after crossing the bridge near Riocentro mall (US$0.30). The entrance to the Parque is a 5min. walk from the main road. ☎2835 356; www.parquehistorico.com. Reservations recommended for large groups. Open Tu-Su 9am-5pm. Tu-Sa US$3 adults, children and seniors US$1.50; Su and holidays US$4 adults, children and seniors US$2.)*

🎵 ENTERTAINMENT

FESTIVALS. Guayaquil's serious disposition is abandoned during its festivals. While national holidays send locals packing to the beach, city festivals are celebrated at home. July is an exciting month, with **Simón Bolívar's birthday** on July 24 and the **anniversary of the city's founding** on the following day. Both involve parades, concerts, fireworks, and beauty pageants. **Guayaquil's Independence Day** on October 9 is celebrated in conjunction with *El Día de La Raza* (October 12) in Durán, across Río Guayas. Guayaquileños join forces with hundreds of other South Americans in the annual *Fería de Durán*, one of the continent's largest celebrations with inexpensive handicrafts, live music, and cultural dances. Guayaquil's **New Year's Eve** festivities are especially unique. In addition to the ubiquitous fireworks display, Guayaquileños ring in the new year by burning *Años Viejos*, life-size dolls resembling well known local and international personalities. This annual ritual symbolizes the old year's completion and the commencement of the new.

MOVIES. For a relatively small city, Guayaquil has a surprising number of movie theaters. *El Universo*, Guayaquil's major newspaper, lists showings for most theaters. In the Centro, **Supercines** (☎2522 054), on 9 de Octubre between Rumichaca and Aviles, plays new releases in English with Spanish subtitles (US$2.60). The new **MAAC Cine,** on the Malecón, shows foreign and art films in a state-of-the-art theater; most films are in English (M-Th US$2.80, F-Su US$3.80). Just south of the MAAC Cine on the Malecón is South America's first **IMAX** theater (☎2563 078 or 2563 079), featuring adventurous films on a gargantuan screen. All shows are in Spanish (M-W US$3.75, Th-Su US$4). **Cinemark 9,** in the Mall del Sol (see **Shopping**, below), is arguably Guayaquil's most modern cinema, with nine screens and a full schedule of new release showings. (☎2692 013. US$4.) Other good options are: **Albocines,** at the Plaza Mayor in Alborada (☎2244 986; US$3); **Supercines,** in the San Marino Shopping Mall; and **Maya** (☎2386 456), at Las Lomas and Dátules in Urdesa. Almost all cinemas showing recent blockbusters offer English-language movies with Spanish subtitles.

SOUTHERN LOWLANDS

SHOPPING. Guayaquil offers two primary and utterly distinct shopping experiences: totally enclosed modern malls and busy outdoor markets. Guayaquil Centro's largest mall, **Unicentro,** in the block formed by Ballén, Chile, Aguirre, and Chimborazo, is still relatively small compared to the newer malls in the suburbs. The **Mall del Sol,** Ecuador's largest mall, is north of the Centro in Vernaza Norte near the airport. Practically every sign and store name is in English, and there's a food court, arcade, supermarket, movie theater, and 24hr. restaurant. (Open M-Sa 10am-9pm, Su 10am-6pm.) **Policentro Mall,** on Kennedy, is another popular option. Guayaquil's several **markets** provide a cheaper and slightly more authentic shopping experience. **La Bahía,** which runs parallel to the Malecón from Villamíl south to Colón, is the city's largest and busiest market. Hundreds of vendors hawk bootleg DVDs, belts, and bras and absolutely everything in between. Bargain actively for the best deal. (Open daily 9am-7pm.) At the southern end of the Malecón is the **Mercado Artesanal** (Artisan's Market), a good place to window-shop for woven bags, wooden jewelery, dolls, and leather goods. (Open daily 10am-8pm). The **Mercado de Artesanía,** at the other end of town on Loja between Moreno and Córdova, near Las Peñas, stocks a wider and generally less expensive variety of traditional handicrafts and art. (Open M-Sa 10am-6pm, Su 10am-3pm).

▓NIGHTLIFE

As the saying goes, spend your days in Quito and your nights in Guayaquil. Unlike the tourist-packed clubs of Atacames and Quito, going out in Guayaquil is a local affair. Clubs and discos in the Centro light the sky in shades of neon until dawn on the weekends, but many downtown areas are dangerous at night, so nightlife should be explored with caution. A better option is to hit clubs and bars outside the town center, which generally attract a younger crowd. Many hotspots lie in Kennedy Mall, opposite Mall del Sol in Kennedy Norte; along Victor Emilio Estrada in Urdesa; on Francisco de Orellano in Kennedy Norte; and in Centro Comercial Albán Borjaín Alboraba. Most bars and clubs charge a cover of US$5-10, which almost always includes *barra libre* (open bar).

BARS

Resaca Bar and Restaurante (☎2263 106), on the southern half of the Malecón, near the intersection with Junín. Resaca's wrap-around windows allow great views of the waterfront, especially in the evenings when the bar fills with a young and lively crowd. TVs showing soccer tournaments and pictures of past visitors on the walls inspires a fun, casual pub feel. One of the hipper bars in the Centro. Happy hour 6-8pm: 2-for-1 shots, 10 chicken wings US$6, nachos US$5. All-you-can-eat crabs and beer M-W 8pm-midnight US$10. Th Mexican night with 2-for-1 tequila. F seafood night. Sa live music, karaoke, and free *piña colada* for ladies. Sa-Su *típico* meals noon-6pm US$1-8. Open M-W and Su 11am-midnight, Th-Sa 11am-2am. AmEx/DC/MC/V.

Chappuc's Bar, Estrada 606, between Ficus and Monjas, in Urdesa. Wooden panelling all around gives this popular weekend hangout a smooth saloon-like feel. Enjoy a beer (US$1.50-2) on the upstairs balcony and people-watch. Open Tu-Sa 7pm-late.

El Manantial, Estrada 520 (☎2382 983 or 2884 288), between Ebaños and Monjas, in Urdesa. A casual place where people stick around after dinner to enjoy drinks late into the evening. Outdoor tables are especially popular. Beer US$1.25-$2.50, cocktails from US$2.80. Open daily noon-2am.

CLUBS

Alto Nivel, in Urdesa Norte, next to the huge TV antennae. 1st fl. room has techno tunes and black leather couches shrouded in fog and neon lights. 2nd fl. is dominated by salsa, red lights, and a large disco ball. Open daily 9pm-4am.

El Jardín de la Salsa, Las Américas 140 (☎2396 083), between the airport and the terminal. This stadium-sized disco is one of the hottest spots in Guayaquil. With a capacity of 6000, it's packed with anyone and everyone—old and young. Countless tables and benches surround the huge dance floor, which may occasionally feel more like a gymnasium floor than a *discoteca.* Occasional live music and free salsa lessons. Kiosks serve meals near the entrance. Pitchers of beer US$3.

Suruba, Francisco de Orellana 796, at Agustin Cornejo, near the World Trade Center in Kennedy Norte. Locals fill this large, wood-decorated flashy disco/bar. Bright flashing lights out front ensure you won't miss the party. Cocktails US$2-6. Open F-Su 8pm-late.

Cafe Olé, in Kennedy Mall. With several dance floors, karaoke, and a variety of Spanish, salsa, and American pop music, Olé attract's Guayaquil's hippest 20-somethings all night long. US$8 cover includes open bar. Open Tu-Sa 8pm-3am.

Jarro-cafe Bar, in Kennedy Mall. Have a snack in the outdoor bar area before entering the dark and smoky *discoteca,* where a large video screen plays music videos to a variety of popular music. US$5 min. bar tab. Open Tu-Sa 6pm-3am.

BOSQUE PROTECTOR CERRO BLANCO

Cerro Blanco has a rather unusual history. It was founded in 1989 by Cemento Nacional, an Ecuadorian cement company interested in the limestone deposits in the area. By setting aside a 3000-hectare patch of forest close to the lucrative rock, Cemento earned both a tax break from the government and unrestricted access to mine the land. Although the tax shelter has since been repealed, the verdant tropical dry forest remains protected and has more than doubled in size. Now managed by Fundación Pro-Bosque, a non-profit conservation organization originally set-up by the cement company, Cerro Blanco faces new challenges. Poachers continue to hunt illegally endangered animals and sometimes set fire to the forest to clear the brush. Fortunately, Pro-Bosque's dedicated volunteers and staff have initiatated a fire-control program and animal refuge center for threatened species. And, though the forest is less lively than Ecuador's most visited parks, it offers great ecological diversity and a tranquil nature escape just 16km from downtown Guayaquil.

AT A GLANCE

AREA: 6078 ha.	**GATEWAYS:** Guayaquil (p. 263).
CLIMATE: Hot and rainy Jan.-May; cooler and drier June-Dec.	**CAMPING:** About 400m from the park entrance. Facilities include picnic tables, bathrooms, and grill. US$3 per person.
HIGHLIGHTS: One of Ecuador's few remaining dry tropical forests. 215 species of birds, butterfly garden, and rescue center for threatened or hurt wildlife.	**FEES:** Entrance US$4, children US$2. US$7-12 for trails (includes guide).

🔢 PRACTICAL INFORMATION

Transportation: From Guayaquil, catch a bus headed to Chongon from the main bus terminal or from José de Anteparra and 10 de Agosto, 2 blocks west of the southwestern corner of Parque Victoria; ask the driver to let you off at the entrance to the park (30min., daily every 20min., US$0.50).

Park Information: Park rangers guard the main gates and collects entrance fees. Pro-Bosque's **information center** is located about 250m past main gates; veer right when the main path splits. Photo ID required to enter. Guides required to hike most trails.

Reservations required for Sa-Su visits, but walk-ins welcome. To arrange group or M-F visits, contact Pro-Bosque's Guayaquil office (☎2416 975), at the corner of Eloy Alfaro and Cuenca, Office 16, in the Edificio Promocentro. For reasons of safety, it's best to take a cab to the office. Park open daily 8:30am-4:30pm.

Maps: Available from the park ranger near the entrance.

Supplies: Potable water available at the Pro-Bosque offices (see above), but bring extra, with food, sunblock, hat, long pants, comfortable shoes, and insect repellent.

Tours: Guides are required for most hikes; hire one at the park (US$6-10, depending on hike). **Metropolitan Touring** (see p. 268) provides organized tours to the park.

Volunteering: Cerro Blanco's volunteers assist in trail maintenance, reforestation projects, guarding against poachers, and wildlife rescue. For more information, contact Pro-Bosque's director, Eric Horstman, at vonhorst@ecua.net.ec. See **Alternatives to Tourism,** p. 74.

◎ ◪ SIGHTS AND HIKING

Cerro Blanco offers four trails, three of which require park guides. The gravel path beginning at the main gates leads to the start of all five hikes. **Avenida de los Aves** (400m) begins just past the main gates and can be traversed without a guide. With a little patience and an observant eye, hikers can see the rare *colibrís* (hummingbirds), most famous for flapping their wings 80 times per sec. Cerro Blanco's trees are home to nine of the 132 registered species of *colibrís*. At the end of the trail sits a small **Jardín de Mariposas** (Butterfly Garden). Nectar-sipping birds share branches with colorful butterflies, whose population in Cerro Blanco ranks the fifth most diverse in South America. From the Butterfly Garden, continue past the main path to visit the **nursery** and **information center.** Fundación Pro-Bosque's offices stock **potable water** and some information (all in Spanish) about the park's ecology. Michael, who has worked for the Fundación for over a decade, speaks fluent English and can share a wealth of information about the park's history. Michael also manages the **vivero** (nursery) which grows many native trees and plants for the extensive reforestation work in the burned-down and pasture areas of the park. Around the corner from the nursery is a small **animal refuge center,** where endangered, threatened, and hurt animals are cared for and treated.

Back along the main path, it's a short walk to the mini-bar, where you can hire guides for the parks three main trails, **Sendero Buena Vista Largo** (4hr., 5096m, US$12), **Sendero Buena Vista Corto** (2½hr., 2588m, US$9), and **Quebrada Canoa** (1½hr., 1177m, US$7). Senderos Buena Vista Largo and Corto begin with a steep climb through primary forest but eventually flatten out to a dry landscape dense with enormous trees. The *ceíbo* tree, with its rough, grayish-green bark, is the most prevalent member of the park's more than 100 tree species. Decades ago, its buoyant fruits were used to make lifejackets. The trees, though occcasionally thin, provide excellent views of the city and coastal mangroves. If you go early in the morning or later in the afternoon, there's a good chance you'll see monkeys, ocelots, peccaries, and tapirs. The shorter Quebrada Canoa trail traverses a wetter environment, offering glimpes of ravine and pond wildlife. Many different species of fish, crabs, shrimp, and birds are frequently sighted.

 A wide variety of animals lurk in Cerro Blanco's dense tropical forest, but the afternoon sun and heat finds most of them sleeping or hiding in the shade. Peak hours for viewing wildlife are either first thing in the morning or around 3pm.

RESERVA ECOLÓGICA MANGLARES CHURUTE

AT A GLANCE

AREA: 50,000 hectares

CLIMATE: Hot and rainy Jan.-Apr.; cooler and drier May-Dec.

HIGHLIGHTS: One of Ecuador's last coastal mangrove areas. Occasional dolphin sightings from the coast.

GATEWAYS: Guayaquil (p. 263)

ACCOMMODATIONS AND CAMPING: Cabañas located within the park US$5 per person, children US$2. Camping US$3 per person, children US$2.

FEES: Entrance US$10, children US$2. Mangrove tour US$15 per boat.

Backpackers who flee Guayaquil in search of more rugged terrain overlook Reserva Ecológica Manglares Churute, a massive national park just 45km southeast of the city. Created in 1979 to prevent shrimp farmers from destroying the area's ecologically valuable mangroves, the reserve now protects nearly 35,000 hectares of some of the nation's only remaining coastal mangroves. The water levels are highest from January to May, when boat tours through the swampy lagoons almost guarantee sightings of rare shorebirds, like ospreys, laughing gulls, ibis, and spoonbills. Bird sightings are more limited from June to December, when the drier climate makes hiking from the coastal wetlands to the hilly tropical dry forest a worthwhile daytrip. Although visiting the park and touring the mangroves is somewhat pricey, conservationists can rest assured that their money is well-spent: all proceeds go toward expanding Ecuador's ecological gems and protecting them from illegal poaching.

🖪 🗷 TRANSPORTATION AND PRACTICAL INFORMATION

Transportation: Many visit the reserve on organized tours to see the mangroves, but you can easily go alone. From the bus terminal in **Guayaquil,** any **bus** to **Machala** or **Naranjal** can drop you off at the park entrance. Tell drivers that the park entrance is just after Km48 on the left side of the Guayaquil-Machala highway, a few km before Puerto Inca. Buses return to Guayaquil frequently all day long; just flag one down on the highway.

Park Information: Park office and **information center** located near the entrance within short walking distance from the highway. Guides (Spanish-only; US$5) required to hike trails. Park open daily 8am-1pm, occasionally open until 2pm.

Maps: Available from the park office near the entrance.

Supplies: Bring sunblock, hat, long pants, comfortable shoes, and insect repellent.

Tours: Contact the **Ministerio de Ambiente** in Guayaquil, Quito 402 and Padre Solano, 10th fl. (☎2397 730), to set up boat tours into the mangroves (US$12 for up to 12 people). **Chasquitur** in Guayaquil (see p. 268) offers organized hikes and mangrove tours with English-speaking guides.

🗗 🎜 SIGHTS AND HIKING

Although the reserve's main attraction is touring the tranquil and ecologically rich **mangroves,** four short hikes offer glimpses of the park's distinct ecosystems. **Sendero Red-letter de la Laguna** circles the 800-hectare Laguna del Canclón in the northeastern region of the reserve. The scenic body of water is named after the *canclón,* a native bird known for its unique calls. **Sendero El Mate** (1½hr.) begins with a rather steep ascent through the secondary tropical dry forest before transitioning into regions of flatter primary forest. With a bit of luck, hikers who tread lightly can observe several species of birds, white-faced capuchin monkeys, *tirgrillos*, armadillos, and more. The shortest and easiest of the reserve's trails is **Sendero El Mirador** (20min.). A brief jaunt leads to a lookout about 80m above sea level, from which visitors get panoramic views of the reserve's contrasting landscapes. **Senderos Cerro Pancho Diablo** and **Cimalón** traverse the primary humid tropical forest along the coast at an altitude of over 300m above sea level. This is one of the reserve's best protected areas and is home to numerous endemic plant and animal species. **Sendero Cerro Mas Vale** gradually ascends to the highest regions of the park, in which monkeys are frequently seen swinging high from the tree branches. The trail also includes a lookout point to a 30m waterfall.

BABAHOYO ☎05

Most travelers whiz by Babahoyo (pop. 80,000), the bustling capital of the Los Ríos province, en route to the more aesthetically pleasing and backpacker-friendly towns of central Ecuador. Although the murky Río Babahoyo was once an important means of transport from Guayaquil to Quito, most of the town's traffic is now limited to the province's rice, banana, cattle, and palm farmers, who make occasional trips to stock up on supplies or catch the bus to Guayaquil, 83km southwest.

☐☑ TRANSPORTATION AND PRACTICAL INFORMATION. Like many Ecuadorian towns, Babahoyo's main street is **9 de Octubre.** Parallel to it are **Malecón** on one side and **10 de Agosto** and **Barona** on the other. Streets are poorly labeled, so ask around for help with directions. **F.B.I. buses** leave from the terminal a few blocks southwest (away from the river) from the green church on Barona for **Guayaquil** (1hr., every 5min. 5am-10:30pm, US$1). **Banco de Guayaquil,** at Malecón and Bolívar, exchanges money and has a Plus/V ATM. (☎2730 029. Open M-F 8:30am-5pm, Sa 9am-2pm.) **Western Union** and **DHL** have offices on Sucre and Malecón. (Open M-F 9am-1pm and 2:30-5pm, Sa 9am-1pm.) Dozens of pharmacies line the streets near 10 de Agosto and 9 de Octubre; try **Farmacia María Elisa** at Rocafuerte and Barona for a wide range of medicines. (Open M-Sa 8am-10pm, Su 9am-noon.) **Cabinas Telefónicas,** at Eloy Alfaro and Barona, offers local, regional, and international phone service. (International calls from US$0.30 per min. Open M-Sa 9am-7pm, Su 9am-noon.) **Conexión Cyber Café,** opposite Cabinas Telefónicas on Bolívar, has some of the cheapest rates around. (US$0.80 per hr. Open M-Sa 9am-9pm, Su 9am-3pm.) The **post office** is behind the bus terminal on Gilbert. (Open M-Sa 9am-6pm, Su 9am-noon.)

☐☑ ACCOMMODATIONS AND FOOD. Lodgings cater mostly to farmers or businessmen passing through; foreign tourists are quite rare. **Hotel Capitol ❸,** at Martín Icaza and 10 de Agosto, has pleasant rooms in a homey building. Pastel-colored walls complement the clean and spacious rooms, all of which have private hot baths, TVs, and phones. A popular inexpensive restaurant is an extra perk. (☎2733 368; fax 2730 446. Checkout 1pm. US$9 per person with fan, US$13.50 with A/C.) **Hotel Cachari Bolívar ❺,** near Bolívar and Barona, opposite the church, is the nicest place in town. Enjoy tastefully decorated and fully equipped modern rooms in addition to a gym, sauna, bar, cafe, and disco. (☎2734 443; fax 2731 317. Breakfast included. Checkout 2pm. Reception 24hr. Singles US$30; doubles US$35; triples US$37; quads US$48.) A few doors down on Barona is **Hotel Cachari ❷,** Bolívar's more economical sibling. Rooms are small and simple, with TVs and cold private baths. (☎2734 443. Singles and doubles US$7; triples US$10.)

Babahoyo has dozens of cheap, family-run joints serving the standard fare. Locals recommend **Restaurant Pizzería Inés ❶**, between Rocafuerte and Barona on 10 de Agosto, for inexpensive Western favorites. (Sandwiches US$1.25. Burgers US$0.80-$1.50. Pastas US$2. Pizzas US$2-9. Open daily 9am-10pm). If you're craving *ceviche*, **Pastelería y Cafetería El Cubano ❶**, next to Hotel Capitol (see above) prepares some of the best *típica* fare in town. (Lunch US$1.25. *Ceviche* US$2.50. Open M-Sa 8:30am-9pm, Su 9am-2pm.)

PUYANGO PETRIFIED FOREST

The Puyango Petrified Forest, 7km from Ecuador's border with Peru, showcases flora and fauna from the Triassic Period. Today, visitors roam through a forest dense with lizards, butterflies, and birds, but its ancient remains are the real attraction. The 2658 hectares make Puyango one of the three largest petrified forests in the world. Scattered throughout are the petrified remains of 120 million years old Arcadia trees, as well as imprints of ancient sea creatures. The stone-cold Arcadia stumps are some of the largest in the world; the biggest, known as *"el gigante,"* measures roughly 25m in length and nearly 3m in diameter. Although they'd be hard-pressed to nest in these trees, over 130 bird species live in this small park. The guide can name many species by sight or song as he takes you along the well-maintained paths (1hr.). Highlights include numerous *tropotas* (enormous blue butterflies), leaf and root impressions, and towering Pretino trees. (Park open daily 8am-5pm. US$1, children US$0.50; includes required guide.)

Travelers can stay in the caretaker's **bunkroom ●** (US$5). **Camping ❷** (US$3) is available by the river; they have no equipment to lend. The house across the street from the park office sells sodas (US$0.40), crackers (US$0.30), tuna (US$0.90 per can), and ice cream (US$0.30-0.90). The few **restaurants** in Puyango do not see many customers but can prepare something substantial if given time. It might be a good idea to place an order, go hike for an hour, and return for the meal.

From Machala, take either the 9:30am or 1:15pm **Transportes Loja** bus to **Bosque de Puyango** (2½hr., US$3). It will be headed for Loja and pass first through Arenillas before reaching the Puyango Petrified Forest. From the military checkpoint at Río Puyango, walk to the park offices (5½km, 1hr.); from there it's another 15min. walk to the park entrance in a white building by the bridge. On Thursday and Sunday, a bus bound for Puyango passes the checkpoint at 1:30pm. To get back to Machala or Loja, hail a bus from the checkpoint. Since buses are sporadic, ask about return times when buying your morning bus ticket. Normally buses head back to Machala at 4, 5, and 6pm.

PIÑAS   ☎07

When discussing the streets of Piñas (pop. 24,000), it's hard to know which adjective to choose: sloping, slanted, or just plain steep. On the other hand, if you ask about life in the city, there's no problem—the only variation possible is the number of *"muys"* that precede *"tranquilo."* In 1825 Spanish geologist Juan José Luís was given a large land grant for his work in the nearby gold mines. Eventually, his big ranch became today's small town. Modern Piñas has few ties to its past; the Virgen del Cisne and a gaggle of other saints exert far more influence than any of Juan's kinsfolk. Indeed, other than valley vistas and tourist-less quietude, the main attraction of Piñas is its prominent piety.

◪◪ TRANSPORTATION AND PRACTICAL INFORMATION. Loja and **Sucre**, which merge on the Machala end of town, are the most active streets. There are two main **bus** companies in town. **Cooperativa Ciudad de Piñas** (☎2976 167; open daily 2:30am-10pm), at the corner of Loja and Sucre, sends **buses** to: **Guayaquil** (5hr.; 3:50, 8:15am; US$5.65); **Machala** (2hr.; every hr. 4:30am-6:30pm, 8pm;

US$2.10); **Quito** (12hr.; 7:45, 8pm; US$10) via **Santo Domingo** (9½hr., 7:45pm, US$9) or via **Riobamba** (9hr., 8pm, US$9) and **Ambato** (10hr., 8pm, US$10). **TAC,** at Independencia 31-10 (☎2976 151; open 24hr.), runs buses to: **Cuenca** (5hr., 1:30am, US$6); **Guayaquil** (5hr., 5 per day 1am-2:15pm, US$5.65); **Loja** (5hr.; 3:30, 7:45am; US$4.75); **Machala** (2hr.; every hr. 4am-7pm, 10:30pm; US$2.10); **Quito** (12hr.; 6:15, 7:30, 7:45pm; US$10); and **Zaruma** (45min., every 30min. 4am-7pm, US$1). **Tourist information** can be obtained in the municipal building across from the Iglesia Matriz on Sucre. (Open M-F 8am-noon and 2-6pm.) **Banco Machala** is just beneath the plaza on Sucre. (☎2976 201 or 2976 225. Open M-F 8:30am-3pm, Sa-Su 8am-1pm.) The **police** (☎2976 134; phone/fax 2976 433) are downhill where Ángel Salvador Ochoa and 9 de Octubre meet. **Policlínico Reina del Cisne** (☎2976 689), on 8 de Noviembre at Loja, offers 24hr. medical services. **PacificTel,** two blocks uphill from the church, doesn't allow collect or calling card calls. (Rumiñahui 29-292976 104; fax 2976 990. Open daily 8am-8pm.) A **branch** is on Sucre under the plaza. (Open daily 7am-10pm.)

▯▯ ACCOMMODATIONS AND FOOD. Residencial Dumari ❷, on 8 de Noviembre at Loja, on top of the hill, may not be eye-catching, but it has what counts—cushy beds, fluffy pillows, and plenty of hot water. (☎2976 118. US$4 per person, with bath and color TV US$6.) **Hotel Las Orquídeas ❷,** at Calderón and Montalvo, in the lower end of town, has a wide range of rooms, some with cable TV. The fancy suites have jacuzzis. (☎2976 355. Singles from US$4; deluxe doubles US$25.) It's easy to find a chicken (live or roasted) in Piñas, but other fare can be tricky. Restaurants with standard meals are scattered on Sucre, Loja, and Bolívar. For something a little different, try **Magic's Pizza ❶,** two blocks up Moreno from the church. After a personal pie (US$1-2.50), have something sweet from the fully stocked ice-cream freezer. (☎2976 697. Cones US$0.50-0.65. Open M-Sa 9am-11pm, Su 10am-10pm.)

▣ SIGHTS. The woodcarvings, metalwork, and unique clock-tower architecture of the **Iglesia Matriz,** on the plaza at Sucre and Gonzales Suárez, are interesting but can't outdo the nearby **Cerro del Calvario de Cristo (Hill of Christ's Calvary).** The red dirt path glitters with mica as it climbs (35min.) past 14 paintings, protected by concrete and glass, that depict Jesus's journey from condemnation to crucifixion. The view from the hilltop cross is spectacular. From the plaza walk downhill on Gonzales Suárez, then down the stairs to the footbridge. The trailhead is at the concrete arch across the river and to the left. Alternatively, take an Orquídea de los Andes taxi from Sucre and García Moreno (15min., US$4) straight to the top.

HUAQUILLAS   ☎07

The town of Huaquillas (pop. 42,000) enjoys a strictly geographic fame on the border of Peru. Prices in Ecuador used to be lower than those in Peru, a fact that brought Peruvian shoppers in droves and transformed the city's main street into a giant open-air market. Today, Ecuador's recent dollarization (and continuing inflation) has reversed the trend: now Ecuadorians flock across the river in droves, and Aguas Verdes (the tiny town on the Peruvian side of the bridge) is experiencing a boom. Both sides of the Puente Internacional are packed with merchants hawking their wares, advertising prices in dollars and soles. The border crossing itself is usually painless but bewildering, and most travelers opt to keep moving.

▮ TRANSPORTATION. CIFA (☎2996 370; open 24hr.), one block east of the street light on República at Santa Rosa and Machala, sends **buses** to **Guayaquil** (4½hr., 8 per day 3am-6:30pm, US$5) and **Machala**—both **direct** (1hr., every

BORDER CROSSING: INTO PERU. Ecuador and Peru are separated by Río Zarumilla, which is crossed by a bridge. When crossing the border, everyone must pass through both Ecuadorian and Peruvian immigration within 24hr. Leaving Ecuador, pass through **Ecuadorian Migraciones,** on the left side of República, about 3½km before Huaquillas. (☎2996 755. Taxi 7min., US$1.50. Open 24hr.) After getting your stamp, take a waiting cab back to Huaquillas. Walk across the bridge into Aguas Verdes, ignore the numerous overpriced transport offers you'll receive, and push through the crowd to the **mototaxis** waiting a few blocks from the border on República del Perú. These can take you the 3km (5min., s/3) to **Peruvian Migraciones** (☎2561 178; open 24hr.), but may try to con you into paying extra for your luggage. After completing customary procedures, **combis** to **Tumbes** (35min., 5am-7pm, s/1) can be hailed on the highway. They run to two destinations: the corner of Tumbes and Abad Puell, and the Mercado Modelo on Mariscal Castilla. Everyone crossing the border in either direction must have a tourist **T3 card** (available at both Ecuadorian and Peruvian immigration offices) and a **valid passport.** Tourists can stay up to **90 days** in Ecuador or Peru. Anyone staying longer must get a visa extension (**see Documents and Formalities,** p. 11). Occasionally, officials ask for a return ticket or for proof of sufficient funds for the expected stay, but this is rare.

SOUTHERN LOWLANDS

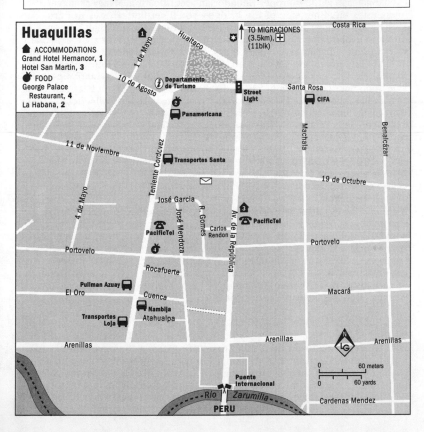

Huaquillas

🏠 ACCOMMODATIONS
Grand Hotel Hernancor, **1**
Hotel San Martin, **3**

🍴 FOOD
George Palace
Restaurant, **4**
La Habana, **2**

20min. 7am-7pm, US$1.80) and **indirect** (1¾hr., every 10min. 4:15am-8pm, US$1.80) via **Arenillas** (30min., US$0.60) and **Santa Rosa** (1hr., US$1.20). **Panamericana** (☎2996 695; open daily 8am-9pm), at Teniente Cordovez and Santa Rosa, goes to: **Ambato** (11hr., 8pm, US$8); **Quito** (12hr., 6 per day 10am-9pm, US$10) via **Santo Domingo** (8hr., US$7); and **Tulcán** (18hr., 4:30pm, US$15). **Transportes Santa** (☎2995 212; open daily 8am-7:30pm), on Cordovez near 19 de Octubre, travels to: **Ambato** (10hr., 5:30pm, US$8) via **Riobamba** (9hr., US$7); and **Quito** (12hr.; 1:15, 7:30pm; US$10). **Pullman Azuay** (☎2996 575), at Cordovez and El Oro, sends buses to **Cuenca** (5hr., 6 per day 1am-6:30pm, US$6). **Nambija** (open daily 5am-3pm), on Cordovez next to El Oro, goes to **Zamora** (8hr.; 6am, 12:30pm; US$7.50) via **Loja** (6hr., 12:30pm, US$5). **Transportes Loja** serves **Loja** (6hr.; 1:30, 6pm; US$5) and **Piura** (3½hr., 2pm, US$5).

🖫🛈 ORIENTATION AND PRACTICAL INFORMATION. Everything of importance for travelers lies along one of Huaquillas's three main thoroughfares: **Machala, Teniente Cordovez,** or **La República.** The majority of the street market lines La República; most bus companies are found on Cordovez. The **Departamento de Turismo,** on the top floor of the municipal building at 10 de Agosto and Cordovez, provides maps of Huaquillas and info on attractions in El Oro. (☎2996 285. Open M-F 9am-1pm and 2-6pm.) Most **banks** in town won't exchange cash without proper Ecuadorian identification. **Money changers** offer lousy rates on either side of the bridge—you'll get better rates in Peru. The authorities suggest having a police officer present when changing cash in order to avoid being ripped off. If you have to change money, be especially wary of fake bills and fixed calculators. Other services include: **police** (☎2996 341), at República and Costa Rica, just before the street light; **hospital,** on República, 11 blocks before the stoplight on the right (☎2996 097; open M-F 8am-4pm; emergencies daily 24hr.); **PacificTel** is on República between 19 de Octubre and Portovelo. (Fax 2995 100. No calling cards or collect calls. Open daily 8am-10pm.) It has a **Branch** on Teniente Cordovez near Portovelo. (☎2997 022. Open daily 7am-9pm.) The **post office** is on 19 de Octubre, near República. (☎2995 311. Open M-F 8:30am-4:30pm.)

🖪🖸 ACCOMMODATIONS AND FOOD. Spending the night in Huaquillas isn't recommended, but travelers arriving late may have no choice. **Grand Hotel Hernancor ❸,** at 1 de Mayo and Hualtaco, has spacious, airy rooms with cable and phones. (☎2995 467. Singles US$10, with A/C US$12; doubles US$12/$14; triples with A/C US$18.) **Hotel San Martin ❶,** on República across from the church, has sizable budget rooms with working fans and bug nets. (☎2996 083. Rooms US$3, with bath and cable TV US$5.) Most locals pick up grub from the numerous **street vendors ❶** that set up shop around the sole traffic light on República. (Entrees US$1-1.50.) For a quieter, indoor dining experience, head to **George Palace Restaurant ❶,** on Portovelo near Teniente Cordovez (open daily 7am-5pm) or **La Habana ❶,** at 10 de Agosto and Teniente Cordovez (open M-Sa 7:30am-9:30pm). Both serve hearty *platos* for US$2-4.

MACHALA ☎07

Locals have proclaimed their city (pop. 235,000) the "banana capital of the world," and that's a title they work hard to maintain—the city, surrounded by banana plantations, takes its fruit seriously. Local newspapers list the value of the banana alongside the dollar and the price of gold. El Bananero, a larger-than-life banana grower carrying a 2½m bunch, greets entering visitors, and

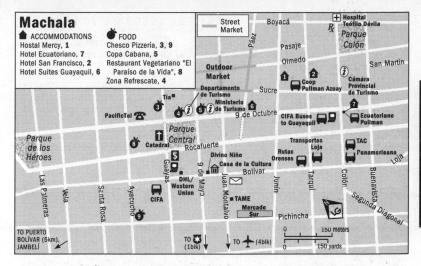

Machala

ACCOMMODATIONS
Hostal Mercy, **1**
Hotel Ecuatoriano, **7**
Hotel San Francisco, **2**
Hotel Suites Guayaquil, **6**

FOOD
Chesco Pizzería, **3, 9**
Copa Cabana, **5**
Restaurant Vegetariano "El
Paraíso de la Vida", **8**
Zona Refrescate, **4**

cartoon-style "banana men" signs dot the town. Locals extol the virtues of the sacred fruit, Ecuador's second-largest export, during the third week in September, when the immense Banana World Fair draws participants from as far away as Mexico and Argentina. Festivities include the selection of one lucky lady to receive the city's highest honor—the coveted Banana Queen title. Bananas aren't all Machala has to offer, though; a lively atmosphere and the nearby waterfront of Puerto Bolívar and beaches of Jambelí make it a good rest stop before crossing into Peru.

⌐ TRANSPORTATION

Flights: The **airport** (☎2930 620) is 7 blocks south of the main plaza on Montalvo. **TAME** (☎2930 139; www.tame.com.ec), on Montalvo between Bolívar and Pichincha, flies to **Quito** (1hr.; M, W, F 9am; US$80) via **Guayaquil** (30min., US$34). Open M-F 8:30am-7pm. DC/MC/V.

Buses: Buses leave from the grid formed by Junín, Bolívar, Colón, and Sucre. **Rutas Orenses** (☎2937 661; open daily 4am-10:30pm) at Bolívar and Tarqui, goes to **Cuenca** (3½hr., 12 per day 5am-5:15pm, US$5) and **Guayaquil** (3hr., every 30min. 4am-10:30pm, US$4.50). **CIFA** has 2 offices: 9 de Octubre 627 (☎2937 074; open daily 4:30am-7:30pm), which goes to **Guayaquil** (3½hr., every 30min. 4:30am-7:30pm, US$4); and at the corner of Guayas and Bolívar (☎2933 735), serving **Huaquillas** (1½hr., every 20min. 6:40am-7:30pm, US$1.80). **Panamericana,** Colón 1839 (☎2930 141; open daily 7am-10:30pm), at Bolívar, goes to: **Ambato** (7hr., 10pm, US$8); **Quito** (10hr., 8 per day 7:45am-10:30pm, US$9) via **Santo Domingo** (7hr., US$6); **Tulcán** (15hr., 6:30pm, US$13). **TAC,** Colón 1819 (☎2930 119; open daily 4am-10pm), goes direct to **Quito** (10hr.; 8:15am, 9:30pm; US$7) and **Piñas** (2hr., every hr. 4am-8pm, US$2.10). **Ecuatoriano Pullman** (☎2931 064; open daily 4am-10pm), at 9 de Octubre and Colón goes to **Guayaquil** (3hr.; 2, 3, 3:45am; every 30min. 5am-8pm; US$4) and **Huaquillas** (1½hr., 16 per day 4am-9pm, US$1.50). **Transportes Loja,** Tarquí 1813 (☎2937 030; open daily 6:30am-11pm), goes to **Ambato** (8hr., 10:30pm, US$6) and **Loja** (5hr., 10 per day 7am-11:30pm, US$6).

Taxis: US$1 within the city.

⚡ 🔃 ORIENTATION AND PRACTICAL INFORMATION

Most activity takes place between the bus area and the **Parque Central,** along the strip defined by **9 de Octubre** and **Rocafuerte.** The busy **9 de Mayo** crosses both to connect the park to the hectic **market.**

Tourist Offices: Ministerio de Turismo (☎2932 106), on 9 de Octubre between 9 de Mayo and Montalvo, 2nd fl., has information on sites and helps arrange tours. Enter through Stephany Boutique. Open M-F 8am-12:30pm and 1:30-5pm. **Departamento de Turismo** (☎09 9984 594), on the 3rd fl. of the Municipal building at Parque Central, has free city **maps.** Open M-F 8am-12:30pm and 3-6:30pm.

Bank: Banco de Guayaquil (☎2963 101), on the plaza at Rocafuerte and Guayas, exchanges AmEx/MC/V traveler's checks for a 1% commission 8:45am-4pm. 24hr. MC/V **ATM.** Open M-F 8:45am-6pm.

Markets: From fresh fruit to kitchen sinks, the **market** around 9 de Mayo and Sucre is a rainbow of shopping value. Open daily from 6am-6pm. **Tía,** Sucre 1123 (☎2931 270), has everything, including **Western Union** service. Open daily 8am-8pm.

Laundromat: Divino Niño, Bolívar 810 (☎2930 099), at 9 de Mayo. US$3 per 12 items. Delicates US$0.20 each. Open M-F 8am-6:30pm and Sa 8am-noon.

Emergency: ☎101. **Fire:** ☎102. **Information:** ☎104.

Police: ☎2933 391. At 9 de Mayo and Manual Serrano.

24hr. Pharmacy: Farmacia Imperial, Boyacá 601 (☎2931 528), at Colón.

Hospital: Hospital Teofilo Dávila, Boyacá 502 (☎2937 581 or emergency 2939 099), at Colón, in front of Parque Colón. Open M-F 8am-noon and 2-6pm for consultations. Emergencies 24hr.

Telephones: PacificTel (☎2937 788), on 9 de Octubre between Guayas and Ayacucho, handles faxes but not collect or calling card calls. Open daily 8:30am-10pm.

Internet Access: The **PacificTel,** on Guayas between Rocafuerte and Bolívar, has Internet for US$0.60 per hr. Open M-Sa 8am-10pm, Su 8am-8pm. **Carplo.net,** 9 de Octubre 614 (☎2936 241), at Colón. US$0.70 per hr. Open daily 9am-6:30pm.

Post Office: Bolívar 733 (☎2930 675; fax 2931 908), at Montalvo. Open M-F 8:30am-5pm. **EMS** (☎2935 669) is at the post office. Open M-F 8:30am-5pm and Sa 8:30am. **DHL/Western Union,** Bolivar 914 (☎2962 444), between Guayas and 9 de Mayo. Open M-F 8am-7pm, Sa 9am-5pm. DC/MC/V.

🏠 ACCOMMODATIONS

Because of the large number of tourists passing through Machala, budget accommodations abound. Be sure to check for window screens, mosquito nets, and fans.

Hostal Mercy, Junín 915 (☎2920 116), at Olmedo and Sucre. Simple but clean rooms with private cold baths surround a tiled courtyard, all in a central location. Courtyard has a few palm trees and no street noise. Kind owners give you a key to the front gate. Singles with fan US$5, with A/C US$6. ❷

Hotel Suites Guayaquil (☎2922 570 or 2934 270), at Páez and 9 de Octubre. Wooden floors and friendly staff. Private, cold water bath, fans, and cable TV. Near the market and food. US$6 per person, slow business US$5, with A/C US$10. ❶

Hotel San Francisco (☎2922 395; hotel_sf@hotmail.com), on Tarquí between Sucre and Olmedo. Offers luxury at affordable prices. Amenities, including an elevator, hot baths, cable TV, and room service, mitigate the maze-like halls. Singles US$10, with A/C US$14; doubles US$18/$22; triples US$21/$26. AmEx/DC/V. ❸

Hotel Ecuatoriano, 9 de Octubre 531 (☎2930 197), above Ecuatoriano Pullman. Clean, dark rooms with shared baths are convenient for catching early morning buses. Singles US$6, with bath and fan US$9, with bath and A/C US$12.50; doubles US$10/ $16/$22.50. ❷

❐ FOOD

If you can imagine it, you can find it (or at least the ingredients) in Machala's sprawling **outdoor market** (see above). More inexpensive lunches and snacks are advertised around town, and provide filling helpings of *comida típica*. Join the locals at **Puerto Bolívar** (see below), only a 5min. cab ride away, for great seafood. The *ceviche* and other coastal specialties at the Malecón de Puerto Bolívar, near downtown, draw hungry visitors from far and wide. Reach it by a west-bound bus with "Pto. Bolívar" in the front window from the Parque Central (12min., US$0.25) or a taxi (5min., US$2.50-3). Get off at Hostal Solar del Puerto, at the corner of Gonzalo Córdova and Rocafuerte; walk two blocks to the waterfront.)

Zona Refrescate (☎2962 777), on 9 de Octubre at Parque Central. A clean, cheery place serving everything from breakfast (US$2-2.60) to burgers (US$2.40-3.20) to mixed drinks (US$3.10) to ice-cream treats (US$2-4.20). The clientele is as varied as the menu, from groups of teens to businessmen. Watch the big screen cable TV in back if the busy plaza isn't entertaining enough. Open daily 9am-10:30pm. ❶

Chesco Pizzería, Guayas 1050 (☎2936 418), with a branch at Pichincha and Ayacucho, serves the best pizza in town. Try the tuna and corn pizza. Large pie US$11-13; pasta US$4-5. Open M-Sa noon-11pm, Su 4-11pm. ❷

Restaurant Vegetariano "El Paraíso de la Vida" (☎2930 218), on Ayacucho between 9 de Octubre and Rocafuerte. Green tablecloths and fruit pictures jive with the city's banana theme. Quiet and calm with a tiny courtyard and fountain in the back. Veggie *menú* US$2. Also sells *carne de soya* by the kg. Open M-F 7am-8pm, Sa 7am-4pm. ❶

Copa Cabana, 9 de Octubre III (☎2923 491), at 9 de Mayo, has a bright, tropical atmosphere and comfortable booths. Specializes in breakfast (US$1.60-2.50) and ice cream (US$1.10-3.50). Open daily 7am-10pm. ❶

❺ SIGHTS

From Puerto Bolívar **boat tours** make full-day trips out to **Isla Santa Clara** (a.k.a. **Isla del Muerto**). From a distance, the island looks like a dead man floating on his back. Between July and September, try to catch a glimpse of migrating **humpback whales.** On the island see diverse fauna reminiscent of the Galápagos. (Make reservations with Geómer Garcia ☎09 4008 605; geomertierramar741@hotmail.com. Find him at the *muelle antiguo,* 200m down Malecón from the spot where boats leave for Jambelí. 1 tour per week leaves from the pier next to Pepe's Sa 7am; returns 5pm. US$20, including lunch. Open M-F 9-11am and 2-4pm.)

The **Casa de la Cultura** displays interesting artifacts from the province of El Oro. Enthusiastic guides explain the historical significance of objects as well as their connection to present-day life. The assortment of petrified rocks and fossils from Puyango and artifacts from the pre-Inca (500 BC-500 AD) Jambelí culture takes no more than 30min. to explore. (☎2937 117. On Bolívar between Montalvo and 9 de Mayo. Museum on top fl., but it might be necessary to find a guide in the Salón Histórico on the 2nd fl. Open M-F 9am-noon and 1-4pm. Free.)

JAMBELÍ ☎07

Festive music, bamboo benches, thatched roofs, swaying palms, warm water, and gentle waves combine to give Jambelí a constant summer feel. This island is about the beach, and modern luxuries such as telephones and electricity (M-Th 11am-4pm and 6pm-midnight; F-Sa 6-9am, 11am-4pm, and 6pm-2am; Su 6-9am, 11am-4pm, and 6pm-1am) are limited. Food stands and ice-cream vendors congregate at the point where the town's one street meets the beachfront sidewalk. Bird-watchers also flock to the island to view the crowded treetops along the main waterways. In spite of Jambelí's eternal summer, some things do change with the seasons: winter (Dec.-Apr.) brings more frequent rains and sandflies, while summer (May-Nov.) sees sunny skies and droves of tourists. Jambelí parties on Friday and Saturday nights to salsa beats that drown out the surf at the open-air dance floors (left of the beach entrance). Look for the biggest crowd and listen for the hottest beats. The party doesn't stop until the lights go out (2am).

Accommodations are expensive and basic. During summer and holidays, rooms fill and prices double. Reservations are recommended during these times, but few locals have phones—leave a message in Máchala or with the operators at **Pacific-Tel.** (☎2964 113. Open M-Th 11am-2:30pm and 6-10pm, F-Su 11am-4:30pm and 7-10pm.) **Hostería La Casa en la Luna ❷,** up the beach to the right at the northern end of the island, offers the largest, best maintained rooms. The owner speaks English and German, runs a book exchange, and offers snacks on the patio (cocktails US$2-4; pasta US $3-4). Additional amenities include bug nets, kitchen, and laundry facilities. Ask here about boat tours around the island or horse rentals. (☎09 7046 049; jambeliluna@hotmail.com. Camping US$2-5 per tent. Singles US$5; doubles US$10; triples US$15. For longer stays, guests can help with **work** around the hostel to receive a discount.) **Acuario Beach ❷,** to the left on the main drag, has rooms (US$5) with private baths on the second floor; the front two have large windows with great ocean views. North from the road, **Cabañas del Mar ❷** has comfy rooms with porches, fans, private baths, and big windows. Cabañas fit five but can be split into doubles. (US$5 per person. Inquire at Restaurant Costañita.) Seafood is Jambelí's perennial specialty. Of the town's offerings, **Restaurant El Niño Turista ❶,** at the beachfront corner of the main street, is the biggest, busiest, and best located. Sugarcane juice (US$0.50) and salsa music restore spirits. (☎09 9623 421 or 09 8296 358. Entrees US$2-6; lunch US$2. Open daily 7am-9pm.)

To get to Jambelí, take a **boat** from Puerto Bolívar (30min., M-F 9 per day, round-trip US$2.40), from **Cooperativa 31 de Julio** on the pier with the "Muelle de Cabotaje" sign, next to Pepe's (see above). To return, just reverse the route (30min., M-F 9 per day). During peak season and weekends, additional boats make the trip. Entrance to the island costs US$0.20.

THE ORIENTE

Off the eastern edge of the Ecuadorian Andes, snow-capped volcanic peaks and wind-swept páramo fall away to equatorial tropical world: blazing hot sun alternating with torrential rain amid a sinewy network of Amazon tributaries and lush rainforests. One road and its offshoot traverses thick junglve and clear-cut pastures at about 1000m, linking the small communities of Equador's last, and quickly disappearing, frontier. Farther cast, having lost all altitude in the stifling depths of the Amazon Basin, canoes are the only means of transportation. The as-of-yet

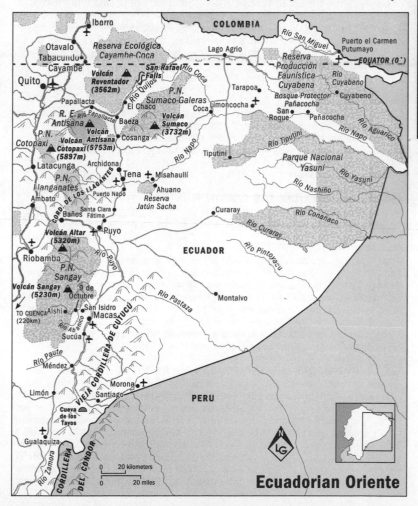

Ecuadorian Oriente

untouched parts of the jungle—gloriously dense, green, and alive—stretch into Peru and Colombia, more than 100km away. This primary-growth rainforest hosts countless varieties of trees, vines, and insect species—as well as larger, rarer animals—including jaguars, sloths, monkeys, and crocodiles.

HIGHLIGHTS OF THE ORIENTE

RAFT the Class II-IV **rapids** in the many rivers around Tena (see p. 295).

RUMINATE on the mysteries of nature deep within **Jatun Sascha** (see p. 304).

DANCE to traditional music at the village of **Runa Huasi** (see p. 303).

Humans have also lived here in isolation for centuries. The remaining indígenas include the Huaorani, Secoya, Siona, Quichua, Cofán, and Shuar peoples. Today, the oil industry has gained a foothold in the Oriente, giving Ecuador an economic boost, while threatening to ravage an incomparably precious ecosystem. Ironically, the infrastructure created by oil companies has allowed ecotourism to flourish, providing new economic opportunities while preserving natural habitats.

BAEZA   ☎06

Though officially part of the Oriente, Baeza's altitude (1900m) and surrounding Andean peaks are more like those of a Sierra hamlet. The village is little more than a crossroads that grew from the so-called Y of Baeza. One road leads northwest to Quito, one south to Tena, and the last northeast to Lago Agrio. If you can't bear the full-day bus rides to and from the Oriente or need a good base for exploring the San Rafael Falls, Baeza (pop. 5000) is a convenient place to spend the night.

▟▊ TRANSPORTATION AND PRACTICAL INFORMATION. Passengers on Quito-Lago Agrio **buses** get dropped off at the **"Y,"** but if you're on a Quito-Tena bus, you should ask the driver to let you off at the Baeza Nueva bus stop. From the Y, walk 35min. downhill from Baeza Nueva, and flag down one of the camionetas heading up the road (US$0.50). Buses pass the Y every 45min. heading to Quito (3hr., US$3.80) and Tena (2½hr., US$2.50). Houses and storefronts line the Quito-Tena road 2-3km from the Y junction going toward Tena. Uphill from the Y (toward Tena), the road first passes **Baeza Vieja** on the right, then twists over **Río Machángra** to become **Av. de los Quijos** in **Baeza Nueva**. Hotels, restaurants, and the town's few services are along the eight blocks of Quijos. There are **no ATMs** in town. **Police** are on 5 de Marzo, across from Hotel Samay. (☎2320 291. Open 24hr.) A little farther along this street is **Hospital Centro de Salud Baeza**. (☎2320 117. Open 24hr.) **Andinatel,** 17 de Enero and Quijos, is in Baeza Nueva.

▛▟ ACCOMMODATIONS AND FOOD. Hostal Bambus ❷, about three-quarters of the way down New Baeza's Quijos coming from the Y, is a squeaky-clean place, with private baths, TVs, and a covered courtyard with a pool table. (☎2320 219. US$8 per person.) **Hostal San Rafael ❷,** farther down Quijos on the right, has hot baths, clean tiled floors, and perks including a video and music room and kitchen, which doubles as a restaurant. (☎2320 114. US$3 per person, with bath US$5.) **Hotel Samay ❷,** also on the right side of Quijos but closer to the Y, has well-lit wooden rooms and a hot shower. (☎2320 170. US$5 per person.) **Restaurante El Viejo ❷,** between Hostal San Rafael and Hostal Bambus has table linens, yellow wallpaper, and postmodern Ecuadorian paintings. (☎2320 442. Meat and the specialty, trout, US$4. Open daily 7am-10pm.)

◪ **CAMINO DE LA ANTENA.** The trail (3-4hr.) follows a steep 4-by-4 road to antennae which overlook the town and surrounding countryside. The many viewpoints are at eye level with clouds and the surrounding cloud forest. Take **Gil Ramirez Davalos,** the street to the right of the church in Old Baeza, uphill. Soon it becomes a dirt road and heads past a **cemetery.** Follow the road across the river and head left up the steep road. Unfortunately, the end is rather anticlimactic.

PAPALLACTA ☎06

When you're exhausted and messy, dirty and drained, it's time for Papallacta (pop. 600). Tucked away in a high, narrow, and beautiful Andean valley 1½hr. east of Quito, Papallacta tantalizes travelers with cloud forest greenery and azure pools of steaming hot water. Like Baños (see p. 150), this hot-springs town is part mountain and part jungle. Unlike Baños, Papallacta is rooted firmly in the Oriente sytle of life. Nearby hikes hold their own, but the luxurious baths with resort-like facilities are Ecuador's best pools for soaking your weary bones.

▐─▉ TRANSPORTATION AND PRACTICAL INFORMATION. Papallacta itself is a handful of small buildings along the Quito-Baeza road. **Buses** from Quito turn first onto Termas de Papallacta. Most tourist facilities line the first 2km of this road. The residential district begins 500m down the road. Buses to **Quito** and **Tena** run frequently along this road and can be easily flagged down in front of the Termas de Papallacta sign or the **police station,** the blue-and-white checkpoint on the right walking downhill from Quito to the town center. (☎2320 430. Open 24hr.)

▐▐▛ ACCOMMODATIONS AND FOOD. By far the best but expensive place to stay in Papallacta is the hotel ◪**Termas de Papallacta ❺.** The well manicured grounds have many private, quiet nooks. The hotel also has a spa (US$15 per day, children US$10; open Tu-Su 9am-5pm) and several hot pools, though it offers free passes to Las Termas. (☎2320 621. Singles US$55; doubles US$85; triples US$97; 6-person cabañas US$89. In-room jacuzzi US$15 extra. IVA included. Ask about mid-week discount of 10-15%. AmEx/MC/V.) Back toward town but a stone's throw from the thermal pools, **Hostal Antisana ❸** provides an excellent shared bath alternative. (☎2320 626. US$8 per person, private bath US$10.) **Hostel Coturpa ❸** is next to the pools of the same name. Follow signs for las nuevas piscinas. Rooms are clean, large, heated, and have private baths with thermal water.

10 REASONS ORIENTE TRANSPORTATION IS SLOW

10. Engine malfunction: Old Bessy doesn't work so well on hills.

9. Construction: It's very hard to drive on a road that hasn't been built yet.

8. Driver breaks for dinner: The call of hunger is a strong one. Restaurant El Amanecer in El Chaco (between Baeza and Coca) is a favorite stopping place.

7. Popped tire: Interestingly, drivers don't use regular jacks. They'll find large rocks or small boulders from the side of the road to prop up the neighboring wheel in order to fix the flat.

6. Felled tree: Not only does deforestation ruin the environment, but cut trees also block the road.

5. Buses play tag: If a bus can't cross a small bridge, another must pick up waiting passengers on the other side—just hope it's on time.

4. GEMA checkpoint: Don't mess with the Grupo Especial Móvil Antinarcóticos—just wait patiently.

3. Not enough water: Low rivers force passengers to drag canoes, not ride in them.

2. Too much water: Heavy rains cause mudslides that relocate car-sized rocks to the middle of the road.

1. Protests: Insurgents have found that blocking major roads to stop all traffic flow sends a loud message.

(☎2320 640. Singles US$12; matrimonials US$20; doubles US$26.) **Hostería La Pampa de Papallacta ❸**, in the white compound on the right just after the road to Las Termas flattens out, has a ping-pong table and two pool tables. Some rooms have fireplaces. (☎2320 624. Breakfast included. Singles US$10; doubles US$20. If vacant, a double may go for the price of a single; be sure to inquire.)

Café Canela ❹, at the Balneario at Las Termas, provides upscalde dining and looks over the pools to the mountains beyond. You might be surprised when you look up; the roof is clear! (Entrees US$6-8. Open Su-Th 8am-7pm, F-Sa 8am-8pm.). The immensely popular **La Choza de Don Wilson ❶**, at the foot of the road to Las Termas, has wide valley views and a ski-lodge feel. Enjoy lunch (US$1.95) or the local specialty, fresh trout (US$3), in this thatched-roof restaurant. (☎2320 627. Open daily 6am-10pm.) Bright and clean, **El Leñador ❶**, just before the entrance to Las Termas, stands out among the small trout shops. (US$2.50. Open daily 7am-7pm.)

⚠ IMMERSE YOURSELF IN NATURE. At the base of the town are the piping hot **Coturpas** pools, also called the nuevas piscinas (new pools). Changing stalls, mandatory hot showers, and baskets for belongings are provided. (Open M-F 7:30am-5pm, Sa-Su 6am-5:30pm. US$2, children US$1.) However, **⛲Termas de Papallacta** offers genuine hot springs 2km farther up. The road to these pools veers to the left off the main highway just before entering town from Quito, and to the right if coming from town (10min; there's a big sign). From here, the walk is 20min. The first half of the walk is steep, but then it flattens out. The public pools are past the *balneario* (health resort, or, in this case, hotel) entrance on the left. The pools are kept at a steamy 36-40°C, but those seeking to cool off need only dip their feet in the icy stream rushing by. Ride horses (US$6 per hr.) at the same complex. (Locker rental US$0.50 with US$5 deposit. US$6, children US$3, seniors US$2.50. Open daily 6am-9pm.) Past the entrance to the pools, the **Exploratorio** houses displays of local flora and fauna. **El Sendero de la Isla** (1hr.; entrance fee US$1) starts here and follows Río Papallacta. Hikers can camp in a clearing beside the trail (US$6). Two longer guided tours (4hr., US$4; 5hr., US$8) head toward the **Cayambe-Coca Reserve.** Contact the Exploratorio or the Fundación Ecológica Rumicocha in Quito, to arrange trips that venture deeper into the wilderness.

ANTISANA ECOLOGICAL RESERVE

These 120,000 hectares southeast of Quito cover a wide range of altitudes and ecosystems. Glacier-covered Volcán Antisana (5758m), the valley of Río Cosanga, and the headwaters of Ríos Coca and Napo reside here. The reserve also protects an incredible amount of biodiversity. Over 550 species (over 60% of all the species of Ecuador) of amphibians, reptiles, and mammals live within its borders. 600,000 residents around Quito even get their potable water from here. Contact Fundación Antisana (www.antisana.org) about two- to three-day hikes through the reserve. Though most of the year is very wet, the months between June and August and December and February are driest. Instituto Geográfico Militar (see p. 97) has a good regional map. From Quito, travel through the town of Pintag to reach the reserve. Arrange a tour with a Quito-based tour group for easy traveling. **Surtrek** (see p. 87) offers daily tours for groups of at least two people. (☎2231 534; www.surtrek.com. Food, entrance fee, guides, and technical equipment included. English- and German-speaking guides available. 4-day US$390 per person; 5-day with climb of Volcán Antisana US$590 per person.)

VOLCÁN REVENTADOR

Clouds often enshroud this 3562m active volcano, located near the southeastern edge of La Reserva Ecológica Cayambe-Coca. On clear days, it is possible to see it from the road to Lago Agrio. On November 3, 2002, Reventador sent a column of smoke and ash 17km into the air, and its upper slopes are prone to lahars (volcanic mudflows) caused by frequent rainfall. Guides warn that no one has summitted since the eruption because conditions are still dangerous at the top. However, hiking the lower slopes on the trail that begins at Hostería El Reventador is possible. **San Rafael Falls** (see below), **Hostería El Reventador** (see p. 295), and the town of **El Reventador** (30min. toward Lago Agrio) can provide guides and more information.

SAN RAFAEL FALLS   ☎06

Las Cascadas de San Rafael are another display of natural beauty on the Baeza-Lago Agrio road and are the highest waterfalls (130m) in Ecuador. They fall about 1km west of the starting point of Río Reventador, about 2hr. east of Baeza on the mostly-paved Baeza-Lago Agrio road. If you ask to be let off at "las cascadas," bus drivers will drop you off on the right at a sign next to a dilapidated hut where the road starts. The trail descends from there, but be careful. It's been washed out and requires some creativity to find. About 200m after the washed-out portion, the trail crosses a bridge over a small waterfall. It then leads to a little house marked "Guardia" where you pay an entrance fee (US$1). Leonidas, who lives there, is very helpful and will let you stay in his extra room. Past the house, the trail continues to a group of **casitas** (small houses). The black arrows to the left of the casitas indicate where the path enters the jungle. From here hike 30min. on a clearly marked trail to Mirador, a lookout point with a couple of benches and a good view of the *cascadas*. For extended viewing, backtrack a few minutes to the campsite and set up a tent. One hundred and fifty meters uphill from the entrance to the falls is the **Hostería El Reventador ❷**. It offers a waterpark atmosphere with a pool and slide filled with runoff from the volcano. The compound includes a roadside eatery. (☎2550 468; cell 09 7582 198. Fish dishes US$2. Dorms US$7; singles with bath US$10. Cash only.) As of June 2004, the Ministerio del Ambiente was instituting a US$10 fee for access to **La Reserva Ecológica Cayambe-Coca,** though it is unclear whether the falls are under this ministry's jurisdiction.

TENA   ☎06

Known as the "green heart of the Amazon," Tena (pop. 30,000), 197km southeast of Quito, sits at the confluence of the fast-flowing Ríos Tena and Pano, part of the headwaters of the Amazon. Life here is a happy compromise between bustling city and tranquil riverside. The pretty city, with its three bridges and shockingly green foliage, is overshadowed by the mighty Cordillera de los Llanganates and engulfed on all sides by a wild and high jungle (500m above sea level), ensuring superb bird and insect biodiversity. Entrepreneurs have already developed a jungle playground, with spelunking, whitewater rafting, kayaking, and every other adventure a cement-weary urbanite could desire. So many exciting options exist that it can be almost overwhelming. Moreover, the beautiful setting, well-lighted streets, friendly locals, and do-it-yourself daytrips tempt travelers to stick around for a while, even after their jungle jaunt is over.

▐▌ TRANSPORTATION AND PRACTICAL INFORMATION

When visible, the mountains to the west are a useful landmark. Roughly speaking, they run north-south. The town center lies at the confluence of **Ríos Pano** and **Tena;** the town as a whole spans both sides of the rivers, connected by a traffic bridge (closed as of July 2004), a footbridge, and a third bridge that reaches **Parque Amazónico La Isla.** Most hostels and tour agencies are on or near **15 de Noviembre** between the footbridge and terminal. The main **plaza** is on the opposite side. Restaurants and bars cluster around both sides.

THE ORIENTE

THE ORIENTE

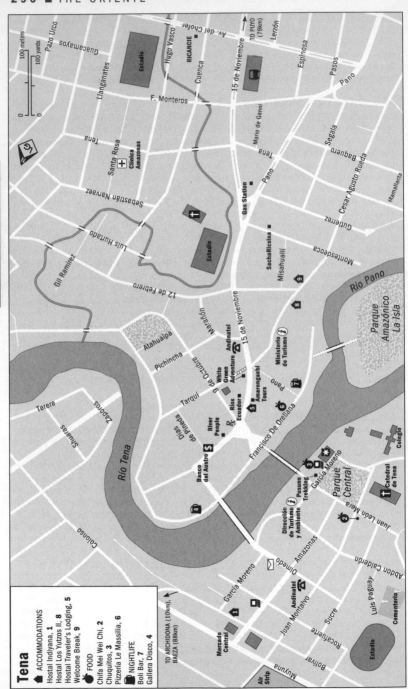

Tena

♦ ACCOMMODATIONS
Hostal Indiyana, **1**
Hostal Los Yutzos II, **8**
Hostal Traveler's Lodging, **5**
Welcome Break, **9**

♦ FOOD
Chifa Mei Wei Chi, **2**
Chuquitos, **3**
Pizzería Le Massilia, **6**

■ NIGHTLIFE
Boli Bar, **7**
Gallera Disco, **4**

TO ARCHIDONA (10km),
BAEZA (88km)

100 meters
100 yards

Pazo Urco
Guacamayos
Llanganates
Tena
Santa Rosa
Clínica
Amazonas
Sebastián Narvaez
Luis Hurtado
Gil Ramírez
12 de Febrero
Atahualpa
Pichincha
Tarquí
Meratión
de Pineda
Dias
Terere
Zapotes
Sinaries
Río Tena
Colonso
Banco
del Austro
River
People
Ríos
Ecuador
Amarongachi
Tours
White
Green
Adventure
Andinatel
15 de Noviembre
Francisco De Orellana
9 de Octubre
Ministerio
de Turismo
Río Pano
Parque
Amazónico
La Isla
Pano
Misahualli
SachaRicsina
Montesdeoca
César Agusto Rueda
Gutiérrez
Gas Station
Mario de Gamii
Tena
Pano
F. Monteros
Estadio
Hugo Vasco
RICANCIE
Cuenca
Av. del Chofer
TO PUYO
(79km)
Lerón
15 de Noviembre
Espinosa
Pasos
Pano
Segala
Baquero
Mamallacta
Estadio
Dirección
de Turismo
y Ambiente
Pusuno
Trekking
García Moreno
Parque
Central
Catedral
de Tena
Colegio
Juan León Mera
Abdón Calderón
Luis Pagüay
Cementerio
Estadio
Olmedo
Amazonas
Juan Montalvo
Andinatel
Rocafuerte
Sucre
Bolívar
García Moreno
Mercado
Central
Muyuna
Air
Strip

Buses: The **terminal** is along the right side of 15 de Noviembre, 1km uphill from the bridges. Main ticket offices are in the circular building, behind the row of stores. Buses go to: **Ambato** (6hr., 11 per day 2am-9pm, US$5) via **Puyo** (3hr., US$2.50) and **Baños** (5hr., US$4); **Quito** (6hr., 10 per day 2am-11:45pm, US$6) via **Baeza** (2½hr., US$2.50); **Riobamba** (7hr., 5 per day 2am-6pm, US$5.50); **Ahuano** (2hr., 9 per day 6am-5:30pm, US$1.50); **Misahuallí** (1hr., every 45min. 6am-7pm, US$0.95; leaves outside the terminal); **La Punta** (2½hr., 8 per day 6am-5:30pm, US$1.50).

Tourist Office: Dirección de Turismo y Ambiente (☎2888 046) offers information on local sights and tour companies. Open M-F 8am-12:30pm and 1:30-5pm. **Ministerio de Turismo** (☎2886 536) and **Cámara de Turismo de Napo** (☎2886 536), both on Rueda next to Los Yutzos (see below), offer maps and contact information of tour groups in Tena. Open M-F 8:30am-12:30pm and 2-5:30pm.

Currency Exchange: Banco del Austro (☎2886 446), on 15 de Noviembre between the bridges. Offers V cash advances. 24hr. **ATM.** Open M-F 9am-5pm. Banks do not exchange traveler's checks, but **Chuquitos,** next to the police station, does.

Volunteer Opportunities: Check out Amarongachi Tours's (see p. 300) work involving Spanish-English translation. Jatun Sacha (see p. 304) also offers opportunities.

Market: On Amazonas and Bolívar. Sells canned and fresh food. Open daily 6am-5pm.

Emergency: ☎101.

Police: ☎2886 101. On García Moreno across from the Parque Central. Open 24hr.

Pharmacy: Farmacia Bellavista (☎2887 511), at 15 de Noviembre and 9 de Octubre. Ring bell at night. Open 24hr.

Hospital: Clínica Amazonas (☎2886 515), at Tena and Santa Rosa. Walk toward the bus station on 15 de Noviembre and turn left on Tena; clinic is halfway down Santa Rosa on the left. Open 24hr.

Telephones: Andinatel (☎2886 105), at Olmedo and Montalvo and at 15 de Noviembre and Marañon. Open daily 8am-10pm.

Internet Access: Sn@lme.net, at Amazonas and Rocafuerte, is the best deal in town at US$0.04 per min. or US$2 per hr. Open M-F 10am-12:30pm, Sa-Su 9am-1pm and 3-9pm. **Cucup@net,** between Pusuno Trekking (see p. 301) and the police station, costs US$2.40 per hr. Open daily 7am-9:30pm.

Post Office: ☎2886 608. At Olmedo and Amazonas. Open M-F 8am-4:30pm.

▛ ACCOMMODATIONS

▓ **Hostal Los Yutzos II** (☎2887 897), on Rueda near 12 de Febrero across from Welcome Break (see below). Spacious rooms with high ceilings and riverfront views overlook the Parque Amazónico. Side-street location makes for a tranquil night's sleep. Rooms have telephones, hot showers, cable TV, and fans. Friendly owner offers Internet (US$1.20 per hr.). Take note that its more luxurious counterpart up the street—Hostal Los Yutzos—is budget only for big groups. Singles US$10; doubles US$18. IVA included. ❸

Hostal Traveler's Lodging, 15 de Noviembre 438 (☎2886 372), just uphill from the footbridge, in the same building as Amarongachi Tours (see p. 300) and Cositas Ricas (see p. 298). Rooms have private baths, fans, cable TV, and orthopedic beds. Overflows with satisfied tourists thanks to a helpful and knowledgeable family. US$5, with hot water US$7-13. IVA excluded. ❷

Hostal Indiyana (☎2886 334), at Bolívar and Amazonas, across the street from the market. Tena's cleanest and most aesthetically pleasing hostel sits in a quiet corner of town. Hot baths, cable TV, and fans. US$8. IVA included. ❷

Welcome Break, Augusto Rueda 331 (☎2886 301; cofanes@hotmail.com), at 12 de Febrero. Simple, clean rooms have bamboo desks, common baths, and kitchen access. Offers a small shaded area and hammocks for afternoon siestas. US$4 per person. ❶

Hostería el Paraíso de las Orquídeas (☎2889 232), 2km north of Archidona on the road to Baeza, is also known as La Isla de los Monos. More than 7 different species of monkeys wander the grounds. Walk through lush forest; visit the oquidearios (orchid garden); ogle at 300 species of birds in the adjoining El Para reserve; or just relax by the pool. Good for families. Breakfast included. 6-person private cabañas US$21. ❹

🖒 FOOD

It's easy to work up an appetite after a long day of water sports or hiking. Tena's quality eateries hug the river and are perfect places to rehash the day's stories.

▨ **Chuquitos** (☎2887 630), at Moreno and Parque Central, next to the police station. Enjoy uncommonly good pollo salteado (US$3.50) while watching the river below. This spacious spot (tastefully jungle-themed) is rightfully popular among travelers and locals alike. Cold beer US$1. Open M-Sa 7:30am-9pm. ❷

Pizzería Le Massilia, at Orellana and Pano. This open-air hut with spectacular mountain views offers hearty portions of tasty pizza, do-it-yourself soft tacos (US$5.75), and tasteful presentation in a relaxed atmosphere. Entrees US$4-6. Open daily 5-10pm. ❷

Cositas Ricas, part of the Hostal Traveler's Lodging (see above) complex. This colorful joint is always busy. Stop in for breakfast (US$1.80), a quick hamburger (US$1.80), or a full meal (US$4.50). Open daily 7:30am-10pm. ❷

Chifa Mei Wei Chi (☎09 7372 573 or 09 4423 180), at Mera and Montalvo below Hotel Amazonas (see above). Fill up on generous amounts of chaulafan (US$2.80) while you watch the passersby along Parque Central. Open daily 10am-11pm. ❶

👁 📝 SIGHTS AND ACTIVITIES

Tena boasts hot days and even hotter daytrips, many of which—though rugged—don't require a guide. If traveling solo, discuss the route with someone knowledge-able and leave a route plan with somebody in town; orientation can be difficult, and getting lost in the jungle is extremely dangerous. For information about choosing a guide, see **Jungle Tours,** p. 300.

CAVERNAS DE JUMANDY. These caves north of Tena, between Archidona and Cotundo, are wide and well-lighted by electric lights. Wade and swim deep beneath the surface of the earth in the small river that flows through these caves. Once inside the caverns, all is quiet except for the trickle of water. Though it's possible to explore the front of the caves alone, guides at the Jumandy complex, including **Manuel Moreta,** lead jaunts into the far reaches of the caverns. (8hr., US$30 per person) You can also camp here for the price of admission. There is a flat clearing with a volleyball and basketball court, as well as access to a nearby resort's bathrooms and showers. *(From Amazonas and Bolívar, catch a local bus bound for Cotundo and tell the driver you are going to "las cuevas" (30min., every 15min. 6am-7pm, US$0.25). If you can only find one bound for Archidona, take a bus from Amazonas and Bolívar (20min., every 15min. 6am-7pm, US$0.20), then catch the bus from Archidona to Cotundo, 1 block down Napo from the plaza, at Jondachi, and ask to be let off at "las cuevas" (15min., every hr. 7am-6pm, US$0.20). ☎2889 185 or 2887 833. US$2, children US$1. Cabins available. Singles US$6; doubles US$10. Tent rental US$3. Open daily 9am-5pm.)*

CENTRO INTERCULTURAL DE ECOTURISMO. Within walking distance of Archidona, this center has cabañas, a restaurant, a short self-guided hike through the forest, and an information center with descriptions of indigenous tribes. Volunteer here for US$10 per day, and get lodging and three meals per day. Contact the Fundación Sinchi Sacha (www.sinchisacha.org) to learn about volunteer opportunities. *(When entering Archidona from Tena, turn left at the sign for Centro Ecoturismo Río Misahuallí. After 1km, you reach the river. The center is on the other side of the bridge. Set up more for big groups. ☎ 2889 044.)*

PARQUE AMAZÓNICO LA ISLA. This 0.25 sq. km island between Ríos Tena and Pano, connects to Tena via a bamboo bridge 50m up-river from the main footbridge behind Hostal Traveler's Lodging (see above). Monkeys and birds inhabit the park's sprawling forest, which melts into soft, sandy beaches. Footpaths wind their way through the trees. Jungle cats bare their fangs (from cages), and a lookout tower affords a panoramic view. *(Open daily 8am-5pm. US$2.)*

EL CAÑÓN DE ÑACHI YACU. Take a bus heading north to Quito or Coca from Tena past Cotundo to Km10. A trail on the right marked by a small sign leads to El Cañón de Ñachi Yacu, also known as La Cascada del Gran Cañón. Try the challenging hike (round-trip 6hr.) through primary forest and waterfals—even one inside a cave—with someone who knows the muddy trail. Guides are available from **Cavernas Jumandy,** or ask around for **Lennin Tanguila,** who lives near the trail. *(Bus US$30 per person from Cavernas Jumandy. Price decreases with larger groups.)*

RESERVA ECOLÓGICO MONTEVERDE. This private reserve (8km from Archidona) is part of Sumaco-Galeras National Park. Hike along well-kept trails to discover caves and natural baths. Or lounge at beaches (with volleyball court). Sites for sport fishing are along Río Hollín, as it runs down from the Sumaco Volcano. Large groups can stay in a cabaña complex; anyone can camp on the reserve. *(☎ 2889 606; www.ecoturmonteverde@hotmail.com. The Monteverde information office is located next to the Residencial Regina in Archidona, 1 block off the plaza on Rocafuerte. Entrance fee US$2. Contact the office at least 1 day in advance for access.)*

CASCADAS GRAN EDÉN. Known by many as the **Cascadas de Latas** (tin waterfalls), these impressive waterfalls lie at the end of a very muddy trail through dense jungle vegetation. Along the way, rushing Río Umbuni runs through narrow rock formations called tobaganes. Relax and enjoy a meal on large rocks at the base, or take a dip in the nearby natural pool. Wear rubber boots on this hike. Rent them from Amarongachi tours (US$2), or buy them from local vendors (US$5). *(Take the Misahuallí bus and ask to be let off at the Cascadas de Latas (40min., every 45min. 6am-7pm, US$0.50). The trail to the falls (30-40min.) begins on the left just before a small bridge at a sign for Cabañas Gran Edén. Entrance fee is collected at a booth 100m up the trail or farther along the trail by the river at the gate just before the falls. US$2.)*

🎵 NIGHTLIFE

The nightlife is centered on the river. **Gallera Disco,** on Orellana and the river just past the vehicle bridge in the Hostal Puma Rosa, is the most popular place to boogie to a mix of Latin and hip-hop beats. Part on two floors with flashy disco balls and a fog machine. (☎ 2886 320. Cover US$1.50 for men includes 1 drink. Open F-Sa 8pm-2am.) Share the day's stories or get the inside scoop from locals at **Malecón Iluminado,** the area bordering the river between the two bridges. Bars in *choza* huts are open daily and give the best views of the river below. Here, the music blasts and the beer flows (US$1). On weekends, dance clubs open. Play ping-pong and pool or party on a small dance floor at **Boli Bar** (☎ 2889 219. Orellana and Pano. Open 6pm-2am.) Other clubs and bars line 15 de Noviembre toward the terminal.

⚠ INTO THE JUNGLE FROM TENA

RAFTING AND KAYAKING. The biggest adrenaline rush in Tena (and maybe in all of Ecuador) comes from killer whitewater rafting and kayaking. Recently the world's whitewater enthusiasts have discovered the river-filled region around Tena. Here, the headwaters of the Amazon rush down from the Andes through canyons, over waterfalls, and past rocky banks. In 2004, pros flocked to Tena for the National Rafting Championship. The unique topography and sheer volume of water provide a density of whitewater rapids higher than almost anywhere else in the world. However, though rapids churn year-round, **river levels can change drastically** based on local rainfall. June is generally the wettest month of the year. Tour guides offer single-day and longer river trips, which include hiking and cabaña stays. Many trips float down nearby **Río Jatunyacu** ("Big Water" in Quichua). Many trails alongside the river lead to hidden waterfalls and enchanting gulleys.

🖺**Ríos Ecuador,** across from Traveler's Lodge, is the most established whitewater outfit in Tena. They offer popular, time-tested routes with professional multilingual guides and modern equipment. The exhilarating, safety-conscious trips come complete with a rescue kayak. One-day rafting trips (US$50 per person) leave year-round with Class II (beginner) and Class III/III+ (intermediate) options. They also offer: a Class IV/IV+ trip (Oct.-Feb.; US$65), 1-day kayaking trips (US$60 per person), a 4-day kayaking course (US$250), and kayak and gear rental sans guide (US$30 per day). In April 2002, Ríos Ecuador joined in alliance with Quito-based **Yacu Amu Rafting.** Make reservations through Quito (☎ 2904 054; www.yacuamu.com) or Tena (☎ 2886 727; www.riosecuador.com. SAE/ISIC discount 10%. Open M-F 8:30am-1pm and 2-7pm, Sa-Su 8:30-10:30am). A cadre of former Ríos Ecuador guides formed **River People,** on the corner of 15 de Noviembre and 9 de Octubre, in 2002. President Gary Dent, once the head guide at Ríos Ecuador, now manages the **Asociación de Guías de Aguas Rápidas (AGAR).** In addition to daytrips (US$50), they offer two- and three-day rafting trips, which include a stay at their cabins and customizable jungle excursions (2-day US$95, 3-day US$130). River People are knowledgeable, friendly, and experienced. (☎ 2887 887; www.riverpeopleraftingecuador.com. Open M-Sa 8am-7pm. Traveler's checks accepted.)

JUNGLE LODGES AND TOURS. For a more tranquil wilderness experience, spend some time at one of the many riverside cabañas. Ask the Ministerio de Turismo in Tena for up-to-date information, as cabañas open and close frequently. The Ministerio de Turismo strongly advises that you **only go with certified guides.**

Amarongachi Tours (☎ 2886 372; www.amarongachi_tours.com) operates out of Hostal Travler's Lodging (see above), and is the oldest, most well known ecotourism company. They take guests tubing and swimming in the wooded rivers west of Tena, and put them up in 2 different cabin complexes with some of the best views in the Oriente. Quichua guides explain local traditions and point out native flora and fauna. Open daily 7:30am-8pm. Tour (US$40 per day) includes 3 meals (including vegetarian options), lodging, transport, and various activities. **Volunteers** (see p. 76) at Amarongachi translate native guides' talks from Spanish to English and also serve as English teachers for local community members. Volunteers get free room and board and sometimes tips. A 1- to 2-month commitment is required. Contact the Tena office to volunteer.

RICANCIE (☎ 2888 479; http://ricancie.nativeweb.org), at Chofer and Cuenca. A cooperative of 9 Quichua communities offers a variety of multi-day jungle excursions. 2- to 6-day programs (US$36 per day) can be customized. Communities offer intercultural exchange, shaman demonstrations, artesanía, hikes, swimming, and scientific investigation. Profits go straight to the communiites and offer an alternative income to intensive agriculture and deforestation. Contact Samuel Pedros Tapuy Vargas through the Tena office to find out about longer stays and volunteer opportunities at Capirona, one of the 1st communities of RICANCIE. Spanish-speaking guides. To arrange for a translator, contact the office before arriving. Open M-F 8am-6pm.

Sacha Ricsina Tours (☎2886 839), on Montesdeoca at 15 de Noviembre, is run by the Cerdas, an indigenous family, and offers horseback riding, jungle touring, and indigenous community visiting. Includes 3 meals with vegetarian options. US$30 per day. Open M-Sa 7am-7pm.

Pusuno Trekking (☎2886 706; pusunotour@hotmail.com), at Moreno and Mera, by the pedestrian bridge, offers hand-tailored treks for beginners and the seasoned. English-, Quichua-, and Spanish-speaking guides lead tours of traditional farms and primary forest. Great **map** (US$2). Tours US$35 40 per day. Open daily 9am-2pm and 3-9pm

THE IMPORTANCE OF RUBBERS In Ecuador, one has to be careful—outside the bigger towns in the Oriente, the preferred footwear is rubber boots (botas de goma). Even on major roads, frequent rains create thick mud and calf-deep rivers. If you're planning on doing a lot of hiking in the Oriente, picking up a pair is essential. They are completely waterproof, which at times (say, in a river) makes them much more useful than your water-wicking hiking boots, and can be purchased (US$5) in almost any Oriente town. **A few caveats:** Best for keeping feet dry, rubber boots lack ankle support. If you are prone to sprained ankles or are planning on a hike with rocky ground, rubber boots might hinder more than help. Most town vendors don't carry very large sizes, so bigfoots should purchase a pair in a larger city.

ARCHIDONA ☎06

Just a gathering of stores 20min. north of Tena on the road to Baeza, Archidona is a good place to pick up supplies on the way to nearby cabañas, camping spots, or area petroglyphs (see p. 301). Local buses bound for Tena or Cotundo and long-distance buses frequently pass through town. Most of Archidona's businesses are at the corner of Rocafuerte and Cosanga, just off the main plaza.

Companies in Tena handle most tourism in the area (see p. 300). The **Hospital Stadler Richter** is a block off the main plaza. (445 Rocafuerte. ☎2889 529. Open 24hr.) **Residencia Regina ❷** offers quiet rooms a little way off the road. (☎2889 144. Dorms US$5; singles with private bath US$7; doubles US$12.) Small **restaurants** and **shops** line the plaza.

PETROGLYPHS

In the Misahuallí Valley, about 200 petroglyphs have been discovered, one-third of which are near the town of Cotundo. Studies of these drawings were done by Padre Pedro Porras, a teacher in Cotundo and at the Catholic Univiersity of Quito. They depict spirals, lines, and figures of humans and animals. The petroglyphs treat subjects such as fertility and visions of the universe. With so many petroglyphs, it's possible to see many in one afternoon. However, since the rocks are spread throughout the hills, they can be hard to find without a guide. Ask for **José Topanta** at the Junta Parroquial in Cotundo (drivers on Tena-Cotundo buses know where this is). The hills around Cotundo also offer spectacular views. Don't forget to bring chalk, which can be used to make the petroglyphs more visible.

The valley of **Río Misahuallí** around Archidona and Cotundo (7km north of Archidona) is rich in artifacts that are hundreds and even thousands of years old. A benign climate and quality soil among gently undulating hills next to the river facilitated the growth of one of the oldest population centers in the region. In the valley near

THE ORIENTE

Cotundo, also known as the **Valle Sagrado,** archaeologists have discovered remnants of earlier cultures. Excavations have uncovered obsidian knives from the pre-Ceramic Period before 2000 BC, as well as granite axes and ceramic vases from around 1000 BC to 3000 BC. Many artifacts are still buried in the hills around Cotundo.

Several other petroglyphs in the valley are accessible without a guide. In **Reten** (2km south of Cotundo), there is a boulder covered with petroglyphs. A dirt road on the right (coming from Cotundo) leads to Reten. Just before the bridge into town, a trail leads up-river, to the right. After 10min., this trail reaches a fence. The petroglyphs are on the other side to the right about 50m away.

The barrio **San Augustín,** just south of Archidona, has a big granite boulder carved with images of monkeys, snakes, and the sun. To reach this site, get off the bus at the partially obscured sign for the Museo Mundos Amazónicos (now closed). Follow the road 300m; the boulder is on the right, in front of the large choza huts. (*Take the Archidona bus from Amazonas and Bolívar (20min., every 15min. 6am-7pm, US$0.20). ☎ 2886 826. US$2. Open daily 7am-5pm.*)

SELVA VIVA   ☎ 06

Forty-five kilometers east of Tena, wander through 13,000 hectares of private forest reserve along Río Arajuno. A Swiss group purchased the land, 75% of which is primary forest, in order to preserve and protect it. The reserve includes an animal rescue center (see below), cabañas at Liana Lodge, the Quichua community Runa Huasi, and Sacha Yachana Huasi Christina, a school for local children. The married couple Angelika Raimann (from Switzerland) and Remigio Canelos (a native Quichua) run the compound and help foster sustainable development with local communities. For information about programs or donations, contact Amazoonico (☎ 09 9800 463; www.amazoonico.org).

▐ TRANSPORTATION. The cheapest and usually the fastest way is to catch the Santa Rosa-bound **bus** outside the Terminal Terrestre in Tena. Tell the driver you are going to Amazoonico, and if this fails say **Puerto Barantilla** (1½hr., 8 per day 4am-6pm, US$2). If going for only one day, take a morning **bus** (6:30, 9, and 10am, US$2) to leave enough time to see everything. Just before Selva Viva, the bus drops you off at a sign on the left. Though it claims that the 1.7km walk to Amazoonico is possible, instead walk through the gate and follow the path to the left down to the water. From here, take a 10min. motorized canoe to Amazoonico at Selva Viva. Call Amazoonico before coming so they can have a canoe meet you (visitors US$4; guests at Liana Lodge free). For a more scenic but expensive route, take a motorized **canoe** directly from Misahuallí (1hr., US$50) or La Punta, near Ahuano (30min., US$15). Travel time varies based on river levels. Prices are often based on how much the driver thinks you are willing to pay. To return, catch the last Tena-bound bus passing through at 5:45pm.

▐ AMAZOONICO. Begun in 1993, ▨**Amazoonico** provides a haven for rehabilitating animals. Some have been saved from the black market where they were sold as pets or meat. Others are wild animals abandoned by former owners. In the end, only one-quarter of the animals return to the wild. Another quarter is in such bad shape that it dies within the first few days after arrival. The rest become too accustomed to human contact that they would no longer be able to survive in the wild. Volunteers (English-, Spanish-, French-, and German-speaking) give hour-long guided tours of the grounds (US$2.50). At Amazoonico capuchin, spider, and woolly monkeys wander freely about the path, and scarlet macaws and white-throated toucans—the largest toucan species in the world—flap about their cages in this grand menagerie. Among the other interesting native fauna here are jaguarundis, ocelots, boas, and capybaras. The gift shop sells artesanía from local Quichua and Huoarani people to help them earn money without exploiting the forest or illegally capturing and selling animals. The last tour of the compound begins at 4pm. **Volunteers** at Amazoonico should be able to speak two languages (English, Spanish, French, or German) and have an interest in biology. They pay US$80 per month for food and lodging. The minimum stay is two months.

⚐ ACCOMMODATIONS. Selva Viva built the **Liana Lodge ❺** to increase revenue to improve animal facilities. Less than 1km downstream from Amazoonico, these environmentally-conscious cabañas offer river views and peace and quiet. None of the protected forest was harmed to build this complex: the cabins rest on previously cleared land and are made of trees that were cleared to build the road to Santa Rosa. The six cabañas, each with two doubles, boast private bathrooms with hot showers and terraces with hammocks, but no electricity. The lodge offers activities that include visits to Amazoonico and nearby Isla Anaconda, guided walks through primary forest, and the opportunity to construct a balsa raft and ride it down the river. (Including meals and tours US$50 per day. July-Aug. call at least 1 week ahead for reservations. Traveler's checks accepted.)

⚐ LOCAL CULTURE. Also located on the Selva Viva land is the Quichua settlement of **Runa Huasi,** a 22-family community part of the RICANCIE network (see p. 300). Arrange visits through RICANCIE or directly through Selva Viva (US$35 per day). A few minutes upstream and across the river from Amazoonico is a small **museum,** which displays Quichua traps, crafts, and instruments. The sign says **Museo Sacha Samay,** but many in the area refer to it as El museo de las Trampas (The Museum of the Traps). If no one is there, make some noise and some one should show up. (Admission US$1.50.)

MISAHUALLÍ ☎06

Monkeys loitering in plaza of Misahuallí (pop. 600) should dispel any lingering doubts that this is real jungle, if the charitably termed "road" into town hasn't already. Here, emerald parakeets and iridescent butterflies flutter among the orchids just outside of town. Except for the occasional intrusion of a tourist boat, the only sound to be heard in Misahuallí is the squawking of wild parrots. Many tours leave from Misahuallí to explore the rainforest and see indigenous villages.

▣ TRANSPORTATION AND PRACTICAL INFORMATION. The road enters town from the west and ends at the **plaza,** where hotels, restaurants, and shops congregate. Away from the plaza, opposite the road into town, is a sandy beach where **Río Misahuallí** merges with **Río Napo.** Most jungle tours depart from this point. **Buses** leave the plaza for Tena (1hr., every 45min. 5am-6pm, US$0.95). The cheapest way to Ahuano and Jatun Sacha is to cross Río Napo in a **motorized canoe** (US$0.25), walk 30min. away from the river (on a dirt track) to the Y de Misahuallí on the Tena-Ahuano road, and flag down a bus headed for **Ahuano Punta** (US$0.70). Ask the bus driver to let you off at Jatun Sacha or La Punta. If going to Ahuano, get off at La Punta, cross the river again (canoe US$0.25), and walk 20min. along the road from the canoe station. Alternatively, motorized canoes travel directly from Misahuallí to **Ahuano** (45min., US$30 per boat). The **police** (☎2890 125) are in the blue-and-white office to the left just off the plaza.

▣ ACCOMMODATIONS AND FOOD. Hotel Albergue Español ❷, on the right just before you enter town, is impeccably clean, with hot private baths and screens on windows. (☎2890 004; www.alberguespanol.com. Laundry service

US$3 per kg. Check-out 11am. US$6-8.) **Hostal Sacha ❶**, past the plaza at the sandy beach where the two rivers merge, is the best deal. It has a great location but is average both in architecture and room quality. (☎ 2890 065. Kitchen access, cold-water showers. Singles US$3, with bath US$4; doubles US$6/$8; triples US$9/$12.) **Hostal Marena Inn ❷**, 50m uphill from the plaza, offers clean rooms with cabinets, hot water, and balconies over the river. (☎ 2889 002. Dorms US$5; matrimonials US$8.)

The **Restaurant Albergue Español ❷**, at the back of the hotel (see **Accommodations,** p. 303), serves a full menu of pizzas (US$4) and choice meats (US$3-5). Uses only boiled water. (Open 7am-8:30pm.) **Peco's Café ❶**, at the far left corner of the plaza, serves tasty Tex-Mex dishes (US$2.50). The owner speaks fluent English. (☎ 2890 081; pecoscafe@yahoo.com. Open July-Aug. 11am-9pm; Sept.-June 4-9pm.)

▓ INTO THE JUNGLE FROM MISAHUALLÍ. Most visitors use Misahuallí as a starting point for jungle tours. For more information on choosing a guide, see p. 41. Except for one, most of the guides in Misahuallí speak little English. ▓**Ecoselva**, on the plaza, is run by the English-speaking biologist Pepe Tapia, who offers *charlas* (informational talks) about local indigenous groups and jungle fauna in the evenings. Ecoselva also has a *mariposario* (butterfly garden) just off the plaza, past El Paisano on the right. (☎ 2890 019. Itineraries tailored to group size and interests. Tours US$25 per day.) **Douglas Clarke's Expediciones,** behind the Hostal Marena Inn (see above), has 0.3 sq. km of private rainforest downriver, including a fenced-in Muestrario, where jungle animals roam in higher concentrations than in the wild. Customized one- to four-day expeditions feature wildlife-watching, tubing, nighttime canoe rides, and other jungle fun. (In Tena, ☎ 2897 584; through Marena Inn, 2889 002. Some English spoken. 3 or fewer people US$35 per day; 4-5 US$20; 6 or more US$25.) **Billy Clarke Travel Agency,** on the plaza, is run by Douglas Clarke's sister and takes groups by motor canoe to jungle cabins. (☎ 2890 006. Group of 3 or more US$25 per person per day, including 3 meals with vegetarian options.) **Albergue Español** runs Jungle Lodge and its solar-powered cousin, Jaguar Lodge, 1½hr. downstream from Misahuallí by canoe amid dense primary forest, and offers a variety of adventures: treks into both low and high primary jungle and visits to an indigenous village, rafting, and kayaking. Albergue Español also organizes a few longer expeditions that go deeper into the forest. (☎ 2890 004; www. alberguespanol.com. US$40 per day.)

JATUN SACHA ☎ 06

Quichua for "big forest," the Jatun Sacha tropical rainforest reserve, 8km east of Misahuallí, is still 80% primary growth. This is a thick forest, deep and quiet, not suitable for trekkers but ideal for introverts and nature-lovers. The 20 sq. km reserve was founded in 1986, and in 1993 was named the world's second International Children's Rainforest. The reserve is also a working biological station and visiting researchers are welcome. Well-trodden and very muddy paths meander through the forest, passing an incredible variety of flora. The self-guided trail lasts about 1hr. Birds love this peaceful place as well—to get a better view of Jatun Sacha's winged inhabitants, ask to climb (with required harness) the station's 30m bird observation tower. Those looking for even more adventure can scale a giant tree (with required guide) to the 30m rope bridge stretching across the canopy. **As of July 2004, the rope bridge was broken.** (☎ 2453 583; www.jatunsacha.org. **Maps** available at the main office. Reserve US$6. Self-guided info packet US$1. English-speaking guides US$10 per day. Open daily 7:15am-5pm.)

From the main entrance, a path across the road leads to a sandy beach by Río Napo (if the river isn't too high). The path starts 20m from the main entrance in the direction of Tena. Just off the road it passes Tamboran, a small bar. It is a 20min. walk to reach the beach. **Be careful wading into the water; the current is quite strong.**

Centro de Conservación de Planta Amazónicas (CCPA) is also part of the Jatun Sacha station. It features a botanical garden and a lookout tower on the bank of Río Napo. CCPA is 1km toward Tena from the main office. There is a sign on the right, just before the bridge.

Facilities can accommodate 24 visitors and 18 long-term residents. Bunk beds in screened **cabañas ❾** with nearby cold baths and showers include three meals and admission (US$28, scientists or students doing research US$20). The new **dining hall ❿** offers three communal meals with vegetarian options (US$2.50; breakfast 6:30am-7am, lunch noon-12:30pm, dinner 6-6:30pm). Those looking for an unconventional Ecuadorian experience can **volunteer** at the reserve. Volunteers work with the local Quichua community on sustainable development projects, help maintain the reserve, and once a week perambulate the forest collecting seeds for the botanical garden. (Volunteers pay US$300 per month for food and lodging, plus a US$50 application fee. Min. 1-month commitment.)

Travelers seeking more comfortable lodgings can shack up at the solar-powered **Cabañas Aliñahui ❺**, 3km down the road to the east of Jatun Sacha. After 25min. of walking, a sign on the left marks the cabañas. Turn left and walk 20min. to the complex. The forest melts away to reveal a wide yard with fruit trees on a bluff overlooking Río Napo. Eight spacious cabins, raised on stilts above hammock-blessed patios, have two rooms that share a cold bath. (Quito office ☎2227 094; www.ecuadorexplorer.com/alinahui. Conference room, bar, and library. US$35, including meals. Profits go to the reserve.) Contact **Fundación Jatun Sacha** to learn more about the **volunteer** program, make research reservations, or simply get in touch with the reserve. (Casilla 17-12-867. ☎2432 240; www.jatunsacha.org.)

For a comprehensive and personal tour of the forest, ask around for **Don Gabriel.** He comes from a long line of shamans (though he is not one himself) and has extensive regional knowledge. He guides hikes and offers charlas (informational talks) about shamanism. You can probably find him at **Laboratorio Dos,** the bar owned by his family, which is a 5min. walk past the main entrance to Jatun Sacha

ON THE MENU

ANTS: THEY'RE WHAT'S FOR DINNER

Every September it's ant mating season, and the princesses must leave the nest to find their Prince Charmings. Too bad for them that humans long ago learned that these inch-long winged beauties make for quite the tasty meal.

People watch the ant nests closely to determine when the princesses will leave. Generally, a good indication is the gathering of soldier ants around the entrance to the nest. Ant hunters wait outside the nest with lights or flames to attract the ants. Just like moths, the ants fly straight into the light. The heat burns their wings, causing them to drop to the ground where they can be easily collected for a meal. Most often the ants are wrapped in leaves and cooked or simply fried in oil. The back half, filled with a mushroom flavored liquid is the true delicacy. What's more, they're a great source of protein.

If you couldn't stomach the above, you may not want to hear that these are not the only ants eaten in the Oriente. Lemon ants, small creatures that taste, well, like lemon, are another flavorful favorite. Locals have found that they are a great way to stave off hunger in the backwoods. The ants reside in the Duroia tree, with which they have an interesting symbiotic relationship. In return for a place to live, the ants clear the ground around the tree of vegetation, so it can grow without competition.

when coming from Tena. The bar is on the right, in a large thatched roof hut with open sides. **Buses** from Tena to Ahuano or Santa Rosa can drop visitors off in front of Jatun Sacha (1hr., every hr. 6am-7:30pm, US$1.25).

YASUNÍ NATIONAL PARK

The 982,000 hectares of Yasuní, in the far eastern reaches of Ecuador's territory, make it the country's largest mainland national park. Created in 1979, it was declared an International Biosphere Reserve by UNESCO for its incredible biodiversity. The park is bordered on the north by the protected land of the Huaroani Reserve. Due to Yasuní's isolated location, any foray into the park takes at least the better part of a week. Access is generally from Coca by motorized canoe. From **Quito,** get to **Coca** by bus (7hr., US$10) or by **plane** (1hr., US$60). It is difficult to see the park without a guide of some kind. Quito-based tour operators can organize trips to Yasuní and surrounding areas. The Yuturi Lodge, 5hr. downriver from Coca, has native guides and translators. The cabañas have full baths and provide a mosquito net. (Amazonas N24-236 and Colón. ☎2504 037; www.ytutilodge.com. Tours leave from Coca. 5-day (M-F) trip US$360 or 4-day (F-M) trip US$280.) Emerald Forest Expeditions has a five-day Pañacocha Program (Quichua for "piranha lake") with licensed English-speaking naturalist guides and the chance to go piranha fishing and see freshwater dolphins. (Pinto E4-244 and Amazonas. ☎2541 543; www.emeraldexpeditions.com. Trip can be extended to 7 days, including camping in the forest. Vegetarian meal options. US$275. 3 or more person group US$250 per person.)

PUYO   ☎03

Just beyond the last foothills of the Andes, Río Puyo passes through the town of Puyo (pop. 25,000). Many buses also pass through this transit town—a logistical stop between Baños and eastern national parks. Unlike other towns in the Southern Oriente, most of Puyo's *indígenas* are Quichua, sharing the same language as their Highlands cousins. In spite of this connection, the town nurtures its jungle image. While accommodations and services are quite comfortable by Oriente standards, the urban core surrenders quickly to the surrounding rainforest.

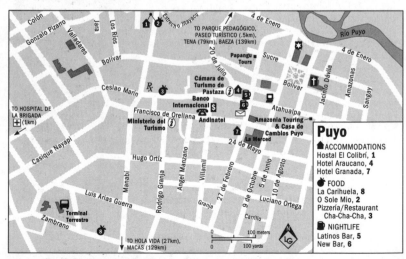

Puyo

⬛ ACCOMMODATIONS
Hostal El Colibrí, 1
Hotel Araucano, 4
Hotel Granada, 7

🍴 FOOD
La Carihuela, 8
O Sole Mio, 2
Pizzería/Restaurant
   Cha-Cha-Cha, 3

🍸 NIGHTLIFE
Latinos Bar, 5
New Bar, 6

⌐ TRANSPORTATION

Buses: Terminal (☎2885 480), a 20min. walk or short taxi ride (US$0.80) from the *centro*. From downtown, take 9 de Octubre downhill from the main plaza and then Atahuallpa to the large intersection with a bronze bust and a pedestrian overpass. Turn right on Alberto Zambrano and follow it 1km. Open daily until 11pm, after which buses stop at the intersection of 9 de Octubre and Atahuallpa. Buses passing through for other destinations may drop passengers on Zambrano a few blocks from the terminal. Buses go to: **Ambato** (3hr., 20 per day 4am-7pm, US$2.50) via **Baños** (2hr., US$2); **Guayaquil** (9hr.; 6:15am, 11pm; US$9); **Macas** (5hr., 13 per day 3am-10:30pm, US$5); **Quito** (5hr., 14 per day 12:30am-8pm, US$5); **Riobamba** (4hr., 7 per day 3:45am-5:30pm, US$3.75); **Tena** (3hr., every 30min. 6am-8:30pm, US$2.50).

Taxis: Taxis charge US$1 between any 2 points in the city.

◼◪ ORIENTATION AND PRACTICAL INFORMATION

The east-bound road from Baños approaches the **terminal**. From there, take a bus (US$0.14) or taxi, or walk 1km northeast into town. The visible mountains lie to the west. The **centro** is defined by the east-west **Ceslao Marín** and **Chunchupamba, 9 de Octubre,** and **27 de Febrero.** Most hotels, restaurants, and shops cluster near 9 de Octubre and Atahuallpa. Muddy **Río Puyo** borders the northeastern edge of town.

Tourist Office: Cámara de Turismo de Pastaza (☎2883 681), at the corner of Marín and Atahuallpa. Provides helpful info on nearby sights as well as maps. Open M-F 8:30am-12:30pm and 2:30-6pm, Sa 9am-noon. **Ministerio de Turismo** (☎2884 655), on Orellana in the bright new Cooperativo de San Francisco building, has limited info on Oriente tourist facilities and a city **map.** Open M-F 8:30am-5:30pm.

Tours: Amazonia Touring (☎2883 219; amazoniatouring@andinanet.net), at Atahuallpa and 9 de Octubre, offers guided tours in English of the Hola Vida reserve and multi-day jungle treks (US$25 per day). Owner Santiago Cordero is the ideal businessman, running tours, exchanging traveler's checks, and offering English lessons, Spanish lessons, and artesanía out of the same store. Open M-Sa 8am-8pm, Su 9am-noon. **Papangu Tours** (☎2883 875), at 27 de Febrero and Sucre, 2 blocks downhill north of Marín, works in community-based ecotourism. Guides lead trips (in Spanish) to Hola Vida, Indichuris, Cueva de Los Tayos, and Sarayaku. (US$35-40 per day.) Open M-F 9am-6:30pm.

Currency Exchange: Casa de Cambios Puyo (☎2883 219), on Atahuallpa between 9 de Octubre and 10 de Agosto, in the same office as Amazonia Touring, exchanges traveler's checks. Open M-Sa 8am-8pm, Su 9am-noon. **Banco Internacional,** on General Villamil between Orellana and Atahuallpa, provides **Western Union. ATM** outside in back. Open M-F 9am-5pm, Sa 9am-2pm.

Market: Mercado Central "La Merced," on Plaza México at Orellana and 27 de Febrero. 2-story indoor market has food and more. Open daily 6am-8pm.

Police: ☎2885 101. On 9 de Octubre, past the park. Open 24hr.

Pharmacy: Farmacia Ferr-ade, Marín 187 (☎2883 892), just past Hostería Turingia. Check the en turno list posted on each pharmacy door for the 24hr. pharmacy on duty.

Hospital: Hospital de la Brigada 17 (☎2883 939), on Marín, 2km from the *centro* toward the mountains. Open 24hr. **Hospital Voz Andes** (☎2795 172), just a few km away in the town of Shell, has the Oriente's best facilities and helicopters to Quito.

Telephones: Andinatel (☎ 2885 140), at Orellana and General Villamil, 1 block downhill from Atahuallpa, accepts calling card and collect calls. Open daily 8am-10pm.

Internet: Centronet@, on Marín between 27 de Febrero and 9 de Octubre. US$1.20 per hr. Open 8am-9pm.

Post Office: Correos (☎ 2885 332), at 27 de Febrero and Atahuallpa. Open M-F 8am-6pm.

⛏ ACCOMMODATIONS

Although there are plenty of super cheap residenciales, quality improves dramatically when hotel prices reach US$3-4.

Hostal El Colibrí (☎ 2883 054; hostalelcolibri@yahoo.es), at Manabí (toward Tena) and Vacas Galindo. From Farmacia Ferr-ade (see p. 307), turn right on Manabí. A bit removed from the *centro,* but all the quieter for it. Clean rooms with private baths. Laundry service and cafe. US$7, children US$3.50. ❷

Hotel Araucano, Marín 576 (☎ 2885 686), at 27 de Febrero. Tries hard for a jungle lodge atmosphere despite the rumbling of nearby bars. Rooms have lukewarm private baths and cable TVs. Go deluxe for a nicer set-up with a refrigerator. Breakfast included. Singles US$6, deluxe US$10; doubles US$12/$20; triples US$18/$30. MC/V. ❷

Hotel Granada (☎ 2885 578), at 27 de Febrero and Orellana, 2 blocks downhill from Atahuallpa, next to the market. A no-frills, low-cost option. Rooms are bare but reasonably clean. US$2.50, with bath US$3.50. ❶

🍴 FOOD

▧ Pizzería/Restaurant Cha-Cha-Cha, Marín 249 (☎ 2885 208), on the right just past the Hotel Turingia. Painted menus on the walls and cardboard cut-outs point the way to pizzas and traditional dishes (US$2-3.80). Open M-Sa 8am-10pm. ❶

O Sole Mio, at the Hostal El Colibrí (see p. 308), has pizzas and spaghetti cooked up by an actual Italian. Soft jazz completes the relaxed atmosphere. Entrees US$3.50. Open 7-10pm. ❷

La Carihuela (☎ 2883 919), on Zambrano, near the terminal. Cloth napkins, a large floor space, and classy decor contrast sharply with the Baños cyclist crowd. Pasta, filet mignon, and other French favorites US$5. "Plebeian" BBQ also served. Open M-Sa 9am-3:30pm and 6-9pm, Su 9am-4pm. ❸

◔ SIGHTS

Travelers will find many institutions dedicated to educating visitors about the surrounding jungle in Puyo.

PARQUE PEDAGÓGICO ETNO-BOTÁNICO OMAERE. The complex, run by an indígena organization, invited native craftsmen to build representative, livable (but not lived-in) traditional dwellings for the enlightenment of the region's cinder-block denizens. The park lies on Río Puyo, up the trail from an iron footbridge, and contains very grown-up secondary forests. Guides explain medicinal uses of plants as well as the cultures of the Shuar, Huaorani, and Zápara. *(Walking away from the plaza on Marín, veer right past Hotel Araucano onto 20 de Julio. At the intersection with the gas station, turn right onto Cotopaxi, which leads straight to Río Puyo. Follow signs for the Hostería Flor de Canela. After crossing the*

*wooden bridge, follow signs to the left for Omaere. 20min. walk. Taxi US$1. ☎09 7095
583. One guide speaks English. Open daily 8am-5:15pm. US$3, with student ID US$1.50,
includes a 1hr. guided tour.)*

HOLA VIDA. Hola Vida provides a self-service jungle experience, including hiking, canoeing, and swimming under the 38m Hola Vida waterfall, and basic cabins (US$3 per person per night), food (US$2 per meal, including veggie options), and primary rainforest in most of the park's 2.25 sq. km. It offers a half-day trip to the **Cascada Escondida,** which requires wading through waist-deep water. Visitors can see Quichua ceramics being made. Contact Edwin Amores at Hola Vida or Amazonia Touring (see **Tours,** p. 307) to go with an experienced English-speaking guide. *(27km south of town. Buses to Pamona leave the Cooperative Centinela In the Mariscal area of Puyo (1hr.; daily 6:15am, 1pm, return 8am, 3pm; US$1.25), and pass the entrance to the reserve. Or take a Macas-bound bus and ask to be let off at "Hola Vida, Km16." From there, it's an 11km walk on the side road to the reserve. Taxi US$15. Puyo ☎2883 219 or reserve 09 9702 209 . 3-day, 2-night tours with Amazonia Touring US$25 per day. Guided trip to Cascada Escondida US$10. Entry US$1.25. Camping for the price of admission, but talk to an Hola Vida official.)*

DIQUE DE MERA. A small stretch of beach on the inland side of the Andes, the Dique de Mera (a.k.a. Complejo Turístico Río Tigre) was made by damming Río Tigre. In the town of Mera, 20min. toward Baños from Puyo, the pool is about 1m deep and 60m long. On weekends, crowds play volleyball and soccer on the banks, or just float lazily in rented tubes (US$1). There are showers and baths, as well as a snack bar. The Dique can be reached by following signs along Velasco Ibarra from the town square in Mera or by way of the Sendero Ecológico, which offers river access along the rivers Alpayacu and Tigre. The trail starts at the bridge over Río Alpayacu 500m before the town of Mera (coming from Puyo). When Río Tigre enters from the left, the trail continues along its banks.

The hills around Mera, in the Anzu River Valley, contain over 90 caves full of stalactites and stalagmites. Frankie Lugo guides full-day trips to explore these caves. One formation looks like the World Cup. While hiking to the caves, make like Tarzan and swing on one of the many vines. Frankie's office is on the road coming from the Puyo-Baños road, just off the main plaza in Mera. The **Jacinto Dávila Museum,** located behind the church in a school of the same name, houses a small collection of archaeological finds, old coins, and handicrafts. One and a half kilometers uphill from Mera is the **Mirador Sighca,** a simple bar with extensive vistas of the twisting tentacles of the Pastaza River and the mountains of Sangay National Park. *(☎2790 148 for Frankie Lugo; frankie_justicia@lat-inmail.com. US$40 per person includes all equipment. Min. 2 people. Dique open daily during daylight hours. Museum open M-F. Bar open daily 9am-7pm. Take any Baños-bound bus (20min., US$0.50) to get to Mera.)*

CABAÑAS CASCADA YANA RUMI. Contact Sergio Tito, owner of the Hostal El Colibrí (see p. 308), to arrange a visit to these cabañas, on 103 hectares of private land with hikes and access to waterfalls. (US$7 per person.)

PASEO TURÍSTICO RÍO PUYO. This 3km walk around the edge of Río Puyo provides a leisurely tour through jungle vegetation amidst the sounds of the river rushing below. Unfortunately, the wildest life to be found here are the children swimming. *(Follow the directions to Omaere and continue over the 2nd iron footbridge to the cobblestone trail, which ends at the highway to Tena.)*

 NIGHTLIFE

New Bar, at 27 de Febrero and Atahuallpa, mixes mellow lights with sizzling salsa. (☎2885 579. Beer US$1.25. Open M-Sa 6pm-2am.) Fridays and Saturdays, the **New Disco** picks up downstairs (no cover). Around the corner, **Latinos Bar** has decent beer (US$1) but not much else. (Open M-Sa 9am-midnight, Su noon-2am.)

MACAS ☎07

Macas (pop. 30,000) is sometimes called the "Oriental Emerald" for its stunning beauty, but travelers who have visited the colonial cities of central Ecuador may not be so stunned. Farther off the travelers' circuit and with less established tourist services than the northern Oriente, Macas maintains the quiet, friendly atmosphere of a small jungle town while offering the amenities of a large city. It also serves largely as a launch pad for trips to pristine stretches of the Amazon, visits to Shuar villages, and longer jungle jaunts that cross the border into Peru. However, much can be learned about the jungle from within Macas itself. Many townspeople are Shuar or part-Shuar and tell fascinating tales of their jungle experiences.

🖃 🞠 TRANSPORTATION AND PRACTICAL INFORMATION

The **airstrip** forms the western boundary of town. The bluff overlooking **Río Upano** borders the town to the east, behind the cathedral. Several restaurants and hotels are at the intersection of **Domingo Comín** and **Amazonas,** the town's busiest street.

Flights: Airport, at Amazonas and Cuenca. Open M-F 8:30am-noon and 1:15-5pm. **TAME** (☎/fax 2701 978), at the airport, serves **Quito** (30min.; Tu and Th 3pm; US$48).

Buses: Terminal, on 10 de Agosto, just west of Amazonas. **Cooperativa de Turismo Oriental** (☎2700 159) goes to **Cuenca** (11hr., 7 per day 5am-10pm, US$8.50). **Cooperativa de Turismo San Francisco** (☎2700 995) goes to: **Ambato** (6hr.; 3, 7am, and 2pm, US$7.50); **Guayaquil** (13hr., 6pm, US$14); **Puyo** (5hr., 7am, US$5); **Quito** (11hr., 6 per day 10am-10:45pm, US$10). **Cooperativa de Transportes Macas** (☎2700 869) goes to **Cuenca** (11hr., 8:30am, 11pm, US$8.50) and **Puyo** (5hr., 6 per day 4am-5pm, US$5).

Tourist Office: Información Turística, at 9 de Octubre and Bolívar on the plaza, is new and still getting organized. Provides guides (US$20 per day) as well as contacts and recommendations. Open M-F and Su 9am-noon and 2-4:30pm. **Ministerio del Ambiente** (☎2953 041), on Juan de la Cruz at Guamate in the same lot as the Ministerio de Agricultura y Ganadería, has info on Parque Nacional Sangay. Pay park entrance fee here (US$10). Open M-F 8am-12:30pm and 1:30-4:30pm.

Bank: Banco del Austro (☎2700 216), at 24 de Mayo and 10 de Agosto. Offers V cash advances when the owner is available. Open M-F 9am-5pm, Su 9am-1:30pm. Open 24hr. **ATM** outside. There is nowhere in Macas to exchange traveler's checks.

Emergency: ☎101.

Police: ☎2700 101. At the bus station. Open 24hr.

Hospital: Clínica Jervés, 10 de Agosto 7-34 (☎7200 007; phone/fax 2701 898), at Soasti. Open 24hr.

Telephones: PacificTel (☎2700 104), on 24 de Mayo between Cuenca and Sucre, services international calls but not collect or calling card calls. Open M-F 7am-11pm. Open 24hr. **Branch** on Bolívar between Soasti and 24 de Mayo. Open daily 8am-11pm.

Macas

🏠 ACCOMMODATIONS
Hostal Casa Blanca, **3**
Hotel La Orquídea, **2**
Hotel Peñón del Oriente, **7**
Hotel Safari, **11**
Hotel Sol de Oriente, **12**

🍴 FOOD
Charlot, **9**
Chifa Pagoda China, **8**
Cinnamon, **10**
El Jardín, **6**

🍸 NIGHTLIFE
Café Bar, **4**
Discoteca Acuario, **1**
K'chos Discotek, **5**

THE ORIENTE

Internet: Cyber Vision (☎ 2701 191), on Soasti between Sucre and Bolívar, has broadband service (US$1.20 per hr.). Open M-F 8am-midnight, Sa-Su 9am-midnight.

Post Office: Correos (☎ 2700 060), on 9 de Octubre, between Comín and 10 de Agosto, 1 block from the central plaza. Open M-F 8am-noon and 2-6pm. **Western Union** and **DHL** (☎ 2701 911), on the corner of Pastaza and 24 de Mayo. Open M-F 8am-1pm and 2:30-4:30pm, Sa-Su 8am-noon.

🏠 ACCOMMODATIONS

Hostal Casa Blanca (☎ 2700 195), on Soasti between Bolívar and Sucre. A stylish, tinted-glass facade mirrors the hip, sparkling-white rooms within. Tile floor, cable TV, hot water, and phone. Breakfast included. Singles US$11; oversized doubles US$20. ❸

Hotel La Orquídea (☎ 2700 970), at Sucre and 9 de Octubre. Clean, airy rooms with cable TV and large private baths. On the quieter side of town with a rooftop patio. Singles US$7, with hot water US$8. ❷

Hotel Sol de Oriente (☎ 2702 900), on Tarqui at Soasti. Special touches like shampoo in the shower and flowers (they're fake, but the thought counts) on the bedside table. Cable TV and hot water. Singles US$8; matrimonials US$15. ❸

Hotel Safari, on Soasti between 10 de Agosto and Tarqui. Bright, clean, tiled rooms include hot private baths and cable TV. Some have balconies. Laundry service. Singles US$7; doubles US$14; triples US$21. ❷

Hotel Peñón del Oriente, Comín 837 (☎2700 124; fax 2700 450), at Amazonas. Nestled between a bakery, ice cream shop, and restaurant of the same name. Large firm beds but inconsistent service. Splurge for the clean deluxe rooms (hot water, phone, and rug). US$6-8, depending on size and location. ❷

▣ FOOD

▨ **Chifa Pagoda China** (☎2700 280), at Amazonas and Comín. Their sizzling platters (US$2-6) are dubbed the best chifa in Ecuador. Open daily 10am-10:30pm. ❶

El Jardín (☎2702 307), at 24 de Mayo and Bolívar. Congenial atmosphere and a good selection of local dishes (US$1.50-3.50). Open daily 7am-10pm. ❶

Cinnamon (☎2700 443), at Soasti and Comín. An eclectic selection of dishes with burgers and fries (US$1.50), large pizzas (US$8), and *ceviche* (US$5, only served M-F). Open daily 9am-midnight. ❶

Charlot, at Bolívar and Soasti, serves cheap local dishes (US$1.25-2.50) and is especially popular with the breakfast crowd. Open M-Sa 7am-3pm and 5:30-9pm. ❶

◉ ♫ SIGHTS AND ENTERTAINMENT

Macas's **cathedral** is a large, modern building with a series of 12 elaborate stained glass windows depicting the story of the Virgen Purísima de Macas, the town's patron saint. Festivals dedicated to the Virgin are celebrated on **February 18** and **August 5.** Five blocks north of the cathedral on Don Bosco, just past Riobamba, is a lush, well-groomed **park** with a river view. The entrance is next to the *biblioteca* (library). Follow 10 de Agosto uphill to the Voz de Upano church with radio tower for additional panoramic vistas. Located in the Casa de la Cultura, on 10 de Agosto at Soasti, the small **Museo Arqueológico Municipal** contains ceramics, tools, instruments, and other remnants of the pre-Upano, Upano, Shuar, and Sangay traditions. (Open M-F 8am-noon and 2-5pm. Free.)

◙ NIGHTLIFE

Macas rages when locals unwind on weekends. Techno-and salsa-filled **K'chos Discotek** ("KAH-chose"), on Bolívar between Soasti and 24 de Mayo, has a true jungle hut vibe. (Open M-Sa 8:30pm-3am.) Dance the night away at **Discoteca Acuario,** on Sucre between 24 de Mayo and Soasti. (☎2700 085. Open Th-Sa 8pm-3am.) At **Café Bar,** on Soasti next to Cyber Vision, enjoy quick eats, karaoke favorites, and a big-screen TV. (Open M-Sa 9am-2am.)

▨ INTO THE JUNGLE FROM MACAS

Macas is the most convenient town in the southern Oriente from which to begin a jungle jaunt. While the northern Oriente sees more tourists, the jungle east of Macas affords some unique opportunities, as hundreds of thousands of square kilometers remain undeveloped. The tourist infrastructure is not fully developed here, so bring important gear because there is nowhere to rent it.

TOUR COMPANIES

Due to the low volume of tourists setting out on jungle excursions in Macas, most companies consist primarily of local and indigenous guides with trekking equipment, transportation, and vast regional knowledge. As a result, they will customize any trip. Tour companies are considerably safer than independent guides. For more information on chossing a guide see **Jungle Tours,** p. 41. The following outfitters have good reputations:

Tsunki Touring CIA (☎2700 724; tsunkimar@hotmail.com or tourshuar@hotmail.com) can by reached via Hotel Peñón del Oriente or Hotel Splendit (see **Accommodations,** above). Shuar owner Tsunki Marcelo Cajecai speaks Achuar, English, Shuar, and Spanish and specializes in rafting and jungle treks to Shuar villages (US$35-45 per person per day). Also offers longer, more expensive 10-day circuit to Peru and back. Most equipment provided. Bring your own sleeping bag—there is nowhere to rent in Macas.

Rodmor Tours (☎2701 328; tw131313@hotmail.com), on Comín at Soasti, offers tours all around the Macas area, including Sardinayacu and Tukupi, a Shuar community. Ethnotourism is the focus at Tukupi where guests stay in typical cabins and get to see a shamanism demonstration. Some English spoken. All-inclusive price US$45-60 per day, depending on group size. Open daily 9am-8pm.

Orientravel (☎2700 371; www.orientravel.com.ec), on 10 de Agosto between Soasti and Amazonas, organizes 3-5 day trips to the Shuar community of Buena Esperanza. US$35 per day. Open M-F 8:30am-1pm and 2:30-6pm, Sa-Su 9am-1pm.

SHUAR COMMUNITIES

This area is home to Ecuador's second-most populous indigenous group, the Shuar. While many Shuar have abandoned their traditions, more isolated communities in the jungle east of Macas continue to live as they have for centuries. Four- to six-day tours from Macas visit these communities, accessible by light aircraft or long river trips. While the Shuar have not expressed distaste for this kind of tourism in the way other *indígenas* have, it cannot help but affect their way of life. If you decide to visit one of these communities, do so with a guide who has a contract that ensures your hosts are accepting your visit. Some guides arrange stays with a Shuar family, while others bring camping gear. Hosts may offer guests **chicha de yucca,** an alcoholic drink made from a yucca plant fermented with the saliva of an older Shuar woman. Don't go on a tour if you are unprepared to imbibe such a cocktail—it is considered rude to reject this token of friendship.

PARQUE NACIONAL SANGAY: ZONA BAJA

Macas offers access to the *zona baja* of Parque Nacional Sangay (see p. 157), which includes the Lagunas de Sardinayacu, Cugusha Falls, and many rivers flowing from the Highlands. Sangay's countless trails climb hills and weave through primary rainforest. Cable cars span the otherwise impassable Ríos Sangay and Upano, and the three-day hike from Atillo to Macas traverses several diverse climate zones. Although it's best to go with a guide, there are entrances with rangers at 9 de Octubre and San Isidro that can be reached by bus from Macas. Guardaparques (park rangers) are great sources of information and even possible rides to the entrance. Unmanned stations are at Palora and Sexta Cooperativa. Discover attractions near the border of the park, but only explore the interior on multi-day hikes with an experienced guide. Sangay's *zona baja* receives far fewer tourists than its Highlands counterpart. As a result, there are fewer well defined, popular routes and fewer people who can help you find them.

LAGUNAS DE SARDINAYACU

Made up of three lakes that act as a large mirror of the surrounding park, Sardinayacu is the most beautiful attraction of Parque Nacional Sangay's *zona baja*. The area is full of jaguars, spectacled bears, and orchids. The lakes are filled with sardines (hence the name) and are great for fishing. (It takes a full day to reach Sardinayacu from Macas, via the town of Playas de San Luis. Guides are available in Macas, and park rangers can provide more info.)

CUEVAS DE LOS TAYOS

Another site commonly visited from Macas, the **Cueva de los Tayos** is an enormous, 85m-deep cave named after the large colonies of oilbirds (tayos) that reside in the cavern. Like bats, the oilbirds are nocturnal fruit-eaters and use sonar to stake out their location in pitch-black environs. They were once captured and their flesh boiled for oil. Other caves closer to Macas, such as Chuwitayo to the north, also once hosted colonies of tayos. Serious spelunkers should contact Marcelo Churuwia, head of the **Sociedad Ecuatoriana de Espeleología** (churuwias@hotmail.com).

GUAPU ARCHAEOLOGICAL COMPLEX

This site, about 1hr. by bus and 45min. more on foot from Macas, contains a group of tolas (hills) and is full of artifacts. There are ceramic pieces and axes dating back to the pre-Upano period (1700 BC). The mounds, which some say form an intimate portrait of a jaguar and a woman when viewed from the air, may mark the area as an ancient ceremonial center. The impressive views of Volcán Sangay on a clear day and nearby Tunants Waterfall contribute natural beauty to the historical significance of the area. The tolas are best seen with a guide familiar with the area. The grass in this field grows very high, making it hard to find the tolas and easy to get lost. Guides can be arranged through the tourist information center or Rodmor tours (see **Tour Companies,** p. 313).

SEVILLA DON BOSCO

A large brick Salesian mission dominates Sevilla Don Bosco, located across the Upano river from Macas. Most townspeople are Shuar, making this is a great place to encounter handicrafts straight from the hands that made them—at much cheaper prices than in Macas or Quito. However, the town has no center of commerce. To find something, ask someone. The Fundación Tsantsa sells artesanía and can find others who do, too. Find postcard-perfect views along the dirt road to Sevilla, across the river to Macas. At the top of the hill across the river (on the way north to Puyo), this is the first right. From town, it is an easy 4hr. hike to Sevilla. Once there, ask almost anyone about hikes to La Cascada (a nearby waterfall) and other, more traditional Shuar communities. **Rayo de Luna** sends red-and-white **buses** to Sevilla (15min., every 30min. 5:45am-7:15pm, US$0.25). The station is at the end of Comín by the airstrip, behind the Mini Centro Comercial "Aeropuerto." **Taxis** also drive the distance (US$5).

TSURAKÚ COMMUNITY BIOLOGICAL STATION AND RESERVE

A new community-based project of the Jatun Sacha Foundation, Tsurakú is a cooperative effort between the local Shuar and Jatun Sacha's volunteers. The main goal of the reserve's 4500 hectares is the preservation and growth of mahogany trees, which are commercially extinct, in order to send seeds and plants to growers and others who need the trees. The town is 2hr. south of Puyo by bus (US$1.75) almost halfway to Macas. Trails wander into the surrounding forest. **Lodging ❺** for visitors is US$25 per day (students US$20), including three meals and entrance to the reserve. Tsurakú has all the modern amenities: running water, electricity, phone service, Internet—but the power occasionally goes out. Volunteers at the reserve teach English to Shuar High students and also work in the reserve clearing trails and tending the medicial plant garden. (To volunteer, contact Diego Dávalos. ☎2432 246; volunteer@jatunsacha.org. Volunteers pay US$350 per month; min. 2-week commitment. Application US$35.)

ALTO MACUMA
This group of waterfalls, just a few hours from Macas, is renowned for its crystal-clear waters. The cascades form natural slides and pools for swimming. The Shuar believe that the waters of one sacred waterfall have powers of purification. Either pack a trip to the falls into one day, or camp overnight in the surrounding primary forest. Fish and hike around Alto Macuma. To get here, travel 1½hr. by **bus** and 1½hr. on foot. Guides are available in Macas. Rodmor (see **Macas: Tour Companies,** p. 313) offers a two-day package, including watching Shuar purification rituals.

LAS CAVERNAS DE LOGROÑO
This extensive cave network is a 15min. walk from Logroño, 2hr. south of Macas. The cave has two main passages. The one to the right goes back 250m and is more easily explored. The left fork follows an underground river back to a 30m waterfall. If there is rain in the mountains, **this route can be dangerous and even fatal when water levels rise quickly.** The entrance to the cave is locked. To get the keys, contact Mario Crespo (☎2702 250), or go to his family's store La Pradera, 1½ blocks south of the plaza on the left. He can act as a guide if you want to explore the caves, but bring your own equipment—helmet, headlamp, rope, boots. The Crespo family runs a little tourist complex (cabañas and bathrooms) outside the caves. Camping is also possible. Either way, bring a sleeping bag.

SUCÚA   ☎07
South of Macas, Sucúa (pop. 9000) is tranquil, pleasant, and distinguished for housing the headquarters of the Federación Interprovincial Centros Shuar. It offers a large-town feel while maintaining small-town nicety. And every year at the end of February, townspeople throw on party gear for their very own Carnaval.

▐ **TRANSPORTATION.** From **Macas,** any Cuenca- or south-bound **bus** passes through Sucúa (1hr., 14 per day 5:30am-8:30pm, US$0.90), disembarking at the central plaza. **Taxis** also run from Macas to Sucúa (30min., US$10). Sucúa's **terminal terrestre** is a 7min. walk from the plaza. Take Comín north from the plaza; follow it to the right of the little grass area; and the terminal is four blocks away on the left. **Turismo Oriental** sends buses to **Cuenca** (9hr., 8 per day 6am-11pm, US$7.50). **San Francisco** goes to **Quito** (12hr.; 8:30, 10pm; US$11) via Macas, **Puyo,** and **Ambato.** Or catch a bus to another destination as it passes near the plaza on Comín at the police station. There is frequent bus traffic.

◪▞ **ORIENTATION AND PRACTICAL INFORMATION.** Well-trimmed shrubs line the road from Macas as it enters town and becomes **Domingo Comín.** Most of Sucúa's services congregate along this road as it passes the plaza, formed by Comín and Edmundo Carvajal, which both intersect with Pastor Bernal and Carlos Olson. Neighboring music stores enliven the plaza with tunes. For helpful information on area attractions or a town map ($1), visit **La Unidad de Turismo,** in the back part of the Municipio on the plaza. (☎2740 211, ext. 206. Open M-F 9am-12:30pm and 2-5pm; afternoons are better.) **Banco del Austro,** at the far corner of the plaza, does not exchange traveler's checks but does have Money-gram service. (☎2740 864. Open M-F 9am-4pm.) There is a **Western Union** one block off the plaza on Olson. (☎2741 162. Open M-F 8:30am-12:30pm and 2-

4:30pm, Su 8:30am-12:30pm.) **Police** are in a blue-and-white building at Comín and Bernal, on the plaza. (☎2740 101. Open 24hr.) **PacificTel**, on the plaza next to Banco del Austro, has fax service in addition to telephones. (Open daily 7am-11pm.) **Farmacia Sucúa** is across the street. (☎2740 389. Open 24hr.) **Hospital Pío XII** is on Comín, three blocks from the plaza on the left. (☎2740 109. Open 24hr.) **Clínica Morales** (☎2740 134), one block off the plaza behind BNF, is open 24hr. **D@m@rys**, across from Delgado Travel at the plaza, offers **Internet access.** (US$1.40 per hr. Open 9-11am and 1-3pm.)

☐☐ ACCOMMODATIONS AND FOOD. Hotel Athenas ❸, on Comín, two blocks toward Macas from the plaza, is tranquil in the already calm world of Sucúa. Paintings adorn the walls; muted blues fill wood and tile rooms graced with cable TVs, hot private baths, and fans. (☎2740 216. Singles US$8; doubles US$12.) **Hotel Don Guimo ❷,** on Comín, one block south of the plaza, is clean and bright. Rooms have fans and telephones. (☎2740 483; bertha_f3@yahoo.es. Breakfast included. US$6, with hot private bath US$7.) **Hostal Karina ❷,** on the far corner of the plaza, has shared baths, comfortable beds, and bare rooms. The common area has a small balcony overlooking the plaza. (☎2740 153. US$4, with TV US$4.50.) Camp in open-sided *choza* huts at **recreation centers** with bathrooms and restaurants. Small eateries serving traditional cuisine speckle the the plaza. **Restaurante Los Arrieros ❶,** on Comín, one block from the plaza, under the Hotel Gyna, serves a typical menu. (☎2741 288. *Almuerzo* US$1.70. Entrees US$2.50-4.50. Open 6:30am-9pm.) For a bit of foreign flavor, head to **Chivon's Bar and Pizza ❶,** on 8 de Diciembre. Go two blocks south of the plaza on Comín and turn right. It has tiki torches out front. International flags and Italian soccer paraphernalia decorate a faux bamboo hut interior. (☎2740 409. Beer US$1. Pizza US$1.50. Open daily 10am-midnight.) **Los Canelos ❶,** on the plaza, serves breakfasts, lunches, and snacks. (Meals US$1. Open daily 7am-midnight.)

◉ SIGHTS AND ACTIVITIES. The Federación Interprovincial Centros Shuar (FICSH) is the center of an organization that attends to the needs of 80,000 Shuar in over 400 communities. Once known as the Jivaro, the Shuar were known in the past for their practice of shrinking heads—a practice that no longer occurs. The Federation can organize visits to closer (there are 20) villages or ones deeper in the jungle. Visits include cultural exchange, shamanism, and artesanía. The village of **Cumbatza** has thermal waters. The **Centro de Formación,** 5min. from Sucúa, has a small zoo and some traditional buildings. Contact the Federation to organize a tour. (Comín 17-38, 4 blocks south of the plaza. ☎2740 108 or 2740 938; ficsh@mo.pro.ec. Open M-F 8am-noon and 2-5pm.) **La Unión** is a rarely visited spot at the confluence of Ríos Tutanangoza and Miriumi. Swim and enjoy the untouched natural beauty of the gold-specked sandy beach here. Locals claim that the river contains medicinal mud. (From the plaza, go 5 blocks south; turn right on 3 de Noviembre; walk a few blocks past the town pool complex on the right and the cemetery on the left. Continue walking along this road to Asunción (20min.). Soon after crossing the river, turn to the right. La Unión is 5min. upstream.) **El Tesoro** has a small **zoo** with tapirs, a toucan, and some other animals, as well as a small **lake** with **canoes** and **balsa rafts.** The restaurant serves *platos típicas*, including *ceviche* fresh from the fish pond and sugar cane juice made on the premises. On weekends, school groups come to enjoy the bar, sports field, and dance floor. (☎2702 276 or 09 9886 675. Any Sucúa south-bound bus (30min., US$0.50). Taxi (15min., US$7). Entrance fee US$1. Tents US$5.) At the **Centro de Exposiciones, Ecoturismo, y Recreación Miriumi** pitch a tent beside trails leading through the forest or pass the night at the restaurant/dance floor, where food is made to order. (Walk 20min. along Olson and Río Miriumi from the plaza, past Hostal Karina and Clínica Morales. Signs are on the right as the road forks.)

MÉNDEZ
☎07

Nestled among green hills with a large, circular plaza, and viewpoints overlooking Río Paute, Méndez (pop. 2500) is a relaxing place to visit. It sits at a crossroads, where the east-west Cuenca-Morona (and the Cueva de Los Tayos; see p. 314) road intersects the north-south Macas-Zamora road. Enjoy the scenery and friendly people; it's a good place to break up a long bus trip.

C TRANSPORTATION. Buses pass through the plaza. Companies have offices in local restaurants. From Restaurant El Reportero (see below), **Cooperativa de Transportes Macas** goes to **Macas** (3½hr., 3 per day noon-8pm, US$2.50) and **Cuenca** (4½hr., 6 per day 8am-8pm, US$6.50). **Ciudad de Sucúa,** across the street from PacificTel, goes to **Gualaquiza** (6hr., 4pm, US$3) and **Limón** (2½hr., 7pm, US$1.75).

⊞⊠ ORIENTATION AND PRACTICAL INFORMATION. The main road, **Cuenca,** passes in front of a stylish church. All traveler services are within one block of the plaza. Lookouts over Río Paute are opposite the church. **Farmacia Pasteur** is on Cuenca, just off the plaza. (☎2760 374. Open 7am-10pm.) The **police** are on the plaza, opposite the church. (☎2760 101. Open 24hr.) **Western Union** is on the plaza. **PacificTel** is one block up Cuenca from the plaza. (Open daily 8am-10pm.)

⌂◻ ACCOMMODATIONS AND FOOD. Hostal Los Ceibos ❷, on Cuenca, one block up from the plaza, provides Méndez's cleanest and most comfortable lodging. (☎2760 133. Reservations recommended. Noisy rooms with common bath US$5; singles with private bath and cable TV US$7; doubles US$12.) **Residencial Vanessa ❶,** on Cuenca next to Los Ceibos, has shared baths and harsh, cement architecture, but the price is right. (☎2760 146. Rooms US$3.) Méndez has quite a few inexpensive food options, including *cuy* from a storefront spit. **Restaurant El Reportero ❶,** on Comín around the corner from the Departmento de Cultura, offers plastic lawn furniture and hearty food, as well as information on Cuenca- and Macas-bound buses. (*Comida típica* US$1.50. Open 7am-10pm.)

◧ ✻ SIGHTS AND FESTIVALS. The hills around Méndez hide some enjoyable spots. **Nunkantay Canyon** is in a Shuar community 25min. from town. The area has trails from which you can admire the waterfalls and nesting parrots. **Río Negro baths** have a few cabins by the water. Information about these attractions is available from the **Departamento de Cultura** (☎2760 416), on the plaza next to the church. This normally quiet town turns into a hotbed of activity during the **annual festival** celebrating the town's founding on July 12, 1913. The party is on from July 10-12, with a concert, parade, and motocross competition. If you plan on attending, make reservations in advance; only so many beds are available.

GUALAQUIZA
☎07

At the southern edge of the Morona-Santiago province, Gualaquiza (pop. 6500) is a growing town surrounded by green hills. Waterfalls, caves, and pre-Inca ruins, as well as the rumored site of the lost city of Logroño de los Caballeros are all within a few hours of town. A castle-like structure marks the central park. Unfortunately, the early Spanish colonists who came here looking for gold and converts discovered that the journey to this beautiful land is arduous. Due to poor road conditions, it takes at least 5hr. to reach Zamora, Macas, or Cuenca. As a result, not many tourists pass through and guides for the sites are rare. That said, adventure awaits the intrepid traveler who does come to explore this mysterious region.

TRANSPORTATION. The **terminal terrestre**, on Pesantez, sends **buses** to: **Loja** (7hr., 11 per day 2am-10pm, US$6) via **Zamora** (5hr., US$3.50); **Macas** (9hr.; 6am, 6pm; US$8); **Cuenca** (via Sigsig 6hr., via San Juan Bosco 9hr.; 9pm; US$7). **Rancheros** leave from the terminal for destinations like La Pradera and San Juan Bosco. Find **taxis** at **Ciudad de Gualaquiza** (☎2780 777), behind the bus terminal.

ORIENTATION AND PRACTICAL INFORMATION. Gualaquiza's businesses are clustered betwen the **Parque Central** and the bus terminal, four blocks down Pesantez. The tourist office, **Unidad de Turismo,** in the Municipal building next to the park, on the second floor, has **maps** of the town and surrounding area, as well as info on nearby sites. It also helps find tour guides. (☎2780 109 or 2780 782. Open M-F 7:30am-12:30pm and 1:30-4:30pm.) The **Centro Comercial Popular** market has three stories of goods. (Open daily 7am-6pm.) The **police** (☎2780 101) are on Pesantez at Altaro. **Farmacia Central** (☎2780 203) is on Pesantez across from the police. (Open daily 8am-12:30pm and 2-9:30pm.) The **hospital** (☎2780 106) is one block uphill from the church. **PacificTel** (☎2780 105), at Cuenca and Moreno across from Hotel Internacional, accepts incoming calls. (Open daily 7am-11pm.)

ACCOMMODATIONS. **Hotel Internacional** ❷, one block from the church at Cuenca and Morena, is the newest, biggest, and best hotel, including hot private baths, cable TV, fans, and phones. (☎2780 637. Rooms US$7.50.) **Hotel Wakiz** ❷, at Orellana and Comín, has walls painted with tropical scenes. Rooms cluster around a well-lighted atrium. The common area has comfortable couches and TV. (☎2780 138. Rooms US$4, with cold bath US$5.) **Hostal Residencial Guadalupe** ❶ (☎2780 113), on Pesantez, one block from the park, offers plain rooms a long walk from the cold shared bath. (Rooms US$3 per person.) **Residencial Amazonas** ❶, on the park, has small rooms and shared baths. (☎2780 715. US$3 per person.)

FOOD. Gualaquiza is heavy on the cheap *comida típica* but still has a surprising number of burger and hot-dog places. **Restaurant Copacabana** ❶, on the corner of Pesantez and 12 de Febrero, on the second floor, serves a *menú* (US$1.50). (☎2780 353. Open daily 7am-10pm.) Grab a quick bite at **Topy Burguers** ❶, across from the terminal. (☎2780 793. Burgers US$1.60; chaulafan US$3. Open daily 7am-11pm.) **Bar Restaurant Internacional** ❶, under the hotel of the same name, has checkered tablecloths, a mural of New York, and paintings of fish. (*Chaulafan, desayuno,* and *almuerzo* each US$1-3. Open daily 6am-10pm.)

SIGHTS. Those with an adventurous spirit can find ruins (speculated to be pre-Inca) in nearby towns. **Las Ruinas del Remanso** were discovered in 1815 by José Prieto. He incorrectly identified them as the Spanish city Logroño de los Caballeros (also known as the City of Gold), but they actually belong to an older civilization. **Las Ruinas del Cady** can be found in Nueva Tarqui. Don't expect to find a guide for either of these attractions; the best plan is to get information from the tourist office. Locals in the small towns near these ruins also offer help. (Rancheros go to La Pradera (1½hr., US$2). From there, it is a 5min. walk up the hill to El Remanso. To visit the Cady site, catch a ranchero (1hr., US$1.50) heading to Nueva Tarqui.)

Stalactites, stalagmites, and a subterranean river await in the 300m long **Dolorosa Cave.** A 30min. hike following a 45min. car ride will reach the cave. Orchids and nearby waterfalls beautify the way. **Cascada del Guabi,** a 50m waterfall to the west of the city, was used in indigenous purification rituals. Visiting these sites requires hiring a guide—no easy feat in Gualaquiza. Contact **Rodrigo Lituma** at the hospital; he guides on the weekends. Also, ask at the Hotel Wakiz (see above). Wide, shaded paths line Ríos Yumaza and Gualaquiza in the **Parques Lineales** that borders town to the northeast. (From Parque Central, walk 10min. past the hospital. The entrance to the park is on the right, just before the river.)

The Salesian mission at **Bomboiza** is a Shuar center near Gualaquiza. Walk down the palm-lined Av. de los Achos and admire the surrounding countryside. The adept shopper can also find Shuar crafts here. (Take any bus bound for Pangui, Loja, or Zamora (35min., US$0.60). The road to Bomboiza is on the left. From here, walk 10min. to the mission and 45min. to the town.)

Enjoy the valley views from the miradors **Portón** and **La Gruta.** To get to the first, walk 1½hr. along the old road to Sigsig. At the crest of a hill, the Gualaquiza, Bomboiza, and Chuchumbletza valleys spread out below. Ask at the tourist office for directions. **La Gruta** is in town, a short walk from the central park. Take 24 de Mayo 500m from the front of the church.

THE ORIENTE

THE GALÁPAGOS ISLANDS

There are few places in the world where humans are truly second-class citizens—the Galápagos Islands is one of them. About four million years ago, underwater volcanoes spewed forth what would become Isla Española and Isla San Cristóbal. Later, animals began to venture toward this undiscovered paradise; those that completed the journey found a large area with little competition. Isolated from the mainland by 1000km and from each other by up to 200km, the islands provided a secluded environment for rapid and undisturbed species expansion.

And expand they did. Slowly and silently, the Galápagos evolved into a treasure chest of endemic species—plants and animals found nowhere else in the world. Although the archipelago was discovered in 1535 accidently by the bishop of Panama, its miraculous beauty would remain a secret until the 1830s, when Charles Darwin set out on a journey around the world. Darwin's astute observations of the exceptional flora and fauna that had adapted to the island's landscapes led to introduced the theory of naturual selection, also known as survival of the fittest, and rocketed the Galápagos to stardom. Darwin discovered the mechanism for evolution, thus securing his title as one of the most influential figures in history.

HIGHLIGHTS OF THE GALÁPAGOS ISLANDS

MAKE OUT the heart shape of Isla Santa Cruz's Bellavista lava tunnel, **The Tunnel of Endless Love** (see p. 337).

SPLASH with sea lions in the waters off **Isla Santa Fé** (see p. 339).

SNORKEL with hammerhead sharks in Isla Floreana's **Devil's Crown** (see p. 352).

DELIVER a letter in person from **Post Office Bay** on Isla Floreana to someone near your hometown (see p. 352).

RIDE the world-class waves near **Puerto Baquerizo Moreno, San Cristóbal** (see p. 340).

Each year, more than 60,000 tourists travel here to admire the lovable Galápagos tortoises, flightless cormorants, blue-footed boobies and waved albatrosses. Meanwhile, giant manta rays, sea turtles, iguanas, thousands of playful sea lions, sharks, and millions upon millions of fish all coexist in an underwater paradise. Dive in and see for yourself; the Galápagos touts some of the best scuba diving and snorkeling sites in the world. Back on land, however, examples of the carelessness of human settlers are many. Even though the Galápagos were declared a national park in 1959, entire species remain threatened by non-native rats, feral goats, dogs, and cats. And despite the National Park Service's efforts to limit immigration to the islands, mainland Ecuadorians continue to move here in hopes of cashing in on the US$80 million-a-year tourism industry. Still, 97% of the archipelago is officially protected by the Park, a sanctuary of living geological and biological history that makes any visit an extended first-hand natural science lesson. Whether it's because they've learned everything they'd ever want to know about marine iguanas' mating patterns or because they've been mesmerized by the sunset over a never-ending stretch of ocean, all who visit these enchanted islands will remember the trip for the rest of their lives.

FLORA AND FAUNA

BIRDS

Birds, the most prominent and diverse type of animal on the islands, aren't camera-shy and allow up-close observation.

BIRDS OF THE SEA. "Penguins only live in Antarctica!" you say? Tell that to the **Galápagos penguins,** which live around the Bolívar Channel between Isla Isabela's western coast and Isla Fernandina. Just 30cm tall, the white-bellied Galápagos penguins are the only penguin species that nest entirely in the tropics and the sole penguin species that reside in the northern hemisphere. Some of the most well known birds in the Galápagos are the three types of **boobies: blue-footed, red-footed,** and **masked.** Blue-footed and masked boobies nest on the ground, encircling their territory with white excrement—an effective enemy defense system. Blue-footed boobies are by far the islands' most commonly observed birds, performing their famous plunge-dive and goofy-looking mating dance for visitors on several different islands. Observing the much smaller red-footed boobies, however, is not as easy, since the tree-nesting species live almost exclusively in the infrequently visisted islands of Islas Genovesa, Seymour Norte, and Wolf. The masked boobies are the largest and most well known for the murderous habits of their nestlings. Although masked boobies always lay two eggs, only one hatchling survives, since the stronger one pushes its weaker sibling out of the nest to ensure that it will get enough to eat. Another famous endemic seabird, the **flightless cormorant,** is found only on the westernmost islands of Fernandina and Isabela. These cormorants, the largest of the worlds 29 cormorant species, were originally a flying species, but the lack of predators or terrestrial food meant that big wings were a waste of energy. Those with webbed feet, powerful legs, and small wings survived—and voilà!—birds that can't fly. To complicate matters, cormorants have light bones, appropriate for flying but not for diving. Rather than resign themselves to the shallows of plankton and lesser seafood cuisine, cormorants swallow small stones that provide the extra umph needed to reach the deep, fish-filled waters.

The largest and most notable birds on the islands are the cleptoparasitic great and magnificent **frigate birds.** Males boast an inflatable red pouch below the beak during mating season—sure to catch the eye of any female. Crowning its attributes, a frigate's wingspan can reach 2.3m, giving it the largest wingspan-to-weight ratio of any existing bird. Mating occurs on San Cristóbal and Genovesa from March to April, and on Seymour Norte throughout the year. The **waved albatross** is endemic only to Española, where the world's 12,000 pairs nest from April to December before vacationing in the South Pacific. They are the largest birds in the archipelago, weighing over 4kg with a wingspan of 2.5m.

BIRDS OF THE SHORE. Flamingos are by far the rarest and most famous shorebirds; a mere 500-600 specimens currently inhabit Floreana, Isabela, Rabida, Santiago, and Santa Cruz. To maintain their pinkish hue, flamingos feast on small pink shrimp larvae and pink marine insects. Other shorebirds include the **Great Blue, Lava, and night herons; American oystercatchers; egrets; gallinoles; turnstones; whimbrels;** and **black-necked stilts.**

BIRDS OF THE LAND. Due to their isolation from mainland bird populations, Galápagos land birds compose 76% of endemic species. Most famous are the 13 types of **Darwin's finches.** These sparrow-sized birds can only be differentiated by beak morphology and feeding habits. Darwin himself didn't recognize them as distinct species until after he'd left the archipelago. While some live on seeds or fruits, the elusive **carpenter finch** uses a stick to dig insects out of trees, and the

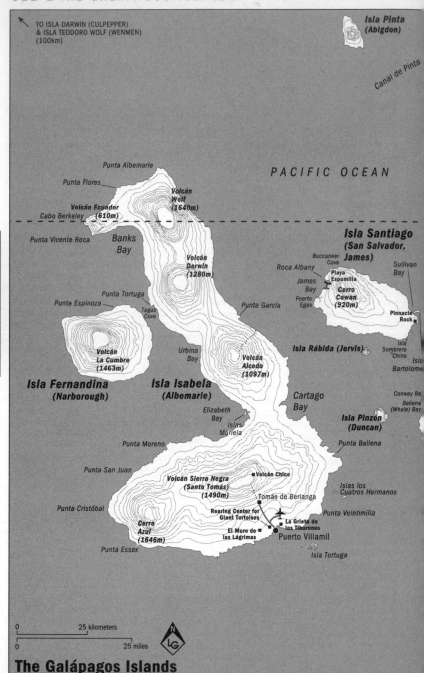

TO ISLA DARWIN (CULPEPPER)
& ISLA TEODORO WOLF (WENMEN)
(100km)

Isla Pinta
(Abigdon)

Canal de Pinta

PACIFIC OCEAN

Punta Albemarle

Punta Flores

Volcán Wolf
(1640m)

Volcán Ecuador
(610m)
Cabo Berkeley

Punta Vicente Roca

Banks Bay

Isla Santiago
(San Salvador, James)

Buccaneer
Cove

Roca Albany

James
Bay

Playa
Espumilla

Cerro Cowan
(920m)

Sullivan
Bay

Volcán Darwin
(1280m)

Punta Tortuga

Punta Espinoza

Tagus
Cove

Puerto
Egas

Punta García

Pinnacle
Rock

Volcán La Cumbre
(1463m)

Urbina
Bay

Volcán Alcedo
(1097m)

Isla Rábida (Jervis)

Isla
Sombrero
Chino

Isla
Bartolomé

Isla Fernandina
(Narborough)

Isla Isabela
(Albemarle)

Cartago
Bay

Conway Bay

Ballena
(Whale) Bay

Elizabeth
Bay

Islas
Mariela

Isla Pinzón
(Duncan)

Punta Moreno

Punta Ballena

Punta San Juan

Volcán Sierra Negra
(Santo Tomás)
(1490m)

■*Volcán Chico*

Islas los
Cuatros Hermanos

Punta Cristóbal

Tomás de Berlanga

Punta Veintimilla

Cerro Azul
(1646m)

Rearing Center for
Giant Tortoises

La Grieta de
los Tiburones

El Muro de
las Lágrimas

Puerto Villamil

Punta Essex

Isla Tortuga

0   25 kilometers

0   25 miles

N

LG

The Galápagos Islands

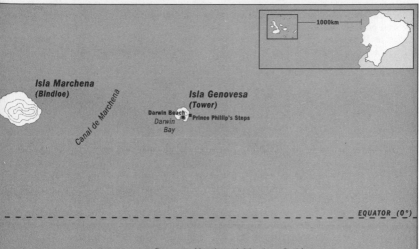

1000km

EQUATOR (0°)

Isla Marchena
(Bindloe)

Canal de Marchena

Isla Genovesa
(Tower)

Darwin Beach   ■ Prince Phillip's Steps
Darwin
Bay

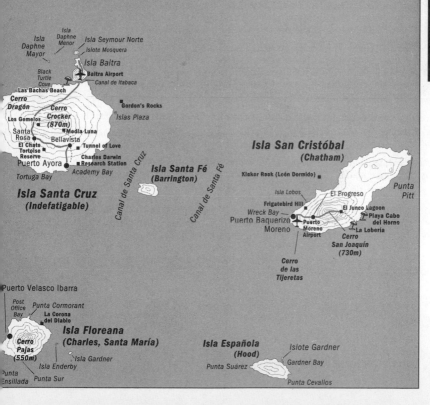

Parque Nacional Marina Galápagos

Isla
Daphne   Isla
Mayor   Daphne   Isla Seymour Norte
         Menor
              Islote Mosquera

Isla Baltra

Black   Baltra Airport
Turtle
Cove   Canal de Itabaca
Las Bachas Beach

Cerro
Dragón   Cerro   Gordon's Rocks
Los Gemelos   Crocker
             (870m)   Islas Plaza
Santa   Media Luna
Rosa
El Chato   Bellavista
Tortoise
Reserve   Tunnel of Love
Puerto Ayora   Charles Darwin
             Research Station   Isla Santa Fé
Tortuga Bay   Academy Bay   (Barrington)

Isla Santa Cruz
(Indefatigable)

Canal de Santa Cruz

Canal de Santa Fé

Isla San Cristóbal
(Chatham)

Kicker Rock (León Dormido) ■

Isla Lobos
                          El Progreso
Frigatebird Hill
Wreck Bay   El Junco Lagoon
Puerto Baquerizo   Puerto   Playa Cabo
  Moreno   Moreno   del Horno
                Airport   La Lobería
                          Cerro   Punta
                          San Joaquín   Pitt
                          (730m)

Cerro
de las
Tijeretas

Puerto Velasco Ibarra

Post
Office   Punta Cormorant
Bay   La Corona
       del Diablo
              Isla Floreana
              (Charles, Santa María)   Isla Española
                                        (Hood)   Islote Gardner
Cerro
Pajas   Gardner Bay
(550m)   Isla Gardner
       Isla Enderby   Punta Suárez
Punta   Punta Sur
Ensillada   Punta Cevallos

"blood-sucking" vampire finch of Wolf Island uses its sharp beak to suck the blood of red-footed and masked boobies. Other notable endemic land birds include the carnivorous **Galápagos mockingbird, hood mockingbird** (on Española), **Galápagos hawk** (the largest land predator on the islands), and the **Galápagos dove.**

REPTILES

TORTOISES. The undisputed king of Galápagos reptiles is the **giant tortoise.** How the big guys (up to 250kg) first came to inhabit the islands is still a mystery. Their closest relative is a species native to Argentina. Sadly, three of the original 14 subspecies are now extinct as a result of human interference, and introduced animals continue to harass the remaining populations. The very characteristics that enabled the turtles to endure millions of years of climate and landscape change have also played a part in the decimation of their population. Sailors and pirates found the giant tortoises excellent sources of meat, especially since the reptiles could live for up to a year without food and thus provide fresh meat for an entire voyage. Even worse, hunters targeted the much smaller, and thus easier to transport, female turtles over the massive males, which further damaged the population's reproductive capabilities. While these tortoises can live to be over 150 years old, they do not reproduce often, and when they do, the vulnerable hatchlings have an extremely low chance of reaching maturity. The Galápagos National Park and the Charles Darwin Research Center (see p. 335) are doing what they can to prevent predation and boost the head count. The largest tortoise population is found on Isabela, concentrated around the crater of Volcán Alcedo. Wild tortoises can also be observed on Santa Cruz (see p. 329) and Española (see p. 353). Captive tortoises reside at the Charles Darwin Research Center on Santa Cruz and the Breeding Center for Giant Tortoises on Isabela (see p. 345).

SEA TURTLES. The **Pacific green sea turtle** calls many of the islands home, breeding from November to January and laying eggs till June. Nesting females plod onto the beach at nighttime, dig an enormous nesting hole in the sand, bury a few dozen eggs, and urinate and defecate on the resulting sand mound to harden the sand and protect the fragile eggs. After about six months, hatched sea turtles quickly scurry to the water, many snatched up by predators along the way. In those few risky moments, they apparently develop a sentimental attachment: after wandering to waters hundreds or thousands of kilometers away, the turtles amazingly return to lay their eggs on the exact same beach where they themselves were hatched.

IGUANAS. One of the most bizarre and unique reptiles of the Galápagos is the dark-hued **marine iguana,** the only aquatic iguana in the world. Related to the land iguanas of the American mainland, marine iguanas eat green algae that grows underwater. They can swim to a depth of 20m, anaerobically lower their body temperatures to stay underwater for up to 1hr. at a time, and are able to rapidly discharge excess salt from their unusually square noses (an amusing spectacle). Less exotic (but also endemic) orangish-green **land iguanas** can grow up to 1m in length. Keep an eye out for the **prickly pear iguanas** on Santa Fé and South Plazas, the rare **hybrid iguana** on South Plazas, and the **crested canolophus pallidus** land iguana species, found only on Santa Fé.

OTHER REPTILES. Long ago, through some heroic feat of seamanship, **snakes** reached the islands. The non-poisonous Galápagos **land snake,** colored brown or gray with yellow stripes or spots, slithers in search of small prey to crush with its constrictive power. Seven species of gray **lava lizard** are also unique to the islands. Females have eye-catching red-orange throats. They are very territorial, but most confrontation takes the form of bouncing up and down on the forelegs; fights between lizards are seldom serious but can be entertaining.

MAMMALS

The superstar mammal of the Galápagos is the **Galápagos sea lion**. Weighing up to 250kg, the lethargic giants occupy what seems like every open speck of beach on the islands, posing for tourists, surfing a wave, belching loudly, sliding through the water with one fin in the air. Although the sleek sea lions are generally playful, beware of the extremely territorial "beachmaster" *machos* (male bulls), which pace the shores guarding their harem of 20-30 female partners. Disguised as a seal, the **Galápagos fur seal** (nicknamed "Galápagos sea bear") is an imposter—beneath its pointed ears and extra layer of fur hides a smaller, more introverted sea lion. Unfortunately, their furry cover has come at a price—thousands of these little "bears" have been hunted to supply the fur industry. The only other mammals that were not introduced by man are **bats** and **rice rats**. However, even rats are not safe from human impact. Before the arrival of the introduced black rat, there were seven species of endemic rice rat; today, only two remain.

MARINE LIFE

While a relatively limited number of species inhabits the terrain, the Galápagos's waters teem with life. The 16 species of **whale** include the **sperm, humpback, blue,** and **killer whales.** The **common** and **bottle-nosed** are the most prevalent of the seven species of **dolphin,** which are concentrated off the west coast of Isabela and are frequently seen jumping and swimming in schools near the bows of tour boats. Twelve species of **shark,** including the **hammerhead** and **black-tipped reef shark,** and five species of **rays** also lurk in these waters. Before El Niño's most recent visit in 1998, **coral reefs** surrounded many of the islands, but the inhospitable temperature extremes caused by this pesky weather phenomenon destroyed many formations. However, most species remained unaffected, including **crabs, lobster, squid, octopus, starfish,** and **shellfish.** The **sea cucumber,** or *pepino,* continues to struggle against its status as a delicacy in Japan. Because of this diversity, the waters in and around the Galápagos (70,000 sq. km) were designated a **marine reserve** in 1986. While the area is protected and fishing is frowned upon, regulated commercial fishing of some species is allowed within the 40-nautical-km protected sea zone; before dropping a line, consult locals or your trusty tour guide.

PLANT LIFE

The Galápagos support seven vegetation zones that are home to over 600 plant species, 170 of which are endemic. The zones range from low and dry to high and moist. Plants that have a taste for salt, like **red,**

IN-RECENT NEWS

GOATS GONE WILD

Although uninhabited by humans, the northern side of Isabela has its share of uninvited guests that threaten island dwellers. In the early 70s, feral goats left on the island got busy and exploded in population. By 1998, 75,000 to 125,000 goats were ravaging the countryside. They consumed just about every type of vegetation in their path, endangering both endemic plant species and the organisms dependent on them. As time wears on and the goat population continues to expand, locals have started to notice ominous climate changes on the rim of Volcán Alcedo, further jeopardizing the fragile island habitats.

In response to these pesky goats, the Charles Darwin Foundation has deemed it necessary to implement an eradication plan, ominously known as the Isabela Project. The plan sends normally animal-loving park rangers into the brush with rifles in hand and instructions to shoot anything about 1½m tall, with four legs and horns—luckily for the rest of the island fauna, these animals tend to be goats. To ensure that only the most humane techniques are used, all the rangers involved in the project undergo professional huntsman training. Whatever the case, at the end of the day, these goats are endangering the few giant tortoises left on the island: someone's got to go, and it ain't gonna be Lonesome George.

black, and **white mangroves,** dominate the **littoral zone,** the area along the coast. The **arid zone** is the driest region, just above the littoral in altitude and dominated by cacti and other dry-weather plants. Next highest is the **transition zone,** where the fragrant **Palo Santo** ("holy stick") trees thrive, annually hailing Christmas with their white flowers. The next zone, the **scalesia,** is ridden with humidity and the endemic scalesia trees. The three remaining zones are the **brown, miconia,** and **pampa zones.** The brown is appropriately named for its prominent **brown liverwort mosses,** while the miconia zone houses the endemic, shrubby **miconia plant.** The highest and wettest vegetation zone is the **pampa,** dominated by mosses, ferns and grasses; few trees or shrubs can brave this hyper-humid region.

ESSENTIALS

The Galápagos Islands are 1hr. behind the Ecuadorian mainland and 6hr. behind Greenwich Mean Time. Daylight Savings Time is not observed. When first arriving in the Galápagos (Isla Baltra or Isla San Cristóbal), all foreign visitors must present a valid **passport** and pay a **US$100** park admission fee in **cash.** Credit cards and traveler's checks are not accepted. Visitors who arrive without the US$100 in cash can enter the islands by leaving their passports with Park officials at the airport, obtain cash in Puerto Ayora, and pay the fee at the National Park Office by the Charles Darwin Research Center in Puerto Ayora. Park officials at the office will return your passport to you when you pay the US$100 fee. Make sure you hold on to the entrance ticket if traveling between islands.

TRANSPORTATION

GETTING THERE AND AWAY

HOW TO GO. Almost everyone flies to the Galápagos, although boat travel is available. Going by boat is generally more expensive, or at least no cheaper than flights. **Boats** usually cost US$150-200 one-way, and the journey from Guayaquil can take anywhere from three to five days. They leave one to two times per month from Guayaquil. Conditions tend to be very basic, and the journey is long. Not many boats make the trip, and many are not authorized to take passengers. The best thing to do is to check with the tourism office in Guayaquil to see what boats are available and about what time they leave. All **flights** go through **Guayaquil.** Consequently, many people take a bus to Guayaquil after flying to Quito because it's slightly cheaper to fly from Guayaquil than Quito. For airlines, schedules, and prices, see p. 330.

WHEN TO GO. Don't be misled by the Galápagos's equatorial location—a trip here is not the tropical steambath of other areas with the same latitude. Temperatures generally hover between 22°-28°C (70°-80°F). The water is fairly cold, sometimes below 20°C (68°F). Low season is May 1-June 14 and September 15-October 31, and everything else is high season. The rainy season lasts from January to April, with decreased winds, warmer sea currents, and heavy rains. March and April are usually the wettest months. The dry season is June to November, when the weather is often cloudy and the islands enshrouded with mist.

GETTING AROUND THE GALÁPAGOS

INTER-ISLAND TRAVEL. There are several ways to visit the Galápagos, although by far the most popular, easy, informative, and cost-effective way to view the islands is on a multi-day boat tour. Travelers uneasy with spending a week on a small boat getting tossed around by rocky waves, however, may choose a more land-based alternative to visit the islands. Multi-hotel package tours visiting different islands are the best middle ground between boat tours and land-only trips. Several agencies offer 5- to 14-day trips visiting various sights by boat but sleeping and eating at hotels on the islands. Multi-hotel package tours, however, are generally more expensive than multi-day boat tours. A third way is to explore the islands at your own pace, relying on inter-island travel and privately arranged tours. EMETEBE **flights** fly between Baltra, Puerto Villamil, and Puerto Baquerizo Moreno. All **inter-island boats** leave from Puerto Ayora and go to Puerto Villamil and Puerto Baquerizo Moreno. (See the **Practical Information** section of each city for more schedules and prices.) This option offers more autonomy but is usually limited to Islas San Cristóbal, Santa Cruz, and Isabela; daytrips to other islands are expensive and often require groups. Budget travelers who economize on accommodations and food and find groups to visit sites on tours may pay less per day than passengers on multi-day boat tours or hotel packages. Lodging and restaurants on the main islands, however, are more expensive than on the mainland, so solo travelers roaming the islands without a guide should plan ahead and research tour options well to determine which of the three main options to visit the Galápagos is the most economical, practical, and complete.

GUIDES. A guide can make or break a trip to the Galápagos, and many travelers will confirm that a knowledgeable, responsible guide is easily the most important asset of a good tour. There are three classes of guides: Naturalist I, II, and III. A Naturalist I guide usually has limited foreign language skills, and his biology training may not be the best. Naturalist III is experienced, usually multi-lingual, and possibly holds a university degree in biology. Naturalist II is somewhere in between. Tour boats and tour agencies should let you know in advance the qualification of their guides. Many tours can also provide guides who speak foreign languages, especially German, French, and Italian.

TOUR BOATS. There are five main classes of tour boats. **Economy** boats tend to be small, with about 12 passengers, multi-bunk rooms, shared or private cold water bathrooms, good, simple food, and a Naturalist I guide (US$80-95 per person per day, last-minute US$55-65). **Tourist** boats tend to be a little bigger (averaging 16 passengers), with cold private showers, greater food diversity, and a Naturalist II guide (US$90-120 per person per day, last-minute US$65-75). **Tourist Superior** is a step up from the tourist class, offering A/C, hot water, larger social spaces, excellent food, diving opportunities, and Naturalist II or III guides (US$110-150 per person per day, last minute US$70-80). **First-class** boats are predictably lavish and have Naturalist III guides (US$250 per person per day, last minute US$115-180). **Luxury boats** offer all the amenities imaginable (US$250-300 per person per day).

FINDING A TOUR. All boats are run by an "operator," a person or company that usually directly manages over one to four boats. Some operators have their own offices for booking tours directly; other tours are purchased through tour agencies that have information about many boats and charge a small commission. To get a list of different operators, contact the Ministerio de Turismo or Cámara de Turismo in Puerto Ayora (see p. 332); both offices have current info on every boat authorized the to tour the islands. Another great resource is Safari Tours in Quito (see p. 86); English-speaking Jean Brown has an extensive database of Galápagos tour boats and provides honest advice about tours, guides, and travel options. Bargaining with operators is appropriate, especially for last-minute prices, which can be as much 50% cheaper than the listed price of the tour. **The closer you are to the sailing date and the boat when you make reservations, the lower the price.** However, keep in mind that those who wait run the risk of not finding a suitable boat. Prices rise during high season (June 15-Sept. 14 and Nov. 1-Apr. 30.), becoming more negotiable during low season (May 1-June 14 and Sept. 15-Oct. 31). Last-minute deals on economy, tourist class, and tourist superior boats are relatively easy to find in the low season, though harder to find in the high season. More luxurious boats are often booked solid months in advance and rarely offer last-minute deals.

Agencies in Puerto Ayora (see p. 329) on Isla Santa Cruz generally offer the best deals on multi-day boat tours. Ask around at hotels, tour agencies, and the tourist information offices to inquire about openings on boats. During the low season, budget travelers won't have much difficulty finding a last-minute deal on an inexpensive or mid-range tour, but in high season groups sometimes wait around Puerto Ayora for up to a week before booking a tour. In the high season, many travelers with less time and patience opt to pay a bit extra and arrange their tour in advance from the mainland. Travel agencies in Quito (see p. 86) or Guayaquil (see p. 267) arrange relatively cheap passage on boats that are scheduled to leave in a few weeks, although last-minute deals may be available on boats setting sail within a few days. Agencies that directly represent their own boats may be able to negotiate a lower price. Contact **The South American Explorers** (see p. 85) or **Safari Tours** (see p. 86) in Quito for recommendations. **Agencia de Viajes Galasam, Central Viajero Travel Agency,** and **Dreamkapture Travel** in Guayaquil (see p. 268) have been recommended by several budget travelers. Get a contract in writing, and if you are unsatisfied, take your complaint to the Chamber of Tourism.

TOUR LENGTH AND ITINERARY. Duration varies from three to 21 days, the most common lengths being four or eight days. The four-day tours begin when you board the plane in Quito, even though you might not set sail until the afternoon, and the fourth day usually ends around 5 or 6pm. If you're considering an eight-day tour, be sure it's not simply two four-day tours being advertised as one: if it is, the fourth day will be spent dropping off and picking up passengers. Verify the itinerary of the tour before finalizing your booking, and ask about what sites on Isla Santa Cruz will be visited. Many boats spend a day near Puerto Ayora visiting the Charles Darwin Research Center, lava tunnels, tortoise reserves, and Los Gemelos. Since these sites are easy to visit on your own from Puerto Ayora, you may want to purchase a shorter, less expensive tour that skips these sites and explore them instead on your own.

TIPPING. It is standard to tip the crew on a tour boat at least US$25-50 per week or US$5-10 per person per day, depending on the quality of the service. Crew members work hard and aren't paid well (especially on economy boats), so be generous. It is appropriate to tip the guide as well; a good guide can get up to half of the total tip. If an anonymous tipping box is not provided near the end of a trip, it is common to pool money with other passengers and give it to the captain for distribution. Some boats give passengers envelopes to leave their tips, which will be divided among the crew and guide.

INDEPENDENT INTER-ISLAND TRAVEL. Independent inter-island travel is irregular, time-consuming, and costly, but it's also a more adventurous choice. Islands can only be reached by guided tour, small boat, or small plane, and independent travelers should not expect to follow rigid itineraries. See the **Transportation** section of each town for more information.

MONEY MATTERS

Locals routinely overcharge tourists; always ask the price beforehand and bargain, especially during low season. Few establishments accept credit cards on Isla Isabela and, to some degree, on Isla San Cristóbal. In Puerto Ayora, however, many tour agencies, restaurants, and souvenir shops widely accept credit cards. Mastercard is preferred everywhere, although acceptance of Visa, Diners Club, and American Express is growing in the Galápagos. The islands' only bank is Banco del Pacifico, which has branches in Puerto Ayora on Isla Santa Cruz and Puerto Baquerizo Moreno on Isla San Cristóbal. Feel free to stock up on cash, since theft is less of a concern than on the mainland, but ATMs and money wiring services make withdrawing large quantities of cash from the mainland fairly unnecessary.

RESPONSIBLE ECOTOURISM

National Park Service rules: stay on trails, don't bother wildlife, don't smoke within the boundaries of the National Park, don't take or leave anything, and respect what your guide says. The perfect photograph is not worth the damage that clumsy feet will have on animals. Recognize that these islands are a unique natural treasure as well as an opportunity for the adventure of a lifetime. For more info, see **Sustainable Travel,** p. 43.

ISLA SANTA CRUZ   ☎ 05

Known also by its English name of Indefatigable, Isla Santa Cruz is as diverse as it is well traveled. With an area just under 1000 sq. km, Santa Cruz is the Galápagos's second largest island, with nearly a dozen visitor sites, the National Park headquarters, and an astounding variety of geology and wildlife. Tourism in the Galápagos revolves around this hub, a convenient first stop for the nearly 70,000 tourists who arrive at the Baltra Airport and make a beeline for Puerto Ayora, the archipelago's largest town. Indeed, Santa Cruz offers a sampling of nearly all that the Galápagos have to offer. Pristine beaches near the southern coast criss-cross with mangroves and lava tunnels, lush scalesia forests in the Highlands teem with endemic birds, and giant tortoises creep on private ranches and reserves throughout the island. Tours and daytrips generally require a hefty budget, but travelers pinching pennies or not keen on spending a week on a pricey, cramped boat tour will be in heaven here—Santa Cruz is one of the few islands in the Galápagos where many sites can be reached without a boat.

 Although an increasing number of shops and travel agencies accept American Express, Diner's Club, and Visa, Mastercard is by far the preferred credit card on the island. Discover Card and traveler's checks are almost never accepted.

PUERTO AYORA   ☎ 05

A constant influx of tortoise-happy tourists has given the port town of Puerto Ayora (pop. 6000) a vaguely cosmopolitan air, a high standard of living, and a carefree attitude. Not surprisingly, tourist dollars have also made the town much more expensive than mainland Ecuador and considerably less authentic. But, despite the number of Galápagos t-shirts and sea lion figurines for sale along its main streets, the town emits an aura of tranquility as only a tropical island can. If nothing else, Puerto Ayora serves as a convenient pitstop for tourists, who stock up on cash, snacks, and film before boarding their boats. Those with spare dollars and extra time, however, will find a night or two in Puerto Ayora well worth their while, as nearby Tortuga Bay, excellent scuba diving and snorkeling, and a laidback nightlife scene promise to complete any true Galápagos vacation.

⌐ TRANSPORTATION

Domestic Flights: The **Baltra Airport** is on Isla Baltra, a small island just north of Santa Cruz. To get to Puerto Ayora from the airport, take the free shuttle bus to the boat to Santa Cruz (10min., US$0.70). A CITEG bus to **Puerto Ayora** (45min., US$1.80) meets passengers at the boat drop-off. Bus schedules are coordinated with flight arrivals. **TAME** (☎2526 165 or 2909 900, airport office 2526 527; www.tame.com.ec), at Darwin and 12 de Febrero and at the airport, flies to **Quito** (4hr.; daily 10:30am, 12:30pm; round-trip US$380, ISIC discount 15%) via **Guayaquil** (2½hr.; round-trip US$344, ISIC discount 15%). Puerto Ayora office open M-F 7am-noon and 1-4pm, Sa 9am-noon. Airport office open M-F 8am-noon and 1-5pm, Sa 9am-2pm. **Aerogal** (airport office ☎2441 950; www.aerogal.com.ec) also flies to **Quito** (4hr.) via **Guayaquil** (2½hr.). Reconfirm flights, and reserve return seats as soon as possible. If you are taking a multi-day boat tour that stops at Baltra half-way through the trip, have your guide help you reconfirm your flight at the airport.

Inter-Island Flights: EMETEBE (☎2526 177, airport office 2521 193, Guayaquil office 229 2494), at Los Colonos and Darwin on the 3rd fl. above Sante Fé Bar and Grill and in the Baltra airport near check-in, flies to **Puerto Baquerizo Moreno** on Isla San Cristóbal (30min., M-Sa 11:30am, US$82) and **Puerto Villamil** on **Isla Isabela** (30min., M-Sa 10:30am, US$82). Schedules and itineraries are not fixed but are fairly reliable; flights generally leave after mainland flights from Quito and Guayaquil arrive. Planes carry 9 passengers each. Reserve tickets at least 2 days in advance. Luggage max. 13kg per person on full flights. Puerto Ayora office open M-Sa 7:15-11:30am and 2-5pm. Airport office open M-Sa 8:30am-2pm. AmEx/MC/V. Cash preferred, although credit card arrangements can be made if necessary.

Inter-Island Boat Travel: Victor Rueda Lira at **Restaurante Salvavidas** (☎2526 418, cell 09 9809 833), opposite the main dock, sends lanchas (small boats) to **Puerto Villamil** on Isla Isabela (2-2½hr.; daily 2pm, return 6am; US$30). The ride to Isabela is usually very rough—be prepared to get a little wet. **Anyone susceptible to sea sickness should take proper precaution or consider flying to Isabela instead.** Purchase tickets 1 day in advance from the restaurant. Victor can also arrange charter boats for groups of 8-10 people to just about anywhere in the Galápagos. Restaurant open daily 8am-9pm. **Ingala** (☎2526 199 or 2526 655), at Los Colonos and Darwin, on the 2nd fl. above Sante Fé Bar and Grill, sends fibras (fiber-glass motorboats) to **Puerto Baquerizo Moreno** on Isla San Cristóbal (2½-3hr.; Tu and F noon, return M and Th noon; US$50.) Open M-F 4-7pm. Inquire with the Capitanía next to the volleyball courts or around the dock early in the morning (6:30-7am) to see if any private boats are going to Islas Isabela or San Cristóbal—those with space are usually more than happy to give you a ride (US$20-40, cheaper if you bargain).

Buses: CITEG (☎2526 232), on Darwin between Herrera and Los Colonos, sends several buses north across the island to the boat drop-off near the **Baltra Airport** (45min.; 6:50, 7, 7:20, 7:30, 9:30, and 9:40am; US$1.80). **Transgalpas** (☎2526 649), next door to the CITEG office, sends 2 additional buses to **Baltra** (7:10, 9:20am; US$1.80). All Baltra-bound buses pass through the Highlands and can let passengers off at any point along the way. Return buses are usually full with passengers arriving from the airport, so don't count on them to stop and pick you up along the highway.

Taxis: Yellow taxis run along Darwin and Herrera, usually serving the Highlands or the other side of the island for a morning or afternoon (US$25-30). **Water taxis** shuttle passengers from the main dock to their tour boats, usually anchored a few minutes' ride from shore (US$0.50, after 11pm US$1).

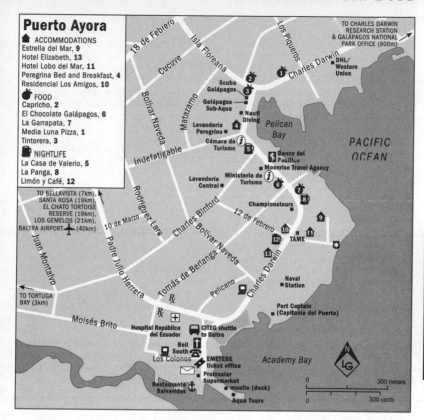

Puerto Ayora

🏠 **ACCOMMODATIONS**
Estrella del Mar, **9**
Hotel Elizabeth, **13**
Hotel Lobo del Mar, **11**
Peregrina Bed and Breakfast, **4**
Residencial Los Amigos, **10**

🍴 **FOOD**
Capricho, **2**
El Chocolate Galápagos, **6**
La Garrapata, **7**
Media Luna Pizza, **1**
Tintorera, **3**

🍷 **NIGHTLIFE**
La Casa de Valerio, **5**
La Panga, **8**
Limón y Café, **12**

Camionetas: White camionetas can be found anywhere in town, especially near the park, Proinsular Supermarket, and the CITEG office (see above). Half-day US$30-35; bargain for discounts if you're with a group.

Bicycles: La Casa del Valerio (☎09 7460 176), on Darwin near Indefatigable, rents bikes. 1½hr. US$1, 4hr. US$6, 8hr. US$12, overnight rental US$15. Passport, US$100, camera, or valuables required for deposit. Open M and W-Su 9am-11pm, Tu 9am-3pm. **Hotel Elizabeth** (☎2526 178), on Darwin near 12 de Febrero, rents bikes (US$1 per hr).

✈ 🛈 ORIENTATION AND PRACTICAL INFORMATION

Most accommodations, restaurants, and tour agencies spread out along **Avenida Charles Darwin,** the main road that runs along the waterfront. The **muelle** (dock) sits at Darwin's southernmost point, while the **Charles Darwin Research Center** is 1½km north. **Avenida Padre Julio Herrera,** which intersects Darwin near the town center and main bus stop, and runs northwest out of town toward Bellavista, the Highlands, and the Baltra Airport.

Tourist Offices: Ministerio de Turismo (☎2527 135; www.vivecuador.com), on Darwin, between Berlanga and Binford, provides slighty out-of-date island **maps** and basic info in Spanish. Open daily 7:30am-noon and 2-5pm. **Cámara de Turismo** (☎2526 206), at Binford and Darwin, is a better option. They have good **maps**, info about tour boats, hotels, and restaurants, and an informative book in English on Isabela. The **Galápagos National Park Office** (☎2526 511; spng@fcdarwin.org.ec), on Darwin just before the Charles Darwin Research Station, near the new statue of a park ranger, offers free **maps** and park information. If arriving by boat, pay the **national park fee** (US$100) here. Travelers who arrived by plane and did not pay the park fee at the airport can pick up their passports and purchase their park entrance ticket at the park offices. Open daily 7am-4pm.

Tours: At least a dozen agencies line Darwin, and most offer similar tours. Be sure to compare prices and bargain with different agencies before booking a trip. Hotels may also set up better deals.

Moonrise Travel Agency (☎2526 403 or 2526 589), on Darwin, across the street from Banco del Pacífico, is a very helpful English- and German-speaking agency recommended by SAE. Daytrips to islands from US$50, bay tours US$15 per person (min. 6 people), Highlands tour US$12-20 per person (min. 6 people), multi-day trips from US$55 per person per day. Open M-F 7:30am-1pm and 3-6pm, Sa 9am-2pm.

Championstours (☎2543 099; cell 09 7067 508; www.wearethechampionstours.com), on Darwin between Berlanaga and 12 de Febrero, is a good place to check for last-minute Galápagos boat tours. Also offers daytrips, trekking and cycling tours, horseback riding in the Highlands, and surfing trips. Friendly, English-, German-, Spanish-, and French-speaking staff. Open M-Sa 7:30am-8pm, Su 8am-noon.

Aqua Tours (☎2526 234), by the main dock, offers comprehensive snorkeling tours of Academy Bay in its exclusive glass-bottomed boat. Sights include the reef sharks at Shark Channel, the golden rays at Franklin Bay, and the sea lions at Isla Lobería.

Galápagos Sub-Aqua (☎2526 350 or 2526 633; 24hr. cell 09 9261 195; www.galapagos-sub-aqua.com), on Darwin between Floreana and Indefatigable. Friendly and knowledgeable Fernando runs the islands' most reputable dive center. Boasts of a 100% safety record, 12 years' experience, and "eco-operator" certification (check www.projectaware.org for more info). Dives are pricey, but you pay for service, safety, and quality of gear and boat. 2 dives in Academy Bay US$80, daytrips from US$140, 2-day trip with 4 dives to Floreana US$300. Intro dives US$120, 4-day certification course US$430. English, German, French, and Spanish spoken. Open daily 8am-noon and 2:30-6:30pm. AmEx/DC/MC/V.

Scuba Galápagos (☎2526 130 or 2526 084; 24hr. cell 09 986 844; Quito office 2503 740), on Darwin between Floreana and Indefatigable, offers a variety of diving daytrips that are generally less expensive than its competitors'. Min. 3 people (from US$105 per person). Also arranges multi-day diving tours on its private yacht, which has 6 double cabins, A/C, and hot private showers. 5-day tour US$590, 8-day tour US$990. Open M-Sa 7:30am-noon and 2-6pm. DC/MC.

Nauti Diving, on Darwin near Galápagos Sub-Aqua, arranges relatively inexpensive diving tours. Intro dives US$80, 3-day trips with 6 dives US$295. Certification courses from open water to dive master also available. Open M-Sa 8am-7pm, Su 2-7pm.

 Snorkeling in the Galápagos can be an extraordinary experience, and swimming at flippers' length from sea turtles, sharks, sea lions, manta rays, and dozens of other tropical fish is one of the most memorable experiences of visitors' itineraries. During the Galápagos summer (June-Dec.), however, the water temperature can get quite cold, and less-than-tropical air temperatures can make any submarine adventure uncomfortably chilling. Bring a **wet suit** if you're susceptible to the cold, or ask if there are any available for rent on your boat. Many crews carry a few extras aboard or can stock up on some in Puerto Ayora with advance notice—expect to pay about US$15-20 per week to rent one.

Bank: Banco del Pacífico (☎2526 282; fax 2526 364), at Darwin and Binford. 24hr. Cirrus/MC **ATM** and V cash advances (4% commission, passport required). Exchanges traveler's checks. Open M-F 8am-3:30pm, Sa 9:30am-12:30pm.

Alternatives to Tourism: The Charles Darwin Research Center (www.galapagospark.org or www.darwinfoundation.org; see below) is always looking for volunteers. Check website or inquire at the Center for up-to-date info.

Supermarket: Proinsular Supermarket, opposite the main dock, stocks snacks, drinks, waterproof cameras, and film. Open M-Sa 8am-8pm, Su 8am-noon. AmEx/DC/MC/V (min. US$20).

Laundromat: Lavandería Central, on Binford, 1 block up from Darwin, charges US$1 per kg. Open daily 8am-8pm. **Lavandería El Peregrino,** at Darwin and Indefatigable next to El Peregrino Bed and Breakfast, charges US$1.40 per kg. Open M-Sa 7:30am-7pm.

Police: ☎2526 101. By the water on 12 de Febrero, next to Lobo del Mar. Open 24hr.

Hospital: Hospital República del Ecuador (☎2526 103), on Herrera near the supermarket, less than a block from the town center. On call 24hr. for emergencies.

Pharmacy: Farmacia Edith, on Herrera, 1 block up from Darwin. Open daily 8am-11pm.

Telephones: Bell South, at Darwin and Los Colonos and Darwin and Indefatigable. Local calls US$0.16 per min., regional calls US$0.19 per min., to US US$0.25 per min, to Europe from US$0.40 per min. Open daily 6:30am-10pm. **La Choza.net,** on Los Colonos, 1 block up from Darwin, charges US$0.20 per min. for national and international calls. Open M-Sa 8am-10pm, Su 3-8pm. **Moonrise Travel Agency** (see above) has AT&T and MCI card service and a fax machine.

Internet Access: Cheapest connections available at **La Choza.net** (see **Telephones,** above) and **Limón y Café,** at Darwin and 12 de Febrero (open M-F 4pm-2am, Su 6pm-midnight). Both charge US$0.80 per hr. More expensive service at **Cybercafe Galápagos,** on Darwin near Naveda, opposite the Capitanía, where you can also download and scan digital pictures onto a CD. US$1.50 per hr. Open M-Sa 8:30am-10:30pm, Su 11am-10:30pm.

Post Office: ☎2526 575. Opposite the main dock, next to Proinsular Supermarket. Open M-F 8am-1pm and 1:30-5pm, Sa 8am-1pm. **DHL/Western Union** (☎/fax 2526 041; servigal@ecua.net.ec), on Darwin between Las Fragatas and Los Piqueros. Open M-F 8:30am-12:30pm and 2-5:30pm, Sa 9am-12:30pm. **FedEx** service available at Moonrise Travel Agency (see above).

ACCOMMODATIONS

Given the number of wealthy tourists who visit the Galápagos, Puerto Ayora caters more toward those seeking luxury, but penny-pinching budget travelers can still find reasonably priced, clean lodgings with great views. The cheapest places generally have cold, shared showers. An ocean view may cost US$5 more, but if you've gone to all the trouble to get here, you might as well go for it.

Peregrina Bed and Breakfast (☎2526 323), at Darwin and Indefatigable. Likely the best budget value in Puerto Ayora, Peregrina is homey and clean with cordial management. 4 spacious rooms are clean and tiled with hot private showers and towels. All rooms open up to a family room with TV. Despite the "and Breakfast" in the name, breakfast costs US$2.50. Laundry US$1.40 per kg. Check-out 11am. Singles US$7, with A/C US$10; doubles US$14/$20. Taxes included. ❷

Estrella del Mar (☎2526 427 or 2526 080), on the water next to the ocean. From Darwin, walk down 12 de Febrero toward the ocean, and make a left at the dirt path by the police station. Estrella twinkles with airy rooms, clean hot baths, a TV lounge, and fantastic views (for a few extra bucks). Breakfast and taxes included. Singles US$17, with A/C or sea views US$22.50, with A/C and sea views US$28; doubles US$28/$33.50/ $39.50; triples US$40; quints with A/C US$50. Traveler's checks and cash only. ❹

Hotel Elizabeth (☎2526 178), on Darwin near 12 de Febrero. Large, bright rooms have a funky 70s feel, with orange paint and retro tiles. Small hot private baths have towels, and most rooms have cable TV on request. Balconies open up to a small courtyard with tables and hammocks. Owner likes to bargain, so try for a good discount. US$8 per person with cold water, US$12 per person with hot water. Excludes 12% tax. ❷

Hotel Lobo del Mar (☎2526 188; fax 2526 569), on 12 de Febrero, near Darwin, down the street from the police station. Recently renovated, this stately hotel offers some of Puerto Ayora's most luxurious rooms. Elegant and comfortable rooms have gleaming baths, A/C, cushy beds, cable TV, and balconies overlooking the bay. Lobby has a fountain, pool, Internet, restaurant, and TV. Travelers on a tighter budget can go for one of the older but still comfortable rooms. Older singles US$15, newer US$35; doubles US$30/$54; triples US$64. Excludes 22% tax. ❹

Residencial Los Amigos (☎2526 265), at Darwin and 12 de Febrero, has small, clean rooms with narrow beds under a corrugated tin roof. You pay for what you get here, so don't expect much. Cold baths. US$5 per person, with private bath US$6. ❷

▶ FOOD

Restaurants in Puerto Ayora are as abundant as pelicans, and most line Darwin. Eateries on the first few blocks from the dock are moderately priced, but those toward the research station are more expensive and cater to travelers ready to splurge on fantastic food. For *comida típica*, head down Herrera to Binford, where locals get cheap, fresh meals from wooden kiosks (US$3-3.50). Of these, **William's** is highly recommended. The best supermarket is **Proinsular Supermarket** (see above), across from the dock.

▨ **Tintorera** (☎09 2457 538), on Darwin and Isla Floreana. Complete your eco-vacation with a meal at this socially responsible and superbly delicious gem. All ingredients are grown, bought, or caught in the islands. Specialties include jam handmade by local fishermen's wives, fresh cheese straight from the Highlands, excellent bread and baked goods made by a locally trained baker, and homemade ice cream. Breakfast served with juice and bottomless organic coffee US$2.50-3.50; smoked salmon and egg sandwich US$4.50; other sandwiches US$3-4.50; chicken curry and rice US$3.50; onion rings US$1.50. Excellent espresso drinks like mint mochas and amaretto lattes (US$2.50) counter instant Nescafe overload. Open M-F 8am-10pm, Sa 8am-3pm. ❷

▨ **Media Luna Pizza** (☎09 9777 340), on Darwin between Piqueros and Floreana. Casual Italian eatery with white stucco walls, paper lanterns, and friendly waitstaff. Offers delicious pizza (small US$4-6.25, medium US$9.20-14, large US$14-21), pastas (US$4.50-6), and sandwiches (US$3.75-5). Try the stellar avocado sub and amazing homemade chocolate chip cookies (US$1.50 for 5). Excludes 22% tax. Open M and W-Sa noon-10pm, Su 6-10pm. ❷

Capricho (☎2526 868), at Darwin and Floreana. Not much *comida típica* here, but the superb organic offerings include spaghetti dishes (US$4.90-7.50), omelettes (US$2.50-4.20), *empanadas* (US$1.20-2.90), great pancakes and waffles (US$2.60-3.50), and take-out lunches (US$6.50). The prickly pear crepes (US$3.50) and fixed lunches (M-F from noon, US$4.50) are popular. International book and magazine exchange. Spanish, English, and German menu. Excludes 10% tax. Delivery available M-F 7am-4pm, Sa-Su 7am-6pm. Open daily 7am-10pm. ❷

La Garrapata (☎2526 264), on Darwin between 12 de Febrero and Berlanga, is locally regarded as the best restaurant in town. The open-air seating area fills up almost exclusively with tourists, especially in the evenings, when live musicians occasionally entertain diners. Expensive, but worth the splurge. Daytime juice bar serves hearty breakfasts

(US$3-4.50), salads (US$2.50-4), some *típico* lunches (US$3.50-4), and, of course, fresh juice (US$1.50). Dinner specialities include delicious pastas (US$5.50-9), seafood dishes (US$5-9), chicken in cognac sauce (US$6), and T-bone steak (US$8). Pilsner *grande* US$2.50; margarita US$4. Open daily 9am-5pm and 6-10pm. ❸

El Chocolate Galápagos (☎2526 759), on Darwin between Binford and Berlanga across from Banco del Pacífico, serves quality meat and vegetable lasagna (US$4.20), fish (US$0.40-5.10), pizzas (US$3.15-4.50), salads (US$3.10-4.20), and warm sandwiches (US$2.70-3.40). Try the specialty—a decadent piece of chocolate cake (US$1.80). Nice breakfast selection (US$3.10-4.50) served with 100% organic coffee (US$1-1.50). Open daily 7am-10pm. ❷

◳ SIGHTS

▦ TORTUGA BAY. This seaside eden gets its name from the large number of **sea turtles** that come here to lay eggs. Pristine fine white sand, giant cacti, yellow warblers, and a scenic, rocky background make it perhaps the most beautiful beach in the Galápagos. The first kilometer of the beach has bright turquoise waters and consistent swells ideal for surfing. Past this beach is a small cove with a much calmer, mangrove-flanked beach more suitable for swimming. As the beach is within National Park boundaries, be sure not to leave any garbage behind. Camping is not permitted. *(To reach the beach from Puerto Ayora (40min.), pass the hospital on Herrera to Binford, turn left, and follow the dirt road out of town for 200m to a Galápagos National Park sign and an observation tower on a cliff. This is the beginning of a pleasant 2½km hike to the beach. Check in with the guard—the passport numbers and names of all visitors must be recorded. Open daily 7am-6pm, but last visitor allowed in around 4:30pm.)*

CHARLES DARWIN RESEARCH CENTER. Just beyond the Galápagos National Park Headquarters, this research station is a storehouse of Galápagos and conservation-related information. Volunteers and staff here coordinate the scientific and technical research fundamental to the park's existence. The station's **library** is open to the public and has a helpful librarian. *(Open M-F 7:30am-noon and 1:30-5pm.)* There is also a tiny but beautiful **beach,** where sunbathers gaze across the turquoise waters of the harbor. A wealth of coral and seashells on the shore make a nice walk in the sand. *(Open daily 6am-6pm.)* Up the road, the **administrative building** has a park **map.** Many multi-day boat tours visit the Research Center on Thursday mornings, so avoid coming at this time if you're on your own. *(☎2526 146 or 2526 147; www.darwinfoundation.org. Offices open M-F 7am-4pm. Visiting area open daily 6am-6pm.)*

Within the research center are different stations, of which the **Tortoise Rearing Center** is the most important. A path from the entrance leads to several pens that contain baby giant tortoises—part of the effort to rehabilitate the severely reduced tortoise population. Scientists estimate that nearly 250,000 giant tortoises once roamed the archipelago. Decades of hunting, habitat loss, and damage done by introduced animals such as goats and pigs, however, have wiped out 90% of the islands' tortoises. Farther down the path, two more pens contain eight adult tortoises. Originally kept by islanders as pets, these animals really like people and rarely retreat into their shells, unlike wild ones. Although it's acceptable to get close enough to pose with them for priceless pictures, touching them is not allowed. Be careful not to walk across or stand on the tortoise feeding platform (a large cement slab covered with partially chewed vegetation); this may contaminate their food with harmful organisms. To be truly awe-struck, get a glimpse of the **albino tortoise.** The center keeps him indoors because of sun-sensitivity, so make a request at the administrative building to see him.

The **Van Straelen Exhibit Hall** has information in English and Spanish on the islands' natural history and the National Park's objectives, focusing on threats to island ecology and on current efforts to counteract them. A short video provides a good overview of the conservation program currently in progress. An enthusiastic staff answers most questions and runs the tourist center. Tourists are encouraged to give donations in the envelopes near the entrance, although some visistors use the envelopes instead to voice complaints about the captive tortoises and other aspects of the Park's management. *(Near the beginning of the path that loops through the Charles Darwin Research Center. Open daily 7am-4pm.)*

◧ NIGHTLIFE

As the hub of the Galápagos, Puerto Ayora offers the liveliest late-night scene. Clubs and bars play everything from salsa to techno, mix a variety of cocktails, and have pool tables. Things really get going on the weekends, when locals join tourists for wee-hour partying. Many tour boats dock at Puerto Ayora mid-week, so expect an especially tourist-packed scene on Wednesday and Thursday nights.

La Panga, on Darwin and Berlanga. Sharks shoot pool, loungers sip cocktails, and jitterbugs grace the dance floor. Live DJ most nights and huge screen on dance floor plays music videos and *fútbol* matches. Jam on the guitar, mic, and amp—if you're good, you'll get a drink on the house. Happy hour 8:30-10pm: 2-for-1 Pilsners US$2, *cuba libres* US$3, and caipirinhas US$3. Th ladies night. Open M-Sa 8:30pm-3am.

Limón y Café, at the corner of Darwin and 12 de Febrero, is a good example of Puerto Ayora's upbeat bar scene. With foosball at one end of the bar, billiards on the other (grab the triangle to call next game), and the ring game off to one side of the small dance floor, there is room for everyone to be entertained. Gravel floor, good music, and friendly staff complete the laid-back mood. Internet US$0.80 per hr. Pilsner *grande* US$2.50, cocktails US$3-4. Open M-Sa 4pm-2am, Su 6pm-midnight.

La Casa de Valerio (☎09 7460 176), on Darwin near Indefatigable. Restaurant by day and laid-back bar by night. At Valerio's *casa,* a couch in the middle of the seating area will make you feel right at home. Salsa lessons M, W, and F 8pm and some of the cheapest beers in town (US$1.75). Organic set-lunch US$3.75, volunteers US$2.75. Cocktails US$2.75. Open M and W-Su 9am-11pm, Tu 9am-3pm.

◧ DAYTRIPS FROM PUERTO AYORA

Daytrips can be broken into two categories: the Highlands and northwestern Santa Cruz. Guided tours of the Highlands generally visit Los Gemelos, the Lava Tunnels, and the Tortoise Reserve. The most stylish way to see the Highlands is atop your very own horse, or by mountain bike; most tour agencies can arrange either mode of travel. Many sites in the Highlands are in National Park territory and, thus, require a guide; inquire at the Galápagos National Park Office about finding one. The far northwestern side of Santa Cruz boasts beautiful bays and beaches that can only be reached by boat. Some daytrips to these areas leave from Puerto Ayora, but they are more often visited as part of multi-day boat tours.

THE HIGHLANDS

EL CHATO TORTOISE RESERVE. Even if you've visited the tortoises at Darwin station, seeing these massive creatures on their home turf is an unforgettable experience. Here, the tortoises are as wild as 250kg reptiles can get, as evidenced by their trails—although slow, these beasts are powerful green bulldozers, leaving behind flattened vegetation and collapsed fences. Approach them slowly, as they are much more shy than their captured friends and will hiss if you get too close. A guide is required to visit the reserve, and doling out extra cash for a knowledgeable one is highly recommended. The reserve itself has two trails: **La Caseta** (2km) leads to a pond, and **Cerro Chato** (3km) traverses a small hill. The tortoises are elusive, but a good guide knows where to look. Hiking through the low, scrubby vegetation can be challenging; bring water and wear sturdy shoes and long pants. *(Guide required. Check National Park Office or one of the travel agencies in town. A Baltra-bound bus can drop you off at the town of Santa Rosa, from where a 3km trail leads to the reserve. Alternatively, inquire at the park office near Santa Rosa about renting a horse to get to the reserve. A camioneta (US$30) can be hired in town to take you to the reserve and back.)*

PRIVATE TORTOISE FARMS. Near El Chato Tortoise Reserve are two private torotise farms, the **Divine Farm** and the **Rancho Primicias.** Since these ranches are privately owned, they can be visisted without a guide for a small fee. The giant tortoises are free to roam the somewhat less dense vegetation, and visitors can get quite close to them for pictures and observe them in their natural habitats. Trails at both farms can get muddy from the mist, so bring good shoes and rain gear. For more information about visiting the Divine Farm, inquire at Moonrise Travel Agency (see p. 332), owned by the Divine family. *(Although most visit either farm on organized tours from Puerto Ayora or as part of multi-day boat tours, camionetas from Puerto Ayora run to either farm for US$30 round-trip. US$3.)*

LOS GEMELOS. These "twins," on either side of the road to Baltra, just 2km beyond Santa Rosa and 21km from Puerto Ayora, are a pair of crater-shaped **magma chambers.** Centuries ago, the craters were completely vacuous, but the heavy overlying rock has since caused them to collapse in on themselves. Nonetheless, each is about 30m deep and filled with lush vegetation, mostly endemic **scalesia forest.** Look for flycatchers, woodpecker finches, and the elusive short-eared owl. *(Guide required. Inquire at the National Park Office (see p. 332) or at one of the travel agencies in town to arrange a tour (see above). Camioneta US$30.)*

LAVA TUNNELS. Santa Cruz is riddled with lava tubes, the remains of ancient magma flows that formed the Galápagos. The outer crusts of these molten streams hardened as they cooled, but the liquid magma within continued flowing. When the flow ceased, these enormous hollow tubes were remained. There are several tunnels around the island, but the most frequently visited is Bellavista's 800m **Tunnel of Endless Love,** named not for what could potentially go on in its dark chambers, but for the heart-shaped hole in the tunnel's roof. A rickety banister provides support, but visitors must tread carefully over the loose rocks when descending. The sheer enormity of this tunnel and the strange, magma-carved designs on its inner surface serve as reminders of Ma Nature's creativity. *(The Bellavista tunnels are 7km outside Puerto Ayora—take the Baltra shuttle to Bellavista (US$1.50) and ask for directions, or take a camioneta directly there (US$30 round-trip). US$4; flashlight US$0.50.)* Another set of lava pathways is **Furio's Tunnels,** off the road to Baltra between Bellavista and Santa Rosa. The tunnels are lighted, but a flashlight may be useful. Divided into different levels, the tunnels are connected by slime-coated ladders. Wear sturdy shoes and prepare to get dirty. Particularly memorable are the entrance and exit to the tunnels, laden with lush tropical vegetation unique to this part of the island. *(Furio's Tunnels can be reached by the Baltra shuttle (US$1.50) or by camioneta (US$30). Contact Restaurante de Furio 1 day in advance; hotels and travel agencies in Puerto Ayora can radio them. Ask at Moonrise Travel (see above) for more information about tours to these sights or other tunnels. Tunnels US$2.)* Many multi-day boat tours visit the tunnels near the Tortoise Reserve and private turtle farms just off the road to Baltra.

OTHER SIGHTS. The verdant interior of Santa Cruz offers a multitude of land excursions, many of which can be visited independently, on foot, or by bike. For those interested in getting a view from above, the small towns of Bellavista (6km north of Puerto Ayora) and Santa Rosa (8km northwest of Bellavista) are ideal starting points for nearby hikes. Two popular peaks are Media Luna, a crescent-shaped volcanic cinder cone 5km from Bellavista, and Cerro Crocker, 3km beyond Media Luna. The trail to Media Luna (round-trip 10km) winds through pastures and bamboo forests and continues deep into dense Miconia and Scalesia forest. The poorly marked trail can get muddy and misty; hiking without a guide is not recommended. The trail to Cerro Crocker (round-trip 16km) offers excellent views—if the sun is out. On a clear day, the mirador offers stunning panoramic views of many nearby islands. The Galápagos species of the Hawaii petrel was once a common sight here, but introduced dogs and rats have severely reduced the population of the rare birds. *(Although it is possible to reach the Media Luna and Cerro Crocker trails via the Baltra-bound bus from Puerto Ayora, Park officials discourage doing these hikes by yourself. The trails are obscure and are within the boundaries of the National Park, so a guide is strongly recommended. Additionally, hikers who take the bus from Puerto Ayora to the Highlands may have difficulty finding return transport, as buses are often full and may not stop for passengers. Inquire at tour agencies in Puerto Ayora or at the Park Office about finding a guide. Camioneta from Puerto Ayora US$15 one-way.)*

NORTHWESTERN SANTA CRUZ

Sights on this part of the island are only accessible by boat and with licensed National Park guides. Most travelers visit them with multi-day boat tours, but day-trips are offered from Puerto Ayora as well.

LAS BACHAS BEACH. Near the Baltra Airport, Las Bachas is a frequent first or last stop for tour boats. Its spectacular white-sand beach and turquoise blue waters make for a refreshing swim, but bring insect repellent to ward off stinging flies and wasps. Also beware of the unusually strong current. Although Las Bachas offers considerably fewer opportunities to ogle wildlife, a small colony of **flamingos** poses for cameras in the **saltwater lagoon,** a brief walk from the main beach. **Great blue herons, frigates, sanderlings,** and **American oystercatchers** are among the other feathered creatures that frequent the shores. On the way to the lagoon, you'll see a cluster of wooden poles, the remains of two barges, poking out from the sand. The vessels were beached and abandoned by the US military when its attempt to occupy Baltra was cut short in the 1940s. The name "Las Bachas" is, in fact, Spanglish for "barges." Additionally, a sizable number of **sea turtles** nest on both beaches between November and January; their sand-covered nests protrude as mounds on the shore until at least August.

CERRO DRAGÓN. On the northwestern coast between Las Bachas and Conway Bay, **Cerro Dragón** gets its name from an imposing hill resembling a bumpy green dragon. Its summit is a 2km climb, and the more popular trail winds through scrubby vegetation, revealing dragons of another sort—monstrous, cactus-eating **land iguanas,** many of which were repatriated here from the breeding center at the Charles Darwin Research Center. Feral dogs introduced by colonists decades ago nearly decimated the once-thriving land iguana population, but canine predators have since been controlled, allowing the iguanas to recover slowly. **Trail finches** and **yellow warblers** also add color to the dry landscape. Visits to Cerro Dragón are often a stop en route to **Isla Rábida,** an island to the northwest of Santa Cruz.

BLACK TURTLE COVE. Tour boats anchor far from the shore, sending their passengers on pangas (small boats) to explore the mangrove-sheltered inlets of Black Turtle Cove. Its proximity to Isla Baltra makes it a convenient last stop before sailing to the airport. Motors hush and tourists ready their cameras for the rhythmic bobbing of countless **marine turtles** rising slowly to the murky surface for air. December to March is mating season, and during the months following, hundreds of tiny turtle hatchlings stumble along the water. Scurrying between the plodding green reptiles are bulbous brown and white **pufferfish,** famous for their ability to swallow water or air to inflate defensively when disturbed or under attack. Considered a delicacy in Japan, the pufferfish have made an impressive comeback following several years of overfishing. The surrounding islets harbor **golden mustard rays, white-tipped reef sharks, spotted-eagle rays,** and various birds including **lava herons, blue-footed boobies, yellow warblers,** and **pelicans.** Black Turtle Cove is visited only from small boats, and snorkeling is prohibited.

THE CENTRAL ISLANDS ☎05

ISLAS PLAZAS ☎05

Of the tiny twin islands off the eastern coast of Santa Cruz, only South Plaza (a mere 1.3 sq. km) is open to visitors and boasts a surprisingly diverse array of wildlife. North Plaza remains off-limits due to scientific research (and the high rocky cliffs surrounding the island). The desert-like interior of South Plaza can be viewed from a rocky trail that winds its way around the sloping island, which was formed by uplifted sea coral from the ocean floor. Travelers to South Plaza are greeted by barking female sea lions and their pups. Beware of the local macho-males—sea-lion bulls, each of which has his own harem of female sea lions. Those males not tough enough to have chicas of their own reside in the bachelor colony on the southwestern side of the island. Here, hundreds of males compete for harems of about 20 females. There are so many on South Plaza that their excrement has almost permanently transformed the hardened black lava into a maladorous white rock. Snorkeling is banned here due to the high concentration of sea lions.

 Sea lion bulls, or *los machos*, bite several tourists each year, making them statistically more dangerous than sharks. Keep your distance.

South Plaza is one of the best islands from which to observe the famous **Galápagos land iguana**, distinguished from the marine iguana by their orangish-green hue and larger size. These endemic reptiles lurk beneath **prickly pear cacti**; the two share a scintillating tale of evolutionary intrigue. Long ago, the reptilian culprits devoured low-growing flowers. The only cacti able to reproduce were the taller, tree-like plants with large trunks that the chubby iguanas couldn't climb. Today, the sky-scraping prickly pears prevail, and the diminutive dragons must wait for their succulent treats to fall to the ground. **Marine iguanas** cluster by the mist-soaked rocks near the ridge feeding on seaweed. From June to November, when vegetation is sparse and temperatures are cooler, you might see the scaly black reptiles feeding on dried sea lion droppings, a good source of calcium that helps warm the marine iguanas. South Plaza is also the best place in the Galápagos to see **hybrid iguanas**—the result of male marine iguanas (smaller with black scales) and female land iguanas overcoming their habitat differences to get freaky. A number of bird species also nest on South Plaza—swallow-tailed gulls, brown noddy birds, red-billed tropic birds, firgates, and the extremely rare lava gull, of which only about 400 pairs remain in the world—swoop down near the windy cliffs.

ISLA SANTA FÉ (BARRINGTON) ☎05

Formed by submarine basaltic lava that rose from the ocean floor over four million years ago, Isla Santa Fé keeps its treasures hidden; a walk along the beach will reveal little animal life beside a handful of playful sea lions. Still, exploring the island can be a great way to see the quieter, more elusive Galápagos critters. One of the best-concealed island creatures, the Santa Fé land iguana, lives nowhere else in the world and, in fact, on no other island in the Galápagos. A sub-species of the famous endemic Galápagos land iguana, the Santa Fé variety is yellowish-green in color and can grow to over 1m in length. Hide-and-seek champions with patience and time stand the best chance of spotting one of these devious creatures, which spend much of their time near prickly pear cacti waiting for their juicy fruits and pads to fall to the ground. Two short trails loop the island. The first is a short 300m path that leads to a forest of giant Opuntia cacti; some of which are over 10m tall. A longer, rocky 1½km trail climbs into the highland region. The short but somewhat steep ascent is a bit strenuous but offers a better chance of seeing land iguanas and an impressive view of the island and shimmering ocean. The trail is also an excellent place to birdwatch for the Galápagos dove and scout the Galápagos snake and rice rat. Both trails are somewhat rocky, so bring sturdy shoes. Santa Fé also features a beautiful, sheltered cove in its northeastern bay. Sea lions, along with flashy fish, often join snorkelers.

ISLA SEYMOUR NORTE   ☎05

North Seymour Island, just off Baltra, is one of the most frequently visited islands. Most boats visit Seymour just before dropping passengers at the airport, so the seemingly ubiquitous sea lion colonies and slow-moving marine iguanas are no longer as jaw-dropping. Nonetheless, this island is a must-see for any devoted ornithologist. The largest colony of magnificent frigate birds in the Galápagos nests in the dry saltbrush near the coast. During mating season, the photogenic male frigates inflate the bright red pouches under their beaks with the hopes of attracting a female partner. Equally sizable colonies of blue-footed boobies and their fuzzy white hatchlings clutter the guano-coated trail around the island (2km). Lucky visitors may catch a glimpse of the beautiful gray-and-white swallow-tailed gull or a few land iguanas, which scientists introduced to the island from Baltra several years ago to test if they could survive.

ISLA SAN CRISTÓBAL   ☎05

Despite its airport, proximity to the mainland, and position as the administrative capital of the islands, Isla San Cristóbal is perpetually a distant second to Isla Santa Cruz in terms of tourism. Mediocre by Galápagos standards, it's one of the few islands you can explore without being on a tour boat. The northern part of the island is dry and rather barren, but the lowlands are kept humid by moist southern winds. Interesting daytrips can be made by boat to Isla Lobos, León Dormido, Punta Pitt, and several other sites. Keep in mind, however, that these daily boat excursions will cost you a pretty penny if you're not part of a large group.

PUERTO BAQUERIZO MORENO   ☎05

The capital of the Galápagos Islands, Puerto Baquerizo Moreno (pop. 5500) supports the seafaring interests of both surfers and fishermen. When December and March bring sizable swells, sea lions share the waves with people at famous surf spots like Punta Carola or After Reef, while the congestion of motorboats and pelicans reveals the port's true nature as a fishing town. Despite the seasonal surfing craze, this town exudes more tranquility than its bustling neighbor, Puerto Ayora.

▐ TRANSPORTATION

Flights: Puerto Moreno Airport (☎2520 111), at the end of Alsacio Northia, about 1km from the town center. Camioneta to town US$1. **EMETEBE** (☎2520 793 or 2520 793) flies to **Puerto Villamil** on Isla Isabela (45min., M-Sa 8:30am, US$127) via **Baltra Airport** on Isla Santa Cruz (20min., US$82) and **Puerto Villamil** (US$119). Additional flights scheduled based on demand. Planes carry 9 passengers each, so book your ticket at least 2 days in advance. Max. 13kg luggage per person on full flights. Open M-F 9am-2:30pm, Sa 8:30am-1pm. MC/V. **Aerogal** (☎2441 950; www.aerogal.com.ec) flies to **Quito** (3½hr., Th and Su 10:40am) via **Guayaquil** (2hr.). Open M-Sa 8am-4pm, Su 8am-noon. **TAME** (☎2521 089) flies to **Quito** (3½hr.; M, W, and Sa 1pm) via **Guayaquil** (2hr.). Open M, W, and Sa 8am-2pm; Tu, Th, and F 8am-noon and 2-4pm.

POACHING IN THE GALÁPAGOS

Fisherman and Tour Guides Alike Need These Islands

The position of the Galápagos, at the confluence of three major Pacific Ocean currents, creates the unique conditions that support the thriving marine life of the archipelago—as well as incites competition for control of this ecosystem.

Recent history has witnessed a series of hostile conflicts between the fishing industry and the organizations aimed at conserving the Galápagos's ecological resources: the National Park Service and the non-governmental Charles Darwin Research Station (CDRS).

The conflict regarding the sea cucumber fishery originated in the late 1980's. A delicacy in Asia and an ingredient in alternative medicinal remedies, the sea cucumbers command a high price from dealers. But they are also an essential component of the ocean ecosystem, acting as "recyclers" of up to 90% of the detritus on the seafloor. Without the vital service provided by sea cucumbers, it would not be possible for the larger and more "charismatic" marine organisms, on which tourism depends, to exist.

Once fished off the coast of mainland Ecuador, sea cucumber, or *pepino*, populations plummeted in the 1980s due to overexploitation and pollution. The relatively pristine Galápagos then caught the eye of mainland fisheries, and the lucrative business of *pepino* fishing became well established in the archipelago by the early 1990s. By 1992, however, concern over the intensity of harvesting and the presence of illegal camps in ecologically sensitive areas resulted in the institution of a moratorium on fishing.

Due to increasing pressure from local fisherman and mainland corporations, the *pepino* fishery was reopened in 1994 for a trial period with a quota of 500,000 sea cucumbers. Ultimately, between five and six million *pepinos* were harvested that year. This extreme over-harvest resulted in the re-institution of the moratorium. Furious fisherman, or *pepiñeros*, called a strike, and a group of fishermen invaded the Park Service Headquarters and the CDRS. Endangered Galápagos giant tortoises were taken hostage and some were slaughtered in an attempt to exert pressure on the government. Poachers continued to harvest sea cucumbers, establishing large camps on the remote outer islands of the archipelago. In 1997, a park ranger investigating one such camp was shot and killed. The park service, with only one boat, was unable to effectively patrol the waters: even when they succeeded in making arrests, the culprits were ultimately released with little or no penalty.

Despite the protests, the fisheries remained closed until the chaotic period of the 1999 Ecuadorian economic crisis. By this time not only Galápagos residents but many mainland Ecuadorians as well had heard of the fortunes that could be made through *pepino* fishing. Many relocated to the Galápagos to try to earn a better living, and many Galápagos natives who were not normally fisherman invested in the equipment necessary to harvest sea cucumbers. The number of boats registered in the Galápagos tripled in less than a decade, resulting in greatly decreased per capita earnings. Fishermen angrily protested what they perceived to be excessively restrictive catch limits. The park service and CDRS offices were again taken over, and ultimately the government raised the quotas. Due to the extreme over-harvesting, the sea cucumber population has drastically declined in the last few years. Although the intensity of fishing has abated somewhat as the increased competition has made *pepino* fishing a less lucrative endeavor, over-exploitation of this vital component of the marine ecosystem continues.

The troubles surrounding the protection of the Galápagos Archipelago are unfortunately not unique to the *pepino* debate. New conflicts between the fishermen and the park service have erupted over recent regulations. Twice in early 2004, fishermen took over the Park Service and CDRS in a protest over restrictions on net-fishing within the Galápagos marine reserve. The result was the complete shut-down of all tourist operations, a virtual disaster for the majority of Galápagos residents whose income depends on tourism. Because of the political pressure exerted by local fishermen and large fishing corporations, however, the government frequently capitulates to their demands: recent strikes have typically ended in raised quotas and lengthened seasons. Thus, the country finds itself in a bit of a Catch-22. The fishermen view restrictive quotas as evidence that the government cares more about animals than people. But without the quotas, those people in the tourism industry would be out of work. And so the conflict continues to rage between the fishermen and tourist companies.

Maren Noelani Vitousek is currently pursuing her PhD in the Department of Ecology and Evolutionary Biology at Princeton studying sexual selection in the Galápagos marine iguana.

Camionetas: 3 different cooperatives—**Coop. La Lobería, Coop. Islas Galápagos,** and **Coop. La Galápaguera**—operate white camionetas. Most line up on Darwin or run along Alascio Northia. To: **airport** (US$1); **El Progreso** (US$2); **Laguna Junco** (round-trip US$30, including 1hr. wait). You can hire a camioneta for the day (8am-3pm) to go to **Laguna Junco, La Galápaguera, La Soledad mirador,** and **La Lobería** (US$40-45).

Boats: INGALA, outside the town center on the road to El Progreso, sails to **Puerto Ayora** on **Isla Isabela.** Ask around at the docks or at **CAPTURGAL** (see below) to find out if any other boats are heading to nearby islands.

Bikes: Nahin Zavala (☎2520 696), at the **Champu** shop on Darwin next to Scuba Bar, rents bikes for US$1 per hr. or US$8 per day. Open daily 8am-noon and 2:30-9pm. If none are available, try **Pirampiro** (☎2520 323), a souvenir shop down the road near Banco del Pacífico. US$1.50 per hour, US$15 per day.

✦ 🛈 ORIENTATION AND PRACTICAL INFORMATION

Puerto Baquerizo Moreno sits at the southwestern tip of Isla San Cristóbal. Parallel to the water's edge is the main road, **Malecón Charles Darwin,** followed by **Ignacio de Hernandez** and the town's second major street, **Alsacio Northia.** The **airport** is at the western end of Northia; from here, Northia runs straight through the town before taking a hard left turn up the water's edge to the **Interpretation Center** at the other end of town. The main street running perpendicular to Northia is **12 de Febrero,** which heads out of town toward **El Progreso** and other nearby sights. Be forewarned that many of the town's shops and restaurants close sporadically or take long breaks around lunchtime.

Tourist Office: CAPTURGAL (☎/fax 2521 124), on Darwin near Wolf, opposite the pier. Helpful staff provides info on nearby sites, bike rentals, local tour operators, and all kinds of transport. Open M-F 8am-noon and 2-5:30pm.

Tours: Several operators offer similar tours of nearby sites and islands, usually as daytrips. Most require a min. of 8 people, so solo travelers and couples may have to visit on their own or pay prohibitively expensive charter prices. CAPTURGAL (see above) usually has up-to-date info about available tours and prices.

Wreck Bay Diving Center (☎09 7545 086; insofacto@hotmail.com), on Wolf near Darwin, is the town's most repuatble dive center and, unlike most agencies, does not require large groups for tours. Daytrips with 2 dives to nearby León Dormido and Isla Lobos US$110 per person. 1-day intro dive US$50-80, 5- to 7-day open-water course US$300, 5-day advanced open-water course US$300, 4-day rescue diver course US$300, 1-day emergency response course US$80, 2-week divemaster course US$600. Also rents snorkels (US$15 per day) and BCDs, regulators, and wetsuits for diving (each US$10 per day per piece). Open M-Sa 8:30am-1pm and 2-7pm.

Rosita's (see below), is popular with groups. 2-dive trips US$110; to El Junco Lagoon, La Galápaguera, and La Lobería US$30, 6-8 person min.; land tours to León Dormido, Islas Lobos, and Playa Ochoa from US$50, 12-14 person min.; to Isla Floreana or Isla Española US$60 per person. Talk to Gustavo (☎2520 106; ghernandez27@latinmail.com) for more info.

Nahin Zavala (☎2520 690), in the Champu shop on Darwin next to Scuba Bar, has snorkeling trips to León Dormido and Isla Lobos in a fiberglass motorboat. US$20 per person, min. 10 person.

Bank: Banco del Pacífico (☎2520 366), on Darwin, between Wolf and Gavilán, gives V cash advances, exchanges traveler's checks, and has a 24hr. MC **ATM.** Open M-F 8am-3:30pm, Sa 10am-12:30pm.

Alternatives to Tourism: New Era Galápagos (www.negf.org or www.neweraGalápagos.org), on Darwin, next to the post office. One of the most popular and reputable volunteer organizations on the Galápagos. Volunteers teach English, manage summer youth camps, conduct environmental awareness activities, organize weekend activities for local youth, and more. Offers free National Park entrance fee, language exchange, accommodation with family or in private apartment, and reduced rates for PADI scuba courses and tours. For more information see **Alternatives to Tourism** p. 74.

Supermarket: Comercial Dos Hermanos, at Quito and Juan José Flores, 2 blocks inland from Northía, has the best selection. Open M-Sa 7:30am-8:30pm, Su 8:30-11:30am.

Laundromat: On Alsacio Northía and 12 de Febrero, near the cathedral. US$4 per load. Open M-Sa 8am-1pm and 2:30-11pm, Su 8am-noon.

Police: Policía Nacional (24hr. emergency ☎2520 101) in the blue-and-gray building on Darwin and Española.

Pharmacy: Farmacia San Cristóbal (☎2520 773), on José de Villamil, 1½ blocks from Darwin. Open M-Sa 6am-10:30pm. In emergencies, call upstairs.

Hospital: Hospital Oskar Jandl (☎2520 118), at Alsacio Northia and Quito. Open 24hr.

Telephones: PacificTel, on Española, just up from Northia, has the cheapest rates for international calls. Local calls US$0.11 per min., to US and Spain US$0.22 per min., to rest of Europe from US$0.39 per min. Open daily 7am-11:30pm. **BellSouth,** at Darwin and Malville, has slightly more expensive service. Local calls US$0.16 per min., to US US$0.25 per min., to Europe from US$0.40 per min. Open daily 7am-10pm.

Internet: Restaurant y Bar Miconia (☎2520 608), on Darwin just past Malville, has slow connections, but it's the cheapest on the island. US$1.50 per hr. Open daily 8:30am-10pm. **EasyNet Cybercafe,** on Quito near Juan José Flores, 2 blocks from Northia, is a bit out of the way but has faster service. US$2 per hr. Open daily 8am-10pm. **Shopping House Arena y Sol,** on Española near Northia, also provides access. US$2.50 per hr. Open M-Sa 9am-8pm, Su noon-8pm.

Post Office: ☎/fax 2520 373. Near the western end of Darwin, just past the 3-story, tan municipal building. Open M-F 8am-noon and 2:30-6pm, Sa 8am-noon.

▛ ACCOMMODATIONS

Puerto Baquerizo Moreno's hotels offer a decent alternative to cramped ship quarters, although many of the town's tourists only stay for a night before flying back to the mainland. Few good budget options exist; expect to pay at least US$12 for hot water. **Camping** is permitted at the Galapaguera beaches; check with **CAPTUR-GAL** (see above). A souvenir shop called **Pirampiro** (☎2520 323), on Darwin next to Banco del Pacifico, may have a few tents and sleeping bags for rent.

Hotel Los Cactus, (☎2520 078), on Quito and Juan José Flores, opposite Iguana Rock in the green-and-white building. Sunny corridor opens up to clean simple rooms with fans and hot private baths. Singles US$12; doubles US$20. ❹

Cabañas de Don Jorge (☎2520 208; cabanadonjorge@hotmail.com), opposite Playa Mann. Follow Northia as it veers left out of town toward the Interpretation Center. Built right on the lava rocks opposite the beach, these rustic, ecologically-inspired cabins are not the newest rooms in town, but the location is ideal. Barking sea lions, instead of roosters, for a change, may provide early wake-up calls. Spacious cabañas have high, tin-roofed ceilings, tempermentally hot showers, fans, and fully-stocked kitchens. Singles US$12-15; doubles US$20-25. Discounts for longer stays. ❸

Hotel Chatham (☎/fax 2520 137), on Alsacio Northia at Armada Nacional, near the airport, has many new rooms with A/C, mini bars, hot water, and TVs. Older but still clean and comfortable rooms also have TVs and hot showers. Enjoy meals in the courtyard (breakfast US$2.50; lunch US$3), and make collect and calling card calls from the office. Laundry US$6 per load. Internet US$4 per hr. Tour info. Older singles US$15, newer US$18, with A/C US$25; doubles US$24/$30/$45; older triples US$30, with A/C $55; quad (only 1 room) US$40. Discounts for longer stays. AmEx/DC/MC/V. ❺

Hotel Mar Azul (☎/fax 2520 139), on Alsacio Northia, just before Hotel Chatham on the way to the airport. Tasteful plants adorn the tiled entryway. Clean rooms have private hot baths, TVs, and fans. Singles US$15, with A/C US$22.50; doubles US$24/$45; triples US$30/$67; quads US$40/$96. ❸

Residencial San Francisco (☎2520 304), on Darwin between Wolf and Villamil, in the blue and white building—the sign is on the 2nd fl. Slightly run-down hallway yields a colorful courtyard. Cold private showers, TVs with remotes, beds, sheets, pillows, blankets, soap for bathing, and fans. Singles US$8; doubles US$12; triples US$20. ❷

🍴 FOOD

Unlike neighboring Santa Cruz, Puerto Baquerizo Moreno offers many cheap restaurants, snack bars, and bakeries. Seafood is the specialty, and several family-owned restaurants on Darwin and Alsacio Northia serve it up fresh.

Albacora (☎2520 712 or 2520 646), on Alsacio Northia and Española. Popular with locals for huge portions of delicious breakfasts (US$2), *almuerzos* (US$2), and meriendas (US$1.80). Special *platos* (US$2.50-3.50) of rice and beans with chicken, pork, or fish with fried plantains and salad served on weekends. Extensive variety of seafood dishes (fish US$3.90-4.40, breaded shrimp US$9.30, lobster US$9.50) is worth the splurge; vegetarians can try the vegetable spaghetti (US$4.50). Spanish/English menu. Open daily 8am-10pm. ❶

Deep Blue (☎252 0990), on Darwin at Española. Bay views complement good típico menu with plenty of meat and fish dishes. Friendly cooks prepare Ecuadorian favorites like *guatita* (pig intenstines) and *encebollado* (fish soup) on M, W, and Sa. Breakfast US$3, set lunch US$2, a la carte plates US$3-4. Open M-Sa 6:30am-7:30pm. ❶

Restaurante Rosita (☎2520 106 or 2520 526), at Villamil and Ignacio de Hernandez, half a block up from the ocean. Outdoor tables and a varied *menú* complement its flag-draped international feel. Caught daily and served in large portions, seafood is the house specialty. Owners also operate a tour agency (see above). Set breakfast, lunch, and dinner US$2.50 each. Open daily 7am-3pm and 6-10pm. ❶

Restaurant Bar Miconia (☎2520 608), on Darwin, just past Malville, caters mainly to tourists. Excellent breakfasts (US$2.50-5), pizzas (from US$8), vegetarian pastas and rice (US$5-8), and a wide variety of pricey seafood and meat dishes (most US$5-12). 2nd-fl. dining room offers spectacular views of the bay. Open daily 8:30am-10pm. ❶

🅢 SIGHTS AND ACTIVITIES

Visiting Puerto Baquerizo Moreno's sights takes just a few hours, but it's easy to while away the day at any of the quiet, cove-like beaches. **Snorkeling** is possible at most beaches; mask and fin rentals are available at **Wreck Bay Diving Center** (US$15 per day; see above) and **Pirampiro** (☎2520 323), on Darwin next to Banco del Pacifico. **Ferremar,** on Malville and Ignacio de Hernandez, sells snorkel gear for US$20.

CENTRO DE INTERPRETACIÓN. The center's architecture and environment are treats in and of themselves: wooden walkways wind through modern buildings amid lush plant life and ocean views. Its informative exhibits, providing some of the best and most comprehensive information about the Galápagos, trace the geological and human history of the islands. Colorful Spanish/English displays explain everything from the evolution of Darwin's finches to chronicles from the infamous pirates and prisoners who once inhabited the islands. A **trail** (15min.) from the Center leads to **Cerro de las Tijeretas** (see below). The center also houses an outdoor stage with occasional **free performances.** *(From the town center, walk down Alsacio Northia and follow it out of town as it makes a sharp left turn. From the turn, the Center is another 5min. walk, past the Cabañas de Don Jorge. ☎2520 358. Open daily 7am-12:15pm and 2-5pm.)*

CERRO DE LAS TIJERETAS. Just beyond the Centro de Interpretación, a well made, rocky trail (round-trip 30min.) allow for incredible views, access to Bahía Tijeretas (a prime spot for photography, swimming, or snorkeling), and observation of a frigate birds' nesting site. Nick-named *tijeretas* (scissors) for the blade-like movements of their tails, the exotic black birds are most well known for their bright red pouches, which males inflate during mating season. An abundance of frigates used to nest here, but, for unknown reasons, their population has shrunk dramatically. Observation decks from the hilltop provide vistas of the ocean and islands, including a nice shot of León Dormido. *(The most popular entrance to the trail is inside the Centro de Interpretación (see above), just past the main exhibit hall. Another trail begins past the Centro de Interpretación on Alsacio Northia, just past the point at which the paved road becomes a dirt path. Both trails take 15min.)*

PLAYA CABO DEL HORNO. Past the Centro de Interpretación, another short trail (5min.) leads to this small, quiet beach trimmed with mangrove trees. Although the sometimes rough current makes swimming dangerous, the lava rock formations along the coast are great spots to watch some of the islands' best surfers ride huge waves at nearby **Punta Carola.** *(Walk past the Centro de Interpretación along Alsacio Northia. A dirt path replaces the paved road beyond the center, and a small opening in the rock wall, just past a sign to Cerro de las Tijeretas, marks the entrance to the trail.)*

LA LOBERÍA. The rocky, remote beach of **La Lobería** offers tranquility, sea lions, and tons of land iguanas. Many tourists visit La Lobería on organized day tours, but it's easy to visit on your own. *(Take Alsacio Northia toward the airport. Turn left at the airport and bear right at all forks in the road. Once on the beach, follow trail signs. Round-trip walk 1hr. Taxi 10min., US$3-4.)*

▶ NIGHTLIFE

The club scene in Baquerizo is rather dull, and most spots open sporadically or only on weekends. **Iguana Rock,** on Juan José Flores near Quito, two blocks from Alsacio Northia, is a laid-back place popular with the town's many foreign volunteers and local university students. Occasional live music, a TV, board games, and cards entertain for hours, although things can sometimes get rowdy with customized *fuerte* (strong) and *suave* (smooth) drinks. (Pilsner grande US$1.50; cocktails US$3.50-4. Open daily 3-7pm and 9:30pm-3am.) The **Scuba Bar,** on Darwin near the pier, offers old-school foosball and billiards while a DJ plays the latest hits. (Open W-Sa 8pm-3am.) The most popular disco, **Neptunus,** on Darwin in the main building on the pier, is relatively quiet most nights. (Open Th-Sa 8pm-3am.)

THE WESTERN ISLANDS ☎ 05

ISLA ISABELA ☎ 05

This sea horse-shaped island constitutes over 58% of the archipelago's land mass. Created by the fusion of six volcano lava flows, Isla Isabela proudly bears its title as the island with an abundance of land tortoises and the greatest number of active volcanoes—four are waiting to erupt at any moment. One can explore much of the island from the tranquil southern town of Puerto Villamil, but the remote western coast is visited only by the longest of tours, making this part of the Galápagos unseen by most visitors.

PUERTO VILLAMIL ☎ 05

Compared to the Galápagos's two other towns, Puerto Villamil (pop. 1200) is relatively free of commercialization and signs of tourism—there is no tourist office, no supermarket, and, in lieu of a newspaper, people make announcements from a loudspeaker in the town center. Many islanders expect an explosion of tourism and, subsequently, infrastructure in Puerto Villamil in the next few years. But until then, prickly pears serve as fence posts, and only the moon lights the town after midnight. Although foreigners are an uncommon sight, numerous hikes, sights, daytrips, and activities in addition to the tiny port's phenomenally relaxing atmosphere make Puerto Villamil the perfect place to unwind and explore for at least a few days. Residents are friendly; expect a *"buenos días"* or *"qué tal"* when starting a conversation, and don't be surprised if an islander invites you in for a chat.

▢ TRANSPORTATION. **Camionetas** bring in passengers from either the airport or the dock (US$1). **EMETEBE** (☎ 2529 555), at Antonio Gil and Las Fragatas, sends **avionetas** to **Puerto Baquerizo Moreno** on San Cristóbal (45min., M-Sa 11:15am, US$127) via **Baltra Airport** for **Puerto Ayora** on Isla Santa Cruz (30min., US$82). Reserve a seat at least two days in advance. Additional flights are scheduled on demand. (Puerto Villamil office accepts cash only, but credit card payments can be arranged. Luggage max. weight 13kg on full plane. Office open M-Sa 7:15am-12:30pm and 2-5:30pm.) A **lancha** leaves daily from the main dock to **Puerto Ayora** on Isla Santa Cruz (2-2½hr., daily 6am, US$30). Several agencies around town sell tickets for the lanchas; inquire at La Choza Restraurant, opposite the main plaza, and Aqua Express, in the PacificTel office on Antonio Gil, near Las Fragatas. Be wary of agencies that tell you they can arrange boat transportation for you to Puerto Baquerizo Moreno on Isla San Cristóbal. All boats go through Puerto Ayora, from which transport to Puerto Baquerizo Moreno is irregular. Talk to **Capitán Darwin Vihalua** (☎ 2529 401), **Señor Ulises** (☎ 2529 146), or **Capitán Checho** (☎ 2529 438) about arranging a boat to Puerto Baquerizo Moreno.

◪ ▨ ORIENTATION AND PRACTICAL INFORMATION. Antonio Gil is the main road through town; **16 de Marzo** and **Las Fragatas** intersect Antonio Gil near the main plaza, which marks the town center. The airport is 3km northeast of town, and the main dock is at the southeastern corner of town. There are **no banks or ATMs** in Puerto Villamil, but if you're in a bind, **MoneyGram** (☎ 252 9462), on Antonio Gil near the Pacifictel office, does international money transfers; bring your passport. (Open M-F 7:45am-1pm and 2-4:30pm, Sa 8am-noon). In an **emergency,** call ☎ 101. The **police** station (☎ 2529 101) is at Antonio Gil and Las Fragatas, opposite EMETEBE. A **health center** sits at 16 de Marzo and Antonio Gil, one block from the police station, in an unmarked peach building. (Emergency ☎ 2529 181. Open M-F 7:30am-noon and 1:30-5pm.) **Pacific-Tel** has an office on Antonio Gil, next door to EMETEBE. (Local calls US$0.13 per min., national and international US$0.25 per min. Open M-Sa 8am-9pm, Su 8am-noon and 5-9pm.) Slightly more expensive phone service is available at **Central Telefónica Isabela,** at Las Escalecias and Los Cactus. (Local calls US$0.18 per min., national calls US$0.25 per min., international calls US$0.66 per min. Open M-F 8am-8pm, Sa-Su 8a-11am and 4-7pm.) Next door is **Easy CyberCafe.** (Internet US$2 per hr. Open daily 9am-noon and 1-6pm.) **Albatros.net,** on 16 de Marzo four blocks inland from Antonio Gil, has a few more computers with somewhat more reliable service. (Internet US$2.50 per hr. Open M-F 8am-9pm.) Puerto Villamil has **no post office,** but EMETEBE office may be able to carry a package to Puerto Ayora or Puerto Baquerizo Moreno.

⌂ ACCOMMODATIONS. Relative to lodging elsewhere on the islands, Puerto Villamil's accommodations are a great value. **Hotel Ballena Azul ❷,** at the edge of town on the road leading inland from the dock, is one of the best budget places in the Galápagos. The hotel offers large, rustic rooms with warm, solar-heated showers in its sister hotel, **Cabañas Isabela del Mar ❷,** which is across the street. Ballena Azul has two rooms with shared baths; those pinching pennies should call ahead and reserve a room. Dora, the Swiss owner, loves to sit down and chat—in English, French, German, or Spanish—and will be more than happy to set up tours, advise you on nearby sites, provide information on the town, or rent tents for camping. (☎/fax 2529 030; isabela@ga.pro.ec. Laundry US$1 per kg. Internet US$1 per 5min. Tents US$10 per day. Rooms US$5, with private bath US$10 per person.) **Hotel Cormorant ❸,** on Antonio Gil a few blocks past the town center, boasts an unbeatable location right on the beach and spacious, clean rooms with tiled, hot private baths and towels. Some rooms have TVs, and the cozy rooms upstairs have wood floors and steepled ceilings. All guests have access to a well-stocked kitchen. (☎2529 129. US$10 per person.) **La Casa de Marita Bed and Breakfast ❺,** a towering yellow-and-red building, is a step up in both price and luxury. Kitchen facilities and ocean views complement 13 rooms, all with unique themes, A/C, large luxurious beds, and tiled bathrooms. Subtle decor, a homey sitting area, and the family-style restaurant complete the pleasant atmosphere at this country villa. Breakfast included. (☎2529 238; www.galapagosisabela.com. English, German, Italian, and Spanish spoken. Rents snorkeling equipment and can arrange beach horseback rides. High season singles US$35; doubles US$60; triples US$70-90. Low season singles US$18; doubles US$30. Excludes 22% tax.)

❏ FOOD. Unfortunately, in Puerto Villamil, the choices are few and the hours irregular. Inexpensive, high-quality meals are served at the several *comedores* near Antonio Gil and Las Fragatas. The best place to eat in town is **El Encanto de la Pepa ❸,** on Antonio Gil, past the police station toward Hotel Ballena Azul. This comfortable patio restaurant is complete with tablecloths, placemats, and romantic lighting. Locals recommended the shrimp (US$7), which is caught fresh and served with a tasty avocado salad. (Breakfast US$2, lunch and dinner US$2.50. Open daily 8am-10pm.) **Bar y Restaurante Caraball ❶,** on 16 de Marzo near Antonio Gil, is popular for *típico* dishes. (Fixed lunch US$2.50. Yucca bread US$1; *encebollado* US$2; *guatita* (pig intestine) US$2.50; shrimp US$4.50. Open M-Sa 7am-10pm, Su 7am-8pm.) The **restaurant ❷** at Hotel Ballena Azul serves high quality local and international meals. Try one of their filling and tasty spaghetti dinners (US$4). Everything is cooked to order, so the restaurant needs advance warning to find ingredients—stop by to order a few hours before you plan to eat. (Open daily 7:30am-9pm.) **La Casa de Marita B&B ❷** has an excellent but expensive restaurant in Marita's family-style kitchen on the third floor overlooking the ocean. Large portions of fresh pasta taste authentically Italian, and the cordial cooks prepare killer seafood dishes. Try the penne with pomodoro (US$3.50), octopus (US$5-6), fish with veggies and rice (US$6), or beef lasagne (US$7.50), with excellent wine (US$15-25 per bottle). (Excludes 22% tax. Open daily 7:30am-9pm.)

◨ SIGHTS. Exploring the several sites near Puerto Villamil can easily occupy a day or two. A 10min. boat ride to **La Grieta de los Tiburones** (also called **Las Tintoreras**) drops you off on a rocky lava trail that looks like a lunar surface surrounded by crystal-clear water. Be careful not to step on the countless land iguanas that scurry out of your way. Small fish swim around the channel's entrance, but **white-tipped reef sharks,** docile creatures that glide in and out of the channel in groups, congregate farther up the waterway. **Sea turtles, spotted eagle rays, manta rays,** and **penguins** occasionally appear as well. Bring snorkeling gear or rent some from La Casa de Marita (see above) if you want to swim with the sharks. It continues to a beach where **sea lions** rest under mangroves. *(Local fishermen bring tourists to La Grieta and guide them along the trails (1½-3hr.). Talk to Dora at Hotel Ballena Azul about finding a boat to La Grieta, or ask around the docks. Min. US$25 per boat, groups of 3 people or more US$7 per person, large groups US$5 per person.)*

Operated by National Park, the **Giant Tortoise Breeding Center** provides up-close encounters with Galápagos tortoises of every size and many different species. The zoo-like turtle nursery focuses on rearing two rare breeds of Isabelan tortoises—the Cerro Paloma species, which are genetically unique from all other Galápagos tortoises, and the flat-shelled tortoises, of which the center's 16 adults have produced over 200 offspring. If you're lucky, you might get to see these massive reptiles mating, which occurs January through May. Viewing this process feels about as awkward as the action looks and sounds, and it can last up to 5hr. Female tortoises at first try to escape during mating, but the stronger males eventually climb on top of and capture their reluctant partners. Watch out for buzzing **wasps**. A small visitors' center has good English and Spanish explanations of the breeding process. *(Follow Antonio Gil past the health center to the edge of town; a National Park sign points to a 1.2km trail that leads to the breeding center. ☎ 2529 178. Open daily 7am-6pm.)* The **Villamil Lagoon**, on Petreles and Flamencos, is a 5min. walk from the town center. Many migratory birds used to frequent this large, murky lagoon, but development has reduced the wildlife population. Better lagoons lie along the trails to the Breeding Center for Giant Tortoises (see above) and El Muro de Las Lágrimas (see below). **Flamingos** and several species of **waders** are common bird sightings.

▐ DAYTRIPS FROM PUERTO VILLAMIL

VOLCÁN SIERRA NEGRA AND VOLCÁN CHICO. After a jolting 45min. camioneta ride and an hour of bruising your fanny on the back of a horse, the mist parts, your jaw drops, and you tell your bum it was worth it. The dark, ominous crater extends in all directions, refusing to be framed by even the widest angle lens. Also called Volcán Santo Tomás, **Volcán Sierra Negra** (1490m) is the oldest and largest of Isabela's six volcanoes. With a diameter of 10km, it's the second-largest volcanic crater in the world—Tanzania's Ngorongora Volcano's 14km crater is the largest. It's possible to hike around the rim of the crater, but the trail is poorly-marked, and fog can settle in unexpectedly—go with a guide. Adventurous trekkers may follow a trail westward along the crater rim to the **sulfur mines,** the only active area of the volcano. Just inside the crater, three levels of sulfur formations bubble and steam. The trip to the sulfur mines is longer and more difficult than the daytrip to Sierra Negra, and those who are planning to do both might consider **camping** at the crater rim, which will allow time to see everything. *(Because this is National Park territory, guides are required; before camping, talk to the park officials in Puerto Villamil (☎ 2529 178), at the park office in the town center on Antonio Gil. Fires are not permitted. Tents can be rented from Hotel Ballena Azul (see above); bring long pants, long sleeves, and a raincoat.)* Most tours to Sierra Negra only ride on horseback along the rim of the crater for about 15min. before dismounting their horses and hiking to neighboring **Volcán Chico.** Much more massive than its name suggests, Chico's immense crater is textured by young lava formations from the 1979 eruption. Walking across the steaming Mars-like landscape, winded trekkers can put their hands near several "hot spots" in the crater and feel the hot vapor from deep under the crater's surface. On a clear day, hikes to the edge of the crater afford fantastic views of Elizabeth Bay and Isla Fernadina. Daytrips can be arranged through Hotel Ballena Azul and usually include a stop at neighboring **Volcán Chico.** *(It's not safe nor allowed to visit the volcanoes without a guide; however, people who rent horses will send a guide to escort the group. Daytrips can be arranged through Hotel Ballena Azul or through the National Park office on Antonio Gil. Hiking to the crater from the Highlands takes about 4hr.; guides can be hired at the National Park office. Richard and Joseph are excellent English-speaking guides. US$25-30, including transportation, horse, and guide. Discounts for larger groups. Lunch and water are excluded—bring your own. Guides charge US$35-40 to hike to the crater.)*

EL MURO DE LAS LÁGRIMAS (THE WALL OF TEARS). From Puerto Villamil, a beautiful 7km trail passes several sheltered lagoons and pristine beaches before heading inland to the Wall of Tears, which commemorates Isabela's former status as a penal colony. In June 1946, President José María Velasco Ibarra decided to move 300 prisoners and 30 guards from Guayaquil to the base of a hill called **La Orchilla,** just west of Puerto Villamil. With no other means of employing the prisoners, the penal colony's chief put them to work constructing a jail with the only substance available: lava rocks, piled on top of each other without cement. The extreme variety of rock shapes prevented efficient stacking, so the result was a 9m pile with sloping sides. The grueling hours in the sun and back-breaking labor broke many men's spirits. Over time, it came to be known as the place "where the cowards died and the brave wept." Construction of this wall of tears ceased when the sadistic chief was discharged and the colony moved to the Highlands. The colony was abolished in 1959 after a major rebellion in which prisoners seized the camps and fled to the continent in a stolen yacht. *(Follow Antonio Gil out of town past the big pink house. At the sign pointing toward the Giant Tortoises Breeding Center, go straight along the sandy path that runs parallel to the beach. 2km down the path, National Park signs point the way to the Wall of Tears. Round-trip walk is 14km, about 3½ hr.)*

ISLA SANTIAGO ☎ 05

Santiago's history has been less than serene. Human commercialism and volcanic activity have disrupted the island time and again. Santiago's volcanic cones, beachfront lava spires, gentle pahoehoe lava flows, and black sand beaches are reminders of the island's explosive past. As if liquid-hot magma weren't enough, four rather amorous goats were abandoned on the island in the 1880s, causing irreparable damage to the ecosystem (see **Goats Gone Wild**, p. 325). The island was further denigrated in the 1920s and 1960s by two salt mines. Nevertheless, Santiago remains one of the most intriguing islands in the Galápagos, with numerous visitor sites chock-full of wildlife.

PUERTO EGAS (SOUTH JAMES BAY) ☎ 05

Puerto Egas, located on Santiago's western shore, packs a lot into one fun-filled visitor site. A black-sand beach, remnants of the island's habitated history, amazing geology, and unique wildlife all cluster in South James Bay. During the 1920s and 1960s, the island shared its wildlife with two salt-mining communities. Miners dug salt from a crater just east of the bay; today the lagoon is frequented by **flamingos.** The salt-mining ventures were short-lived, but the national park decided to portray the scraps of their towns as "industrial archaeology." The island's more natural landscape, however, features brown layered tuff stone and black basalt volcanic rock that creates apertures, crevices, and natural bridges. Tours begin on a trail that runs along the coastline near an old road to one of the best tidal pool areas in the Galápagos. The black lava towers, basins, and craters are filled with crystal-clear seawater. Sea birds, such as **great blue herons, lava herons, ruddy turnstones, oyster catchers,** and **terns,** often gorge enthusiastically on the tasty shellfish, crustaceans, and small fish that reside in these accessible tidal pools. The lava rock along the tidal area is very slippery, so be careful.

Past the tidal pools, water laps in and out of the **grottoes,** where deep pools, belonging to a connected system of collapsed lava tubes, are constantly filled and refilled by the open sea. One pool, appropriately dubbed **Darwin's Toilet,** fills with a particularly noisy "flush." The grottoes are a good spot to find **Galápagos fur seals.** Once hunted to the brink of extinction for their thick, insulating fur, these diminutive sea lions have now made a comeback. They are excellent climbers and use the shady grotto ledges to keep the sun off their extra-thick fur.

PLAYA ESPUMILLA ☎ 05

Trimmed with verdant mangrove trees, Playa Espumilla's long, golden-sand beach is one of the Galápagos's most idyllic spots. Get there via a wet landing at the northern end of James Bay. An inland trail (2km) is good to observe bird species such as **Darwin finches, Galápagos hawks,** and **vermilion flycatchers.** The long, sandy beach is also great for **swimming.** Be careful where you step; **sea turtles** lay their eggs here. Behind the beach are several saltwater lagoons. Flamingos were former residents of the lagoons, but floods in the early 1980s sent them to other islands.

SULLIVAN BAY ☎ 05

Sullivan Bay's unearthly topography is what fascinates most visitors. This eastern shore of Santiago consists of a 120-year-old balsatic pahoehoe lava flow, producing solid black-rock fields that look as if they just cooled yesterday. *Hornitos* ("little ovens")—gas pockets trapped beneath the lava's surface—have erupted as "mini- volcanoes," producing intenstine-like wrinkles that break up the barren, moon-like black landscape. The roughest lava formations are nicknamed *aa lava*, to mimic the squeals made by fearless tourists that traverse the trail barefoot. Also notice the kipukas, tuff cones that were once autonomous rocky isles before the sudden attack of lava, and the shiny crystallized volcanic "glass" along the 2km trail that loops around the bay (40min.). The only signs of life that interrupt the plateau of hardened lava are the colonizing Mollugo carpetweed, rare lava cactus, and occasional black marine iguana that adeptly blends in with the terrain.

BUCCANEER COVE ☎ 05

Located on the northwestern side of Isla Santiago, Buccaneer Cove is named for the renegade pirates who frequented this area to hunt for meat and to stock up on firewood in the 1600s and early 1700s. Fresh water was often available in lava rock depressions, and the cove was a convenient place to keep boats. Although today tour boats don't land in the cove, many pass by slowly, letting passengers enjoy the area's towering cliff walls and impressive rock formations—try to identify the "elephant" and the "monk" formations. The shoreline is now populated by **feral goats** that do as much damage to the landscape as the pirates did on the high seas.

ISLA BARTOLOMÉ ☎ 05

Although only 1.2 sq. km in size, Isla Bartolomé's vivid geology makes it one of the most stunning islands to visit—deep reds, blues, and shimmering blacks mingle and shift, creating a kaleidoscopic landscape. Dominated by a geologically young volcano, the island consists of ash and porous lava rock, on which colonizing plants are just beginning to grow. You'll likely recognize the view from atop the summit of the volcanic cone, as it's the archipelago's most photographed landscape. The island has two visitor sites. The first is a short lava trail to the summit, accessed by a dry landing. The magma rock meets two sandy crescent **beaches** on either side of the island. **Pinnacle Rock** (also called Los Torres) leans into the bay at one end of the north beach, where tropical fish, penguins, and sea turtles swim with snorkelers. You'll have to stay on dry land at the southern beach, where snorkeling is prohibited, but sharks and nesting sea turtles are often visible from shore.

THE SUMMIT ☎ 05

A dry landing often occupied by sea lions leads to the trail (20min.) to Bartolomé's summit. Wooden steps aid visitors climbing the 114m tall volcanic cone. Along the trail, **lava lizards** dart back and forth. Observant hikers will notice that the rare **lava cacti** have slowly begun to colonize the barren lava landscape. The plant's banana-shaped stalks show the relative ages of different parts of the plants: the oldest are gray, the younger green, and the youngest bright yellow.

A fitness-testing climb takes you to a lookout where the view on a clear day reveals the archipelago's expanse. A 180° turn while standing on this peak reveals why Bartolomé is often compared to the surface of the moon—unearthly craters coated with black ash surround the volcano. Looking down into the ocean, an almost perfectly circular submarine crater is visible from shore.

THE TWIN BEACHES ☎ 05

Boats make a wet landing at the North Beach, where **Pinnacle Rock** (also called Los Torres) leans into the bay at one end of the beach. The massive rock formation owes the formation of its twin towers to a practice bomb dropped by the United States during WWII. This "rock" is made up of tightly packed sand shaped by wind and sea. As with everything in the Galápagos, Pinnacle Rock is still changing; the Swiss-cheese holes caused by the wear-and-tear of the elements will eventually send the rock crumbling into the sea. Before it tumbles, take a moment while swimming to stop beneath the rock, throw on a snorkel and mask, and relish the sight of brightly colored tropical fish, **sea turtles, white-tipped reef sharks,** and the occasional **Galápagos penguin** wandering among the submerged formations.

A short trail (5min.) through mangrove-covered sand dunes framing the northern beach leads to the southern beach. Snorkeling is prohibited to protect the marine life—including at least a dozen white-tipped reef sharks—swimming in the sometimes-powerful tides and currents.

ISLA RÁBIDA ☎ 05

Although Isla Rábida, just south of Santiago, is certainly not conspicuous in size, its striking color, central location, and wide variety of wildlife keep it from being overlooked. Visitors make a wet landing onto a remarkable maroon sand beach, which owes its unique color to centuries of erosion from the reddish volcanic cliffs to the west. **Sea lions** and **marine iguanas** rest close to shore, while **brown pelicans,** some of the Galápagos's largest birds, nest in the saltbush area behind the beach. Behind this vegetation lies a small lagoon hemmed in with mangrove trees. **Galápagos flamingos** used to breed here, but the recent growth of the sea lion population has driven them away. A short but somewhat steep trail from the beach leads to a peak overlooking the ocean, lagoon, and striking scarlet cliffs. The trail winds back to the beach passing through a neat forest of the aromatic palo santo trees. This portion of the island is also a great place to see **blue-footed boobies, white-cheeked pintail ducks,** and **black-necked stilts.** Clear and calm water, amazing reef fish like surgeon fish and pufferfish, and elusive **sharks** and **manta rays** make Rábida's beach an ideal **snorkeling** area.

THE SOUTHERN ISLANDS ☎ 05

ISLA FLOREANA (SANTA MARÍA) ☎ 05

Although Galápagos visitors today may distinguish the islands from one another mainly by their animals and landscapes, the unique history that has developed since the discovery of the archipelago gives many of them a unique personality beyond the lava formations and boobies. Isla Floreana is the first inhabited island, and more than a century of human impact on this area is plainly visible today.

PUERTO VELASCO IBARRA ☎ 05

With about as many people as a mid-sized hotel, the town of Puerto Velasco Ibarra (pop. 70) is quiet and unassuming, even with the occasional influx of tourist ships. While accommodations are sparse, visitors can stay at the small **Pensión Wittmer ❷.** Rooms with hot private baths and an ocean view are much cheaper than their equivalent on other islands. The owners also serve all three meals (US$1.50-2).

GALÁPAGOS ISLANDS

Four generations of Wittmers, one of the original German families to inhabit Floreana, reside under this friendly hotel's roof. Pensión Wittmer also sells autographed copies of Floreana, a book written by an original inhabitant, and it stamps letters for the post office barrel. (☎2521 026, Guayaquil 04 294 506. Rooms US$5.)

Just outside of Puerto Velasco Ibarra is the **Asilo de la Paz,** the site of the island's original settlement. A number of mysterious, hand-carved "caves" were hewn out of this mountainside by arriving settlers, but their purpose is uncertain. Also look for the **medium tree finch,** found only on Floreana, usually near Asilo de la Paz.

POST OFFICE BAY ☎05

In 1793, a British whaling captain erected a post office barrel on the quiet bay of the then-uninhabited island. For years, this barrel was the only postal facility for hundreds of miles. Whaling ships from around the world left their letters in the barrel and picked up those that they could deliver during their travels. Although the first barrel is now long gone, the tradition is maintained by the island's thousands of visitors each year, who arrive via a wet landing at a mahogony beach on Floreana's northern shore. Today's barrel is quite different from the original: no longer content to leave letters, numerous visitors have added signs, pictures, and other wooden messages to this growing piece of public art. Drop off a postcard, letter, or hastily scrawled note and see if any are addressed to an area near you. When you return home, deliver them in person if possible, or just drop it in the mail. The barrel isn't all there is to check out; a 5min. walk farther along the trail past the barrel leads to a 100m **lava tunnel** with an underground salt-water pool. Bring a flashlight and sturdy shoes or sandals for this short adventure, and be prepared to wade thigh-deep through cold sea water.

PUNTA CORMORANT ☎05

While many people come to Floreana for its history, they go to Punta Cormorant for other, more colorful reasons: glistening green stones, red mangroves, gray hills, pink flamingos, white sand, and blue water. Visitors arrive on a wet landing at the northern end of the island, on a beach littered with thousands of tiny green crystals. This unique mineral, called olivine, formed centuries ago from the erosion of pyroclastic volcanic cones. Olivine gives the sand a subtle greenish tinge; scoop up a handful and you'll easily see the smooth, green crystals. A short walk inland leads to one of the largest flamingo lagoons in the Galápagos. The rare **cut-leaf daisy,** a flower that grows nowhere else in the world, can be seen here as well.

At the other end of the trail sits **Flour Beach,** named for its strikingly soft, fine white sand. Shadowy gray **ghost crabs,** bright red **sally lightfoot crabs,** and green **sea turtles** frequent nearby waters. The main attraction, however, is the opportunity to see the numerous **stingrays** that lurk in the shallow waters near shore panning for sand crabs. Stay alert when entering the water, as the stingrays are somewhat dangerous, but chances of getting stung are slim.

LA CORONA DEL DIABLO (THE DEVIL'S CROWN) ☎05

Just off the coast of Punta Cormorant, this underwater crater formation was once a fully submerged volcano. Subsequent eruptions and the powerful ocean have eroded the cone into a jagged ring of black lava spires rising from the sea floor. The area's sharp drop-off and strong currents attract fish of all sizes, making for great **scuba diving** and some of the best **snorkeling** in the islands. These currents can be dangerous, however; snorkelers should be cautious. **Sharks** are perhaps the biggest attraction of La Corona del Diablo, and the probability of seeing the elegant creatures is high—both **white-tipped reef sharks** and **hammerheads** frequent the area. Swimming with **parrotfish, sea lions, surgeonfish,** and **triggerfish** is also quite likely.

ISLA ESPAÑOLA   ☎05

Española's isolated position as the Galápagos's southernmost island may be its greatest asset. Its remote location has prevented genetic flow between Española and other islands; as a result, many of its animals are found nowhere else in the world. Española's most unique fauna are its birds; conspicuous colonies of the **waved albatross,** one of the Galápagos's largest and most comical birds, make this island a highlight of the archipelago. Also expect to find hundreds of gregarious **marine iguanas** and **sea lions,** making for a complete Galápagos experience.

PUNTA SUÁREZ   ☎05

Visitors arriving on Española's southern tip (dry landing) may well have to dodge the lolling **sea lions,** which lounge on the sand and surf the rough waves near the rocky beach point. Beware of the aggressive beachmaster pacing the shallow shores—this male sea lion is protective of his harem of 20 to 25 females and will fight for his territory. Considerably more easy-going are the dozens of **marine iguanas** that warm themselves on the black rocks partitioning the two small beaches. Although young and female iguanas are all black, adult males have a reddish tinge and develop an additional greenish hue during breeding season. The **Española mockingbird,** has a longer, curved beak and is the only carnivorous mockingbird species; they feed on sea lion placentas, sea turtle hatchlings, marine iguana eggs, and insects. With no natural source of drinkable water on Española, the intrepid birds have even been known to drink the water-rich blood of baby boobies. Farther along the trail are more unique bird species, including **blue-footed boobies** and **swallow-tailed gulls,** one of five seabird species endemic to the Galápagos.

However, the most famous wildlife spot on the island is the nesting area of the **waved albatross.** Almost all 12,000 of the world's pairs breed here (Apr.-Dec.), combining elements of grace, ungainliness, and sheer comedy in a way only the albatross can. These yellow-beaked curiosities have quite the mating dance, a spectacle that can last up to five days and involves strutting, stumbling, honking, and a good deal of thumbwar-like beak-fencing. The main trail around Punta Suárez also passes the island's famous **blowhole,** where incoming waves are forced out of a narrow volcanic fissure in the rock. A seaside cliff on the southern end of the trail provides the perfect vantage point from which to watch spray soar over 25m into the air. From the cliff, visitors can also chuckle at the albatross's clumsy attempts to land and take off. Since their awkward webbed feet make it impossible to take flight from inland, they must first walk to a cliff in order to take off.

GARDNER BAY   ☎05

Gardner Bay, on the northwestern side of the island, is a white-sand paradise. If seaside bliss isn't enough of a draw, dancing **sea lions** offer another source of entertainment at this pristine beach. Divided into two sections by an outcropping of lava rock, the long, open shoreline is one of the few places in the Galápagos that is completely safe to explore without a guide (although park regulations require your guide to stay nearby). Venturing past the rocky partition to the other beach, however, is prohibited. Feel free to **snorkel** in Gardner Bay, or go to nearby Isla Tortuga for better visibility and more diverse marine life. Keep an underwater eye out for **sea turtles, stingrays,** and colorful **parrotfish.**

APPENDIX

HOLIDAYS AND FESTIVALS

Consult the **South American Explorers** (in USA, ☎607-277-0488; www.saexplorers.org) or the tourist office in each city for the dates of art exhibitions, theater shows, music festivals, and sporting events, when hotels fill up quickly and banks, restaurants, stores, and museums may close. When traveling around these dates, reserve accommodations in advance. Check with tourist office when you get to a new city or town, since small local festivals are common. Holidays listed below are only a small sample of the many fiestas that take place almost every week.

Most nationally celebrated holidays in Ecuador are Roman Catholic. Rural celebrations frequently feature days of nonstop feasting, dancing, and traditional rituals. **Semana Santa** (Holy Week), immediately preceding Easter, brings the most celebrations. Quito is the biggest party-mecca on Good Friday, but its processions are rivaled by those in Chimborazo province towns, such as Chambo, Chunchi, Tixán, and Yaruquies. However, festivals can be found in most cities, especially in the Highlands. **Navidad** (Christmas) on December 25 is another religious holiday of great importance, featuring processions of the Christ child. **Carnaval** celebrations occur the week before Lent. **Día de los Difuntos** (Day of the Dead; Nov. 2) combines the Catholic tradition of All Souls' Day with *indígena* burial rituals. Offerings of food, along with figures of people and animals made from bread, are laid on top of the graves of relatives. Many Highland towns also hold a **Corpus Christi** (Body of Christ) celebration in early June, most notably in Cuenca.

Not all regional celebrations are rooted in Catholicism, however; especially in the Highlands and jungle regions, locals continue to honor non-Christian deities. In September, there are harvest festivals throughout the nation. The **Fiesta del Yamor** is celebrated at the beginning of the month in Otavalo, when townspeople prepare a potent liquor called chicha. Most towns celebrate an **Independence Day** associated with the date on which they were liberated from Spain. Quito's (August 10), Guayaquil's (October 9), and Cuenca's (November 3) are Ecuadorian national holidays and entail concerts, sporting events, parades, and other spectacles.

SPANISH QUICK REFERENCE

PRONUNCIATION

Each vowel has only one pronunciation: A ("ah" in father); E ("eh" in pet); I ("ee" in eat); O ("oh" in oat); U ("oo" in boot); Y, by itself, is pronounced the same as Spanish I ("ee"). Most consonants are pronounced the same as in English. Important exceptions are: J, pronounced like the English "h" in "hello"; LL, pronounced like the English "y" in "yes"; and Ñ, pronounced like the "ny" in "canyon." R at the beginning of a word or RR anywhere in a word is trilled. H is always silent. G before E or I is pronounced like the "h" in "hen"; elsewhere it is pronounced like the "g" in "gate." X has a variety of pronunciations: it can sound like English "h," "s," "sh," or "x." Spanish words stress an accented syllable. In the absence of an accent, words that end in vowels, "n," or "s" receive stress on the second to last syllable. For words ending in all other consonants, stress falls on the last syllable.

Spanish has masculine and feminine nouns, and gives a gender to all adjectives. Masculine words generally end with an "o": *él es un tonto* (he is a fool). Feminine words generally end with an "a": *ella es bella* (she is beautiful). Pay attention—slight changes in endings can cause drastic changes in meaning.

LET'S GO SPANISH PHRASEBOOK

ESSENTIAL PHRASES

ENGLISH	SPANISH	PRONUNCIATION
Hello.	Hola.	OH-la
Goodbye.	Adiós.	ah-dee-OHS
yes/no	sí/no	SEE/NO
please	por favor.	POHR fa-VOHR
Thank you.	Gracias.	GRA-see-ahs
You're welcome.	De nada.	DAY NAH-dah
Do you speak English?	¿Habla inglés?	AH-blah EEN-glace
I don't speak Spanish.	No hablo español.	NO AH bloh cho pahn-YOHL
Excuse me.	Perdón.	pehr-DOHN
I don't know.	No sé.	NO SAY

SURVIVAL SPANISH

ENGLISH	SPANISH	ENGLISH	SPANISH
Again, please.	Otra vez, por favor.	I'm sick/fine.	Estoy enfermo(a)/bien.
What (did you just say)?	¿Cómo?/¿Qué?	Could you speak more slowly?	¿Podría hablar más despacio?
I don't understand.	No entiendo.	How are you?	¿Qué tal?/¿Comó está?
What is your name?	¿Cómo se llama?	I am hungry/thirsty.	Tengo hambre/sed.
How do you say... in Spanish?	¿Cómo se dice... en español?	Is the store open/closed?	¿La tienda está abierta/cerrada?
Good morning/night.	Buenos días/noches.	I am hot/cold.	Tengo calor/frío.
How much does it cost?	¿Cuánto cuesta?	I want/would like...	Quiero/Me gustaría...
That is very cheap/expensive.	Es muy barato/caro.	Let's go!	¡Vámonos!
What's up?	¿Qué pasa?	Stop/that's enough.	Basta.
Who?	¿Quién?	What?	¿Qué?
When?	¿Cuándo?	Where?	¿Dónde?
Why?	¿Por qué?	Because.	Porque.

YOUR ARRIVAL

ENGLISH	SPANISH	ENGLISH	SPANISH
I am from (the US/Europe).	Soy de (los Estados Unidos/Europa).	What's the problem, sir/madam?	¿Cuál es el problema, señor/señora?
Here is my passport.	Aquí está mi pasaporte.	I lost my passport.	Perdí mi pasaporte.
I will be here for less than six months.	Estaré aquí por menos de seis meses.	I have nothing to declare.	No tengo nada para declarar.
I don't know where that came from.	No sé de dónde vino eso.	Please do not detain me.	Por favor no me detenga.

GETTING AROUND

ENGLISH	SPANISH	ENGLISH	SPANISH
Does this bus go to (Tierra del Fuego)?	¿Va este autobús a (Tierra del Fuego)?	¿How can you get to...?	¿Cómo se puede llegar a...?
Where is (Moreno) street?	¿Dónde está la calle (Moreno)?	Where do the buses for (Quito) leave from?	¿De dónde salen/paran los buses para (Quito)?
When does the bus leave?	¿Cuándo sale el bús?	What bus line goes to...?	¿Qué línea de buses tiene servicio a...?
I'm getting off at...	Bajo en...	Where does the bus leave from?	¿De dónde sale el bús?
Can I buy a ticket?	¿Podría comprar un boleto?	I have to go now.	Tengo que ir ahora.
How long does the trip take?	¿Cuántas horas dura el viaje?	I am going to the airport.	Voy al aeropuerto.
How far is...?	¿Qué tan lejos está...?	Continue forward.	Siga derecho.
I would like to rent (a car).	Quisiera alquilar (un coche).	The flight is delayed/cancelled.	El vuelo está atrasado/cancelado.
I lost my baggage.	Perdí mi equipaje.	Do you have change?	¿Tiene cambio/suelto?
Where is the bathroom?	¿Dónde está el baño?	I'm lost.	Estoy perdido(a).
How much does it cost per day/week?	¿Cuánto cuesta por día/semana?	Does it have (heating/air-conditioning)?	¿Tiene (calefacción/aire acondicionado)?
Where can I buy (a cell-phone)?	¿Dónde puedo comprar (un teléfono celular)?	Where can I check e-mail?	¿Dónde se puede chequear el email?
Could you tell me what time it is?	¿Podría decirme qué hora es?	Is there anything cheaper?	¿Hay algo más barato/económico?

DIRECTIONS

ENGLISH	SPANISH	ENGLISH	SPANISH
(to the) right	(a la) derecha	(to the) left	(a la) izquierda
next to	al lado de/junto a	across from	en frente de/frente a
straight ahead	derecho	turn (command form)	doble
near (to)	cerca (de)	far (from)	lejos (de)
above	arriba	below	abajo
traffic light	semáforo	corner	esquina
street	calle/avenida	block	cuadra

ACCOMMODATIONS

ENGLISH	SPANISH	ENGLISH	SPANISH
Is there a cheap hotel around here?	¿Hay un hotel económico por aquí?	The shower/sink/toilet is broken.	La ducha/pila/el servicio no funciona.
Do you have rooms available?	¿Tiene habitaciones libres?	I am going to stay for (four) days.	Me voy a quedar (cuatro) días.
I would like to reserve a room.	Quisiera reservar una habitación.	Are there cheaper rooms?	¿Hay habitaciones más baratas?
Can I see a room?	¿Podría ver una habitación?	Do they come with private baths?	¿Vienen con baño privado?
Do you have any singles/doubles?	¿Tiene habitaciones sencillas/dobles?	I need another key/towel/pillow.	Necesito otra llave/toalla/almohada.
I'll take it.	Lo tomo.	My bedsheets are dirty.	Mis sábanas están sucias.

EMERGENCY

ENGLISH	SPANISH	ENGLISH	SPANISH
Help!	¡Socorro!/¡Ayúdeme!	Call the police!	¡Llame a la policía/los carabineros!
I am hurt.	Estoy herido(a).	Leave me alone!	¡Déjame en paz!
It's an emergency!	¡Es una emergencia!	They robbed me!	¡Me han robado!
Fire!	¡Fuego!/¡Incendio!	They went that way!	¡Fueron en esa dirección!
Call a clinic/ambulance/doctor/priest!	¡Llame a una clínica/una ambulancia/un médico/un padre!	I will only speak in the presence of a lawyer.	Sólo hablaré en presencia de un abogado(a).
Don't touch me!	¡No me toque!	I need to contact my embassy.	Necesito contactar mi embajada.

MEDICAL

ENGLISH	SPANISH	ENGLISH	SPANISH
I feel bad/better/fine/worse.	Me siento mal/mejor/bien/peor.	I have a stomach ache.	Me duele el estómago.
I have a headache.	Tengo un dolor de cabeza.	I think I'm going to vomit.	Pienso que voy a vomitar.
I'm sick/ill.	Estoy enfermo(a).	Here is my prescription.	Aquí está la receta médica.
I'm allergic to...	Soy alérgico(a) a...	It hurts here.	Me duele aquí.
What is this medicine for?	¿Para qué es esta medicina?	I have a cold/a fever/diarrhea/nausea.	Tengo gripe/una calentura/diarrea/náusea.
Where is the nearest hospital/doctor?	¿Dónde está el hospital/doctor más cercano?	I haven't been able to go to the bathroom in (four) days.	No he podido ir al baño en (cuatro) días.

INTERPERSONAL INTERACTIONS

ENGLISH	SPANISH	ENGLISH	SPANISH
What is your name?	¿Cómo se llama?	Pleased to meet you.	Encantado(a)/Mucho gusto.
Where are you from?	¿De dónde es?	I'm (twenty) years old.	Tengo (veinte) años.
This is my first time in Ecuador.	Esta es mi primera vez en Ecuador.	I have a boyfriend/girlfriend/spouse.	Tengo novio/novia/esposo(a).
Do you come here often?	¿Viene aquí a menudo?	I love you.	Te quiero.
Do you have a light?	¿Tiene fuego?	What a shame: you bought Lonely Planet!	¡Qué lástima: compraste Lonely Planet!

EATING OUT

ENGLISH	SPANISH	ENGLISH	SPANISH
breakfast	desayuno	I'd like to order the eel.	Quisiera el congrio.
dinner	comida/cena	lunch	almuerzo
dessert	postre	drink (alcoholic)	bebida (trago)
fork	tenedor	knife	cuchillo
napkin	servilleta	cup	copa/taza
spoon	cuchara	Do you have hot sauce?	¿Tiene salsa picante?
Where is a good restaurant?	¿Dónde está un restaurante bueno?	Table for (one), please.	Mesa para (uno), por favor.
Can I see the menu?	¿Podría ver la carta/el menú?	Do you take credit cards?	¿Aceptan tarjetas de crédito?
This is too spicy.	Es demasiado picante.	Disgusting!	¡Guácala!/¡Qué asco!

APPENDIX

ENGLISH	SPANISH	ENGLISH	SPANISH
Do you have anything vegetarian/without meat?	¿Hay algún plato vegetariano/sin carne?	Check, please.	La cuenta, por favor.

NUMBERS, DAYS, AND MONTHS

ENGLISH	SPANISH	ENGLISH	SPANISH	ENGLISH	SPANISH
0	cero	20	veinte	last night	anoche
1	uno	21	veintiuno	weekend	fin de semana
2	dos	22	veintidos	morning	mañana
3	tres	30	treinta	afternoon	tarde
4	cuatro	40	ouarenta	night	noche
5	cinco	50	cincuenta	month	mes
6	seis	100	cien	year	año
7	siete	1000	un mil	early/late	temprano/tarde
8	ocho	1 million	un millón	January	enero
9	nueve	Monday	lunes	February	febrero
10	diez	Tuesday	martes	March	marzo
11	once	Wednesday	miércoles	April	abril
12	doce	Thursday	jueves	May	mayo
13	trece	Friday	viernes	June	junio
14	catorce	Saturday	sábado	July	julio
15	quince	Sunday	domingo	August	agosto
16	dieciseis	today	hoy	September	septiembre
17	diecisiete	tomorrow	mañana	October	octubre
18	dieciocho	day after tomorrow	pasado mañana	November	noviembre
19	diecinueve	yesterday	ayer	December	diciembre

MENU READER

ENGLISH	SPANISH	ENGLISH	SPANISH
grilled	a la plancha	pastry with fruit	kuchen
steamed	al vapor	milk	leche
oil	aceite	vegetables/legumes	legumbres
olive	aceituna	lime	lima
water (purified)	agua (purificada)	lemon	limón
garlic	ajo	lemonade	limonada
clam	almeja	abalone (white fish)	locos
rice	arroz	steak or chop	lomo
rice pudding	arroz con leche	syrupy dessert	macedonia
sandwich with chicken and avocado	ave-palta	corn	maíz
sandwich with beef and cheese	Barros Luco	seafood	mariscos
beefsteak	bistec	orange	naranja
crab with onions, eggs, cheese	bundín de centolla	cream	nata
coffee	café	soup of various shellfish	paila marina
eel and vegetable soup	caldillo de congrio	bread	pan
hot	caliente	a common heavy bread	pan amasado

QUICHUA PHRASEBOOK

ESSENTIAL PHRASES

ENGLISH	QUICHUA	ENGLISH	QUICHUA
Hello.	napaykullayki	distant/close	karu/sirka
Goodbye.	ratukama	down/up	uray wichay
How are you?	allillanchu?	How much?	maik'ata'g?
please	Eallichu	What?	iman?
Thank you.	yusulpayki	Why?	imanaqtin?
yes	arí	water	unu
no	mana	food	mihuna
Where?	may?	lodging	alohamiento

NUMBERS

ENGLISH	QUICHUA	ENGLISH	QUICHUA	ENGLISH	QUICHUA
1	uc	8	pusacc	60	soccta chunca
2	iscay	9	isccon	70	ccanchis chunca
3	quimsa	10	chunca	80	pusacc chunca
4	tahua	20	iscay-chunca	90	isccon chunca
5	pichcca	30	qimsa chunca	100	pachac
6	soccta	40	tahua chunca	1000	huarancca
7	Ccanchis	50	phichcca chunca	2000	iscay huarancca

GLOSSARY OF USEFUL TERMS

aduana: customs
agencia de viaje: travel agency
aguardiente: strong liquor
aguas termales: hot springs
ahora: now
ahorita: "now in just a little bit," which can mean 5min.-5hr.
aire acondicionado: air-conditioned (A/C)
a la plancha: grilled
al gusto: as you wish
alemán: German
almacén: (grocery) store
almuerzo: lunch, midday meal
alpaca: a shaggy-haired, long-necked animal in the cameloid family
altiplano: highland
amigo/a: friend
andén: platform
anexo: neighborhood
arroz: rice
arroz chaufa: Chinese-style fried rice
artesanía: arts and crafts
avenida: avenue
bahía: bay
bajar: to go down

bandido: bandit
baño: bathroom or natural spa
barato/a: cheap
barranca: canyon
barro: mud
barrio: neighborhood
biblioteca: library
bistec/bistek: beefsteak
bocaditos: appetizers, at a bar
bodega: convenience store or winery
boletería: ticket counter
bonito/a: pretty/beautiful
borracho/a: drunk
bosque: forest
botica: drugstore
bueno/a: good
buena suerte: good luck
buen provecho: bon appétit
burro: donkey
caballero: gentleman
caballo: horse
cabañas: cabins
cajeros: cashiers
cajeros automáticos: ATM
caldera: coffee or tea pot
caldo: soup, broth, or stew
calle: street
cama: bed

camarones: shrimp
cambio: change
caminata: hike
camino: path, track, road
camión: truck
camioneta: small, pickup-sized truck
campamento: campground
campesino/a: person from a rural area, peasant
campo: countryside
canotaje: rafting
cantina: drinking establishment, usually male-dominated
carne asada: roast meat
capilla: chapel
caro/a: expensive
carretera: highway
carro: car, or sometimes a train car
casa: house
casa de cambio: currency exchange establishment
casado/a: married
cascadas: waterfalls
catedral: cathedral
centro: city center
cerca: near/nearby
cerro: hill
cerveza: beer

ceviche: raw fish marinated in lemon juice, herbs, veggies
cevichería: ceviche restaurant
chico/a: boy/girl, little
chicharrón: small pieces of fried meat, usually pork
chuleta de chancho: pork chop
churrasco: steak
cigarillo: cigarette
cine: cinema
cima: peak, top
ciudad: city
ciudadela: neighborhood in a large city
coche: car
colectivo: shared taxi
coliseo: coliseum/stadium
comedor: dining room
comida típica: typical/traditional dishes
con: with
consulado: consulate
correo: post office
cordillera: mountain range
corvina: sea bass
crucero: crossroads
Cruz Roja: Red Cross
cuadra: street block
cuarto: a room
cuenta: bill/check
cuento: story/account
cueva: cave
curandero: healer
damas: ladies
desayuno: breakfast
descompuesto: broken, out of order; spoiled/rotten food
desierto: desert
despacio: slow
de turno: a 24hr. rotating schedule for pharmacies
dinero: money
discoteca: dance club
dueño/a: owner
dulces: sweets
edificio: building
email: email
embajada: embassy
embarcadero: dock
emergencia: emergency
entrada: entrance
estadio: stadium
este: east
estrella: star
extranjero: foreign/foreigner
farmacia: pharmacy
farmacia en turno: 24hr. pharmacy
feliz: happy
ferrocarril: railroad
fiesta: party, holiday
finca: a plantation-like agricultural enterprise or a ranch
friajes: sudden cold winds

frijoles: beans
frontera: border
fumar: to smoke
fumaroles: hole in a volcanic region which emits hot vapors
fundo: large estate or tract of land
fútbol: soccer
ganga: bargain
gobierno: government
gordo/a: fat
gorra: cap
gratis: free
gringo/a: North American
guanaco: animal in the camelid family
habitación: a room
hacer una caminata: take a hike
hacienda: ranch
helado: ice cream
hermano/a: brother/sister
hervido/a: boiled
hielo: ice
hijo/a: son/daughter
hombre: man
iglesia: church
impuestos: taxes
impuesto valor añadido (IVA): value added tax (VAT)
indígena: indigenous, refers to the native population
Internet: Internet
isla: island
jarra: 1L pitcher of beer
jirón: street
jugo: juice
ladrón: thief
lago/laguna: lake
lancha: launch, small boat
langosta: lobster
langostino: jumbo shrimp
larga distancia: long distance
lavandería: laundromat
lejos: far
lente: slow
librería: bookstore
lista de correos: mail holding system in Latin America
loma: hill
lomo: chop, steak
madre: mother
malo/a: bad
malecón: pier or seaside thoroughfare
maletas: luggage, suitcases
máneje despacio: drive slowly
manjar blanco: a whole milk spread
mar: sea
mariscos: seafood
matas: shrubs, jungle brush
matrimonial: double bed
menestras: lentils/beans

menú del día/menú: fixed daily meal often offered for a bargain price
mercado: market
merienda: snack
mestizo/a: a person of mixed European and indigenous descent
microbus: small, local bus
mirador: an observatory or look-out point
muelle: wharf
museo: museum
música folklórica: folk music
nada: nothing
niño/a: child
norte: north
obra: work of art/play
oeste: west
oficina de turismo: tourist office
padre: father
pampa: a treeless grassland area
pan: bread
panadería: bakery
panga: motorboat
parada: a stop (on a bus or train)
parilla: various cuts of meat, grilled
paro: labor strike
parque: park
parroquia: parish
paseo turístico: tour covering a series of sites
pelea de gallos: cockfighting
peligroso/a: dangerous
peninsulares: Spanish-born colonists
peña: folkloric music club
pescado: fish
picante: spicy
pisa de uvas: grape-stomping
pisco sour: a drink of pisco, lemon juice, sugarcane syrup, and egg white
plátano: plantain
playa: beach
población: population, settlement
policía: police
pollo a la brasa: roasted chicken
pueblito: small town
pueblo: town
puente: bridge
puerta: door
puerto: port
queso: cheese
rana: frog
recreo: place of amusement, restaurant/bar on the outskirts of a city
subir: to go up
taximetro: taxi meter

INDEX

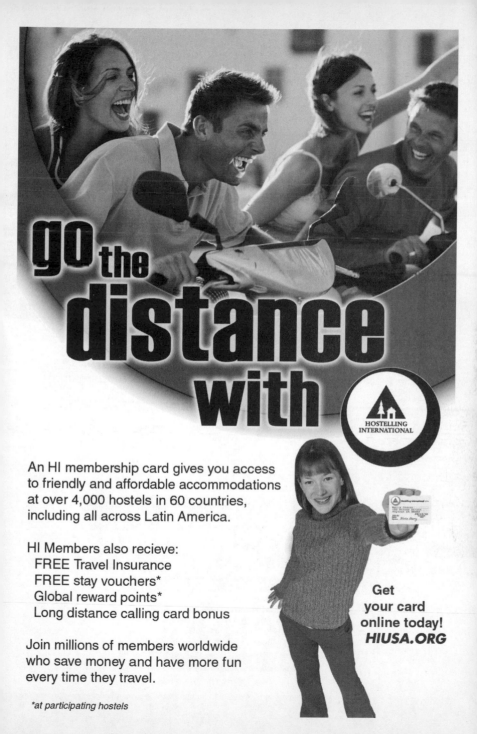

MAP INDEX

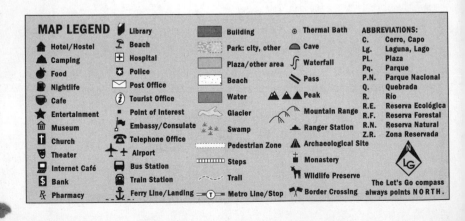

MAP LEGEND

📚 Library		🏢 Building	◉ Thermal Bath	**ABBREVIATIONS:**
🏠 Hotel/Hostel	🏖 Beach	Park: city, other	⌒ Cave	C. Cerro, Capo
▲ Camping	✚ Hospital	Plaza/other area	∫ Waterfall	Lg. Laguna, Lago
🍴 Food	🚓 Police	Beach	⬿ Pass	PL. Plaza
🍺 Nightlife	✉ Post Office	Water	▲▲▲ Peak	Pq. Parque
☕ Cafe	ⓘ Tourist Office	Glacier	Mountain Range	P.N. Parque Nacional
★ Entertainment	■ Point of Interest	Swamp	▲ Ranger Station	Q. Quebrada
🏛 Museum	🚩 Embassy/Consulate	Pedestrian Zone	▲ Archaeological Site	R. Río
🏚 Church	☎ Telephone Office	Steps	✝ Monastery	R.E. Reserva Ecológica
🎭 Theater	✈ Airport	Trail	🏵 Wildlife Preserve	R.F. Reserva Forestal
💻 Internet Café	🚌 Bus Station	Metro Line/Stop	⧫ Border Crossing	R.N. Reserva Natural
💲 Bank	🚂 Train Station			Z.R. Zona Reservada
℞ Pharmacy	⚓ Ferry Line/Landing			

The Let's Go compass always points NORTH.